GOING
TOO FAR

By Tony Hendra

GOING TOO FAR

(Editor)
OFF THE WALL STREET JOURNAL

(with Sean Kelly)
NOT THE BIBLE

(Editor with Christopher Cerf and Peter Elbling)
THE 80'S: A LOOK BACK

THE SAYINGS OF AYOTOLLAH KHOMEINI

(Co-Editor with Christopher Cerf)
NOT THE NEW YORK TIMES

GOING TOO FAR

TONY HENDRA

A DOLPHIN BOOK
Doubleday
NEW YORK
1987

THE AUTHOR GRATEFULLY ACKNOWLEDGES PERMISSION TO EXCERPT MATERIAL PROVIDED BY THE FOLLOWING: Interviews conducted for and published in *Something Wonderful Right Away* by Jeffrey Sweet (Limelight Editions, 1987). Used by permission of the author. Covers of *The Harvard Lampoon* 1965 and 1969 *Time* parodies, used by permission of *The Harvard Lampoon*. Transcript of "A Little Tea with Goldie" sketch from *The Smothers Brothers' Comedy Hour* (February 25, 1968). Used by permission of Thomas Smothers. Versions of the Second City sketches "Great Books" and "Museum," by permission of The Second City. Political posters by Rick Meyerowitz, used with permission of the artist. Illustrations of "Bulgemobiles" and "R.M.S. Tyrannic," by Bruce McCall, used by permission of the artist. Selected panels from the *MAD* comic parody "Howdy Doodit," © 1954, 1982 by E.C. Publications, Inc. Used by permission of *MAD* magazine. Material from the Compass Theater scenario "Enterprise" and from the Second City sketch entitled "Businessman," both by Roger Bowen. Used by permission of the author. Illustrations by Jules Feiffer used by permission of the artist. Illustrations by Robert Crumb, © 1987. Used by permission of the artist. "The Censor," published in *The Mason Williams Reading Matter* (Doubleday and Company) © 1969 by Mason Williams. All rights reserved; used by permission of the author. *Wide World of War*, copyright THE COMMITTEE "CABARET INC.", written and performed by THE COMMITTEE. Excerpts from "Positively Wall Street," "Colorado," "Highway Toes," "Lonely at the Bottom," by Christopher Guest. Used by permission of the author. "The Big Muddy," words and music by Pete Seeger, TRO—© copyright 1967, Melody Trails, Inc., New York, New York. All rights reserved, including public performance for profit. Used by permission. Excerpts from songs by Tom Lehrer, used by permission. Excerpt from "Lecture on the Universe," by Severn Darden, used by permission of Severn Darden. Excerpts from "Lawrence Welk Trumpeter," "How to Talk to Your Colored Friends at Parties," "The Tribunal," "Thank You, Masked Man," "Religions Inc.," "MCA and Hitler," "Father Flotsky's Triumph," and "The Defiant Ones" by Lenny Bruce. Used by permission of The Douglas Corporation.

Designed by Peter R. Kruzan

Library of Congress Cataloging-in-Publication Data
Hendra, Tony.
Going too far.
"A Dolphin book."
Includes index.
1. American wit and humor—History and criticism.
2. Comedy programs—United States—History. 3. Comedians
—United States—Interviews. 4. Theater—United States—
History—20th century. I. Title.
PS438.H39 1987 817'.54'09 87-13721
ISBN 0-385-23223-3

This book is for Sean Kelly,
whose idea it was,
and for Carla,
without whom it wouldn't exist.

Acknowledgments

My thanks are due to many many people for their assistance with this book. First and foremost to all those who agreed to be interviewed, and provided me with materials and contacts, especially Matty Simmons, Alan Myerson, and Mason Williams.

My thanks also to Peter Occhiogrosso, for a gargantuan work of research; also in this respect, to Valerie Vaz. To David Barber and Robert Heusinger, for an equally gargantuan job of processing my words—all of them several times. To John Boswell, who guided the project from its earliest beginnings, and to Patti Brown for her kind advice. Thanks also to Casey Fuetsch, for her sane and much-needed editing, which curbed my worst excesses before it was too late, and of course to my editor, Paul Bresnick. Paul's generosity and enthusiasm kept me going through the hard parts, but his most important quality (one authors prize above all others) was an almost limitless patience.

Contents

Author's Note

This book covers a period of more than thirty years from the mid-fifties to the late eighties. It also sets out to make general observations about that most particular of tastes—humor—and what's more a relatively specific form of humor.

It's inevitable on any of these counts that many artists do not appear in this book or have not been examined in depth. Some of these artists will feel slighted because they have not been included. (Others, however, may very well be delighted.) A general apology is in order to all of those who have been left out, as well as to readers who might be puzzled or offended at the absence of favorites.

Further, the simple pressures of deadlines and timetables have meant that several people key to the central premise of this book were unavailable for or not contacted for interviews. Their presence in these pages is therefore secondhand, which is deeply regretted.

Here, in no particular order, are just a few of those who, for one reason or another, were not included. This list too is far from all-inclusive: Those whose careers began substantially before the period from 1955 to 1960—however brilliant—do not appear here. This, alas, means the exclusion of such giants as "Your Show of Shows" graduates Neil Simon, Mel Brooks, and Carl Reiner. Similarly, those comedians of the traditional school, such as Buddy Hackett, Alan King, and Jackie Mason, and extending even to the eminently respectable Mr. Dangerfield. In general, situation comedies are not dealt with here, in part because of the book's focus, but also because the subject of sitcoms is so vast that it needs its own volume to do it justice. In general, too, literary satirists receive short shrift, chiefly because their work is critically assessed elsewhere and better by others. Nonetheless, this has meant only the most passing mention of such great writers as Nabokov, Southern, Roth, Friedman, et al.

Six of the funniest men (and women) in the English-speaking world—the cast of "Monty Python"—are also absent, along with most of the practitioners of Boomer humor from the other side of the Atlantic. American readers interested in remedying this lack are unequivocally recommended to the excellent book *From Fringe to Flying Circus* by Roger Wilmut (London: Methuen, 1980), which covers the period from 1960 to 1980 in England and includes all major milestones from *Beyond the Fringe* to "That Was the Week That Was," "Fawlty Towers," and to the Pythons' best film, *The Life of Brian* (1979).

The collective work of Woody Allen is not dealt with, partly because Mr. Allen is adverse to interviews, and partly because his work, too, is widely examined elsewhere. The work of Richard Pryor is similarly absent for some of the same reasons. (A businesslike biography of Mr. Pryor has been published, however, called *This Cat Has Nine Lives* by Fred Robbins and David Ragan, Delilah Books/G. P. Putnam, New York 1982.)

Apologies also to Steve Martin, whose work is barely mentioned here, and to Albert Brooks, ditto—if for no other reason than that his superb *Lost in America* should have been. Apologies also to my good friends Reni Santoni and Pat McCormick, both of whom gave me excellent interviews, as did the multitalented Buck Henry. Somehow there just wasn't room for everybody.

One of those artists I most regret not having been able to interview because of crossed messages and other exigencies of the age of communication is Lily Tomlin. If anyone should have been in this book, she should have.

Lastly and most importantly, apologies to those dozens of writers and artists who helped to make the *Lampoon* what it was, but were not mentioned in my account of it; in particular, my good friends Danny Abelson, Peter Kaminsky, Ted Mann, Gerry Sussman, and Ellis Weiner.

Regrettably, in a key chapter of this book—its first, concerning Mort Sahl —little of the seminal artist's material appears, beyond random quotes. Initially Mr. Sahl agreed to permit the inclusion of certain portions from two of his best-known albums, *Mort Sahl at the hungry i* and *Look Forward in Anger,* both from the fifties. As the book was being readied for the compositor, however, he decided after all to withhold this permission, feeling that exclusive concentration on material from the fifties would militate against his contemporary image.

Chapter 2 of this book concerns itself with the origins of the Compass Theater in Chicago and of its distinguished offspring, Second City. An overwhelming proportion of the interview material presented in this chapter is drawn from the definitive history of Second City, entitled *Something Wonderful Right Away* by Jeffrey Sweet. New York: Avon, 1978; (reprinted) New York: Limelight Editions, 1987, Sweet's account of the quarter of a century that Second City has been in existence is based on in-depth interviews with almost all its principals. The interviews are both informative and funny, and any reader wanting to know more about this unique satirical and theatrical phenomenon is recommended to Mr. Sweet's book, to date the only serious work on the subject. Chapter 2 should be regarded as only the barest of introductions to it. My gratitude for his generosity in the use of this invaluable material.

—Tony Hendra
April 1987

A joke is not a joke when it deals with the sacred goods of the nation.

—JOSEF GOEBBELS

GOING
TOO FAR

Introduction

In the twenty-five years immediately preceding the election of President Ronald Reagan, there occurred in the United States an almost continuous explosion of comedy. Whether in print, the spoken word, or on-screen, humor of all kinds—high, low, witty or witless, satire, parody, lampoon, pastiche, slapstick, pure schtick, sitcom, ethnic, beatnik, precious or presidential—has been inflicted on the American people with a frequency unmatched in its history. Not that the American people have had any great objection. From its earliest days, this period's dominant form—television—has favored comedians and comic actors; in all visual media, in fact, humor's only serious competitor as a form of entertainment has been violent death.

This is not to suggest that at some unspecified point after the Second World War, America suddenly discovered humor. Both radio and movies made extensive use of comedy—indeed, the earliest practitioners of motion pictures, like those of television, were almost exclusively comedians. And they in turn were preceded by a comic tradition that, if not quite as secure in its attitudes toward authority and institution as its older European equivalents, was at all times alive and well. Nevertheless, in frequency, variety, and intensity, the impact of humor over the last three decades has been extraordinary and the effect of this bombardment immense. Clowns are no longer the lowest of the low in the class structure of performance. On the contrary, what they specialize in is regarded as eminently desirable in fields far removed from mere entertainment. Not to put too fine a point on it, getting laughs can get you elected. To have reached that stage is historically unique, and the means by which we have arrived at it is a vast cultural phenomenon.

Within this phenomenon, however, another smaller and more precise one has had a disproportionate effect on the whole. This is the rise of a humor peculiar to the postwar or Baby Boom generation, a generation everyone purports to be able to describe but whose provenance is as confused as its goals. It includes people conceived during the war out of panic, those conceived after it out of relief, and those conceived for the next few years because no one had invented the Pill yet. The humor of this vast group—which we shall call *Boomer humor*—has been at various times described as "black," "radical," "underground," "tasteless," "sophomoric," "gross," "Communist," "anarchist," and a host of other contradictory labels, but the one label that still sticks, as it did when it first appeared in the mid-fifties, is "sick." "Sick" was a term invented to denigrate the earliest manifestations of Boomer humor by those it denigrated. It was subsequently adopted by the Boomer humorists themselves, partly to make those they denigrated madder still, and partly because it expressed the ambiguity and ambivalence that is at its heart. Thus the term could be (and still is) one of both opprobrium and approbation, as in: "That is (you are) really sick."

Boomer humor never has been, in any understandable sense, sick. (Certainly not as much so as the routine depiction of violent death.) What the original coiners meant by the term back in the fifties—a decade intrigued by calibrating and improving mental health—was that such humor could only be the product of a sick mind. Only a lunatic would want to rock a boat so firmly on course; only a madman would want to smash the windows of such an august century-old edifice; only a disturbed child would want to break into a country club exclusively reserved for grown-ups with Big Things on their minds.

Always assuming that the boat *was* firmly on course and that it *was* a boat, that the edifice *was* a century old and those *were* windows, and that the grown-ups in the country club really *did* have Big Things on their minds.

If, on the other hand, it turned out that the boat was a cardboard box in the desert, that the edifice was a hastily erected movie flat and that the grown-ups were actually just as obsessed as the next person about whether their penises were too short, or their breasts too big, or whether anyone really liked them (not that these are not Big Things, they're just not the official Big Things), then the rocking, stone throwing, and breaking and entering, far from being sick, would be healthy for all concerned.

It was the informing quality of Boomer humor that it indulged, quietly or noisily, directly or obliquely, in such violent escapades. From a historical point of view, Boomer humor dealt for the first time with subjects that had hitherto been completely off-limits in popular comedy. Furthermore, it dealt with them aggressively, challenging rather than confirming attitudes and assumptions. Thus, for example, where the previous generation had made jokes at the expense of blacks, now it was white prejudice that became the butt (in every sense of the word). The cozy ethnicity of the great radio comedians, important in its own way and in its own day, was replaced by self-questioning about the same ethnicity and its social and religious roots. The "traditional" values that family comedy had always affirmed became themselves the object of satire. Stereotypes were no longer familiar cartoons but disturbing caricatures. Titillation was not the object of this comedy—but rather the sexual attitudes that made titillation necessary.

Needless to say, those in society who had appointed themselves to oversee such subjects did not take kindly to this intrusion of their airspace. A category of performers whose social status had up to this point been roughly equivalent to that of professional masseurs had suddenly abandoned their traditional function of kneading the public into a pleasant torpor. Instead, they were doing quite the opposite—disturbing people, making them sit up abruptly when they should be lying down, and what's more doing it in ways that were at least as interesting as those of the self-appointees, and far more fun. These people were pirating their public, trespassing on their territory; these people were Going Too Far.

Tommy Smothers was once told during the period immediately following the cancellation of the highly successful and controversial "Smothers Brothers Hour" that he was "incompetent to make social comment." The person who made the remark was the owner of a television station in the Midwest. Regardless of the merits of the Smothers' opinions, which in this context had mostly to do with the war in Vietnam, what this arrogant nobody was saying was that merely by the expense of capital he had become competent to judge a matter of life and death to the public, but Smothers, who had proved on innumerable occasions that the public was only too delighted to hear what he had to say, was not. Clowns do not comment on wars; clowns make you laugh. Clowns who did comment on wars were stepping out of their floppy shoes and baggy pants, were becoming indistinguishable from station owners, were Going Too Far.

What's important to stress here is that the comments in question were not preachments stuck inappropriately in the middle of a routine. On the contrary, one of the continuing elements in the Smothers' television success was the ability to deal hilariously with public affairs, in particular President Johnson's conduct of the war. In these terms, Smothers proved his competence every time he got a laugh. No other performer except the politician is as sensitive to public reaction as the satirist. He needs no poll to tell him whether he has correctly expressed what his audience thinks and feels about a given issue. If he chooses to comment on such an issue, then he had better get it right, for he is solely responsible for its content, and there is no rejection as devastating as dead silence.

Boomer humor has had to contend throughout its history with station owners, night club owners, theater owners, record company owners, publishing house owners, and studio owners and the owners of those owners. In many ways, the history of Boomer humor has been simply one of struggling to be heard. And once heard, to be accorded the respect that any art should enjoy. However difficult and dangerous it is to create and perform comedy, and however rare real comedic talent may be, people always seem to have trouble thinking of comedy as an art. It's as if the ironic trivialization that lies at its core is in some way infectious or must be turned back by the audience on its creators. The distinction made by old-time vaudeville bookers between the "comedian" and the "artists" (meaning every other kind of performer) persists, no matter how profound the scope of his piece, or how brilliant its execution, or how far removed it is from two guys hitting each other with umbrellas. It's impossible not to notice how often Boomer humor, usually when it's at its most daring and innovative, has had to contend with such judgements as "childish," "immature," "adolescent," and above all, "sophomoric" (a word Michael O'Donoghue, one of its more daring and innovative practitioners, once defined as "liberal for 'funny' ").

Now Boomer humor isn't all ground-breaking stuff, nor thank God is it all powerful satire* on weighty political themes. Many humorists of the Baby Boom generation are excellent comedians and comediennes of a traditional bent, groups and individuals span every category of comedy and every conceivable subject, and the generation's humor is no less derivative, imitative, or just plain felonious than that of any other age. The operative principle is "Whatever works," rather than "Whatever changes the world."

Politics in the strict definition is a relatively rare preoccupation among Boomer humorists; indeed, many of its boldest exponents stress that their work is apolitical or nonpolitical. And yet just as disobeying a stop sign may be a political act, so too is mentioning the hitherto unmentionable in public, whether it's farts, freedom, or funeral parlors. Boomer humor was born in the era of kindly old Senator McCarthy, whose foam-flecked crusade had as much to do with the anti-intellectualism (and of course Mrs. McCarthy's inadequate toilet training) as it did with any grasp of an alternative view of

* Wherever possible, terms describing different modes of comedy will be used precisely throughout this book. Thus words such as "satire" and "parody," often used interchangeably by those who should know better, will only be employed where they are accurate descriptions of the form and/or intent of a humorist. Satire, for example, is defined as intellectual judo, in which the writer or performer takes on the ideas and character of his target and then takes both to absurd lengths to destroy them. This is the most mischievous of all forms of humor, the most radical use of irony. (It is also the most easily misunderstood, since taking on the character of one's target—a bigot, say—can lead the uninitiated into thinking that you actually share the target's ideas. Saying the word "nigger" in character can get bricks thrown on your head—and not by bigots.) Satire is not a gentle process, and the more sacred the belief or person whose mantle it assumes, the more effective it is.

Parody is a far gentler version of the same process, by which the target's style is assumed and slightly exaggerated. The intention here is of paramount importance, since it is usually playful, mocking rather than destructive, and relying as much on recognition alone, as recognition and disapproval. Parody is central to Boomer humor, and not just in verbal form. TV has tremendously widened the scope of what was once a largely literary game—gesture, inflection, facial tics, everything that makes up on-camera behavior are all part of parodiable style. Parody, in this sense, comes perilously close to those dread badlands of modern thought—semiotics.

It is acknowledged that a parody can sometimes have satirical force, as indeed can a lampoon (which is not a parody, containing usually a far greater element of direct ridicule).

Despite this footnote, a glossary of useful terms will *not* be found at the back of this book, nor will the Oxford English Dictionary—which has never had to appear in a nightclub full of drunks—be regarded as the final court of appeal.

the Industrial Revolution. Boomer humor was thus from its birth political by the mere fact of being intelligent. When it wasn't intelligent, it was still informed, and when it was neither of those, you could at least still say that it was well-educated.

Well, overeducated.

But the most important sense in which Boomer humor has always been political is that from its inception it was Not the Official Version. Until relatively recently, it was humor that defined itself against the Official Version, whether the Official Version dealt with an international crisis or the way teenagers were supposed to date, or what God looked like, or indeed what comedy looked like. It was a humor of the street, of the stage, of the underground, of the page; a live humor, not a taped one; an unpredictable, often improvised affair fraught with danger for all concerned.

Boomer humor has both mirrored and helped to express the tremendous movement of dissent that characterized so much creative activity in America since the end of World War II. Contrary to the thinking of the current orthodoxy, this movement has rarely been "liberal" in any accepted sense, being far too probing and artistically explosive for so featherweight a term. Nowhere has this been truer than in its satire. (It's hard, for example, to see how *Catch-22* could be described as "liberal".) Boomer humor has always had a tendency to disparage liberals, partly because they seem to take a masochistic pleasure in being trashed, partly because a liberal satirist is a contradiction in terms—an orange with an apple core. Satire is inherently unfair, and although it may be unfair to any form of authority, or any form of hypocrisy, there is no such thing as an even-handed joke. Satirizing a military cretin or corporate banditry doesn't make you a liberal any more than satirizing some self-important wishy-washy makes you a neofascist. Of course, it is perfectly possible for an ideology to get laughs at the expense of an opponent—but that is ridicule, a potent weapon of humor, but not satire. Satire functions on the gap between reality and fantasy; its dynamic is to reduce pretension and presumption to the tangible and recognizable. A satirist who espouses one ideology over another is saying in effect that he is superior—and that makes him satirizable. The satirist believes only that there is no such thing as being half-pregnant or half-nuked. From the point of view of authority, satire is thus the most inimical form of free speech there is. (Indeed, satire dramatizes better than any other use of it, the inherent contradiction of free speech—that it functions best when what is being said is at its most outrageous.)

All this, however, is as true of Aristophanes as it is of Lenny Bruce. What caused the particular outpouring of satire and other forms of irreverent comedy that occurred from the mid-fifties until the early eighties? (It should be pointed out here that satire is reactive art—it needs goading, a prior cause, be it aberration, repression, or pretension. Explanations of dissent as the end product of over-lenient authority just won't do. The satirist doesn't ply his trade because he's privileged, or got taught the wrong things, or because his folks were just too darn permissive. Swift didn't write *A Modest Proposal* because he was a spoiled brat.)

The Great Deal

From a strictly pragmatic point of view, the postwar years hardly seemed an ideal breeding ground for dissent. World War II was a triumph. In Europe, at least, the fantastic human cost had been borne by the Allies, overwhelmingly by the Russians, leaving the United States relatively unscathed and economically dominant. America was quite literally on top of the world.

Capitalism had finally adapted to democracy, and hand in hand they defeated fascism, a horror unthinkable before the twentieth century, which combined high technology with black magic, supersophisticated media with the darkest filth of demagoguery; a system that asserted that the consent of the governed could reside in one man.

The distinction between capitalism and democracy is important historically. (This distinction is one modern Americans are apt not to make—with some reason.) Nonetheless, capitalism—whatever its opponents say—is not a form of government and democracy—however much it costs—is not an economic system. As we shall see, the distinction will help explain the society that nurtured our ingrates and therefore shaped their humor.

The distinction between capitalism and democracy was extremely clear at the beginning of World War II to large numbers of Europeans and a substantial number of Americans. Indeed, the war was fought to preserve those political systems that allowed at least an ostensible exchange of power between the people and the government (systems which deferred from ally to ally, ranging from American-style democracy to Soviet-style socialism) rather than permanently concentrating all power and force in the hands of one man or group—something traditionally associated with capitalism.

Capitalism at the beginning of the war was in bad shape. A mere decade before, it had Gone Too Far, blowing itself up in an accident (the Great Depression) that not only almost killed it but injured innumerable innocent bystanders. Its future was far from assured.

Even in its native land, England, and its adopted one, America, capitalism was regarded with considerable caution—even suspicion. It didn't help its image much by approaching the European dictators with distinct ambivalence. A great deal of the pressure for appeasement of Hitler came from international capital, which didn't really care how socialism was stopped—just so long as it was stopped. When Hitler, like all "strong men," turned out to be a lunatic, this was conveniently forgotten.

Ironically, it was the war against the very champions it had groomed that rehabilitated capitalism. World War II was the most industrial war in history. It was a war in which huge machines in huge numbers, requiring staggering amounts of support—oil, coal, food, clothing, metals, chemicals, and explosives—lumbered around the globe, blowing one another to bits. Instant replacement could only be managed by round-the-clock operation of belching furnaces, bustling factories, dust-filled mines, humming plants, racketing shipyards. Fortunes were made supplying one type of bandage to one branch of the services, one type of rivet for one type of aircraft, one form of packaging for one kind of dried food. The frenzy of activity included those left at home. The business of everyday purchase became a vicarious patriotic effort, in which merely by making Jell-O you associated yourself with the brave boys who consumed it as power food before they flew off to smash fascism. Open any magazine from 1942 to 1945 at any page and you will be swept up in a swirl of victory through purchase—the button-popping message: *Every dollar spent is more profit in the coffers of freedom.*

And, of course, it worked. People bought the Jell-O, the gadgets, and the gum, still more furnaces belched and factories bustled and plants hummed and yards racketed, and the result was victory. World War II galvanized American industry from the top down and the bottom up. It was by far the largest—and perhaps the last—smokestack war in history.

Capitalism, which had gone into the war under a cloud of suspicion, emerged at the other end a hero. Not only had it left in place a vastly increased producing capacity, but it had created an economic model that seemed to assure perpetual prosperity: *Spending wealth creates more wealth.* Of course the idea that consumption rather than thrift led to prosperity was not a new one—it was a basic Keynesian principle espoused by FDR—but victory dramatized it as the New Deal had never been able to. It also helped overcome a deep-seated prejudice against consumption left over from immigrant assumptions that wealth meant saving and avoiding debt.

This psychological shift was crucial, since the principle would only work if a substantial majority believed it. And they did. The notion that spending was good for the country at wartime, very easily led to the notion that spending was good for the country at any time. And not just on basics like food, shelter, and clothing, but on anything, large or small, luxury or superluxury.

It worked yet again. Fueled first by the GI Bill and associated postwar aid programs, and then by ever-increasing private debt, America began to develop into a consumer society of unimaginable prosperity. The glimmerings of suburban paradise which had appeared spottily in the twenties now became reality in most major urban areas. Jobs soared, goods and manufacturing soared, owership of single-family homes and family automobiles soared. Cheap oil and the interstate highway system (started in 1956) ensured the triumph of the automobile—by far the most expensive form of mass transportation ever devised, but therefore, of course, the best yet for the economy. This created, in turn, a commuter work force and, in turn, a massive real estate and construction boom. Practically anything that could be manufactured was manufactured, and anything that was manufactured was bought somewhere by someone, whether they needed it or not. What that ensured was a vast new expansion of the advertising and packaging industries in order to induce the consumer to make the right choice between an ever-proliferating number of products. Finally, higher education came to be within the reach of the middle and working classes, not only guaranteeing that the last vestiges of those class distinctions would disappear in a future generation, but also that Baby Boomers stayed in school and unmarried far longer than in previous ones.

For its part, capitalism became wealthier than it had ever been when it held its capital in very few hands. The economic activity made it prosper as it never had before. It had learned the lessons of the first half of the century well. The answer was democratization.

Rather than battling to maintain a system that ensured staggering personal wealth to a tiny group of entrepreneurs, capitalism cut the rest of society in on the action. Making credit universally available meant spreading the risk inherent in speculation, especially when new technologies (e.g., labor-saving electronics) or social experiments (e.g., surburban developments) meant colossal investment. Everybody became in effect an entrepreneur, with a scaled-down version of the risk and a scaled-down version of the rewards. The "Us" versus "Them" dynamic of the Depression era—in which social revolution, or at least upheaval, was a very real possibility—was defused. For capitalism, this sharing meant no real loss of power or wealth. It simply meant that these passed from individuals into the hands of the huge apparati needed to manage and maintain and police the new order—the corporations. And the fifties and sixties were preeminently the era of the corporation.

None of this is supposed to imply that there weren't still entrepreneurs, or the killings weren't still made on the stock market or that widows and orphans weren't from time to time foreclosed by mustachioed bankers. Nor that there had never been large corporations or that the concept of personal debt had not previously been used to fuel the economy. All these were and are inherent in capitalism.

But the universality of the process in the America after the war was peculiar to the period and was its most profound social innovation.

This was the world to which the Baby Boomers were born, the world that shaped them and their culture—and their humor. Indeed, despite inevitable challenges, upheavals, and setbacks, it remains the world in which they have grown to maturity. (From a socioeconomic point of view, the Reaganite assertion that the past three decades have been dominated by the welfare state is a flat lie, made either out of ignorance of what living in a welfare state is like or for some more sinister purpose.) By any objective standard, international or historical, it has been capitalism—aggressive, imaginative, adaptive, diversified, and unprecedentedly egalitarian—that has been the prevailing orthodoxy of those years. If their parents grew up with the New Deal, the Baby Boomers grew up with the Great Deal.

But like all Great Deals there were some catches. A lot of little ones and one Big One.

The Big Catch

Once you had moved to your single-family house in a new suburban tract, what happened to the community you left behind in the city, a community that in many cases was a microcosm of the country your parents or grandparents had come from? (For that matter, what happened to your parents?) What did you say to your neighbor—who might easily have come from an utterly different community, hundreds or even thousands of miles away? Now that you lived on relative isolation in your dream house, with neighbors not of your choosing and only your family to talk to, what did you say to your wife, or your husband, or your kids, or parents? What were proper kinds of behavior in this new ad hoc community, the limits of pretension, the rules of social intercourse?

Who decreed what was normal or abnormal? Permitted or Going Too Far? How did you feel about your job now that you worked in a corporation dealing with paper and the spoken or written word, rather than like your father and grandfather, with tangible hard-edged products? Now that you spent a third of your waking day in a car, what did you think about? Now that rent, with all its carefully prescribed rights, was replaced by a monthly mortgage payment with its equally clear obligations, just how secure were you? How did long-term debt affect your mind and soul—and sleep? How did you measure self-worth and professional advancement? Was that a promotion or a kiss-off? In so vast and anonymous a group, who could tell if you were winning? Was it not more likely that you were a loser? For in so big a race there could only be one winner—and many losers.

Now that you had labor-saving devices, what did you do with the resulting leisure time? How did you feel about owning things that were identical to the things other people owned? (For in a consumer economy, singularity is not profitable, but uniformity is.) How did you distinguish yourself? How much or how little did you believe what the new persuaders told you about their products? Without your parents, or their community, how would you know who to believe?

Now that your kids spent so little time at home, and so much in the hands of people you barely knew, how could you be sure that what they were learning was not some hideous corruption of what you had been taught? Now that they stayed in school far longer than you or your parents had, what became of those terrible sexual desires of your own youth? How could they be controlled? Should they be?

And if you were one of those kids, how could you avoid seeing how confused your parents really were? How preoccupied with trying to find their footing, their relationship to one another, and you, and all the things they owned? Why, at the time you most craved stability and routine, were things always changing? The house, the car, the gadgets? And why, even though they were always changing, did they always look more or less the same? Why were there so many "hallowed" traditions about behavior, dress, customs, and authority in places you knew had only been built last year? And what did you do with the lump in your pants or the lumps in your sweater? Why were they so wrong when they felt so good? If they were wrong, why did God stick them on you?

And last but far from least: What about those black people who were always on TV or downtown? Who seemed to have nothing, yet lived exotic lives you were forbidden to know about? Why were they only allowed in your homes as silent menials, or on wild, thrilling, crooning, wailing, thumping, lump-exciting records?

Boomer humor has, for all its young life, addressed—obliquely or directly —such contradictions. For contradiction—the gap between promise and reality, between expectation and what you actually get when you open the box, between the cherished belief and behavior of the believer, is the breeder reactor of humor. And the period in which Boomers grew up had breeder reactors up the wazoo.

Alienation, conformity, repression, anonymity, and noncommunication are recurrent themes of Boomer humor, the themes of a middle class that at least knows where its next meal is coming from. This isn't the whimsy of a leisured class, or the cozy reaffirmation of ethnic humor, nor for the most part is it the humor of an underclass. And if all this sounds terribly earnest, it must be added that the saving grace of Boomer humor is above all else a self-deprecation, an awareness of itself, sometimes bordering on self-destruction, that doesn't take its essential seriousness too seriously. But even that is part of the questioning, part of the same satirical process. One's own assumptions are held up to ridicule as part of the establishment the satire seeks to challenge.

Where classical satire expresses revulsion at the departure from widely held standards, Boomer humor seems to operate in the other direction, rejecting standards, searching for new ones, experimenting with limits, pushing taste, and—more often than not—Going Too Far. Even when it deals with perennial subjects of humor—sex say, or, family tensions—it does so in a special multilevel way. As portrayed by Boomer humorists, sex is as often as not the lack of it, and the lack of it within a rigidly regimented and bafflingly moralistic world; satire of family tensions deals as much with the gap between an ideal of family and the reality as it does with traditional conflicts between father and mother, daughter and son. It could be said that the history of the Baby Boom generation has been one of seeking stability out of chaos, the chaos that was the underbelly of postwar prosperity, and which was made even more confusing by having all the hallmarks of stability but none of the substance.

It is what gives Lenny Bruce and the other New Comedians, Second City and its companion improvisers, the free-form stand-ups of the midsixties (George Carlin, Lily Tomlin, Woody Allen, et al.), *The National Lampoon* and its underground predecessors, and "Saturday Night Live," their special edge, their characteristic quality of dealing with more than they're willing to

admit, however trivial the primary subject matter may be. In this context—
the context of resistance and dissent, however unpolitical in a formal sense—
practically everything Boomer humor does and expresses has political force.
Stop signs are being disobeyed at all times and at every conceivable speed.

What the preceding observations don't quite explain, however, is the tone
of Boomer humor, its occasional fury and its frequent rankness. Boomer
humor has always copped a great deal of attitude. The special social confusion from which it sprang might explain its edginess, but not its edge. There is
nothing confused about the tone of Boomer humor. It doesn't know the
meaning of the phrase "all in good fun." It's out to get someone. And that
doesn't match its origins. That can only come from another source, the dop-
pelgänger of capitalist utopia, the Big Catch.

The Big Catch, of course, is the Bomb—but not *just* the Bomb; it is that
along with capitalist utopia must go a massive peacetime military. The Big
Catch is part of the landscape for the Baby Boomers, something we have
grown so accustomed to in everyday life (and annual budgets) that it never
occurs to us to question the equation. Actually, there is no reason why capitalist utopia must also involve a vast military machine; indeed, the only system of thought that insists there is an inherent and inevitable connection is
Marxism.

The military machine which has been in place since World War II and
which has grown to such mind-numbing proportions since is quite without
precedent in American history. During the twenties and thirties, at a time
when a neighbor with whom we share a virtually indefensible border, Mexico,
was the scene of a violent upheaval, and when America itself came as close as
it ever has to parallel upheaval, the size of the military was a mere fraction of
what it has been since 1945, a period of far greater domestic and proximate
tranquility. Yet Baby Boomers have been expected to accept, approve, and
respect this self-perpetuating behemoth without question, and in every sense
—moral, physical, financial, and occasionally with their lives—to pay for it.

This, of course, would be fine if the military did what it said it did. Actually, its war record since 1945 hasn't been that bad—Drawn 1, Lost 1, better
than, say, Argentina's—and its commercials have been uniformly inspiring.
A few rumbles in the Caribbean have come off quite well—usually against
heavily armed chicken farmers, or more recently in Grenada, seven hundred
Cubans with shovels—not bad value for a forty-year total outlay (in 1987
terms) of roughly seven thousand billion dollars. Aside from these triumphs,
the military has time and again had to duck involvement on behalf of U.S.
interests (Hungary, the Congo, Angola) because it is simply too big, slow, and
clumsy. Since U.S. foreign policy is dominated by military priorities over
corporate or mercantile ones, this is a formula for almost continuous embarrassment.

Nowhere was the obsolescence of the greatest fighting force on the planet
more clearly dramatized than in Vietnam. Bombing Vietnam back to the
Stone Age was impossible, since this would destroy our allies and our own

forces, as well as the enemy. So much for deterrence. The fabulous new gunships—however sexy the word "gunship" and however many thousand rounds they might fire a minute—were nothing but a liability in populated areas where the support of civilians was more important than the death of a few guerrillas. Tanks and heavy artillery found themselves defeating not the enemy but water buffalo and next spring's rice. The stars of the show, B-52s, were largely ineffective, thanks to the wily North Vietnamese ultramodern high-tech defense of digging tunnels in the earth. This war could not be fought on radar screens with ultrasonic jets; it was a political war, a civil war fought not on battlegrounds but in people's minds. With dread and terror certainly, unjust and brutish, but psychologically far more powerful than the most powerful piece of industrial or technological matériel. These vast machines may shove over a few houses, crush a few crops, but they come and go like the dollars that accompany them. Your neighbor, on the other hand, may have the power of life and death over you and your loved ones within a week, and forever.

The course of military strategy in our times is not within the scope of this book. But since we are dealing with contradictions and the U.S. military is a welter of contradictions, how our protectors have arrived at this state of muscle-bound impotence is not completely outside our sphere of interest. Especially since the means by which they maintain it involves—as it has all our lives—massive psychological manipulation, entrenched official subterfuge, institutionalized corruption in the name of national honor, and a system of lunatic paradoxes. All these radical assaults on an open society have by now achieved the status of "hallowed traditions." And perhaps this is not surprising, for they date all the way back to the end of World War II.

The huge network of connections that had sprung up between the military and industry during the war had brought unparalleled profits to certain corporations (e.g., the Hughes corporation). It also had created millions of new jobs and brought prosperity to many areas of the country, particularly California, and more particularly Southern California. Victory, of course, would bring an end to this terrific arrangement.

Keeping the Spruce Goose laying golden eggs wasn't going to be easy, however, with Hitler and Tojo down the chute. What was needed to keep war profits rolling in was a new war—or at least a new enemy. Happily for all concerned, there was Stalin, whose fine mix of dementia and rabies had inflicted at least as much damage on his own people as Hitler had on his.

There was work to be done, however. Just a few weeks earlier, Stalin had been an ally, sitting next to FDR at Yalta—and with good reason. The incredible sacrifice to which he had—mysteriously—inspired his people had done as much as any other ally, if not considerably more, to smash the Wehrmacht. Partly for that reason, Stalin was not acting like a really hot property, enemywise. Twenty million Russians had perished resisting Hitler (the figure accepted by the West; the U.S.S.R. claims it was nearer 24 million). Practically every family in Russia had lost a father or son, a daughter or mother. The percentile of the work force lost was naturally far higher. Not that there was much for the work force left to work in—the Nazi invasion and Stalin's scorched-earth response had between them destroyed a tremendous amount of the Soviet's brand-new, fragile, and not very extensive industrial base. In short, this bear was exhausted. For a blood-crazed killer of the wild, he was spending far too much time sitting in the corner of his cage, licking his wounds.

Furthermore, the chances of Stalin actually attacking the United States were zip. Stalin had occupied previously Nazi territories in Eastern Europe (Hungary, Poland, Czechoslovakia, and so on,) with false guarantees of self-determination and was getting ready to subvert his former allies' colonies in Africa and Asia, but the United States just didn't seem very high on his hit list. Something had to be done.

On August 6, 1945, something was done. The United States became the first and, as of this writing, the only nation in history to use a nuclear device on human beings. Of course, these weren't really human beings at the time (and they certainly weren't a couple of seconds later); they were dirty Japs who stuck safety pins in the nipples of Red Cross nurses and who therefore deserved everything they got. Feisty President Truman—who later said he never lost a night's sleep over this decision—declared that thousands of American lives had been saved that would have been lost on the Japanese beaches. The Emperor surrendered, the war was over, and everyone went down to Times Square.

There is an alternative view to the official excuses given by Truman, however: the Japanese—completely drained of time, money, and energy, far from being able to defend their nation in street-to-street fighting—were on the point of surrender. (There is evidence that the Emperor had already made overtures of surrender before the first nuclear device was detonated.) The Tokyo firebombing in March 1945, numerically just as devastating as the A-bomb attacks, had sent a perfectly adequate message to the Japanese of what Uncle Sam had in mind; therefore the detonation of "Little Boy" and "Fat Man" (the cutesy names given to the two bombs by their "parents") had some ulterior motive. That motive was to draw the battle line in an as yet undeclared war between democracy and the Red Menace, particularly in its fur-hatted and slanty-eyed versions. The Bomb wasn't dropped on the Japanese to teach them a lesson. It was dropped on the Japanese to teach the Russians a lesson.

For the next four years, despite horrific accounts of what "Little Boy" and "Fat Man" had done to Hiroshima and Nagasaki, respectively, the U.S. military pressed ahead, developing higher and higher yields. The Russians, of course, had no nuclear capability during this period. Furthermore, the United States had spirited away some rather brainy Nazis in the general celebrations of victory, chief among them a kid named Werner von Braun,† who had made his name by randomly slaughtering British civilians in the last days of the Reich. This casually sloughed-off piece of opportunism was evil of a depth even Stalin didn't stoop to.

Not for the time being. He learned his lesson well. In 1949, the plans for that special American baby, the atom bomb, turned up on his doorstep, thanks in turn to another Nazi lowlife named Klaus Fuchs.

These events are worth recounting for two reasons: 1) because the fact that the U.S. military and its civilian allies initiated the early years of the Cold War has been conveniently forgotten in the panic and terror of escalation; 2) because at the time and ever since the wisdom of strapping ourselves, so to speak, to a nuclear weapon and daring the other side to blow us up is not clear. The two geniuses of the Manhattan Project, Robert Oppenheimer and Edward Teller, went through a fierce personal and public battle in the late forties over the development of nuclear weapons. The issues the two men raised have never changed. As it was, Oppenheimer, the scientist who called for sanity and restraint, was beaten and thereafter reviled as a coward and a pinko. The ghastly Dr. Teller is with us still, the living corollary of the truth that the good die young, still subverting democracy to his own inconceivably crazy ends, a Frankenstein whose monster outstrips every boundary of imagination, (including most recently the X ray laser, heart and soul of Star Wars,) and most relevantly for our purposes, the model of that classic of Boomer humor, *Dr. Strangelove*.

Once Stalin had the Bomb, the self-fulfilling pattern of U.S. foreign/military policy was established. The U.S.S.R., able now to respond in kind to the U.S. "threat," did so, claiming defensive needs. Claiming that this was *offensive* and thus required heavier defense, we went farther than they did, then we did, then they did, then we did, and so on in a nice tidy package of deadly absurdity.

This absurdity rounds out the world to which Boomer humor was born. The effects on us, in terms of simple anxiety, have been incalculable. The effect on our belief in authority and our potential for skepticism is similarly incalculable, since we have only ever had "Their" word for it that this vast, tottering, inverted pyramid of terror would not tip over. We had no experience to judge whether "They" were telling the truth (any more than "They" did)—only a radical choice between assuming "They" were lying, or blind faith. Finally, this war would be like no other in history—certainly not the one our fathers had fought in and won. This war would be the ultimate existential joke—to win it, everyone had to die.

Boomers have thus grown up with some fairly hilarious contradictions about the institution that claims to protect their homeland and its cherished ideals and freedoms. Now the military of every nation has been the butt of

---

† Hollywood, handmaiden of national security, made a movie of this thug's life called *I Aim for the Stars*. Mort Sahl amended the title with the words: ". . . But Sometimes I Hit London."

humorists throughout history, for it takes a certain kind of animal to end another man's existence, and expect only food, drink, and lavish praise in return. But the U.S. military has surprisingly rarely—even during Vietnam—been portrayed satirically by Boomer humorists. When it has, the portrayals have been classics—*Catch-22,* for example—but more often than not, the sheer vastness of its duplicity and above all the vastness of its threat of extinction always hovering over every individual has been too much to grasp. Instead, the frustration has manifested itself in a tone of voice, or urgency (must get this joke out before the Bomb drops), an edginess, a tortured impatience that is the sound of Boomer humor. You might say that just having the military around has made us hostile.

But there are many other indirect results of forty years of militarily induced tension and all of them are the stuff of Boomer humor. Our language bristles with militarese—some of it so deeply embedded that we no longer recognize it as such. People "set their sights," "occupy the high ground," "take the offensive," "regroup," "provide themselves with ammunition," "shoot down arguments," and praise associates for being "good soldiers." This is probably the first society in history in which the word "aggressive" is a compliment. People have a soft spot not just for a uniform but for regimentation. Especially in commerce military qualities are highly prized. There are few greater accolades for an executive than that he is "an ex-Marine." This is odd. Being trained to obey orders without question and if necessary kill or be killed in the process hardly seems consistent with the qualities traditionally considered necessary for commerce—qualities such as initiative, flexibility, survival, and salesmanship. "Make a deal or I'll kill you" has never been a great way to do business. And such attitudes evidence the threat posed by regimentation to democracy—and to the individualism that's supposed to be its glue. Democracy is the one system no good soldier can ever comprehend.

This is not to lay all social evil at the feet of the military. They are neither demigods nor evil monsters but ordinary Americans. But these ordinary Americans have been allowed to acquire incredible power over the rest of society. And of course this power has been granted to them by other ordinary Americans, which is to say Congress. On the issue of the military and its weaponry, not to mention its budget, the bipartisan system is impregnable. If there's one thing Democrats and Republicans can agree on, it's extinction.

Forty years of no recourse on the issue of the military has thus bred in Boomers something that goes way beyond the healthy skepticism any democrat should feel towards his government. We have grown up with a sense of impotence, that on the one issue unique to our generation we could do and say nothing. Nor is it just the Bomb. We have also watched as time and again our democratic institutions are embarrassed by military or paramilitary or mock-military operations. The U-2 incident, the Bay of Pigs, Watergate, the Iran-Contra debacle, to name just the obvious ones, all have the same component. The cynicism Boomers feel for their public institutions is therefore not only self-perpetuating—for abstaining in a democracy is a pretty good guarantee that you will remain out of power—but is completely at odds with everything we were quite rightly taught about them. It's not surprising if the resulting gap has often been filled with raucous laughter.

And Now . . . the Box

But even if the Big Catch is what is uppermost on your mind, not to worry. Kindly old Father Physics has come up with another miracle to keep your mind off it. The Box.

The Bomb and the Box are symbiotic. The Box narcotizes us to the immanence of the Bomb, and in so doing may even be preparing us for its imminent use.

The Box is more than soma, more than a drug, it's a hallucinogen that becomes reality. It externalizes hallucination, puts it into a tangible machine, a real thing in our real living room. Therefore it must be reality, and what happens inside that magical world, far from being fantasy like the movies, far from being a dream like drugs, takes everything we think and care about and gives it back to us the way we want it to be: fantastic, provocative, intelligent, manly, feminine, informative, sexy, violent, gritty, speculative, scientific, titillating, fluffy, anything we like.

The continuum of TV is its giveaway. There is no dramatic structure to its entertainment, for in the middle of a tragedy you can be moved to a commercial for a hardware store. There is no logic to its sequence, when news contradicts what we are seeing being portrayed in a drama, where religion can be back to back with sex, or a flip of the remote away. This is the mind made external, the streams of consciousness (the continuum of each channel) and the levels of consciousness (the channels themselves) reflecting back at us our own preoccupations.

TV is a pictoral version of a reverie—like seeing in flesh and blood what you think about while you're driving. Indeed, if what's on TV is something that doesn't fit with your thinking, or triggers unpleasant associations, or refers to a grid outside our experience, we reject it instantly. If many others agree, it will be removed forthwith from the continuum. TV is almost entirely reflexive. It can only present what has already been considered, and to a large degree, already accepted. If everything on television was new information presented in unusual ways, we would never watch it. Thus even news must fit into what we can tolerate. There is almost no possibility, except when the medium gets out of control of its managers, that we can be shocked or repelled by what we see. This happens less than it used to, as news managers have become more adept at presenting one-time experiences. Compare coverage of the assassination of JFK with that of the shuttle explosion, for example. For the most part, the news is as repetitive as a sitcom, a familiar cast of characters, all of them basically good guys or basically bad guys and in familiar locations, dealing with familiar issues, on which we usually already know where we stand.

How can we not be hypnotized by these miraculous hallucinations? This machine gives back to us the one thing we know to be the most important thing in the universe—us. Surely what it's giving us must therefore be reality. Those are real faces on the box, real voices, real people, places. And isn't that real . . . laughter? They are not illusions exactly, for they match what is already on our minds. There is no need to suspend disbelief, just simply believe. Henry Kissinger and Krystle Carrington exist in the same world.

■   ■

It was in the narrow strip of ground between the reality of the Bomb and the reality of the Box that Boomer humor first began to sprout. From the beginning the humor was live in at least two senses. Rejecting both the terrifying impersonality of the Bomb and the hallucinatory self-absorption of the Box, it quite literally went out, collared the nearest human by the lapel, and started talking. Nightclubs and small theaters were the loci of the first appearances of Boomer humor.

Secondly, it rejected the patter and sketches of the previous generation of comedians, material which for some performers had lasted them, unchanged, for a lifetime, and instead started improvising, alone or in groups, a new kind of material that was never the same two nights in a row. This was live on a level unheard of even in the theater—if you weren't there that night, that was it. It was also dangerous for performer and audience, for both could be embarrassed if the comedian blew a real sour note, but the danger gave the whole affair an added thrill when it worked.

Boomer humor's other turf, print, while it could hardly support improvisation, was similarly transformed. Free-form styles mirrored the riffs of the live performers, and a new shaggy blitzed-out kind of character entered from stage left in novels such as *The Ginger Man, Stern, Catch-22,* and *Lolita.* And not surprisingly, along with both came a distinct lurch toward the demotic.

All this coming from people with—as we have seen—a lot on their minds was not something designed to fit nearly in any corner of the Box. Nevertheless, Boomer humorists, then as now, had a highly ambivalent attitude toward television. (Throughout the three decades of its existence, in fact, Boomer humor has kept circling the Box in the same cautious, fascinated, and hungry way a raccoon circles a garbage can.) For its part, too, it should be noted that at the birth of Boomer humor, television was also very young. While CBS and NBC (ABC was just a sparkle in its father's eye) were hardly bongo-thumping nonconformists, there was a natural tendency on the part of Boomer humorists, however cynical they might pretend to be, to see television as another rebel with a cause. TV for its part was still in its adolescence, veering wildly from stimulus to stimulus. Thus it could bring down McCarthy without really meaning to, but almost died every week or so, mainlining massive doses of cuteness. In addition, the fact that it was still live gave it the illusion of running in the same pack as Charlie Parker and Lenny Bruce (when actually it had to be, and always was, home by midnight).

Conventional media progressives now see Boomer humor as ultimately having had a "beneficial" effect on television, forcing it to change its stodgy ways and liberalize its standards, thus creating the wonderful, diversified, and intensely responsive medium we enjoy today. What this analysis assumes is that the underground will always be assimilated into the overground to the mutual benefit of both. The underground finally gets to earn a decent living and the overground gets new blood. Things get better all the time. While this neat construct would seem to be refuted by empirical evidence (if it were true of human life, for example, there ought to be a large number of incredibly old, incredibly perfect people running around the planet), it is pervasive. Many of the humorists interviewed for this book evinced it in describing the course of Boomer humor over the last decade. This is not surprising, considering the optimistic view they doubtless wish to take of their life's work, but unfortunately it does not square with the facts.

The most obvious false assumption in the things-get-better theory is that of an underground and an overground, and the gradually diminishing antagonism between them. Actually, the antagonism between Boomer humor and television has ebbed and flowed throughout its relationship. It is certainly true that for most of its history Boomer humor has had to keep two outfits in the closet—one to wear when it was doing the real thing and another to wear when it went on the Box. This history is thus littered with tales of censorship, "You can't do that on television" is a recurrent cliché of the generation.

It is true, too, that Boomer humor developed its skills in loci traditionally associated with an underground, but generally speaking, this underground regarded the political and judicial establishment—the traditional overground —as its antagonist. Television, for all its faults, for all the controls it endured, was not necessarily part of the establishment. Mort Sahl, Lenny Bruce, Mike Nichols, and Elaine May, for example, all used television with varying degrees of success to expose their work and those who put them on knew quite well what they were doing. As late as the turn of the seventies, even the most radical of Boomer humor's practitioners thought the compromises they would have to make to appear on television worthwhile in the light of the audiences they could reach. They still thought of television as a means of communication—one controlled by antagonistic forces, certainly—but a vehicle for ideas, just as a printing press was, or a bullhorn.

By 1970, though, much had changed for both TV and Boomer humor. Television had done a great deal of thinking about itself—had grown into a very serious young man. One thing it had learned for sure was that whatever else it might be, it wasn't a mere means of communication, an open mike between viewer and viewee. Both dealing with and avoiding dealing with

Vietnam had taught it that it could be a means of controlling communication, even absorbing it, perhaps even making communication unnecessary.‡

For its part, Boomer humor had already surprised itself by how far it was willing to go, and it was preparing in the pages of *The National Lampoon* to go even farther.

The National Lampoon was about to turn on the one last thing that remained sacred to it—its own generation. In doing so, it may have sowed the seeds of its own destruction, but this was being faithful to one of the more admirable traits of Boomer humor, that it was always willing to include itself in the danger, strap the dynamite around its own head, as well as lighting sticks under others. This was no bow-tied geek sneering from the sidelines. If you're Going Too Far at someone else's expense, it's only fair that you Go Too Far yourself. Feet first. In the arm. Off the cliff.

In its *Lampoon* form, Boomer humor went off the cliff in several directions at once. Almost all of them were self-destructive, not the least a gleeful probing of its own past that led (it seems now inevitably,) to nostalgia, and thence to wealth beyond Woodstock's wildest dreams.

At its outset, though, the *Lampoon* had many claims to be the ultimate expression of Boomer humor. The people it brought together were from all different walks of Boomer life—literary, underground, heartland, Brahmin, Canadian, British, gay, and feminist. It defined itself once it found its voice as the ultimate hip. It defined itself against television—presenting an advanced form of Boomer humor that simply wasn't available anywhere else. It was New York rampant on a field of targets. It was post-radical, post-Woodstock, post-rock, post-almost-everything, and yet in the character of its most brilliant and least predictable editor, Doug Kenney, self-deprecating in the finest tradition of the Boomers. Confronted with the above list of post-weightiness, Doug might have added ". . . and post-Toasties."

Transformed, as its collective ambition and background required that it be, to the perennial Boomer preserves of album, stage, and radio, the *Lampoon* scooped up practically every major comedic talent of the seventies. It did so by a ratification processs which paralleled that of the political underground. First *Radio Dinner* (the *Lampoon*'s first album, on which scabrous parodies of Lennon, Baez, and Dylan appeared) convinced the cast of *Lemmings* to come to New York—in particular, a bearded lunatic from Second City named

‡ For an intelligent and cogent discussion of the shortcomings of television as a means of communication, the reader is recommended to a recent book called *Amusing Ourselves to Death"* by Neil Postman. (New York: Viking-Penguin, 1986). Professor Postman's thesis is that far from being a medium of communication, television is a medium of entertainment, which tends to convert into an entertainment *any* material it presents, whether it's trivial or weighty. Television is therefore insidious to precisely the degree that what it purports to communicate is indeed serious and important information (e.g., news and political debate), and not merely because it reduces matters of vital concern to charades or spectacles, but because people have been convinced that their participation in these events is a "learning" process, that they have been "communicated" with, when in fact they have simply been entertained and actually *diverted* from the seriousness of the material. Needless to say, Professor Postman hasn't sold a whole lot of books on television.

John Belushi and a wandering preppy cad named Chevy Chase. The success of *Lemmings* then convinced the balance of Second City's best and brightest that the *Lampoon* and its "Radio Hour" were the place to be.

In the critical years surrounding the humiliation and downfall of Nixon, it was. Boomer humor was doing its best in network television and getting raves for doing it, with "All in the Family," "The Mary Tyler Moore Show," "M*A*S*H," and "Mary Hartman, Mary Hartman." Back East, though, the *Lampoon* was assembling the television cast of the future to do what could never be done on television. Aside from Belushi and Chase, there was Gilda Radner, Bill Murray, Harold Ramis. All of them added to the contributing stalwarts of the *Lampoon:* O'Donoghue, Beatts, Kenney, and Chris Miller. In the background were John Hughes, who would one day—in every sense—outgrow them all, and Ivan Reitman, who would—in every sense—outgross them all.

The *Lampoon* was successful in the first half of the seventies precisely because in every issue it published, it could be relied upon to Go Too Far. It was the apotheosis of Going Too Far. It had plenty to work with. Not only its own solid canon, the Boomer humor staples of suburban values, sex, and chaos, the educational establishment, and the military, but a whole newly fashioned group of butts, those who it had identified in the Woodstock generation, the new hustlers, the new preachers, the new contradictions, the new gaps between promise and delivery, expectation and reality.

And above all, parody. The *Lampoon* at its height used parody as a lingua franca, a shared secret between it and its readers, a vocabulary all its own, with nothing to do with television. *The National Lampoon* insisted—unlike *Mad,* even at its best—that print was its proper means of expression, that the vehicles for its humor were comics, newspapers, magazines, junk mail, tickets, greeting cards, photo albums—anything that could be printed on a piece of paper. In so doing, it always defined itself instinctively against the dominant medium.

Parody, in short, was the *Lampoon*'s nightclub—the turf it called its own, the place where you could be certain that there would be no punches pulled, no words forbidden, no ideas too outrageous.

On or about the Ides of March, 1975, two things happened to Boomer humor. Doug Kenney and Henry Beard, founders of the *Lampoon,* were bought out by management for the astronomical multiple of the magazine's annual earnings. At the same time, producer Lorne Michaels signed a deal with NBC for a dangerous new departure in late-night television called "Saturday Night Live"—a revue whose cast and staff included many of the *Lampoon's* brightest lights.

Most accounts of "Saturday Night Live" proceed from the notion that nothing happens except on TV—that nothing to do with the expression of ideas and attitudes is validated until it reaches vast numbers of people. From the point of cultural history, if we are to assume that Boomer humor's ideas and attitudes have any effect at all on public life, this makes very little sense.

The conservative administration that coincided with SNL's period of greatest success, highest ratings, and highest visibility saw a return to the very ideas against which Boomer humor originally revolted. If Boomer humor was at its most influential in the mid- to late seventies, thanks to SNL, why did America go for Carter, a conservative Christian, and then Reagan? (This is not dissimilar to characterizing the fifties as conformist, corporate, and conservative and then having to explain how Kennedy got elected.)

No, the much more likely observation, and one that fits the facts a little better, is that SNL actually represented the end, the last final flourish of Boomer humor before it died. This is a conclusion unpleasant to accept, and which takes a little more thought to expound, but it is in the end far more persuasive.

Getting Boomer humor on television was an understandable urge in 1975. But getting it on television also involved trading away its most unique characteristic, its fundamental attitudinal message: "We don't agree." It's significant that Lorne Michaels made so much of his generation being the first to grow up on television. The facile next step would be to conclude that all his humor was going to be about television. But that wasn't what he meant, nor was it either the background of either his cast or staff. Although they had grown up with the constant pressure to accept the world presented by television and the vocabulary of television as a perfectly good substitute for the real one, they had, to a tremendous extent, and in common with most Boomers, revolted against the pressure. They trained themselves in live situations; they idealized personal contact over televisual. That's the message of Woodstock, in fact. Real people, live music, actual events, one time only.

That's one of the reasons why Michaels was so insistent, ludicrously so if one pauses to examine it, on the fact that his show was live. But, alas, a live television show is a contradiction in terms. You are hundreds—even thousands—of miles from the performer. You are watching with an inconceivably large number of people, who could never all be gathered together at one time to witness one event and experience it together. (How would one perform live for 34 million people?) Furthermore, you are watching it alone, on a relatively small machine, in the corner of the room. In what sense is anything that happens on that screen, even if the screens are so blown up that the images on it are life-size, live?*

If television is a parallel reality, not a means of communicating ideas, if it is your own mind given back to you, then the success of SNL can only mean

* Another thought on the word "live" as used in relation to "Saturday Night Live." The principal reason for SNL's uniqueness was that it was broadcast at 11:30 P.M. on Saturday night, the traditional middle-class night out. Ratings were insignificant on Saturday late-night. One of Herb Schlosser's intentions in sticking with SNL was to change that. And one of the extraordinary things about SNL is not just that at its height it got so large a share of the homes viewing but that it changed viewing patterns. People stayed home to watch it, or came home to watch it. Where before they had left their televisions behind to go out and dance, drink, eat, talk, get laid, get high, fight, or whatever, with other people, live things with live people, now they stayed home to watch a "live" television show.

that the ideas and attitudes its promoters thought were so revolutionary were actually already in the minds of a large number of viewers. The viewers were delighted to see this part of their minds illuminated finally, for it had been in shadow before, and they weren't sure what it contained, but once the switch was thrown, they recognized everything they saw. They knew about dope, they knew politicians were dangerous assholes, they knew the Army sucked, they knew every reference to sex or deviation and were no longer puzzled by them, they copped the attitude, that "fuck-you" tilt of the head, that certain edge and edginess.

SNL changed nothing. It had already been changed. Boomer humor became part of that delightful continuum, that reflection of us: TV. And probably for that reason there were surprisingly few voices raised in objection. Those executives in the halls of NBC might have been shocked five years before if someone had offered them a toke in the elevator. By 1975, they'd not only heard about it, some had probably offered someone a toke themselves.

Indeed, in the case of SNL it was not the money or the drugs that brought Boomer humor to a well-earned and possibly permanent vacation, but the nature of the beast it chose to lie down with. It was TV's relentless appetite and its equally relentless approval that exhausted this—perhaps the strongest —strain of postwar dissent. Television—and by television here we mean the amalgam of executive and audience—shows little restraint once its hunger is aroused and none at all in showing its gratitude when you toss it a few bloody morsels from your life and times. But it wants more and gets gratefuller and then still more and gets still gratefuller, until pretty soon it's eaten your whole head.

Historically, the force—and failure—of SNL was that its participants were of such high quality, were such uncompromised Boomer humorists. They clearly felt the obligation to try to recreate the unrecreatable flash where fear, fury, pain, lust, or something worse find a crack and the god is on your tongue, and you're Going Too Far. And to try to recreate it every week. It's an impossible task of course, and SNL found (as Monty Python and the *Lampoon* did also) that Going Too Far can be the biggest trap of all. There's only one thing worse than doing the same show night after night, and that's having to top yourself night after night.

Going Too Far can only be tolerated when it is the involuntary by-product of some deeper priority, where by virtue of your own outrage or insight you exist briefly in a world of different values. The minute Going Too Far becomes a self-conscious, planned course of behavior, you forfeit your satirical license. The need to outrage your audience outweighs the outrage inside you.

This may sound a great deal like drug dependency and the two may go hand in hand, but the pressure to Go Farther Than Too Far comes as much as anything else from the pressure to produce and keep producing way beyond the capacity of any single human. It is a corruption indeed, but a corruption of integrity—in this case, satiric—and as such infinitely better than having no integrity in the first place.

Thereby, of course, hangs the final part of our tale, the two who were at the heart of Boomer humor's most glittering public demonstration, *Animal House*, the two who went too far by a long chalk, Doug and John.

Whether Doug Kenney jumped or fell, whether Belushi shot or was shot up, really isn't the point. Both were pushed. Drugs may be the agency of self-destruction, the occasion of the sin, but they are never the cause. Only drab little fearful minds—like that of the drab little petty criminal who currently heads the Justice Department—really believe that people could be that drab and little. No—the simple fact is that John and Doug, having Gone Too Far in one blinding flash of commotion recollected in tranquillity, were expected to do it again and again. People gave them money even—not that much, relatively speaking, enough to take good care of their folks—and then stood back waiting for the beast to repeat the trick.

Both of them, poor fellows, gave it their best shot. Jumped, fell about, twitched, made faces. And naturally it didn't work. *Animal House* was really all they had to say about the subject. One time only. All the way. Flat-out. That's what going to college is like in America, folks. Let's move on.

They weren't allowed to move on. And neither was Boomer humor.

Animal House, like the *Lampoon* and SNL, came out of nowhere. This may have been because the plant managers didn't know what was going on, or that they didn't want to know, but once Boomer humor had connected with its audience, they had no choice. That didn't mean, however, that they were about to lose control of the plant. Confronted finally with Boomer humor in all its naked glory, without the baffle of a cineast (e.g., Stanley Kubrick) or traditional talent (e.g., Jack Nicholson), but right there, grunting, smart, educated and farting, hundreds of millions of dollars' worth of it, Hollywood was going to tread very carefully.

It's significant that our memory of *Animal House* has been largely conditioned by its so-called imitators. These vary enormously, from *Porky's*, say, to *Fast Times at Ridgemont High*, but all of them take what they exhibit to be the *Animal House* formula of adolescent sexual energy versus dumb authority. This distortion is endemic to almost all of "adolescent" comedies that have poured out of Hollywood ever since. And it's hard, given its obviousness, not to conclude that it was deliberate.

Actually, the backbone of *Animal House* are its villains. It is against the dirt in high places that all of *Animal House*'s energy—sexual or not—defines itself. This ranges from the social—the fraternity system that wants the Deltas out—to the official—the Nixonlike dean, who is in league with the fraternity and furthermore with the local Mafia scumbag who runs the town. And through all of it runs the ROTC, the military, kicking the shit out of everyone, organizing the parade, and enforcing every detail of every law—including the educational ones.

Furthermore, its sexual predicament, truer to Boomer history, is that of college-age adults expected to maintain a ludicrous continence well past their ability to do so. These are not adolescents discovering the sweaty world of sex for the first time, but young men and women made horny by a combination of educators and moralists. And of course the authors of *Animal House*— Boomer humorists deluxe—had no illusions about where all this led. In the epilogue, the ROTC villain, Neidermeyer, gets fragged in Nam and Bluto becomes a U.S. senator.

Every one of these elements is typical in some respect of Boomer humor. Beneath the apparent flatulence of food fights and toga parties, there is a crazy balance to the movie that while it may have seemed crude at the time, is in reality quite dramatic. The Deltas, in a world where every outlet is denied to them, sometimes by corruption, sometimes by force, sometimes by sheer lack of numbers, simply go nuts. But they don't go nuts without cause. The causes are carefully arrayed. Step by step we learn with "the wimp and the blimp" the facts of life beyond home and high school. The world is full of fakes. College doesn't exist to bend your brain but to teach you how to shut up and conform, and worst of all, you can't get laid. Girls won't let you and even if they want to, someone else won't let *them*.

This degree of skepticism was of course what the massive audience that went to see *Animal House* adored. Nothing was truer of their lives than what they saw of that college. Not the Delta frat house—which is not the only thing *Animal House* was about—but the college, its enforcers, and the world beyond. This was not a formula—this was quite the opposite, a point of view, crude maybe but total. The America of Boomer humor in microcosm. Whatever their reasons may have been, and as we shall see the motives behind them were extremely mixed (for example, the executive in charge of the project at Universal was an ex-activist), this was clearly not something Hollywood could duplicate. Or perhaps wanted to. However much "the kids" might like it, there wasn't much future in encouraging this attitude. What happened if someone else got the idea to make a similar movie about their first glimpse of a corporation? Or their tour of duty in the armed forces? Or, God forbid, their first jobs in the media? They'd be portrayed as the same kind of scumbags as the dean and the mayor. Yikes!

Hardly surprising then that college became, in the resulting Hollywood formula, a high school. Much more manageable, much lower stakes. The dean could become the nutty old (or young) principal. These alarming ROTC characters, the Deltas' own contemporaries, became good old boys or big-bellied cops. And of course the kids are just as nuts because kids are, well, just nuts. Without any cause. Go figure them.

Within a movie or two, Hollywood had made the unique blend of anarchic energy and skepticism of *Animal House* into a formula of conformist rebellion against unthreatening authority, converting its ebullience into the familiar dreary celebration of misogyny and titillation.

Those fun, fun days of youth. Your youth. The one you will have and like it.

Theories of media conspiracy are no more valid or invalid than any other theories of conspiracy. This book does not set out to construct such a theory.

As we hope to show, the evidence is far too complex to be reduced to a nice, simple good-guy bad-guy fable, and in any case far too ambiguous in its own right. If it weren't, it wouldn't be funny.

There could be no worse tribute to the wild multiplicity of Boomer humor, its insistence on being different, dangerous, not the same as it was yesterday, anti-official, and anti-ideological, than to freeze its history with some dumb construct such as: "We were young and innocent and bought our virtue with their baubles."

Selling out is like any other contract. It needs the consent of both parties. And show business, like democracy, is a two-way street. You can't get laughs without the consent of the governed. Or the drunks in the front row.

That said, however, something has passed. A certain attitude, a series of unique moments, a procession of brilliance. Unlike its close relative, rock and roll, Boomer humor has received scant attention as a homogeneous phenomenon, one with its own roots and special sounds, its own internal history and lineage. This book is an attempt to start the process of chronicling that phenomenon.

Therefore, almost certainly it's doomed. It can't be comprehensive—indeed, there is so much ground to cover, so much work and so many individuals to acknowledge, that it can't even concern itself with the cream, only with the peaks in the cream. And since it doesn't intend to write just another chapter in the history of television—quite the contrary, in fact—some of these peaks have been judged not on the Benthamite standards of how many people were witness to them, but just for themselves, on their own merits.

This then is not a comprehensive chronicle of everything that everyone said, everywhere, in the last three decades if they were in the business of being funny. It is a selective account of the moments which, in this author's opinion, moved the body of humor forward and which best represented the uniqueness of the phenomenon.

And one thing this book cannot be is a friendly collection of jokes. Boomer humor burned holes in people's minds when they first heard it, and to live again it must burn holes in these pages. However much those who abhor dissent will abhor them, these words existed, these laughs were brought forth, these ideas were thought. Boomer humor may have passed, its exponents exhausted, bought off, silenced, converted, fattened up, or dead, but the reasons for its outrage have not. The same foolish faces, the same grim unrealities, the same fatuous lies surround us, as they always have. Indeed, if anything, they loom larger, press harder, use even more makeup. Under such circumstances, we should remember that once we knew them for what they were.

And laughed our asses off.

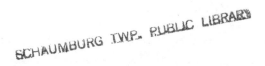

PART ONE

FISSION

⅂

Number 1—Mort Sahl

Nineteen fifty-five was a good year. Commissar McCarthy's long siege of America had finally been lifted and Uncle Joe consigned to the file in which he'd placed so many others: Where Are They Now? Two of the more interesting American males of the age, Sebastian Dangerfield and Humbert Humbert, made their debuts, albeit in Paris. In Montgomery, Alabama, a solid black citizen named Rosa Parks took care of some business left undone since FDR's second term, and declared herself too tired to go to the back of the bus. Perhaps coincidentally, perhaps not, the first records of Mr. C. Berry, Mr. B. Diddley, and Mr. L. Richard blared from bulbous radios. In Chicago, a pipe-sucking hedonist named Hefner pored over nude pics of the girl next door. In New York a Democrat-bucking upstart called Dan Wolf started printing a nickel rag called *The Village Voice.* Arthur Miller and Sam Beckett fought existence very nicely, thank you. Robert Rauschenberg painted his bed, Allen Ginsberg howled, and Brando's brow drove everyone wild. Far away in a mysterious part of the Orient called Vietnam, a little place called Dien Bien Phu was firmly in the hands of the people who lived there. It was not all bad that year.

On the nation's thirty-nine million TV sets (four fifths of the world's total) fully half of the top ten shows were classified as comedy. Among these was the only comic genius created by the medium to date, Sid Caesar, still holding his own despite the fantastic greed of NBC who had broken him away from fellow genius Imogene Coca in the apparent belief that this would make the network twice as rich; the wondrous Golden Ham, Jackie Gleason, bringing situation and comedy to situation comedy, a flesh-and-blood American male the like of which had not been seen since W. C. Fields, and would not be seen again until the arrival of Archie Bunker (and, in the case of John Belushi, the tradition's natural heir, alas, never); finally perhaps the funniest of them all, new old-timer Phil Silvers proving weekly that the real asset of a peacetime military was that it put corruption within everyone's reach.

A new generation, born in war, were sprouting into their teens, sending up flares for one another, tentatively drumming out messages in the night, leaving notes in hollow trees: "I too am a Martian."

In fact, despite the cultural advances of that year like the opening of Disneyland, the introduction of Thorazine, and TV dinners; despite cars modeled so closely on the female form their rear fenders looked like buttocks and their front bumpers like brassieres, despite the religious fanatics who divided the nation by insisting President Eisenhower add "under God" to "one nation indivisible," despite the oatmeal-faced Dulles brothers who between them controlled both the State Department and America's new secret police, the CIA; despite the relentless efforts to separate young people physically, alienate them spiritually, encourage them to compete with each other at an age when it was natural to reach out, experiment, and explore, despite the bafflement of adults only a generation or two away from bustling immigrant life transplanted to silent, suburban dormitories, despite the four thousand A-bombs the United States now boasted in its bulging armpit, the country was alive and well, bursting with dissent and creativity and democratic resistance to the ill effects of government.

Nowhere was this more true than in Chicago and San Francisco, two hot spots that have always given Babbitt a hard time. In both cities trouble was brewing that would soon add countless new expressions to the faces America made at itself in the bathroom mirror. If anything as traditional as humor can ever be said to have been born, it was in these two places that Boomer humor first wailed.

Morton Lyon Sahl was, like several in our story who came after him, born in Canada.* Like many others he was raised in Los Angeles, with unlimited access to dreams of stardom and none at all to material goods. In this respect he is not unlike another father of Boomer humor, Lenny Bruce, with whom Sahl had some differences as to its upbringing. Both men also shared the experience of serving in World War II, which they had in common with several important contemporaries (e.g., Joseph Heller) and therefore of course do not strictly qualify as Boomer humorists. (Sahl was twenty-eight in 1955.)

Nonetheless, the influence of them both on Boomer audiences and there-

---

* He can therefore never be President. It's unlikely he would want to be though, since Sahl sacrificed a large chunk of his career and fortune trying to persuade the American public that its thirtieth President was assassinated by an agency of its own government, the CIA, a theory no less absurd than the one contained in the Warren Report. The possibility that Sahl is himself a CIA operative, whose job is to make proponents of the CIA-killed-Kennedy theory look like obsessive conspiracy buffs has, however, never been exhaustively explored. The possibility that this author is a CIA operative whose job is to discredit Sahl with the last sentence has never been explored at all.

fore on Boomer humorists was enormous. In the case of Sahl it was unique in several additional ways—personal, professional, and above all political.

The first and most important thing to know about Mort Sahl is that he was, in every way, *the first*. He came from nowhere, out of left field, with no warning and few antecedents. Where contemporaries like Bruce had complicated ties to vaudeville and burlesque, or Second City to the Federal Theatre Project and European cabaret, Sahl had none. He made it up all by himself. He told jokes of a sort and he stood on his feet, but there the resemblance to stand-up comedians ended. He worked clubs that had previously booked only music, and he was the first man to put spoken funny words on the hitherto musical twelve-inch LP. He probably invented the comedic "riff," that extended free-form metaphor that explores all the possibilities of a preposterous premise or paints the details of a verbal picture based on one, a technique which became an indispensable creative tool of all modern comedians—indeed, which has passed into everyday conversation.

Before him the closest thing to this was the extended fictitious sketch in which one actor played several different characters, or, in everyday conversation, the joke. Sahl was the first person to substitute an idea for the supposed event of an anecdote, and the first to take tremendous license in leaping about from one aspect of that idea to another, as he pleased, until its possibilities were exhausted. He thus not only discovered new tools, but educated his audiences to suspend their disbelief in a new area. He challenged the audience to follow his train of thought; then, having got them to trust him, turned their assumptions upside down, exposed the illogic of official logic, and used its rhetoric to destroy itself. At a time when vast new vistas of absurdity and mass manipulation were opening up, Sahl was a pioneer of them; a man who ventured where none had gone before, he was the Captain Kirk of Boomer humor.

Sahl started out as a hanger-on at Berkeley, where he spent nights in the back of a 1936 Buick and lived on leftover pies from a diner run by a friend. He decided sometime in 1953 to try his hand at becoming a comedian and, since he didn't own a tuxedo, set his sights on North Beach, then the bohemian area of San Francisco. (Sahl defines the words "bohemian area" as meaning "a lot of Jewish people acting like Italians.") The place he picked was a dive called the hungry i—the "i" stood variously for "intellectual" or "id"—and was run enough by a splendid, beret-toting Italian called Enrico Banducci.†

The hungry i was quite literally a dive—down a long flight of steps—and tiny (eighty-three seats). Sahl auditioned and caught Banducci's attention immediately. This was 1953. The McCarthy subversion was at its height, and the fear and paranoia in the air were palpable. People were committing suicide, going into exile, losing careers overnight. It was not a time to say smart

---

† Space does not permit a tribute to Banducci, whose name and club appear several times in this chronicle. The author will have to confine himself to saying that of all the nightclub owners in North America in the fifties and sixties, Enrico was the hardest to get paid by.

things about the senator—which is why most brave souls waited until he'd drunk himself to death—and certainly not in public.

Sahl knew different. Banducci booked what he later called Sahl's "terrible" act on the basis of one joke. It involved a detailed description of the then popular Eisenhower jacket, a garment lavishly equipped with zippers in all kinds of unexpected places. Sahl suggested that an improved model of it should be marketed, a McCarthy jacket, with an extra zipper across the mouth. Mild though this may seem, at the time it was roughly equivalent to defecating on the flag and mailing it to the DAR. It was dangerous, for there was no way in 1953 of knowing how far Uncle Joe's assault on democracy would go. A comedian of the time *might* have made a reference to McCarthy but without a doubt it would have been a joke at the expense of his victims, not of the senator.

Sahl papered the house for his first show at the hungry i with loyal friends from Berkeley, and did sufficiently well to persuade Banducci to let him stay. His early material reflects this campus-oriented audience.

One of his better-known routines at the time involved a group of students who decide to hold up the Fairmont Hotel in San Francisco. They pass the classic note to the hotel cashier who unfortunately is also a student. The hold-up note reads: "Give us all your money and act normal." The cashier passes it back with one of his own: "What do you mean by normal? Define your terms."

Intellectual though this routine was, it was not academic. His early material may have appealed primarily to students—and that in itself ensured the growing prosperity of the hungry i—but it was not of the kind that left you gasping if you hadn't read your Sartre.

Sahl was interested in ideas. And especially that area where ideas intersect with self-interest, and where they affect people of all backgrounds and classes —politics. Sahl's preoccupations were ideas that were just as much on the mind of Joe in the corner bar as they were on his. That he never really got to talk to Joe much might have been his own fault, or it might have been the fault of those who sat between them. Nonetheless, on the evidence of his work there was little that was not comprehensible to anyone who cared to keep himself reasonably well informed. But if you took the chance of listening, you had to accept that everything you knew about and certainly everything you assumed would be twisted into knots.

Increasingly, Sahl's work became a running counterpoint to the absurdities and contradictions of Official America, a cocky little pirate vessel peppering the ship of state. Of McCarthy's fellow Red-snappers, the House Un-American Activities Committee, he said: "Every time the Russians throw an American in jail, the HUAC retaliates—by throwing an American in jail." (Occasionally substituting in this joke for HUAC was the brand-new young Vice President Richard Nixon, who had rocketed to stardom in the elections of 1952 because the Republicans needed a strong anti-Communist on the ticket to balance Ike's pro-Moscow leanings.) When the Atomic Energy Commission initiated what was in effect a public trial of J. Robert Oppenheimer, and revoked his security clearance, Sahl imagined a scene in which the AEC confronted Oppenheimer like a sheriff with a recalcitrant deputy: "Okay, Doctor—turn in your brain." When the debate over the abolition of capital punishment was raging throughout California, Sahl arrived at a definite position: "You've got to execute people. How else are they gonna learn?" But he had a special word for religious groups pushing for the death penalty: "They should remember, however, that they once made a Very Big Mistake."

Increasingly too, the people came. Within a year of Sahl's opening at the i, which had become and would remain his base for rest of the decade, Banducci opened a large club (which typically he remodeled, rebuilt, sandblasted, and poured cement for by himself), and Sahl was up to $1,000 a week. CBS had come up from Hollywood to sign him to a contract—although, having done so, they confessed that they had no idea what to do with him because he was too "intellectual"—and tiny though his forum was, he was beginning to be noticed.

The hungry i was becoming, thanks to him and his insistence on political comment, a sort of watering hole of the intelligentsia; Sahl developed contacts with newsmen like John Chancellor of NBC and through him met Adlai Stevenson, the Democratic candidate for President in 1956, who was to become a longtime friend. Quite literally, no one else in America was doing what Sahl was doing, and he was getting better at it all the time. His commentary began to range more freely, going beyond a stacked series of one-liners into much more extended pieces that started off with a distinct premise and then appeared to drift off into an unconnected flow of observation which nonetheless ended up triumphantly where it began. He also began to posit himself as the loyal, credulous American, buying the official line and working faithfully from it to an absurd conclusion. A typical piece was his response to the Berlin crisis.

Sahl starts the routine as a loyal patriotic ready to go to war if his country calls. As a member of the Air Force Reserve, he reports for duty and insists on getting a full list of the reasons for the crisis from his group commander. This is not because he needs any motivation—on the contrary it's so that he can write the "reasons" down and paste them in his helmet. That way when he gets posted overseas and his morale gets low he can always refer to them. The group commander rattles off the usual list of grievances—oppressed East European satellites, Soviet anti-Semitism, Siberian labor camps, and Sahl dutifully writes them down. (Characteristically, he drops out of character to make an aside to the audience *in re* Soviet anti-Semitism. The Russian people were anti-Semitic before they became Communists and there are *some* things they just can't ruin.)

So Sahl has his reasons and he's ready to lay down his life for freedom. Imagine his chagrin when only three days later, the papers announce that there's suddenly been a thaw in the Cold War and that Vice President Nixon is going to Russia. People are dashing around in the streets, incredulous, says

Sahl. One or two ask hopefully if Nixon's intending to stay. And so the piece moves on through subsequent political events, with Sahl maintaining his simplistic character and throwing off lines about every concievable aspect of them. (E.g., he notes that Nixon flew to the Soviet Union with a team of Presidents and CEOs of multinational corporations, so that the Soviets "could see what we're really like".) He describes Nixon's trip to Russia—including the famous kitchen debate—and by simply repeating the official version, faithfully mouthing the propaganda, destroys it. Winding up back home in the USA, he parrots the prevailing view that Nixon's trip showed him in a new role, and gets in a sideswipe at Ike—that he'd been in a new role also, having been totally in charge of the country while Nixon was away.

This piece is typical of his method. While it has a subtly narrative quality, and an easily graspable character at its core, it's both too long to be an anecdote and too wide-ranging to be a routine. And since the basis for the narrative is not his own experience, real or fabricated, so much as universally available information—the news of the day in its approved form—its impact is immediate and broad in appeal.

The free-form approach to what was on his audience's mind had much in common with a similar movement in jazz. Sahl's method was to establish a theme as a jazz musician did and then ring changes on it, wringing every possible phrase or comment out of its inherent absurdity until the possibilities had been exhausted, very much in the same way that a jazz soloist would handle a solo. It was natural that both jazz musicians and their audiences would feel at home with his method.‡

This led to his being booked at jazz clubs that had never previously presented anything but music, notably Storyville in Boston which he first played in 1956. While there he was approached by one Oscar Marienthal who owned a club called Mister Kelly's on Rush Street in Chicago, and later the same year he opened there—another first for a comedian. Not only did this give him a second base (he worked at Mister Kelly's for thirty-one weeks) but it brought him into contact with both the rapidly expanding comedic underground of the University of Chicago, and a man with whom he would have a long and complex relationship, Hugh Hefner.

An interview with Sahl appeared in *Playboy* in 1956, and helped to establish his nationwide credentials as a voice of resistance. Sahl was perfect for the fledgling *Playboy* ethos—young, single, in full cry against the political fatuities of the time, obsessed with cars, women, and the technology of recorded music. Suspect though *Playboy*'s reputation may still have been in 1956, the explosive growth of its influence in the ensuing years indubitably helped to make Sahl not just a national figure, but the embodiment of a new, well-informed, you-can't-fool-us spirit in the land.

---

‡ Sahl's only prop onstage was a newspaper, which he would use as a starting point for many of his riffs, and also as a kind of continuity device in hopping about from one subject to another. Jazz friends like Dave Brubeck used to refer to the ubiquitous newspaper as his "axe."

And just as *Playboy* backed the new technology of recording as a means of disseminating this attitude, so did Sahl. From 1955 to 1960 Sahl's albums were his most important achievement. Not only were they the first LPs to present live comedy performances, but their content had a profound effect on the way the new generation began to think of its leaders. Objectively it would have been quite possible for anyone to have made the first recorded comedy albums and it would have been a breakthrough right there. That the first albums were recorded by a man who was also the foremost satiric commentator of the time was the most happy coincidence.

Sahl had good reason to resent contemporary attempts to pigeonhole him. He was definitely a new comedian but he had little in common with the New Comedians who followed him (who, to do them justice, had little in common with one another either). And to be compared to Will Rogers, as *Time* did in its cover story on him in 1960, drove him nuts. As he explained the difference, Rogers assumed the role of yokel who questioned the common sense of the educated men managing the country, while he was an educated man questioning the sense—if there was any—of the yokels in government. The surface arrogance of this epigram belies a deeper and worthier conviction central to Sahl's work: not only that he defined himself against his antecedents first and foremost by being intelligent, but that the audience—any audience, not just a nightclub full of Berkeley students—was equally capable of understanding what he had to say. This simple assertion had several reverberations in practice. Audiences were drawn to him if for no other reason than that they were flattered, after so many years of pap, to be offered solid, well-prepared and -seasoned food. Second, it gave him a powerful populist stick with which to beat the condescension of the media. Sahl told the New York *Times* in December 1958: "I am not denying that suppression [of satire] exists, but the ultimate taboo is not against racial jokes or off-color jokes but against intellectual content."

What intrigued Sahl more than anything was the rhetoric and logic of all kinds of official utterances, political or cultural. The nuances of official America fascinated him, as it did other Boomer humorists. For example: "Eisenhower says he's for integration but gradually; Stevenson says he's for integration but moderately. It should be possible to compromise between those extremes."

As Sahl said later and with some justice: "One of the great tools comedians don't use is the English language."

Sahl was obsessed with language and concepts. He delighted in banging them together in unexpected ways, juggling them, almost dropping them, but always reaching a happy conclusion. Implicit throughout his work is a fury that certain terms are being used to make people feel comfortable with ideas that should be questioned. He reserved his most ferocious sarcasm for the introduction of military priorities into public life and the droning insistence on the military's central role in government, even though his contemporaries grew up in the Depression and most of them thought of government as something to do with jobs and utilities. (A meddler perhaps but not a military one.) He was, however, unusually reticent about his motives for this anger, insisting only: "I'm not so much interested in politics as I am in overthrowing the government."

(A phrase in itself fraught with official semantics, since the political aim of Communists, according to the Communist Control Act, was the violent overthrow of government.)

Sahl was not partisan, and he was at pains to emphasize this. He operated during his peak years, however, in a Republican administration, and willy-nilly his targets were mostly Republican. Since he was a pioneer as far as strictly political humor was concerned, people might be excused for thinking that he must be a Democrat. Try as he might he could not get away from this assumption, and his close association with Kennedy didn't help, although he valiantly attacked the young senator and his Dad to keep things even. (Kennedy was quoted as describing somewhat ruefully Sahl's "relentless pursuit of everybody.") To call Sahl a Democrat, though, is like calling him a Will Rogers. It does no one a favor and the cause of overthrowing the government a great disservice.

The most obvious and important result of Sahl's nonstop needling of the established order was that by the time the 1960 election came around, he was in a position of considerable media influence. In addition to much other media attention at that time, for example, Sahl was extensively quoted in the *Time* coverage of the 1960 Democratic convention, was the subject of a *New Yorker* profile—a signal honor—and on August 15, less than a fortnight later, was on the *cover* of *Time*. Clearly, whatever else the media thought about in that election year, they included Mort Sahl in their thinking.

Sahl was also important to those whose business it was to sell the two candidates. This was partly because he was highly quotable—his observations, especially for the Kennedy team, seemed tailor-made for campaigning. The august patriarch Joseph Kennedy personally called Sahl "to write stuff for Johnny" and as a result Sahl banged off a continuous series of bon mots, which were faithfully picked up by couriers like Pierre Salinger and Peter Lawford from wherever Sahl happened to be.

What was significant for both sides was the fact that Sahl was speaking with a new voice and that new voters and voters-to-be were lapping it up. With respect to the sound of Sahl, the quoted excerpts cannot convey how dramatically different he sounded to his contemporaries when compared to the love-me tone of the comedians who had preceded him. A constant refrain in reviews and articles about him is his "fury," his "lupine smile," his "savaging" of targets, and so on. Sahl was and is a definitely abrasive personality, and married to a cause as his nature was after the assassination, it became something of a liability. Under control in the late fifties, it made people sit up as if they'd had cold water thrown on their brains. Our perception today is clouded too by the degree to which he influenced the voice of those who imitated him and took it further (Woody Allen, for example). Even Bruce, who would have gone cold turkey rather than admit it, was influenced by Sahl's jerky, nervous, inclusive manner of speech—the very urgency of his free-form delivery has passed into the style of almost all who came after him.

This was new in the worst way in 1960, and *Time* magazine, by putting a comedian on the cover for the first time in their history, was practically acknowledging that the torch had already been passed. *Time* was not the only one. Here's Kennedy historian Arthur Schlesinger, Jr., on what Sahl represented: "A mounting restlessness and discontent, an impatience with clichés and platitudes, a resentment against the materialist notion that affluence is the answer to everything, a contempt for banality and corn—in short, a revolt against pomposity. Sahl's popularity is a sign of the yearning for youth, irreverence, trenchancy, satire, a clean break with the past."

This was what most interested the vulpine new breed of political managers pressing forward over the inert bodies of the Eisenhower era—this mysterious unprogrammable youth Sahl had captured, and captured with their own tools.

Who were they, how many of them were there, how could they be programmed? If Sahl was anything to go by, they were not about to buy much of anything the current system had to offer, on either side of the aisle. They certainly weren't interested in continuing the Cold War, or the home-front sacrifices of freedom it demanded. Affluence, as Schlesinger noted, didn't seem to get them particularly hot, and they appeared to have an apolitical disrespect for duly elected authority. Civil rights was the only political issue that brought them to their feet. This was fine for the Boston liberals but boded no good for the Democrats as a whole, for they were split right down the Mason-Dixon Line on integration.

In voicing a certain lack of enthusiasm for the Democratic party, Sahl spoke for many young people. He seemed to know what they wanted, who they liked and didn't. Thus, during the 1960 campaign, arguably one of the more significant in postwar American history—Sahl became a sort of unofficial favorite son of this constituency, a privileged observer from a nonaligned territory that had not yet applied for statehood.

The Democratic convention in Los Angeles in 1960 was the most televised to date. *Time* consequently did a long section analyzing the effectiveness of the coverage (and concluded that while much of it was good, much of it was also bad). That obligation aside, they then ran this:

"Of all the seasoned infighters who appeared in Los Angeles last week, probably none was more combative than the man in the cashmere sweater who said: 'I like fun, but we don't have time for jokes. We have to overthrow our government.'

"This was Morton Lyon Sahl, delegate from everywhere and nowhere . . . a side show considerably brighter than the main attraction.

"Senator Kennedy, Mort suggested, was a natural for 'Father Knows Best,' and he noted that Kennedy's appearance on 'College News Conference' made sense because 'kids like to talk over problems with someone their own age.'

Sahl pictured a lineup of war heroes getting their medals from President Truman in 1945. Harry, by Sahl's account, made the usual claim that he would rather have that medal than be president, and 'all the boys agreed, except this thin lieutenant from Massachusetts.' "

By Sahl's own account, he conducted a sort of satiric guerrilla campaign throughout the convention—striking at will, leaving few tracks, hopping from one alternative means of comment to the other while the networks were ponderously establishing their bona fides as responsible journalists.

The impact Sahl had was due to the fact that the convention was still strictly a live affair whose outcome could be influenced by outspoken (or very soft-spoken) individuals and which, for all the planning and rigging that went on, was still democratically messy. Television's role was still to report, or at best overhear, what went on. Its reality had not yet begun to supplant that of suites and streets, caucus rooms and convention floor, nor were people aware of it except as a novelty or a nuisance. Wild cards like Sahl could thus still disturb the best-laid plans. To the extent that the Kennedy team were fascinated by Sahl they were also alarmed by him. The last thing the fragile Kennedy drive wanted was someone as engaging and quotable as Sahl in Los Angeles, slinging around one-liners about the Democratic platform and JFK's youth: "You shouldn't send a kid up on a plank like that."

At any event, Kennedy was sufficiently intrigued by Sahl to initiate an arm's-length relationship with him. What *Time* omitted from its story was that after the Butler banquet, Kennedy invited Sahl to fly back to Palm Springs with him. According to Sahl, a conversation ensued in which the senator more or less turned the tables on Sahl, demanding to know what he *meant* by the material he was doing—especially as it related to the Kennedy fortune. "What does that mean," Sahl has Kennedy asking, "how much do you think my father has?" Sahl's response was "four hundred million." Kennedy looked at him as if he were retarded and explained how much the Rockefeller brothers (Republicans, of course) were worth. "Liquid, about ten billion. Now, *that's* money!"

A singular version of the underdog theory.

The very fact of Kennedy's openness to someone capable of doing him a lot of damage prefigured a basic tactic of the Kennedy administration toward dissent: to contain it by measured approval, even respect, to defang it by admiring the length and whiteness of its teeth. Sahl's relationship with candidate Kennedy became one of mutual fascination, and his access to the Kennedy inner circle considerable (due also in some degree to his friendship with Sinatra and Sinatra's fellow Packrat Peter Lawford).

Sahl never again reached the prominence he did in the summer of 1960. Whether, as he claims, the White House was responsible for his decline after Kennedy was inaugurated, or whether he became too closely identified with the Kennedy campaign to be a credible skeptic once it triumphed, his role in the 1960 election should not be the measure of his worth. Had Mort Sahl never gone near Los Angeles in July of 1960, his contribution to the birth and nurture of Boomer humor would still register in the red zone. He single-handedly created a nightclub circuit out of jazz clubs that had never before booked anything but music, not only opening them up for those who followed, including his arch-rival Lenny Bruce, but also associating humor for the first time with the idea of hip. He played the first college concert to include the then unfamiliar package of a comedian followed by a group (with Dave Brubeck in 1953) and he pioneered albums of the spoken word, in particular the live spoken word. Here's Woody Allen, who rarely gives interviews and never comments on other comedians, on Mort Sahl in 1963: "It was that he had *genuine* insights. Without him there wouldn't have been Beyond the Fringe or Newhart or [Vaughn] Meader. He made the country receptive to a kind of comedy it was not used to hearing."

Sahl revivified the tradition of live dissent at a time when the dominant media, on the airwaves and in print, banned dissent. He was first and foremost a live performer, one whose rapport with the audience created material, one who took the risk that a relationship established at the beginning of a set might be different by its conclusion. In an era when weapons of monstrous size and screens of minuscule absurdity obsessed almost everyone, Sahl sought out an audience averaging between five and six feet in height, powered by proteins and oxygen. He was ill served by those who criticized his work as all head and no heart. It lacked the passion of Bruce and the weird embrace of Jonathan Winters and the glittering rapport of the early improv companies —it was demanding and it kicked you in the head rather than the gut; but for all that, Sahl went out in the dead of night without support or encouragement, laid down the outline of the structure—along with exits, entrances, and room for expansion—and did it all by himself.

Last and most important, Sahl made no bones about what he had to say. He didn't pretend to be a harmless clown, or an eternal kid, or a wacky kook too zonked to read the papers. He went right for the only thing that mattered —the half-wits in charge. By doing that he set the agenda for Boomer humor for years, not merely by being good and funny but by challenging others to challenge. He may have dug his own grave by doing just that, for he gained no friends with such standards and the very medium he most wanted to conquer, television, was by its nature inimical to such consistency. But for all that, Sahl was no radical naïf. He knew the score. The best anecdote with which to leave him summed up his attitude to everyone and everything who stood for orthodoxy of any kind in those fabulous fifties. The occasion was an Eddie Fisher show in 1957. Eddie Fisher at that time was the embodiment of everything good, clean, wholesome, and brainless about the American Way of Life. His show ruffled its surface no more than a straw would a milkshake. It was also live.

Fisher gave Sahl an effusive introduction, the burden of which was that Sahl was one of the funniest people alive, and then said, "Say something funny, Mort," whereupon Sahl strode purposefully front and center, stopped, glared at the camera, and said, slowly and distinctly, "John Foster Dulles."

2

Number 2—Second City*

While Sahl was busily subverting the masses eighty-three at a time out in San Francisco, something else was aborning in a storefront in Chicago's Hyde Park that would have an even more far-reaching effect on the nature and attitudes of a generation.

It was 1955 again, that fat fulsome fifties year, and it was summer.

The University of Chicago, sometimes known to its enemies as Red U., was run at the time on the quaint and dangerous notion that higher education actually meant education and that "higher" was not pronounced "hire." The college was open to anyone who could pass the entrance exam, classroom attendance was not required, and grades were established on the basis of one annual exam. Not only did this system ensure a brilliant and inquisitive student body, it encouraged—through its lack of rigid scheduling—all forms of original experimentation. Moreover, as has always been the case with genuine institutions of learning, it attracted a concentric circle of free spirits for whom the mere smell of culture cooking was enough to make them swarm.

Two of these products of U. of C.—one enrolled, the other not—were Paul Sills and David Shepherd. Sills and Shepherd, who were to become the Romulus and Remus of improvisational humor, had discovered each other in the bustling on- and off-campus theatrical underground of the university. Both men were directors and (in June 1953) they had founded a repertory group called the Playwrights Theater Club† which presented for the first time such

* As mentioned in the author's foreword, interview material in this chapter is drawn from *Something Wonderful Right Away* by Jeff Sweet, with permission of Mr. Sweet.

† Playwrights' first theater was a converted Chinese restaurant—so was the location of the hungry i. No one has ever explained this sinister and subversive "coincidence."

twinkling future stars as Mike Nichols, Ed Asner, Elaine May, Barbara Harris, and Tom O'Horgan.

Like Sahl, neither Sills nor Shepherd is a Baby Boomer; unlike him, they are not, strictly speaking, even humorists. All three men, however, were driven to explore that territory which lies between live performers and a live audience, a place fraught with the dangers of incomprehension, mistrust, and rejection but which can suddenly be transformed into a common ground of self-realization for any who venture deep enough into it.

Especially when the means by which it is explored are real ones, of real concern to all concerned. Sahl had replaced traditional rituals of humor with a coruscating flood of observation about things which impinged on the interests of his audience—and in so doing, intentionally or not defined himself as a new kind of spokesman.

Shepherd and Sills, too, were obsessed with developing this same piece of real estate, although each man's motives—and achievements—were very different. Their influence was also far more widely felt, not just on humor but on the American theater of the last three decades because of their contributions to the theory and practice of improvisation.

Beyond this they also represented the dichotomy in progressive thought of the time. Shepherd leaned toward the collective and communal and Sills to the existential and personal. In more practical terms this meant that Shepherd's emphasis was on the audience side of the performance experience, while Sills's was on that of the actors, which further meant that Shepherd tended to stand for what should work, and Sills for what actually did.

Shepherd's earliest vision of what came to be called the Compass was a community theater presenting ever changing plays that reflected the concerns and life of the streets:

"I wanted to rejuvenate the theater . . . which I found had been captured by Giraudoux and Shaw and Ionesco, who turn it into a distorted picture of life. Instead of being about what's happening in the streets of Chicago it was about love affairs in Nice fifty years ago. I thought it was obscene for the theater to be dominated by French and English people. I'm a WASP. I want a WASP theater. And you can't get that on the East Coast because it's dominated by European culture. So I went to the Midwest . . ."

By which he meant the University of Chicago. The social atmosphere he found when he got there was:

"Very mixed and flowing. There were hard hats and intellectuals, steelworkers and students, professors and homosexuals. And a lot of these people were in and out of the university, whether they were fifteen years old or forty-year-old paratroop veterans . . .

"This is what Compass came out of . . . a popular theater [where] you let people come and go and smoke and drink, be comfortable and not think of the theater as something holy and untouchable . . . a theater where everybody would come. Literally everybody. Not only theatergoers but non-theatergoers, which meant 95 percent of the people who lived in Chicago, whether they were steelworkers or college students who don't have the money to go . . . or Japanese, or black . . . Whoever they were I wanted them in my theater . . . instead of being in the Lyric watching Westerns. I wanted them in my theater watching stories about Hyde Park . . ."

These were worthy sentiments and Shepherd was deeply committed to them—so much so that his first impulse was to take his theater concept to the people, rather than waiting for the people to come to him. What he wanted to do was present live theater to workers right in their own environment—the stockyards and steel mills in and around Chicago. He actually approached union representatives about this (encounters which must have been somewhat satirical in themselves, since Shepherd was not only a bespectacled English major from Harvard but one of the Vanderbilts), and was roundly rebuffed. Undaunted, he set about raising his theater where it more properly belonged, on the polyglot University of Chicago campus, at a hole-in-the-wall bar called the Hi-Hat on East 55th Street. This was renamed the Compass and amalgamated with the storefront next door, which became the actual Compass theater. The net result was a tiny, ninety-seat theater connected to a working bar.

Familiar though this arrangement later became at the dozens of theaters and clubs spawned by the Chicago school of Boomer humorists, at the time it was a complete innovation. For this was not a nightclub, where a jazz group or band might play in relaxed surroundings, but a theater, with a resident company of actors whose job was going to be to suspend the disbelief of an audience with access to alcohol and nicotine. And most unusual of all, to the actors themselves. The only comparable arrangement anyone could think of was that of the prewar cabarets of Weimar Germany, but for the United States it was next door to revolutionary.‡ The tone of Shepherd's manifesto for what was to be expected on his stage reflected this:

"We won't use any sets or special lighting or curtains, and the casts will be small. We'll need strong stories with a lot of action in them—songs, fights, games, and orations. We'll encourage pantomime and an intensity the stage hasn't known since Ibsen . . .

"As we develop a new kind of play and audience we may have to develop an entirely new style of acting."

In that last sentence of course lay an enormous problem. The problem was that while Shepherd had everything together regarding his concept, his commitment to live theater, his manifesto, his physical ambience, even his function in the community, he still had an ultimate reality to face. What would be

‡ Conventional wisdom has made this comparison with many loci of Boomer humor (e.g., the Establishment in London), but it's neither very accurate nor very optimistic. It does of course bring a frisson of danger and doom to the act of attending underground satire, but as historical insight, it's worthless. (For one thing you didn't have to bring the price of admission in a wheelbarrow.) The Weimar cabarets were mostly formal, owed as much to European vaudeville as they did to the theater, and were obsessed by sexual deviation. Besides which it would be four elections and many years before the Chicago police got their storm-trooper act together.

said and done on his stage? Who would create these things? And how would they represent everyone involved, not just the playwright, not just the actors, but everyone—including the audience, which changed every night?

The territory was for the most part virgin. But there were a few hints as to which paths to follow and what to expect, and Paul Sills knew what they were.

Sills is less the father of improvisation than its son. His mother, Viola Spolin, deserves the credit if anyone does, although it must be said for the record that one of the oddest paradoxes about improvisation is that its very development was improvised, new forms and techniques being discovered by the very same process of trust it demands in all its phases.

To detail Spolin's contribution to the theater is beyond the brief of this book* but at its core is her invention of various "theater games" intended to develop trust between two or more performers and to draw from them characters and concepts they contain within themselves, often without knowing that they do. Generally speaking, these techniques involve combining a simple dramatic situation with ritual or repetitious rules like those of a children's game. For example, two performers are given a situation and characters to go with it, say a customer and proprietor in a Chinese laundry. They begin to play the scene. At a given signal, a third performer enters the scene with the instruction that what he or she says must completely change the situation (and therefore the characters). The change must be complete—in other words the new arrival must change the situation: for example, to a submarine in a combat zone. It is not sufficient that he or she enter the Chinese laundry as a fireman to announce that it's burning down. The new scene now proceeds with all three performers in new characters exploring its possibilities. At an appropriate moment one of the original two performers finds a reason to exit. Then a fourth performer enters with the same instruction, to completely change the situation (and characters), and the new scene proceeds until the second of the original characters finds an exit, whereupon a fifth enters and so on. This continues for as long as the director keeps sending new performers into the scene. In a very short time, therefore, the original Chinese laundry can have been transformed into the Kremlin or a motel room full of rock musicians—wherever the preoccupations and abilities of the performers takes it.

The exercise forces the players to adapt abruptly to the new reality imposed by the new arrival, and change their characters accordingly. On one level this obviously develops versatility and awareness of the other performers' intentions (a process known simply as "listening"); but the mysterious thing about such a game is that in having to observe the rules, the creative powers of a performer are unexpectedly opened up, in a way which would never happen if he or she were just told to play through a scene from beginning to end. It may be that having to observe the rules dissipates the natural reserve or fear of

* Her book *Improvisations in the Theater* is a classic of theatrical instruction.

failure the performer might feel, but the theory of improvisation goes further, holding that it is trust in one another that allows performers to find new personalities and realities in themselves. Here's Sills on the beneficial effects of improvisation:

"True improvisation is a dialogue between people. Not just on the level of what the scene is about, but also a dialogue from the being—something that has never been said before that now comes up, some statement of reality between people. In a dialogue, something happens to the participants . . . a discovery. As I say, you can't make this discovery alone. There is always the other."

Placed before an audience allowed to suggest characters and situations, this process now includes them as participants. The preoccupations of the audience help to determine the boundaries within which the performers must improvise. It shares with the performers both the experience of exploring the characters and situations and an ignorance of where they will lead. If a "statement of reality" is successfully discovered by those onstage it will be as much that of the audience as it is theirs. Sills can thus say:

"I think theater comes out of consciousness of the community. If you look at the theater of ancient Greece, it came out of the necessity of the Greek community to handle its spiritual reality in a public form. Theater has always been concerned with this, so why should contemporary theater be any less so? Theater is concerned with reality. Now, reality is not to be defined as what is real for you alone. Reality is shared. And reality of the moment can occur only with spontaneity."

Improvisation can therefore be an instant and remarkable means of arriving at a collective reality—a consensus between performers and audience of how they feel about a certain subject, group, or issue. In theory at least, Sills's access to improvisation provided the solution to Shepherd's problem, that "new style of acting." It was also a practical solution, for in the uncontrollable mix of preoccupations and aims inherent in the idea of a community theater, it concentrated on the one controllable element—the actors.

Theories of art put into practice, like political ideologies and British cars, work about half the time. Shepherd and Sills were cautious in moving from the written script to the terra incognita of improvised performance. The basic unit of material which the Compass presented at first was a sort of halfway house between the written and the improvised called a scenario.

One of the most important members of the original Compass company was Roger Bowen. A scenario of his first gave Shepherd the tangible evidence that what he was proposing to do at the Compass was possible. The scenario was called simply "Enterprise" and it was presented at the University Theater in May of 1955, directed by Shepherd. The scenario was the model for those which began a month later—a tape of it convinced Sills to become involved—and a rough version of it is presented below.

(In performance the scenario would have been pinned backstage in a sparser form than this with only a list of scenes, and within each scene a one-line description of each character's intention and motivation—i.e., where he or she had to start and end in each scene. In this version a synopsis of the back story has been added to introduce the action; also included are the written handbills that accompany it from time to time.)

JUNIOR ACHIEVEMENT
(Enterprise)

THE STORY

Five teenage boys own an automobile in common, an old Ford that barely runs. One day a used-car dealer's advertisement is placed on the windshield of their car, offering to buy it. They drive to the dealer's lot, but once there they find that the bargain is not as attractive as it seemed. They trade their car in for one larger but equally old and useless, for which they are to pay an additional hundred dollars in weekly installments. Meeting the payments is too difficult for the boys but just as they are about to lose their car, they discover an even more promising advertisement from another dealer. On their way to his lot, however, they smash their car up.

They are now forced to work to make up their deficit, and go into the handmade jewelry business, using as raw material the junk from their smashed car. At last they pay for it, but still they have no car, when suddenly they are singled out to receive a junior achievement award. The prize is a new car. Just as they are about to ride off in it, they find still another advertisement, and as the play ends they are undecided whether to be content with their lot or to try to improve their luck once more.

THE CHARACTERS

The chief characteristic of the *group of boys* is that no statement, even the most trivial, can be made without encountering an argument. There is a continual struggle for leadership in the group, and this struggle will be decided by the actors themselves.

The *used-car dealer* is a master of many roles. He is at once fatherly and avaricious, a perfect confidence man.

The *Junior Achievement Committee* is a group of glowing businessmen and PTA women, full of enthusiasm for the enterprise of these boys, which is, after all, what has made America great. The chairman of the committee is the used-car dealer.

SCENE I
The boys and their original car

A minor repair is needed on the car, and a loud argument is raging about who will bear the cost. Each of the boys recalls some incident in which he underwent a great personal hardship on behalf of the car. (If a real car is available, many effects will take place. A door won't shut. Finally several good slams are successful, but these cause the window to fall down. Efforts to raise the window by hand come to a halt when someone puts his foot through the running board.)

It is revealed at last that regardless of whose obligation it is, there is no one who has enough money for the repair. At this point they discover a way out of their difficulties. An advertisement has been placed on their windshield by a used-car dealer. One of the boys reads it aloud.

"I must have two hundred used cars by Friday. I will pay up to twice the value of this car. You may even receive a new car plus cash for your present car. Don't ask me why, I'm crazy."

Another argument begins. The tough-minded faction of the group laughs pitilessly at the dealer's plight. It is clear that they really have this dealer over a barrel and are anxious to capitalize on it. The milder view that they should play fair with the dealer and not take advantage of him is suppressed by the argument that one has to be tough to get along in the world.

SCENE II
The dealer's lot

The boys are vastly impressed by the wonders they see at the dealer's lot. Some argue for foreign cars, although the members of this segment cannot agree on a model. Others argue for Fords, Plymouths, or Buicks. Evidence of speed, pickup, mileage, economy, and appearance is introduced.

The dealer himself joins them, awing them completely. He deprecates their car, blames the state of business, slings mud at his competitors, and describes his own unhappy circumstances which shames them into discarding their low, profiteering motives. The dealer becomes fatherly and generous, taking the group into his confidence, and professes that his liking for the boys has corrupted his good judgment and that he has a deal to propose that is very much to their advantage.

SCENE III
The boys and their second car

The boys have traded in their car for another one in similar condition. They must also pay five dollars every Friday for twenty weeks. It is now several weeks later, on a Friday, and the weak points of the car have by now been revealed to the disillusioned group. Some have a tendency to blame, some to defend the dealer. They describe the difficulties of meeting the payments, since the allowances they receive from their parents are just enough to pay for gas and maintenance. A collection among them nets exactly five dollars and four cents, but some of this is borrowed money, and the prospects for next Friday are black. The horrors of part-time employment are described at some length, and the boys are shocked by this possibility into a state of near panic. Some are for giving the car up. Any wild scheme might be proposed.

But suddenly a way out of their difficulties arises. They see on the windshield a note from another dealer containing an offer even more fantastic than the first.

"If I don't get three hundred used cars in the next five days I will go broke. I have paid up to a thousand dollars for a car just like this, and will continue to pay triple and quadruple prices. Come and take the shirt off my back. [signed] Crazy Sam."

Their speculation now runs high. They will sell their present car to the new dealer and with the profits they will not only pay off the first dealer but will have enough money left for a really good car. They regret their lenience with the first dealer and decide that their circumstances are sufficiently desperate to override any sympathy they might have for the dealer's business difficulties.

They jump into their car to drive off to the new dealer's, but as they start they become loudly preoccupied with a pretty girl passing by on the sidewalk and run into a tree.

SCENE IV
The boys without any car at all

Their car is a complete wreck, although they have escaped without injury. Now they have no car and must still meet their payments. The necessity of working has been imposed on them by parental command, and their allowances have been shut off. As they go through the inventory of their talents and skills they find themselves completely barren of any money-making possibilities. Joining the army, leaving town, and other romantic notions are argued vigorously but defeated.

At last someone comes up with an idea. In metalworking class he has learned how to make jewelry from scraps of tin. Why not cut up their smashed car into earrings and pins? Then each one can sell this junk to the parents of the others and the money for the car will soon be paid. This is agreed upon.

SCENE V
The same, weeks later, four of the boys

The enterprise is successful, and the last of the money has been paid. It seems that their efforts have coincided with a juvenile fad for the jewelry. Horrible-looking examples of their work are demonstrated. Their allowances have been restored as a reward for their enterprise, and the boys resolve to be patient and wait until they have saved enough money for another car.

The fifth boy joins them. He has received a letter, and the five of them are to receive a junior achievement award for their little business. This elates them, but their elation is all in terms of the possibility of receiving a car as a gift from their proud parents.

SCENE VI

The boys and an audience of proud parents at the Junior Achievement Awards. The chairman of the Chamber of Commerce makes a speech. Needless to say, the chairman is the first used-car dealer, Crazy Jake. The chairman's speech:

"Ladies and Gentlemen: It is a privilege and an honor to come before you to pay tribute to these five boys whose courage and enterprise have gained them this award. When we see the shocking crime rate and read in the papers of the growing wave of juvenile delinquency, we say, 'Is this the youth of America?' It is boys like this who show us that the answer is 'no,' that America can depend on her youth, and that they are fit to carry on her promise.

"These boys are a lesson for us all. When we ourselves fall behind and say, 'there are no new worlds to conquer,' that 'the frontier is dead,' we have only to look at these boys and see that the road to success lies everywhere and that many a trash can conceals a fortune. Look at this jewelry [he shows a piece of jewelry]. Who would believe that this beautiful piece of jewelry was once a hubcap? Or that this handsome paperweight was ever a radiator ornament? [It is all too easy to believe it.] This, ladies and gentlemen, is the American spirit.

"Who says we are behind Europe in artistic accomplishment? Here is the art of America. In America, the beautiful, the useful, and the profitable are all combined. That is the American way. Look at our automobiles. The whole story is told by the American automobile. I am proud that I sell automobiles. Whenever I sell an automobile, I know that someone's life has been enriched. You'll always find me, right there at 2230 South Richmond Street, open till nine on Fridays.

"We have a prize for these boys. It's outside, and they'll see it after the official part of the ceremony is over. But first we will give them this plaque. Let me read what it says on this plaque: 'From the citizens of today to the citizens of tomorrow. Courtesy of the Forthright Jewelry Company.' Here you are, boys [gives plaque].

"In conclusion I would like to say that in plain words what we're honoring today is hustle. It is not the laggard who will win the day, it is those who have the true American spirit of hustle. America is a nation of hustlers. Thank you."

SCENE VII

A road in the park

A new automobile is parked at the curb, just offstage right.

The prize is a new Ford. The boys are overwhelmed. The used-car dealer congratulates them and leaves. Immediately a squabble breaks out about who will be the first to drive it. The importance of breaking a new car in right is stressed by all. In the midst of this argument a third advertisement is discovered on the window of the car.

"They say I'm crazy and they're right. I cannot stay in business if I don't get a thousand used cars by next week. To do this, I must give away my new Buicks and Cadillacs in almost even trades. Don't wait! I may be in a mental institution in five days. Just ask for John the Madman."

A new argument breaks out. Shall they be satisfied with what they have or try to better themselves? The argument continues as the curtain falls.

THE END

What was remarkable about this scenario—and many others that followed it—was that familiar though its content might seem, it came out *funny*. On the face of it, it might be interpreted as an improving slice of life, a tableau which might conceivably be presented by the local Chamber of Commerce itself. Yet presented by young actors grappling through improvisation with how they really felt about the idea of "enterprise" to an audience equally aware of what that idea meant to society in general, unhysterically, realistically, without didactic symbolism or ideological fanfare, it made everyone laugh.

Clearly there was a large gap between the reality endorsed by the Chamber of Commerce—a reality that included exploitation of gullible youth and rewards for self-extrication—and the reality of the street. What Bowen—and Shepherd and Sills—discovered was that merely by telling the truth, without a moralistic conclusion or a neon sign flashing the word "message!", they could make their audiences wet their pants.

It was this principle which made the Compass, and later the Second City, the success they became. Neither Shepherd nor Sills set out to create a satiric theater. Each in his own different way was committed deeply to the idea of community theater. When they put young actors onstage with a sympathetic audience and supplied them with a technique that stripped away the learned for the actual, they had on their hands an exclusively satiric theater. The most dynamic theatrical manifestation of Boomer humor—one which gave us many of our seminal actors and directors and writers—was not in its genesis a comedy store. It was a continuing experiment which, because of the techniques of release it invented and the times in which it existed, created satirists.

On July 5, 1955, the Compass opened, and was an immediate hit. Its basic program included a scenario, usually directed by Shepherd, Sills, or Elaine May; a "Living Newspaper" which had performers taking news items from the day's paper and then rendering them as playlets, and on top of that, improvising scenes on suggestions from the audience. The evening began at 9:00 P.M. and though it was supposed to end at midnight often continued until one or two in the morning if the audience demanded it. The pace was extraordinary largely because of the involvement of the audience, which was allowed the license of determining how long the performers stayed onstage.

Sets, costumes, and lighting effects were minimal, ideas from both sides of the footlights defining the action. When lags occurred there was always someone ready with music or pantomime to bridge the gaps. Actors doubled as waiters and waitresses serving those lucky enough to gain access to the actual performance area. The sidewalks were always packed with the not-so-lucky. Little material, alas, survived this chaos of activity, for it was not written down, but Bowen's recall is invaluable:

"There was one called 'The Fuller Brush Salesman.' In the first scene we see a young man off the street, a kind of aimless fellow, who goes in and answers an ad for Fuller Brush salesmen. The manager—I played that part—explains to the young man what it's necessary to do to be a Fuller Brush salesman. He equips him with a box of samples and gives him a sales pitch, dresses him up, and sends him out. So the young man goes from door to door and he can't master the sales pitch. He sort of stupidly holds out the samples and the people grab them and they take the things that aren't supposed to be samples and they order a lot of things they never intend to pay for. Halfway through, he realizes that everyone's taking advantage of him—all the housewives—and he says, in effect, the way it is in this society, you either screw or be screwed and he's not going to be screwed anymore. So then we see him visiting all the same women, but this time he comes on like a high-powered salesman. He's learned his lesson the American way and now he's an ace salesman, and he swamps them with brushes that they haven't the faintest use for. The actor, Andy Duncan, had marvelous ingenuity in coming up with weird kinds of brushes. In the end, he is now the sales manager and he's interviewing the new young man who comes in.

"Then there was one that Elaine [May] wrote called 'Georgina's First Date.' It's about a fat, unattractive girl. On a bet from his friends, a very handsome guy invites her to the senior prom. Everybody thinks she's ugly and fat and she sort of knows it. He's got a bet with his friends that he's going to take her out and screw her—ten dollars, twenty dollars, whatever. But what the play is about is how all of society pushes her into this date because it's a 'winner' date. He's a 'winner' in society. So now her parents are delighted that she's got this great date, and they tell her to stay out as late as she likes. At the prom, all the guys are sniggering and taunting behind her back. It's quite ugly. And one of her friends explains what to do if the date tries to make out. Eventually they leave, and he screws her, which is now a very unhappy thing for her. But when she gets home, her mother is waiting up, and Georgina, crying her eyes out, insists she's had a great, great time. Just a great time!"

In the fall of 1955 Compass moved to a new location at 6473 South Lake Park, where fifty more people could be accommodated, and new infusions of talent occurred at that time with the arrival from New York of Mike Nichols, Severn Darden, and Shelley Berman. (Sills and his then wife Barbara Harris left for England that fall and Shepherd brought many new people both as directors to fill his shoes and as increments to what was becoming a theatrical phenomenon.)

It's worth noting that very, very few of those involved started out with any idea of ending up an actor. Mike Nichols says:

"Right down to when Elaine and I auditioned for the Blue Angel we knew we weren't going to be in show business. It was just something to make a living until we decided what to do. For the first year in which we ended up on television and everything else (i.e., Broadway) we thought it was a big joke . . . Everybody back in the Compass had that mentality of . . . I don't know . . . oddballs, who didn't know what they were going to do, but knew it wasn't going to be the theater."

This attitude was shared by other founders of both Compass and Second City. Roger Bowen had no thought of becoming an actor although he participated in every major improv group of the fifties and sixties. Bill Alton first got involved as a lark. Tony Holland knew that whatever he did, it wasn't going to be performing. In short, a majority of the most important participants in the creation of a satiric center and the techniques it invented did so outside the legitimate or conventional theater. It was almost as if show business was something else to be rebelled against, another facet of the established order, and as absurd as all the others. This was equally true of the English branch of the family—the Beyond the Fringe team and the Cambridge Footlights—and certainly informed the *Lampoon*'s originators. Show business and its acceptable humorists were regarded as legitimate targets—and not just to parody, but to search out and destroy.

Many of the basic forms that would later become those of Second City were established at the Compass between 1955 and 1957. Partly because the actors could not keep up with the pressure of rehearsing and creating a new scenario (they were generally forty minutes long or more) every week, the show began to concentrate on shorter pieces, the product of successful improvisations, which were repeated, refined, and "set" as sketches in the repertory of the company.

One of these was a piece originated by Mike Nichols and Elaine May called "Teenagers." "Teenagers" was historic. The first example of what would become a major theme of Boomer humor, the counterpointing of the officially approved version of teenage sexuality with reality. Says Nichols: "It's hard to describe. It's just two kids screwing around in the backseat and getting their arms tangled up, talking about what they talk about, and it had the line in it when she says, 'If we went any further, I know you wouldn't respect me,' and I say, 'Oh, I'd respect you like *crazy!* You have no idea how much I'd respect you!'"

In a decade that found *Never on Sunday* a salacious movie, this kind of material was risqué. And in presenting the reality behind the desperately clean and controllable image of teens presented on television and everywhere else in the official media, it appealed immensely to the young audience who saw it. It became one of the most requested scenes at the Compass.

In this respect, of course, the scene was also at odds with the whole notion of an improvised cabaret. How, if improvised material was the core of the performance, new and raw and ever changing, could a scene be requested? Therein lay a paradox that would be one of the factors in the dispersion of the Compass players, and that would haunt Second City all its days. However sincerely the group adhered to the principle of improvisation, inevitably in the process dominant material and dominant performers would be bound to emerge.

Within the company Nichols and May found a distinct rapport. Nichols recalls that in the final analysis he could never "do it" with anyone else the way he could with Elaine: "It depended on a certain connection with Elaine and a certain mad gleam in her eye or my eye when we knew something was starting and then the other would jump in and go along."

Inexorably, the two became the core of the group. (There were other pairings but none that could hold the audience in quite the same way.) The rules and techniques which all had learned became most dramatically realized by the team.

In spring 1956 Compass moved to a still larger location some distance away and, before winter, had closed. A friend of the company, Ted Flicker, proposed to Shepherd that they open a New York Compass, but this proved difficult to finance and one was opened in St. Louis instead. Nichols and May and others migrated south to be in this company but in 1957 it too closed, and the new team headed east to New York and stardom.

At one time or another Compass players or Compass theaters operated in several cities—New York, Philadelphia, Washington, again St. Louis, and a rather successful one in Hyannisport in which Alan Alda made his debut. This was in line with Shepherd's original desire to have Compass theater spring up spontaneously wherever people felt the need—as if it were a sort of beneficial herb. Like most of Shepherd's ideas it was only partially successful as indeed were the companies. Shepherd himself says of the Compass: "I lost track of the fact that what I was trying to do was based on the audience, not the performers. I should have been building audiences out there, training audiences to improvise and direct and write and get into the act. But I was blinded by the success of some of my friends. I thought that if they were able to make a living at the industrialization of gags, I should be able to, too."

Not only is this little epitaph revealing of Shepherd's messianic character (he later, according to Bill Alton, decided to concentrate his energies only on amateurs, not professionals, teaching them the technique of improvisation so that they could enjoy theater "right in their living room"), but it is typical of the feelings of most of the original members of the Compass at the time, as they watched the extraordinary success of Nichols and May and then of Shelley Berman. There is, too, a clear undercurrent of purism, an implication that those who became stars subsequent to their experience of the Compass were exploiting it for their own gain.

The moral niceties of this problem need not concern us—although they recur again and again throughout the history of Boomer humor—but the accusation helps obliquely to demonstrate the value and limits of improvisation. Improvisation was a remarkable phenomenon, profoundly of its time, and far from confined to theater. As Robert Brustein pointed out in a subsequent article in *The New Republic* (May 1963), reviewing the Premise and Second City together, improvisation was—aside from its obvious relationship to jazz—also at the core of "action painting" and much of the literature of the day. If no other example were needed, Kerouac's work in toto was a form of improvisation in print. But as Brustein also demonstrates, improvisation, especially improvisation before an audience, is not an art form, or a substitute for theater. This is something that has largely been forgotten by improvisation's modern exponents who seem to think that calling for complex suggestions from the audience for a place, a time, a mood, a dramatic style, etc., and then improvising a scene that fits is somehow an end in itself. While there is a certain Houdini-like spectacle involved in watching performers extricate themselves from the apparently inescapable bonds of audience suggestion, this is neither true improvisation nor theater. Improvisation is a process. Ironically, Shepherd, by implying that those who went on from the Compass to fame and fortune were somehow betraying their improvisational roots, may well have been making the same mistake of regarding improvisation as something sacred, an end in itself.

It was hard in the late fifties not to be a true believer. Despite its foreshadowing in the Stanislavsky/Method school of acting (Method-ist par excellence Marlon Brando improvised scenes in *On the Waterfront),* improvisation as a functioning creative technique was "discovered" at the Compass. This must have been pretty exciting, for it was an expression of revolt, symbolic and actual, discarding accepted theatrical forms and, what's more, demonstrating that the result was dynamic and original.

It was also an antidote to the perceived poison of television, which dehumanized drama of any kind by erecting a panoply of technology between performer and audience and cramming the result into a piece of furniture in the living room. Improvisation was thus a banner under which many different kinds of people could gather—not all of them humorists nor, as we have seen, by any means professional actors. The excitement at the Compass in 1955 was inchoate, a spontaneous discovery of community, as well as an expression of dissent and distaste with the prevailing repression. Andrew Duncan, one of the original members of both Compass and Second City and one of the best, said:

"We were doing some very outspoken things on sex and politics, saying 'shit' onstage, calling a spade a spade. A lot of what we did was very negative in that we were satirizing the establishment's institutions. But a lot of it, too, was an expression of how we wanted to live, crude and pioneering as it was."

Improvisation, in this particular mix of people, actualized satire. The kind of material it produced sprang from concern, not ideology. These were not Brechtian heroes and villains, but ordinary middle-class characters caught in the various binds of an overcontrolled society. The scenarios it performed concentrated on salesmen, tax evaders, parents, priests, teachers, and exposed them not by frontal assault but by taking on their characteristics, gently judoing them into absurdity.

This is what improvisation did for the Compass. It would do something very different for Second City.

■   ■

From 1957 to 1959 Nichols and May went from strength to strength, deepening and consolidating their pieces and appearing on most of the major variety shows of the time. They recorded a highly successful album and began to appear in major print media such as *Life* magazine: they also caught the attention of Jack Paar, whose show gave major exposure to those who were called "The New Comedians." Television and the new humor did not click right away. Nonetheless, Paar always claimed to have "discovered" Nichols and May. Here's Tom O'Malley who booked the show at the time:

"Jack Rollins came around with these two people that he'd just brought in from the Compass in St. Louis. And they would ask secretaries: 'Think of a place, think of a Shakespearean actor,' and they would play these games in the office and they were just great. There was an entire day of Mike and Elaine just going around and performing at the Hudson Theater. I went in and said, 'Jack, they are just sensational.' Then . . . we made a mistake, and it was everybody's fault. It was so new, improv, at the time. They had set pieces and they could have done a couple of those and then gone into an improv, but they said, 'Let's really shoot the works. We'll *just* do improv.' In the Hudson Theater, where people line up at 43rd Street near midnight!

"So I wrote this glowing intro and they came out and they were improvising, on live television, and they died! They just died! Right after the commercial Paar comes into the control room and says, 'They are awful, my God, they are awful, Tom! On that introduction I read, I can't go out there.' And I was laughing and saying, 'They are fantastic, we shouldn't have done it this way.' [Paar says,] 'Don't ever bring their name up to me again.'

"And the next morning Paar came in around noontime and I said, 'Now, Jack, about last night,' and he said, 'Don't ever mention their name to me again! Don't ever mention it.' And I said, 'Jack, they are wonderful.' And he said, 'I'm only telling you one time more, don't ever mention Mike and Elaine to me again.' So O.K., I didn't. They went on to 'The Perry Como Show,' they went on to 'The Steve Allen Show,' within a couple of months they had a huge spread in *Life* magazine. That was the final certification, validation.

"I took the *Life* magazine and I laid it out on Jack's desk opened up to Mike and Elaine, the sensational new comedy team. And he looked at it, I was sitting right next to him. And he said, 'Would Mike and Elaine come on the show?' And I said, 'They are out of our category now, Jack. They are getting five thousand dollars for Perry Como, five thousand dollars for Steve Allen.' And then he said . . . 'You mean to say they won't come on with me even though I discovered them?' Later, after he went to 'The Tonight Show,' he had them on a number of times and every time his introduction to Mike and Elaine was: 'Here's a couple of kids who came to me a few years ago and I put them on their very first appearance on television.' "

Hard on the heels of Nichols and May came Shelley Berman, a much less likely candidate for success. Berman had been an import at the Compass, with no ties to the U. of C. and not many more to academia. His first impression of the Compass players was blunt: "They were a bunch of smart-asses . . . [and] . . . extremely young." Nonetheless he remembered being intimidated by their intellectualism:

"Some of our sessions together, which we called rehearsals, were largely intellectually steeped conversations. I was never really intellectually oriented. I had worked more viscerally, intuitively. All I wanted to do was to get up onstage and explode, you see. But these sessions were good because I learned a great deal from those people . . . more than the craft of acting and comedy. I learned on an academic level things I never knew. I thought I'd read everything there was to read, but I hadn't read what they'd read. I tried to catch up, to at least have some acquaintance with much of what was being said. I'd never heard of Kierkegaard. I wasn't by any means unschooled, but they had a more specific knowledge. It was esoteric and I wanted to be part of that and so I tried."

He did try and, for the most part, it didn't work. Berman had not only his own intellectual insecurity, but he was an aggressive and ambitious professional. In an atmosphere where many, as we have seen, never thought of themselves as performers, this was alien; additionally, although everyone who worked with him is highly complimentary of his improvisational skills, the group-think that improvisation demanded ultimately had no place for his combative individualism. He wanted intensely to have such a place, and on sheer talent emerged as one of the more powerful of the original company. Even so, he could not seem to develop a relationship like that of Nichols and May—although the three of them actually talked of forming a trio. Rather than fade back into the group as less driven colleagues might have, Berman went forward into solo improvs. The very first of these contained within it the seeds of what became his classic telephone monologue style.

"It was a soliloquy. I opened with a brief telephone conversation in which I found out there'd been a party last night I hadn't been invited to and that the girl who'd stood me up [last night] was at the party. I hung up the phone and then did this thing to the mirror in which I sold myself to myself—talked about the good qualities I had. And it was rather moving and interesting. I think then I went back to the phone to call my friend and tell him to go to hell. The only reason I used the phone was to establish why I felt disliked and why I felt there must be reason to dislike me. I didn't feel, since my idea was selling myself to myself rather than selling myself to somebody, that it would be a good idea to have another person to improvise with. Yet I had to establish my plot. Although improvisation isn't playwrighting, you still have an action to pursue and it has to be clear.

"Anyway, I was doing this scene at the Compass, and the phone conversation was getting more involved every night. It got to be a little better and a little longer, and one night, when I finished the phone conversation, the audience applauded as I hung up. So I stopped right there. And that became my first actual telephone monologue."

Later on during the same season (on New Year's Eve, appropriately), Berman had an opportunity to do another of these. The audience suggestion was "the morning after the night before."

"I set my hangover by having the worst possible headache. The first words out of my mouth were: 'Oh God, God, God, God . . .' and I felt around for the rest of my head. 'Oh God, where is my Alka-Seltzer?' Then the pantomime of the Alka-Seltzer and water. 'Don't fizz!' Then I got on the phone, dialed my friend, and found out what I'd done to his household. Well, on the first night I did it, it was just that I threw a lamp through his window and vomited on his rug. That, I thought, was a little strong, to have thrown up on his rug. A rather tasteless idea. So on future occasions I took that out.

"One night, after I'd done this two or three times, Severn Darden came to me as I was just going out to do it again. 'Not his lamp,' he whispered, 'his cat.' So I said, 'Okay.' What the hell? I had nothing to lose. And so I threw the cat out the window. And it became one of the most requested routines that I have in my act today. People are still requesting 'The morning after the night before,' or they say, 'Do the hangover,' or sometimes, 'Do the one with the cat.' How casually it was said: 'Not a lamp, Shelley, a cat.' Just whispered in darkness. How casually that became a routine which earned me great, great sums of money and considerable importance in a difficult field."

In its first two widely recognized successes—Nichols and May and Shelley Berman—the Chicago school of Boomer humor was doing something it would do for the next thirty years. By subjecting talented individuals, not necessarily actors, to the neutral discipline of improvisation, it enabled them to tap into their reserves so they developed their own deeply personal sense of comedy and voices. This was a spiritual process, involving a profound awareness of self and of others.

Nichols and May and Shelley Berman were the first proponents, followed by many others from both Compass and Second City, of what came to be known as the Second City style. In one sense this is a misnomer, for it has always been their very differences from one another, their properly realized uniqueness that has set these particular Boomer humorists apart. In another sense, though, the perception of a style was accurate. To the outside world there was something Nichols, May, and Berman (and the others who followed) had in common. However different their material might be in form and content, they all had the same level of intelligence. It could be an intellectual intelligence in the case of Nichols and May or one that wasn't intellectual at all, as in the case of Berman, but it was the same supple entity at work—an intelligence stripped of fat, proud of its musculature, in well-developed control of its inflection, gesture, and phrase.

This was not style—which carries with it the implication of learned behavior, or even uniform behavior—so much as a quality which informed many different styles. That quality was at the time quite tangible to those who booked television shows, signed record contracts, and produced Broadway shows, all areas in which Nichols and May and Berman prospered quickly. Like Mort Sahl, they found audiences hungry for encounter with well-conditioned minds and only too delighted to question the sleazy propaganda that was being sold to them. Even if the questioning was as gentle as throwing the traditional American family cat out of the window, that was fine. That was an attitude people found refreshing. Out the window went faithful pets and with them the official mechanisms designed to keep people busy, preoccupied, nervous, frightened, and certainly far from free.

What interested Paul Sills was this business of being free. It had interested Shepherd too, and his dream of community theater was his way of trying to release ordinary people from their social bondage. The trouble was, however much Shepherd's missionary fervor might have originally galvanized the Compass, Compass hadn't survived. It hadn't even—at least in the sense he dreamed of—had a community function. When all the smoke cleared and the house lights went up, there was not much left in the theater but a very new and special kind of performer. That stripped-down intelligence. Men and women prepared to experience the paradox of irony—to let the problems of lust, arrogance, fear, bigotry, loneliness, hatred, or frustration flow from them and find in the resultant absurdity a mysterious but satisfying solution. It was these people—not actors, exactly, but not ordinary humans either—who headed Sills's agenda.

Some people have suggested that it was the success of Nichols and May that prompted Paul Sills to found Second City, but this makes little sense in the overall pattern of his life.†

Far more likely that their success had quite the opposite effect—prompting him to redouble his exploration of what could never be accomplished in the world of mass entertainment. The closing of the Compass must have been frustrating, especially as he had not exactly shared Shepherd's theories of its aims; part of him must have felt simply that it was his turn to drive.

In some ways he was in an enviable position. Shepherd's political fervor had smashed down doors which Sills, left on his own, might only have leaned on. And where Shepherd had stumbled blindly off into the darkness, Sills was

† Nothing Sills, one of the half dozen most important figures in modern American theater, has done indicates any desire for conventional success, financial or otherwise. The hardest-nosed thing he ever seems to have done is selling out his interest in Second City to Bernie Sahlins, for $25,000. An Amadeus-sized sum of course, except that Salieri Sahlins can hardly be accused of profiteering himself. After thirty years of remarkable stewardship of the nation's greatest comedic oil field, Sahlins realized a massive $1.8 million from current owner Andrew Alexander, which averages out at $43,000 a year; he would have made a good deal more renting out the Second City Theater for revivalist meetings.

left with the opportunity to explore the new territory, find out where he was, what could be built and how. He was no less committed than Shepherd to the idea of change and personal freedom, but it was through the more achievable methods of self-regeneration and example rather than political agitation:

"[The purpose of theater is] . . . liberation of the people. The possibility of this country liberating itself. I'm not talking about tearing down buildings and things like that. I'm talking about personal liberation. People suffer from fantastic restrictions on their self-understanding or their ability to affect. They're graded, stacked in categories of excellence, measured against all kinds of nonsense standards with the result that their personal selves are locked inside them. The confirmation of their own existence must come to people or else they find it in negative ways such as delinquency or apathy or reactionary behavior, the shrinking of the person from the common good, cynicism, denial, and so on. To me it's very important the people get a little heart and spirit back. Now I can't go up to some guy who's putting in a lot of dead time with his life and say, 'Look, you're screwing your own existence.' But if the actors hit it, everybody will pick it up."

On December 16, 1959, Second City opened its doors for the first time, at 1842 North Wells Street in a converted Chinese laundry.‡ It was barely bigger than the Compass (120 seats as opposed to 90) and was even smaller in the performance area. It's name was sarcastic; the phrase came from an A. J. Liebling article about Chicago, in which that arch-Manhattanite did a cut-and-slash job on the city of Big Shoulders. Considering how much would proceed from its tiny stage in the new few years—and how little by comparison from New York—it was a juicy piece of prognostic irony.

Sills's business partners in the venture were Bernie Sahlins and Howard Alk. Sahlins had been a co-producer of the Compass precursor, Playwrights Theater, and Alk was an ex-Compass member. Their business arrangements were simple and minimal. (According to Second City veteran Tony Holland, Sills had been in two minds up until a short while before the founding of Second City, whether to invest his nest egg in it or in a hamburger franchise called Mr. Swiftee.) The pay scale, variously recollected as either $100 or $150 a week, was by current theatrical standards quite generous. (This was at a time when Off-Broadway still paid a mere $35 a week.)

The cast consisted of Compass stalwarts Roger Bowen, Severn Darden, Barbara Harris, Andrew Duncan, Eugene Troobnick, and Alk. There was only one newcomer, a brilliantly funny airhead called Mina Kolb. Until quite shortly before the opening the most important planned element in the show had been a long, improvised scenario just like those originally presented at the Compass, built around an average guy who experiences various dehumanizing forces in the course of his daily life, dreams of overcoming them, and finally dies and goes—happily—to heaven. The scenario, which was too

‡ Cf. the hungry i and the earlier Playwrights. The sinister part played by the Chinese in the development of modern satire must not be underestimated.

clumsy to work, was dumped but several of the scenes it had generated survived in the opening show, including a great piece by Bowen called "Businessman," which would become an early Second City classic (Businessman—capitalism's superhero—was performed by Eugene Troobnick):

BUSINESSMAN*
(A Satire)

NARRATOR: The most recent trend in entertainment has been to take what was originally a juvenile form of entertainment and upgrade it for the adult taste. In the last few years we have seen the adult western, this year television is featuring the adult eastern, and tonight, for the first time, we would like to present the adult middle-western.
Faster than a speeding ticker tape! More powerful than a goon squad! Able to leap loopholes at a single bound! Is it a bird? Is it a plane? No! It's *Businessman!* Yes, Businessman, who in the guise of mild mannered Pierce Fenner, ace reporter for the *Kiplinger Letter,* fights unfair business practices. The scene is the boardroom of a giant corporation. The directors are in an uproar. *(Uproar backstage. Three directors walk on, make despairing gestures, and leave.)* What can be done about Japanese competition? Unnoticed, Pierce Fenner slips from the room.
FENNER: This is a job for . . . *(voice deepens)* . . . Businessman! Quick. Out of my Ivy League suit. Into my Bermuda shorts. Then it's up, up, and away! *(Businessman removes trousers with difficulty, then strikes flying pose.)*

BLACKOUT

(The scene is a factory in Japan.
Two Japanese are inspecting a sports car)
SATO: *(Obsequiously)* Truly, Director of Research Mori, this is a wonderful automobile you have designed!
MORI: *(Arrogantly)* Your words of praise are like a whispering waterfall beneath a grove of pine trees.
SATO: Look at those low, sleek lines. (He pantomimes a car two feet high.) An engineering marvel. It will capture the American market. Everyone will want to own a Mark II Haikupet Sports Car.
MORI: How much will it sell for in America?
SATO: *(Using abacus)* Let's see . . . we'll sell two million the first year . . . buy them back for junk value the second year . . . Brilliant idea of yours, designing a car that's obsolete before it leaves the factory . . . The price will be forty-nine dollars and ninety-eight cents. But tell me, Director of Research Mori, how will this superb engineering marvel run without a motor?

* Copyright 1960 by Roger Bowen

MORI: Watch. (*He claps his hands. A laborer enters, pantomimes lifting the car like a rickshaw, and carries it to the other side of the stage.*)

SATO: Brilliant! We will not only solve the foreign exchange problem but the population problem as well.

MORI: And the low cost of technical assistant will be an additional inducement to the American buyer.

BUSINESSMAN: (*Coming to earth*) Hello? What's this? Ah! My old "friends," Sato and Mori. What deviltry are you up to this time?

SATO: Stay right where you are, Businessman! One more step and you will violate the Commerce and Navigation Pact of 1954.

BUSINESSMAN: What is this gimcrack you are attempting to foist off on the American public? I warrant you'll not succeed.

MORI: We will this time, Businessman. We will import the Haikupet into America under the Balance of Payments Agreement signed by your chief executive last week. Come ahead, Sales Manager Sato! (*Businessman starts piling huge blocks of air in front of them and the progress of the Japanese is arrested.*) What are you doing, Businessman?

BUSINESSMAN: What you had forgotten about, Mori. The Haikupet is a product of slave labor and a threat to the American Workingman. It must be kept out. I have constructed a Tariff Wall!

SATO: Curses! Businessman has defeated us again! (*The Japanese commit hara-kiri, bow, and shuffle from the stage.*)

BUSINESSMAN: Another victory for sound business principles. Then up, up and away! *Businessman flies away after bumping head on Tariff Wall.*)

(*A manager enters, pursued by two angry strikers. They are shouting.*)

STRIKER I: Look! There's Businessman!

STRIKER II: He'll help us!

MANAGER: Businessman! The United States Steel Company needs your help! These workers object to the new company policy!

STRIKER II: They cut our coffee break!

STRIKER I: Yeah! By one hour!

BUSINESSMAN: What you workers must realize is that the United States Steel Company is one of the great corporations in the world. When it does something, you can be sure it has a pretty good reason for doing it. Sometimes it's not wise to explain these reasons. You, on the other hand, are simply working men, and no one expects you to have the same broad perspectives as the company officials. I appeal to you, as one good American to another, get back to your machines.

STRIKER II: Scab!

STRIKER I: Fink!

STRIKER II: Down with Businessman!

BUSINESSMAN: Since you take this unpatriotic attitude, I myself shall operate the entire production line!

STRIKER I: Don't let him through!

STRIKER II: Close the picket line! (They link arms and sing: "Oh, you can't scare me, I'm stickin' with the union . . .")

BUSINESSMAN: *(While they are singing)* I don't wish to hurt them. After all, they are American workingmen. I have it! This is a job for my Businebreath! *(Businessman puffs up his cheeks and exhales loudly, sending the strikers flying from the stage.)*

MANAGER: Congratulations, Businessman, you've broken the strike! With the help of five freight car loads of our good neighbors from Mexico, we'll have the production line running again tomorrow. Name your own reward, sir.

BUSINESSMAN: I shall not refuse the customary stock option, but if you *really* want to show your gratitude, hire those men back with a decent American coffee break!

MANAGER: Of course, Businessman!

STRIKER I: *(Returning to stage)* God Bless you, Businessman!

STRIKER II: Businessman, stay for the company picnic!

BUSINESSMAN: Relax and enjoy yourselves, for *Businessman,* there can be no rest. Then it's up, up, and away! *(All cheer.)*

BLACKOUT

NARRATOR: Tune in next week when Businessman brings peace to the troubled island of Cuba.

END

In many ways, Second City was taking only a very cautious step forward from what had worked at the Compass four years earlier. There was a different organizing principle at work (or perhaps just an organizing principle, period). However cautious the content, however tentatively Sills moved forward, he kept every element that could be controlled under control. The result was a show very distinct from its chaotic progenitor. Here's Andy Duncan:

"What was evident at Second City was the completeness of the presentation. Rather than the anarchy which reigned at the Compass, Sills planned every second from the minute the light dimmed to the applause and bows. Also, whereas in Compass scenes would start without introductions, at Second City they would often be set up. I don't know where we got that convention of making introductions, but somehow it fell on me to come out and say, "Good evening. Welcome to Second City. Tonight we'd like to bring you our show, 'Too Many Hats'—or whatever the title was. Sills insisted very strongly that the audience get to know the actors very early in the show, so that by the end of the first act they could identify who the people were and pretty much what they did—who was the kook, the square, et cetera. The first act would have a lot of group numbers; then at the end of the first act I'd come out and say something like, "That completes the second part of our program. After a brief intermission we'll bring you the first part." The second act would have more of the heavy stuff. The people scenes were always second-act scenes. The stuff that relied on character and place, when you knew the audience was really with you. Part of the fun then was to turn the audience's expectations upside down in terms of what they anticipated from the individual cast members. Like Barbara [Harris] would come out and play old ladies. But very rarely would we start the show with people playing something very far away from themselves. Sills wanted a variety of cast and a balance of cast.

"We had a pretty rigorous schedule. We were open six days a week. We'd come to the theater at ten o'clock and work till about two, then have lunch and come back and work till about six or seven—sometimes right up almost until nine, show time—get a quick bite and then do a full Second City show, then take an intermission, and come back and do improvs. So a normal day could be fourteen, fifteen, sixteen hours. Saturday worse. You didn't usually have a rehearsal on Saturday, although there were times we did. Saturday night we did two full shows. We were open Sunday so we'd rehearse on Sunday. Monday was off. You'd fall into a rhythm, and sometimes it was easy because of that rhythm. It was almost like going to the office. Your perceptions were out in terms of what was going on—reading papers. And you'd be thinking of ideas for scenes, storing them up for the improv set."

What we see at work here of course is a director with a shrewd sense not just of what will persuade or jolt his audience but of what will entertain them. The traditional concern with making it clear to the audience which performer fits their preconceptions (the kook, the straight, the gay, the sexy blonde and so on), was the instinct of a showman. For all his profound commitment to the beneficial effects of improvisation, Sills was not about to proselytize his audience on that score, nor did he have any intention of leaving more to chance than he had to. Improvisations that worked, in fact, were noted, pulled into rehearsal, refined, further improved by further improv, and if they stood up to all this testing, found their way as set pieces into the next three-month cycle.

And restrictive though these concerns and disciplines might superficially seem, that group function was their ultimate goal. Only by becoming so totally focused on their theatrical purpose could the actors liberate themselves an individuals, liberate themselves even from being actors.

For Sills was not interested in founding a "theater" or training "actors." He was impatient with even *that* form of pretense. Andy Duncan: "Sills would say to us, 'Goddamnit, we're not a theater where you go out every night and give the same performance by the numbers, and the audience has a certain relaxed assurance that the actor knows what he's doing. The whole point of Second City is the unexpected. You've got to have your creative juices going. *Do* something onstage.' 'Don't drop your pants,' he'd say, 'but if you do, make sure your ass is painted blue.' "

This directorial approach drew a fine but crucial line between the two meanings of the verb "to act"—between "acting" in the sense of mimesis and "acting" in the sense of doing. Sills preferred the latter. It was presence over pretense every time—unrepeatable action over reproducible illusion.

In practice this gave Second City performers an intensity that startled audiences accustomed to the sprightly upbeat patina of revue and comic theater. The semiritual stock figures of these forms, whose actors were required to play *in front of* the audience and whose comedy relied to a large extent on what the audience expected of the stock figures (including occasionally dropping their pants) were discarded in favor of a much more comedically effective approach directed *out* to the audience, including them in the process and challenging them to enter the common and unpredictable reality (in which asses might conceivably be blue). But this was more than just letting the audience in on the joke—it was allowing them to see the essential machinery at work. The performer's reality preceded the actor's magic. Thus, when Second City played stock figures (for however modern their manifestations may be, there is no such thing as a new character type; the dizzy blonde, nerdy youth, or mad professor have been and will be with us forever), those figures themselves were, subtly, targets of the humor. The performer conveyed to the audience that he or she was now *acting*. The audience could thus enjoy both the character that was being played, and the fact that they knew a character was being played. And not the smallest part of the audience's enjoyment was that it was flattered to be let in on the process.

On December 16, 1959, the Second City opened its doors for the first time to an overflow crowd.

The company was an instant and enormous success.

Partly this was due to simple novelty; partly it was because Second City filled a social need for the new self-consciously educated and aware young audience from Chicago's suburbs—the prototype Boomers. There was, too, another element in their performance that struck a chord in the late fifties. Perhaps because they were improvising and therefore hesitant, or perhaps because they were just as neurotic as their audiences, there was a brittle, nervous quality to the early Second City companies that spoke directly to a generation preoccupied with psychoanalysis. A running theme in Second City material of the time—echoed elsewhere in humor of course, especially in print—was analysis, neurosis, and related disorders. Nor are these just the usual psychiatrist sketches. At least two major surviving pieces from the first couple of years of Second City's existence deal with Oedipus. One of them was a classic Second City group piece called "Great Books":

> *(The scene is a classroom in an adult education center.*
> *Enter a woman, Melva.)*

MELVA: Well, hello there.

ROCKWOOD: Are you a member of this Great Books course?

MELVA: Yes, I am, but what are you doing here?

ROCKWOOD: Well, Mr. Crenshaw, your regular instructor, is ill, I'm afraid. I'm filling in for him. My name is Rockwood.

MELVA: Oh, that's too bad. My name is Melva Stratford. My, these chairs are arranged strangely.

ROCKWOOD: Yes, well, so are we all.

SCOTT: *(Entering)* Hi! Great Books?

ROCKWOOD: Great Scott.

SCOTT: Hi, Melva. Sorry I'm late. I was working down at the agency and I . . . don't recognize you. You're new, aren't you?

ROCKWOOD: Not terribly. I'm thirty . . .

SCOTT: My name is Peregrine. Scott Peregrine the Third. *(Shakes hands.)* Bit greasy.

STELLA: *(Entering)* Hi!

MELVA *(to Stella):* You left a price tag on your purse.

STELLA: Yeah, I think I'm gonna return that. The season's over. I don't think it's me, you know?

SCOTT: Oh, I think it's you. It's a lovely bag.

ROCKWOOD: My name is Rockwood. What is yours?

STELLA: Dallas. Stella F. Dallas.

ROCKWOOD: Hi! How are you tonight?

GHENGIS: *(Entering)* Hi! How are you?

STELLA: You've been sick, haven't you?

GHENGIS: Yeah, Mummy and I both had the flu.

SCOTT: Your mummy's not coming tonight?

GHENGIS: No, she's at home tinting her hair blue.

ROCKWOOD: Excuse me, Mr. Peregrine. Is this the entire class?

SCOTT: Oh, well, there were a lot more in the class when we started, but *War and Peace* came along and wiped us out.

ROCKWOOD: Well, I trust you've all read every page of tonight's assignment from Mr. Crenshaw, *Oedipus Rex* by Sophocles.

SCOTT: Boy, I'll say.

ROCKWOOD: Just what is it about this great book that makes it truly great?

SCOTT: Well, actually I was wondering about that.

ROCKWOOD: Well, how is that, Mr. Peregrine?

SCOTT: Well, it's interesting, it's racy, it's spicy and God knows how it gets through the Post Office, huh? But it's not really a book, it's a play.

ROCKWOOD: Yes, but we've discovered that if you take a play and put it between covers it becomes a book.

MELVA: You mean . . . Are you trying to say that anything between covers is a book?

ROCKWOOD: No.

(General uproar)

ROCKWOOD: Ms. Dallas. I wonder if you'd perhaps be good enough to get the ball rolling, as it were, by giving us your opinion of this great book?

STELLA: I'd be delighted. I'd like to say first of all that I believe it's a great book because it's so old. Very difficult to follow, a little sickening here and there and it has a message . . . that I missed.

MELVA: That was wonderful, Stella, sweetie.

ROCKWOOD: Certainly a significant appraisal. Now, could we go on?

MELVA: Well, I thought it was very dizzy. Highly obtuse. And, everybody, I had my first catharsis.

(General congratulations)

MELVA: It wasn't much. It was a small one, but that's a start.

GHENGIS: I wonder if the class knows that the *Poetics* of Aristotle, the Greek philosopher, was based at least in part on *Oedipus Rex* and in the *Poetics,* Aristotle says that the plot is the soul of a tragedy.

SCOTT: You'll find that Ghengis here does a lot of reading on the side.

ROCKWOOD: Oh?

STELLA: He cheats!

GHENGIS: Well, despite the class's hostility, I would like to say that Mummy and I went to Greece last summer where we visited Mount Cithacron, where Oedipus was abandoned to the mercies of the elements. Mummy and I go everywhere together. It's always Mummy and Ghengis, Ghengis and Mummy.

ROCKWOOD: Well, you and your mother must have gotten a good deal of special significance from this play. Now, fascinating parallels could be drawn between the reactions of the Chorus in the play and the public controversy stirred up not too many months ago by Prof. Leo F. Kogh at the University of Illinois on premarital sexual relations.

SCOTT: Aren't you straying a little bit from your subject matter, bringing that up in here?

MELVA: You think that just because this is the University of Chicago Downtown Branch, you can say anything you want?

SCOTT: After all, you're not our family doctor.

GHENGIS: Nor mother for that matter . . .

In many ways this sketch is typical of the output of Second City in the first few years of its existence. It is mildly academic, its characters are upwardly mobile middle-class professionals, and it has a teacher-pupil relationship as its core. In the first two respects it is significantly different from Compass material at the same stage, which was not at all academic and tended to observe lower-middle-class mores rather than identify with middle-class ones. Certainly in comparison to the Compass scenarios quoted earlier, it appears to be expressing the actual interests and insecurities of the performers themselves more than making a point about people at large in society. (As for example in Bowen's "Enterprise" scenario.)

The teacher-pupil relationship appears in an overwhelming number of the sketches that have survived from this period.† This is sometimes a quasi-academic relationship as it is in "Great Books," but in its most obvious form the teacher-pupil relationship occurs in the far-ranging lectures of Severn Darden's timeless character Dr. Walter van der Vogelweide:

DR. WALTER VAN DER VOGELWEIDE *(heavy German accent):*

Now why, you will ask me, have I chosen to speak on the universe, rather than some other topic? Well, it's very simple . . . *there isn't anything else!* Now, the universe we examine through what Spinoza has called "The Lens of Philosophy." He calls it this because he was a lens grinder. Heaven knows what he would have called it if he had been, for example, a pudding manufacturer. So, into three branches is philosophy divided: ethics, aesthetics, and metaphysics. Now, ethics is the branch of philosophy which is neither aesthetics nor metaphysics . . . I think you follow.

This evening, I have decided to take the jump to metaphysics. Now, in the universe we have time, space, motion, and thought. Now you will ask me, what is this thing called thought? *(Long pause)* That is thought.

Now you will ask me, what is space? Now, this over here . . . this is some space. However, this is not all space. However, when I said that was time, that was all the time there was everywhere in the universe . . . at that time.

Now, the early Egyptian astronomers—there were no late Egyptian astronomers—looked up at the stars and with ease they measured time. But the Greeks were very exact—sometimes to the point of tediousness. They alone asked this question: Is time a measure or, conversely, is motion a measure of time? Well, I have in my hand a stopwatch . . . imaginary . . . and coming through the room is a railroad train . . . also imaginary . . . because if it was a real railroad train, it would kill us . . . Now, with the arrival of the twentieth century and Planck's Constant and the theory of Quantum Mechanics and with Heisenberg's Uncertainty Principle, I think . . . we still don't know. However, we might now easily turn to the pre-Socratic philosophers . . . who are always good for a laugh . . . Now, take Heraclitus. He went home to his wife Helen and he said, "Time is like a river which is flowing endlessly through the universe and you couldn't step in the same river twice, Helen." And she says, "What do you mean by that, Heraclitus? Explain yourself." "That means you could go down to the Mississippi River, for example, and you could step in and you could step out, and then you could step in again. But that river that you stepped in has moved downstream, you see? It's here. And you would only be stepping in the Missis-

† There are two albums from the first years of Second City, *Comedy from the Second City* and *From the Second City* both released in 1961, but containing material performed from its inception, in December 1959.

sippi River because that's what it's called, you see? But if something were on top of the water, for example a water bug, it would be downstream . . . unless of course it were swimming upstream. In which case it would be older and it would be a different bug." And she said, "Don't be an ass, Heraclitus. You could step into the same river twice. If you walked downstream."

He was amazed. So he went down to the agora, or the marketplace, where there were a lot of unemployed philosophers, which means philosophers who weren't thinking at that time. And they went down and had a few drinks first and went down to the river and into the river they threw a piece of wood, just to test how fast the river was going. And so Heraclitus saw how fast the wood was going, so he stepped into the river and ran and stepped and ran and stepped and ran and finally he ran into the Aegean Sea and was drowned. So much for time . . .

The teacher-pupil relationship often crops up more obliquely in scenes that have nothing to do with academia—those which were known as "people" scenes, or scenes of encounter. In "Blind Date," for example, which is about a young man getting ready for a blind date arranged by his sister, the sister begins to instruct him first in character as the date and then in character as the date's mother—on how to behave during the coming ordeal. And in one of the greatest Second City pieces, a scene known as "Museum," created by Alan Arkin and Barbara Harris, Harris as a neurotic art student encountering beatnik Arkin in a museum, first instructs him on the meaning of the art works and in turn is instructed by Arkin on how to express herself freely.

GUIDE: If the tour of the Art Institute of Chicago will kindly step this way. You will notice that this painting here is not really a painting at all, yes? It's what we call a construction. The young artist who made it, Mr. Harry Moore, has taken various bits of metal and crammed them willy-nilly in the frame and painted them.
STUDENT: I don't like it.
GUIDE: Well, you're wrong . . . Now, shall we go see the fish?

BEATNIK: *(Sings.)*
Here I am in Chicago
Sittin' in an art gallery.
I just fell in from New York City
In a driving rig.
And it's a bad scene in New York
But I swear it's a worse one in Chicago.
That's why I'm gonna split
For Denver, Colorado
Where my buddies are.
And that's the end of my story
And that's the end of my song.

STUDENT: I don't want to sound like a prude, but you're going to get kicked out of here.

BEATNIK: I don't care. I gotta speak my mind.

STUDENT: Oh, well that's healthy. I mean, as far as I'm concerned. Of course, it's all right with me. Actually, I know who you are, so . . .

BEATNIK: How do you know who I am?

STUDENT: Well, I mean I know who you are generically. You see, I took a Humanities course last year and I read quite a few of this generation's writings. I read *On the Road*.

BEATNIK: Yeah, Jack Kerouac.

STUDENT: Well, I read *Howl*, Allen Ginsberg.

BEATNIK: You know he's my buddy.

STUDENT: I didn't know that.

BEATNIK: I said yes. When we're in New York, we mess around.

STUDENT: Oh, how totally exciting.

BEATNIK: You know something about Allen Ginsberg? He's nuts.

STUDENT: Oh, well actually I didn't know that. That's very interesting. Well, you know, it took us all a week and a half to analyze that poem. While we knew it was profound, we just weren't sure why. There was one line in particular, though, that was totally enigmatic to us all and since you know him, maybe you could enlighten me and I could go back and tell the class . . .

BEATNIK: I could try.

STUDENT: Oh, wonderful. How nice of you. It came just about in the middle . . . let's see . . . "Oh, America. When will we deserve your fifty thousand Trotskyites?"

BEATNIK: Yeah, that's a line in that poem.

STUDENT: Now, I know it has a lot of different meanings to it, but what was he trying to say there?

BEATNIK: He don't know what he's trying to say there. See, he writes very fast. Sometimes he don't even look . . .

STUDENT: Oh. Well, thanks . . .

BEATNIK: Hey! Excuse me. You know a lot about art and everything . . . ?"

STUDENT: Well, yes . . . no . . . well, I'm insecure. Is there something that you'd like to know about?

BEATNIK: Well, I don't know about art. You know, that stuff . . .

STUDENT: This is a collage. There's a tin can, a pie plate, a fish structure . . .

BEATNIK: Well, now, looking down I can see that. That's not hard to see, a fishbone. What I was wondering more . . . do you dig it? That's what I mean.

STUDENT: In this context what do you mean by that?

BEATNIK: In this context that means does it grab you?

STUDENT: Oh. What an interesting idea. Where?

BEATNIK: Where does it grab you? Somewhere around in the guts?

STUDENT: Oh. Oh, for heaven's sake. Well, I have gas, I can't be objective.

(The beatnik expresses his reaction to the "art" by improvising a free-form song. The student is amazed by his spontaneity.)

STUDENT: A hundred art courses and you couldn't get that kind of freedom . . .

BEATNIK: Well, where I come from, anybody knows how to sing a song. But you know, I could take somebody who had never done this before, sit them in this chair right here and in two minutes' time, they'd be wailing away and wouldn't know what was going on.

STUDENT: Well, I doubt that very much.

BEATNIK: I could do it. I could do it to you.

STUDENT: Oh, no. I couldn't . . .

BEATNIK: Yes, I could.

STUDENT: Oh, no, no, no. Some people observe and others participate.

BEATNIK: How do you know which one of those you are until you try it?

STUDENT: No, I can't. I have the worst problems in the area of spontaneity.

BEATNIK: But you know what President Eisenhower said about that?

STUDENT: What?

BEATNIK: He said there was nothing to lose but fear itself . . . I'd be happy to give you a lesson.

STUDENT: Well . . . I'll might as well try it.

BEATNIK: What the hell, right?

STUDENT: What the hell.

BEATNIK: You know, we only live once or twice. We might as well make the most of it. Okay, now the first thing is, don't be afraid that you're gonna say dirty words. See? 'Cause you're gonna. And then, next . . .

STUDENT: Excuse me. I'm going to say dirty words?

BEATNIK: Oh, yes. That's right. And the next thing is, the very second—

STUDENT: Well, does everyone say dirty words?

BEATNIK: Yeah, oh yeah. See, you got to get rid of all that misery and frustration and everything. That's the way to do it. Now, the next thing is . . .

STUDENT: Well, I guess I'm human.

BEATNIK: Yeah. The very second that I start to wail . . . You listening to me now? The very second that I start to wail on my horn here, you got to come right in, see? You understand why?

STUDENT: No.

BEATNIK: Well . . . That's so you don't have the time to think about nothin'. And it just comes right out. Okay? Here we go.

(Music)

BEATNIK: You're too late.

STUDENT: I confess, I was thinking of a dirty word there . . .

BEATNIK: That's what I told you not to think about, wasn't it? And you was thinking about it. Okay, let's try it. Let's go on and head right with it . . .

(Music)

STUDENT: All right. Let's see. *(tries singing; warms up)* "Throw away all your material possessions. The whole system is corrupt . . . and the, um, social status is . . ."

BEATNIK: Wait, now see . . . where do you see that up there? See, that's not in that painting, you know what I mean? See, you writing a speech with them kind of words. You want to know the key or something? Okay, try that for size, now.

(Music)

STUDENT: "Oh, freedom, freedom, freedom."

BEATNIK: That's right.

STUDENT: "Rebellion, rebellion, rebellion. Oh, blue green orange yellow. Oh, I hate my aunt. Oh, freedom, freedom. Oh . . . *SWEAT!*" *(Laughs)*

BEATNIK: Hey, now. That's very good. You ever do that before?

STUDENT: No.

BEATNIK: Well, that's fine for the first shot. Listen, you know, you keep workin' on that for about a week and you're gonna have somethin' really good? That's right. I've been doin' this for a couple of months. I know about it. Listen, that's why I think that to keep up with development of everything like that, what should happen is this: I'm gonna come up to your pad for a few days, see? And we'll work on this, and we'll work on a couple of other things I got in mind . . .

No doubt the age of the cast was one reason for the frequency of the teacher-pupil relationship in early Second City material. Most were still in their twenties, and teaching or being taught was still the most familiar means for them to exchange information. Then too, a teaching relationship is rich in comic possibility, since one party is in authority, giving it ample opportunity to correct, rebuke, or even ridicule the other, while the other, being subordinate, has equal opportunity to rebel, miscomprehend, or just plain screw up. Many frequently used improv situations are simple in the same way: the interview, for example, with its close relatives the job application and the press conference; or the demonstration in which an action or object (e.g., a dance or machine) is demonstrated. Close to the latter is another common one, the sales pitch, similar in dynamic to the teacher-pupil relationship in that one party is in control while the other by definition is at its mercy.

What is unique about the teacher-pupil relationship, however, compared to the others, is that it is fraught with implications of human weakness: the desire to appear superior on the one hand, and the fear of ignorance or being uninitiated on the other. This is what makes "Museum" so good—and touching—a scene: the universal yearning to know how another person functions.

By insisting that his cast reach down into their own personalities and discover what they really felt, Sills was constantly releasing this basic impulse to learn and explain. "Museum" was the kind of scene that typified Second City's best work under Sills's direction, and for which it became best known.

Arkin created several of these and they became Second City classics. Among them was another teacher-pupil scene called "Camp Counselor" with Tony Holland in which Holland played an ultra-repressed child at camp who is painfully painting tiny, repressed figures and whom Arkin, as the liberal camp counselor, tries to encourage to splurge with fingerpaints. This scene was secretly taped by persons unknown during a performance and turned up several years later as a teaching tool in a child psychologists' course.

Holland, in turn, created with Bill Alton yet another classic scene called "Lekythos" (after a type of Greek vase), in which two old college chums meet at a ten-year reunion. One, Alton, used to be the radical hero on campus, but has now become a highly successful stockbroker, while the other, Holland, has never left college, becoming an impoverished archaeologist. The scene revolves around the lekythos, an irreplaceable Greek vase which is Holland's only possession; it is thus that they discover how utterly their values have changed, and how dead is their love and respect for each other. As he leaves, Alton accidentally knocks over the vase and it smashes to the ground in a thousand pieces, a priceless piece of history gone forever. "Can I write you a check?" he asks Holland blithely.

Things had come a long way in five years from the meandering scenarios of the Compass, whose most precise aspect was their political intent. To the extent that scenes like "Museum" and "Lekythos" were exquisite observations of modern types, they were also social commentary, and their shape and conflicts had a social relevance. Where improvisation had, for the Compass, released a broadside of discontent with false values, official regimentation, and repression, for Second City it released a much more precise skepticism, a more detailed and personal and less conclusive attitude of dissent. Under Sills's relentlessly improving eye, the performers were encouraged to refine all the time, mining their own personalities for ever finer and more permanent germs of truth.

And yet what Sills gained in personal intensity and timelessness he may have lost in satirical impact. "I know that person" you might say to yourself, watching Alton turn his back on his youth and idealism or Harris trying to sing free-form protest, but the recognition was an end in itself, not a means of changing your mind. Whether such recognition can in any theater have a mind-altering effect is a never-ending debate, but for some the refinement Second City represented was not necessarily progress. Roger Bowen: "Compass seemed to have a theme—how society molds people into the shape it wants them to take. Now this is interesting because it characterizes society as an intelligent force with direction. Whereas the kind of picture you got of society at Second City a couple of years later was that society was a blind, meaningless, unintelligent automaton and people would just get lost in it. Second City was about alienation. It was about 'How do I get out of this?' About people talking to machines, machines talking to them, everybody lost, everybody looking for a way out, and how it all didn't make any sense."

Part of the reason for the change was the sheer scope of Second City's success. In the first half of 1960 it began to attract people from all over the country, and not just those who had already done a stint at the various Compasses. Unlike most of the original Compass people, many were professional actors with an eye on future careers. Alan Arkin, for example, who joined in 1960, was only interested in an acting career, and as charter members like Bowen and Darden took sabbaticals, their places were taken by still others. One of these was Del Close, who actually replaced Sills for a while in 1960, during a period when "communication" between the founding director and his company "had broken down." Close, who over the years has emerged as one of the great survivors of improvisational comedy, was a brilliant anarchist with plenty of ideas, a lot of them highly satirical. His General Clevis character represented one of the first of a long line of military buffoons in Boomer humor. Says Close: "The clevis is the least essential piece of military equipment there is. It's the little ring you hang up a mess kit with. The first time I used General Clevis was in an interview near the Berlin Wall. He's being interviewed about Communist brainwashing techniques, which he's warning against. But during the course of the interview, it becomes apparent that he has been brainwashed himself. He tells the interviewer that the way you teach the men to resist brainwashing is to teach them brainwashing techniques. 'How do you teach them?' the interviewer asks. 'You pound it into their heads, day after day.' THE INTERVIEWER: 'After one of your recruits goes through your anti-brainwashing school, what'll you have?' 'Pabst Blue Ribbon,' says Clevis."

The satire party, however, was never very strong at Second City at any time from its inception. Most of its members probably shared some approximate sense of social purpose—but few if any ever seemed to feel that what they were doing at Second City would "make a difference."‡

‡ There is a presumptive fallacy here in any case. All too often in the history of Boomer humor, these implied aims—social upheaval, mind-alteration, cataclysmic change—are assumed to be synonymous with satire. In other words, satire is by definition revolutionary or left-wing. Historically, there is no evidence of this. The great satirists of the past (e.g., Swift, Voltaire, Waugh) were all profoundly conservative. Certainly most American satire has been directed against the immediate or residual effects of aberrant capitalism; it does not follow, however, that satire is part of Moscow's plan for world domination. Writers like Mencken or Nathanael West may have deplored the ravages of capitalism on modern society, but they did so from the basis of earlier standards of tolerance, decency, or literacy, not because they were advocating revolution. Bowen's satirical scenarios for Compass were attacks on sleaziness and dishonesty newly promoted as desirable social qualities. That doesn't make him a revolutionary. If anything, it makes him a traditionalist.

Alan Arkin says: "Tony Holland did a monologue at one point on satire and the great influence satire has had on the world. He said, 'Here's a letter from Mrs. Jerome Whatsis from West Jesus, North Dakota. She says, "Dear Sir: I don't know what I would do without satire. When my husband is home sick in bed and my children are screaming for food and there's no money, I thank God there is such a thing as satire!' " And then he said, 'Well, this is only one of the influences of satire. We all know how much satire did to stop the rise of Hitler in Germany in 1931.'

"No, none of us had any effect, nobody was paying any attention to us at all, except the audience laughing. I don't think any of us were terribly deluded about the great social impact we were having or that the world was going to be a better place because of us. It was a release valve . . . a way of screaming endlessly and getting paid for it."

Unlike anyone or anything else, Second City crops up again and again in the history of Boomer humor, and therefore will do in the pages of this book. (Indeed, more of its story, including a bloody internecine battle, appears in a later chapter.) But this is the moment—1960 and its first glory—to leave it and to pay it and its progenitor the Compass theater the tribute they deserve. No other single enterprise produced so many of our generation's funny and talented men and women as the axis created by Paul Sills and David Shepherd between the years 1955 and 1960. Across one tiny stage or another passed Alan Alda, Jane Alexander, Alan Arkin, Shelley Berman, Roger Bowen, Jack Burns, Severn Darden, Paul Dooley, Andrew Duncan, Ted Flicker, Larry Hankin, Barbara Harris, Dick Libertini, Elaine May, Paul Mazursky, Mike Nichols, Diana Sands, Anne Meara, Jerry Stiller, David Steinberg, John Belushi, Joan Rivers, Bill Alton, Dan Aykroyd, Sandy Baron, Peter Boyle, John Candy, Del Close, Melinda Dillon, Bob Dishy, Brian Doyle Murray, Gail Garnett, Catherine O'Hara, Valerie Harper, Anthony Holland, Robert Klein, Linda Lavin, Eugene Levy, Lynne Lipton, Ron Leibman, Shelley Long, Andrea Martin, Martin Short, Bill Murray, Joe Flaherty, Tom O'Horgan, Sheldon Patinkin, Gilda Radner, Harold Ramis, Eugenie Ross-Leming, Paul Sand, Richard Schaal, Avery Schreiber, Dave Thomas, Eugene Troobnick, Larry Tucker, Fred Willard, and Jules Feiffer. If one includes the natural children of this extended family—the Committee in San Francisco, Ted Flicker's Premise, and Elaine May's Third Ear—the list includes others like George Segal, Buck Henry, Howard Hesseman, Rob Reiner, Leigh French, Renée Taylor, Peter Bonerz, and Reni Santoni. The master list includes scores of other names, not so well known, of talented and brilliant people who perform, act, direct, write, or produce a sizable proportion of our daily entertainment. And this list is only the regulars. No record has been kept of those who merely dropped in, hung out, or jammed, but there are very few people in Boomer humor who have not.

Looking back on Compass–Second City, one thing is clear: Neither Shepherd nor Sills ever quite achieved what they set out to achieve. To their credit this was mainly because neither allowed theory to interfere with reality.

Whatever the differences between them in aims or skills or temperament, both were committed to respecting individual freedom. On all levels from the mundane to the artistic, people were free to come and go, enter and exit, say something or nothing. The result was constantly changing companies, consequent shifts in balance and output and emphasis, a kaleidoscope of comic vision and talent.

Compass–Second City's fundamental innovation, improv, was in fact not just a means for individuals to expand and explore their own capacity for freedom, it was and is a living metaphor for Boomer humor's limits and potential. Whatever you take with you onstage, you can never know what you will leave with. So it was with Compass–Second City. Everyone got a little of what they wanted, some a little more, but no one, not even Sills and Shepherd, everything. It was, at all times and in the best sense, a fine old democratic mess.

3

Meanwhile,
Back on the Printed Page . . .

In good old 1955, fully 17 percent of Americans were willing to admit that they had read a book during the preceding twelve months.

Deplorable though this might seem by standards of national literacy, book-readers had their reasons. Old Uncle Joe had savaged publishers and authors, along with everyone else. The bipartisan pack of rats that poured through any hole he punched gnawed almost as eagerly on literary eggheads as they did on scientific ones or those in the entertainment media. Shut-up-shut-up-and-play-the-game was the rule in publishing. Books—amazingly enough—were burned, and even modestly impudent masterpieces like *Catcher in the Rye* were condemned as un-American. (Then as now, those who don't actually need to read books to know they're subversive routinely listed Salinger's book *Catch Her in the Rye* and banned it as pornographic.)

Part of the result was also part of the reason for that deplorable 17 percent. A certain hush fell over those authors who had not headed for the hills, or Mexico or Paris. When individual perceptions felicitously expressed might, by virtue of their very individuality and felicity, be interpreted as taking dictation from Moscow, people trod water. And while the bastions of publishing, offended as much by the sleaziness of the new order as by its politics, protected their established authors, none was too keen on Research and Development. The first half of the fifties saw an understandable tendency toward safety and security—a publishing philosophy which might be summed up as "duck 'n' cover."

Then, too, publications come in all colors packaging all kinds of dirt. *Red Channels* (1950) was a bestseller in its time, as was *Peyton Place* (1956). It would be pleasant to think that every one of the books read by every member of the deplorable 17 percent was an act of self-defense against the intellectual terrorists abroad in the land. No such luck. Publishing in a free society has always produced a substantial number of books supporting maniacs who would end their right to write. William F. Buckley's *McCarthy and His Enemies* (1954) was one such piece of potential self-excision.* Another 1954 classic, Frederic Wertham's *Seduction of the Innocent,* similarly embraced a principle that taken to its logical conclusion might have jeopardized its own existence. Similarly, too, it took a highbrow approach to a lowbrow subject—something that gained it a certain amount of support from highbrows who should have known better. But unlike Buckley's bootless boosting of the bicameral bully, *Seduction of the Innocent*'s naked assault on the First Amendment was successful—resulting directly in the Comics Code, an unconscionable regulation of a truly American art form.

Unlike the voluntary ratings system of the Motion Picture Association of America or the Standards and Practices guidelines of the major networks, the Comics Code is law. Outside of rules governing classified information, it is the only piece of prior restraint censorship to be so honored. The Comics Code Authority can prevent by law the publication in comics of anything it considers unsuitable in a wide variety of areas, from the way characters dress to their "depiction"—in other words, everything they say and do. Not all comics or strips are covered by the code, it is true, but all newsstand product is; how this power of censorship came about is as germane a part of our story as its effect.

When comic books were born in the mid-thirties, the bulk of their material was either an extension of the comic-strip form popularized in newspaper syndicates (e.g., "Mutt and Jeff"), or frame-by-frame versions of pulp novel adventures (e.g., "Sheena of the Jungle"). With the arrival of Superman in 1938, comics acquired their first home-grown hero. Superman and his offspring—Batman, Captain Marvel, etc.—brought to comics cohesive stories that were best told through the comic form, along with adult relationships, adult concerns, and an ever more sophisticated approach to framing, effects, and layout. These were the first hints that comics might actually be an artistic form of narrative, and not just something to keep the kids in the backseat quiet.

Such creative developments largely went on hold during the war, but comic books expanded enormously as a form of entertainment, embracing all kinds

---

* The emergence of William F. Buckley—a sometime humorist—in the mid-fifties (he started the *National Review* in 1955) is fascinating, because his ultramontane Catholicism and his polysyllabic pretension wouldn't appear to have had a chance in so determinedly yahoo a period. Part of his success seems to have arisen from the occasional perception in the Anglophiliac Northeast that he was somehow associated with the British Isles. This was and is frustrating for Britishers, for whom his maloccluded delivery is as incomprehensible as his version of modern European history. Anglo-American Steve Vinaver, a veteran of "That Was the Week That Was" and director of the Off-Broadway hit *The Mad Show,* was once asked in this writer's presence the recurrent question: "What part of England does Bill Buckley come from?" to which he replied without hesitation, "The new part."

of material from detective to religious, and making a great deal of money, especially for National Periodical Publications, a.k.a. DC Comics. Like other popular stars, the superheroes were enlisted in the fight against fascism, and became jocular symbols of Allied might (ironically, in some ways, since Superman's invincible male power was an uncomfortably fascist notion; his name of course is a literal translation of the Nietzschean term *Übermensch*).

After the war, comics began to expand and develop in previously unimaginable ways. This was partly because of increased competition, not just among the multiplying number of publishers, but also from the new contender, television. (The first days of television, from 1946 to 1950, were dominated by children's programming; children were still the major—and certainly the official—audience for comics.) But the effect of such competition can be overestimated. First, comic books were a very different form of entertainment; second, they were still only a dime apiece, almost nothing in postwar America compared to the Depression dime of ten years before, when radio was just as free as, and a far more pervasive competitor than, television. As the movie industry was to find, the audience's capacity for entertainment was not a fixed quantity, divisible into ever smaller portions depending on the number of competing calls on it, but tended to expand to accommodate new forms of entertainment if they were attractive enough.

Comics were attractive enough. The decade from the end of the war to the adoption of the Comics Code—1945 to 1955—is referred to by comic buffs as "The Golden Age." While such hyperbole is to be expected from people who spend much of their time reading boldface italic hand-lettered captions, it is an accurate reflection of just how good comics were becoming. New artists and writers, many of them fresh out of the service, and the lively journalistic infrastructure that grew up in the armed forces during the war were entering the comic book industry, bringing new skills to the rigidly paneled page, experimenting with graphic equivalents of movie techniques, creating sharper characterizations and stories with quirky premises and twisty endings. These were comics far removed from prewar pulp. At a deeper level, many of the new writers had actually been exposed to the complex ironies of flesh and blood "adventure"—war gave their concepts an edge Buck Rogers fantasy could never match.

One such artist was a young New Yorker named Harvey Kurtzman. Significantly, Kurtzman's early work from 1943 to 1950 alternated between action-adventure and humor. In 1950 he joined a fast-growing young company called E.C. (for Entertaining Comics, formerly Educational Comics), run by publisher William Gaines, which was doing extremely well thanks to horror titles like *The Crypt of Terror* and *The Vault of Horror*. Kurtzman's first major contribution to E.C. was his editorship of its war-comic titles, *Two-Fisted Tales* and *Frontline Combat*. What he brought to them was a desire for realism, a raw, you-are-there focus on the common soldier confronted with his death or that of an individual enemy. There were no stupid glorifics, no gritty posturing, no cigar-chomping machismo. Nor were they romanticized, desanguinized versions of World War II. These were stories about Korea at the height of the Korean War—the new order's first outing against the new enemy, sort of. In context there was a certain sardonic quality behind these intensely serious works; by bringing home the absurdity of men, all in a day's work, trying to kill one another, they were an implicit comment on the propagandist twaddle personified by draft-dodging capons like John Wayne who'd never heard a bullet whine in their lives.

These war titles contributed to E.C.'s growing success, although it was their horror titles that were the profit leaders. In 1952 Kurtzman and Gaines added a further title, a humor comic book called *Mad*. Actually its full title was *Tales Calculated to Drive You . . . MAD*, with an added cover line: "Humor in a Jugular Vein." Its cover showed a familiar horror vault with a man and a woman, both petrified at a dark shadow in front of them, screaming "That Thing! That slithering blob coming towards us! WHAT IS IT?"

A tiny child at their feet says, "It's Melvin!"

E.C., of course, was parodying itself. Every reference on *Mad*'s cover was to their own horror comics. Conventional wisdom might have suggested that this wasn't too hot an idea with a faithful readership already in place, but the faithful readership lapped it up. *Mad* was an immediate success and under Kurtzman's editorial direction took the art of self-parody to ever greater lengths. Many of the subsequent covers of *Tales Calculated to Drive You MAD* had similar crime/detective or horror references, often featuring a busty bonde in wildly hazardous situations of which she is quite oblivious. Inside, similar parodies abounded in full-length six- or eight-page form.

This policy was significant, as was its obvious appeal to the new magazine's readers. By any yardstick the coexistence of E.C.'s horror comics (many of which were truly scary and therefore taken seriously) and a humor comic (which didn't take them seriously in the least) suggested quite a sophisticated audience. In theory, readers of comics like *Tales from the Crypt* and *Mad* might have been entirely different but in practice the chances are that there was a lot of crossover. Only a readership that had access to, and cared about, the real thing was going to appreciate its being parodied.

Mad didn't, of course, confine itself to parodies of other E.C. titles. Kurtzman used his magazine both to broaden the uses of parody and to range widely in search of new targets. Comics had long been experimenting with uses of framing, based on artists' familiarity with movie techniques, equating the comic frame with the screen. It was logical, therefore, to use the comic page to attack not just movies but the new screen arrival, television.

Most importantly, a great deal of what Kurtzman edited, wrote, and occasionally drew during the first three years of *Mad*'s existence was pretty tough stuff. If its prevailing tone was lunatic, youthfully exuberant—mad, in fact—its tone could occasionally be quite savage. The sardonic and passionate attitude of his war comics was just as present in *Mad*. He also had access to some of the finest comic artists of his time—the example chosen was drawn by Bill Elder. It's called "Howdy Dooit!" (1954) from *Mad* No. 18. In it, Kurtzman presciently points out that it was "Buffalo Bill" and his sponsors who practiced the true "seduction of the innocent."

No sooner has Buffalo Bill got his charges under his control than Howdy Dooit launches into a commercial, insisting that the kiddie viewers go and fetch their moms for the pitch:

Commercial follows commercial and the puppet becomes more obnoxious each time. Final panels show Buffalo Bill chatting with members of his audience. One little monster produces a pair of scissors, and cuts Buffalo Bill's puppet strings, revealing him to be just a puppet, also.

This piece was to have numerous imitators—or, depending on your degree of discretion, "echoes" and "resonances"—later in the decade and beyond. Both Lenny Bruce and Bob Newhart incorporated similar kiddie-show satires in their repertory (as indeed did Ken Shapiro in *The Groove Tube)*.

Kurtzman, like many others, is now reticent about his motivation for starting *Mad*—and for causing such pieces as this and many others to become flesh. At the time, however, there were pressing reasons for the young comics company to spread itself around. Rumblings were beginning to be heard in the land, directed at the blood- and slime-drenched horrors of E.C.'s *Vault* and *Crypt* titles and their ever proliferating clones at other companies. Most of these rumblings came from that ubiquitous force for good in American society, parents' groups. In 1954, these defenders of other people's children found their own superhero, a psychiatrist called Frederic Wertham, and a bible in his book *Seduction of the Innocent.* The good doc had studied comics and found them to engender not just violence, but every clinical psychotic disturbance known to medicine. Locked in the bathroom or beneath the sheets with flashlights, the little darlings were turning into monsters. Hair sprouted from their brains each time the moon—or a page—turned.

As usual with such quackery, the aim was control, not protection. Unlike radio and television, comics enjoyed a certain freedom of expression, if they cared to exercise it, from federal regulation and sponsor bias. So long as they stuck to fantasy adventures and invincible men battling crime, this freedom went unhampered. But as soon as they began to expand into something closer to reality, the stupidity of war, irreverence, however lowbrow, and crime as a social fact rather than the product of religious evil, something had to be done. (Actually the E.C. crime and horror comics, more often than not, were rather neat short stories with a de Maupassant-style twist at the end. Beneath the blood and slime, plots centered around family relationships and the crimes they could engender: husbands who hated wives or vice versa, strange children with strange powers, dead aunts and ancestors with family secrets, and so on. Bubbling under the Norman Rockwell ideal of family was a caldron of weird and violent possibility which both reflected the non-Norman reality and was as traditional as folk tales.)

There certainly was plenty of trash in the industry. But as the success of *Mad* indicated these unprotected kids were perfectly aware when they were being scared. Far from leading to juvenile delinquency or worse, what this suggested was the much more dangerous possibility that kids were capable of thinking for themselves. They were not, as the good doctor's title suggested, sweet little vessels simply waiting to be filled with the correct information.

Nor were they all kids. Not only were many readers well out of the preteen range, a considerable number were in the armed services, a traditionally large market for comic books. Antiwar comics could be construed as a clear and present danger to the republic. Antiauthoritarian ones were not much better.†
Going after such specific items, however, would be bound to attract attention to the real purposes of the anticomic crusade. Especially when it came to the armed services, sticky questions could arise, and there were always Commie lawyers waiting in the bushes for just such cases. Armed with its medical "evidence," the anticomic movement went after the industry as a whole—not just the trash, but everything, good, bad, funny, scary, or indifferent. And rather than tangling with specific questions of audience and content, they went after the most sensitive and sensational point in the industry's defenses —kids, a.k.a. innocents.

In 1954 the New York State Legislature convened a special investigation into comic books. (Comics even rated investigation by a subcommittee on juvenile delinquency of the U.S. Senate.) The hearings attracted a colossal amount of publicity, and were conducted, not unlike the McCarthy hearings, as a trial. Attorney for the prosecution Wertham won hands down. An "independent" Comics Authority and a code were passed into law, banning horror comics outright, the depiction of criminals in any "glamorous" way, and among much else demanding that all characters be dressed in a manner "reasonably acceptable to society"—which raised the interesting possibility that Buck Rogers and Tarzan might have to grace future comics in three-piece suits. (A few comics publishers—notably Dell and Classics Illustrated—were exempted from the Code's jurisdiction, but only because they were already in accord with its strictures.)

The lack of support the comics industry received from other segments of the publishing world was almost as depressing as the legislation itself, and seemed to arise as much as anything from the perception that since they had no class, comics weren't protected by the First Amendment. Their demise was widely predicted, and although comics were reborn better than ever in the sixties, the industry was utterly crippled for the balance of the decade.

† No demographics exist for these readerships and Kurtzman himself is adamant that he has never written anything for a particular audience, but first and foremost for himself. Either a lot of *Mad*'s readers were kids with a quasi-adult sense of humor (which is by no means impossible or unlikely) or they were old enough to relate to Kurtzman's work (he was 28 in 1952). Or they were a mixture. In all three cases this was a smart audience.

E.C. in particular was more or less destroyed. (It tried to launch half a dozen new titles, actually classified as "New Direction" and which were supposed to be more mature. One of them was *Psychoanalysis Comics.*) But there was one crucial survivor, *Mad.*

By converting *Mad* to a larger-sized, black-and-white magazine (up to this point it had been a comic), Gaines and Kurtzman put their publication outside the Comics Code. *Mad* not only continued with the editorial policies it had already established, but gathered under its banner all the artists and writers whose work had previously been dispersed around many other titles. The array of talent was awesome and the result was a huge body of satirical, parodistic, and straight-ahead funny work that became a sort of passbook of Boomer humor.

Wertham and his hordes unwittingly created a vacuum which *Mad* filled with a vengeance. By concentrating it all in one place, and more or less forcing it to be satirical rather than narrative, he became something he would have given back all the blood and slime to avoid—another father of Boomer humor.

Kurtzman and Gaines quarreled after only five or six issues of the new *Mad,* and Kurtzman left the magazine. This is something he now regrets, although he went on to many other publications, most notably *Trump* magazine, a lavish satire effort that resulted from Kurtzman's friendship with the ubiquitous Hugh Hefner. (Brilliant though much of it was, it only lasted two issues.) Kurtzman remains one of the recurrent influences on Boomer humor and, like several other progenitors, reappears elsewhere—particularly in his connections with the underground comics of the late sixties.

But *Mad* was his most important achievement. In the harsh climate of the fifties it is now possible to see there was perhaps room for only one magazine, one fountainhead of impudent print humor. Had Kurtzman remained at its head, there is no telling how much better it might have become than it did. As it was, *Mad* continued to grow throughout the period, becoming one of the great success stories in American magazine publishing, and certainly helping to set the stage for the arrival fifteen years later of *The National Lampoon.*

•   •

In 1955 two New Yorkers named Ed Fancher and Dan Wolf published the first issue of a community newspaper called *The Village Voice.* From its relatively limited original scope the *Voice* quickly became an influential organ of what might best be described as popular left thinking. Aside from its reportage of Reform Democratic affairs in the metropolitan area, the *Voice* was a natural vehicle for avant-garde criticism and literary comment. Since New York is a cosmopolis and the paper had little competition at the time, the *Voice* also served as an outlet for major artistic talent, becoming in toto a most unusual newspaper, and forging a national and international reputation for itself and its contributors far beyond the actual reach of its circulation.

Two of the better-known of these contributors were Norman Mailer, whose column later formed the basis for his book *Advertisements for Myself* (1959), and a young cartoonist whose influence on Boomer humor and his own profession was to be profound, Jules Feiffer.

In the history of cartooning, Feiffer's innovations fall into two broad categories: his unashamedly intellectual approach to a form traditionally short on thought and long on cuteness, and his radical experimentation with line and space. In one category or the other he has influenced artists as varied as Garry Trudeau, British cartoonist John McGlashan, and French satirists like Wolinski, Reiser, and Bretecher.

Feiffer is and always has been a chronicler of behavior, a man seeking to tell the truth about what men and women do to each other and why, an observer of the small, intimate ways in which people express the larger forces at work on them. In other times, that need to chronicle might have produced a very different result. But as at Compass–Second City (with whom Feiffer developed close ties), the urge to dig into people's true behavior, into their true motivations confronted with the peculiar terrain of Cold War America, produced—a satirist.

More explicitly than any other practitioner of Boomer humor, Feiffer deals in contradiction. The contradiction between the learned and the human, the imposed and the human, the official and the human. At the most basic level his strip reflects contradiction, the twin lines of speech and picture always in tension, the inner voice exposing the outer face, the outer voice being exposed by the inner face. Feiffer is never satisfied with explanations, between lovers or between parents and kids, presidents and the press or, for that matter, the press and you. Since he is both a spare and witty writer, and—increasingly so over the years—a remorseless caricaturist of both types and individuals, he has a special way with self-justification, and the unhappy people who practice it.

But for all that he deals with the little lies about family, sex, kids, and the orthodoxies surrounding them, his perception of contradictions ranges wide. He is at home at home, or on any other battlefield. Thus, more than most of his satiric colleagues, Feiffer makes critical connections between the large and the small, between the living room and the halls of Congress. Feiffer's work is shot through with the conviction that everything we do is political, and politics affects everything we do. Even if you spend your life in a monastery or munching madeleines, there are consequences to your decisions, and self-deceptions. There is a continuing urgency to this conviction: "One thing I don't want as I advance through my middle years is to mellow," he says. It has kept him aloft while others fell back to earth or blew up in midair. Feiffer is dead clear about what he thinks, perhaps because three decades of reducing it to a terse six or eight panels has taught him the worth of the right word, and equally lucid about his hatred for officialdom and officialness. He's serious, passionate, and blunt. He talks of purpose, rarely of entertaining. The standard humorist's cop-out—"strictly for laughs" is never on his lips. Feiffer says: "I think everything's political. I think that in those years, certainly, whoever you hit was an appropriate target. You know, there could hardly be a wrong target. That doesn't mean that the targets all agreed with one another. But they all represented authority, with very repressive social and political structures. So whether it was Mom or your boss or your teacher or your President, there was no confusion in targets. They were all the enemy. Because—and this is about language—they were all lying to us. They were all saying things they didn't mean. They were all using language as code. Certainly what my work was about in the beginning was about people saying one thing and meaning something very different.

"It was a direct reflection of the society we lived in where on every level, from one's parents to one's teachers to one's leaders, one learned automatically to decode what was being told you. And so automatic had it become that it took years to find anything wrong with this. You know, to feel outraged.

" 'Hypocrisy' is too mild a word. The blatant, mischievous disinformation practiced on us from birth seemed like such a norm that you didn't know you had a right to expect anything different. And so, often when you did complain, it was turned around on you as if there were something abnormal in expecting something other than that, just as Huck Finn felt foolish and self-conscious for feeling loyal to Jim when he should have turned him in. The rules of society were so corrupt and so cynical . . . that anybody pointing out the obvious was considered the cynic instead."

Feiffer's earliest ambition—one he describes as "having begun shortly after birth"—was to write and draw a syndicated newspaper strip. This was in 1930 in the depths of the Depression and at the height of popularity for the comic strip, then securely in the hands of masters like Milton Caniff and George Herriman. To a poor kid in the Bronx with an unemployed father and overworked mother, such a dream was one of glamour and money, attention and approval.

Feiffer's very first published strip, drawn when he was only eighteen, certainly demonstrated little in the way of satire. It was called "Clifford" and first appeared in 1949 in a Sunday supplement masterminded by artist Will Eisner (Harvey Kurtzman's longtime collaborator). Although it prefigures Feiffer's lasting preoccupation with kids (and his belief that they are the ultimate proletariat, locked in a timeless class struggle with their parents), it is touching rather than funny, wistful rather than satiric.

Predictably enough for an artist still in his teens, its style is derivative but the premise was, for its time, original. Based on this showing one might have projected modest syndication glory, a line becoming gradually looser and wittier, middle-of-the-road humor, page four of the Sunday funnies, a comfortable career. The U.S. Army changed all that:

"By dint of being drafted [during the Korean War in 1950] I was forced to convert my talents in another direction, simply as a survival tool. It was my first all-out battle with the system. I saw from the beginning that my enemy was not the Koreans but the United States Army. And they seemed to understand that, too. I did all sorts of battle (with my superiors) but no more than anybody, however noncombative, would have if they questioned the logic of the system. If you question the military, it all comes unglued because it doesn't make any sense. Although I had no education it was clear that the people over me, who also had no education, were quite stupid and quite defensive about their stupidity and so would use authority in the most repressive or crudest way possible.

"What the army really taught me that was very useful was to trigger my rage, which was neatly under wraps because it was not allowable in the confines of the Jewish family nest. With all the outrages going on (in my family), with all of the hypocrisy, the double messages and double whammies . . . my mother had enough skill to cut any anger off at the pass, or to turn it around, or turn it against me, or turn it toward my father. My mother was a genius at catching whatever bullets I had to throw at her, off her bracelets like Wonder Woman and hurling them back. One never laid a glove on her. When I went into the arena with my mother, it always ended with confusion and self-doubt and self-hate.

"But the army justified real rage. You couldn't ever think for a moment that the army, like your mother, meant for your best, that the army was out for your interest. The army was basically out to kill you—it didn't care whether it did or it didn't. So it gave me a wonderful outlet when I needed one."

It is characteristic that this confession implicitly compares two very different kinds of violence, domestic and military—the kind of irony Feiffer has explored all his life. What makes Feiffer so exceptional is his more disturbing admission that his rage came not from the army but was released by it, that the violence may proceed from deeper deceptions parents practice on their children, deceptions upon which parasites like the military might feed but which are not, in the first place, of their making.

Feiffer's resistance to the military took predictable forms—gross insubordination, deliberate flunking, flirtations with the stockade—all this in wartime —but the most lasting one was called Munro. Munro was Feiffer's first excursion into satire, written almost entirely while he was still completing his tour of duty. It is the story of a four-year-old boy who gets drafted into the army and, because the system cannot have made a mistake, is put through basic training as if he were a normal-sized and -aged recruit.

Munro passes all the tests. But in the process he is brutalized and decides to try to appeal to the authorities. Good luck . . .

The sergeant still did not look up. The way to always tell its a sergeant is if he doesn't ever look up. Finally he said

IT IS THE
OFFICIAL
POLICY OF
THE ARMY
NOT TO
DRAFT MEN
OF FOUR.
ERGO YOU
CANNOT BE
FOUR. ERGO
YOU ONLY
THINK YOU
ARE FOUR
GO ON
SICK CALL.

Munro accepts the inevitable and decides to give the Army his best try . . .

He would march with the best of them

He would shoot with the best of them.

And, if need be, he would go to war with the best of them.

One day a sergeant picks out Munro as an exemplar for some new recruits. "That's a soldier," says the sergeant proudly . . .

All the men looked

"WE'RE GOING TO
SEPARATE THE
MEN FROM THE
BOYS!" said
the sergeant

And Munro began to cry.

Munro cries and cries. A succession of officers attempt to staunch this unmanly cowardice until finally a general intervenes:

And then finally he said:

I RULE THAT **THIS** IS A LITTLE BOY.

Everyone nodded in agreement. "WHO COULD EVER THINK THIS WAS ANYTHING BUT A LITTLE BOY." they said. And they made out it was all a big joke.

Munro gets a message from the President: "I hold no fear for our nation's future when even a mere lad of four is stirred strongly enough by our cause to enlist himself in the service of his country."

He was awarded a medal, a set of military brushes, and a whole box of toy nuclear weapons. Munro was a hero!

Munro is a relative of Clifford, but the fury of its image of powerlessness is an utter transformation. Even here we see the glimmerings of an understanding that different forms of brutality are linked, for Munro's parents are not exactly on his side and the whole environment in which that brutality is contained—the children's book, the child-like drawings—is itself a brutal comment. This was a man for whom cute had been shot in the head.

For a variety of reasons, Munro was not published until 1959, well after Feiffer's much more commercial success, "Passionella." Feiffer tried for some time to get Munro published after leaving the army (in 1952) only to find himself in a classic trap of the innovative artist. Editors, unable to categorize the work as either adult satire or a children's book, advised him to do more and come back later. The implication was that if he was better known they might take the chance but they couldn't give an unknown so risky a shot. In short, they could make him famous if he were already famous. Feiffer didn't think at the time—"in my innocence" he calls it—that there was a blacklist at work even though, in the period he was trying to sell Munro, its politics were extreme; certainly both the excuse that "we love it but we don't know what it is" and "we'd risk it if it weren't so risky" are familiar editorial cover-ups for feeling queasy about courageous writing.‡

Faced with the leanness of integrity Feiffer decided to write another story, this time with the avowedly cynical purpose of getting published. In order to do this he had to write something that merely appeared to be a satire. Actually, as he says, "it was really about big tits."

‡ It was later made into a short and won a 1961 Academy Award. (Feiffer also won a Pulitzer Prize for editorial cartooning in 1986.)

"Passionella" was the story of a chimney sweep who dreams of having a great body and a resultant movie career and who gets her wish (with some strings attached). Published in *Pageant* magazine, it was an immediate success and resulted in publishing offers.

The ear for official mendacity, the eye for the telling encounter, and the new naïf style of drawing were opening up vistas of possibility. Feiffer now turned not just to prohibitions of sex, family, and authority for material but also to his own generation. The new lingos, the new officialese, the new lies fascinated him as much as the old. He gives some examples:

"Sociologists referred to contemporary college students as 'the silent generation,' to my own age group as 'conformists,' to my elders as 'status seekers' or 'organization men.' We were told we were 'affluent.' One of the most serious problems was 'the leisure problem.' Another problem was 'alienation.' Also 'anxiety.' Not to overlook 'apathy.' "

The result was that in the years immediately following his military service, Feiffer began to develop a body of cartoons called "Sick, Sick, Sick." This was the first time the word "sick" had been used in an explicitly ironic sense. The postwar period had seen much interest in psychoanalysis, no doubt to assuage the guilts of affluence and the terrors of Armageddon as well as more clinical disorders, and the word "sick" had acquired a contemporary connotation of neurosis rather than psychosis. And certainly the target protagonists of Feiffer's world displayed all manner of modern neuroses. But the title of the cartoons held a deeper irony: You say we are sick, and we are, but the reasons lie outside us as much as in ourselves. And since they do, it may well be that those whom orthodoxy labels sick, those who behave rebelliously, "antisocially," or even just naturally or elementally are healthier than those who condemn them.

This was where the *Voice* came in. Figuring shrewdly that if he was published in a paper every New York editor was reading he might have better luck with them collectively than individually, he accepted the fledgling journal's generous pay rate (a big zero) and was on his way.

"Sick, Sick, Sick" was Feiffer's tribute to what he calls the "Ike Age," those chillsome days of the Great Deal and the Big Catch, the Bomb and the Box. He began by observing the trickle-down of these vast realities on his own kind—Greenwich Village men and women, anxious parents, Madison Avenue poseurs, TV organization men, capuccino addicts, modern dancers, the sweater-and-sandal I-just-got-back-Paris crowd, the lefties, the lofties, the nifties, and the softies. But he soon discovered that:

"These characters, self-obsessed as they were, could not live independently of Dwight D. Eisenhower, the President of their existence. Eisenhower's presidency surrounded me and mine, not in its politics—the wise among us shunned politics—but in a Cold War mood of muted anxiety and isolation that bled out of the White House into the offices, bars, coffeehouses and bedrooms. We took Ike to work and to bed. He gave us complacency and a bad stomach."

In short, Feiffer couldn't help that his strip engaged the great as well as the small. However familiar the situation of a given episode of "Sick, Sick, Sick," it resonates with further meaning, refers somehow to a wider and unresolved conflict. Many interpretations of Feiffer—and in particular his strip, which was and remains the backbone of his work—seem to ignore this level. There is a tendency—correct but inadequate—to concentrate on the humanity of his eye and pen at the expense, in this writer's opinion, of his extraordinary ear for language. From the beginning Feiffer was a master at spotting the give-away word or phrase, the repeated opinion, the brand-new cliché masquerading as an insight.

The following examples from "Sick, Sick, Sick"—a title that was changed after a couple of years to simply "Feiffer"—are all from the late fifties. They seek to demonstrate that gift first and foremost, for artistically Feiffer had not yet developed the certainty of line he would develop later; in fact in some of them the style occasionally lurches about so much that only the acuity of language tells the reader that the same artist is at work in all of them.

Perhaps the most remarkable thing about this sampling is the range and precision of Feiffer's voices (he was twenty-six when the strip started to run). Many of these strips shocked and startled readers of all ages not just by their power of mimicry, but by the mere fact of such matters appearing in a strip. And not the least of those matters was a subject never far from a twenty-six-year-old mind—or any other: sex. For—outside of avant-garde literature—sex, as distinct from titillation or frustration, was still in 1956 a grand taboo. Feiffer again:

"It came as a shock—the notion that there could be serious humor about young men and young women coming together for the purpose of fucking, rather than the purpose of innocent necking or fooling around. Or that the end of a cartoon on sex would not be somebody looking foolish or mortified. I mean there was a lot of mortification in what I did but it was mortification based on people's real experiences, where getting laid was clearly the object."

And getting laid in 1956 in the Village meant Bernie—Bernard Mergendeiler, the first horny mega-nerd of American humor—and his bed-hopping nemesis, Huey. Here's Bernie and Huey at their most quintessential, and Feiffer with his ear tuned to high and low frequencies:

In one of the strips's most famous episodes language no longer works, no longer stirs any emotion.

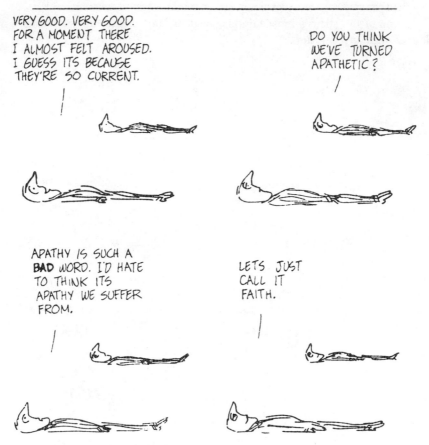

It was in addressing concerns like conformism—essentially superficial if it concerned you in the same ways and words it concerned everyone else—that Feiffer found himself, involuntarily perhaps, digging deeper. And finding as he did so that he was discovering connections and depths even he had not suspected existed. As he says, "I scared myself by my anger and my politics. I scared my readers." The following demonstrates his arrival at a rather alarming place:

LATER ON I WAS IN THE MILITARY
SERVICE. IT WAS MY JOB TO
CLASSIFY PERSONNEL. I DIDN'T
LIKE TO SEND MEN TO WAR.
BUT THOSE WERE MY **ORDERS**.
I HAD NO CHOICE.

AFTER SERVICE I HAD TROUBLE
FINDING MY NICHE. FOR AWHILE
I WAS REALTY AGENT FOR A SLUM.
THE TENANTS DIDN'T UNDERSTAND.
I WAS JUST DOING WHAT I WAS
HIRED TO DO.

NEXT I WENT TO WORK AS A WITNESS.
I APPEARED BEFORE DOZENS OF
CONGRESSIONAL COMMITTEES. I DIDN'T
LIKE THE WORK. BUT I **HAD** TO DO
WHAT I WAS BEING PAID FOR.

AND NOW I'VE REACHED THE **PINNACLE!**
I'VE GONE TO WORK IN A STATE PRISON.
I DON'T NECESSARILY BELIEVE IN
CAPITAL PUNISHMENT BUT **SOMEONE**
HAS TO PULL THE SWITCH.

What constantly delights about Feiffer, though, is that however total his satire may become, he can always bring it back to earth—and with no loss of effectiveness. The same attitudes that control the Cold War can be found in bars—in sex games and brawls:

...

NOW LISTEN TO ME. **ALWAYS** LOOK OUT FOR
YOURSELF. YOU LOOK OUT TOO MUCH FOR THE
OTHER FELLOW AND WHEN **HE GETS** TO
THE TOP HE'LL ONLY KICK YOU IN THE
TEETH FOR THANKS.

NOW **LISTEN** TO ME. LEARN TO BE
WATCHFUL. NEVER TRUST ANYBODY -
NOT EVEN ME! THE WORLDS OUT
TO **GET YOU.**

NOW LISTEN TO ME. DEVELOP SINCERITY.
LEARN A STRONG HANDSHAKE AND A
GOOD EYE STARE. ALWAYS BE ATTEN-
TIVE TO STRANGERS. THEY MIGHT DO
YOU SOME GOOD.

NOW LISTEN TO ME. DON'T **EVER** FEEL
SORRY FOR YOURSELF. YOU'RE EATING
GOOD AND YOU'VE ALWAYS GOT A
CHANCE. WITH THE RIGHT MENTAL
ATTITUDE YOU CAN TAKE **ANYBODY.**

And where does all this begin? Feiffer returns time and again to his favorite subject, kids. This strip is a classic:

NOW FOR CRYING OUT LOUD **LISTEN** TO ME. DON'T DO FAVORS! DON'T BE A PATSY! THE **SMART** GUYS **LAUGH** AT THE NICE GUYS. NEVER EXPECT TOO MUCH AND YOU WON'T BE DISAPPOINTED.

WILL YOU **PLEASE** LISTEN TO ME. **NEVER** TALK POLITICS. YOU ONLY MAKE ENEMIES AND NOTHING YOU'RE GONNA SAY WILL EVER CHANGE THE WORLD.

C'MON NOW YOU'RE NOT **LISTENING** TO ME. RESPECT **EVERY** GIRL LIKE SHE WAS YOUR MOTHER. BUT WHEN YOU **GOT** TO FOOL AROUND DO IT OUT OF THE NEIGHBORHOOD. NEVER PLAY IN YOUR OWN BACKYARD.

YESSIR, WE'LL PUT OUR HEADS TOGETHER AND MAKE A MAN OUT OF YOU. YOU LISTENING, BOY?

This of course is Feiffer's saving grace. It's kids over concepts every time. Feiffer is only liberal in the sense of supporting liberation. Otherwise, a liberal lie can be as oppressive as any other. Such clarity of vision often made him enemies. Certainly this last example must have been a voice unique to the point of lonesome in 1960 New York:

"Sick, Sick, Sick" broke ground in several directions at once. Like Sahl and Compass–Second City, it brought not-funny social and political issues to a profession which had been—with exceptions like Al Capp and Walt Kelly—acutely aware of the parts of the park to which it was restricted. Like Sahl and Compass–Second City and unlike any other strip, it avoided punch lines (i.e., gag final panels). The focus was on the thoughts and attitudes expressed throughout the strip rather than on a neat resolution. Like Sahl and Compass–Second City, the word flow was crucial to the action, the internal slapstick of a mind tying itself in knots replacing the graphic farce of "biff!",

"Yow!", puffs of smoke, and speed lines. Unlike any cartoonist before him Feiffer threw away the rules, letting his characters float on the page, without frames, sometimes even allowing his image to remain identical in all the panels. And by opting for an apparently slapdash style rather than the controlled conventional line he started with in "Clifford," he conveyed a nervous flow-through energy to each episode, leaving the reader with an impression that he had been drawn in a wild burst of insight.

Obviously both in its liberated style and its emphasis on flow over form, this looked a lot like jazz, a lot like improvisation. And while his line actually was anything but slapdash—representing more a restless, painstaking drive to convey minutiae of gesture and expression, a certain set of the hand, foot, or head—the totality was utterly of its time. Like Sahl's lean and hungry synthesis of information and rage, like Compass–Second City's driving overlapping rush of frustrated intelligence, Feiffer was right on the airfoil of the bulbous shiny new jet that was the fifties: urgent, urban, edgy, and smart. Every strip grabbed you by the collar, was preceded by unspoken incredulous "Look at this! Listen to this!", dove headlong into contradiction, conflict, pain. No cars drove up to doors in Feiffer's opening panels, no pies were placed on kitchen tables, there was no setup, no scenery. The strip was Feiffer's mike and stool, his postage-stamp stage, as live as a page could get.

It was inevitable that Sahl, Compass–Second City, and Feiffer would one day find one another. This being the mid-fifties, however, that took time. It's hard for people of the eighties who live lives in pervasive and complex communication to imagine how such vitally similar organisms could coexist without being aware of one another. For a surprising length of time, however, this was the case. It's a measure of how controlled information and its exchange was—and of how tremendously the fear of seeming different suffused society. Time and again in talking to those who grew up or matured in the fifties this writer has encountered the same recollection: young, lonely people who thought they were mad or weird until they read or saw or listened to a kindred spirit, and couldn't believe that there was someone else who felt the same way, that they weren't crazy, twisted—or sick.

It's even harder for us to believe that one of the means by which those lonely voices made themselves heard was sometimes television; that there was ever a time when television did not repackage our thoughts and feelings so completely that new, raw ones could still find their furtive way through the system. But there was, and for Feiffer it was a revelation. His is an eloquent version of a common fifties experience:

> I remember the first time I saw Mike and Elaine . . . on "Omnibus"—I could not believe that I was watching this stuff on television—that first of all I was watching stuff so close to what I was doing and secondly that there it was on the air on this medium. It just seemed to be some kind of miracle. I remember being so astonished that I couldn't laugh—although I knew that what I was watching was hilarious.

I felt an immediate colleagueship with Nichols and May. When I went to Chicago to push my second book of cartoons (in 1959) somebody took me to Second City, which I'd never heard of before. I couldn't *believe* what was on that stage!

You did get a sense watching Sahl in nightclubs, or Nichols and May —but Sahl and Second City most strongly because they were the most political—that you were a member of some kind of underground, a privileged political social movement, and that something was happening. That the laughter was a laughter of real humor but also of defiance, that there was anger here. That these perceptions were necessary in order to breathe. It wasn't just about being funny, it was about being true.

If one reads [Milan] Kundera's book *The Book of Laughter and Forgetting,* even though the Czech government was obviously more repressive than anything I lived under, I immediately understood what he was writing about. Those are the feelings that I had in a society that seemed to also to "forget" officially, and to translate reality into different things with no problem at all.

If you told the truth—I found this with the cartoon and when I went to see Sahl and Second City—people would come over (to us) and say, "How do you get away with that? That's the way we talk among ourselves, but nobody says that in public. You *just don't do that!"* People hadn't read this stuff, it hadn't appeared in print, so when it did there was this immediate identification, "somebody is out there speaking for me" and what a relief and what a release!

The unrepresented Feiffer was speaking out, finding others who felt the way he did but were too inhibited—socially, educationally, or however—to do so. The unrepresented was becoming himself the representative.

When people are dimly aware or benignly or *unconsciously* aware that the reality of their own lives is in contradiction to the official version they get in the media, the official version they get from their teachers or their family or their leaders, and yet their own version isn't articulated, when someone starts defining it . . . they—just—go—crazy!"

And little by little they were going crazy. The audiences like the artists were beginning to make connections, were beginning to realize that there was something abroad in the land, not just down at their friendly neighborhood satirist's. In the last couple of years of the fifties, the various trickles started to flow together into a substantial body of water. People began to draw strength from the simple awareness that they were not alone.

The subversives were exchanging handshakes all over the place, as nightclubs proliferated, comedy album sales soared, banned books were passed from hand to hand. Old Uncle Joe's worst fears were being realized. The things were coming out from under the bed, but instead of slipping six frames of Lenin into the latest Doris Day movie, they were doing something much worse—they were laughing. And what's more they were laughing at *him* and his cherished vision of a rigid-with-fear, screwed-shut, dumbly obedient, boot-in-the-mouth America. He was probably too far gone to hear the laughter, though, and in 1958 he, or rather his liver, gave up the ghost. He died like so many he drove to death and despair—forgotten, discredited, a barroom drunk who'd grabbed the microphone for a few moments and entertained the patrons by belching the national anthem.*

Creators like Feiffer, who only a few years before had felt so isolated and alienated, found new mates for cross-fertilization. At Second City, Sills and Feiffer formed an alliance that a year later produced a Second City show based on Feiffer's book *The Explainers* (a collection of *Voice* strips first published in 1960). Doubtless the favorite satiric mode of Compass–Second City, the teacher-pupil relationship, found an echo in Feiffer's fascination with those who *explained*—whether it was themselves or "the rules" they were explaining. The relationship between Feiffer and Second City was cemented, drawing him ultimately into a second career—the theater and movies—which would last for many productive years (e.g., his screenplay *Carnal Knowledge,* directed by Mike Nichols, and the Off-Broadway hit *Little Murders).*

Other nexi sprang up. Feiffer was ubiquitous. Unsurprisingly, Hefner brought Sahl and Feiffer together in his magazine *(Playboy* published a lavish version of Feiffer's original *Sick, Sick, Sick* book under the title of *The Conformist).* Feiffer also became a regular at the salon of George Plimpton, whose *Paris Review,* was a direct line to the new and highly dangerous American expatriate literature being produced in Paris.

In 1958, a book originally published there in 1955 by the infamous Olympia Press was finally allowed past customs. Vladimir Nabokov's *Lolita* was an instant classic of black humor, satire mainlining down America's arterial highways. Another 1958 Olympia Press production, not allowed through Idlewild, was smuggled in and around New York: Terry Southern's hilarious *Candy.* Donleavy's *Ginger Man* followed, as did the crypto-satire *Naked Lunch* by William S. Burroughs.

All this activity could not fail to attract the attention of *Time* magazine. On July 13, 1959, it published a Show Business lead story that—maybe intentionally—put the word "sick" on the map for good. Although only a short piece, it was widely quoted and was an important checkpoint in the progress of Boomer humor.

Time's piece identified what it called the "sickniks."† Under this rubric,

---

* He is now in hell.

† The use of the suffix "-nik" during the fifties and sixties, especially by Time-Life, is a revealing scrap of trivia in the history of propaganda. The suffix is a Russian diminutive (as in Sputnik), and was consciously attached to identifiable groups of dissenters, as a subliminal smear, suggesting—good-naturedly of course—that such groups were dupeniks of Moscow. Hence, beatnik (beats called themselves beats, never beatniks), folknik, and (a little later) peacenik. Two of these stuck, beatnik and peacenik, and the suffix has now passed into colloquial American with

Time grouped an assorted collection of humorists ranging from Sahl to Don Adams and including such disparate performers as Jonathan Winters, Shelley Berman, and Nichols and May.

The operative paragraph ran as follows:

"What the sickniks dispense is partly social criticism liberally laced with cyanide, partly a Charles Addams kind of jolly ghoulishness, and partly a personal and highly disturbing hostility toward all the world. No one's flesh crawled when Jack Benny carried on a running gag about a bear named Carmichael that he kept in the cellar and that had eaten the gasman when he came to read the meter. The novelty and jolt of the sickniks is that their gags ('I hit one of those things in the street—what do you call it, a kid.') come so close to real horror and brutality that audiences wince even as they laugh."

One aspect of this, obviously, is that some Timenik wanted to tell a sick joke, and this was a respectable way to do it. (Interestingly, their example is not credited to anyone, nor to this writer's knowledge does it survive in any contemporary's recorded material, so it was probably a current street gag.)

Overall the piece acknowledged the arrival of a chorus of disturbing new voices, but by lumping them all under the "sicknik" banner *Time* left the impression—at least to anyone who knew who they were talking about—that the only precise meaning to the term "sick" was "different." *Time* tied itself in definitional knots with Nichols and May ". . . the wistful social desperation of Elaine May and Mike Nichols, who are barely sick at all . . ." (so why were they included?), and gave a chunk of space to Don Adams, a traditional comedian whose only connection to the subject was that his act at the time included a very unfunny routine *about* "sick" humor:

"Adams does a take-off on a sicknik who is telling jokes about a plane crash and suddenly looks out into the audience: 'Sitting over there I see Mr. Thompson. He lost his wife and two children in the crash. Stand up and take a bow, Mr. Thompson. Let's give him a nice hand . . . No tears now. Just take your bow and sit down.' "

Berman's contribution to the sicknik corpus was as follows:

"Have you ever, when you were out playing, had to listen to your mother's voice calling, 'Sheldon?' " Pretending to talk to his sister on the telephone, he will say thoughtfully, "Marge, tell my nephew he's a boy—he doesn't know. Don't wait until he grows up and makes an arbitrary decision."

And, significantly, one of the decade's purest and most uncompromising satirists was represented by this verse from his *Mad*-magazine-style "Masochism Tango":

> I ache for the touch of your lips, dear,
> But much more for the touch of your whips, dear.
> You can raise welts

---

little knowledge of its origin or the original purpose of its use. There's no reason to suppose, however, that we are ever likely to see such terms as nukenik, right-to-lifenik, or Reaganik.

> Like nobody else
> As we dance the masochism tango.

Tom Lehrer, a quiet, courtly mathematics instructor from Harvard, had been writing his poisonous words and music since 1953. Most were a lot tougher and more disturbing than this:

> We will all go together when we go
> All suffused with an incandescent glow.
> No one will have the endurance
> To collect on his insurance.
> Lloyd's of London will be loaded when they go.

> When the shades of night are falling
> Comes a fellow ev'ryone knows.
> It's the old dope peddler
> Spreading joy wherever he goes . . .
> He gives the kids free samples
> Because he knows full well

> That today's young innocent faces
> Will be tomorrow's clientele . . .

> I wanna talk to Southern gentlemen
> And put my white sheet on again.
> I ain't seen one good lynchin' in years.
> The land of the boll weevil
> Where the laws are medieval
> Is callin' me to come and nevermore roam . . .

> Soon we shall be out amid the cold world's strife
> Soon we'll be sliding down the razor blade of life.
> But as we go our sordid sep'rate ways
> We shall ne'er forget thee, thou golden college days . . .

Most of the songs from which these lyrics are drawn had been copyrighted in 1953 or 1954. Lehrer's quiet academic demeanor, tinkly Flanders & Swann melodies, and impeccable Ivy-Leagueness made him very acceptable to the East Coast Time-Life in-crowd, but this piece chose to quote one of his nonpolitical songs. Nowhere in fact does the piece refer to the obvious political and social thrust of the "sickniks" (Sahl was not quoted at all—just his then current salary: $300,000 per annum). There was clearly a lot more that disturbed the voice of the "center" than their breezy tone suggested.

The only interpretation put on "sickness" was a boilerplate quote from Nelson Algren: "This is an age of genocide. Falling on a banana peel used to be funny, but now it takes more to shock us. And there is no more fun in the old comedians. People nowadays would rather be hurt than bored."

Moreover, *Time* made no reference to the manifest intelligence of the new humor and attempted no distinction between it and the very definite late-fifties phenomenon of sick jokes, of which it was clearly aware.

Sick jokes, like the example quoted in *Time* about running over a kid, were a new, odd, and widespread cult at the time. Most of them took the form of a two or three-line exchange of dialogue as in:

"Mommy, Mommy, why am I going around in circles?"
"Shut up or I'll nail your other foot to the floor!"

Or:

"Mrs. Smith, Mrs. Smith, can Jimmy come out and play?"
"No, dear—I can't get his iron lung through the door."

Or:

"Mrs. Smith, Mrs. Smith, can Jimmy come out and play?"
"You know he doesn't have any arms or legs."
"We want him for third base."

As far as research can show, none of the humorists named in this chapter (or in *Time*'s piece) ever used such jokes publicly. The jokes were not those of a professional humorist. They seemed to have originated in the beat underground, and to have been passed around by word of mouth. There were a few paperback collections of them in circulation at the time and up until the early sixties.

The overwhelming proportion of sick jokes at the time dealt with kids as victims of horrific situations, while a few referred to other untouchable subjects such as the Crucifixion or the Holocaust.‡

While there was a superficial similarity between much of what the new comedians were doing, in that it dealt with death, disease, the Bomb (the not-funny subjects), and sick jokes, there was a world of difference in the treatment. For example, Sahl was quoted earlier in a line about capital punishment

‡ Eugene Troobnick recalls Feiffer hanging out at Second City around the time Adolf Eichmann had been extradited by Israel (1960). Someone came into the theater wearing a button that read, "I like Eich." This effort was greeted with general hilarity, except from Feiffer. He was called on his lack of reaction: "Come on, Jules—don't you think that's funny?" to which Feiffer responded, "Only up to the first five million."

a saying that its religious advocates should remember that they once made "a Very Big Mistake." While this is a reference to the Crucifixion, it is in no way the same as this (which was usually acted out by its narrator):

> Two Roman soldiers come up to Christ on the Cross. It turns out that he's been reprieved by Pilate. He's free to go. The two soldiers shinny up ladders and remove the nails from Christ's hands. Christ couldn't be happier. Then he very slowly starts to topple forward. "The feet!" he screams. "The feet!"

With sick jokes, shock was the intention and the end result. Sick humor was the trappings of satire without the purpose. And while sick jokes operated in the same areas of taboo, there was no apparent further purpose to them. "Shut up or I'll nail your other foot to the floor" had no objective meaning and therefore no objective purpose. Without knowing who initiated the jokes or why, it's hard now to assess what their purpose was although it is clear that people laughed at them and they enjoyed a wide vogue.*

It may be that their appearance had something to do with the perceived insensitivity of the fifties affluence, that sick jokes were a new version of *épater les bourgeois;* however, it could just as easily be argued that a beat called Bob started them one afternoon in San Francisco to see if they'd get as far as New York.

The *Time* story, which caused quite a stir in the "industry" in the summer of 1959, satisfied no one. Lumping Winters with Sahl, Berman with Lehrer, Nichols and May with Don Adams, and everyone with dead kids seemed to betray nothing so much as a desire to defuse the whole thing, and write it off as just another crazy show biz phenomenon. Certainly the real satirists, Sahl, for example, were appalled by the label "sick"; by the same token more traditional comedians were terrified that it put them in some weird pinko bag. For all that, from this time on the term stuck to Boomer humor like a tick.

Feiffer, who had probably been the first person to use it on the printed page, was never mentioned. The reason for this omission might have been that Feiffer had changed the title of his strip a year earlier from "Sick, Sick, Sick" to just "Feiffer," having got fed up with explaining the complex irony of its use. Or it might have been that *Time* did not want to deal with the disturbing aspects of his work. Admittedly, the notion of "It's not us that's

---

* Gratuitously sadistic (or sick) jokes disappeared for a long period in the sixties and early seventies—perhaps because their apparent insensitivity was construed as playing the system's game. But in the late seventies they began to reappear, usually in a new, shorter, question-and-answer or definition form. Such jokes are now so prevalent that no disaster can go by without a rash of amazingly cruel one-liners emerging almost simultaneously. Consider the jokes that have arisen, for example, in response to the Ethiopian famine, terrorist attacks, nuclear accidents, the Shuttle explosion, and so on. Far from the sick jokes of the fifties, which could at least lay claim to some vestigially bohemian purpose, these simply affirm brutality, insensitivity, and racism—the jokes of, not against, a thuggish collective mind. They might make Rambo laugh—but not Rimbaud.

sick, it's society" was by 1959 teetering on the edge of cliché, but Feiffer was then three years into the process of demonstrating the notion rather than talking about it.

But there was one person *Time* could not let get away by damning with faint praise. So much space did they spend on him (one column out of three), and so much disapproval, that a case could be made for the whole piece having been set up to get him. The voice of the establishment might be confused about who was and wasn't included in their own definition of sickness, but they had no doubt whatsoever about "the Newcomer": ". . . a kid who thinks he's a comedian but succeeds only in spouting his miseries . . . who merely shouts angrily and tastelessly at the way of the world . . ."

His "extremes," his "weird routines," his "vicious barrage" might be explained, says *Time* smugly, by "his own checkered background (the son of divorced parents, he ran away from home at twelve)."

Time cannot believe the naïveté of this cultural lout. (On religious leaders: "They have missed the boat. Thou shalt not kill, they say and then one of them walks comfortingly into the death chamber with Caryl Chessman . . .).'' And in any case, "San Francisco *Chronicle*'s celebrated columnist Herb Caen" says the kid is "a bore."

For all *Time*'s careful condescension toward the new laughniks, this was someone who made them sick.

Lenny Bruce went much, much, much too far.

4

Et Tu, Bruce!

In every period of genuine innovation one person gradually works his way to the core of the activity, circling at first, sneaking a little here and there, jostling people to get farther in, eclipsing some, linking up with, then dumping others, all the time growing stronger and more obvious—and often less liked. One day he is indisputably at the center, representative of the whole but none of its parts—the voice, look, and symbol of the entire phenomenon.

Lenny Bruce was not like that at all.

The literature that has sprung up around Bruce is packed with comparison to great artists in other fields, at other times. Picasso and Balzac are frequent guests. So are Charlie Parker and Mozart. His biographers and hagiographers are also fond of comparing him with his contemporaries, almost always to their disadvantage. The implication of both tendencies is clear: Lenny was a giant among great men, the Beethoven of Beats, the Jesus of Jazz, *primus inter pares,* the Führer of Fifties Fury, the Earl of Angst, the Duke of Dissent, the One Who Said It All.

Certainly his contemporaries regarded him with awe, and claimed him for their own. And without question the places he led future followers, and the voices and rhythms he inspired in them, were extraordinary, and without precedent. But what is striking in retrospect is how different he was from his contemporaries, not how alike.

Lenny Bruce stands alone. And he is not just "head and shoulders" above the rest. He is off by himself, in a world essentially closed. The ring of his observation, even when it was off-center or mistaken, is inimitable. The most sedulous scholar would find it nearly impossible to demonstrate that he owed anyone anything. And while his imitators were—and still are—legion, not one of them ever produced anything in the way of form or content like him. Comedically Bruce grew by himself in his own meager soil. It was watered and irradiated and polluted by the same things that affected his contemporaries, but where in them it produced weird growths common to them all, in him it produced a most exotic and monstrous plant, a fabulous fungus, a wonderweed.

Bruce was a comedian. (So, at various times, was his mother, under the name of Boots Malloy.) This immediately cuts him out from his peers, for he was a true down-and-dirty nightclub comedian who'd cut his teeth the hard way, introducing strippers, silencing drunks, attacking an audience into attentiveness. (He calculated one laugh every twenty-five seconds for a period of not less than forty-five minutes.) This grounding in "traditional" comedy was crucial in forming his style, and it gave him a common touch none of his contemporaries could command. Bruce was a rowdy. He was definitely in show biz. This was the world he knew, the way he dealt with reality. And while he shared with the others their rebellion, their dismay and disgust at the world their elders and betters had bequeathed them, his rage expressed itself in show biz forms. The result was something far less cognitive and intellectual, far more vulgar and appealing and dangerous than the rest of Boomer humor to date. The stop signs Bruce ran were on Broadway and Sunset Strip, the true heartland of America.

Leonard Alfred Schneider was born in 1925 in Long Island. He was the product of a shotgun marriage between Jewish parents, his father from somewhat snotty English stock, his mother from distinctly the wrong side of the tracks. His father, who sold orthopedic shoes, cosseted and spoiled his only child. His mother was, all Bruce's life, a back-slapping buddy, his best pal. Not to put too fine a point on it, his father was his mother and vice versa.

In 1933, when Bruce was eight, his parents divorced. His father remarried in 1936, to a highly conventional woman, far more to the parental taste; Bruce was brought up from then on in a highly conventional way, in a highly conventional house—still in highly conventional Long Island.

In 1942, at the age of seventeen, Bruce enlisted in the Navy and spent the next two years lobbing shells at fascists in places like Anzio. Tiring of this kind of action by 1945, he went to the medical officers and claimed to be obsessed with homosexuality, and with the idea of putting his obsession into practice. A dishonorable discharge followed quickly.

Rejecting a sensible offer from his father to go into the twisted foot business, Bruce plunged instead into the equally twisted world of comedy. New York in 1946 was flooded with young comedians and times were not easy. Perhaps this is why Bruce started not as a comedian but as an impressionist.

He wasn't a very good impressionist, but he got a shot on an early TV show called "Arthur Godfrey's Talent Scouts" in 1948. Godfrey and/or his talent scouts had a knack for being unimpressed by genuine talent (they passed over both Carol Burnett and Jonathan Winters), so accepting Bruce was a kiss of death that left lipstick on his collar for several years. Bruce's routine consisted of a scene in which Bogart, Cagney, and Edward G. Robinson spoke in German accents. He made a sufficient mark to get a few bookings, which took him nowhere. Nonetheless this experience, typically, melted down into his central core, and reemerged a few years later in his classic movie parodies. The very weirdness and inconsistency of Bruce's "impressions" of movie stars in his maturity was one of the more delightful in-jokes of his humor. For all his apparent impatience with convention and form, Bruce was a squirrel of technique. He never wasted anything.

By the early fifties Bruce was solidly in the toilet. Or more accurately, what he called "the toilets"—two-bit bookings in the fag ends of the great night-club era of the thirties and forties. In one respect he couldn't have cared less. Baltimore had in 1951 brought forth his wife, a long, luscious redhead who went by the name of Honey Harlow. Honey was a stripper. She and Bruce were the loves of each other's lives, although their marriage ended some seven years later in a drug-addled divorce. They toured around together for a bliss-ful year or two, she stripping, he quipping. For a while they even appeared as a song-and-patter team, in an act written and directed by Bruce, ending up in early 1953 in Los Angeles, where Bruce now united his and his wife's worlds and started working the L.A. area as a strip club emcee.

It's possible to see even this unsalubrious episode of his life as a positive influence. His love for Honey and the places that it took him in particular could be said to have "saved" Bruce from a more conventional and more initially successful course. From the outside, though, it seemed as if he was headed in the worst way down the razor blade of life. (Aside from working grungier and grungier strip joints in L.A. and the Valley, he was working on a tidy little drug habit.)

Without question, the five years Bruce spent hustling his way down the ladder of success during the early fifties gained him firsthand knowledge of what life looked like and what mattered most to the lowest and largest class in white America. This was stuff University of Chicago students and *Village Voice* subscribers could only read about. Professionally, too, there couldn't be a much tougher training ground than trying to wring laughs out of guys with erections; and if this didn't give Bruce much scope to explore his talents as a writer, it did encourage a sense of abandon. Working essentially as a mobile prop separating various nude bodies, Bruce had no option if he wanted atten-tion than to be outrageous, to go as far as the situation demanded, too far if necessary. Taking your clothes off is infectious. The conventional kid from Long Island was stripping too, slowly and laboriously peeling off layer after layer of restraint, learned standard, preconception.

Most conventional kids from Long Island would either have skidded rap-idly down the short sharp blade or quit. But Bruce had a very special drive. Half of it was sheer ambition, the other half was the same rage felt by his contemporaries that things were not the way they'd been told. Possibly be-cause he had no politics, learned or self-taught, and a limited formal educa-tion, Bruce's rage took more elemental forms than that of his contemporaries.

Bruce, after all, saw the reality underneath the Norman Rockwell America every night. For him the we're-not-sick-it's-society tag didn't need verbalization. There it was, right on the other side of the footlights: nice guy, happily married, father of two, sweating, twitching, half smashed, with a hat over his crotch.

This gave him the license to lash out in all directions. He would make "phone calls" from the stage pretending to call up the guys' wives; he would fall down in the middle of a routine and froth like an epileptic; he would turn the stage curtain into a huge floppy hand puppet giving him head.

Finally, one night in the summer of 1955, as a line was forming around the block outside the Compass, Mort Sahl was walking onstage for his second show at the hungry i, Fancher and Wolf were putting a *Voice* to bed, tens if not hundreds of thousands of future hippies, draft resisters, Beatle fans, and Peace Corps volunteers were snuggling under the covers with their first issue of *Mad* magazine, Bruce hit bottom. In an appalling dump in the San Fernando Valley, Lenny Bruce, master of ceremonies, sashayed out from the wings—and into show biz legend—bare-ass naked.

As what was happening sank through the audience's smutty, sodden reverie, the place began to go wild. Bruce, studiously jacking up applause for the stripper who'd just left the stage, affected to be unconcerned. "What's the big deal? This is what you came for, isn't it?"

Had it been anyone else, this might have been written off as the flip-out of a washed-up jerk, the end of the road, the final fuck-you before a long and permanent vacation. (It certainly wasn't normal—strip clubs operated in a very narrow corridor of official tolerance; the slightest deviation brought the L.A.P.D. around like bees at a picnic.) But in the light of Bruce's subsequent success, this outrage deserves a little more attention, for it was prophetic. (As if sensing this, the national grapevine buzzed with the news, something it would never have done for any other obscure emcee in a strip joint. The retold and embroidered story passed quickly into Bruce lore; three different versions were recorded for this book alone, one of them so confused that the narrator described the event as having happened not at a strip club but at a club on the Strip.)

Bruce had done the one impossible, unthinkable thing. Within the community of voyeurs he had crossed its only boundary of taste. He didn't put on a biretta and pretend to say mass, he didn't try to out-obscene the proceedings.* He simply took off his clothes and became the exact opposite of what they wanted to see—a nude male. (The only thing that was taboo, the one thing calculated to make those tiny brains begin to smoke.)

Chronologically this simple animal gesture serves to mark the calendar, for in an elliptical Bruce-like way it really was the beginning of his subsequent

* Prevailing community standards were exact. If Bruce had whipped it out no one would have been shocked so long as he remained clothed. One of Bruce's older contemporaries, a comedian called B. S. Pulley, actually made something of a name for himself this way. The spine of his act was a standing threat to urinate on the front row.

success; it's entirely true to paradoxical form that he would initiate his career at rock bottom, by taking off his clothes in a sleazehole.

From 1955 to 1957 Bruce worked in Los Angeles at a number of clubs, most notably one called the Crescendo, developing a local reputation as an ultrahip comic, and a following among the avant-garde of then moribund Hollywood. This was the period of germination for Bruce, when he began to build a repertory of pieces and attitudes that would sustain him for the rest of the decade. It was also a time during which he allied himself with the hip—that tenuous but distinct cultural tradition which until the fifties was largely black and largely musical; but which in the fifties because of the disaffection felt by a sizable segment of white society toward its own officials began to spread far beyond its original elite, creating a society within society of people who "understood" (the hip), consciously allied against those who didn't (the squares). The arts were where this collective psyche principally manifested itself, not just in music but in show business at large. Thus, even on television Ernie Kovacs and Steve Allen (who played jazz piano) were hip, but Milton Berle and Lawrence Welk weren't.

One of Bruce's early routines explores this gap:

And now, a tribute to the greatest living Polish artist in America today —Lawrence Welk. It's a half hour before the Welk show goes on the air. Lawrence Welk is hung for a new trumpet player for the band—twenty minutes left before show time . . . fifteen minutes . . . and the new trumpet player finally shows up.

WELK: Awright. Send in da new boy! . . . Hullow, sonny. How're you? My name is Larry Welk. The agency, Mr. Glazer, told me all about you. You're gonna be perfect boy for my band—you're deaf! Now, the rules are: Cooking in the dressing room; Fern does the laundry, fifteen cents a pound, fluff dry; you fold though. That's it.

"Ve go right on the road. We gotta lotta college dates—mostly industrial colleges—vatsamatter vit you, sonny? How come you don't talk to me?"

MUSICIAN *(Nodding out—he's so stoned):* Ah, like hello man, ah . . . know . . . alotta cats put you on, Mr. Wick, but, ah . . . you really something else, sweetie, ah . . . you're the best banjo—or whatever your ax is—you swing . . . that's it, sweetie, swing with your ax . . . I got Byrd's ax, man, he gave me his ax, you know, like, and you're pretty wild, Mr. Funk, and, ah . . . I really wanna make the scene with you baby, you know . . .

WELK: WHAT THE HELL ARE YOU TALKING ABOUT?

MUSICIAN: Hey, I don' wanna bug you but . . . er . . . could I get a little bread in front?

WELK: You hungry? You wanna sandwich?

MUSICIAN: No . . . I need some money to . . . er . . . take my aunt to the hospital . . . look at her, man. She's out in the car throwing up . . .

WELK: WHAT ARE YOU SCRATCHING YOUR GODDAMN FACE FOR?

MUSICIAN: Cause I'm allergic, man . . . don't come on corny that way . . . I'm a nervous cat, man . . .

WELK: Awright, I'm gonna sign you, 'cause I'm a good judge of character. You're honest boy. I can tell by your eyes—they're so small! Yeah . . . nice boy. That's a funny instrument—all them spoons there! You do novelty act?

MUSICIAN: Hey, I hate to cop out on myself, Mr. Wook, but, ah . . . I better tell you in front, baby, that . . . I got a monkey on my back . . .

WELK: Oh, that's all right—we like animals on the band. Rocky's got a duck. They'll play together.

Among other Boomer humorists only Sahl could really be considered hip; his preoccupation with politics, however new and jazz-associated his presentation, actually militated against him somewhat in this regard. For while hip was another face of Cold War despair and disgust, it tended towards the apolitical, the nihilist. Politics smacked of solutions, and the hip had no place for solutions other than their own awareness of the problems. Sahl therefore, for all his brilliance, tended toward a hipness that was never more than attitudinal.

Bruce's was behavioral. Not only did he run with jazzmen and their drugs, he experimented with extremes. This lack of inhibition would stand him in good stead once he'd groped his way to a moral purpose for exploring them. For the moment, however, the result was an element in his performance that could only be described as sick and whose purpose was at best shadowy.

The Crescendo, by comparison to any of the joints Bruce had inhabited to date, was a "nice" place. It was on Sunset Strip, and it was a genuine nightclub with a big gameroom and a more intimate lounge upstairs. The mix included the hipsters, the jazz-cool crowd with shades and a working knowledge—or a reasonable facsimile—of which drugs went where; along with nervous suburbanites newly prosperous from the hotshot defense and aerospace industries, out for a night on the town. The latter were in the majority and tended to exhibit that perennial schizophrenia of wanting to look cool but hoping they wouldn't have to sit next to any Commies.

Bruce, identifying with the former group, had a tendency to lash out at the latter. In a modified form this was only doing what he had done by taking his clothes off in the strip joint; the suburbanites were the meat and potatoes of the Crescendo and the owners wanted to keep them happy.

It was only natural therefore to do things like this: Bruce would pin a couple in the audience and ask them if they had a baby-sitter back home. In front of them, he'd then actually call the baby-sitter and tell whoever it was that he was very, very sorry but their employers had just been killed in a fiery freeway accident.

The in-crowd loved it and Bruce gained his first real notoriety. Since it appears to be amazingly cruel, it's worth asking why anyone, hipster or otherwise, would laugh at it. The reasons go deep into the contradictions of the fifties. However twerpy they might have looked, the hipsters were not just watered-down mid-century bohemians. "Square" was a vital term at the time, charged with layers of attitude; it meant someone whose mind was closed, someone who thought in neat fields and identical suburban tracts, in the modes of physics and technology, in grids, squads, neat columns, rules and right angles. The most obvious manifestation of square values were their ideas of family, parenthood, religion, and work.

The simplest way to challenge such values was to chuck a conceptual grenade at them, postulate the untidy realities of death, disease, and disaster the squares supposedly had trouble fitting into their grid. This was pretty crude stuff, and there was a definite element of cultural snobbery in it. The hipsters looked down on suburbia because that was increasingly where the power and money was, just as a previous generation of cognoscenti had looked down on farmers when *they* were where the action was. "Shock the hicks" was a lot of it. What Bruce did therefore was even discriminatory, since he pinned his couples essentially on the basis of the way they looked, their skin color, the way they did their hair, and so on, something he would never have dreamed of doing two or three years later.

But the squares left themselves open. Treating kids as innocents until the day they left home, and in the same breath ordering them to duck under their desks because the Russians were coming to crisp them (especially when at the outset that was a lie) was a pretty sick joke itself.

None of this shows any sense of the content of what he was doing. It had a simply rebellious purpose. The reality implied was obviously not a factor with Bruce, for he now had a two-year-old baby girl. These jokes were not intended to be at the expense of kids.

Once again, had he stopped here he could have been written off merely as a satiric terrorist. As it was he was on the brink of what was probably the best and most creative part of his career. While he didn't back off or compromise any of the reflexes he had developed in this period, he vastly expanded his challenges to all kinds of social assumptions. What began to appear in his work was a real sense of the moral issues his subjects raised. From shocking the squares, he progressed at an amazing speed to the point where the need to explain the good and bad of people, to get it right—to teach, almost—started to shape the choices he made. Hilarious, rowdy, and destructive though his humor was, this growth was palpable.

In January 1958, Bruce opened at a gay club in North Beach, San Francisco, hard by the hungry i, called Anne's 440 and—finally—took off. As it had been for Sahl and would be for the Committee, San Francisco was the hothouse, the transformation factory. What went into Anne's in the winter came out the following summer barely recognizable. Lenny Bruce learned all he knew from Long Island and L.A. but it took San Francisco for him to know what he'd learned. By the time he left for Chicago the next fall, to open at a new club called the Cloister, Bruce had acquired a solid following, a vociferous champion in the press (Herb Caen of the San Francisco *Chronicle)*, a record deal—crucial to the virtually untelevisable Bruce—but most importantly, a repertory of major pieces which were some of the finest of his career.

His progress from his booking at Anne's 440 to the time of JFK's inauguration was spectacular but largely uneventful, at least for the purposes of this overview. It included a television appearance, in 1959, one of Bruce's very few, with Steve Allen. Although this made NBC very, very nervous, it was chiefly remarkable for Bruce's exemplary behavior.

More ominously, in the summer of 1959 Bruce was busted in L.A. for narcotics. He bargained with the L.A.P.D. to stay out of jail by turning in a number of dealers he knew. The ethical trauma of this situation—for Bruce was ambivalent in the extreme about his addiction—undoubtedly added another level to his ever deepening preoccupation with what was and wasn't moral. By now his satirical sense was secure—he was light-years beyond indiscriminate flailing at social stupidity. When he did a piece that cut, he knew who the villains and the victims were. Moreover, he was acquiring that essential satirical skill: becoming your enemy in order to destroy him. Here's one of his best pieces, which he premiered in March 1960, called "How to Relax Your Colored Friends at Parties":

BRUCE: This is the typical white person's concept of how we relax colored people at parties—the white guy (Dennis) and the black guy (Miller) establish themselves at "some spread" of a party:

DENNIS: I never saw you around this neighborhood. You live around here?

MILLER: Yeah, on the other side.

DENNIS: Yeah, I was wondering about that. *(There is an awkward pause)* That Joe Louis is a hell of a fighter. They'll never be another Joe Louis. Hey, you got a cigarette on you?

MILLER: Yeah.

DENNIS: Oh, the one *you're* smoking? Here, I'll put that out for you. I don't know these people too well. Are you familiar with them? I think they're Hebes . . . you're not Jewish, are you?

MILLER: No.

DENNIS: No offense . . . some of my best friends are Jews. We have them over to the house for dinner. They're all right, but some sheenies are no good. You seem like a white Jew to me. Yeah . . . that Bojangles, Christ, could he tap-dance! You tap-dance a little yourself?

MILLER: Yeah.

DENNIS: All you people can tap-dance. You people have a natural sense of rhythm. What's that, born right into you, I guess? Yeah, boy, the way

I figure it, no matter what the hell a guy is, if he stays in his place, he's all right. That's the way I look at it. That's what's causing all the trouble in the world. Everybody's uhhh . . . well . . . *(Raising his glass)* here's to Joe Louis. Joe Louis was a guy, the way I figure it, who just knew when to get in there and get out of there, which is more than I can say for alot of you niggers. No offense. I guess I must have had a few on the way over here. You're all right. You're a good boy. Did you have anything to eat yet?

MILLER: No, I haven't yet.

DENNIS: I can see if there's any watermelon left, or fried chicken, or dice, or razors . . . I want to have you over to the house, but I got a bit of a problem. I don't want you to think I'm out of line or nothing, but I got a sister, and I hear that you guys . . . well, I'll put it to you a different way. You wouldn't want no Jew doing it to your sister, would ya? And that's the way I feel. I don't want no coon doing it to my sister. I mean, no offense . . .

MILLER: Yeah, sure, sure.

DENNIS: And as far as my sister's concerned, shake hands you won't do it to her . . . You won't do it to her? . . . I hear you got some perfume you put on them that makes them do it to you. That's not true? There's no perfume you put on them? They just do it to you? . . .

It is supposed to be a virtue of great hunters and trackers that they can think the way their prey does; if this was true of Bruce he sometimes projected himself so well that reviewers mistook him for the animal. The response in the press to "How to Relax" was universal disgust—Walter Winchell's column dubbed Bruce "America's Number One Vomic," confusing Bruce's brilliant depiction of Northern bigotry with endorsement of it. Again, Bruce was swimming against the current; 1960 was the first crest of the civil rights movement, and the full force of liberal self-righteousness was directed against that good old bigot in the white sheet, with the obvious corollary that everything was all right up North where people enjoyed social integration and Colored Friends. The perception that mere physical juxtaposition would not eradicate racism overnight wasn't a truth the self-righteous wanted to face.

Bruce's deft characterization of a specific figure that disgusted him couldn't be equated with his earlier and much less secure victimization of symbolic targets. One thing "How to Relax" wasn't, was sick. It made little difference at this point to Bruce's rise—and the piece was unusual for him. For in this most political year, he did little about politics. True to form he was swimming upstream, nobody's spokesman, seeing beyond and beneath what others felt certain of. One of his best pieces of the period, and one of his most famous, has nothing whatsoever to do with politics. It is about his own business, and even about himself.

The piece demonstrates (and in this it is typical of his routines at the time) how he had begun to see his own business as a microcosm of society, how he was making it his metaphor for reality, his reductio ad absurdum. In this his instinct was impeccable, for from this distance we can see that in taking show business as his overriding preoccupation he may well have understood, at the profoundest, even at a completely unconscious level what it was that drove his generation.

So here's the sad tale of Frank Dell, "Dean of Mimicry and Satire." This piece is about pretension and comeuppance, but the way Bruce chooses to demonstrate it is classic. Frank, a two-bit Vegas comic, is tired of working the toilets—he wants to play a "class" room or upmarket nightclub. What better venue than the world-famous London Palladium? His agent, Bullets, tries desperately to dissuade him but he threatens to quit the agency and eventually the booking comes through. After a riotous send-off from the comedic establishment at the Lambs and Friars Club, during which every conceivable form of coprophiliac joke is mingled with heartfelt appeals for crippled kids, Frank arrives in London, at the Palladium rehearsal. The music director, outwardly charming, mutters to himself in disgust as he reads the music cues for Dell's appalling impressions (" 'Cue: now let's go up to musical heaven and meet . . . Eddie Cantor' Oh God! The same bloody thing every week") and we have a premonition of disaster.

That night, Dell waits nervously in the wings for the interminable act that precedes him—singer Georgia Gibbs. Georgia, the Grand Old Lady of the music halls, has been on for forty-five minutes already, and she has the audience eating out of her hands, alternately cheering and weeping as she belts through numbers like her "Tribute to Harry Lauder." (One of the most delicious things Bruce tosses off in this sketch is his picture of the English. It is not at all the usual cliché, but a people as vicious as they are charming, happily obsessed by their own past glories.)

Dell bounces out with his utterly out-of-place routines, which of course he hasn't even had the sense to adapt ("I just flew in from Lost Wages, Nevada") and bombs appallingly. He is throwing up in his dressing room afterward when in comes Val Parnell, the house booker. After Dell, Parnell is the best character in this piece—a smooth-as-velvet British killer, with a vast knowledge of show biz on both sides of the Atlantic, he is repelled by this sleazy jerk. He suggests politely but firmly that Frank board the next boat back to New York. Nothing doing. This booking is everything to Dell. His pleading with Parnell is a masterpiece. It ranges from wild bluster, "I gotta union, ya know," to sobbing, begging, and groveling, "I don't want to have to work shit-houses all my life." Eventually Parnell relents and agrees to let him do the second show.

Second show. It's even worse than the first. Georgia's now on her tenth encore. When it's over, she gets quiet and serious and asks the audience for a very special favor—a moment of silence for the boys at Dunkirk, the dead boys at Dunkirk, the dead boys at Dunkirk who won't be coming back.

On goes Dell. "I just flew in from Lost Wages" . . . and into the toilet.

The audience is an oil painting. He tries going to musical heaven to meet Eddie Cantor. Forget-it city. Mount Rushmore out there. Desperate now, he tries something different. "SCREW THE IRISH," he yells at the audience. Finally there's some response. "That's the funniest thing you've said all night!" comes a voice from the balcony. "You're right! SCREW IRELAND!" In seconds the place is in an uproar, people screaming "SCREW THE IRISH" at the top of their lungs and ripping up the seats.

Of course he's back in his dressing room, throwing up again, when in comes Parnell. "Oh goddamn son, you're a bloody Mau-Mau," says Parnell, incredulous. This time Dell has to sign the release, and Parnell undertakes to get him out of the country alive. True to form, Dell still protests, begging for one more chance; he'll do "hip smoker-reefer" material, anything. The piece has no real end, but when it was over Bruce would always say, "That's the bit. The bit is, naturally, part me."

Bruce used to be called "the comedian's comedian" by other comedians as if by this chuckling, knowing, finger-rapping-"funneee"-on-the-table term they could include him in their brotherhood. And he did do comedy about comedy. But they were not in-jokes so much as examinations of himself. Being funny was part of his metaphor for life—far from playing to other comedians with a nudge and a wink, he encompassed their world, turned it over, poked it, bounced it, spun it around on one finger. He shared the absurdity of being funny with the audience, whoever they were, and made his world familiar to non-comedians. If anything this tended to *include* the noncomedians and *exclude* the comedians, to whom it was a threat. The joke was on them. And him.

He belonged to no one. Only in one area was he unified with other humorists of his time (and many more since), and typically it was one he treated with an abandon none other of them dared to.

Almost all the principals of this phase in the development of Boomer humor—those who gave it its roots, spirit, and sound—are Jewish. Sahl, Berman, Nichols and May, Kurtzman, Feiffer, a preponderance of charter members of Compass–Second City,† Sills himself, and of course Leonard Alfred Schneider.

This ethnicity was echoed in the slightly older generation of Sid Caesar (not Italian as some people believed), Mel Brooks, Carl Reiner, Red Buttons, Buddy Hackett, and of course the Jack Benny–Georgie Jessel "establishment." There were historical, psychological, even temperamental reasons for this dominance of early Boomer humor by Jews, but the indications of it were covert until the arrival of Bruce. Sahl made no mention of it whatsoever, nor any use of Yiddish, nor did Compass–Second City. Feiffer, though eloquent about the presence of Jews in a movement turning on the perception of official

† Despite the fact that there were obvious exceptions—e.g., Duncan, Alton, Holland—one of Sills's favorite ways to calling his cast together at showtime was: "Okay—Jews onstage!"

absurdity, nonetheless was subtle about his own references. As he says—although there is nothing to indicate it particularly in his drawing or writing:

"I always knew that Bernie was Jewish and Huey wasn't . . . Probably the first Jewish mother humor was in my cartoons, but if anybody had called specifically for a Jewish mother, I probably would have backed off from it. And . . . if one looks at the work of Mike and Elaine in those years, well, clearly the mother that Elaine played . . . was a Jewish mother . . . again they never clearly pointed out any such thing. And if one had asked them at the time, they would have just said something privately, but I don't think they ever would have admitted it. One didn't do it, I think, until—probably until Roth, which was some time later. And Philip came along close to ten years later (in the late sixties).

"I remember having a Jewish girlfriend in the late fifties, who, unlike me, had a strong, unambiguous Jewish identity. And whose friends, whom I was introduced to, were very much like her. It seemed to be very normal. And I, who came out of another time, another class, was simply bowled over by how usual this was to them and how unusual and intimidating it was to me. I mean, it frightened me at first because I had grown up in an atmosphere where you didn't wear your Jewishness on your sleeve, because you were essentially among enemies. That's what I was taught by my mother and that's what I was taught by the culture that I lived in."

Until Lenny Bruce, Jewish characters and the Yiddish they spoke were a private culture among comedians. Left to themselves in Lindy's, the Stage, or the Carnegie Deli, everyone was a schnorrer or a schmuck, a gonif or meshuggener, the world was full of tsuris. The putz-punim-tuchis school of character depiction was in force, the only thing that could really crack them up.

In the outside world, though, such characters and language were unthinkable. In public performances, characters were strictly neutral from an ethnic point of view, and the language was pure English—as indeed were their names (Allen, Hackett, Burns . . . as the saying went, "Briddish not Yiddish"). Drawing attention to one's Jewishness was not done, even if the characters you depicted—Henry Youngman's wife, for example—were to other Jews obviously Jewish. Thus by the late fifties, being Jewish or using Yiddish onstage had become a social taboo even it it had once had the entirely pragmatic purpose of concealing ethnic origins in a racist and violent environment.

And therefore, for Bruce, an irresistible target. With him a dam opened. Nor was it a question of a crack and a trickle. His Jewishness was loud and clear, joyous and contemptuous, right off the street corner, deli-counter ranting, babbling Yiddish his vernacular, the language he returned to in extremis, the root and branch of half his characterizations, an in-joke with himself, his own hip within Hip.

Bruce used Yiddish everywhere—everywhere in his act and everywhere in America, with reckless disregard for who might be listening: Klansman, Cossack, neo-Nazi, or just plain members of the New York Athletic Club. It crept into every corner of his routines. Whether it made any "sense" or not, characters were always using Yiddish words in the most outrageous places or turned out to be Jewish, whether they were politicians or vampires or cowboys. "Goddamn!" says the Cracker of the Lone Ranger. "The masked man's a Jew!" Yiddish was part of Bruce's lexicon of hip, blazing out from its bizarre backgrounds for all the goyim to see, try to decipher, and occasionally understand. You got it or you didn't. You didn't, too bad. Bruce actually got people to think of Yiddish as hipper than Briddish. "Fuck" was a word he used to show how words were used; what he did in bed was *schtup*.

There was no intent in this, no preconceived purpose. Yiddish just bubbled out of him along with the junkie rap, the intellectual bric-a-brac, the encylopedic backlog of Mid-Americana, brand names, B-movies and trailer-park glitz. One of the things that remains startling about Bruce long after many of his references have sunk back into the primeval mud they came from is this spontaneity of flow, its directness and lack of premeditation. There seemed to be an open pipeline between the audience and his subconscious, and up it came a whoosh of observation, insight, recall, experience, impression, mimicry, parody, pain, contempt, and pity, equally arresting whether clear as crystal or hopelessly jumbled. The man vomited genius. And a large chunk of it was Jewish genius. Yet what would have been weird or even offputting in other mouths makes perfect sense in his, because of the company it keeps. Thus, if a little old Jewish lady suddenly starts talking like a junkie, it somehow doesn't matter. Or come to that, if Eisenhower suddenly starts talking like a Jewish mother in a Cabinet meeting, that doesn't either.

One routine, "Ike, Sherm, and Nick," concerns itself with a scheme to get the heat off the Eisenhower administration during a crisis by sending Vice President Nixon somewhere to get assassinated. Nixon resists, and the President starts berating him, "guilt-tripping" him into going. Ike: "Is that a nice way to talk to me? Create a monster is what I did? The boy I helped? *I capped your teeth . . . !*"

Involuntary, unreflective, spontaneous, explosive, the Jewish part of Bruce operated on several levels and operated in several directions. One observable effect was that the sudden appearance of an unashamedly Yiddish-spouting comedian—especially one who talked like a strung-out horn player—scandalized many, Cossack and comedian alike. For his peers, an ethnic taboo that permitted one thing in private but forbade it in public was shattered. His lack of shame was a clear message of rebellion to those who constituted his surrogate authorities, what he called "old show biz" the largely Jewish, support-my-disease-but-nobody-else's comedians who had been young and struggling in the Depression and were now a fat, complacent, meretricious establishment. One of his routines of the period, called "The Tribunal," put Frankie Laine, Sophie Tucker, and the newly converted Sammy Davis, Jr., on trial for the obscene salaries they commanded:

I feel some guilts. The fact that my salary exceeds twenty-fold school-teachers in states like Oklahoma. They get $3,200 a year, which is a disgrace! Just think . . . Zsa Zsa Gabor will get $50,000 a week in Las Vegas and a schoolteacher's top salary is $6,000 a year. This is really sick to me. That's the kind of sick material that I wish *Time* had written about. I'm not that much of a moralist. I'm a hustler. As soon as they give, I'll grab. But I know that someday they're gonna have a tribunal. We'll all have to answer. They'll line us up, the guys in the black shrouds;

JUDGE: All right, line 'em up! All the offenders there. State your names and your salaries and sentences will then be meted out. The first offender. What is your name, there?

LAINE: Frankie Laine.

JUDGE: How much do you make a week, Mr. Laine?

LAINE: Ten, twelve thousand dollars a week.

JUDGE: Remarkable! What do you do to earn ten to twelve thousand dollars a week?

LAINE: *(Sings.)* "To spend one—"

JUDGE: Burn his wig! Break his legs. Thirty years in jail! Line 'em up here. Here's the next one. What is your name?

TUCKER: Sophie Tucker!

JUDGE: And how much do you make a week, Miss Tucker?

TUCKER: Twenty to thirty thousand dollars a week.

JUDGE: What do you do to earn twenty to thirty thousand dollars a week?

TUCKER: I'm the last of the red, hot—

JUDGE: Burn her Jewish records and jellies and the crepe gowns with the sweat under the arm. Get rid of her! Back 'em up. Here's the next one. The one that's worshipping the bronze god of Frank Sinatra. What is your name?

DAVIS: Sammy Davis Junior.

JUDGE: And how much do you make a week, Mr. Junior?

DAVIS: Twenty thousand, sometimes thirty thousand dollars a week.

JUDGE: What do you do to earn twenty to thirty thousand dollars a week?

DAVIS: *(Sings.)* Hey, ding, ding, that old black magic—

JUDGE: Take away his Jewish star and stocking cap and the religious statue of Elizabeth Taylor. Thirty years in Biloxi.

Here Bruce, for all his idiosyncrasy, was replicating the attitudes of his contemporaries. This was a point at which he and his fellow humorists intersected. For Bruce, "old show biz" and its second generation—the momma's boys and teacher's pets of his own age who aped them, and the enormous pyramid of agents, public relations men, press, hustlers, assorted hype artists and good solid money that spread out beneath them—was his version of officialdom. What parents were for *Mad,* what social idiocies were for Compass–Second City, what Ike was for Sahl and the army for Feiffer, "old show biz" was for Bruce. They were his starting point, the easiest targets, the closest to home, the Mom and Dad who'd taught him the rudiments but couldn't handle them half as well or fast or smart. He was first and foremost interested in exposing their hypocrisy, he wanted to shock them, nail their greed and mendacity, ridicule their motheaten ideals of goodness and courage and moral responsibility.

And if Sophie Tucker and Georgie Jessel and the whole panoply of performers that stretched historically from Eddie Cantor to the Rat Pack seem like flimsy or unworthy targets for so formidable a satirical talent, it should be pointed out that this establishment was no mere symbol, no cloud of heart-lifting stardust that settled gently over the hardworking masses when their day was done.

These were real people in a real power structure, with unlimited access to the media, constant visibility, carefully maintained individual and collective images, and a monolithic political orthodoxy.

In all respects "old show biz" reflected the most basic aspects of Cold War American society, and sustained both its message and its emotions. For the most part its members had grown up in, or experienced, the Depression—and like other American parents, they had largely forgotten the collective sacrifices that had lifted them out of it. Like them, they were now bent on an orgy of acquisition; unlike them, its results were not only conspicuous but trumpeted from coast to coast. When their own industry was attacked from outside by McCarthy, they had, for all their avowals of solidarity and the comradeship of greasepaint and sawdust, cravenly accepted the blacklist and turned in, and on, their own. Onstage and offstage (which meant onstage in some other forum like print or television), they spouted the rabid militaristic messages of the times, usually in their silliest forms. Far from being big-hearted buffoons and big-voiced cockle-warmers, "old show biz" were the spokesmen and salesmen of orthodoxy, ratifying its attitudes toward children, women, work; endlessly regurgitating its sexual, religious, and racial prejudice; relentlessly equating happiness with money, fulfillment with obedience, love of country with war; and above all—something no one but they could do —manipulating, exploiting, narrowing, and conditioning the public's emotions, keeping things simple, ladling out happy endings, big finishes, good guys win, ain't she something, and kids are the darndest.

Bruce understood that this establishment was not the mindless, harmless, meaningless thing its enemies said it was, but a central and pernicious chorus of false values and induced feelings; in a word, bullshit. And he knew, as perhaps his peers didn't, that it could not be cured, counteracted, or replaced by something else. Bringing up everyone on Kierkegaard, or even Charlie Parker, was not going to undo the damage. The lure of the package these false values and feelings came in was irresistible—the glamour, the lights, the excitement, the laughter, the music, the high of it all—in fact, he loved it as much as anyone. But what he could do was expose it, ridicule it, burn holes in its dress, puke down its tux, torture its overfed little pets to death.

In a word, dissent. Point out what was really meant, the gap between the real and the official. Decode the messages from the Ministry of Everything's Okay. To do that he had to speak the language, be fluent in show biz. And he was. Bruce was a scholar of sleaze. No one before or since in Boomer humor had an ear for cliché like Bruce. Wherever it came from, a movie or a news story or barroom wisdom, or your mother's mouth, the cliché rings throughout his work, the flow and juxtaposition his particular sound, his way of handling the instrument of language.

Bruce knew about clichés. He knew that a shared cliché always gets a laugh. He also knew that a cliché means trouble, a sure sign that a thought has been repeated, a feeling received, the start of an untruth. And he knew that celebrity and cliché are inextricably mixed. That when somewhere in the dusty library of the culture, in an obscure movie or song or routine, in the mouth of some forgotten celebrity, everything we say or think has already been said and thought, that's not comforting but absurd, even horrifying. It means we have relinquished the freedom to think and feel for ourselves and ourselves alone, instead delegating that right to entertainers, stars, show biz and allowing a crust of familiar emotions and familiar beliefs—mouthed and repeated by those we imagine are merely amusing us—to form over our lives.

In his day people were simultaneously delighted and puzzled by Bruce's apparent obsession with show business—delighted instinctively because he was so funny at its expense, puzzled on reflection at his depth of interest in so officially trivial a part of American life. They would perhaps have preferred their satirical hero to come through with some heavier stuff directed at weightier targets.

Bruce did deal with heavy-duty subjects, all the time, but his audience got their fix in the form of parody or some odd or more offbeat show biz riff; and even when he took on the big guys frontally, show biz kept nudging its way back in. In retrospect, this only confirms his status as a genuine artist, one who sees before the others.

What Bruce grasped, unlike his contemporaries, was that the crust of cliché, of show biz, of delegated beliefs and emotions, was spreading. Spreading by feeding on its own importance, and ratified by the celebrity of its spokesmen. Sahl might amuse the politicians with his pyrotechnic display of informed wit, he might even help to undermine a President of a traditional heroic mold; Compass–Second City might brilliantly translate middle-class anxieties in a brand-new form to the traditional stage; Feiffer and the other young dissidents of the printed page might reinvigorate its forms; but at the end of the day America's attention was elsewhere.

What Bruce understood was that America received its values from the screen, from its media—and, more importantly, loved to. Its values were no longer passed on from person to person or from parents to children but from movie to movie, from star to star, from show to show, from illusion to illusion. It wasn't so much that people preferred being entertained to hearing the truth, so much as that they increasingly got their truths in the form of entertainment.

It was against this, on his dishcloth-sized stages, mike in hand in front of flesh-and-blood humans, that Bruce directed the force of his rage. He tore at apparently innocuous characters and sentiments, apparently meaningless phrases, from the most unpromising corners of show business, tearing away at them, ripping and demolishing them, until suddenly something emerged, ugly, absurd, hilarious, dangerous.

One of Bruce's best and most haunting pieces was "Thank you, Masked Man." In it, he explores the meaning of a seemingly innocuous character, the Lone Ranger. The consistency, the relentless instinct goes just about as far as it can to a final and horrible absurdity. And when we get there, Bruce includes himself as part of the absurdity. Bruce tries to unravel the mystery of illusion, the real meaning of a fiction, how a seemingly mindless phrase actually resonates with loneliness, need, paradox. It is evidence too that what took Bruce so far beyond anyone else of his time was a mind that could not stay away from the dark at the end of the tunnel.

"Thank You, Masked Man" is about a good man—a man who was "better than Christ and Moses." The Lone Ranger. Bruce's choice immediately operates on several levels. The Lone Ranger is a childhood dream, a man in white —totally, absurdly good; an image you can identify with and who also protects you; by definition lonely, the idol of an only child. At the same time ridiculous, moral on the level of Victorian melodrama (rather than of Christ and Moses), therefore perversely hip; at the same time an unworthy target and a perfect one.

We find out what Bruce is up to immediately. No parody this. He cuts without ceremony to the whole question of what it means to "do good":

"The Lone Ranger was so good that he never waited for a thank-you."

Bruce mulls over the consequences we don't find in the average episode. As the Masked Man leaves town, having cleaned it up, we hear a down and dirty New York voice:

"What's with that putz? The schmuck didn't wait! Momma made a cake and everything! I got my hand out like some jack-off—he's on his horse already! What an asshole! I'm standing there with the mayor and a plaque and everything. I'm gonna punch the shit outta him if I ever see him again!"

Another voice comes in, this time with a different angle:

"You don't know about him. He's going through analysis. He can't accept love."

"The whole town," says this voice, "knows about the Lone Ranger's problem, they just go along with his delusions to make him feel good."

"Nice guy?" asks someone else. "How come the asshole uses bullets, then? A nice guy leaves bullets for kids to fool around with?"

This puzzles almost everyone, until someone else offers an explanation. The magic (silver) bullets have a Freudian significance. Symbolically, they mean syphilis. At some level, the Lone Ranger is saying the whole world has syphilis. Hi-yo, Syphylisssss!

In a few deft swipes, the facile perfection of the Lone Ranger is in ribbons. Bruce's method is dizzying. It is the aural equivalent of the screen's quick flashes of voices and faces, each with some point to make, all of them the other side of the story, and the moral equation, we never get to see. The townspeople decide, on the basis of this discussion, to ride after their erstwhile hero, apprehend him, and "rap the shit out of him!" By the time they catch up with him, they have mysteriously become Southern. Now a redneck speaks to the Lone Ranger:

"Boy, you think you're pretty goddamn smart—you're hot shit, ain't ya, buddy? Look at these kids, made up a hamantash and a song, 'Thank you, Lone Ranger' " [why the redneck's kids are Jewish is without explanation].

Some hero. A man that's too good to accept a thank-you from little children. He's going to have to explain or "get the shit whupped outta him." The Lone Ranger—who sounds like the tenor in a musical comedy—obliges, "Supposing just once I did wait for a thank you?"

A cartoon kid's voice, horribly cute, is heard: "Thank you, Masked Man."

The Lone Ranger pauses just this once. He relishes the gratitude of a little child. He loves it. He repeats, "Thank you, Masked Man," over and over. He's captivated, enchanted—in fact, hooked. Now he's got to have a "Thank you, Masked Man" every goddamn day! And he does.

Suddenly, the Lone Ranger is old. He can no longer ride, but he's got those memories of the "Thank you, Masked Man" 's of days gone by. He's become a junkie for gratitude. It's five in the afternoon, and the man with the "Thank you, Masked Man" hasn't come. He's desperate. He whimpers, "You have a 'Thank you, Masked Man' for me, don't you?"

There's no "Thank-You-Masked-Man" forthcoming. "I thought it would last forever," he whispers in despair. An old junkie, no chops left, no connection . . .

"I have led a very flamboyant existence," he confesses. "I pissed them all away. Just give me one," he begs, "till I get to the next town."

A voice of biblical authority, plummy and definite, is heard:

"There are no more 'Thank you, Masked Man's. The Messiah has returned. All is pure."

"What has this to do with me?" quavers the Lone Ranger.

"Well, you see," says the new voice, "men like Jonas Salk [inventor of the polio vaccine], Lenny Bruce, and J. Edgar Hoover . . . these men thrive upon the continuation of segregation, violence, and disease. The purity they protest a need for, they just feed upon."

"You mean—?" says the Lone Ranger in his most melodramatic bass.

"Yes," comes the crisp answer, "without polio, Salk is a putz."

Bruce now brings us back, reminding us that this is a scene within a scene, the Lone Ranger explaining to the redneck *why* he never wants gratitude. We are back with the two of them, and the redneck is admiring:

"Goddamn Masked Man, you can talk your ass off, buddy! Phew! I don't know what the fuck you're talking about, all this Commie horseshit. Wilbur here, he's got blue balls. He's gotta get back to the base . . . You got me dizzy with all that shit!"

There's more to the piece, of which, typically with Bruce, there were as many versions as there were times he performed it, but this is its core, a trip from the triviality of a kiddie Western to the fundamental problem of evil, in a few broad and hilarious steps. Here, Bruce combines everything he did best: wild, dramatic variety, an immediately recognizable cast and landscape. And the profoundest of insights. This is far from his only work of art, but it is the quintessence of his method.

During Bruce's best period (1957–61) his recurrent theme, in the broadest sense of the term, was show business. And not merely show business but what he called "hustling." "Hustler" was one of Bruce's favorite words.‡ It covered everyone from politicians to Popes to pop singers to the putz who sells you shingles.

For Bruce showmanship and salesmanship were virtually indistinguishable, forming a continuum that could stretch from Gielgud playing Lear on one end to Holmes Tuttle flogging Fords in Los Angeles on the other. Whether Gielgud was doing a good job selling Shakespeare or the sleazebag in Southern California was doing an equally good job playing an utterly trustworthy

‡ There is a revealing quote in Sahl's autobiography, *Heartland* which unwittingly measures the distance between him and his greatest contemporary: "I believe that Lenny was funny when he was a comedian, but he was wholly ignorant politically. He used to say to me that he wondered why I found Stevenson preferable to Eisenhower, because, after all, they were both hustlers." There was a fascinating quasi-class consciousness that existed between Sahl and Bruce. Bruce was generous about Sahl in his Carnegie Hall concert; Sahl did not reciprocate as we can see from this. He thought Bruce was a lout for having little awareness and feeling, little urgency about politics. In fact Bruce knew far better at a deeper, more tribal level what was happening to politics. More and more, politics and show business were becoming indistinguishable. Sahl may have known the issues but Bruce knew where the action was.

king among men, the gig was the same. Creating an illusion on a nine-to-five schedule. Running some kind of scam. Hawking some kind of dream. Call it show biz, call it hustling, call it Bruce's Continuum. It's all one, even the most sacred biz of all.

BRUCE: I take you now to the headquarters of Religions Incorporated. Seated around the desk on Madison Avenue sit the religious leaders of our country. Religion's big business. We hear the chairman addressing the tight little group.

THE CHAIRMAN: Good evening, gentlemen. I'm glad to see so many guys here tonight. Many of you religious leaders I haven't seen in many years. I just was talking to Billy [Hargis] this afternoon. I says Billy, we come a long way, sweetie! Who would of thought back in thirty-one, when we was hustling baby pictures? And shingles and siding was swinging? We didn't know what the hell to do. You know, and just like that we came on. The Gideon . . . Bop! . . . and there we were! The graph here tells the story. The first time in twelve years Catholicism is up nine points. Judaism is up 15. The big P—the Pentecostal—is starting to move finally! And now, gentlemen, we've got Mr. Nitaya from our religious novelty house in Chicago. He's got a beautiful seller. The genuine Jewish star, lucky cross, and cigarette lighter combined. And he's got the "Kiss Me in the Dark" mezuzah. And these wonderful little cocktail napkins with some heavenly sayings, "Another martini for Mother Cabrini." Now, here is the greatest holy roller in America today. Oral . . .

ORAL [Roberts]: Well, thank you very much. Here, have a snake! Gentlemen, tonight is thrill night! Gentlemen, why is it thrill night? Is it thrill night for the teenagers, the Elvis Presleys? No, gentlemen, it is thrill night for me because tonight for the first time in seven years I am talking to men in the industry. For the first time in seven years, gentlemen, I am not going to look into a one honest and sweaty Lockheed face! Not one thick red neck! I said, "Oral, tonight you're going to talk to men," and I said, "What would I talk about?" And it came to me! The heavenly land! Well, gentlemen, tonight, tonight, where is the heavenly land? I'll tell you one thing, my friends. The heavenly land is *not* in the cheap neighborhood bar. The heavenly land is *not* in a burlesque house. The heavenly land is *not* in dreamland. The heavenly land is *not* on Wall Street! Well you might say to me, "All right, the heavenly land is not on Wall Street, you tell us it's not in the cheap neighborhood bar. Gentlemen, did you wonder if tonight I knew where the heavenly land is? Well, I do, my friends."

(Depending on the version, the heavenly land usually turned out to be a choice piece of local real estate.)

"Gentlemen, I know what some of you are thinking out there. I know what is going on. Some of you gentlemen who have never seen me before are saying, "Uh, that man up there! This modern-day prophet, there! Look at him ranting and raving. He's so smart. Well, maybe, gentlemen, I'm not that smart. Maybe I'm dumb. That's it. "That old dumbbell up there. Yes, I'm dumb. I got two Lincoln Continentals. That's how god-damn dumb I am! Now, gentlemen, (noticing someone trying to get his attention)—What is it, what's that?

ATTENDANT: You have a long-distance call that just came in.

ORAL: I'll take it in there. I'll talk to you boys later. *(He picks up the phone.)* Yes, operator, this is 610. Yes, operator, I'll accept the charges. *(He speaks into the phone.)* Hello, Johnny [Pope John 23rd]. What's shakin', baby? It's really been an election month, hasn't it, sweetie? Well listen . . . yeah, the puff of white smoke knocked me out! We got an eight-page layout with Viceroy. "The new Pope is a thinking man." Listen, I hate to bug you, but they're bugging us again with that dumb integration. No, I don't know why the hell they'd wanna go to school either. Yeah, that school bus scene. Yeah, we had to give them the bus, but there's two toilets on each bus! They're bugging us. They say "get the religious leaders, make them talk about it." I know it, but they're getting hip. They don't want no more quotations from the Bible. They want us to come out and *say things*. They want us to say, "Let *them* go to school with *them!*" No, I already did "Walking Across the Water" and "Snake into Cane." They don't wanna hear that jazz anymore. And that stop-war jazz every time. The bomb scares! Yeah, they don't want the bomb. Sure they're Commies! No, I ain't getting snotty, but we gotta do something! Billy, you want to say something to him? Billy wants to know if you can get him a deal on one of those Dago sports cars? A Feraroo or some dumb thing? When you coming to the Coast? I'll get you the Sullivan show the nineteenth. Yeah, send me some eight by ten glossies. It's a good television show. Wear the big ring."

Religion is in show biz—and every time Jerry Lewis hosts a telethon, show biz is in religion. (In another piece from this period, "Christ and Moses," Christ and Moses appear on earth to check out the state of organized religion, ending up in Saint Patrick's at a Mass celebrated by Cardinal Spellman. Suddenly, to the Cardinal's horror, hundreds of lepers appear, drawn to the messiah, and also of course the redoubtable Sophie Tucker and Georgie Jessel, in there with the best of them hustling for charity, and themselves.)

This is not the sneer of an outsider, nor the reductio of a partisan. This is someone who cares enough to dare. Bruce's metaphor faces in two directions —neither side, show biz or religion, is guiltless. And as with religion, so with politics. For all Sahl's condescension, Bruce didn't need a detailed knowledge of the differences between Ike and Adlai to get to the heart of the matter. Politics too was in show biz, but uncannily so was show biz in politics. And who better to illustrate the point than Bruce's favorite, the very wonderful, very talented, Adolf Hitler?

After all, hadn't Hitler hustled his way to power, wasn't he the first media leader? A scummy little corporal who'd rewritten his own personal history and that of his country, almost entirely by a relentless use of the press, radio, and film? Who, by wearing the right uniform, designing his look, training his voice, pressing the right verbal buttons, transformed himself from a scratchy-voiced asthmatic runt into a mythical figure of immeasurable size, capable of transforming geography and history in a measurable number of years? On what level did this Hitler exist? Only in German ears and minds, in German eyes and on German screens. Only on that other level where stories came out all right, where emotions could flow one at a time, where great exploits from the dawn of history and stretching to the heaven of the future could actually be played out, uncomplicated by the reality of a scrofulous sex-starved bully, or the fact that his immemorial nation of destiny had existed for exactly sixty years, or that at the business end of the dream was a club, a bullet, a baby with its head stove in and blood-spattered glasses in the gutter. Hitler existed in a story, in a movie, in a loudspeaker, in a digestible five-minute radio speech—a convenient, new, exciting, beautifully designed, superbly tailored, hip, happening place. Hitler was in show biz:

BRUCE: How Hitler got started. We take you to Bremerhaven, 1927—the largest theatrical office in Germany: M.C.A. . . . Mein Campf Arises. We listen to two German talent agents:

AGENT 1: *(Sighing)* What is this? Do you realize what's happening?

AGENT 2: Do I realize? I realize one thing—that we have forty-eight hours to find the dictator. It's a freaky business, isn't it?

AGENT 1: You know what a hell it is? Last week if you needed to find a dictator, everybody. But now everybody's working.

AGENT 2: Just for the hell of it, I called up central casting. Maybe? Who can know? Maybe there is some dictator types who we'll screen.

AGENT 1: All right, switch on the intercom. *(Agent 2 does)* Miss Peron, send in the dictator types, sweetie. All right, they're coming in now, the actors. Yes. Sit down, fellas. Everyone relax. My name is Ben Melser and I am the agent here. We are trying to find a dictator today. We have no script, a couple of pages. We don't know where the hell we're going with the project ourselves. We wanna see just how you guys move, you know? Just ad-lib it for a bit, all right? Okay, we call up the first fellow. Van Eisler, Benny? Come over here. Just ad lib it today and maybe we put a few bucks behind you if you work out. All right. Benny? You look famil-iar. Did I do Schlitz Playhouse with you once? Did I? No? All right, then, just sort of do the bit.

(Van Eisler reads the lines with an extremely thick, heavy, overexaggerated German accent. Agent 1 interrupts him abruptly.)

AGENT 1: *(Outraged)* Ach, that Method crap! Get out of here! That Brando jazz! You kidding with that? Okay, Paul Schneider. Paul? All right, Paul, just do the bit there.

(Schneider reads the lines in an effeminate way. Agent 1 cuts him off before he can even finish his first sentence.)

AGENT 1: Ugh! Too faggy! Next. All right, all of you gentlemen, get out of here! That's right! Get out! Out! All of you! We will call all of your agents. *(Turning to Agent 2 and crying)* You fink, you! This is all your fault! Don't ever look at me again. I'm going to go out on my own personal management. I don't need you.

AGENT 2: Don't get mad at me! It's not my—

AGENT 1: It's not your fault? That we don't have a dictator? That we didn't have the Kaiser on paper? I'm finished with you! *(He begins to cry again.)* I can't stand you! The whole Reich is depending on me!

AGENT 2: Hey . . .

AGENT 1: Don't bother me with "hey." What is it?

AGENT 2: Don't look now, but dig the guy on your right that's painting the wall.

AGENT 1: Where?

AGENT 2: Don't look right away. He'll think you're putting him on. The zhlub in the white uniform and the cap on.

(Agent 1 begins to nonchalantly whistle and sing.)

AGENT 1: Sonny, put down that painting. You'll do that later. Come here, come here, that's right. Look at this face! Is this an album cover? Oh, this is a hero. What's your name, my friend?

HITLER: Adolf Schicklgruber.

AGENT 1: You're putting us on.

HITLER: What are you guys talking about? Just leave me alone. I wanna go back to my painting.

AGENT 2: That's your name, Adolf Schicklgruber? That's a hoof and mouth disease, no?

HITLER: Hey, c'mon you guys. Don't fool around with me. You trying to make a jerk out of me? I know you show people. You fool around and make a fool out of somebody.

AGENT 1: We're not going to fool around. I like Adolf, that's sort of hip and offbeat, Adolf. But give me a last name. Adolf what?

AGENT 2: Menjou?

AGENT 1: Shut up! What a moron you are! That's your dumb sense of humor. Let's see. I like Adolf. He should have something that's really gonna hit the people.

AGENT 2: Hitler! Hitler!

AGENT 1: Hitler . . . Hitler . . .

AGENTS 1, 2: *(In singsong unison)* Adolf Hitler . . . Adolf Hitler.

AGENT 2: Yeah. *(Spelling out and beginning to count)* A-d-o-l-f H-i-t-l-e-r

. . . two—three—four—Yeah, five and five for the marquee. It is perfect. That's it!

AGENT 1: Adolf, my Adolf! Mein Liebchen! You are my Adolf Hitler! Adolf, you are going to make more money in a minute than you make with this Kemtone jazz in a year! No my friend, you will rise with The Third Reich. Yeah! Get the designers up here. Get him something not too hip, two buttons and a natural shoulder here. A little heel, but no pockets because of this Freudian thing. Adolf?

HITLER: *Ja?*

AGENT 1: We're going to make a lot of money with you, sweetie. *(To Agent 2)* We should give him a different act. Put a little rhythm section behind him. Call up maybe Leonard Bernstein and get some tunes for him. A nice opener. *(Singing "Poland, how I love ya, how I love ya, Czechoslovakia here I come . . .")* Yes, we will need one more thing for the arm. We haven't done the armband bit for a while. Something lucky the squares will dig. Four sevens? Ja, four sevens. Adolph, my friend, tomorrow we will be going on the road, my friend, as soon as you sign on the paper right there. *(Hitler signs.)* There, that's good! I won't be screwed the second time! Adolf, we see you tomorrow.

On the surface, this is just another sick joke—Jewish agents were behind Hitler's rise to power. But as we have seen, sick with a purpose was satire with a vengeance. Sure, you could write this piece off as just a great after-hours in-joke—especially if you were an agent—but the image remained, the metaphor had been stated, nothing whatsoever to do with Jewishness or recent European history. Its force lay in the connection, that it was the agents' job to find a dictator, that politics relied on show biz, was hired by it, was even subordinate to it.

Where did that perception lead? To the logical corollary that politics was not where politics was debated, show biz was where politics was debated, and above all—for this was at a time before television had become the forum for all ideas great or small—in the movies. The old generation might force its values on the new through the assembly line of education, the draft, the pyramid of corporate reward, but they made them stick through the movies.

Like so much else in this decade of supposed stability, Hollywood was in turmoil. Reeling from McCarthy's Luddite frenzy, the dream factory was in shambles. Its own greed-heavy infrastructure was falling apart; the small screen seemed infinitely more vital and popular than the large. As a result, throughout the latter half of the decade, it was a battlefield of ideas. Not the least of the ideas was whether movies *should* be a battlefield of ideas. Even movies that were not officially about anything ("wholesome family entertainment") were beginning to be seen as just as political as *On the Waterfront* itself a rat's nest of political meaning, made by a McCarthy collaborator [Elia Kazan] starring the quintessential rebel [Brando] about how unions *should* work but don't, in the supercapitalist mid-fifties). For a movie cannot be about *nothing,* mere sound and lights and pictures. However innocuous a Doris Day/Rock Hudson movie may be, it reflects essentially political phenomena: what occupations the characters are in, for example, or whether Doris decides to get married. Any movie approved by the Catholic League of Decency was full of hidden messages about sexuality, conformity, social priorities, however "tasteful," "inspiring," "family-oriented" or other polite ways of saying "propagandist"—a Catholic term—were used to describe it. And for the most part these were messages against which the entire movement of dissent was in rebellion.

On the most basic level this was what Bruce's best material was about: what was left out, the parts omitted from the morality plays that people attended in order to be "entertained":

BRUCE: A prison picture. It's the break, right. Cut to the warden, Hume Cronyn.

WARDEN: All right, Dutch. This is the warden. You've got eighteen men down there, prison guards who have served me faithfully. Give up, Dutch, and we'll meet any reasonable demands you men want, except the vibrators! Forget it, you're not getting them, Dutch! Can you hear me? This is the warden.

DUTCH: *(Making loud, crazed noises)* YADAYADA! YADAYADA Warden!

WARDEN: Never mind those Louie Armstrong impressions! Dutch, you punk! You're pushing me too far! You better give up!

DUTCH: YADADA YADA!

WARDEN: Shut up, you god-damned nut, you! I'm sorry I gave him that library card now. I don't know what the hell to do. Maybe if we just kill a few to set an example. That may do it. That's right! Kill about seven hundred down there! Go ahead, I said it's all right, now kill 'em! C'mon, don't get snotty, you guys! You gonna kill 'em now?—the ones in the gray shirts. The bullets? Look in the back of my brown slacks. Forget it! This cockamamy prison here! No one wants to help you! I'll kill about six of you with my police special!

FATHER FLOTSKY: (broad Irish brogue) Wait a moment! Before there's any killing, I'll get down there.

WARDEN: Oh no, not you, Father Flotsky!

FATHER FLOTSKY: Yes, I'm going down there.

WARDEN: Will you come down off the Pat O'Brien bit now? Father Flotsky, you don't understand. These guys are monsters! They're vicious criminals! They got knives and guns!

FATHER FLOTSKY: Son, you seem to forget, don't you, that I've got something stronger than a gun.

WARDEN: You mean . . .

FATHER FLOTSKY: That's right—jujitsu!

BRUCE: Cut to the worst part of the last mile—a real Uncle Tom scene—Death Row. The first cell.

BLACK PRISONER: All aboard! Well, well! Soon I gwine up to heabbin' on de big riber boat! Then when I gits on up there, I gonna gits me a lot of fried chicken and some watymelon! *(Proudly bursting into song)* Fried chicken and watymelon! Fried chicken and watymelon! Dat's what I gonna get when I get on up to dat big riber boat in heabbin'! Goddamn, yes sir, boss! You don't mind dying if you got a natural sense of rhythm! Ha, ha!

BRUCE: Another guy is going to the chair. It's the last mile.

INMATE 2: So long, Marty! Here's my playing cards, kid. Here's my mezuzah, Juan! And there's that door! I don't wanna go in there! I don't know what to do! I don't know what to do!

BLACK PRISONER: Don't sit down, master!

BRUCE: Back to the yard with Father Flotsky.

FATHER FLOTSKY: Hello Dutch! You're not a bad boy, Dutch! Killing six children doesn't make anyone bad now. Now, Dutch, I told them up there in the tower that I would take the gun away from you, and I'm gonna do it, Dutch. Now come on. *(Calling toward the warden confidently)* He's going to give it to me. Now c'mon, Dutch, give me the gun now. C'mon, *(aside)* you schmuck! Give me the gun!

DUTCH: YADDI YAH YAH! YADDI YAH YAH, Father!

FATHER FLOTSKY: You're right. He's a goddamn nut! They're no good, the lot of them. Pour it in [i.e., shoot them all].

WARDEN: You men, the prison guards. I know this smacks of an insalubrious deed. I've got a job to do and a pension I'm not going to screw up. I know it's cold, guys, but what the hell, you know what this gig is! It's dog-eat-dog!

(The Warden gives Dutch three seconds when suddenly:)

KIKI: *(Very gay)* Dutch, listen to me, booby!

DUTCH: Who is that?

KIKI: It's Kiki, the hospital attendant. The one who gave you the bed baths! Give up, booby! Don't screw up your good time.

DUTCH: Kiki, you nut you! Kiki baby, I'll give it all up for you!

KIKI: Did you hear that! He's giving it all up for me. Ha! I feel just like Wally Simpson! I don't believe it. He's giving it all up for me! Did you hear that, you bitches in cell block II. *(He laughs.)* My nerves! He's giving it all up for me! Did you hear, Warden?

WARDEN: I heard him, you fruit!

DUTCH: Watch it, Warden, don't outstep your bounds now! Are we going to get all our demands?

WARDEN: What do you want?

DUTCH: A gay bar in the west wing.

WARDEN: All right! You'll get it, you'll get it. What else?
DUTCH: I wanna be the Avon representative of the prison.

Sorry, folks, the warden doesn't shoot rioters because he must obey the higher good of social justice over individual rebellion—he does it to protect his pension; the mad-dog killer doesn't give up his gun because Karl Malden or Spencer Tracy persuades him to make peace with the Man Upstairs—he gives it up for his homosexual lover. Happy ending, anyone?

"Father Flotsky's Triumph" goes beyond a mere parody. As a matter of fact, Bruce contemporaries in Boomer humor—with the exception of *Mad* magazine—disdained parody, perhaps because largely speaking they disdained "popular" culture. Parody was a mainstream game, played on television, a cog in the mechanism of adulation—if a movie or star was big enough then he, she, or it was parodiable. Neither the form nor the target was of much interest to, say, Compass–Second City, who were busy developing their own new forms. In terms of his own generation, this left the field pretty much open for Bruce. It grew organically from his background as an impressionist; more important, it was a solid foundation, a firm base in shared information from which to launch the ferocious instinctual energy of his insight. Without the familiar landscape of parody, Bruce would have appeared a very wild beast to an audience in the late fifties; when later he began allowing that raw instinct to roam at will, he became much harder to both follow and swallow. Bruce needed a foot in reality or he went so far he was out of sight.

It was this mix, chock full of specific references, in-jokes, and broad characterization, that made Bruce so special, able to be both the darling of Hollywood chic and a surprisingly ecumenical comic. What was so fascinating and hypnotic about him was the totality of his instinct. He really didn't seem to know where to stop. Certainly if new Hollywood thought they were going to be let off the hook, they were mistaken. The kind of movie that emerged from the battlefield of ideas was equally likely to get savaged. The following is Bruce's satire on a film called *The Defiant Ones,* which was a prison break film also about a white prisoner and a black prisoner who escape from jail but remain shackled together. Heavy symbolism.

WHITE: *(Heavy Southern white accent)* Come on, Jane! Come on, Jane.
NEGRO: Whaddayou keep callin me Jane for?
WHITE: You don' wanna be called "boy," do ya?
NEGRO: No.
WHITE: You know, I tell ya somethin'. Randy. You know, buddy, when us broke outta here, I just couldn't stand to look at you, I jus' hated you. Boy, if my Daddy ever heard me say this he'd sure whup me good—but Randy, I wanna tell you one thing, buddy *(almost crying),* Randy, standin' next to ya like this, and being chained to ya an' runnin' away from all them hounds, well, it's, it's taught me a lesson—it's, it's opened

up mah eyes, Randy, standin' nex' to ya like this has really shown me somethin'.

RANDY: What's that?

WHITE: I'm taller than you . . . An' Randy, being taller than you is a lesson in equality itself.

RANDY: Speakin' of equality, I wonder will there ever be any equality?

WHITE: Well, it is, Randy—don't forget: To Play "The Star-Spangled Banner" It Takes Both The White Keys And the Darkkeys. Someday, Randy, up theah, up theah in Equality Heaven, they'll all be theah, Randy, the people who believe in it—Darryl Zanuck and Stanley Kramer. Thass why they make them pictures *(voice trembling with emotion),* cause they believe in equality, Randy, and up theah, it's gonna happ'n, cause they caused it, an', an', an' then you gonna be livin' in Zanuck's house with all yo' colored friends, and next door to Kramer on his property in Malibu, you'll . . . you'll be helping them people, Randy—polishin' their car . . . Yeah, you—yessir, I'm gonna tell you, buddy, it's gonna be a, it's gonna be a Message World, Randy, that's what it'll be, Randy, a Message World . . .

This piece now descends into passionate gibberish as the two cons repeat the magic word "knish" over and over as if it were the talisman of racial harmony. They wax rhapsodic about going all over the world (even to "Rooshia" and Nikita Khrushchev) to bring everyone the all-powerful message of "knish" happy ending:

WHITE: An' then, Randy, it won't matteh, it won't matteh anymore even if you are colored and I'm Jewish, and even if Fritz is Japanese, and Wong is Greek, because then, Randy, we're all gonna stick togethuh—and beat up the Polaks!

Always punching through the parody was that insight, leaping on absurdity like a Doberman—directors like Kramer or producers like Zanuck no more had freedom in mind than the KKK. Bruce's instinct here shows itself at its best, entirely consistent, going after pretension as swiftly and surely as it did after selective morality. The line "To play a piano you need the white keys and the darkkeys" explodes in seven different directions at once. One certainly is that many probably just laughed out of shock at hearing the word "darky" in a supposedly liberal setting. That was a paradox that Bruce always lived with, that people often laughed at only part of what he had to say. As with the part, so the whole—what seems most lasting about *The Defiant Ones* is the deep and disturbing message that however worthy or well-intentioned the belief or emotion, don't rely on show biz to say or feel it for you.

These two parodies, "Father Flotsky" and "The Defiant Ones"—and there were others—are no ordinary parodies. They are vehicles for satirical comment as savage as—and, with all requisite respect, much funnier than—anything else of their time. Not until *The National Lampoon* would parody be used like this, going beyond the mere mockery of style to expose the rubbish at its center. But Bruce's medium was his message too. It was not just what the people in the movies said, it was the movies themselves, why people went for them, believed them, loved them. There was much to this complex, contradictory, idiosyncratic and solitary man, but this was at his core. Show biz, pretense, had, for this lonely, conventional Jewish boy, been the road to love, attention, and respect, even a taste or two of glamour. He was thus honorbound to expose it. This was why even at his most savage he was also at his most vulnerable; even when he was scooping out garbage by the handful he was at his most beguiling. He knew that whatever was in America's head, show biz, the delightful lie, was in its heart.

Show business was, after all, about to enter the political arena with an intensity it never had before. Right behind Kennedy, arms linked in emotional solidarity, was new Hollywood, the new celebrities, the new purveyors of belief and feeling: Paul Newman, Marlon Brando, Shirley MacLaine, Natalie Wood, Frank Sinatra, Harry Belafonte, actors, dancers, singers, directors, producers, writers, all those on the sparkling new edges of the crust. The effect this had on the reputation of a relatively unknown, largely untried second-term senator was extraordinary. And while there were many reasons, traditional, cyclical, political, and in every sense economic, why Kennedy was elected, in terms of electoral history, showbusiness was the new kid on the block. No presidential candidate in history had enjoyed this kind or degree of support. Certainly not Ike, certainly not Truman, not even FDR. And certainly not Nixon. Since Kennedy was elected by a hair's breadth, this support and the aura it lent him probably gained him the White House. Kennedy's election was the first instance in American politics of government by celebrity, the first time the two branches of American aristocracy—Eastern political money and Hollywood, long highly suspicious of each other—shook hands and decided to get down to something serious. The first inkling that the business of America would one day be show business.

In a way this was quite natural. The new Hollywood—sincere, committed, articulate about their identification with his proposals for change—identified with him at a deeper level. They knew what he was about. For Kennedy was a man who existed as much on the screen as he did in real life. A man you voted for less because of his accomplishments, his expertise, his verifiable political history than because of the accomplishments and expertise you could assume from his image on screen, the commitments you could deduce from a certain kind of face and actions. Story surrounded him, narrative could be projected from him. He was the young D.A. of old money but public spirit, championing the poor, good in bed, triumphing in the final courtroom scene over the sleazy crooks from City Hall. Feiffer refers to him as The Sundance Kid. Arthurian legend would soon, and more than half seriously, be adopted on his behalf by the most intelligent people around him. Kennedy was as much a personality as a person. He was part of the crust, the noosphere of show biz values, a place as much in the mind as on the ground, where people were tidier, had easy-to-group characteristics, where even if things looked hairy for a while you felt fulfilled that weighty matters like racism and poverty were being dealt with, and that a clean jawline, a shock of hair, and sheer goddamn eloquence would win out in the end.

So deep are we now into this process that it's hard to imagine a time when its appearance was new and startling. Exciting, yes, but by the same token odd, distasteful, even unfair. There were aspects to it that disturbed people immensely, often in ways they couldn't put their fingers on, often uniting those of the old-line right with the old-line left. Kennedy's politics and those he was supposedly replacing were not quite the point. It was the method that mattered.

The end we might all agree on, but did it justify the means? However many fabricators and propagandists huddled behind Ike hoping no one would notice them, Ike was real. He wasn't a story. He had done his enormous bit for his country and the cause of freedom. The facts were in place, messy, moving, equivocal, with some bad bits including tearing off a piece of English ass on a regular basis. Try as you might you couldn't turn Ike into a story. He didn't work on screen. He looked like a genial lizard, and he stuttered when you asked him tough questions—perhaps, although we'll never know, because he knew too much and had experienced too much to give a quotable answer. And he was old. His time was past, his accomplishments firm. He couldn't be forced into a new mold, unlike his malleable young veep—the political Pillsbury Doughboy. He wanted to play golf and that was that. And whatever horrors were perpetrated in his name or under his banner, on his departure he would make the single most important political speech of the Cold War then or since, in a single phrase, "the military-industrial complex," undercutting all the hard work his flunkies had done, identifying and condemning the men who strove to rule the nation. He was simply impossible. The gap between what he was and had done was practically nil. Ike was all fact.

With Senator Kennedy, though, there was a comfortable amount of room for fiction. Since he had accomplished little and been before the public for so short a time, the voters—including those who laughed with Sahl at Ike and at his Chamber-of-Commerce society in Chicago—could supply whatever fiction fit.

You want vigor? Forget golf. You've got touch football. You want youth and beauty, match Jackie with Mamie. You want class over Kansas, what's classier than Boston? You want emotions over platitudes, let freedom ring. You want the beginning of the movie, not the happy ending? Here are issues, issues, issues. You want mind over muscle? Harvard versus West Point. You want a king, not a general? You got—Camelot.

The truth, of course, was somewhat different. There was no reason to suppose Kennedy would be a crusader. His father had bought him a fairly safe Senate seat, and he'd done little with it but run for the Democratic nomination. He was a Cold Warrior from a state that was right up there with

California and Texas when it came to defense budget time. Anyone who thought freedom had ever been a factor in the broken-head turmoil of Massachussetts Democratic politics was nuts. There was nothing new or exciting there. The only thing that was relatively new about Kennedy was his father's money, acquired largely by pushing liquor across the Canadian border during Prohibition. Joe Kennedy had spent his Volstead Act fortune acquiring, as fast as possible, all the un-American Europhile trappings of class, intellect, fabricated lineage, and all the things and places that went with them. The Kennedys were instant aristocrats. Just add wealth, and mix vigorously.

In short, a new officialdom was being formulated. There was a different gap between reality and illusion. The new President could exist in a world of apples where facts were oranges, irrelevant. In a story, in an illusion, on a screen, where from long experience of screens you could be fairly certain you would know what to feel, who was right and wrong, how things would turn out. And he came through. Those debates! He was so good-looking, so in charge, compared to old sticky-lips Nixon. And as soon as he was elected, that press conference! Funny, witty, quick, pat answers when he wanted to answer, amusing evasions when he didn't . . . What a relief!

The aura of boundless possibility that attached itself to Kennedy was almost tangible. Old-time politicians like Johnson and Humphrey couldn't understand it. It didn't seem fair that so much psychic power could attach itself to a man who hadn't labored long years in the muddy fields of politics to earn it. Those who were busy building this new power grid, on the other hand, erecting the scaffolding of the mediacracy to come, who scarcely knew yet how much or how little they had on their hands, were delighted. Delighted that without accomplishing any deeds of political valor, other than having been born with a courageous profile and a fortune, their first experiment was an instant hero. It only validated their efforts that so many stories were attaching themselves to him, that people expected impossibly too much of him.

Even Sahl, for all his knife-like wit, was beguiled, drawn to the Kennedy he cut and diced because he was above all a star, hopping on a plane with him as much because it was headed for Palm Springs as because it carried a presidential candidate. From the barroom scuttlebutt that he'd bedded Marilyn Monroe to the heart of the Rat Pack where his own brother-in-law ran, the new President was borne aloft by illusion. John Fitzgerald Kennedy was in show biz.

Bruce had little to say about Kennedy—as indeed he'd really had little to say about Ike—beyond a brief passage in his Carnegie Hall concert, in which he mused about the fact that Kennedy's term would see a child born in the White House, and that he had never been able to imagine Ike kissing his wife —at least not on the lips.

But with that eerie extra sense Bruce sometimes exhibited, an odd piece of flotsam floated up from his volcanic unconscious. In the same passage he told a joke, an actual joke introduced as such, about Kennedy's recent inauguration. The point of the joke was that Kennedy was unable to make the acceptance speech because he had a virus. Kennedy's men are flipping out when someone mentions he knows a guy in Boston who's a ringer for the President. The only trouble is, the ringer is a burlesque comic who works real toilets. The comic is located, and the resemblance is amazing. The Kennedy men put him on, and true to form, having made a formal opening, the comic President goes into a sleazy impression from his act. It's a funny joke, and the association of JFK and show biz is interesting. What burns through the tape, though, is the conversation of the politicos as they discuss whether they can risk putting the fake Kennedy on the inaugural dais:

"Does he drink?"
"No, it's just a little speech. He'll memorize it, that's all."
"Can we trust him?"
"Don't worry—we'll kill him after the show."

5

Jesters in Camelot

Now we at the Bureau are well aware
that you just sold over four million albums.
You, sir, are the bestselling President of all time!
—VAUGHN MEADER,
The First Family, Volume 2

Shortly after John F. Kennedy's election, the humor magazine *Help!* featured, full-page, a news photo of Grace Kelly smiling adoringly up at JFK. There was a thought balloon over her head. It read: "To think I settled for that schnook Rainier." The *Help!* staff included artists Mad Will Elder and Jack Davis, its covers were photographic, featuring, in addition to Sahl, comedians such as Ernie Kovacs, Jackie Gleason, and Jonathan Winters. It also made use of famous photographs, like the one of Grace Kelly, to which rude and incongruous comics-style speech balloons were appended. This simple satirical technique was used for the first time in this magazine. It would soon become the continuing front-cover policy of the British satire weekly *Private Eye* (beginning in October 1961).* *Help!* was edited by Harvey Kurtzman.

The new Administration was giving the impression to everyone of an opening up in the culture—a new freedom of thought and speech, quite unlike the leaden commodity, Freedom, apparently for export only, that had been peddled by the Eisenhower administration. And one of the most evident signs of this was a surge in ever more adventurous forms of Boomer humor.

In 1959 there had been other vernal stirrings, portents of renewal. God, working in His mysterious ways, had appointed the earthy and lovable John XXIII as His personal representative—a brilliant public relations move that

---

* *Help!* was the origin of many formats and careers. The then gag writer Woody Allen was an early contributor. Gloria Steinem was an assistant editor. *Help!* gave their first popular exposure to many fledgling cartoonists, including Gilbert ("Wonder Warthog") Shelton and Robert ("Fritz the Cat") Crumb. A little later under its aegis, another contributor, Terry Gilliam, would meet up with guest funny face John Cleese, thus ensuring Monty Python's inimitable graphic continuity.

did much to counteract the current rumors of His death. The Supreme Court finally saw fit to allow domestic above-the-counter dissemination of that powerful post-Victorian aphrodisiac, *Lady Chatterley's Lover;* and, just in time to profit from the instant outbreak of lust, G. D. Searle developed Enovid, otherwise known as the Pill.

Something revolutionary was going on in art, as well. Pop was as threatening to the reigning school of Abstract Expressionism as Castro to Batista. The work of Jasper Johns, Claes Oldenburg, and Robert Rauschenberg was irreverent, witty, and even—remarkably—about something. Allan Kaprow was even more dangerous. In the sacred name of Serious Art, he staged the first "Happenings," goofy, spontaneous, improvised events. Flashing lights, weird noises, nudes, and jokes.

In the garden of New York's Museum of Modern Art in the fall of 1959, Jean Tinguely had exhibited his *Homage to New York.* Before an audience of critics, a bizarre-looking piece of machinery whirred, smoked, blinked, clanked . . . and destroyed itself. Kenneth Tynan, the first English writer to enthusiastically champion the work of Lenny Bruce, was delighted by Tinguely's piece of resurgent Dada, and happily explained to a puzzled onlooker, "It means the end of civilization as we know it."

In 1959, American art said "Zap" and "Pow" and thumbed its nose and was willing to try something new, and for a while the avant-garde was actually avant instead of guarded.

There were other omens. Buddy Holly's plane went down, and the music died. Well, some of it. But that made room on the charts for the new wave of folkies. One began to hear songs that were also about something—even, sometimes, *wittily* about something.

The Kingston Trio and other clean-cut strummers and pickers, like the Chad Mitchell Trio and the Limeliters, mixed songs of satiric social comment or protest with their record and concert repertoires. Shel Silverstein, arguably the farthest-out and certainly the raunchiest of the folkies, was quickly adopted by *Playboy* magazine as satirist-in-residence. *(Playboy* had tried to recruit editor Paul Krassner for the job, but Krassner preferred the independence of his scabrous new magazine, *The Realist.)*

Abroad, there was also a major outbreak in tradition-tweaking taboo-busting humor. In Italy, Fellini released *La Dolce Vita,* a film featuring a hilarious brand of blasphemy only an ex-Catholic could produce. In Germany, Günter Grass published his novel *The Tin Drum,* which was, among other things, a violently tasteless satire on the unspeakable topics of Nazi collaboration and the postwar boom. Spanish playwright Eugène Ionesco sent his slapstick totalitarian *Rhinoceros* stampeding across the stage to the shocked laughter of audiences.

In France, the Olympia Press issued *Naked Lunch,* written by expatriot American William Burroughs. Banned in the United States, copies were smuggled through customs and passed hand to hand, American samizdat. The novel's subject matter is everything a vice-squad cop could hope for—

perversion and addiction. Its tone is deadpan apocalyptic. The characters are outlaws, con men, and madmen. And in the technique of its composition—what Burroughs called "fold-in," the random splicing together of stream-of-consciousness monologues and episodes. *Naked Lunch* feels as improvised as a jazz solo, a Happening, or a Bruce set. (And to its credit, the Supreme Court allowed it in anyway in 1962.)

In 1959 in London, producer Joan Littlewood staged an impossibly formless, anti-establishment music-hall farce-tragedy, *The Hostage.* Ostensibly it concerned the capture of a young English soldier by the Irish Republican Army, and his eventual execution. In practice it was a collection of jokes and songs, with something to offend everyone from patriots to cynics. It was written by, sometimes starred, and was constantly and drunkenly interrupted by, Dublin's Brendan Behan.

No two performances were alike—Behan would barge out onstage and update his material (an American moon shot, for example, inspired him to insert the plaintive ditty, "Don't muck about with the moon"). *The Hostage* was an enormous popular and critical success, as it was again in 1960 when it came to Broadway, well publicized by Behan's Dionysian carousings around New York.

At Cambridge University, the Footlights Club, whose annual comic stage revue was scarcely renowned for its biting topicality, presented, in 1959 (to the marked displeasure of the undergraduate audience) a show titled *The Last Laugh.* It was uncharacteristically satiric and explicitly antinuke. Like *Footlights Revues* before it, *The Last Laugh* traveled down to London for a brief "legitimate" run. More appropriately entitled *Here Is the News,* it won a rave notice from the arbiter-of-taste Alistair Cooke in *The Guardian.* Great things, he said, might be expected from the show's director and stars, among them young Peter Cook.

By 1960 Cook had teamed up with another Footlighter, Jonathan Miller, and two opposite numbers from Oxford, Alan Bennett and Dudley Moore. The result was a show called *Beyond the Fringe,* probably one of the single most important settlements on the English bank of Boomer humor. By 1962 it too was a Broadway smash.

All these cultural ICBMs hit the United States during the Kennedy years; what they had in common with their targets was an unrestrained disrespect for authority of all kinds; not the least an implicit hope that the dreary, fearful tough guys responsible for the Cold War could be ridiculed out of existence. Kennedy, the King Arthur of the Cold War, soon dashed these hopes, but what did survive was an internationalism, for which his administration deserves much of the credit. Simply by trashing the sleazy cultural priorities of Nixon, replacing catsup and cottage cheese with Casals, by flying out of Fortress America to far-off lands—England, Ireland, France, Germany—Kennedy and his wife did much to defuse the cartoon propaganda pushed by the U.S. military establishment that there was just "Us" and "Them" and a bunch of disposable foreigners in between.

This internationalism was one of the best things that had happened to America—and for that matter to Europe—since World War II. And as if on cue, bringing a wealth of healthy disrespect to the mythology surrounding World War II itself, Joseph Heller published in the first year of the Kennedy administration another major milestone of Boomer humor, *Catch-22* (a book that was as successful in the European countries the U.S. military was supposed to have saved as it was in the United States itself).

Catch-22 hardly needs any further critical exegesis. It is a major classic, not just of American satire, but of American literature—and a world-class one to boot. A couple of points about it are worth making in passing, however, which might help to illuminate the ways in which the book both shared in and further shaped developing trends of Boomer humor. The first addresses itself to the often-heard and simplistic summation of *Catch-22* as an "antiwar" book. It's not antiwar so much as antimilitary. At the core of its humor is Heller's wild depiction of the military mentality and its circular, murderous logic. *Catch-22* is less about tragedy and inhumanity as about absurdity. For Yossarian and his fellow pilots, it is their own officers who—given the reality of the war—are out to kill them. And the impregnable stupidity of their commanders, the supreme lunacy of their lack of concern for life, is what drives them crazy. That indeed is why *Catch-22* has passed into everyday language as a synonym for absurd paradox.

Second, *Catch-22* is in an extended form a "service comedy." The service comedy, which ranges from *South Pacific* to "Hogan's Heroes," always features a wacky bunch of guys and their bumbling commanders creating happy mayhem in the greater Mayhem, making light of the whole darn mess. It's bad food, bad orders, good fellowship, and great dames all the way. So it is on both sides of the command line in *Catch-22:* a wild multiplicity of character and frenzied abandon of behavior. This gave the book a subliminal familiarity (although it's in no way a parody) to readers conditioned to service comedies; since it's hardly Bali Ha'i or Bilko we have here, it also gives the book an additional level of savage sarcasm.

Where were they Now?

For the groundbreakers of the fifties, the opening doors were mostly useful in the expansion and consolidation of existing reputations: Feiffer toward an Academy Award and international acclaim; Nichols and May separately toward careers as directors, in Nichols's case, of course, a spectacularly successful one.

Second City went national, opening on Broadway in 1961, and moving to a permanent stand Off-Broadway a little later. There was also an international company which toured England—among other places Cambridge—where it played to a rapt audience of Footlighters. This cross-fertilization continued a couple of years later, when Tony Holland and Andrew Duncan became the first two American regulars on the landmark British satirical show "That Was the Week That Was." One result of this activity was that the original Chicago company changed constantly. One of the new directors was named Alan Myerson.

Myerson was probably the most politically committed person to arrive at the birthplace of improv since David Shepherd. His efforts to steer his company in the direction of these commitments became a major bone of contention, particularly for Second City stalwarts, Del Close and Bill Alton, and in effect pitted politics against improv for the first time at Second City. Producer Bernie Sahlins put it this way: "We all objected to certain simplistic political notions of Myerson's. We didn't agree with him that the world is divided into just goodies and baddies, and we didn't buy the sentimentality of the have-nots being good and the haves being bad. So we were always editing him in one way or another. We weren't ready to hand over total control of a company to him to follow that approach."

Myerson found his own way to respond to the "editing" by leaving and founding his own company, the Committee, in 1963 which will be dealt with at length in Chapter 7. But this contretemps exposed some problems Second City was experiencing at the time as the Boomer humor boom expanded. One was the tremendous proliferation of imitators and offshoots during the early sixties, as improv, semiimprov, or just plain revue companies sprang up all over the country.

These ranged from Ted Flicker's the Premise, and its various offshoots (notably the predominately black Living Premise, which included among others Diana Sands and Godfrey Cambridge) to Elaine May's The Third Ear (which actually opened in 1964, after the assassination) and included Louise Lasser, Renée Taylor, Reni Santoni, and a large, dangerous-looking bartender from the East Village, Peter Boyle.

The second problem was that to many of the Second City family, Kennedy and his officials approximated what they were looking for politically and it's hard to satirize what you mostly agree with. One of the then newer members of the family, Avery Schreiber said: "With Eisenhower we had a perfect target. It was a classic setup: we were young, he was old. Youth versus age. And Everett Dirksen was hours of fun with his poems, his flowers, and his wonderful stentorian voice. We had a terrific time with him.

"Kennedy was a different story. He was very close to an age we could communicate with. The only way you could make fun of the man was on the subjects of his accent, his wealth, and his social activities. It wasn't easy. We sided with what the man wanted to do."

In itself the proliferation of Kennedy imitations bordered on the ludicrous. Almost every group had a Kennedy imitation, and every other comedian attempted one—even, amazingly, Jackie Mason. If the best version that remained was Second City's parody press conference with both Kennedy and Khrushchev, it was no longer exclusive territory.†

Indeed, these problems were compounded by a third, namely, that Kennedy was himself a witty man who turned the odd quip in his own press conferences, without question the only President in living memory willing or able to get a laugh in public.

Whether this was a conscious decision or just part of his style, it constituted something of an end run around anyone inclined to deal roughly with him on a satirical level. Only a true believer of the right or the left could have found him demonic enough to present a lampoon of him, and in any case this would have looked like bad sportsmanship—pros taking aim at a gifted amateur. In consequence, as Schreiber noted, the satire was of style rather than substance; even in situations like the Bay of Pigs or the Cuban Missile Crisis, where many were equivocal about Kennedy's actions, there is no record of anything very cutting having been written or improvised.

One instance of all these tendencies rolled together was the appearance of a pair of highly deferential and massively successful comedy albums called *The First Family* (1962) and *The First Family,* Volume 2 (1963). Starring one Vaughn Meader, who did a standard-issue Kennedy impression of the time and actually bore a gnomish resemblance to the President, the albums chiefly confined themselves to domestic life in the White House, a situation comedy about Camelot, or more succinctly, a sitCam.

Most of the material on the albums was of short duration, a minute or so. Two of the better-known bits will serve to illustrate this.

A quarrel erupts between John-John and Caroline over whose bath toys are whose, and the nanny is unable to settle the affair, so the Chief Executive steps in. He specifies very clearly and at some length which of the large number of toys belongs to whom. He then pauses and adds: "The—er—rubber duck, is—er—*mine.*"

Somewhat later good-nights are heard between Jackie and the President. They are clearly in their bedroom. Jackie says she treasures these rare moments of privacy and says good-night. The President also says good-night. Then so do Bobby, Teddy, Rose, and so on, the entire Kennedy clan.

It's all pretty much like that.

The albums in effect came as close to Kennedy propaganda as to anything else. Their affectionate rah-rah of the First Family, far from serving any purpose of dissent, actually contributed to what cult of personality he already enjoyed. *The First Family* albums could not have done Kennedy more good if they had been written by Arthur Schlesinger, Jr.

But for two of the trailblazers, things were not quite so hunky-dory during

---

† A typical question at the Off-Broadway version of Second City might go like this: Question: "Would Mr. Kennedy comment on the slogan 'Better dead than Red'?" Kennedy: "These are obviously both extreme positions. I have tried to keep my government on the solid middle road between them. That is to say—half dead and half Red."

the thousand days of Camelot. If he is to be believed, Sir Mort Sahl was knavishly treated by his Arthur.

According to the wronged knight, it was precisely the show biz element in the Kennedy entourage that did him in, in the person of rat packer Peter Lawford, and their common agency William Morris. In *Heartland,* Sahl claims that word was got to him through his manager, Milt Ebbins, that Joseph Kennedy disapproved of the new satirical attacks he was mounting on Kennedy, and wanted to know why he "didn't know the meaning of the word loyalty" and that Lawford once yelled at him that if he didn't cooperate (in other words, tone down his material) "the ambassador [Kennedy senior again] said he'd never work again in the United States." Lawford apparently had by then an office in or above the William Morris building on Beverly Drive in Beverly Hills, and Sahl says, the work indeed began to dry up. Inquiries to the agency were met with kiss-offs that he wasn't available or he was sick. Eventually, the new owner of the Crescendo, the club where both he and Bruce had been such hits, told him that "the White House would be offended if I hired you and I'd be audited."

True, false, or exaggerated—it's hard to check given the extreme death of most concerned—it's certainly true that Sahl's star sank lower and lower in the sky during these years.

Bruce's was still high, but he had problems of another kind. He had already been busted in 1959 in Los Angeles for narcotics; in September, he was busted for the same charge—this time in Philadelphia. Returning to San Francisco in October, he was busted yet again for obscenity. Much of his subsequent time was then spent shuttling between coasts to appear in court. Then, incredibly, between October and November of 1962, he was busted three times in three weeks, at a hobby shop in the San Fernando Valley for narcotics, at the Troubadour in Los Angeles for obscenity, and finally in Chicago at the Gate of Horn, also for obscenity. That made a grand total of six busts, nicely proportioned between sex and drugs, two subjects about which, in proportion to the whole body of his work, he'd always had only a moderate amount to say—and actually not very much at all when it came to drugs.

The details of Bruce's cases have been dealt with many times in many places, most entertainingly, by Albert Goldman.‡ They need not concern this narrative, although some of the transcripts, especially those of the San Francisco trial, are almost as funny as anything Bruce did onstage. What is important is that he began more and more to discuss the obscenity and drug charges in his act. This may have pleased those who were looking for a champion of these causes, but it seriously cut into the scope of both his material and performance, because a lot of what he had to discuss was done not in character or premise, but didactically straight out to the audience. In

‡ *Ladies and Gentlemen, Lenny Bruce!* with Lawrence Schiller (New York: Random House, 1971.

addition, he was making a classic mistake of strategy, choosing to fight and debate on grounds chosen for him by his adversaries. Not only did this interfere with the impact of his act, the range of its subject matter, the wild humanity of which he was capable in performance, but it also led him further and further into the arms of the converted.

For them, his fight was worth it; for them his adversaries had organized to bring him down on these issues and these issues alone. It seems unlikely though that there was any conspiracy between the various police departments involved, other than the fact that police departments, like most people, have a need to keep up with the Joneses (or in this case people *with* Joneses). It seems equally unlikely that the police anywhere saw themselves as fighting either a rear-guard or a vanguard action on the issue of freedom of speech. Bruce gave them plenty of opportunity to bust him, either by goading them, as he did in San Francisco and at the Troubadour, or by being pretty offhand about using and scoring drugs.

The arrests obscured the fact that if there was any cohesion to Bruce's persecution on obscenity charges, it was that always mixed up with them, perhaps carefully hidden in them, were others of a specifically political or religious nature. *Variety* said of the Chicago trial for example: "The prosecuter is at least equally concerned in Bruce's indictments of organized religion as he is with the more obvious sexual content of the comic's act."

The police captain who transcribed his act in Chicago, a Catholic called McDermott, evidently took most exception to what he called Bruce's "mocking of the Pope." Ad hoc censorship of public discussion of religious hypocrisy would seem to be at least as important as that of bedroom politics, in a world where stinking-rich fundamentalist scum scream at millions that poverty is the result of sin, and celibates rule that hopelessly deformed babies (in Bruce's day thanks to Thalidomide) be born to a life of unimaginable misery. But the defenders of the F-word either didn't get it or wouldn't have it, and obscenity became the issue on which these cases and one climactic future one were fought.

Whatever he may have thought of himself, Bruce's genius should have influenced people by more than just talking dirty.

Despite their individual troubles (and differences), however, Bruce and Sahl had opened the way (with the help of Winters and Berman) for a whole new New Wave of nightclub comedians, for whom the joke-barking style of George Jessel and Fat Jack Leonard was a distant memory. The Kennedy years incubated almost all the most distinctive voices of Boomer humor in stand-up comedy, which for the next twenty years would bring every manner of innovation—personal, verbal, sexual, racial, dramatic, and political—to a once moribund form. Whatever each performer's ultimate destination, these years, with their relative freedom of speech and thought, were everyone's departure point; whatever professions or denials of dissent individuals made, the intellectual and social ferment of the day challenged them all to be both aware and distinctive. And something of what you are the first night you walk onstage will be with you till the day you shuffle off. Even those whose self-assessment is utterly apolitical or nonpolitical cannot shake the a-changin' times from which they sprang. What shaped them was a movement barely a decade old, whose distinguishing features were intelligence, vitality, nonconformity innovation and experiment. Many of this great generation of comedians, men and women, are now the foremost "entertainers" of our time; but their very range and distinctiveness was a product, above all, of the special and highly charged forces of the early sixties. There were no assembly-line comics in this lot.

One riptide in the new New Wave was that the overwhelmingly Jewish pioneers of the fifties were being emulated by those of all persuasions. The first out of the box, and one of the most enduring, was a neat young man, nervous to the point of self-apology, and terminally conformist in appearance, the very model of the modern accountant he had trained to be, Bob Newhart.

Newhart's actual start, like that of so many others, was in Chicago, where he did a weekly radio show; the album that propelled him to stardom was largely made up of pieces he developed on it. It was named *The Button-Down Mind of Bob Newhart* and it sold so many copies, it was second only to Berman's number one hit, *Inside Shelley Berman*. But beneath what was mechanically dubbed his WASP exterior (actually he's Catholic), the button-down mind was fairly hot under the collar:

"My routines came out of things I considered outrageous, that you *had* to make fun of. It was the only weapon I had, or any of the other people. It was more outrage than anything else. Outrage, in my case, at the large corporation, the large impersonal corporation that it looked like I might very well be going into. That was what was facing us. Going with a corporation and being transferred about twenty-five times in twenty-five years and getting your retirement unless a large company took over and somehow furloughed you so that they got your retirement.

". . . The Abe Lincoln thing,* which is probably the best piece of writing I've ever done, I think, that I'm most proud of . . . was really a result of Vance Packard's book, *The Hidden Persuaders*.

"I did this thing on a retirement party, the guy getting the watch after fifty years with the company and I remember someone coming up and saying, 'How can you make fun of that poor man?' And I said, 'Well, that's the whole point, not to make fun of him but to make fun of all of it. To make fun of impersonal corporations who would treat him as outrageously as they did.'

". . . I think that probably where humor is, is the approaching of that line of being outrageous—and how close you can come to it without crossing it and the nervousness of the audience as you come close to that invisible line. It really varies for everybody. I mean my line was certainly different from Lenny's, but he was able to cross that line and in certain ways I was able to cross

---

* A brilliantly economic piece which has a Kennedy-era political manager coaching a reluctant Lincoln in a speech which has been written to upgrade his image—the Gettysburg Address.

my line. I guess there's where the laughter comes from, how close you can come to that line.

". . . The fact that they would pay you for [being a comedian] was nice but humor was the only way I could retain my sanity. I saw these indifferences around me and the only thing I could do was make fun of them. And once you'd made fun of them, you could go on to the next inconsistency. That again is from the outrage at those things. It really is for your own sanity that you become a comedian."

Newhart's version of outrage might appear to have been more a case of mild irritation, but the force of his comedy was enhanced by the anonymous middle-everything manner with which it was delivered. In his routines, Newhart appears as a cog in someone else's machine, a nameless executive or functionary from some invisible corporate nowhere, the flat voice of the middle echelon—ridiculing the invention of baseball, looking for ways to make money out of the Wright Brothers, unable to find the instructions for dealing with a gigantic gorilla climbing the Empire State Building. Newhart's character never rises to the occasion. This persona struck a deep chord at the time and ultimately took him further than almost all his contemporaries.

Noises in the Street

Newhart, of course, was still of the same fraternity which had originally established Boomer humor: middle class, college-educated, jazz-oriented, urbane, post-ethnic. But in the early sixties, new voices began to be heard. Voices from downtown: harsher, cockier, and more assertive. The most obvious and dramatic of these—though by no means the only ones—were black, and the leader of the pack was Dick Gregory:

I wouldn't mind paying taxes—if I knew they were going to a friendly country.

I sat at a lunch counter nine months. When they finally integrated, they didn't have what I wanted.

We put Kennedy in. Voted six or seven times apiece. Made up for all the times we couldn't.

They say Governor Pat Brown's pink and Nixon's yellow. Does my heart good to see two colored fellows doing so well.

I'm going to open a nightclub called Nigger. Then whenever people say it, they'll be advertising my place.

I love America. Where else would I ride in the back of the bus, have a choice of the worst schools, the worst restaurants, the worst neighborhoods—and average five thousand dollars a week just talking about it?

Newsweek said of Dick Gregory in December 1962, "From the moment he was booked into the Playboy Club [in Chicago], in 1961 . . . Jim Crow was dead in the joke world."

By the time Gregory joked himself out of the joke world a few short years later, Jim Crow was dead in few other places too, in no small part to his efforts. Gregory was one of the very few Boomer humorists who got the opportunity to actually put his craft on the line for a real life-or-death issue. And when he got it, he rose to it magnificently.

He also was the first genuine black satirist. He was sometimes touted, in fact, as the "black Mort Sahl" (obviously by people unfamiliar with Sahl's low opinion of black brainpower)—and thus opened the door for many others. Just as humorists of the fifties were sometimes lumped together with the younger old-timers who shared none of their attitude of dissent, so Gregory, too, was lumped with other black comedians, like Nipsey Russell and George Kirby, troupers of an older form, who had little or nothing in common with him. Often in the first year or so of his explosive career, he was credited less with being a formidable and savage commentator than with his ability to cross the color line, and "be accepted" by white audiences. There was a certain obtuseness to much of the early commentary about him, as if he were doing his almost exclusively black-and-white material to ingratiate himself with white audiences, instead of making them squirm. *Time*'s response to his emergence, in fact, was that his pioneering work would then once more make it possible to get lunch going with a few of those good old nigger-wop-kike jokes: "What makes Gregory refreshing is not only that he feels secure enough to joke about the trials and triumphs of his own race, but that he can laugh in a sort of brotherhood of humor with white men about their problems, can joke successfully about the N.A.A.C.P. as well as the P.T.A. Gregory's emergence suggests that there may be a relaxation in the long-standing, well-meant but dreary taboo against 'racial' or 'ethnic' humor, and that it is once again possible to tell a Jewish, Italian, or Negro joke without being regarded as a bigot."

Gregory certainly got his professional start the hard way. On that night in January 1961, the Playboy in Chicago called him at a few hours' notice to replace the scheduled comic who was sick. For Gregory, who'd been scraping a living for the previous three years in and around the city, it was a big break. When he got there the manager apologized to him, not having realized at the time that the club had been booked by a convention of frozen-food executives from the South. In 1961 this wasn't exactly a captive audience for a sassy, young, Northern black. In fact, the audience was likely to see the captive relationship quite the other way around. Playboy said it would replace him, pay him, and promised him a future date.

Gregory wasn't having any of it. He was cold, mad, and broke. He went on, endured a lot of initial insults, but eventually won the audience over, and by every account brought the house down, mostly with the kind of material quoted here. Hefner caught his second show, immediately signed him to a three-year contract, and he was an overnight coast-to-coast sensation. Even in sixties Chicago, where comedy was a heavily traded commodity, Gregory's rise was startling. From fifty and a hundred dollars per week, he went to five thousand. He earned half a million dollars by Christmas, an enormous amount at the time for a comedian. The most immediate reason was that he was black, and black with Kennedy warming up the White House was on everyone's minds. And Gregory was exciting; at that time no audience had ever heard anyone talk the way he did about race, and what made it truly dangerous was that this guy was a "Negro."

I'm really for Abraham Lincoln. If it hadn't been for Abe, I'd still be on the open market.

There's no difference between the North and the South . . . in the South they don't mind how close I get so long as I don't get too big; in the North they don't mind how big I get so long as I don't get too close.

To a heckler who called him a nigger, he replied he got fifty bucks extra every time it happened and invited the whole audience to stand up and call him it. To another, he suggested a trip to Arkansas, "Tell [Governor] Faubus his son says hello."

On Paar he finished one smash appearance by saying sweetly to the viewers, "If you actually like me, you'll invite me to lunch when it *isn't* Brotherhood Week."

In the Blue Angel (a ritzy New York nightclub) he said mock-defiantly, "Hell, I won't even work the south of this room!"

To audiences mute with either guilt or hate over the racial issue, and to whom the most sophisticated form of black humor was Jack Benny's uppity serf Rochester, this was cut-to-the-bone stuff. What made it palatable—just— was the fact that Gregory was, not unlike Newhart, a soft-spoken, smooth performer who exuded a sort of raffish innocence that masked the fury in his material.

He had plenty to be miffed about. Born to rock-bottom poverty in St. Louis in 1932, during the absolute pits of the Depression, he had had his share of shoe shining, no meat for months on end, backbreaking child labor, de facto segregation both official and unofficial, an absentee father, and casual beatings and humiliations at white hands. In other words, the perfectly normal, unremarkable, childhood of a second-class American citizen of the thirties and forties. He pulled himself up, not by his bootstraps, but by the laces of his track shoes, becoming a star athlete in high school and thus winning an athletic scholarship to Southern Illinois University where he repeated his performance. Drafted in 1954, he was chronically insubordinate (but funny) and was eventually given the choice of winning a club talent contest for his unit or being court-martialed. He won the contest (with jokes like, "When I lost my rifle, the Army charged me eighty-five dollars. That's why in the Navy the captain goes down with the ship.") and soon found himself in Special Services doing an army tour. He had become an official army comedian. At such things as this the Army is very good.†

This seems to have left a sufficient impression on him so that returning to college didn't do much for him,‡ and he launched on the hardscrabble career in two-bit clubs that eventually brought him before the national public's eye. Despite all his time spent in college, which had more to do with athletics than with business administration (his major), he was very much of the people. And it was his people by 1962, after his first full year of stardom, that most concerned him.

Civil rights of course was *the* issue in the Kennedy years. This was several long years before vast amounts of federal money and imported French revolution had got everyone in a hysteria of confusion; the issues were still simple ones, black and white in every sense—the right to vote, access to public facilities, and nonsegregated housing and education. Nor was the outcome of the struggle at all certain. Many black performers, especially "crossover" ones, were very nervous about getting involved for fear of alienating the white portion of their audience. A fat check to the NAACP from time to time took care of commitment—otherwise it was show business as usual. Gregory could certainly take this route—apart from the top club circuit in New York, Los Angeles, San Francisco, and Chicago, he started playing Las Vegas in the beginning of 1962—and that year alone made him a millionaire. What's more, he had the advantage of appearing to be deeply involved in the issues anyhow, simply by virtue of the material he did. No one was going to include him on any list of Uncle Toms.

But, as he says in his autobiography, *Nigger* (like the restaurant earlier, it was supposedly advertised every time someone used the word), "the old monster is still hanging 'round, he's not satisfied yet. [The old monster is Gregory's image of the drive for freedom, incoherent, but unstoppable.] You got to work for him too." Working for the monster meant benefits, insisting on nonsegregation clauses in his contracts, shows for CORE and the NAACP. As he did these, he came into contact with the civil rights leaders of the day, Roy Wilkins, James Farmer, and Martin Luther King. "I kept pushing my material further, more topical, more racial, more digging into a system I was now beginning to understand better and attack more intelligently . . . I was learning that being a Negro doesn't qualify you to understand the race situation any more than being sick makes you an expert on medicine."

One of the results of his sharpened awareness of the battle was that as things got hotter in the South during 1962, he had a way of coming up with a memorable line about breaking news events that got him widely quoted.

† The Army has always had an eye for comedic talent; both Jack Paar and Sid Caesar became major stars while serving in the Army.

‡ He did do a brief stint in the post office, where he was fired for routinely sorting mail for Mississippi into the "Foreign" bin.

When James Meredith, escorted by tens of thousands of National Guardsmen registered at the University of Mississippi on October 1, 1962, Gregory said, "It took 16,000 soldiers to put one man in school. Probably the only time in the history of the world that an army joined a man." When President Kennedy (the best-known graduate ever of the Evelyn Wood speed-reading method) signed a housing desegregation order which he had said at the outset of his administration could be accomplished "by the stroke of a pen," Gregory responded, "It took 22 months for the stroke of that pen! For a man who reads 1,200 words a minute, Kennedy sure writes slow." When the possibility of a black astronaut was first mooted by the Kennedy administration, he exulted, "We made it from the back of the bus to the moon! Now the hard part—getting him [across the South] to Cape Canaveral."

His lines might not have been gut busters, but they were right on the money, and just what his people and their partisans wanted to hear. Gregory was putting his satirical wit in the service of the cause and thus becoming its most quotable spokesman.*

But it wasn't enough for Gregory. The upheavals in the South were crystallizing around a massive drive to register black voters in time for the 1964 elections. This was the one thing the white Southern politicos most feared, for blacks were largely disenfranchised and this could mean dramatic changes in elective power. So people were being shot up, fire-hosed, jailed, beaten—and bitten—by dogs and other agents of law and order: "Hell, so long as any man white or black isn't getting his rights in America, then I'm in danger. Sure, I could stay in the nightclubs and say clever things . . ."

But . . . not enough. In April 1963, the real drive began. Gregory opted for satire over show biz and headed south. For the next six months, he was constantly in evidence at registration rallies, church meetings, demonstrations, marches. The press predictably followed him all over the place, for he was great copy. The papers were full of Gregory and his taunts, Gregory being led away to jail, Gregory showing where he'd been clubbed. And while other black stars took part too, notably Lena Horne, there was something special about Gregory's grinning face, his cocky attitude, and his comic aura which turned the tables on the authorities. His very presence made them look ridiculous. This was serious police business and here was this comedian marching toward them, rolling his well-practiced eyes and mouthing off. It made them look like clowns too, and brought the whole segregationist system down to his level of absurdity. Not surprising then that they jailed and beat him, but when they did, they looked even worse. Beating a comedian?

For Boomer humor this was a landmark. Not before or since has any of its practitioners actually gotten down into the fray on which they built their material. And Gregory, for all that he was attacked and intimidated (and misreported), kept the monologue coming, flying back and forth to dates

* It was Gregory in fact who is responsible for the golden oldie: "Shouldn't be no race problem; everyone I meet says, 'Some of my best friends are colored.' "

during demonstrations, effectively reporting from the front to the audiences "back home," and getting sharper all the time.

In Birmingham, Alabama, he drew a jail sentence of 180 days for "parading without a permit." Gregory's reaction: "The Judge said, 'I'm not giving you 180 days because you're a Negro. I just hate comics.' "

"Birmingham," Gregory said, "is a nice place to demonstrate, but I wouldn't want to live there."

Talk of the Southern moderates in the wake of the murder of Medger Evers, brought this: "You know the definition of a Southern moderate? That's a cat that'll lynch you from a low tree."

Of the quarter million people at the Washington civil rights rally in August '63: "Kennedy was so impressed he called in the Negro leadership, asked him if they'd organize a march on Cuba."

Of the signs of progress and victory (and there were many as the year wound down to fall): "A top man in the Ku Klux Klan called me up. 'I want to be the first to congratulate you,' he said. 'I gotta admit you did it. I want to take my sheet off to you.' "

Gregory's role in Boomer humor continued long past the voter registration battles of 1962 and 1963. But he became far more involved in the ever-multiplying issues which the movement as a whole generated, and as he did so, developed a much more serious tone. He never lost the incisiveness of his phrasing or his powers of insight, but they were less often used in the service of humor and more in that of the passionate advocacy he brought to his causes. As the black rebellion grew, he seemed often to be more a teacher or a preacher, and less often a comedian. In the history of Boomer humor, Gregory is a seminal figure. He demonstrated par excellence how effective political humor could be, at the right time, in the right hands. He challenged once and for all the age-old contention that getting laughs has nothing to do with real life, or that it's "just entertainment." He demonstrated in every sense that it could indeed affect people and events, especially if accompanied by the actual body weight of the comedian himself. He opened doors for all who followed him, most notably a superb comedian and actor named Godfrey Cambridge, and two other young comics scuffling around the Village at the time, Bill Cosby and Richard Pryor. And he established a new voice, a new sound for black comics and satirists, one that had never been heard coming from them before—not aggressive so much as noningratiating, less challenging than unapologetic, and therefore more real and more confident, in every sense, looser. Everyone who came after Gregory owed him a little piece of this. Until he came along, there was no black Boomer humor.

White Noise

From a very different direction but in very much the same spirit came a comedian whose career would become one of the longest-lived and least compromised of Boomer humor. At the same time, his origins and development have elements common to almost all humorists of his age. George Carlin is not only a minor genius—he's a typical minor genius.

Carlin was born and raised in the forties and early fifties in an ethnic enclave of New York that no longer exists. On Manhattan's West Side, stretching south from 125th Street, then the boundary of Harlem proper, to the nineties, the area was a relatively harmonious racial stockpot which included not just Columbia University, St. John the Divine, and a thriving Catholic community, but a predominantly lower-middle-class Irish population living side by side with working-class blacks, foreign students, classical musicians, recent Hispanic arrivals, and Jewish intellectuals. The resulting street life—and especially its black component—laid the foundation for Carlin's approach to life and comedy. Carlin says:

"I was attracted by the freedom blacks had. The most ironic thing is that being the least free in society, they were the most free with their bodies, their attitudes, and their street personalities. There was a freedom that whites didn't have . . . talk about uptight WASP, I mean uptight Irish are just the same. And the culture, the music, and the dance that came from it! By dance, I mean the types of make-out dancing that we were able to get into as opposed to what the nuns preferred. Those were things that both attracted something that was already in me and confirmed it, reinforced it for me, and set me on the path with a little more assurance. It gave me the feeling of, 'Yeah, this feels good, to be on the outside.' It was a way of exercising some of the rebellion without having to be a lawbreaker. It was a silent revolution going on within me.

"Then on the street corner, it was very verbal because we picked up the Duzins from the blacks and you had to be fast to exist on the stoop with any self-respect. I wasn't a fighter. I could dance my ass off, but my way of being part of the guys and earning my keep was to be a court jester . . ."

As for so many others, the armed forces were lying in wait for Carlin. To get out of school and beat the actual draft, he joined the Air Force and got an immediate taste of military madness:

"We were an experimental squadron. Our flight of seventy men was an experimental flight because they were testing the spreading of germs in a barracks. Isn't this great? They would plant cultures in our throats once a week and study the spread. One guy would get it and the other three would get a harmless culture and at the end of the week, they would see who else had it. So we got out of a lot of duty. We didn't have to get up early and go to reveille or anything. It was fun, but we were always in the hospital! So I whistled my way through basic training. I didn't have to rebel in the early years of the Air Force. Later on when I ran into hard-nosed sergeants and section chiefs and even COs, I would go tell them to take a flying fuck. You get court-martialed for that. So, I wound up with three court-martials."

Just like Gregory, Carlin's tangles with his elders and inferiors achieved a truce thanks to show business. Stationed in Shreveport, he tried out for a local radio station as deejay—a career he'd set his heart on—and landed a job. Carlin says: "Then it got easy for me. They liked the fact that I worked downtown, representing the Air Force in a positive light. I wasn't impregnating women and spreading diseases."

As with Gregory, this was not only a career move, but a further step in his enlightenment: "I had my own show from eleven to one during the day, and then later I got the afternoon drive spot. What was great was [that] I was a teenager playing teenage music for teenagers. The rest of the guys were older and they were from the Tommy Dorsey era and they really hated the Elvis Presley shit. I had a feeling for it. I didn't like the white encroachment into black music, but I understood it at least and I understood why the kids were shaking their asses. And, I knew they were being politicized. I didn't know that word then, but I knew something was happening to them politically because what was going on was nothing short of a revolution. You could sense that and feel that, especially in the white South."

But if blacks and his knowledge of and empathy with them had been the governing factor to date in Carlin's development, the next one would come from the other side of the Kennedy-era compact—a brilliant young Boston-Irish actor-comedian named Jack Burns. Having reached an agreement with the Air Force that theirs was not a marriage made in heaven (and acquiring a general discharge with honorable conditions in the process), Carlin put in a little more time in Shreveport, but when an opening came in Boston, headed Northeast. He didn't last long in Boston (among other things, he stole a mobile news unit and drove it to New York to score pot, and he cut Cardinal Cushing and his rosary program off the air during the fourth sorrowful mystery to play an Alka-Seltzer commercial). But he did meet Burns. It was "instant comic affinity." The two became inseparable and began developing comedy pieces and characters, in particular a blowhard West Side/Irish bigot whom Burns later used in the famous taxi cab scene he developed with Avery Schreiber.

Finding themselves, thanks to the vagaries of radio employment, in Fort Worth some time later, they actually started appearing in a local beat coffeehouse performing ad-libbed sketches. Carlin was already aware that Boomer humor was shifting. It wasn't Nichols and May, or Berman or Newhart, or even Sahl that he and Burns wanted to emulate. Says Carlin: "There was some other element in what we were doing that was born in that coffeehouse in Fort Worth. It represented more of an edge. Not an edge in the sense of making a point, but some sort of coarser cloth. Dick Gregory was what we would have liked to have been."

Just as important for Carlin, however, was exposure to Burns's political ideas: "I had this really conservative streak, you know . . . but Jack was the first person from whom I learned some of the facts of politics. In my home Westbrook Pegler and Joe McCarthy were gods, and I picked up a lot of that. I mean I just assumed it was correct in the early fifties. "Of course they're Communists, and if you were a Communist, wouldn't you try to get into the State Department?

"But Jack opened the door. I began to realize that the right wing was interested in things and the left wing was interested in people, that one was interested in property rights and the other was interested in human rights. I began to see the error of what was handed to me through the Catholics, through the Irish-Catholic community, through my mother, through the Hearst legacy in our family. It was automatic. It didn't take any reasoning or any thought process for me. 'Of course,' I said, 'that's how I feel, of course these are the assholes who've been keeping me down. Of course this is what all my bad feeling has come from.' "

Burns and Carlin got tired of sitting in their underwear in Forth Worth fantasizing about being on Paar's show. They decided to take the plunge and, as Burns put it, "give Hollywood one last chance." They had the luck of the Irish comedy team upon arrival and were booked into a Hollywood coffee-house. The means by which they climbed the next professional rung in their brief career together is fascinating in what it says about how established Boomer humor had become by the time Kennedy was inaugurated. For what gained them instant notoriety were not the street-oriented tough guy characters they were developing, but two impressions—and brilliant ones at that—that Carlin did in the act. The two impressions were of Mort Sahl and Lenny Bruce: "I could do Lenny and I could do Mort. Now to imitate them in your act in 1960 was an act of defiance.

"The Mort I did was political about Eisenhower flying into Tokyo, and these people, these leftists were going to get out on the runway and block him and he says we weren't going to land anyway 'cause we really got to impress these people. 'Right, onward.' And in the Lenny one, I think I did the genie in the bottle joke of the Lower East Side candy store.†

"Then one night, in comes Mort Sahl. Mort watches us, says, 'Good, good cerebral duo, right, that's what they are, it's a cerebral duo. A duo of hip wits.' That was eventually what *Playboy* called us; 'a duo of hip wits!' A few nights later, in came Lenny Bruce with Honey. We didn't know the legendary quality of this encounter at the time, but we knew how important he was to us and what he represented. You know, I came across his records in Shreveport when I was down there. I heard *Interviews of Our Time‡* and I was changed forever. That meant so much to me! The defiance inherent in that material and the brilliance of the mimicry and the thought, you know, the way he put it all together."

† Bruce's first album.
‡ An actual Bruce routine from the album *The Real Lenny Bruce.*

To their credit—especially the acidulous Sahl's—both of Carlin's mentors took kindly to the impressions. Bruce arranged for his agency, GAC, then a giant in the nightclub booking field, to handle the young team, and Sahl carried word of the "cerebral duo of hip wits" to Chicago and Hefner, whose patronage of the comedic art was by then reaching Rennaissance proportions. The team was on its way.

Burns and Carlin were never a big hit, although they did very respectably in Chicago and in sizable nightclubs elsewhere and did achieve their fantasy of appearing on Paar's show a few months later. And in some ways they were very typical of their time—smart and cocky "hip wits," in fact, following what were by then, if not paved highways, well-trodden footpaths. But the new edge of which Carlin speaks, the rawness of their characters, their origins in the street were a distinct signal that Boomer humor was expanding way beyond those of its roots that were sunk in the college campus. The attitudes it fostered were beginning to permeate the generation without regard to education or privilege. The authority figures Burns and Carlin tended to portray were immediate and everyday, rather than political or judicial: cops, bartenders, priests, and businessmen. That trend would find many expressions later in the decade, as the term "street" itself began to mean many different things. In one form it appeared in Peter Boyle's extraordinary character "Joe"; in another in the comics of R. Crumb; in a third the funky anarchy of John Belushi; and in its most obvious commercial form, the redoubtable Archie Bunker.

The conclusion that this strand of humor owed more to Lenny Bruce than to most of his other contemporaries is obvious; equally obvious was that the most lasting thing about the team was its launching of Carlin. (They broke up in 1962, and Carlin went solo.*) And Carlin is one of the two or three Boomer humorists who can truly be said to have descended directly from Bruce and to have kept his spirit alive. He has Bruce's same fascination with words and clichés and how they are manipulated; he is, if anything, a better mimic. But it took him many years, and a lot of anguish and self-doubt, to even approximate Bruce's mad freedom of thought and insight. In that journey and the discoveries he made along the way, he was symbolic of his generation, and not just of its humorists. But when he got where he wanted to be, as we shall see later, he became one of the best.

---

* Burns went on to a glittering stint at Second City, where he hooked up with Schreiber. The team enjoyed a brief and meteoric career. Burns then became a successful television writer-producer.

What Were You Doing
the Day Comedy Was Shot?

On the afternoon of November 22, 1963, in New York, Terry Southern and Lenny Bruce were sitting in Bruce's hotel room smoking dope. They were faced with a difficult problem: At his concert that night, how would Lenny deal with the subject of Kennedy's assassination? Most of the shows in town —and certainly all the comedians—had chosen to cancel performances out of respect for the fallen President. Lenny, however, had decided that the show must go on—not out of desire to commit sacrilege—but more out a desire, a need even, to grapple with this moment of national trauma, while it was still fresh.

Having made that decision, however, the question became how to implement it. There was no question of pandering to public grief. That after all would make him appear just like Georgia Gibbs in his own famous London Palladium routine who annihilates the comic who follows her, by insisting on a minute of silence for "the boys at Dunkirk."

On the other hand, however many options the richly collective mind of Southern and Bruce could invent, there was little point in being lynched by two thousand heartbroken New York Democrats.

Then, too, the other personalities involved were still somewhat out of focus. Jackie was no fit subject. LBJ, though he must have appeared promising, was behind closed doors, doing and saying very little; Oswald, still alive at that point, was very shadowy. And over everything, the simple reality was that JFK, who had been brazenly, "vigorously" present and alive two days before, was now neither. The shock of that was, in strictly professional terms, untoppable. No comedic response, however unthinkable, could be more unthinkable than what had happened in Dallas. A Mannlicher-Carcano had written the sickest joke of the century.

When Southern left late in the afternoon, the two had not yet arrived at a solution. But Lenny found one. To find it he had to reach all the way back, past "prurience," past sick, all the way back to his deepest roots, in Hip. Lenny's response to the assassination was supremely that of a good old fifties hipster. Smart, inside, in a superheated atmosphere, quintessentially cool. And, once again, it sprang from the perception that politics and show biz were just two sides of the same hustle, that one hustler always scratched the back of the next.

As two thousand people watched apprehensively, many of them no doubt wondering if this was finally going to be it—the point at which the head guru would be unable to rise to the occasion, would finally go too far, would finally, even, succeed in disgusting them, Lenny walked out slowly onstage, shook his head in massive feigned sympathy, and said:

"Phew—Vaughn Meader!"*

According to Southern, his destination when he left Lenny was a screening of his scabrous new film satirizing Cold War politics, *Dr. Strangelove.* The film, which was being screened with a view to U.S. distribution, had been deemed so controversial even in screenplay form that director Stanley Kubrick chose to move the production to London just to get it shot. Its plot —how a weak link in the chain of nuclear command, specifically a psychotic Air Force colonel, can precipitate Armageddon—revolved naturally around the character of the President of the United States. Southern—who as screenwriter should know—claims that in this version of the film, the climatic scene between the President and the Russian ambassador erupted into a furious cream-pie fight that left both sides devastated by multiple strikes of gooey filling. Although Peter Sellers' portrayal of the president as an apologetic Milquetoast was a far cry from the vigorous JFK, studio executives were appalled when in the course of this exchange, the President was hit in the head by a particularly gummy pie.

"My God," says George Scott as joint chiefs chairman. "Our young president struck down in his prime!"

The cream-pie sequence was considered the height of tastelessness and consigned forever to the cutting room floor.

The next day in London, on that week's episode of the hit satirical BBC series "That Was the Week That Was" (or TW3), David Frost decided to take the Georgia Gibbs route. The entire show was a bittersweet, sometimes sentimental tribute to Kennedy in film clips, monologues, and, of course, song.

---

* Meader was indeed ruined. He was at the very point of bringing out his latest *First Family,* a Christmas album whose thread was JFK reading "The Night Before Christmas" to Caroline in bed. Meader tried several comebacks as himself, one notable one as a stand-up comic with partner Reni Santoni, but somehow it didn't spark. As one Bleecker Street club owner is said to have responded to his agent with probably unintentional irony, "I need this act like I need a hole in the head."

Frost, always adept at sensing barometric changes in public attitudes, may well have been exhibiting for the first time a talent that would make him one of the sixties best-known TV personalities. For him, "The Tribute to Kennedy" was TW3's finest hour. For some of his cast, however, mere actors uninspired by Frost's long-range transatlantic ambitions, the show was ludicrous. Better to have stayed off the air than pay such hypocritical tribute to a man whose brinksmanship they had been pillorying since the show began and whose domination of the craven Tory party was a favorite theme. Raspberries and ill-concealed guffaws greeted many of the tribute's more lugubrious passages.

At the same time in San Francisco, Alan Myerson, director of the new improvisational group called the Committee was experiencing a not dissimilar ambiguity about Kennedy's murder. Small wonder then that when John Brent a member of his cast called Myerson with news of the assassination their reaction had less to do with the loss of Kennedy than with the idea that a beast had been loosed. "From now on," said Brent, "dark people from dank places will be pulling out their guns from the floorboards and emerging into the light for the first time."†

The assassination had a subtle but devastating effect on the New Comedians. Overnight, the young men and women who had helped create (and benefited from) the Kennedy administration's hip young and smart image were out of a job. With Camelot's king went his wit, and with it, his court jesters. For some, like Mort Sahl, it was disastrous. Sahl became an assassination buff and spent the next decade explaining to anyone who would listen his theory that the CIA was behind Kennedy's death. For others, Shelley Berman or Jonathan Winters, for example, the fall was more gradual but no less inexorable. Partly this was to be expected—a nation in mourning was not likely to want to laugh as it had. At a profounder level, however, the challenging, the questioning, the probing, the impudence about America's way of life, heroes, and history that was an essential component of the New Comedy seem to make people profoundly uncomfortable. In the two years following the assassination, sales of comedy albums plummeted (becoming specialty, rather than pop items),‡ as did attendance at the nightclubs that had given the New Comedians their most vital forum. By the end of 1964 clubs like the Shadows

---

† The Committee was probably the only improv company in the United States that "went on with the show" the night of the assassination. According to Myerson, the company limped through its opening number—a series of man-in-the-street interviews—to depressed silence from the audience, until cast member Larry Hankin entered. He was asked an obscure question about the restoration of the Palace of Fine Arts and replied, "Jesus! Don't you realize the President's been killed?" and walked off. This got a large laugh and the show proceeded smoothly.

‡ Comedy LPs had begun denting the billboard charts in the late fifties with records by Mike Nichols and Elaine May, and *Inside Shelley Berman,* which entered the charts in mid-1958 and hit number one in 1960 after more than forty weeks in the Top 50. (Berman was a genuine smash hit and remained on the expanded charts—the Top 150—for over two years.)

By July 16, 1961, in the top "150 bestselling monaural LPs," there were over a dozen comedy albums, half of them in the Top 40. Beside Berman (then coasting at number sixty-seven after 116 weeks chartside), Nichols and May, Jonathan Winters, Dick Gregory, and Bob Newhart (with

in D.C., the Crescendo in L.A. and even the hungry i in San Francisco were experiencing serious financial difficulties. The college circuit, a major source of income for comedy acts in the first years of the decade, shifted to an emphasis on music. The few inroads that had been made into television were pushed back or closed off. "The Jack Paar Show," on which Nichols and May, Jonathan Winters, Shelley Berman, and many others had been regulars, was canceled in 1965. The U.S. version of TW3, although it has gone down in show business myth and legend as a groundbreaker, was actually a pale reflection of the U.K. original, and it was canceled in its second season after a string of poor ratings.

For the time being, satire had closed. Not on Saturday night, but on Friday, November 22, 1963. Bruce's mock sympathy could be extended a lot further than Vaughn Meader. The whole gang was in trouble. The court jesters had become unemployed and disenchanted *ronin*. But none of them would come to so tragic an end as that lone samurai, Bruce himself.

Although major metropolitan police departments regarded him as a kind of traveling hunting trophy, there was evidence by the end of 1963 that he was winning his personal battle with the boys in blue and with noses of the same color. The climate of the times was very much in his favor before the assassination, at least in the increasingly liberal interpretation courts were willing to make of existing obscenity laws.

But while that liberalization continued after Kennedy's death, the persecution of Lenny intensified. Clearly some other force was at work. And nowhere was it more obviously at work than in New York, in April 1964. What happened to Lenny during his two-week stint at the Café au Go-Go on Bleecker Street indicated both the profound mood shift that had occurred in the three months since the assassination, and the institutional intolerance it brought in its wake.

The guilty decision handed down by a three-judge panel after Lenny was arrested for obscenity during this booking can now be seen to have contained the seeds of his destruction—both in the sense that Lenny was clearly not arrested for obscenity so much as joking about sacred matters and that the decision was so arbitrary and personal that it gave Bruce what appeared to be the grounds for a crusade. The tragedy was that the crusade was about the wrong issue.

Bruce thought he had been arrested for obscenity. In fact he had been arrested for being funny too soon after the assassination of a President. And since he was determined to be vindicated by the law and since he was so

two LPs, *The Button-Down Mind* at number eighteen and *The Button-Down Mind Strikes Back* at number thirty-one), all had bestselling albums.

By November 23, 1963, the *Billboard* charts had added Allen Sherman (*My Son, the Nut,* number twenty-one) and three Smothers Brothers LPs.

By September 11, 1965, barely two years after Dallas, the only Boomer humor album remaining in the 150 bestselling LPs was Bill Cosby.

From then on, while the occasional Cosby or Smothers LP popped up from time to time, comedy albums had peaked for good.

obviously right on the merits, he was doomed to consume himself. In retrospect it would have made little difference if he'd gone all the way to the Supreme Court and won his fight on the obscenity rap. His career, like so many of the other New Comedians', would have been over. In this sense he was not unlike Mort Sahl. He could not see just how profoundly the assassination had destroyed him. What the CIA became for Mort Sahl, his obscenity rap became for Bruce.

The difference was that Bruce's persistence and brilliance made him irresistible to the powers that were. Being the smartest, the hippest, the rudest, the most dangerous, and the most visible of all the smart, hip, rude, and dangerous young performers, he was the one "they" had to get. So they did; at the Café au Go-Go in New York in 1964.* And it all had very little ultimately to do with obscenity.

Bruce's act at this time was as good as ever. Although elsewhere he had already begun to evidence an alarming inclination to lecture extensively during his act on the intricacies of obscenity statutes, here he seemed to have pulled himself together as if getting ready to take some major step. Much of what he did was familiar, although no two shows were ever the same. He seemed to be taking a delighted look back, an exuberant "Best of Lenny Bruce" twice a night, and the audience loved it.

There was a new routine that very few audiences responded to. Bruce was clearly obsessed by the interpretation *Life* magazine had put on clips from the Zapruder film showing the presidential car immediately after the firing of the shot—or shots. Jackie Kennedy was sprawled on the trunk as if trying to get out of the backseat. *Life*'s version was that she had been going for help. Since the limousine had already speeded up and a Secret Service agent had seconds later rushed to cover her with his body, this seemed like a somewhat unlikely motivation. The official line seemed to be that the President's wife would never do anything so unsaintly as try to save herself from further gunfire. Nonetheless the clips gave the lie to that pious assumption. Or, as Bruce put it, she appeared to be "hauling ass to save ass." He added, quite justifiably, who wouldn't? The fatuity lay in *Life*'s trying to persuade the public that what their eyes told them had happened had not happened at all, and that what they were seeing was something that fit into the prevailing hagiography.

He'd tried this observation out in various ways on the nights preceding the first bust and had received at best a puzzled response. Some brave spirits went along but in general it was not something even the most sympathetic audience wanted to hear only ninety days after Dallas. No one though had any objection. The insight was valid and this *was* Lenny Bruce. The night of the first bust the show proceeded as usual with its familiar content of pissed-in sinks, Eleanor Roosevelt's bared breasts, and sexually satisfied chickens. The

* My partner Nic Ullett and I were present at Bruce's 1964 Café au Go-Go engagement. In fact, we were his opening act. This meant not only the opportunity to be present at every single one of Bruce's shows, but also at *both* his arrests. (During this two-week booking Bruce was arrested regularly once a week.)

N.Y.P.D. Theatrical Crit Squad was there from the start taking notes. They had good reason to conceal their exact motives for arresting Bruce. Although he had performed roughly twenty minutes of what was later described as obscene material of no redeeming social importance, the cops hit the stage very shortly after Bruce finished saying that Jackie had "hauled ass to save ass." The next week they busted him before he could even get the hideous sacrilege out of his mouth. But by then of course the Theatrical Crit Squad knew his act by heart.

In his subsequent trial in New York the judges enumerated a dozen instances in which Bruce was deemed to have "appealed to the prurient interest." All except one had to do with sex. That one is Jacqueline Kennedy "hauling ass at the moment of the President's assassination."

The inclusion of an example having nothing to do with sex or obscenity is highly significant when coupled with the timing of the first police assaults. The confusion of the subsequent decision adds fuel to the interpretation that they had more on their minds than obscenity. Although Bruce was supposed to have appealed to the prurient interest (in other words, got people sexually aroused), his monologues, according to the three-judge panel, were at the same time "nonerotic," "not lust-inciting," and did "not arouse sex."

The judges' decision included the contradictory view that his performances, on all twelve counts, were "lacking in redeeming social importance" —arguable when applied to Uncle Willy and his discussion of a twelve year old's "apples" but somewhat misplaced when applied to a major publication's palpable lie in covering the actions of a president's wife during a disaster of incalculable proportions. A profound similarity exists between this tactic and the one that had been used against him in Chicago, when religion was clearly on the prosecutor's mind, but obscenity was the pretext. Here, what seems to have been uppermost in the judges' minds is that they didn't want this sort of thing going on right then. Or perhaps at any time. In a period bracketed by the publication of a book like *Candy* and the trial of *I Am Curious Yellow*, it seems unlikely that the judges, especially in a liberal city like New York, were really worried about the public being turned into sex maniacs by hearing the words "come" or "piss" on the stage of an expensive and avant-garde nightclub. But they represented the emerging view that such humor was no longer proper, and that its most extreme practitioner was an appropriate target for their disapproval.

Although at the time there was a tendency on the part of his audience and of the judiciary to treat Bruce as a special case, we can see now that his downfall was similar to that of his less daring contemporaries.

Where they adapted or faded gracefully away, Bruce fought back. Alas, it was the wrong battle at the wrong time. No one really cared anymore about obscenity. The last time Bruce appeared in San Francisco was at a topless club in North Beach where he would expound at length on the legal minutiae of the obscenity laws to handfuls of drunk conventioneers who would much rather have heard a few obscenities. They used to leave the club grumbling that they didn't understand what he was talking about. Why didn't he talk dirty like he was supposed to? They'd come to see naked hippy girls and a guy who said "fuck" right onstage. Instead they got flat-chested mothers of two waiting tables and a fat junkie who mumbled about due process.

If those who hounded Bruce to this sorry end had really cared about obscenity or public morality neither the mothers nor the junkie would ever have appeared in public. But that doesn't seem to have been their true concern. What the guardians of decency and propriety cared about was that this humor get back where it belonged—underground. They did their work well. By the time Bruce died of an apparent overdose in his L.A. home in 1966, humor like much else in their culture had become polarized.

But as the bullet left the Mannlicher-Carcano America did not stop laughing. On the contrary, the taste for smart hip young humorists flourished. It was just that the focus and character of the humor—and its practitioners—changed considerably.

Nor did the New Comedians disappear overnight while performers such as Shelley Berman, Bob Newhart, Jonathan Winters, et al. fell back in the field, Woody Allen and Bill Cosby, in particular, became the big front-runners.

What these two apparently disparate comedians had in common was that, unlike the premise-oriented routines of their early sixties counterparts, their comedy tended to center on themselves. It had been rare before this that the New Comedians brought their own experiences or personal history so intensely to their material. Almost all of Allen's routines, on the other hand, had his own inadequacies—physical, sexual, and psychological—as their fulcrum. Not surprisingly, they centered on his growing up, home life—if it could be called that—and his parents. Here is some typical Allen self-depreciation:

(March 1964—from *Woody Allen*)
When I was younger I wanted a dog and we had no money—my father at that time was a caddy at a miniature golf course. They finally opened up in my neighborhood in Flatbush a damaged pet shop. They sold damaged pets at discount, you know, you could get a bent pussycat if you wanted, a straight camel, you know. I got a dog that stuttered—so that cats would give him a hard time and he would go "B-b-b-b-bow wow!
Or this:
(April 1965—from *Woody Allen,* Volume 2)
I was, I would say, overdisciplined, which is really humiliating—I hadda be home by nine-thirty Prom night. Made a reservation at the Copacabana for five o'clock—I took my date and we watched them set up.

Cosby was much kinder on himself but his recollections of childhood were also the most popular part of his act. This is the characteristic Cosby tone:

I started out as a child and grew up in the streets of Philadelphia playing street football and everything, had a marvelous time . . . We didn't have any sneakers, there was only one kid in the neighborhood that had a pair of sneakers, his name was Rudy. I'll never forget it, Rudy came running by us so fast . . . "Wha wuz that?" "I dunno, but it was something fast."

And he came up. "How ya doin', gang, how is everything?"

"Whaddya got on?"

"I got on sneakers. See that, they can make you run fast. You can run, stop on a dime—I'll give you nine cents change—and you see these little rubber balls on the side there? Well, they keep me from makin' sparks, settin' my pants on fire, cause I run so fast."

This inward-looking comedy was not altogether new but in combination with sophisticated attitudes it broke new ground. Both Allen's and Cosby's comedy seemed to strike a deep chord in their audiences, and the reason may have been a yearning for some kind of innocence which the Boomers had lost in Dallas. Or it could be that people wanted to go further than that—regress to the simpler concerns of childhood.

In any event, the gentler humor's replacement of the outward-looking, knowing, and hypereducated stuff of Camelot is highly significant. From this time on until the end of our story, growing up, childhood, and adolescence became ever-growing elements in Boomer humor.

At the time—from 1964 to 1966, the period when both Allen's and Cosby's stand-up careers were at their peak—their self-oriented material was widely imitated. Richard Pryor, in particular, launched his career with an almost slavish pastiche of Cosby.

And by 1965 an ever-growing group of young comedians was beginning to emerge from the early sixties hatcheries of Greenwich Village, North Beach, and Old Town. For these young spirits, their own personal histories gave them a means to create material that had the edge and intelligence they had been trained with, and at the same time ingratiate themselves with audiences who were growing more and more nervous about social humor.

They had good reason to be nervous. The year 1965 saw race riots, more assassination, and a war in Southeast Asia that seemed to have a mind and a life of its own. In the relative security of the Kennedy years, it had been possible to ridicule authority, probe preconceptions, challenge racial attitudes. In the chaos that his death had appeared to precipitate, it simply added to the clamor. In the climate of the time, "personal" material was cocky enough to appeal to the "Us"-"Them" chauvinism of young audiences without giving older ones nightmares about such subterranean monsters as drugs and the draft.

Put another way, it meant they could get on television.

For television more than ever was the name of the game. The New—now not so new—Comedians had made a reasonable living from a combination of college concerts, albums, and nightclub dates where they could develop new material and get paid for it. Now it was not so easy. The folk acts, which almost always had a comedian to open for them, were giving way to rock groups. There was little room in that blistering new environment for a lone unaccompanied voice. Even radio stations were playing less comedy. Unless one was willing to live in a garret and starve for one's comedy, getting on television was crucial.

Television had other ideas. It was in no mood for anything even remotely subversive. Conversely, it seemed to be actively avoiding any reflection of the growing turmoil. As women began to break free from the cocoon of fifties paternalism, "Bewitched" hit the air. The smoke that drifted over St. Mark's Place and the hocus-pocus that rose from Golden Gate Park found their only echo in "I Dream of Jeannie."

Most grotesquely, at a time when young marines were finding out the hard way what ignorant fools their Parris Island mentors were, "Gomer Pyle" was "Sorry, Sarge"-ing his way through season after season of basic. And these sitcoms looked positively avant-garde compared to the variety shows where comedians sought employment. The largest audience a comedian could be exposed to was via "The Ed Sullivan Show." This weekly grand circus was at least live (hence its sometime nickname, "Night of the Living Ed"), but it was hideously shot and featured the embodiment of every conceivable form of prudery—Catholic, Protestant, and Jewish—all rolled into one.

Other shows, although better produced—for instance, the superslick "Kraft Music Hall"—were not much more exploratory than Ed when it came to limits of taste. Perry Como didn't exactly rush in where Ed feared to tread. An important exception was "The Merv Griffin Show." During these dark days of humor, Merv's fledgling syndicated show, then produced out of the Little Theater next to Sardi's in New York, provided a sort of halfway house for young comedic runaways with no place else to go.

The roster of young men and women assembled by producer Bob Shanks and an adventurous team of writer/talent scouts (including Tom O'Malley from the earlier Paar show) is impressive. There were not just the already established Boomer humorists, but Lily Tomlin, David Steinberg, Joan Rivers, George Carlin, Richard Pryor, Peter Boyle, and many, many more.† For most it was the first time they had found a television show sympathetic to their humor; for some it was their *first* television show. This combined with a policy of creating "regulars"—performers who appeared every two weeks or so for an unlimited period—gave people the chance to learn skills and develop characters on-camera with a live audience. In the high-pressure, sanitized, and occasionally hostile atmosphere of network variety such latitude was unthinkable. In the intimate Little Theater, experimentation was expected—and a blown joke got as big a laugh as the real thing.

Safe haven though it was, however, "The Merv Griffin Show" was no place

† Including a somewhat uneven young British comedy team called Hendra and Ullett.

to be dangerous. It was, after all, television, and liberal though the producers were about taking passengers on board, no substantial rocking was allowed.

In the context of the mid-sixties this posed a distinct dilemma for young performers who identified with their own generation. Simple economics compelled them to look to television for a decent living but television forbade them to discuss or even allude to the preoccupations of their contemporaries unless it was to denigrate them. You could always get a booking if you owned a Beatle wig, a toy guitar, and did a fair impression of Bobby Rydell. Sexual freedom, politics, the war, the draft, new religions, racial attitudes, and drugs were all forbidden territory. To make the dilemma more acute, the growing revolt was not just against "the system" but also its chief surrogate, television.

Censoring oneself to appear on television in the mid-sixties therefore involved a triple whammy. You were not being faithful to your roots, you weren't joking about things that interested you, and worst of all, you were appearing on television.

And yet unlike its older, noisier sibling, rock and roll, Boomer humor now had few other outlets. Rock and roll could express the same feelings in its very own medium, records. It had its own means of production and distribution and could afford to be far less inhibited. (And for a far greater profit.) What objections there were came from a fairly weak sector of the establishment—radio—where it was not difficult to undercut or overwhelm any attempts at censorship.

For comedians, the result was frustration and schizophrenia, a general sense of being what used to be known as "a weekend hippie." For most, the all-important aspect was to find common ground permitted by the authorities on which to communicate with their contemporaries. The most obvious one, as we've seen, was that of shared recollections, and the "safe" traumas and taboos of childhood. (Ironically, the pioneers of this approach left nightclub stand-up as quickly as they could—Allen to movies, Cosby to the greener pastures of television and international mayhem in "I Spy.") But for a lunatic few there was an easy way out. Say what you want to say, laugh at what you want to laugh at. But forget about the bucks.

7

Humor by Committee

The Committee, the San Francisco offshoot of Second City, spans roughly the period from the death of Kennedy to the bloodless assassination of Richard Nixon ten years later. More than any other group or individual it kept the cutting edge of humor sharp during the mid-sixties. Its uniqueness lay not in the number of stars it fed into the mainstream (as Second City did), but rather in the fact that it continued to shine brightly when almost everywhere else the fires were burning dangerously low. It was typical of San Francisco at the time and indeed was deeply involved in both the rock explosion there and the birth of underground publishing.

During its glory years (1963–70), the Committee cooked with whatever had San Francisco cooking. Its dilemmas were very much the current dilemmas whether they had to do with excess or success. Even its internal conflicts, however specific to acting or humor, reflected similar conflicts in the worlds of rock, political activism, and art. Its proximity to Los Angeles gave it an advantage over Chicago and New York in terms of access—and if its influence on television and motion pictures was not that direct, its indirect influence was pervasive. Not only did the Committee break new ground and make new connections, but its impudence was aid and comfort to what rebellious souls there were down south in "plastic land." When cracks in the dam of television comformity did begin to appear, its members were right there with the crowbars.

The story of the Committee is here told for the very first time, its part in the development and survival of American satire finally fully acknowledged. That role hasn't been credited up to this point because in conventional show biz terms, the Committee eventually bit the dust. As we shall see, however, there was a certain catch-22 at work here. An unabashed and relatively successful collective, its nemesis was precisely the individualism it sought to escape and the values it tried to transform. It broke up on the very rocks from which it had set sail. Its career was a portrait in miniature of the massively influential West Coast counterculture that insisted on raising its shaggy head under Governor Reagan's bombastic tutelage. Its fate dramatized predicaments Boomer humor would face time and again. In one respect, grotesquely. As it had already for the New Comedians in the person of Bruce, and as it would for both the *Lampoon* and "Saturday Night Live," success for the Committee involved the death of one of its most popular and talented players at an early age.

The prissy revisionists of the eighties notwithstanding, San Francisco in the mid-sixties was a vital element in the nation's mental health. No more drug-crazed or nut-packed than any other major urban center, it differed from most by remaining committed to dissent at a time when it was widely assumed that the need for *real* dissent had disappeared with Eisenhower, and that so long as the Democrats remained in charge nothing could go badly wrong. What's more, the vituperative crud that has coagulated on such institutions as the Fillmore, People's Park, and Haight-Ashbury should not be allowed to conceal the intelligence with which San Francisco presented its challenges to the mainstream. The generation for whom the city was such a magnet during those years was the most knowledgeable in American history. The notion that its members went there exclusively in search of sex, drugs, and rock and roll—as if on some endless spring break—has arisen partly from the generation's own self-disillusionment and partly from the relentless polemic of those who missed out on the excitement. The historical evidence proves otherwise; written and recorded material is above all articulate. From Mario Savio to *Ramparts,* the most dangerous thing about San Francisco was not that it was running amok on illegal substances but that it was well informed. The Berkeley campus alone was a continuing source of innovation— an open laboratory of cultural R and D, some of whose breakthroughs are now so deeply ingrained in our assumptions we don't even remember that they were once experimental.

The theme was sounded time and again that San Francisco was "free," that people felt liberated from their fifties childhoods. While some of this can be explained as generational restlessness, it doesn't explain why so many felt the physical need to "head west," nor their profound interest in alternative ways of living when they got there. That came from the deeply and widely held belief that all was not well with the places they'd come from.

Small wonder that many preferred the communality and tolerance they found in Northern California and judged America's standards of normalcy as more rather than less bizarre than those of San Francisco or Sausalito.

The San Francisco of the mid-sixties was certainly not interested in over-throwing freedom, on the contrary, the whole idea was to investigate just what freedom meant, what its extent and limits were, how far one could go. That in itself was a profoundly American tradition.

When social fundamentals are widely held to have been seriously departed from, satire will flourish. For better or worse, the satirist is the most morally active of the various types of comedic artisan. Where others get laughs making themselves ludicrous, or by creating mayhem around them, the satirist gets his by mocking the betrayal of principles. It doesn't matter what those principles are—they can be Shiite, Trotskyite, or all-American. But if you're mimicking a Shiite, a Trotskyite, or an All-American who falls short of his own principles, and there's one other person in the room—and he's laughing —that's satire.

It's a serious business, and Alan Myerson, founder, director, and in several senses chairman, of the Committee, is an extremely serious man. This is his analysis of the prevailing relationship in the early sixties between the players and the audience at Second City: "For their part, the players had a charming kind of hubris based on . . . their sense of one-upmanship, while the audience thought it was very smart because it got the jokes, or . . . perceived the references. Based on that it applauded and thus became a collaborator."

For Myerson, while there was some value to treating the audience as "smart" since traditionally comedians had built their acts around the assumption that it was dumb, there was a certain smugness in the air, the whiff of elitism. He remembers nothing at Second City at the time that could conceivably be described as provocative on any level—political, social, or emotional.

Very little disturbed the cozy bond between the smart performers onstage and the smart audience in the theater. What political material both the Chicago company and the one in New York presented had a predictable tendency to allude to issues rather than to engage them. To be aware of such issues was enough to establish the bond, to get the laugh of recognition. Going further into the significance of a personality was unnecessary. It came as no surprise for Myerson, when he tried to get the cast to participate in the first General Strike for Peace in 1961, that they enthusiastically agreed to picket City Hall during the day, but by the evening they were all at work.

Myerson likes to pretend that his only motivation in founding the Committee was to make a living. The record reveals a lot more than this "just-a-job" self-deprecation. The time, the place, the cast he chose, and above all the content of the show were brilliantly calculated.

In 1962 Myerson married a member of his Second City cast, Irene Rierdon. The couple quit the company and headed west to meet their respective in-laws. An extended honeymoon brought them to San Francisco, then in the twilight of its beatnik heyday and still several years away from the electric storms of the Summer of Love. But even in this time of cultural watershed, San Francisco exhibited a characteristically rambunctious version of the liberal optimism that prevailed elsewhere in the nation. And while the Ferlinghetti brigade had ossified (it was practically impossible by now for an outsider poet to crack the coffeehouse circuit), the Bay City's cutting edge was still sharper than most, immeasurably hipper than the leaden Elysium to the south.

San Francisco had always tended toward hedonism, its public faces, good or bad, staunchly polyglot; Los Angeles, from the time of its founding, had veered more to Protestant respectability reinforced by the white-knuckled fundamentalism of the Okies and the massive immigration from the Germanic Lutheran heartland. Long before the beats or the hippies, San Franciscans had regarded their southern brothers as stodgy and slow-witted. Los Angeles's response was simply to become more so, and good decent folks continued to fill its apparently limitless bowels, like a heavy meal. Respectability had attacked and defeated the wicked glitter of the movie community, eliminating first sex and drugs through the Hays office and then, through HUAC, its artists and free spirits, mostly Jewish, who had resisted the Teutonic invasion in good Euro fashion by turning Communist.

Throughout the forties and fifties the raffish first wave of film stars was replaced by a carefully cultivated crop of smooth and controllable personalities—among them Ronald Reagan, who wrote of himself in *Photoplay* in 1942: "I'm a plain guy with a set of homespun features and no frills . . . I like to swim, hike and sleep eight hours a night . . . Mr. Norm is my alias . . . I love my wife, my baby and home . . . Nothing about me would make me stand out on the midway . . . Average will do it."

Reagan didn't succeed with this transparent twaddle at the time, but transformed into a political persona twenty years later it played big. San Francisco, and specifically Berkeley, were what birthed Reagan's political career. As his biographer Lou Cannon recounts: "He . . . observed [during the 1966 campaign for governor] to an aide that 'this university thing comes up each time I talk.' " "The surveys taken for Reagan at first showed the demonstrations at UC to be a minor issue, but Reagan did not believe them. Eventually the polls . . . caught up with the candidate and found that public concern about demonstrations at the U of C was indeed the animating issue of the campaign."

There was no more perfectly symbiotic antagonism in the sixties than that between Governor Norm from Disneyland and the Fabulous Furry Freak Brothers from San Francisco. And the Committee was the latter's comic voice and satirical (and often physical) center, its informing spirit of irreverence. If Myerson had little idea of what would erupt in the next five years, he was certainly in the right place to find out.

And the right part of the right place. North Beach, the most melted of San Francisco's pots, was a cracked corner of town where Mafia strip joints mingled with Chinatown overflow, and buck-a-night flophouses with beatniks, all of it nestling a mere bomb's throw away from Nob Hill. From North Beach on a clear day, you could see Alcatraz.

It was here, a hop, skip, and stagger from the City Lights bookstore, the hungry i, the soon-to-be-topless Ciro's, and the horrible, cheesy Swiss American Hotel, from whose second floor window Lenny Bruce would one day fall, that Myerson found his theater. He raised the requisite cash, and in April 1963 the Committee opened its doors.

From the start Myerson says, ". . . I was much more interested in statements and positions . . . in real political theater more than Second City had been or any theater I knew of, with the possible exception of the Group Theater . . . We did stuff from the very beginning that was . . . consciously provocative to an audience . . . that we assumed would not please an audience in a traditional fashion."

This holds up as a minimanifesto of the Committee's attitude to satire, and its various casts stuck pretty much unflinchingly to the principle that shock therapy could be good for you. Nowhere more so than their opening night. (The cast was composed of Larry Hankin, Gary Goodrow, Bob [Hamilton] Camp, Scott Beach, and Kathryn Ish.)

Typical of the material presented that night were two sketches that would not have been found on any other improv stage in America in the spring of 1963. One dealt with race, the other with feminine sex, both still touchy subjects in front of a white liberal audience. White audiences might laugh at castigation from a black comedian such as Dick Gregory, but similar material in the hands of a white would make them very nervous.

The scene in question was a party. Gary Goodrow, who was (and still is) white was duly introduced and made small talk to the other guests. In the course of this chatter the host threw an arm around Gary's shoulder and announced to the assembled company that he was a Negro. There was an audible gasp of horror from the audience. And another when the guests then changed as abruptly as before and then began fawning on Goodrow, bubbling with such fraternal sentiments as "I just *love* Ray Charles." Goodrow turned the tables and began baiting them mercilessly in the standard litany of black oppression.

Such a scene might not appear very shocking in the eighties, but at the time it took the audience deep into racial questions they had only just begun facing. It was clearly going beyond the merely liberal. The scene forced the audience beyond the prevailing orthodoxy, first into white hypocrisy and then into black exploitation of white guilt. There was even an added level of impudence for liberals—that a white was playing a black.

And while "The Pill" scenes were epidemic, female orgasm was just as likely to set the audience on its ears. This sketch was performed by the two women in the cast, Jessica (Irene) Myerson and Kathryn Ish. They played two girls who had been best friends all through high school but who had gone to separate colleges. They were coming back after their first year away from each other; Jessica has gone to Bennington and Kathryn to a more traditional school. Greetings and reminiscences over, the two began to talk about losing their virginity. Once again, such a subject was shocking—especially from the mouths of women.

Both, it seemed, had mislaid the cherry. The Ish character didn't want to discuss it, while the Myerson character did—a lot. Ish, drawn out, admitted that it hadn't done much for her. She had "been there" was all. But the Myerson character had much further to go. She'd had an orgasm and was still high from it.

Myerson could not get his wife to say "come" onstage. But the scene called for it and both director and actress were determined to go the extra mile—too far. When she finally got to that point she said: "Well did you . . . er . . . didja . . . didja didja . . . [at the top of her voice and all rolled together] . . . DJACOOOOOOOM?"

It stopped the show. People turned red, protested, or even left. There were nervous giggles from some of the men, but from the women, according to Myerson, screams. Of shock, of delight, perhaps just of recognition.

It was precisely the kind of reaction the director had been looking for, and precisely the kind that was unknown at Second City. Here was a group that went *looking* for taboos and forbidden places. Their tightropes were stretched across waterfalls, snake pits, piranha-filled pools—and they walked them blindfolded while cooking omelets.*

To its credit San Francisco took to them immediately—in particular the San Francisco *Chronicle* and its head hipster Ralph Gleason.

Within weeks the Committee was a bona fide hit. Thanks to the support of the intellectual community, it had also taken the first step toward becoming a local institution. It began establishing itself as the local chapter of the brotherhood of improvisational teamsters that now spanned the nation. Word began to filter back to Second City and Bleecker Street that something was happening in San Francisco and that it was something new. This was not yet another rearrangement of second- and third-generation Sills graduates or the umpteenth company of the Premise. Second City stalwarts such as Roger Bowen, Avery Schreiber, and Del Close began to visit. Opinions were divided as to whether it was what it claimed to be. For some, like Bowen, the political element Myerson had infused into the process was just the ticket. For others, it was a smoke screen behind which more of the same continued to be produced—a view echoed the next year by New York critics when Myerson made the mistake of bringing his first string to Broadway.

The Committee also began to attract people from outside the improvisational community. One of these was a young man finishing out his patriotic stint as a company clerk in Fort Leonard Wood, Missouri, named Carl Gottlieb.

Gottlieb was like many of the Committee—and unlike many of the Chicago biggies, most of whom were born before the war—a "child of Ike." He also was classic comedic raw material—an only child who had grown up

---

* A further feature of the opening night was a performance of Dylan's "Hard Rain" by Hamilton Camp. Dylan had given it to the group exclusively before he recorded it himself, so this was its first public appearance. The nine-minute testament to nuclear-age angst went over like a failed space-shot, but even it was in line with Myerson's urge to provoke rather than please. Either way it is proof that Dylan—once and future arbiter of what was "hip and happening"— considered the Committee the right place for it to be showcased.

clever and lonely at a time when grease and group stupidity were considered neat. He likes to characterize his career at the Committee as a second adolescence which was necessary "because the first one didn't take." While this is an inadequate self-description (for Gottlieb turned out to be the most professionally shrewd of all the original Committee members), it does convey the excitement San Francisco and the new company had at the time.

In 1961 the Army claimed him for its own and he began a two-year stint in the service of his country. While the experience was a peaceful one, for Gottlieb, this helped authenticate the antiwar satire for which the Committee later became known, mostly because his direct experience and fascination with minuscule regulation gave him an enviable command of militarese.

In 1962 a Compass theater company visited the Crystal Palace in St. Louis. Gottlieb, stationed in Kansas, had bused in to catch the show and was surprised to discover in the cast an old friend from the Village, Larry Hankin. He began to hang out at the Crystal Palace on weekend passes and was thus exposed to improvisation—for the first time. He liked what he saw. When in the spring of the next year, Hankin, by then a charter member of the Committee, urged Gottlieb to come up to San Francisco to check out the new action, he jumped at the suggestion. He went to San Francisco on two weeks' leave, spent almost all of it at the Committee, and fell in love with San Francisco. During this visit he became part of the company for one of its concert bookings. Lacking a stage manager, they offered him the job when he was discharged later that year. He accepted.

The Committee was by then very hot, as successful in its milieu as the Compass and Second City had been before it, and it was lighting fires all over the Bay Area. Scenes were becoming tighter and more focused, moving further away all the time from the social commentary of Second City and into a kind of political comedy designed for a specific purpose and challenging the audience to react. Those points were made directly, not elliptically. Scenes tended to be of the you-are-there rather than the we-were-there variety. And since a lot of the issues roused violent passions, or were more simply about violence, there was a good deal of violence onstage, both verbal and physical.

One well-known example Gottlieb recalls was a scene concerning capital punishment, then still legal in California. A typical improv company sketch would have been likely to take as its target media coverage of an execution, or official double talk or religious hypocrisy. Not the Committee. They got right to the death cell. Hankin, as the condemned man, is led to the chair by a priest, a warden, and a guard. He is strapped in, raucously abusing the authorities, and the switch is thrown. Nothing happens. Hankin becomes obnoxiously arrogant, hurling insults at the three representatives of state and calling them schoolyard names. They confer and throw the switch again. Still nothing. Hankin starts cackling with glee, doubly abusive. They throw it yet again. Nothing yet again. Hankin then demands to be set free—he can't be executed more than once, they're a bunch of assholes, double jeopardy, nyah-

nyah, etc., etc. Totally desperate, the three confer once more, check that they're alone in the cell, and kick Hankin to death.

This sketch was performed once at a jail benefit at Vacaville (now the home of Charles Manson). Jail audiences tend to be enthusiastic but this one could not believe what they were seeing. Identifying with both Hankin's abuse and the death-reprieve cycle of the repeated attempts at execution was a cocktail which would have sent even Molotov crazy. Long before the blackout, the audience was out of control, screaming with joy and joining in with the abuse. At the blackout a riot broke out. It took prison guards some time to restore order among the stamping, cheering, dancing prisoners—and they no doubt did a little kicking along the way themselves.

Understandably such reactions—and there were similar experiences in the regular shows at the theater—convinced the company that its political emphasis was correct. During this seminal period the Committee formed not just its *raison d'être,* but a remarkably pure sense of the collective. Even more than most improvisation companies—and all encouraged group-think rather than star-think—the Committee members submerged their individual personalities. While this worked superbly for the company and its internal discipline and development, it set the stage for individual frustration. Ironically, Gottlieb, in an episode that both prefigured and affected the group's ultimate fragmentation, was the first to feel the chill effects of collectivization.

Free collective though the group may have been, it was not above collaborating with the enemy just a little bit—if the price was right. Late into the first heady year of its existence, the Committee decided to emulate the highly successful Stan Freberg and organize a subsidiary to do comedy commercials for television. It was to be called the Committee Commercial Company and the idea was that since all actors are created equal, all would share equally in the profits. The question immediately arose as to whether the more proletarian members of the company, specifically the stage manager and the music director who did not actually perform onstage, should also share equally in the profits.

Gottlieb, the stage manager, presented his case to the politburo, using the persuasive argument that stage managing an improvisational company is as creative a job as appearing in one and that his commitment to each show was as total (physically as well as comedically) as that of any other of the individual.† The Committee's party committee grappled with this ideological dilemma at great length and after much self-criticism delivered its decision.

No.

---

† The stage manager is essential to any theatrical enterprise, but in improvisation he or she plays as creative and unpredictable a role as any of the actors. Lights, sound, effects, and props must follow the action closely and might even in some cases lead it. The stage manager thus becomes an improviser too and must be adept at sensing the direction a scene is taking. Above all, he or she must know when to hit the blackout, ending a scene. Theoretically, the blackout should be the true end of the scene, the point of it, and the biggest laugh. Hit the lights too soon and you have angry actors; too late and you have a sleepy audience.

Tiny enslaved Gottlieb had no choice but to grind his teeth and go back to the gulag. But he never forgot the collective's arbitrary decision and when six years later, a similar but far more destructive situation arose, the worker got his revenge on the intellectuals.

In 1964 Arthur Cantor, erstwhile producer of *An Evening with Mike Nichols and Elaine May* and *Beyond the Fringe,* brought the Committee to Broadway. Expectations were high. Myerson told the company, "We're going to be bigger than the Beatles." This rash prediction was soon dashed to bits on the rocks of reality—in the shape of New York reviewers.

Although the One That Counts, the New York *Times,* was pickily enthusiastic, liking this but not that ("Some [subjects] are pierced through the heart; others are sprayed with scattered fire that draws hardly any blood"), none could be described as "money" reviews. Several, including the *Times,* demonstrated a certain unease with satire manifesting itself in the guise of boredom. Many reviewers seem to have seen the Committee as interchangeable with Second City or the Premise.

The obvious perception that the Committee's style was the same as that of its parents was contradicted in most reviews by universal praise for the "Negro Party" scene (the one where Goodrow is lionized by white liberals), and further so by universal condemnation of the death cell scene and Jessica Myerson's sketch about orgasm (the latter of which clearly rattled both the *Times* and *The New Yorker).* None of this material would ever have found its way into the Committee's counterparts' repertoire. The only sketch about which everyone universally raved was a mime ensemble of an orchestra playing a nursery rhyme, a hoary old improvisational standby. Thus the company was (1) accused of being just like the rest, (2) condemned when it made substantial departure from them, and (3) praised when it was most like them. A no-win situation.

One reviewer, in the long run the Only One That Counted, smelled something different about the Committee in both its style and its content. Harold Clurman's review in *The Nation* made some quiet points, obvious to anyone who had bothered to listen: "Several of the sketches have real point—for example, the caricature of the frequently peculiar white self-consciousness in personal relations with Negroes—often nearly as bad as the former condescension. There is a savage scenic 'epigram' on capital punishment—more violent than is customary in such entertainments and on that account most welcome.

"The whole evening strikes an engagingly friendly note. Still one feels an intention actually more political and specifically critical than is common in some of this show's Greenwich Village counterparts . . ."

Having gotten "as big as the Beatles" out of its system, the Committee returned to its spawning ground to settle in. While the company had been in the East, a replacement company had kept the theater warm. Directed by Gottlieb, this cast included Avery Schreiber, who had moved on from Second City; Dick Schaal, husband of later cast member Valerie Harper; Hugh Romney, later to be reincarnated as Wavy Gravy, the awakening angel of Woodstock; a young comedian from Minnesota via New York, Peter Bonerz; and, as stage manager, a local boy from the San Francisco café world, Howard Hesseman.

Of this new group Bonerz and Hesseman were to become the most deeply involved in the ongoing life of the Committee and their provenance is worth describing. They are also, along with Gottlieb, the other two Committee members who later made substantial names for themselves in Los Angeles. (Bonerz, for example, in the first Bob Newhart series as Jerry Robinson, and Hesseman in "WKRP" as Johnny Fever.)

Bonerz, unlike many of his peers, came from a relatively placid background in Milwaukee, something that seems to have helped him exercise a moderating influence on the company as he moved into a position of influence. As a child, he was afflicted with a chronic stutter and this was to prove his passport to comedy. Finding himself unable to communicate in a normal way, he developed a line of physical tomfoolery that got him social acceptability in the eyes of his schoolmates. He also found that his stutter disappeared when he used a character voice. A wise teacher encouraged him in this course and suggested that he prepare and perform a routine of some kind for the class. He did, became a hit in school, and was hooked on laughter thereafter.

After a stint at Marquette, he headed for New York. There he mingled with the rest of the 1960 comedic crowd playing clubs and cafés in the Village. His odd solo, which would alternate from Tatilike pantomime to intellectual fantasy such as Freud interviewing Oedipus, attracted the attention of George Segal, which brought him to Ted Flicker, then riding high on the Premise.

He got a spot in one of the Premise companies and responded well to the pressure of improvising topical humor, but as usual, the Army raised its head in 1961 and Bonerz found himself in the Signal Corps in Long Island City across the East River from Manhattan. If one had to be drafted, this wasn't the worst place in the world to be stationed, but for Bonerz it was a mixed blessing.

He could work at the Premise by night and by day shoot training films in the company of fellow draftee Paul Bartel. But being drafted deepened a vaguely liberal distrust of authority into a profound loathing for the military mentality. For Bonerz, the glue that held the Army together even in peacetime, and even in the Signal Corps, was fear. Kennedy-era recruiting programs and Phil Silvers notwithstanding, what he discovered for the first time in Long Island City were human beings who related to other human beings only through the threat of force.

This experience clearly prepared Bonerz for recruitment into the Committee. Well before the horrors it inflicted on the nation later in the decade, the military managed to sow the seeds of radical activism in this thoughtful, moderate, and not very political Midwesterner.

Bonerz's perception and experience were very much that of the Committee at large. It helps to explain why the company became so central to the anti-war movement. The Committee insisted that the war, and the hatred and suspicion it engendered, was a function of the general lack of trust among Americans. Time and again its comedy explored the idea that if the audience could experience the same trust among themselves that the performers did onstage, the problem would be on its way to a solution. This wasn't presented as a naïve belief in "love," but as a practical alternative to the alienation and fear people felt. The trust among the performers onstage was a metaphor for a properly functioning society. And just as that trust existed not necessarily because the performers liked one another but to ensure the safe operation of the whole enterprise, so it could in the audience and the society at large.‡

For Bonerz, for the Committee, for the Bay Area antiwar movement and the generation of draftable males who gradually came to realize that a government willing to risk their lives in an inexplicable adventure far from home did not necessarily have their best interests at heart, the military command—not the Viet Cong was the enemy. It should be emphasized that in the chain of causality that led to widespread resistance, the military and its civilian managers were the prime movers. This obvious point needs belaboring only because our revisionists would have us believe that a wave of self-indulgence, outside agitation, or just plain cussedness brought about the extremism of the mid-sixties and therefore of the humor that expressed it. Wishful thinking, alas. The simple fact of the matter was the war caused the satire, not vice versa.

With Hesseman, the Committee acquired a bona fide connection with the burgeoning rock scene in North Beach and Haight-Ashbury. He came to the company from a job managing the Coffee Gallery, one of the many locations where such luminaries as David Crosby, Dino Valenti, Marty Balin, Hoyt Axton, and Janis Joplin were to be found.

Hesseman was also emcee at a number of the concerts which began to be a feature of the rock underground in the Bay Area throughout 1965, in particular the Family Dog concerts, organized by Luria Castell and Ellen Harmon. Other Committee members started to appear at these concerts also, either as emcees or individual performers, notably Larry Hankin and Garry Goodrow.

In one respect the relationship between the Committee and rock bands was simply a matter of space. As one of the better-equipped functioning stages in the North Beach area, before the Fillmore and the Avalon got going, the Committee theater was a natural place for experimentation. While he was still stage manager Hesseman began producing Monday Night concerts at the theater (Monday night the regular show was dark), usually in company with another member of the cast.

A Committee appearance in the late summer of 1965 was the first time that

‡ One of the most basic improv exercises is called "Trust." It involves being blindfolded and then led around guided only by the voices of the rest of the company. After only a few seconds the subject is so confused that he or she completely follows the guiding voices and can accomplish weird feats of dexterity and balance.

the Charlatans had appeared in San Francisco since their riotous booking at the Red Dog Saloon in Virginia City, Nevada, an event widely considered to have been the official inauguration of the San Francisco sound. They were followed by the Great Society (from which Gracie Slick would join Jefferson Airplane), the Warlocks (soon to be the Grateful Dead), and Quicksilver Messenger Service.

Throughout the years between its return from Broadway and the establishment of a Los Angeles company—roughly from 1965 to 1968, the period of the group's most intense creativity and of its greatest influence on its immediate surroundings—the Committee's ties to the rock world were numerous and complex. In this it broke new ground. Up to this point comedy's ties, whether those of the New Comedians or the various improv companies, tended to be with the folk or jazz worlds. A typical bill at the Café au Go-Go in New York, the Shadows in Washington, or the hungry i around the corner from the Committee might have a comedian like Woody Allen or Godfrey Cambridge, and a jazz group like Ahmad Jamal or a folk act like Judy Henske. The improv theaters rarely hosted groups of any kind—and in terms of personal taste their members probably tended more towards jazz. Although by 1965, following Dylan's infamous lead, many folksingers had been buying pick-up mikes for their Martins, there was no comedian or group following them either in spirit or to the new places they were finding audiences.

This is not to say that the Committee had no interest in folk music or jazz. On the contrary, not just the Monday Night concerts but the regular show itself provided a stage for the likes of Arlo Guthrie, who first sang his anthem "Alice's Restaurant" in between sets, and Joan Baez, who was a regular guest performer. (Baez's sister Mimi Fariña became a regular member of the Committee cast.) Dylan headed for the Committee when in town and his companion, mentor, and sometimes guardian angel, Bobby Neuwirth, was a close member of the Committee family. Several members of the company produced jazz concerts on Monday nights where such people as Keith Jarrett were often on a bill.

But these tastes and events were unexceptional at the time. What was exceptional—and in the light of the controversy surrounding the electrification of music in the mid-sixties, even controversial—was the Committee's unabashed embrace of the raucous new popular music. Hesseman feels it was rock's "spirit of anarchy" that appealed to them most, and certainly the chaos and speed of change that characterized the rock scene in the years 1965 and 1966 was nothing if not anarchic.

More important, the spirit of independence and taste for abrupt change that the music itself symbolized was identical to the Committee's. Whether or not it was expressed politically, a generational consensus was emerging that, in the light of recent events, there had to be a better or even completely new way of doing things. In one form this feeling became the urge to get back to basics (perhaps in order to find out where the system had gone wrong), in another, the need to make a clean break and create an entirely new monster.

In some cases this could be one and the same thing. Jerry Garcia, for example, was a revolutionary musician profoundly rooted in traditional blues. (He'd once spent a sizable chunk of time roaming around the Deep South just to pick up "new" licks from old blues guitarists.)

And when the old was expanded by the burgeoning possibilities of amplification, it became what Pigpen called "the electric blues band"—a colossal and exciting new beast. We have grown so used to this initial premise, and the sound it created, that the simple artistic leap the Dead and other bands made now seems commonplace. At the time it was made in the dark with no particular guarantee of success and only some friendly hands to hold onto. The result was a revolution in music and an appreciable shift in artistic possibility—a new reality. In this respect it was very much the same process as that which improvisers experience, the same search for new conclusions by throwing away the script, the same blindfold jump off the same window ledge.

As Hesseman says: "The magic thing about improvisation is that you and [another] go onstage with our own realities, and create a third one with far greater possibilities both for the two of us and everyone who witnesses it."

Widely different though these two approaches to performance may be— there is not on the face of it much in common between taking the licks from some gnarled old fingers and slamming them through a Marshall amp and taking a cherished belief out of its secret place and poking it till it cries "uncle"—they share one crucial thing: a willingness to take risks, to drop the rules if they obstruct the experience. In the relatively small enclave of North Beach and the Haight in which all of this took place, where everyone was pretty much aware of what everyone else was doing, such a willingness was both infectious and symbiotic. Both had the same taste for danger.

The central paradox of the San Francisco phenomenon was that by exploring the limits of personal experience, this relatively small group of people, pretty much confined to one urban area, terrified an entire nation. These were people who, for the most part, were as apolitical a bunch as generation upon generation of Americans had been before them. They weren't coercing people at gunpoint or subverting them, on behalf of alien powers. They were just making an incredible amount of noise in dusty old ballrooms and tinkering around with their own internal chemistry. The word "head" did not become so universal and all-purpose a term in these times for nothing. One of Garcia's favorite terms for what he did was "indoor anarchy." Most of the action *was* taking place indoors—all the way indoors, between people's ears. Nonetheless, whatever was going on in there was regarded by outsiders to be as great a threat to national security as Moscow's missiles. As Jack Nicholson says in *Easy Rider* (scripted by Terry Southern): "Don't ever tell anyone they ain't free, 'cos they're gonna get real busy killin' and maimin' just to prove they are . . ."

That was the trap: you took the guarantees of freedom, which you had been brought up to believe in, lived where you liked, as you liked, with whom you liked, worked to live rather than lived to work, and generally respected other people's right to do the same, whether the fashion was identical to yours or quite different. But the very same people who had taught you that you were free reacted to your behavior with horror. Perhaps it was envy, perhaps it was fear, but in practical terms it came down to the same thing: prohibition, hatred, and finally violence.

One of Bonerz's favorite pieces developed during his stint as director addressed exactly that paradox, and for him was an epiphany—the first time he can remember thinking that he had participated in the creation of material that mirrored vital national issues. The scene was a sports event. The entire cast of eight is assembled onstage, in a row of bleachers. As the strains of the national anthem begin, all stand except one. At the time, it should be recalled, people would sometimes refuse to stand for the national anthem if they were against the war. As the soloist proceeds over the sound system, those standing, hands over their hearts or saluting, sing along with varying degrees of accuracy. The protestor sits stubbornly, arms akimbo.

Gradually the folks nearest him get riled by his nonparticipation and try to nudge him to his feet. This process soon involves the whole row with a lot of squeezing and pushing to get at the object of their patriotic wrath, and their attempts to get him on his feet become more violent. (On some occasions the protestor would resist, on others go limp, and so on.) Nothing will make him acknowledge the anthem and as it continues they begin pummeling and throttling him in the effort to get him to conform. Eventually, as the song winds down to "the land of the free . . ." they stomp him noisily to death (singing extra loud to cover up his screams).

This was the kind of thing that made people take sides in 1965, and audiences often did. The piece would as often get boos and walk-outs as cheers, and one local reviewer, Stanley Eichenbaum, wrote a fierce review asserting that this time the group had gone "too far" and that they were "too angry"— an interesting concept in itself. For Bonerz, however, "this qualified me for a bachelor's degree in political satire."

By this time the Committee had become a rallying point for political activity in the Bay Area. The theater itself played host to such exotic visitors as Ram Das (Richard Alpert of the old-established Harvard acid firm of Leary and Alpert), the Diggers, and various groups like the Red Guard (from Chinatown). The Angels hung out at the Committee, in the days when Sonny Barger called the shots, as did the legendary San Francisco Mime Troupe.

These were heady days for the company, for its members were the point people for what was happening in San Francisco above- and belowground. If their visceral ties were to the Family Dog and the Fillmore, their intellectual ones were to the artistic and political communities. As the company became more secure about itself, it would often allow cast members the opportunity to make speeches to the audience and invite the audience to respond. Sometimes the audience needed no invitation, particularly when the subject matter involved the Vietnam War. This happened on many occasions, especially when there were military personnel in the audience; on one occasion a piece called "60,000 Come Home," which addressed the first large-scale return of military personnel from Southeast Asia, caused a riot in the theater.

The piece was harsh. Amid great celebration three GIs are greeted at the airport by parents and the fiancée of one of them. With lots of raucous bonhomie the boys are brought back to their motel, where they suffer a flashback and go berserk, killing the parents and group-raping the fiancée. According to Myerson, on this occasion the three GIs were particularly funny in the first part, with lots of predictable stuff about the war, getting home, and what they were going to do now they were back. The audience was appreciative, apparently expecting a service-comedy-type sketch. Predictably they stopped laughing and when the lights went out, the theater erupted. Rather than continue the show Myerson put up the lights, gave money back to anyone who wanted it, and announced an impromptu town meeting on the war. Most people stayed while the cast simply sat onstage and either moderated or took part in the debate. There was no doubt that the piece had made people both laugh and think. Myerson remembers one lady in particular. She announced that her son had been in Vietnam; she said, "He killed a lot of people, but *never never* raped anyone."

These discussions became more common as questions were raised about the war and the government's management of it. Many who came into the Committee were tourists or other kinds of visitors to San Francisco. (The Committee essentially survived off street trade and it was located more or less centrally in a popular tourist area.) In consequence, the Committee had to put up with some violent responses to its material, but to its credit it doesn't seem ever to have moderated any of it for that reason.

There are several opinions about whether these sessions or the material itself changed anyone's mind. For Bonerz, the company didn't change anyone's mind, but then, as he points out with heartland logic, "they didn't change ours either." He adds, though, that the often tragic response they would get to their material—when, for example, the parents of men who had lost their lives were present—"only quickened our satirical desire rather than blunted it." It was their way of resisting the war that was killing people's children. The more people were plunged into the nightmare, the more the satire had to bring the nightmare home.

For Gottlieb, these evenings did have an effect. Along with Myerson he cites innumerable occasions on which he has been approached by people who claim that their lives were changed by seeing the Committee or by being present at an informal town meeting. Gottlieb also feels that the prevailing opinion of the group was valid—that people would never look quite the same way at public figures or politically sensitive situations once they'd laughed at them.

While the company was unabashed about proselytizing against the war, their feelings about the military itself were more mixed. This was not a group for whom the rosy glow of pacifism was untroubled by actual experience.

Those who'd done their time had a salutary effect on those who'd managed not to, if for no other reason than that they'd been on the inside. The Committee rarely made the mistake common in the antiwar movement of despising anything in a uniform.

On the other hand, people who'd been unimpressed by Kennedy's brand-name bravado were not likely to be suckered by LBJ's generic kind. One could sympathize with soldiers but still hate the military. The latest crop of muscle-bound generals, unmanned by a decade of inaction and prodded by the fervent patriotism of a defense industry anxious to clear its warehouses, had found themselves a winnable war. The most immediate victims of this happy occasion (after a couple of million Asian peasants) would be the ordinary guys who were expected to go out and take care of the details.

This antimilitary/prosoldier attitude, however commendable, ran into some serious practical problems. For one thing, Oakland was a major port of embarkation for points east, so that North Beach was always crawling with grunts whooping it up their last night out, or returnees whooping it up their first night back. Inevitably a lot of them ended up in the Committee whose real-people you-are-there style of material more often featured GIs in the jungle than commanders in remote offices. As can be seen from "60,000 Come Home," this was not always what either grunts or anyone else expected to see. The place would regularly get ripped up by guys in uniform, who, depending on their condition, were either invited to make a statement or wrestled out the door by the bartender (who happened to be an ex-marine). Myerson claims that often when the cast found themselves being echoed in antiwar sentiments during an open session with the audience it turned out to be a Vietnam vet.

A lot of the military milling about San Francisco, though, were not in any frame of mind for sanity of approach. They were simply too gung ho, or they had bought the basic propaganda line that when walking around San Francisco they were just as much surrounded by the enemy as they would be in Quang Tri. Once, Gottlieb was sitting with some fellow Committee men in Enrico's, an old beatnik sidewalk café run by original hungry i owner Enrico Banducci. Gottlieb was wearing his buck sergeant shirt from the Army. He wore this shirt with a perverse pride, as if proclaiming to the peaceniks around him that he knew what he was talking about when it came to peace, that he was a better, older, and wiser peacenik than they.

This cut no ice with the two officious young MPs who screeched to a halt outside the café and strode impressively to his table. Here's Goodrow's version:

MP: Let's see your ID.
GOTTLIEB: Fuck you.
MPS: Show us your ID or we're taking you in.
GOTTLIEB: I'm not in the service. Fuck you.

The MPs, a little shaken by the insubordination, regroup and make a call in their car. They return to the table.

MPS: You can't wear that shirt.
GOTTLIEB: Fuck you. I got it at Fort Leonard Wood, Missouri. It's mine.

The MPs are now completely confused. The clientele is drinking in every word. The MPs retire again to the car. A lot of conversation ensues with unseen advisers. They return to the table.

MPS: You can wear the shirt but you have to take off the stripes.
GOTTLIEB: Fuck you. Do it yourself.

One of the MPs, purple with embarrassment, produces a penknife. Larry Hankin, who is sitting with Gottlieb stands to attention. Every patron in the café does likewise. A trumpet is produced from behind the bar and someone plays "Taps," as the unfortunate young MP breaks Gottlieb to the ranks. Gottlieb then demands a receipt for his stripe.

From the time it returned from New York (very approximately the beginning of 1965), until it left for Los Angeles in 1968, the Committee's staple was antiwar satire. This can be said of practically no other stage, forum, or medium of the time.

The Committee, on these grounds alone, deserves credit for keeping the powder dry at a time when all around had fled. Either Mr. Wizard was explaining guava bombs to little Tommy, or a desperate teenager was trying the Helleresque argument on a military doctor that the very fact that he would endure induction meant he was crazy enough to get a 4F. Here is their best-known Vietnam sketch, ABC's "Wide World of War":

THE WIDE WORLD OF WAR:

RED 1: Hi there, sports fans! It's a beautiful, clear, sunnyshiny afternoon here on the Mekong River Delta, where elements of the 101st Airborne Division tangle with North Vietnam's crack 7th Division. Both teams undefeated and untied so far this season. The playing field is directly in front of us here. It's a marshy rice paddy surrounded by trees with hills up in the background. Looking over those hills I see here come those HU1BR Huey helicopters of the 101st! And they're coming in low and fast, raking that landing zone with fifty-caliber machine-gun fire as they windmill down for a landing, and now they are on the ground and it looks like it is the third brigade of the 101st, led by Col. Billy Slocum. And they're landing out there, trying to dig in and set up that defense. There're no signs of Viet Cong . . . Yes, yes . . . Charlie is here and he's got mortars! He's dropping mortar shells at regular three-second intervals. And I see one, two, three, whoops! Let's make that four helicopters down and burning and the rest are headed for a roll! And it looks like Charlie is slowing down . . . Charlie is bogged down now! He's stopped at the line of the scrimmage. Well, Red, what did you think of the action out there so far?

RED 2: Well, both these teams are in tip-top shape for this one. In the case of the 101st, that's due in no small part to the coach, Col. Billy William Slocum. Everything they're doing out there, the way they come busting out of those helicopters, the way they begin shooting long before they've actually seen anything! This is not to take anything away from the Viet Cong, though. They're a rugged opponent at any time. They've had a wonderful season and they've got a bumper crop of rookies this year.

RED 1: Thank you, Red. Now back to the action down on the field. Both sides are taking advantage of this time-out to drag the dead and wounded from the field. I see that Colonel Slocum is over by the field command radio of the 101st and this leads us to believe that they may be taking to the air on this next play, and, sure enough, here they come over the hills—F102 Phantom Jets from the USS *Air Enterprise* and they're coming in low and fast. And now they're dropping five-hundred-pound antipersonnel bombs and I see a dozen oxen down and kicking on the field! In for the second pass this time, it looks like napalm! Flaming black pajamas from the trees to my left and right! It smells like Charlie's hurting down there! And here comes the leader back over from the third pass, and it looks like napalm once again! Oh my God, right on top of the 101st! Well, the field is full of penalty flags on that one, Red!

RED 2: *(Interrupting)* And here come those battlefield hotline tally sheets with the scores for today's contest. In this game, the Viet Cong have 407 killed or injured while the 101st casualties were light to moderate. Why don't you try to size up what happened?

RED 1: Well, I think it's obvious that the way that napalm came sneaking in there, it gave our boys at the 101st a little incentive, a hotfoot, if you will, to gain back some badly needed lost yardage! And it seems as though Charlie got his signals crossed in that last play. From up here, it looks as though those battle-hardened veterans from the North have been wiped out right down to the last woman and child. You know, I'd like to add that ever since the President authorized the televising of these games live, via satellite, his popularity has climbed one tenth of one percentage in every major poll in the country! It certainly makes you proud to be an American, doesn't it? Reminds me and Red of a saying that goes, "If you can't play in a sport, why not be one?"

The company was more than delivering on Ralph Gleason's advice to them that satire "must go past the venturesome into pure risk—they've got to go on what Ken Kesey calls 'trips,' elbowing the reluctant angels out of the way . . ."

Which brings us to the drugs.

So much has been written about psychedelia and San Francisco, and so tight is the noose of fear and ignorance being drawn once again around the whole subject (ironically, by the same gang that did the same thing in California in the sixties), that it is next to impossible to separate historically the real from the imagined.

There is, too, an inherent fallacy, akin to the intentional fallacy of lit-crit fame, in trying to interpret what someone wrote, sang, played, or drew in terms of the substances they were ingesting at the time. It is no more valid to award, say, *Surrealistic Pillow* a special place in the rock pantheon because the Airplane was probably ripped on acid when they wrote and recorded it, any more than it is for some neo-Know-Nothing to dismiss the album for the same reason. Either it's babble or it stands up and that's the only way to judge it.

Specifically with regard to acid, that curare in the spearhead of West Coast counterculture, it's worth making three points, none of them new but all of them forgotten. First, lysergic acid diethylamide came with impeccable intellectual credentials to the San Francisco scene. Whatever happened to its image later, in the hands of the paisley-and-light-show brigade, it was first promoted by a major English writer of the twentieth century, Aldous Huxley, actively touted by two Harvard professors, Drs. Alpert and Leary, and embraced in San Francisco itself by a major American writer of the twentieth century, Ken Kesey. None of this was lost on a class-aware and well-educated generation of middle-class kids, properly scared by the ravages of heroin. Second, whatever twaddle may have been spouted in its name there is no evidence that acid caused or has caused any major physiological damage. This was well known at the time and its users can be forgiven for resenting the blanket repression that lumped it together with hard drugs. Third, and largely as a result of the repression—which was as much a prime mover here as the military was in causing resistance to the war—dropping acid was a political act. So was the wearing of long hair and different clothes, the creation of new music and art, and resistance to the Anglo-Saxon work ethic. (Resisting that doesn't mean you're lazy—just that you don't think Brits and Krauts are necessarily your best role models.)

The Committee seems to have been tolerant of drugs but not missionary about them, users but rarely abusers. From 1965 on, drugs, especially acid, were as much a part of the nutritional scene in North Beach as good Chinese food. It would have been impossible for the company not to have been exposed to acid—and equally so, given their propensity for jumping off cliffs hand in hand, for them not to have tried it.

Once or twice or—at most—three thousand times.

Two members of the Committee's first string personified the company's relationship to drugs. One was John Brent. Brent was the dark angel of the Committee, a huge subverted intelligence out of control. He was also a smorgasbord junkie. Brent's coat of arms read: have head will travel. But while he would take any drug at any strength, or in any combination, he always seemed to know down to the last twitch or milligram what the chemical consequences would be. And while his experiments on himself were of legendary proportions, one always got the feeling that he had entrusted himself to himself and that he was in good hands. The car he was driving was always going to be driven within some obscure but well-displayed speed limit.*

Early in late 1964 or early 1965—no one can remember for sure—a dark slight teenager started to appear regularly in the audience on Friday nights. Soon he was coming twice or more every week. Cornering him one night, the company said there was no need for him to pay to get in, and thereafter he became a fixture. His name was Chris Ross. He was a rare case. His groupie fervor was actually matched by his talent. Slim, curly-haired, but with a face that belonged in an aviary, Chris soon became a member of the company and since he was much younger, its collective kid brother. He became known as "the Egg."

In a company where some members were rapidly reaching the dread age of thirty, a bubbling brilliant teenager was a healthy injection. Over the next couple of years Chris came up with several of the Committee's more memorable scenes and developed for himself a particularly funny character named Danny di Marco, the world's oiliest lounge singer, whose debut came in 1967 at the hungry i, where he opened for Flatt and Scruggs.

Chris was also very interested in drugs. In the Committee that meant being very interested in Brent and frequent Committee visitor Del Close. By all accounts Chris was seriously discouraged from unhealthy pursuits but persisted anyway, regarding them as some kind of examination which, if he passed, would permit him entry to the inner sanctum.

Another, if more intermittent, drug influence came in the shape of Hugh Romney (already mentioned as the later Wavy Gravy of Woodstock). According to Gottlieb, Romney was "too outré even for the Committee."

He was more of a comedian than would fit comfortably into the company, although the kind of work he did stretches the term "comedian" to its limit. The sets he, Tiny Tim, and occasionally Sandy Bull would do either on Monday nights at the theater or wherever they decided to make contact with the Earthlings, were weirder by all accounts than anything a city accustomed to weirdness had ever seen.

Hesseman recalls one memorable set Hugh/Wavy performed at the Committee: "Hugh had decided for reasons of his own that he wanted to do his set in a meat jacket. Together we safety-pinned cold cuts to a jacket (we'd found out that tape didn't work), moving on from pressed ham, when that ran out, to salami and bologna. It took a great deal of time. Rather than use a clock to

---

* John Brent was found dead in his apartment off Santa Monica Boulevard on Thursday, August 15, 1985, by Gary Goodrow, just a few days before he was to be interviewed for this book. It was not drug-related, as he had been clean for several years.

measure the length of his act Hugh decided to use a candle. The set was long —he was out there a couple of hours. By the end of it, he was in much better shape than his jacket. Hugh became aware of this, looked at the candle, and said, 'Well, it looks as though my time is up. The old clock on the wall has melted.' "

Romney's true home, in fact, was with Ken Kesey's Merry Pranksters of which he was a charter member. The Trips Festival in January 1966 was the coming-out ball for the Merry Pranksters and Romney was much in evidence as he was on Kesey's *Acid Test* album.

The Trips Festival deserves elaboration, partly because it was a benchmark for the San Francisco Experience of the 1960s (for Jerry Garcia, for example, "the Trips Festival was as good as it got"), and partly because for all the energy and epiphany surrounding it, it had a very serious purpose. The Merry Pranksters could call themselves by a semantically funny name but they were missionary about the effect acid could have on modern society. And here they and the Committee, who were in the final analysis real satirists and therefore real skeptics, parted company.

Hesseman says it: "I did want to believe that my mythological belief system was sweeping the nation [he means drugs and peace and freedom]. Thank God I was in a situation . . . that allowed me to look at it a little more closely and see what was absurd about it . . .

"I could point out as an actor the difference between what we said we were doing and what we were really doing—a rich trough of humor . . .

"Due to the pressure of Myerson and the group, I couldn't hold on to these cherished notions . . . I was quite willing to abandon them to get a laugh— are you kidding? I'm as revolutionary as the next investor, goddamnit!"

This attitude was not just a saving grace—it came with the territory. And it says a great deal about the company's intelligence with regard to drugs. Certainly every member of the company used them and knew intimately what they meant and could do. But in no way were they or their humor dependent on them. Where others had either to hold on to a drug mythology long past its relevance or appeal, or go, so to speak, cold turkey not just on the drugs but on the beliefs they had espoused along with taking them, the Committee had the sense to treat the extremism of the drug culture like any other kind of extremism.

One of Gottlieb's crisper pieces addressed the widespread philosophy that if everyone smoked dope there wouldn't be a war. In it a traveling salesman picks up a young hippie girl who is hitching. As he chomps away on his cigar the subject of grass comes up and the girl spouts familiar dicta concerning the good old weed. The salesman is intimately familiar with it and agrees about its great effects. He smoked it when he was in Korea. He launches into an ecstatic description of getting loaded while spotting shells and firing tracer, ending up with the question, "Ever killed anyone when you were high? GRRREAT!"

There were also the predictable pieces about getting busted—like "FBI" where Goodrow is beaten up by two narcs who break into his house without a warrant. This sketch had one truly memorable line. Goodrow fighting off two agents, makes it to the window, flings it open, and yells, "Help—police!"

But the most fascinating piece was one originated by the Egg—Chris Ross. It was called "Acid" and it was as much about breaking the fourth wall as it was about drugs.†

The sketch begins with one actor onstage, clearly getting ready for an acid trip, waiting for the drug to kick in. A second actor enters—his roommate who will be his guide. His first words are, "Did you take it yet?"

Dialogue proceeds as the drug takes effect, with the first actor describing how he feels as his mind "expands," a fairly familiar "Oh-wow" litany, played for laughs.

Then the first actor takes a brilliant step. Under the "influence" of the drug, he jumps off the stage into the audience. His "guide," locked into the stage reality, acts as if he has disappeared. And when his colleague tries to talk to him from the audience, he refuses to recognize his presence.

FIRST ACTOR: I haven't disappeared—I'm in the audience!
SECOND ACTOR: There is no audience.
FIRST ACTOR: Then who do you think is laughing?
SECOND ACTOR: It's just a sound coming from the air shaft.
FIRST ACTOR: Oh, you think I'm in the ventilator? *(Putting just his head onstage)* Now can you see me?
SECOND ACTOR: DON'T DO THAT! Don't walk through walls like that.

The sketch then proceeds with the tripping actor free to roam the audience and the theater in general, and the straight actor, who would not break, "trapped" by the four walls of stage reality. On any level this was a noncensorious and nonpromotional exploration of altered reality (which was of course "normal" reality) and its relationship to "normal" reality, in this case stage reality.

To add a final twist, the first actor would then disappear from the audience

† The lineage of this sketch was distinguished. According to Gottlieb:

"Rob [Reiner] had dropped some acid and was an hour or two into it . . . flashing. Albert Brooks came over. [Albert had not taken acid at that time.] At first I thought Albert was being Albert, was being funny . . . but he was genuinely interested and he was asking Rob things like, 'How do you feel? Some people get depressed. Then they get deeper and deeper into the depression. So, like are you depressed yet? And these carvings on the walls—these gargoyles—do they look *horrible* to you? Because they're really grotesque . . . do they look like monsters? Do they come out of the walls at you?'

"These were incredible downer suggestions on Rob who was trying to stay on his trip. It was real psychedelic bad manners! So what happened was later—in a workshop situation—this story was being told by Chris Ross, and we decided to do it as a scene. Someone who has just taken acid is bummed by his roommate, who asks all the wrong questions, who behaves with psychedelic bad manners. When it came to performance, someone, either Chris or Howard, made the step."

also and reappear onstage as the "guide" reversing the original roles. His first words as he comes onstage are of course, "Did you take it yet?" Blackout.

What makes this a quintessentially "Committee" sketch is both its completely accessible physicality and its elegant and intelligent use of the theatrical metaphor to give the audience some idea of what it was like being inside an acid trip looking out (if that's what they wanted to take from it). While it was nonjudgmental, it was also not in the least naïve, a tolerant but skeptical look at something around which a considerable amount of rhetorical gunk had collected. It was the apotheosis of "you are there."

By 1967 the company was becoming a very extended family. Dozens of people were involved in the operation of the Committee. As a San Francisco institution, they hosted many visitors both from the improv fraternity and the underground, and inevitably their paths crossed with almost anyone who had the slightest interest in state-of-the-art comedy. These could be as diverse as Chris Cerf from Random House (and *The Harvard Lampoon),* who was Richard Fariña's editor, and therefore after Fariña's death on close terms with his widow, Committee member Mimi Fariña. Or American Nazi *Führer* George Lincoln Rockwell, who was invited to use the theater as a local forum. (He came to look it over but declined.)

"We were the theatrical editorializers of the city," says Bonerz, "[the press] demanded of us that we dramatize the confusion." This they did with gusto; when Nureyev and Margot Fonteyn were busted in the Haight on marijuana charges, the Egg had a fully choreographed ballet version of the party, the bust, and the rooftop chase ready by the next evening. John Brent ran for mayor against Alioto on the campaign slogan Anything You Want. Kathryn Ish ran as a candidate for Miss San Francisco, holding a well-attended press conference at the St. Francis where she posed with Gary Goodrow's kids, a dog, and a three-hundred-pound, shaven-headed black Committeeman called Pedro Cowley who distributed chocolate crucifixes to the press and issued the following statement: "I think it would be great if a white woman who knew a Negro was to be crowned Miss San Francisco." No one dared not to print it. And they ate the crucifixes.

Los Angeles began to show interest in various ways. Fred Roos, later Francis Ford Coppola's producer, and at the time a talent agent, began booking Committee members for parts on various TV series, ecstatic, according to Gottlieb, at having discovered an untapped pool of highly trained comic actors who would work for scale. Two kids from Beverly Hills High, Rob Reiner and Richard Dreyfuss, would regularly drive up north to hang out at the Committee. Reiner was enthralled by their skills and their values; by the next year he would be a member of the company. Dreyfuss later would move from being an accomplished film actor to a major star in Gottlieb's version of Peter Benchley's *Jaws.* For now, Committee members with TV gigs in LA would bum rides down south from the two kids.

Two other perhaps not quite so welcome visitors were a fledgling comedy team called Cheech and Chong. According to Goodrow, several of the Committee's standard pieces (one in particular that he performed with Dick Stahl where the two of them commented on humanity, sexuality, and other truths from the point of view of two mutts) mysteriously became cornerstones of Cheech and Chong's act. They were unabashed about this, saying in a subsequent *Rolling Stone* interview that they did mostly Committee material because no one was doing that stuff in clubs.

But a certain frustration was beginning to build in the company. Charter members had been working at the same job with essentially the same people for four years. Others like Bonerz and Goodrow had families. The need to put down roots and build some degree of security was beginning to temper the initial fervor. None of this seems to have been particularly disruptive—the sense of collective responsibility remained strong, and the Committee was a highly successful venture, whose financial arrangements, however arcane, took care of everyone. But the work was hard and there was boredom. "Fighting boredom," Myerson remarks, "is like fighting getting old." However satisfying the twin challenges of improvising and dealing with a rapidly changing world might be, there had to be a point at which the actor realized that satisfaction was finite. As several sources admitted, "I got to the point where I said to myself, I know how to do this now."

There were other problems also, ones peculiar to political satire. As the war expanded, and resistance became more familiar, as the authorities fell back on extreme justifications for their abuse of power and its victims made more and more connections between the various results, two things happened. On the one hand reality began to be so close to satire that making the effort to keep ahead seemed worthless. Goodrow had been alarmed back in 1965 the day Lyndon Johnson ordered the troops into the Dominican Republic, to find that a character he created the same night (an American corporate spokesman who ranted on about nineteenth-century concepts of manifest destiny and the Monroe Doctrine) was identical (down to his words), to a real corporate spokesman quoted the next morning in the *Chronicle*.

Less than a year later, satire was again overtaken by reality when Ronald Reagan was elected governor of California. It says a lot about the company's commitment to political issues that they didn't view this election with glee, exulting in so rich and easy a target. They simply found it depressing. It meant that what they were doing hadn't worked. Here was a superhawk—the noisiest advocate of genocide in Southeast Asia—who'd never carried a gun, in fact who'd removed himself from danger in the only war he could have fought in.‡ Here was the strongest advocate of family values in California politics, who was also its first divorced governor in history. Here was a crusader against waste and corruption in government whose defense, oil,

‡ Reagan was called up in 1942 but was excused from active service on the grounds of nearsightedness. Curiously, though, he managed to play football for his high school, work for a long period as a lifeguard, appear in many movies, and be photographed extensively as the president of SAG without ever having to wear glasses. Contact lenses became available to the general public in 1960.

auto, and agribiz backers didn't even bother to conceal themselves, so super-confident were they that the state was theirs.

There was no possibility of satiric tension in dealing with such a man. The truth was more satirical than reality.

There was the other side of the coin. As Myerson puts it, "What gave us notoriety was becoming more available." To the extent that they had been successful, more people were now accepting and less surprised about what they had to say. This put an added burden on the company. "We had to run ahead or be submerged in the consensus," says Gottlieb. Then, too, their unique satirical voice was beginning to be echoed elsewhere. Country Joe and the Fish, of all the possible groups operating out of San Francisco, were the first to have a bona fide national album hit with *Electric Music for the Mind and Body,* a political and satirical work which eventually sold almost five hundred thousand copies.

None of this can have been lost on the company. All around them, rock commercialization was arriving in the city by the limo-load. Record compa-nies were snapping up groups like the Dead, the Airplane, Moby Grape, and Quicksilver Messenger Service (in the case of the Airplane, for twenty-five thousand dollars, an unheard-of sum). The Monterey Pop Festival blossomed just down the coast.

Perhaps most important, Tom "Big Daddy" Donahue ("three hundred pounds of solid sounds") was inventing a radio form that provided the same groups with an outlet they could live with: underground rock FM. The idea was really simple: play album cuts, not Top 40. Nothing could have suited the anti-Top 40 groups better. Used to cutting numbers that could go on for far longer than the rigidly circumscribed 45s on AM, they found Donahue's KMPX a safe haven in a harsh world. His format became widely copied and album sales rather than single sales took over as the basic unit of music, an unimaginably lucrative one.

Donahue's original lineup of on-air talent was himself, his wife, Rachael, and Hesseman, soon to be joined by Sunday afternoon wax-spinner Gottlieb.

The Committee might be excused for feeling a trifle envious of all this action. They had, after all, paid their dues with the best. Although no one seems to be willing to take credit for suggesting it, or can clearly remember how such anathema began to gain widespread credence, the idea of starting an L.A. company took hold.

This is not to say that starting a L.A. company was a sellout. On the contrary, contacts with L.A. had been frequent and necessary, and there was the feeling abroad that L.A. was ready for the Committee rather than vice versa. But the impulse may have come, too, from the conclusion that what could be done in San Francisco had been done, and that it was time to look for wider audiences, for other fourth walls worth breaking. As if in prepara-tion for this, in early 1968 the company produced a piece that has gone down in people's recollection as one of its high points.

The occasion was LBJ's final State of the Union message. Hesseman, Myerson, and Goodrow, along with Mimi Farina, had watched this performance the previous night on television. In it, the President outlined both his plans for committing more troops to Vietnam and for eliminating the scourge of LSD from the face of the planet.

Hesseman was much incensed by this—especially the last bit—and asked Myerson to come up with a scene for him to do. Myerson obliged. When he explained it to the cast the next night, they refused to do it. Myerson threatened to quit, and reluctantly they agreed. Even at this late point in their collective career, the group was willing to take leaps off dark cliffs.

And it certainly worked. Here's Myerson: "Howard came out in all his tie-dyed splendor, hair down past his nipples, and began: 'Last night Lyndon Johnson gave the State of the Union Message. I watched it. I don't know how many of you did but this was part of it.' The lights dimmed and Bonerz, wearing a Stetson, stepped into an imaginary television. Goodrow and Hesseman sat down to watch Bonerz. The rest of the cast stayed onstage. The stage manager read a portion of the State of the Union message while Bonerz mimed LBJ. Hesseman moved toward the set and had to be restrained from kicking it in. The speech continued in the background. Hesseman asked Goodrow to turn off the TV, which Goodrow did. Bonerz, however, continued to speak, saying, 'You can't turn me off—I'm you.'

"Bonerz's instructions were to continue this LBJ mantra throughout the scene. Howard now spoke to the audience.

" 'The man made me crazy. I found that I was consumed with hate for him. I've spent most of my consciousness in the last five years trying to get rid of hate, trying to embrace love as a motive force, trying to make hatred and the desire to kill not a part of my being. When I watched Lyndon Johnson I discovered that I had been completely unsuccessful and that all that rage and all that desire to kill was brought out by him. And you know something—IT FELT GOOD!

" 'It felt good to have someone as hateful as LBJ to hate. And I know that everyone here in the audience also hates him. We've all experienced hate for him and you may not have admitted it as I have and some of you may have admitted it but you all hate this motherfucker.' "

Hesseman's instructions were to get the audience to express their hate in the most extended way they could. The rest of the cast lined up behind Hesseman and began to chant in unison, "It's fun to hate, it's fun to hate," and Hesseman began to exhort the audience to hate Lyndon Johnson, adding, "If we hate him enough we might be able to kill the son of a bitch."

People were either laughing or screaming back at the stage, "Don't make me do this, I don't want to do this," but Hesseman was brilliant at relating one to one with an audience, and they began to chant, dance, scream, pound tables. The sense of hatred was so powerful the walls seemed to be moving in and out. Bonerz was still chanting his LBJ mantra, "You can't turn me off—I'm you," and the cast was still going in unison, "It's fun to hate, it's fun to hate."

Myerson had a sense that the audience "saw a cliff coming and were going to put on the brakes." He gave a prearranged signal and everything except the Bonerz mantra stopped dead. Hesseman went down again one on one with the audience and said: " 'There. Didn't that feel good? But obviously hate doesn't work. You can't kill anyone that way. But maybe, just maybe if we try hard enough we can love the bastard to death.'

"The company had been instructed to express love for one another however they actually experienced it. [For instance, Mimi Fariña and Hesseman were going together at the time, so they could express physical love but no one else could express it in the same way.] The audience picked up on the idea and began expressing a vast range of love for one another. Within thirty seconds the whole thing had been turned around and the theater went from a cataclysm of hate to one of love. People were sighing, swooning, laughing hysterically, kissing, making out, chanting—a vast orgy of joyous feeling.

"It was even more incredible than the hate. People seemed to be literally collectively coming. The roof was lifting off."

At this point Myerson gave a second signal and the lights went out. This time everything stopped, including Bonerz's mantra. It was like being hit by a bucket of ice water. In the dark Mimi's high piercing voice screamed one word: "VIETNAM!"

According to Myerson, the audience wouldn't leave the theater. No one seemed to quite know what had happened. But whatever it was they wanted to remain a part of it. Even though they eventually left, their experience kept them talking, wondering deep into the night. Similarly, with the cast. No one went to bed that night. The piece was never repeated—in part perhaps because it called for what Myerson identifies as "so insistent and determined a vulnerability on the part of the performers." And though the show went on, and the L.A. cast was soon in place four hundred miles to the south, it was somehow the final assault on that villainous fourth wall that kept them from total involvement—the logical extension of what they stood for.

And of course it worked. Just three short months later Johnson quit.

Death by Committee

People have a need to hear the truth
—but not so much and not so often.
—ROB REINER

The cancellation of "The Smothers Brothers Comedy Hour" by CBS occurred on the first Good Friday of the first Nixon administration.

The show probably made a more lasting impact in death than it would have in gradual decline and decay. Tom Smothers says, "We became bigger celebrities by being fired than by being kept on."

The cancellation was regarded as a spineless capitulation to the forces of paranoia in the new Congress. The furor it caused was remarkable. However successful the brothers were, in the end theirs was a television variety series. Intoxicating then, to be the darlings of such hoary thunderers as the New York *Times*'s editors, who on Easter Monday, 1969—dewlaps purple with indignation—declared the Smothers to be "expendable lambs sacrificed on the altar of Congress to save the golden calf." Phew.

The lambs, Tom and Dick, were sired in 1937 and 1938, respectively, by West Point graduate Thomas Bowen Smothers. Their first years were spent in the Philippines as Army brats until the outbreak of war, when they were evacuated while their father remained to fight the Japanese. He subsequently died in a POW camp.

Their mother remarried and settled in California where the lambs gamboled and grew to sheephood in the lush meadows of Redondo Beach and San Jose State College. Quintessential children of Ike, they seemed unmarked by their military provenance and their father's ugly death. According to Tom, they were first galvanized into political skepticism by the U-2 incident. The clumsy official handling of this episode and the institutional deception it revealed shocked Tom, made him aware for the first time that his country was not necessarily right all the time.

But if this skepticism existed and was fed by subsequent assassination, murder, and riot, it certainly didn't show up much in their early work. Their act—which might be characterized as folk-yok—was innocuous and undemanding. Dick was the smart kid, Tom the yo-yo (although offstage Tom was the brains while the younger Dick was very much the follower), and the guitar and bass fiddle they plunked more props than extensions of their musical talent. After a mandatory stint in low-paying low dives (the West Coast version: San Jose and San Francisco), they went east to "The Jack Paar Show" in 1961, hit the medium-big time, and became stalwarts of the college concert circuit.

For the first half of the decade the Smothers could be relied upon to provide a pleasant and funny evening whose gentle romps through Americana were no more threatening than the folksy ditties they jollied their way through. If they were exceptional, it was that in the trim, clean-cut Kennedy years they were even trimmer and cleaner-cut than most. To that vast majority of student bodies west of the Delaware and east of the Rockies—who had heard that there was something blowing in the wind but were nervous about booking it lest it turn out to be too scruffy or too Jewish—the Smothers Brothers were perfect, the first two thirds of the proverbially ordinary trio of Tom, Dick, and Harry. They were not alone in packaging the excitement of the folk scene of Middle America—groups like the Kingston Trio and the Limeliters worked on much the same principle, as did lesser lights like the Lettermen and the New Christy Minstrels. Unlike them, though, the brothers were also funny. Thus they cleaned up two ways. They were folksingers from some vaguely wicked coastal area *and* they were college-educated comedians who hung out with the likes of Newhart, Dick Gregory, and Shelley Berman and said cocky things about stuff in textbooks. It was not surprising that their calendar was so full or that they commanded top dollar (between five thousand and seventy-five hundred dollars a night).

Ken Fritz, who started out as the Smothers' road manager (later graduating to actual manager in partnership with Ken Kragen, of later Live-Aid fame) had ample opportunity to assess the brothers at all stages of their sixties career. He says that unlike some of their contemporaries in the satire game, the Smothers had an appeal that went far beyond the college-educated audience. Without being aggressively all-American, or resorting to bucktoothed rusticity, they were universally appealing. Down-home, suburban-style. (Fritz says that to costume his act he would take a hundred-dollar bill and go down to Carroll & Co in Beverly Hills, returning with two red blazers and thirty dollars' change.) And their problems were completely familiar and familial, "Mom always liked you best," stutter-splutters Tom, "you got a bicycle but I got a chicken."

Says Fritz: "They were big brothers to little people, contemporaries to teens, sons to the people who had sons, grandsons to the people who had grandsons." Their material was open to different interpretations by each level —naughty, conspiratorial, or delightful.

Wherever they went, Fritz recalls, there was almost always a mother, father, or both backstage with a photo of Smothers look-alikes—their own sons. These would be called things like the Other Brothers, or the Mother's Brothers, but they were always the same—two boys, one funny looking, the other stern and admonishing.

None of which was lost on CBS. In 1965 it gave the Smothers their first series, a sitcom of the then-popular "Magic Show" type which had come into being after the success of "Bewitched" and "I Dream of Jeannie." The brothers' version was a creepy comedy in which Tom drowned at sea and returned from the dead as an angel to play tricks on his square brother.

After a strong showing to start with, bad scripts and the frustration of not being their own masters caused the series to slip—and happily perhaps—fall to its death. For a while the Smothers returned to touring, but although they now enjoyed far greater recognition thanks to the series, things were changing in the concert scene, as rock and pop groups began to dominate. One thing did happen while on the road, however, which Tom remembers as being his next step down the yellow brick road of political awareness.

At a concert in Elkhart, Indiana, there was a dispute over the gate receipts with the local promoter and the cops were called. In the ensuing scuffle, Tom was arrested and got his head split open by a cop. What made this an eye-opener (or eye-closer depending on which end of the nightstick you were on) besides the violence of the attack was the fact that all their money was stolen. "What really turned my head around," says Tom, "was . . . in jail. Someone said [of the cop who'd hit him], 'You're lucky you aren't dead.' These were new, dangerous values. Whatever was happening out in Indiana was happening all over, and it looked bad. "About this time in 1965," continues Smothers, "I became aware that I as an artist could make statements."

For reasons of its own and with little inkling of what it would be getting, CBS gave him the materials. The 9 to 10 P.M. slot after "The Ed Sullivan Show" had always been a black hole for the network. The motherless brothers of the Ponderosa had ruled the roost for so long on NBC that they seemed as much a part of America's Sunday evening as ice cream or Ed himself. Whatever or whoever CBS threw into the hole—Judy Garland, Perry Mason, "The Real McCoys"—disappeared without a trace. The most recent sinker had been old-line talk show host Garry Moore. Perhaps with the rationale that where mature age hadn't worked, retarded youth might, CBS handed the slot in mid-season (February 1967) to Tom and Dick. To everyone's amazement the bouncy off-center show was a smash. Before they knew what hit them, the Cartwrights were reeling beneath the onslaught of two skinny folksingers who couldn't even ride or spit (although they did have a mother). By the end of the season a few months later, the brothers had secured the slot and CBS, hindsighting like mad, was solemnly congratulating itself as the first network to hold a youth audience in prime time.

That audience of course was not entirely composed of youth—or the "under twenty-five" crowd. Any prime-time audience, especially on Sunday, would have to appeal to other age groups to get ratings the Smothers commanded. That was why the shorn, shaved, and shiny image the brothers presented to the world was of such value to the network. As Murray Kempton commented later, they could not have done what they did "if they had not originally been so appealing to nice old ladies." What this really meant was that the brothers managed to appeal to, or at least not alienate, the moms and dads of the under-twenty-fives.

These good folks, the backbone of any decent rating, had already been thoroughly alarmed by the noisy, unkempt people they saw burning flags and displaying their dental work in close-up, and while they might suspect that in some way the Smothers were connected to such animals, those cheerful dopey faces topped with a mere fuzz of hair, and the cheerful dopey banter of their sibling rivalry were a pleasant relief. They fit comfortably within norms of behavior, taste, and background established a decade or more before. Nothing about the brothers' appearance, performance, or relationship conveyed any disturbing subliminal messages. Their fanatically neat collars and ties were code for a certain set of opinions. Their nutty fraternal bickering was shorthand for shared assumptions about family and the social fabric.

But nonetheless the brothers managed to command instant and intense loyalty from the notoriously fickle youth audience—that new swing vote in the democracy of entertainment. How did they do it? Partly by simply being the age they were and having their own show on the Sabbath when the sanctified airwaves were usually entrusted to old guys, like Ed or Red. But mostly they were tapping into new information spread by music, rumor, or just plain instinct. From the angle of the network, the brothers were unconventional but airworthy performers, reaching out to attract a new and dynamic segment of the audience. From the brothers' angle, on the contrary, they were the champions of that audience fighting for its right to be heard, for its fair share of the nation's attention. Any way that could be accomplished—frontally or by subterfuge—was allowable. The youth audience understood and agreed.

At the outset it was all wine and roses between the brothers and the network. They were lunch buddies with Zeuslike chairman William Paley and CBS president Dr. Frank Stanton who routinely helped Tom with minor production problems and expedited solutions for him through the network's internal bureaucracy. Such attention was unusual to say the least. They were knocking off an American television institution,—but under other circumstances with other performers it seems impossible that relations would have been quite so cozy. Paley and Stanton were at the very pinnacle of network power. Their preoccupation was with running the country, telling the President how he was doing, choosing the next president, and so on, not with some lowly variety show out of Los Angeles, which for the most part wasn't tremendously different in format, guests, or content than half a dozen others were.

But these men hadn't got where they were by ignoring the scents coming downwind. Tom and Dick, for all their fanatic fifties neatness, came from uncharted territory where they commanded untold forces. With amazing ease these striplings had unhorsed a rival supposedly so representative of everything good and fine about America that merely to challenge it had been futile —if not actually treasonous. No other show had come near to doing that. This phenomenon was more than just a ratings victory—it proved what they had been suspecting for some time—there was a new force in the field.

The new force was skittish and unreliable, but huge. It appeared to have its own system of communication—for its drums had got the word out fast—and on this outing at least it didn't seem to have much taste for traditional American values such as patriarchy, enormous wealth, and the judicious use of deadly force. Paley and Stanton clearly sensed that the emergence of these shadowy hordes was, as much as anything else, political.

Whether Tom came to the show with a political forum in mind or (what seems more likely) gradually became aware of both his opportunity and obligation to act as a spokesman for his contemporaries, two things can be stated with certainty. First, the brothers were ultrashowmen. Years of experience had taught them that there is no editorial license in one-to-one humor—the room gets cold fast if the audience thinks they're being preached to. Entertainment comes before all else. Second, however blue-eyed Paley and Stanton found these boys to be, they weren't about to get the run of the place. Tom and Dick might make Bobby Rydell look like a beatnik, but there was no telling what would happen at full moon. They might sprout facial hair or start eating their draft cards. So the brothers had been saddled with Saul Ilson and Ernie Chambers, two standard-issue producers, who could be relied upon to keep the network's interests (and where their next job was coming from) uppermost in their minds.*

Ilson and Chambers were amiable enough but their previous experience had been of the Red Skelton sort, and the writing staff they hired was heavy on the old-timers. The only members of it that fit the Smothers mold were Allan Blye, a major warning blip on the radar of an impending Canadian comedic invasion, and Mason Williams, a brilliant off-center folksinger and jack-of-all-arts from Abilene, Texas. This duo became known as the Kantor and the Kowboy. They were the only two windows in an unbroken wall of "experience" which surrounded the Smothers. This frustrated Tom, who wanted and been promised creative control, but somehow the mix worked because, as Fritz points out, no one knew the rules. It was everybody's first shot at network TV, and their very naïveté meant they didn't waste time second-guessing the authorities. The authorities booked the show with familiar faces that helped the brothers make the transition into major ratings getters. And for the moms and dads, the familiar faces, even if they were

---

* From the point of view of survival Ilson and Chambers knew what they were doing. When "The Comedy Hour" was finally canceled in 1969, its slot was taken over by "The Leslie Uggams Show." Guess who produced "The Leslie Uggams Show."

saying, singing, and doing things they'd never said, sung, or done before, were reassuring.

This formula worked wonders. The Smothers, instead of droning on about the generation gap, played with it. Seeing George Burns with Herman's Hermits or Kate Smith singing Sergeant Pepper as a Salvation Army number with Tom, let all the generation in on the joke.

In their very first show, the brothers gave an indication of what they were going to do with variety conventions. It was approved network dogma at the time that the premiere of a variety had to have a "walk-on" by a major star. This tedious device meant only that the star "happened" to be in the studio while the show was being taped and "happened" to walk on the set or into a sketch, to the creakily feigned surprise of the host.

Tom and Dick's version went like this: Tom explains the obligation to have a "walk-on" to Dick and with tremendous fuss introduces "someone really important to us both." A complete unknown called Pat Paulsen shambles on and is introduced to America as Arty Bowzer the guy who parks cars down at the Coconut Grove. Dick remonstrates with Tom, but Tom wants to introduce just one other person, please, just one. Okay, says Dick. Out comes Judy Henske in a moth-eaten fox stole as Tom's girl, "Natalie." That's it, says Dick, no more. This is dumb, very dumb. Tom tries hard to get the last person, but Dick is adamant. Tom goes over to the wings crestfallen and tells Danny Thomas his brother won't let him on the show.

It was gentle stuff, but by the standards of Sunday night variety, positively experimental. Nobody but his equals turned Danny Thomas away. Not only could these acceptably bad boys get away with it, but by doing so they smoothed the way for performers who would never otherwise have come near such a show—or been booked by it. Elaine May was a good example. Her hilarious sketch about movie censors in April 1967 was considered so tasteless by their compadres in television that it was lifted in toto from the final tape.

Everyone was somewhat surprised to find that the press picked up this piece of censorship with such gusto. (The New York *Times* printed a story detailing the offending sketch the next morning.) Not the least CBS, who was used to having such problems routinely taken care of behind closed doors. Not since TW3 had there been publicity about censorship on this scale. If some cynics pointed out that it did the show's ratings no harm to be involved in controversy, it irked the network that Tom proved so adept at milking the situation. He got better and better at it—and this turned out to be just the first firefight in a two-year guerrilla war that left him the Che Guevara of the American media jungle—and with about the same job prospects.

It should be noted before more is said about censorship that no one involved can have been a stranger to the Program Practices Department.†

† The Program Practices Department of CBS (Standards and Practices at NBC) is essentially a checkpoint on the content of what the network puts out on the air. In real life this means monitoring sex in drama, violence in children's shows, false claims in advertising, and just about anything in comedy.

Tom Smothers and Mason Williams insist that the censorship problems arose simply because they barreled ahead with what they wanted to do, not knowing the extent or nature of the limitations the network would put on them. This is hard to believe. The Smothers had been doing network television since 1961 and were as aware as anyone that comedians check their First Amendment rights at the door. They may have been two innocent kids just trying to have fun, but if so they very quickly lost their virginity.

Perhaps time has caused some confusion between Tom's onstage and offstage persona. Certainly CBS must have felt the same confusion back in 1967; Tom's two personalities were positively schizophrenic. Offstage, the lovable yo-yo you could tell off and push around became a shrewd, articulated, and opinionated fighter. And he had plenty on his mind.

The show left the air that summer rated with or just ahead of "Bonanza." When it came back in the fall of 1967, it had changed. The self-confidence of good and climbing ratings was combined with a determination to be the voices of the new generation. "We reflected the same consciousness that was occurring in the country at the time," claims Tom, and Fritz adds, "We were definitely headed for more confrontation." One reason was that the group had become exposed to Bobby Kennedy. They didn't limit themselves to the senator—they got to know the family and the Kennedy entourage as well. Fritz remembers breakfasts at Pierre Salinger's house in Beverly Hills, mostly easygoing stuff, hanging out, discussing issues, playing comedy albums. But Tom in particular was much taken with Kennedy's various stands on the issues of the war, the draft, and poverty. And the fact that an election campaign would begin in the middle of the upcoming season was lost on no one.

Tom wasted no time once the show was back in production. This was the beginning of their first full season (1967–68) and Tom was picking up speed. He pushed for and got a booking calculated to make any network see red.

Pete Seeger, pinkest of the pinkos, whitest of the doves, most blackly blacklisted, a singer so identified with pacifism that if war ceased to be, he, probably, would also, had not been allowed to broadcast in his native land for seventeen years. Not since 1950, the year CBS became the first television body to institute a loyalty oath, had that reedy voice been allowed to howl its subversive canon "All together now!" Tom was going to give him the chance. The times they were a-changin'.

But old Pete wasn't a-changin'. He was going to make just as much trouble as ever. He had a new song out called "Waist Deep in the Big Muddy," and it was ostensibly about an infantry platoon in World War II. Of course it hadn't anything to do with World War II. Here's the sixth stanza:

> Now every time I read the papers
> That old feelin comes on
> We're waist deep in the Big Muddy
> And the big fool says to push on

Not a lot of ambiguity there. As the *Times* subsequently—and tactfully— put it: "Some critics have interpreted the ballad of being critical of President Johnson's conduct of the Vietnam War." CBS hit the roof and lopped the sixth stanza out of the tape.

The significance of the episode—and there were several similar ones after it —is that it was very different from the week-to-week wrangling that went on over a sketch about drugs or race or the draft or lung cancer (the network still "accepted" cigarette advertising). Those involved the basic problem of being allowed to joke about the things the brothers and their audience had on their minds. It was simply a question of being allowed to communicate and therefore, at least from the brothers' view, get better ratings.

But there were different aspects to a controversy like the Seeger one. There must have been an element of planning involved on Tom's part. Seeger was not, after all, Dylan or even Buffy St. Marie or Tom Paxton. He was a grand old man of folk and respected wherever he went, but his ratings potential was nil. And only a tiny fraction of the brothers' audience would appreciate the significance of Seeger's return from blacklisting, let alone applaud it.

By contrast, the vast majority of people in the broadcast and print media appreciated only too well the significance of Seeger's appearance, and that he was likely to sing something controversial. Thus it was a no-win situation for the network. It could either (1) forbid the appearance (bad press), (2) cut the song (ditto), or (3) let it air (White House calls at three in the morning). For exactly the same reasons, it was a no-lose situation for Tom. Either he got his message across about the war—which was good—or he made the point that his network was pro-war which was almost as good.

Tom may not have had a master plan to subvert the network, perhaps only a conscious ongoing effort to push it as far as possible. With the constant baffle of Ilson and Chambers to contend with, such planning was not easy, and a deal of subterfuge was needed. This is one of the reasons why through- out the fall of 1967—the period of the show's greatest climb in the ratings—a subtle atmosphere of secrecy characterized the relationship between the per- formers and the audience. The laughter of the audience was increasingly knowing. They and the brothers knew what was being accomplished even if everyone else involved in the show didn't. It was Hip at its most traditional— and dangerous.

By January 1968, the Smothers were consistently in the Top 20 shows and often much higher. On a typical week, for example (January 8–14, 1968), they were twentieth with 23.9 rating. "Bonanza" the same week was twenty-sec- ond with a 23.3 rating.

Tom was always looking for ways around what he regarded as his staff's second-rate writing. It was time to tap into other sources. San Francisco had always been Tom's natural habitat, and it was equally natural that he would gravitate to the Committee. There was kinship with them. "Their social and political point of view was totally in keeping with mine," he says, "they were marvelous." For Fritz there was an opportunity to "get involved with that seminal vehicle, that free thought . . . they were our kind of people . . ."

Not even the most optimistic of producers could envision putting the Committee on Sunday night television—somehow ABC's "Wide World of War" just wouldn't play. But there had to be some way to suck up something from this rich well. Something that wouldn't be complete political anathema to the network, and yet would begin to swing the show a little further toward the new consciousness.

At the time, the show had been looking for a woman character and had been interested in Kathryn Ish. But she had left town for a brief time and was not available. Onstage at the Committee, however, Fritz and Tom found someone else, "a really cute little girl, a magic impish person," whose star turn was singing "Does God Live Near Daddy in Heaven?"

Her name was Leigh French, and she would one day be Alan Myerson's second wife. For the time being, however, she appeared in the audience of the Smothers' show in January 1968 as a flower-haired hippie to give a hilariously Martian lesson on gardening. Or something. Many people in the audience and at home thought she was for real, so lifelike was her performance. Thus Goldie O'Kief of "A Little Tea with Goldie" made the first of many bridges between San Francisco's cutting edge and that of television.

For months Goldie garbled on with impunity undergoing little or no censorship from Program Practices. She was the best-kept secret of all. Everyone under twenty-five knew what she was talking about, but no one in the network had a clue. It was weeks before anyone even figured out that her name was two names for marijuana. Every one of her routines was shot through with symbols and codes. Odd though it may seem now, such subterfuge was necessary—peace signs could start riots and V had to be for, well, vegetables.

According to Mason Williams, with whom she worked on many of her routines, the magic impish person of Fritz's description was as tough as nails when it came to commitment. She might be using the character of the zonked out flower child but her motives were conscious and specific. The environment and women's rights were but two. Goldie was the Smothers' show at its best: a genuinely funny character who drove points home without preaching. Here she is on a few random topics:

"A LITTLE TEA WITH GOLDIE"
("The Smothers Brothers Comedy Hour," February 25, 1968)

ANNOUNCER: (*Voice-over*) Share "A Little Tea with Goldie"—a program for you, the woman of today, a program designed to keep you above what's happening.

GOLDIE: Hiiii, ladies! To start the show off today, I'd like to show you all an item, for all of you who live in the city, an item that you will all soon be wearing . . . you can look forward to this . . . it's a gas mask!

So get ready, girls, *this* is the look of tomorrow.

But for those of you who just wouldn't be caught *dead* wearing one of these unsightly, old, gray gas masks, we have something very feminine and charming for you. *(Holds up gas mask decorated with flowers.)* Isn't this lovely? I love mine. Why, just think of all the money you're gonna save on cosmetics. We'll be right back with a little Kitchen Quickie right after this word from our sponsor.

ANNOUNCER: *(Under a "psychedelic" rendering of the word "love" we hear the following voice-over replete with echo.)* Love. L-O-V-E.

GOLDIE: Wow-ow! What a groovy sponsor we have! Isn't it nice to be brought to you by "love." Why not use it? You'll dig it. And of course, it's guaranteed.

Now, ladies, it's time for our little Kitchen Quickie. And you know, oh, this one was sent to us by Mrs. Elwood Roe, of Wiener, Arkansas. Far out! I was hitchhiking through there once. Mrs. Roe says, "I made a fantastic discovery last summer when my husband and I went on our vacation. He decided not to shave for four weeks . . . and so did I! Now my husband shaves twice a day."

You know, ladies, I think of you out there and I want to bring you something of interest to the shoppers, y'know? I think I've found the product for *you*, ladies. It's called Home Foam. It's an all-purpose foam for the home! It's far-out, too. I really love my can!

DAN ROWAN: *(Cut away to an insert of Rowan and Martin on the set of "Laugh-In." Rowan speaks confidentially to Martin.)* We couldn't ever say that on "Laugh-In."

GOLDIE: . . . you know, one of the nice things about it, it has no special ingredients. It's just plain old foam. You can do an infinite number of things, and more . . . and I can blow my mind with it half the time. You know, one of the far-out things, you can *paint* with it. Look at that. *(She draws a picture of the peace symbol on a three-foot piece of poster-board.)* Isn't that beautiful? I love it! And you know, you can decorate a whole room, in fact you can *fill* a room with it if you want to and then just get in there and *play!* So remember, ladies, the next time you and your husband have an argument, just put it all over each other, and you'll end up laughing and loving each other . . .

On January 25, 1968 (just a few days after the Committee's night of Love and Loathing), the New York *Times* carried a story on the Smothers' show under the head, "Smothers Brothers Winning a Long Battle with Censors." The gist of the piece was that after a year of battling with the Smothers, CBS had made some substantial concessions. The *Times* quoted Tom as saying that Mike Dann, the senior vice president in charge of programming, had met with them the previous week. "He told us we were in a pretty position, that the show was doing exceptionally well, and that controversial social satire was a fresh approach to TV humor. He told us to stand strong; we'll be with you as far as we can."

The *Times* added that Dann declined to comment. As well he might.

Whether or not he had been misquoted, the thrust of the article put some-thing of a gloss on what had become a Byzantine relationship. Not the least of the complicating factors was Tom's increasing adeptness at using the print media to embarrass their video colleagues. Within the same article he man-aged to protest a couple of routine clashes with the network over sexual innuendo (one of which—removing the designation of a men's shoe store as a "gentlemen's recreation parlor"—seemed to reflect more on the censor's sex-ual preferences than the brothers') and also to make an invidious comparison between NBC's standards vis-à-vis "Laugh-In" which had premiered three days earlier, and those of CBS. Tom: "I hear they're way ahead of us in what they can say. I think they'll make it easier for us, just as we made it easier for them."

Tom had ample evidence that his show was subject to a double standard when it came to program practices. For example, the brothers had tried to book Everett Dirksen, the diapason-bass senator from Illinois and Republican minority leader of the Senate, who for reasons of his own had begun a singing career. Although Dirksen was welcomed with open arms on other variety shows, CBS banned him from the Smothers' show on the grounds that his appearance in their company singing a Beatles' song would be "too political."

The arrival of "Laugh-In" gave Tom an instant means of checking whether NBC's standards were more relaxed than those of CBS and since on the face of it they were, another stick to beat his network with.

To its credit, the *Times* took such disputes seriously; where it could easily have dismissed them as bickering between inconsequential bystanders, it al-lotted them due space in the ongoing if implicit debate on censorship. This was after all, the time of the Tet offensive. Accurate information was a matter of life and death—specifically the lives and deaths of American soldiers. The murderous duplicity of the White House and its supposed subordinate Wil-liam Westmoreland would not be allowed on the record for well over a de-cade, but many in the news media suspected that such duplicity was going unchallenged. They regarded censorship in any form as the thin end of a wedge the war party would use to waste or jeopardize still more young lives.

The *Times* television correspondent, Jack Gould, in his review of "Laugh-In" on January 22, 1968, went as far as to herald the new audacity of the satirical community with, for him, audacious fanfare:

"Rowan and Martin, and the Smothers Brothers, could represent the deep-est TV change of the current season. The sacred cows of today's society no longer are immune to the irreverence of the newer school of comedians, and it will be important to see how far their influence and ingenuity may spread. In a recent syndicated radio program, Alan King, the comedian, suggested that one reason some viewers might be turning away from TV was its isolation from the realities of the surrounding world. The restless humorists ironically may be the instrument for gradually and subtly bringing TV into the main-stream of modern concern. And the Establishment may possibly have more to fear in the long run from the contagion of the laughter than from the more publicized stern protest."

Gould sensed something else about these two shows that was unconventional, if not actually without precedent: the affinity they felt for each other. Far from taking the conventional approach that a competitive show on a competitive network was a natural enemy, the brothers welcomed the newcomers with open arms. There was a sense of solidarity between the two shows. Both were unconventional in format. Both were openly satirical. And if there were significant differences between them, they were more alike than other comedy shows on their respective networks.

"Laugh-In" yanked open the door Tom and Dick had so laboriously wedged their foot in, and through it poured a flood of on- and off-camera talent that finally looked and sounded like 1968. With the exception of Arte Johnson, the performers were complete unknowns, their provenance random. If producer George Schlatter followed any rule in picking his writers and performers, it seemed to be that they delivered, rather than they had a great track record. Even Rowan and Martin were unfamiliar—being far better known to Vegas low-rollers than to the network audience. Similarly his prodigious and constantly changing staff of writers came from all over, significant among them being a large Canadian element, which included luminaries like "Hee Haw" producers-to-be Frank Peppiat and John Aylesworth and a young man who seven years later would take a giant step, Lorne Michaels.

For all its glitter and energy, though, "Laugh-In" was doomed to be inconsequential. However pointed its intentions and in the welter of material there were many indications of such intentions—the very elements that gave it its appeal meant that nothing would stick.

Most of the "scenes" in "Laugh-In" were ten seconds or shorter; many flash-cuts or reaction shots were a fraction of that; as a consequence, the show was anchored to the verbal. Jokes—good or bad—were the basic unit of its humor. The better these were, the more interchangeable they became—they had nothing to do with the character who spoke them. The characters were necessarily two-dimensional, limited to a catchphrase or repetitive action, and although great fun, they hardly conveyed much of a message. (By far the most popular character on the show was Arte Johnson's Nazi—a character straight out of that most grotesque of network reactions to the war, "Hogan's Heroes.") These factors combined to cause the show's most obvious lack— any true sense of relationship. Great pains were taken to try and establish relationships, but prefacing a one-liner with "Hey, Judy . . ." or "You know what Goldie thinks . . ." hardly did the trick. The technical imperative of the show (which required performers to record a large number of catchphrases, reactions, one-liners, and so on alone to one camera) further impeded the process. The togetherness implied by the title's pun (Love-In/ Laugh-In) and which the show's sheer kinesis tried to create was illusory. The cast of "Laugh-In" was a group only in the sense that a battery of chickens is a group.

However talented these chickens were (which was immensely: if "Laugh-In" did nothing else, it launched two of the greatest comediennes of our time in Lily Tomlin and Goldie Hawn), the battery they were kept in more or less guaranteed they would be harmless.

While superficially similar, "Laugh-In" and "The Smothers Brothers Comedy Hour" represented their time in profoundly different ways. Schlatter presented the new generation as a collection of lovable kooks who expressed their freedom in a variety of weird ways, betting their bippies, socking it to you, hollering, "Boring!" or wielding killer purses, but who beneath the anarchy were just a harmless bunch of young folks out for a good time. The Smothers presented themselves—and their most important sidekick Paulsen—as apparently harmless young folks apparently out just for a good time but beneath whose normal exterior lay some very weird ideas. If not outright dangerous convictions.

By defanging the new generation's impudence toward its elders and betters, Schlatter got all the goods and none of the grief. The climb of "Laugh-In" to number one in the ratings was phenomenal. But despite the closeness between the two shows and the tendency of reviewers to put them in the same bag, "Laugh-In" actually began to prepare the ground for the Smothers' subsequent interment. On the most basic level, just as "Saturday Night Live" would later do to the *Lampoon,* they robbed the Smothers of their uniqueness. "Laugh-In" complicated the brothers' toughest problem—censorship—enormously. For example, to a casual glance these two items might appear to be of equal satirical weight. (1) On its opening show "Laugh-In" had a joke that suggested that the bombing of the Central Highlands of Vietnam would stop once the Viet Cong reached the outskirts of Paris. (2) One of Tom's more celebrated lines concerning Vietnam was his response when Dick told him that the President was thinking of restricting foreign travel. Tom leaned into the camera and said, "Okay, you guys in Vietnam—come on home!"

The "Laugh-In" quip is a joke pure and simple—it says little about where its teller stands on the issue other than that he is cynical about the way the war is being conducted. Tom's attitude is transparently antiwar, and pro-draftee, yet at the same time disarmingly typical of his yo-yo character. Yet Gould quoted the "Laugh-In" joke in his review as evidence that the new show and its elder brothers were of one and the same temper.

The problem was the censor could always point to "Laugh-In" as evidence that a perfectly good joke could be made about the subject without hackles being raised. CBS West Coast chief Perry Lafferty had always complained that the brothers' better satirical forays "just weren't funny." So long as they were the only satirical show on TV that opinion could be challenged on the grounds of his personal taste in humor. Now, however, he had some good boys on the air to compare the bad ones to.

In the winter of 1968, however, things looked rosy for the Smothers. They were often in the ten top-rated shows, they were at the top of their form, they were presenting acts never seen before on television. On one level, dealing with censors was just plain accommodation by both sides—Tom remembers playing a regular game of Ping-Pong with one of the Program Practices men. Two out of three to Tom meant a disputed line stayed in, two out of three for the censor meant it got cut. Tom had also realized over the months that the censors felt the need to cut something, anything, from a Smothers script. He obliged by putting things in that they could remove. At other times glaring no-nos were inserted in the script as decoys to distract attention from stuff they really wanted in. And sometimes they just had a bit of fun. The most notorious occasion of this involved a young executive called John Kaye, who was installed in the second season by the network with some fanfare, supposedly to give the Smothers a more sympathetic ear in program practices but in reality, conjectures Ken Fritz, to get close to the core group and give the network early warning of whatever foul subversion the brothers were plotting. Says Fritz, "He wanted to be a double agent—the guy had 'spy' written all over him." The brothers decided to pull Kaye's string.

Williams inserted an item in the script with this exchange: "What do you think of her?" "I don't know but, she's 'rowing into Galveston.'" At the script read-through, the entire staff was instructed to giggle lasciviously when the (quite meaningless) phrase "rowing into Galveston" was read. They did. Although he obviously had no idea what it meant, so did Kaye. For the next two days Kaye went crazy trying to find out what ghastly Texan perversion "rowing into Galveston" referred to—without success. He tried to work it into conversation, tried to take people aside to explain it, but all he ever got was a burst of dirty laughter. Eventually he gave up; and on script change day the word came down—"rowing into Galveston" must be cut owing to its "clearly salacious intent."

But censorship was a serious question. To be sure, it did seem as though the Smothers' struggle was veering in their favor. In February '68, CBS relented on the Seeger song, and all six stanzas of "The Big Muddy" made it on to the airwaves. There is some difference of opinion as to whether this had something to do with the increasing number of rumors that President Johnson would not seek reelection. Fritz feels that it didn't, but he is a cautious man; and every step backward by LBJ was one forward for Bobby Kennedy. It can not have been lost on the network that the Smothers enjoyed a close relationship with the senator and his family. The likelihood RFK would seek the Democratic nomination was increasing all the time, in fact the show had a running joke called "the ring," into which various hats representing different candidates were thrown. Bobby was represented by a beanie with a propeller on top which jerked indecisively in and out of the ring. The Kennedy family, which was officially opposed to an RFK candidacy, was not amused by this byplay. Fritz recalls getting a call from Ethel Kennedy one Monday morning in which she said that the jokes at the expense of Bobby's indecisiveness the previous evening had reduced her to tears. (The senator himself, however, had been highly amused). Kennedy was in fact invited on the show but refused to appear in any political capacity—he did say that he would come on if he could do an antismoking spot.‡

(In case Senator Helms et al. see the Kennedy connection as further evidence of CBS's unfairness in media, it should be mentioned that "Laugh-In" evened the score. Paul Keyes, the head writer of "Laugh-In" was an old friend of Richard Nixon and a regular contributor to his speeches. There were no Nixon jokes on "Laugh-In" during the 1968 campaign and it did the Republican nominee no harm to appear on the nation's top-rated show intoning the prophetic question: "Sock it to ME?")

The Smothers' chief contribution to the election year was presidential candidate Pat Paulsen. Even this harmless and not altogether unprecedented put-on riled the network. Serious objections were raised by CBS regarding the question of whether other candidates would also have the right to free airtime. CBS may have simply been using this legality to frustrate Tom's ongoing campaign to bring intelligence to entertainment. The idea was not simply to get a few quick laughs out of running an absurd candidate, but to satirize all comers, taking positions on the issues, attack and defend and maneuver with the best. The candidate would even have a bona fide campaign manager (Tom hired ex-California governor Pat Brown's actual campaign manager, Don Bradley—a sarcastic choice for actor Paulsen in that Bradley had presided over Brown's massive defeat in 1966 by actor Ronald Reagan.)

Nineteen sixty-eight was already a politically tumultuous year. The Democrats, still the majority party, were caught between their conscience and their trigger finger. They were saddled with a war that was a fantasy fulfilled for the military and their bipartisan fans in labor and management, but a deadly nightmare for an equally bipartisan generation of young men and their families. The Republicans, with nothing to lose after their vast nose-wipe four years earlier, were busy sending seductive signals from their new stronghold in California that the certainties of the fifties would calm all the turmoil, if only greed, bigotry, and repression were once more thought of as natural phenomena. For a small but highly visible few, escape into the mind was an answer. For others, the answer lay in mad dreams of romanticized revolution. Possibility was everywhere, change was on everyone's lips. New pleasures proliferated along with pain and sudden death. There were stars in people's eyes and blood on the sidewalks.

Abnormalities abounded. In a normal year the President would run for reelection. This President made people shudder. In a normal year the other side would field a strong candidate looking to build a base for next time. Nixon was a two-time loser who everyone thought had slunk off to die wher-

‡ Antismoking skits were another of the Smothers' annoying little ways. At a time when cigarette companies still spent hundreds of millions of dollars in TV advertising, such material got CBS so nervous they had to light up. Example: Paulsen drags an enormous cigarette onstage, coughs, and explains that this new seven-month cigarette represents a major breakthrough. Inside are two midgets who inhale all the tar and nicotine before you do. Another big advantage —the box these cigarettes come in. You can use it as a septic tank or you can be buried in it.

ever sleaze deceases. Eugene McCarthy, that strange nebulous being who had somehow spirited himself through the chain-link fence around national politics, led a Children's Crusade to nowhere. Romney had his brain washed. Bobby—the old scaredy-cat—worried about having his blown out.

In such times it wasn't that crazy to run a lunatic for President. Especially a responsible one like Paulsen. (Paulsen incidentally was a conservative, and probably a Republican, who lived in Orange County, California.) Here's what Mason Williams, the chief hatcher of the plot, had in mind: "The thing we wanted to do was a satire that made people interested in the political process. The feeling . . . was that there were a lot of bright people who found politics boring and that would vote if it was more interesting. We wanted to create a campaign that both sides would want to be part of. We thought that humor was a unifying force. We used to talk about the fact that there were no songs that people sang together anymore. The thing we were looking for was a point of common knowledge."

Lofty sentiments. And probably in anyone else's mouth fatuous. But one of the disarming things about the Smothers group—and about Tom and Mason in particular—was their ability to convert such unpromisingly serious stuff into good solid laughs. The Paulsen campaign was the longest, strongest, and best written joke of the entire Smothers Brothers show.

The electorate went for the all-party candidate in the worst way. Bumper stickers, buttons, posters, and the inevitable book wouldn't stay on the shelves. The spectacle of this pie-faced loser crisscrossing the country for votes appealed enormously to all sections of put-upon, or put-down, or put-up-or-shut-up public. Paulsen socked it to everyone, while "Laugh-In" just talked about it. PAULSEN FOR PRESIDENT bumper stickers could be seen alongside CLEAN FOR GENE signs as well as those that urged drivers to LOVE IT OR LEAVE IT. The Paulsen for President ninety-seven-cents-a-plate dinner at the Ontra Cafeteria on Rodeo Drive attracted many of the biggest names in show biz who trampled one another to get their spaghetti and meatballs, individual pineapple upside-down cakes with MADE IN JAPAN American flags stuck in them—and of course their all-important souvenir urine sample glasses with the legend Pat Paulsen for President.

Interviewers could not crack Paulsen—and often became quite angry when he would not let them in on the joke but continued to insist that he was a true candidate for president. (Says Fritz, "I'm not sure that at some point Pat didn't actually believe he *was* running for President.") At one Kennedy benefit in Washington, a slew of celebrities were interviewed giving their opinions deadpan on the Paulsen candidacy. Last of all was RFK himself. Kennedy launched into a hilarious attack on Paulsen, accusing him of being divisive, self-indulgent, a carpetbagger, an amateur, exploitative, too liberal, too cynical, everything the media, his opponents, and his own party had accused the senator of. It was precisely what Paulsen's function had been intended to be.

Try as they might CBS could not control the Smothers' candidate. They tried to edit him, but Tom had him shift around a lot when he recorded a piece so that he not only looked shifty but in those days of primitive editing could not be clipped. The candidate appreciated these attempts to silence him or modify his message. As he said in one of his campaign statements, "Freedom of speech in no way guarantees freedom of hearing." The final blow came the night before the election. Hubert Humphrey's last-ditch appeal to the public ran opposite a Pat Paulsen for President special. Paulsen outdrew the unfortunate Democrat by a large margin.

As the Smothers Brothers' second season (actually their first full season) drew to a close, they were on top of the world. "Bonanza" was headed for the archives. CBS held Sunday evening from eight (with Mister Ed, the Talking Corpse) to eleven, when "Mission Impossible" sent America off to bed knowing that another bunch of dumb foreigners had been ingeniously outwitted.

Tom could pretty much write his own ticket. More and more frustrated by the confines of traditional variety, he needed control of his own show. In the democracy of television, the Smothers Brothers had won high office; they were astride the generations, with a record of fighting for what they believed in but not losing their sense of humor. Sure they made trouble, but at least their hair was neat. They might be freaks but they were our freaks.

But it was time to move on. There was competition on the air and change in it. People were learning from the Smothers. Not just on "Laugh-In" but elsewhere, producers and performers were beginning to experiment. As unlikely a place as Greg Garrison's "The Goldiggers" was using alternative comics like the Times Square Two, and Stanley Myron Handelman. Johnny Carson was pushing the censors all the time. On screens large and small breakthroughs were occurring. Slow motion, accelerated montage, split screen, improved sound were all processing information more dynamically for the viewer.

As part of their 1968 renewal deal with CBS, the Smothers were to produce their own show in the forthcoming season. Beside being given control over booking and staffing, they were to have discretionary power over scripts and all other creative elements. Also included was a then-standard provision entitling them to use their Sunday time slot during the summer to produce a replacement series. Tom decided to use this as a testing ground for his new powers as producer.

"The Summer Brothers Smothers Show" was a shrewd piece of work. Tom was determined to prove himself and turn out a tight, disciplined, state-of-the-art mainstream show. He suggested Glen Campbell as star of the new series. The network was delighted to accept.

Campbell was a finely tuned choice. He was an established singer, a respected musician, and as straight as Wonder Bread. His greatest hero was John Wayne. He was one of the first passengers on the pop bandwagon which was just beginning to trundle down the white line between rock and country. He was also smart. One thing he wasn't going to be, he said, was Son of Smothers.

That fit Tom's plans perfectly. The last thing he had in mind was hiring the

Smothers Show staff. The writing staff of "The Summer Brothers Smothers Show" was a roster of good things to come. The Committee expanded its presence with Rob Reiner and Carl Gottlieb. Steve Martin made his first appearance in the big time, John Hartford, Lorenzo Music, and others all made their network debut with Campbell. Only the Kantor and the Kowboy remained from the original Smothers show. The show was a resounding hit, laying the foundation for Campbell's subsequent stardom and the sparkling writing staff, for all its youth and inexperience, turned in an exemplary performance. Tom played by the rules, this time in the big league. (It wasn't all peaches and cream—Campbell would apologize at his concerts for being associated with "radicals" [applause]; and the writers routinely referred to him as "Joe Palooka.") From the network's point of view he was going into his all-new fall series with a solid vote of confidence.

But much happened that summer. Far too much.

On June 5, 1968, in Los Angeles, Bobby Kennedy was shot dead. Happily there seemed to be no organized effort behind his murder—just another of those good old lone gunmen with working firearms, no known means of support, an uncanny sense of time and place, and the convenient knack of getting caught quickly and without a struggle.

For Tom it was the time he lost his sense of humor. As he puts it, "I discovered later that I'd started acting like Jane Fonda." He had some reason —not for acting like Jane Fonda since she was still on *Barbarella* posters— but in feeling that things had become a trifle too serious. Along with many other people, Tom had the feeling that he might be next. The assassins, lone or organized, were the tip of some kind of iceberg. They were the ones who had completed their Mission Impossible whether for their own internal authorities or for some crazed weekend Caudillo. But who knew how many others were still on the job? They might have anyone in their sights—and Tom was certainly about as visible as any one. According to Mason Williams: "Tom used to come to me and say, 'There's something wrong with me . . . I don't feel funny anymore, I'm afraid.' He thought he was going to be next. People were leaving notes on his car . . . One was kinda funny. It read, 'We won't come to terms with worms.' "

There was more. The Democratic convention in Chicago, which was supposed to be a return to party normalcy where the party machinery, set in motion by the President, would nominate the party's natural heir, Hubert Humphrey, turned into a three-day riot.

But the riot was not a simple one in which the rioters rioted and the police put them down. Quite often the rioters rioted all by themselves and the police put down anyone they could find—including Democratic delegates. Sometimes this happened in the park, sometimes it happened in the convention hall. For everyone who wasn't in the park, at home, the hall, or somewhere else in Chicago, it was all happening on television. Cameras were everywhere. Cameras were not just covering the riots, they too were rioting. They were clouted by the police, they intruded where they didn't belong. And when cameras were where they were supposed to be—shooting the host of the convention Mayor Daley, he was screaming at them and waving them away as if *they* were the enemy.

One of the more extraordinary documents of the Chicago convention was a movie directed by Haskell Wexler called *Medium Cool*. The original inspiration for the movie was a novel dealing with the predicament of a television newsman who realizes that he is a professional voyeur. A kid is dying in a burning building—but his job is to report on it not to fetch buckets of water. Wexler's concept for *Medium Cool*—a sarcastic inversion of McLuhan's famous dictum—was to take this premise and place it in the context of a political convention. Without any advance knowledge of what might occur in Chicago he had selected the Democratic convention as his setting. His hope was that the irony of the voyeur newsman confronted with real issues of war and resistance would be bound to provide him with the raw footage of a documentary that was at the same time a compelling fiction.

For this he needed actors able to deal with the challenges of street encounters without a script—in short, improvisers. Along with costars Robert Forster and Verna Bloom, he chose Peter Bonerz of the Committee. Bonerz recalls:

"It's nine in the morning—we're supposed to go over to Grant Park where a demonstration is going to take place . . . and so I get my nice little movie suit on and here's Abbie Hoffman and all those people speaking . . . We were going to use that as a background for a love scene. We're walking up and I notice that we're walking past thousands of policemen and National Guards. We start to film the love scene and someone shimmies up the flagpole and burns the flag—which was happening all over the country at that point. The police saw this and they said, 'This is it—we're gone.' En masse thousands of police started pouring across this field with their truncheons out, throwing tear gas and beating people over the head. I don't mean that they were beating hippies over the head: these were schoolteachers and old people—and kids—and me! It was shocking. It provided some real interesting and dramatic footage for the movie but it was very shocking that in the course of my art I could be physically assaulted."

It would be hard to find quite so dramatic an apotheosis of the Committee's you-are-there style.

That of course was what Wexler wanted to explore. *Medium Cool* drives home the point again and again that however cool the medium might be it is *not* the message. Standing back from real events, real people, real pain, real moral issues is itself a moral issue. Turning yourself into a passionless, guiltless observer is not only probably impossible, it is a denial of your humanity. Forget why these people are here, why these events are unfolding and you will become lost in a maze of unreality.

After Chicago, everyone immediately forgot why the people were there. The issue became the media, whether it had done its job, whether it had been out of control, whether it had caused the violence, and so on. Retreating into this promising maze of unreality neatly avoided having to deal with the fundamental issue—the war. The kids were not in Chicago because they and their contemporaries were being expected to die in a war that had nothing to do with them or their country's vital interests—they were there to manipulate the media. The cops were not on the streets because Daley felt, with some justice, that if you wanted a vote at the Democratic convention, you joined the party and paid your dues—they were "sending a message to the nation." All everyone really wanted to do was to get on television.

The one indisputable conclusion the country drew from watching the events in Chicago was that the Democrats were in chaos, unable to control either their dissidents or their party-liners, and with no idea what to do about the war. Not true, rumbled many senior Democrats, among them the Senator John Pastore from Rhode Island, it must have been the media what done it. The time had come to talk—*regulation*. But not until after the election was won, of course.

For the Smothers group as for most draftable Americans, the message of Chicago was contained in the face of Mayor Daley screaming at the cameras. If they were looking for relief on the life-threatening issue of the war from the party of John and Robert Kennedy, they could forget it. They were as welcome in the Democratic party as they had been in Grant Park.

Says Fritz: "We came out of that summer ready to go, ready and loaded . . . we were going to give it back to him [Daley]." They were not fooled by the handwringing about the media's role in Chicago. The issue was still how to stop the killing.

If ever there was a bipartisan issue, regulating the media was it. No matter who ended up in the White House, come January it would be dealt with. The Republican nominee, after all, had little to thank the media for, even if he had come back for them to kick around. As *The Nation* commented wryly, "Nixon promises he'll end the war, but what does he plan to do about the Smothers Brothers?"

"The Smothers Brothers Comedy Hour," as the new series was called, had a lot going for it. Tom had held over the writing staff from the Glen Campbell success (Reiner, Steve Martin, Gottlieb, and so on) and a slew of new and hitherto unexposed talent had been lined up. Music would include the likes of Cream, Eric Clapton, the Doors, and the Who. The Beatles would contribute "Revolution" and themselves as walk-ons. New comedians like David Steinberg and David "LBJ" and "Nixon" Frye would finally reach a prime-time audience.

As would the Committee. According to Williams their appearances—they were on the show several times during this season—had a certain significance:

"The show had worked its way up to the point where it could be a forum for them . . . it was an evolution. Having them interested in it, and having the show able to accommodate them in prime time was a pretty good indication that we were going someplace."

The *Times* (Mr. Gould, natch) was pleased with the Smothers premiere but included a significant warning: "Tom and Dick Smothers began their third year of network television very quietly at 9:00 last night on the Columbia Broadcasting System. An introductory song offered reassurances of their concern over the war in Vietnam, racial discrimination, poverty, and censorship on TV. Harry Belafonte had one solo, which was not nearly enough.

"A satire of 'Bonanza,' their direct competition on the National Broadcasting Company, seemed primarily designed for the climax of having Roosevelt Grier, the Negro football star, play the long-missing Ma Cartwright who kisses his white daughter, played by Cass Elliott. The only trouble was that the sketch in the meantime dragged badly . . ."

Gould wasn't to know that a lot of the funnier lines had been cut from the "Bonanza" parody—Mama Cass playing Hoss, was called Hass in the sketch, hence there was a lot of stuff like, "Don't grab Hass," and "Don't be smart, Hass," which the censor felt would offend America.

What Gould also didn't know was that his thirst for more Belafonte could have been slaked, had it not been for the censor. The show had a lot going for it—and a lot going against it. As Fritz puts it: "CBS were getting themselves into battle position, they were getting ready for a long hard fall . . ."

Belafonte's "Don't Stop the Carnival," a bouncy calypso in his most typical vein, had been intercut with scenes of the rioting in Grant Park, Daley, beatings in hotel lobbies, the whole hideous carnival of the Democratic convention. By all accounts it was a professional piece of work, funny, sarcastic with no sides taken—right on the money for all segments of their audience, and the centerpiece of the opening show.

CBS cut it *in toto* and sold five minutes of the resulting gap to the Nixon for President Committee.

The battle lines were drawn. CBS, fearing the worst from Chicago and its interpreters in the Democratic party, was battening down the hatches. Whether Humphrey or Nixon became President, neither of them would look kindly on the Smothers Brothers. Hearings on regulation (either by the FCC or a self-imposed version through the NAB) looked like a certainty. When that happened no CBS executive wanted to be in a Senate hearing defending a montage of the Chicago follies. Things had gone too far. No matter how popular the Smothers might be, CBS was beginning to distance itself from one of its own most visible shows.

Increasingly too the Smothers Brothers and their staff found themselves the target of rank-and-file resistance. Performers, especially musicians, would complain about being hassled and heckled by the studio crew. There was the usual crap about not being able to tell the boys from the girls, but there was more virulent stuff from time to time: threats of physical violence, the kind of rhetoric that might be expected on the street from the Joes of the world, but not expected in a TV studio where everyone was "in the biz." Things eventually came to a head according to Williams during the taping of the Los Angeles company of *Hair,* a show produced by the Smothers. In the scene that had been selected for air where the draftee is given the American flag before he goes off to be inducted, the flag hit the ground several times during the taping. The cameramen on the show objected. The cast was multiracial and they sure had hair, and here they were desecrating the flag. The cameramen and crew walked off the set and retired to the CBS canteen.

Tom decided to go down and talk to them. He had no beef with his crew. In the canteen he confronted the cameramen, they were adamant. They were not going to shoot any show in which the American flag was defiled.

Tom was at the end of his rope. "Okay goddamnit!" he spluttered, yo-yo Tom getting mixed up with producer Tom. "Let's have it out right here. Who wants to wrestle?" Tempers were high. One of the cameramen locked horns with skinny old Tom and they fell to the floor. It was hilarious, Tom yelling away and wrestling a beefy technician. Within seconds everyone was beside himself with laughter. No one could remember or cared what the whole dumb dispute had been about. The champs were separated and everyone trooped back upstairs to get on with the job.

But there were irresistible forces building outside the studio Tom couldn't control with his goofy integrity, even outside the network whose respect for him was becoming so ambiguous. In November Richard Nixon defeated Humphrey by a narrow margin. The issues of war and peace, youth and age, freedom and responsibility, were now further complicated by a president who appreciated far better than LBJ just what good and evil could be accomplished by the miracle of television.

For all intents and purposes, Nixon's election, according to Tom, was the end of the road. He likes to think that the show could have stayed on the air for two more years if Humphrey had been elected, but no one else either now or at the time agrees. Senator Pastore had delivered on his rumblings and was calling industry executives into his subcommittee on communications (of the Senate Commerce Committee) to chat informally about sex and violence, specifically violence and specifically the kind that showed kids beating their heads savagely against innocent cops' nightsticks.

No one was fooled for a second about what the Democratic senator's job was. He was supposed to pay back the networks for having shown Chicago in all its glory and lost the election. That was okay and his subcommittee could do whatever it liked. What really worried the networks was Nixon.

The media knew how much he hated them, and the previous year had been sufficiently bizarre that almost any attack on the Bill of Rights would look reasonable in 1969.

The "Smothers Hour," compromised by the success of "Laugh-In," produced by a known radical rather than network trusties, and which insisted that the war was still an issue when everyone knew that Kissinger would take care of the gooks, looked like a good dump. CBS could please the dangerous new administration and avoid federal meddling in its internal policy.

According to Tom, there was another factor. Paley and Stanton both coveted the post of Ambassador to the Court of St. James. The only other candidate for this swinging job was Walter Annenberg, publisher of *TV Guide,* a

Neanderthal right-winger and true hater of the Smothers. One way or another, without losing their immortal souls, Paley and Stanton had to find a way to kill the brothers.

They did. Here is a chronology of how they did it:

March 10. Tom tapes a show with Joan Baez and Jackie Mason—who has a Broadway show starring himself. Joan wants to sing a song for her husband, David Harris, who is in a federal penitentiary. She insists on introducing her song, "The Green Grass of Home," with a tribute to David in which she says, "I'd like to sing a song for my husband, David, who is in jail in Texas for draft evasion and who is organizing the prisoners against the war."

CBS censors the intro. Tom lets the edit stand and it is made ready for air with Joan saying, "This is for my husband, David, who's in jail in Texas," . . . followed by a black hole and then the song.

CBS cancels the airing of the show.

March 25–27. The brothers are renewed over Tom's objections for 4.5 million dollars.

March 30. The Baez/Mason show is rescheduled for the air. With the cuts.

April 3. Tom delivers the April 13th show starring Nancy Wilson, David Steinberg, and Dan Rowan. In view of a previous problem with Steinberg's material, the network asks for an advance copy of his routine and wants it deleted in its entirety. Tom complies.

April 4. Robert Wood, president of CBS, cancels the Smothers show.

April 5. The New York *Times* decides to put news of the Smothers cancellation on its front page. " 'The Smothers Brothers Comedy Hour' has been canceled for next season by the Columbia Broadcasting System, bringing to a climax months of argument over the program's content.

"Robert D. Wood, President of the CBS Television Network, notified Tom and Dick Smothers that they had committed a breach of contract by having failed to submit tomorrow night's program in time for a screening by the network and its affiliated stations last Wednesday. Mr. Wood, who made the announcement last night, said a program seen November 10 would be substituted.

"In Hollywood, Tom Smothers denied CBS's charges and said that the program originally planned for tomorrow had been seen by network reviewers there on Wednesday.

"Mr. Wood said that the network had reason to believe the Smothers Brothers had planned to include in the program a monologue that would have been regarded as 'irreverent and offensive.' It would have been inappropriate, he indicated, even if this past week had not been marked by the funeral by General of the Army Dwight D. Eisenhower and Sunday were not Easter. The monologue, CBS said, was to have been delivered by David Steinberg, the comedian, and was described as, 'a sermonette' on Solomon and Jonah. The text was not available.

"In disputing CBS's contention, Tom Smothers said that Mr. Steinberg's monologue had been voluntarily deleted in advance and that he and his brother had no knowledge that their show would be scheduled after General Eisenhower's funeral on Easter Sunday.

"The program, he said, complied completely with all legal obligations and the CBS protest was just a pretext to 'get us off the air.' "

And that really was just about it. A tremendous amount of print was expended on the various issues involved but when it ultimately came down to issues it was the show that counted. The loyal Mr. Gould found little to object to, and he called the censorship spade a spade:

"If the show still happens to be the thing in television, the Columbia Broadcasting Systems' cancellation of Sunday night's 'Smothers Brothers Comedy Hour' was a silly and suspect move. The program chanced to be one of the best that the Smothers Brothers have offered all season, imaginatively topical, and genuinely amusing, and the 'Sermonette' challenged by the network was not worth all the managerial jitters.

"David Steinberg, the satirist, has done variations on his 'Sermonette' on other TV stations, and why CBS should have been aroused by his version of Solomon and Jonah is difficult to understand.

"In Steinberg's monologue, Jonah was said to have sailed on a ship 'that was commandeered by twenty-three Gentiles' and that the Gentiles, as is their occasional wont, threw a Jew overboard and Jonah was swallowed by a 'giant guppy.'

"In their argument over what the fish really was, Mr. Steinberg said, 'The New Testament scholars literally grab the Jews by the Old Testament . . .'

"In a serious vein Mr. Smothers asked for remembrance of the anniversary of the assassination of the Rev. Doctor Martin Luther King, Jr., an occasion, incidentally, that no commercial network thought worthy of a special . . .

"All in all, the Smothers show was a contemporary variety of modern style and taste to which there could not be the slightest objection. The real reason for the break is the Smothers Brothers teased on content matter and CBS got fed up, only to invite the conclusion that the way to foil Senator Pastore was to go him one better in censorship . . ."

The slow strangulation of Tom continued throughout the spring and summer. Print would give him all the space he wanted and he used it, passionately arguing his cause, replaying the issues of censorship over and over again. In the end he was a victim not just of a paranoid executive within CBS, but of the new order. The first Californian President had come to office, and the name of the new game was form not content, how rather than what, doers over believers. Advertising men were in the Oval Office, carving reality up into ten second spots. Nixon had always been amoral. Once in power he would bomb Cambodia and sit down with the Chinese. None of it made any difference so long as it played, so long as it could be sold. Even LBJ had not been that cynical. The Kennedy era was over for good. Passion, commitment, and the hypocrisy that could be satirized because it was a departure from them, all became overnight white elephants. The censors had won.

Here's Mason Williams:

The Censor sits
Somewhere between
The scenes to be seen
And the television sets
With his scissor purpose poised
Watching the human stuff
That will sizzle through
The magic wires
And light up
Like welding shops
The ho-hum rooms of America
And with a kindergarten
Arts and crafts concept
Of moral responsibility
Snips out
The rough talk
The unpopular opinion
Or anything with teeth
And renders
A pattern of ideas
Full of holes
A doily
For your mind.

P.S. Walter Annenberg became ambassador to the Court of St. James.

9

I Left My Art in San Francisco
The Committee Breaks Up

There was a sad epilogue to the downfall of the Smothers Brothers—that of the Committee.

In 1968 during a visit to London, Tom Smothers had caught a perennial British hit of the BBC called "Top of the Pops." This show, in some ways an advanced derivative of "Your Hit Parade," presented top songs of the week, good, bad, or abysmal, but often in an adventurous way, using considerable technical expertise with camera, lighting, and effects.

The format and tone appealed to the Smothers' group's desire to expand its operations and experiment with new forms of television. Throughout the 1968–69 season they developed a series concept based on the core of "Top of the Pops" but with some very important additions of their own.

The show would combine the very best of rock shot "in concert" (with real fans rather than a studio audience) with satirical comedy performed by a resident group as continuity. Both elements would be top of the line: the music, the biggest and the best groups—the kind the Smothers were introducing to prime time in their last season—Cream, the Doors, Janis Joplin, and so on. The resident group linking the various music items would be the Committee. The show was entitled "Music Scene" and a pilot was shot.

When the Smothers Brothers were canceled, Kragen and Fritz decided to call it a day and go their separate ways; Kragen to the hard rocky road of management which would one day make him the Peter Uberroth of major-league charity; Fritz to more television production, including the hot little rock and comedy format that ABC had bought on the strength of the pilot. The Committee's formidable network of rock contacts was tapped in the early summer of 1969, to line up the megagroups. The San Francisco connection meant a lot more than just cutting-edge comedy. The Committee could get to groups Hollywood could only dream about. (It didn't hurt that Carl Gottlieb and Howard Hesseman had been DJs on Donahue's ground-breaking FM radio show.) Groups who wouldn't even take calls about appearing on television would go on for the Committee. And they did.

The roster lined up for "Music Scene" included names from both sides of the Atlantic that would have caused the average rock promoter to gaze up at the night sky in Malibu and start gently massaging his crotch. The Beatles. The Stones. Crosby, Stills, and Nash. Janis Joplin. Hendrix. Anyone managed by Albert Grossman—possibly even Dylan—whose relationship with the Committee went back to its opening night in 1963.

"Music Scene" was set to be a breakthrough show. And since all the comedy was the Committee's and a lot of the music would be thanks to them, the show was in a very real sense theirs.

Hardly surprising then, that when the terms of the deal came to be finalized, and ABC announced that it would retain final authority over the casting, choose who from their extended family would become the "Music Scene" regulars, the Committee collectively froze.

Gottlieb says: "ABC wanted a rep company of actors—like the "Laugh-In" "zanies"—the conventional wisdom of the time being that people tuned in television to see familiar faces doing familiar things. (A philosophy that has persisted down to this time.) The Committee on artistic grounds insisted that the Committee was a collective entity and that they would say who was going to be on the show.

"Well, on that rock the deal foundered. ABC would not do a show on which they didn't know who the regulars were; and the Committee would not do a show in which they couldn't control who would perform Committee material."

Says Myerson: "They [ABC and Fritz] had verbally committed to this principle: that out of our performing company of about twenty-five people, we would name who would perform on the show from week to week. Literally the day we went over to sign the contract, [ABC] reneged."

"ABC insisted they were very clear that for them the issue was they needed the authority to be able to create stars. And that whatever our principle of equity or democracy was, it got in their way."

There could scarcely have been more of a classic standoff. It was star-think versus group-think, entrepreneurial comedy versus collective comedy, overground versus underground, predictability versus improvisation, entertainment versus satire, live theater versus television, even in a broad sense Los Angeles versus San Francisco. Fritz's credentials as one of the stand-up-and-be-counted Smothers team were unassailable, as were Myerson's and the Committee's in their sphere, but in the crunch they had diametrically opposed creative philosophies.

The stakes were high, or certainly perceived to be. Given the music the show could command, and the size and resources of the Committee in terms of material, experience, and performers, the potential was considerable.

Nonetheless, in the confrontational atmosphere of mid-1969 it was unlikely that a conflict of this kind would be resolved through compromise, and it wasn't. Even as Hesseman, Hankin et al. were in London, filming promo spots for "Music Scene" with the Beatles, the Stones, and others, the Committee pulled out.

Myerson says: "It was a very painful internal event. Once the deal fell apart, the producers began to woo individual members of the group. The performing repertory company for 'Music Scene' was not going to be called the Committee, but initially it was going to include *all* Committee members.

"There was a lot of very harsh rhetoric tossed around, and hurt feelings; Larry [Hankin], Chris [Ross, the Egg], and Carl [Gottlieb] opted to join the 'Music Scene' and to leave the Committee.

"It was a different kind of leave-taking than any previous one had been. The Committee had personally and through consensus all agreed that we were going to stay together. Some who were also very ambitious, Howard [Hesseman] for example, were very torn. Howard elected to remain with the Committee and was very bitter about what he regarded as a betrayal."

According to Hesseman: "It is true [that a lot of the acts lined up as the result of the Committee's involvement backed off]. From Albert Grossman's office, I recall receiving a pledge of support in terms of a boycott action. And I remember calling the Rolling Stones office in London, and talking with them . . . and also talking with Derek [Taylor of Apple]."

The Committee's wrath when aroused was clearly not to be underestimated; Gottlieb discovered this in another way and dealt with it in his own fashion.

Gottlieb says: "The rest of the company was bitter. We had split, we had divided the ranks, we were aesthetic scabs. There was a lot of bad feeling. I don't know why I did it, but such was my loyalty to the collective—I remember flying to San Francisco to a meeting of the entire Committee. It turned out to be a purge trial in which we [Gottlieb and Chris Ross] were confronted with the accusations of many angry people. I was severely criticized for my defection, at which time I reminded them of the meeting in 1963 [re: the Committee Commercial Company] when the stage manager was not included in the share of the proceeds."

As Myerson notes, there had been leave-takings of all kinds before, but the departures here were qualitatively different. Not only was the disruption forcing people to take sides, but the resultant suspicion and destruction of the trust that obtained in such a company demonstrated to even the most loyal and unswerving members that in a crunch the collective will could not enforce solidarity. This breach marked the beginning of the end. One by one senior members began to move on, especially those in Los Angeles. By 1970 Myerson himself had taken an extended leave of absence to direct a movie for Jane Fonda and Donald Sutherland called *Steelyard Blues.* Bonerz and others began to disappear into the various thickets of television, movies, and the theater. Back in San Francisco (the L.A. company closed in 1970) the group continued, but on a downhill slope, and in 1973, as Gottlieb puts it, "collapsed in a fog of dope, junk, and lesser performances."

And what of the scarlet woman who caused all this commotion, "Music Scene"? The show was not even a moderate success. The producers did not persuade any other Committee members to defect, but the cast which was eventually assembled was remarkable: Hankin, Ross, comedian David Steinberg and a young comedienne, Lily Tomlin. The writing staff consisted of Gottlieb as head writer, Tom Whedon, and Richard Schaal. The show began under a shadow, and the backout of several major groups, especially the British ones, was a major blow. There was a further internal problem, at least for Gottlieb—Fritz's coproducer and the show's director, Stan Harris. Says Gottleib: "Stan had a hearing aid and didn't like pop music. We were anti everything he understood. He had directed the first couple of years of "The Smothers Brothers Show"—and the Smothers disliked him so much they paid him off for the entire second season."*

It was old-line television coming up against the cutting edge. The cutting edge broke first. Although the show had some memorable moments like Crosby, Stills, and Nash ambling into the ABC studios in Silverlake and raving to the company about this great rock festival they'd just come in from in a little upstate New York place called Woodstock, it was a creative disaster. Matters were not helped by the fact that ABC decreed the show should run an unprecedented forty-five minutes (from seven-thirty to eight-fifteen on Monday night) and was opposite a half hour of "Gunsmoke" and a quarter hour of "Laugh-In." After a heavily front-loaded premiere in which almost every major group that had not pulled out appeared (advertising promised the Beatles; what the viewers actually got was a video of John and Yoko in a Rolls while a tape of "Revolution" played), the show lost all form and most of the remaining major rock bookings. By the fourth or fifth show, it had become essentially a version of "Your Hit Parade." Incredibly, in light of what they'd sacrificed, Hankin and Ross were dumped after the second show. Tomlin held out for one more, was snapped up by "Laugh-In", and rode off into history. By the fifth show, the only surviving cast member—now the star of the show—was Steinberg. A little later, ABC applied euthanasia.

The only significance of this little bomb was the extraordinary destruction it wrought on the Committee. For the Committee men who had opted for the star machine, it was especially agonizing. They weren't stars and they couldn't go home. For Hankin and Gottlieb this was a temporary setback—both had hacked things before on their own. Hankin had even had a large movie role already in *Viva Max* with Peter Ustinov, and Gottlieb was plan-

---

* According to Gottlieb, Harris has an entire well-appointed room in his house, which he built on the proceeds from this buy-out, called "The Tom Smothers Library."

ning to get married. For the much younger and more fragile Ross, however, things were very different.

Gottlieb says: "Up until that time, [Ross] had lived in the big house on Queen's Road [a huge old Hollywood mansion on Sunset Strip which the Los Angeles Company shared], and in San Francisco he had lived in the Committee compound in Osgood Alley. He always lived in a communal situation. It was a comedy collective. We lived together more than most of the other companies did, certainly more than Second City.

"Chris felt doubly strange. He had gotten fired from 'Music Scene.' The Committee wasn't going to take him right back anyway. He was a hot young actor, with a lot of talent, and a lot of promise, and it was not working."

Ross stayed with Gottlieb and his future wife for a while in their house in Hollywood. It was essentially as communal as any other Committee dwelling, but when they decided to marry, Ross took an apartment by himself. When he removed himself from the nurturing group spirit, there was no one to tell him to stop it.

"It" was drugs.

Says Gottlieb: "He was chippying [occasional heroin]. He'd go to the Troubadour and score. He was also doing reds. He'd get a little loaded and watch television till morning."

By the middle of May, Ross had found a more stabilizing situation with a brilliant group called the Credibility Gap, which did a daily, mostly improvised local radio show. One morning in May he didn't show up at the radio station. Gottlieb says: "They called us and asked if he was there and we said no, he's at his new apartment. We wondered if he was okay; it wasn't like him not to call in. So we went over, and we saw his car in the garage. We knocked on the door and there was no answer, so we went around the side—it was a little bungalow court apartment, little one-room stucco bungalows, and I looked in the window and I saw him on the floor. I kicked the door down and there he was."

Something had gone wrong with Ross's usual cocktail of a few drinks, a little chippying, and a couple of reds; perhaps, Gottlieb conjectured, the smack had been too pure or he'd miscalculated, or something else wasn't quite in its normal proportions. There was no point in trying to revive him.

The Egg was dead.

PART TWO

FUSION

10

1970—Threat or Menace?

The height of the sixties, 1970, went out with a bang. Especially if you were Cambodian or enrolled at Kent State. Grown men wept at the demise of the Beatles and for that time, once, when there was a way back homeward. In Chicago, a mean old man named Judge Hoffman presided over the trial of eight young hotheads, including another Hoffman, Abbie, to whom he was doubtless, way back in the old country, related. To ensure a fair verdict, His Honor ordered the black member of this rabble bound, gagged, and shackled whenever he was in court. The good burghers of Los Angeles thrilled to the daytime "Chiller Theater" of the Manson trial and searched the oleanders by night for other pairs of burning, drug-crazed eyes. The hot rumor of the spring in Southern California was that the Manson gang had shot a home movie down on the beach at Trancas (or Zuma) in which a brown- (or red-) haired hippie girl was decapitated right on-camera. Those spirits of the surf, the Beach Boys, Governor Reagan's wife's favorite group, were somehow implicated. And at Altamont, the Stones' answer to Woodstock, beer-sodden hogs stabbed a man to death at Jagger's feet.

Both sides—all sides—suspected connections in these events. Conspiracy was in the air. And yet cooler heads among the hot were beginning to realize that freedom involved death as well as love, that releasing passions meant releasing the good and the bad, that violence could not always be blamed on external force or conspiracy, that it was perhaps just as intrinsic to human nature as joy.

Whatever the sixties were by 1970, they were growing up fast. It was about time. Resistance and dissent were now so widespread as to be uncontainable. From Leonard Cohen to Leonard Bernstein, from Justice Douglas to Daniel

Ellsberg, the magic spores of doubt were spreading day and night. Far beyond humble beginnings as an ad hoc revolt against the draft, dissent was now challenging the most fundamental assumptions of the Great Deal and the Big Catch—not to mention the Box.

New questions were being asked that quite literally had never been heard before. The environmental movement, far from being a rear-guard action on behalf of a few endangered species, started from the posit that economic and industrial growth could not disassociate itself from the ecology on which it depended. The idea of unlimited growth had to founder on the hard facts of what the planet could sustain, or the environment would change in ways that would modify, if not eradicate, the benefits of economic growth. Wealth could not thus be "created." Nature would one day present the bill for unlimited prosperity in the form of uninhabitable habitats, cancer, radiation, drastic climate change, or desertification—unless a healthy shot of agnosticism was administered to the theology of technological miracles, and technological saints.

Such ideas were unrecognizable to the managers of the plant—they simply went too deep. Nor were they, for all the wishful paranoia of the managers, Communist-inspired, for they challenged the whole underpinning of the Industrial Revolution and therefore Marxism as well as capitalism. Indeed, in one sense this thrust was profoundly conservative—insisting that technology had to be reassessed, controlled, and braked before it crushed its own creators.

The trouble was that these questions were so new and so far-reaching that even those who understood their significance often had as much difficulty grasping the proposed solutions as those who didn't. The net result throughout many areas of cultural life was a combination—peculiar to the time—of brilliant insight and extraordinary naïveté.

Perhaps the best published example of this odd mix was an enormously popular 1970 bestseller, *The Greening of America* (how the youth revolution is trying to make America livable) by Charles Reich (New York: Random House, 1970). Reich, a law professor at Yale and former clerk to Justice Hugo Black, was one of the more brilliant legal scholars of the day and possessed a brain as big as the Ritz. *The Greening* comprised a devastating analysis of the nature of the modern industrial state, based on a fusion of both anticonservative and antiliberal thinking. Reich identified traditional laissez-faire as Consciousness 1 and New Deal managerial technocracy as Consciousness 2. His discussion of the character of what he called the Corporate State, its radical modification of personal liberty, the "consciousness management" by which it imposed and sustained its will, and the consequent effects on the ontology of the individual was incisive, scholarly, frigidly clear, and deeply compelling. His conclusion was that Consciousness 1 and 2, parents of the Corporate State, could be superceded by Consciousness 3, an incredibly vague mush of adolescent mysticism, muggy self-indulgence, and wishful political thinking that he seemed to have developed mainly from talking with his students at Yale.

Current revision of this fascinating period in modern American history holds that the laughability of the conclusion invalidates the eloquence of the case. Such assertions are as silly as the excesses they condemn. Reich's analysis of the Corporate State stands, a corpus of thought too profound to be unthought, simply because the State finds it distressing, or because the State's flunkies and trimmers deem its manifestations to have been indecorous. That Reich's analysis was embraced by people who needed a bath doesn't render the analysis meaningless, any more than René Dubos's ecological manifesto was discredited because a sophomoric coprophile dumped sludge in a power company's lobby; any more than Buckminster Fuller's notions of fundamental redesign were unworkable because urban teenagers froze their nuts off in geodesic yurts.

Historically, the years immediately before and after 1970 were a time of intense cultural excitement. An enormous generation was more or less simultaneously reaching that point in its development where it simply had more energy than it could use up. If you had been born between 1940 and 1955, you were horribly young in 1970. This was a biological phenomenon as much as a political or cultural one (and not therefore subject to revision).*

The sense of community that connected Boomers by 1970 was dramatic. Overly trusting it may have been, but for the moment the trust worked. It was not just a matter of appearance. Certain signals conveyed a community of attitude. It was as if people exuded cultural pheromones, alerting one another to their affinity, their common state of mind. At a stop sign, in a bar or airport, at a party or hitching a ride, getting information or buying food, the signals were exchanged and attitudes were assumed about basic issues: the war, the President, the media, the nature of the community and its future.

Contemporary commentators might like to characterize these upheavals as the squalling of a mob of coddled brats, obsessed with sex, drugs, and rock and roll. But they simply weren't. While sex, drugs, and rock and roll were part of the rebellion (and why not, since provided they didn't interfere with the right of others, they would definitely seem to be covered by the term "pursuit of happiness"?), the seriousness of what was on their minds is not normally associated with brattishness. And, as a result, by 1970 they had large numbers of sympathizers too old to be brats, including what George Wallace

---

* The question of just how many young men and women were involved in all of this seems to be something that deeply disturbs current right-wing commentators. It's hard to understand why. Whatever was happening here—whether it was truly happening or whether it was perceived to be happening—there was no question about what was on people's minds. The most raucous right-wing voice of the time, Governor Reagan of California, spoke in 1970 of silencing youthful dissent "If it takes a bloodbath . . ." Bloodbaths are generally conceded to involve more than a few scattered individuals. Beyond that the numerical approach to historical phenomena is never very illuminating. In what sense is a plane crash in which five hundred people die more significant than one in which three hundred die? Especially if, for example, all of the three hundred are right-wingers?

called "pointy-heads,"† meaning fifties academics and intellectuals, significant segments of the Catholic Church and of the scientific community, much of the military rank and file, the vast majority of black, Hispanic, or Indian citizens, and of course the usual hordes of artists, writers, actors, composers, directors, sculptors, and other habitual troublemakers.

There was an element of danger in belonging to this extended family, for its solidarity was as apparent to the nonsympathizers as to its members. In the summer of 1970, packs of vigilante hard hats, organized by their own union, roamed through Manhattan, beating up anyone whose hair or dress offended them. They were noisily applauded by the Vice President Spiro Agnew, recently retired from a career in the two-bit bribery business as governor of Maryland. His loftier task as Veep was combing Roget for alliterative terms of xenophobia with which to incite the citizenry against its long-haired and liberal enemies, especially those in the media (he called them "nattering nabobs"). Quite what old Thesaurus Rex wanted the citizenry to do about this threat wasn't clear—he stopped short, perhaps because it made him uneasy, of suggesting that his enemies should be sent to jail. For the Nixon White House, it also served another purpose, familiar to students of right-wing tactics: By unleashing a loudmouth farther to your right, you can appear moderate.

My Lai was the moral nexus of the year, ambivalence dripping from it like blood. The photos of the dead expressed all that was both thrilling and chilling about a spectator war—bright, crisp, sharply focused, death in living color. The bodies lay in a heap like dogs shot by some woozy hunter at the end of a bagless day. William Calley, who had given the order to fire on these civilians, symbolized the ambivalence. Was he one of our brave boys or what he certainly appeared to be—a pudgy, inhuman slob? Richard Nixon, who still wore his panties manfully loose, rose to the moral challenge of the situation and embraced Calley as a hero. But somehow it didn't wash. However much people might secretly thrill to the spectacle of a bunch of dead gooks in a ditch, they couldn't buy Calley. The grin on the fat little face, far from reflecting the radiance of heroic deeds, made it only too clear why civilians got killed. Calley squeezed the trigger because he was allowed to, because he could get away with it. People were hip to that grin. They knew Calley loved killing those folks, probably had a beer or two afterward, probably made some sneering unfunny crack about the heap of dead meat he'd left behind him. Calley forced into people's consciousness the fact that when war is trumped up, when home and loved ones are not threatened, when territory and life are not at stake, there is only one reason why men will kill—for pleasure. The ranks of Official America closed around Calley, but he was a bad mistake. He was in appalling taste. He oozed the moral turpitude the war

---

† George Carlin commented on this term in a 1970 "Ed Sullivan" appearance as odd coming from a guy who tended to spend his evenings in a conical white hood.

was creating and to wrap him in official glory only created still more, for Calley soaked through anything you wrapped him in—even the flag.

And if Nixon's embrace of Calley had the purpose of inspiring youth, by giving the war a younger face than Westmoreland's, that too backfired. Kids knew Calley better than anyone. They knew him from the schoolyard. "That creep a hero? Gimme a break." The intrinsic absurdity of glorifying the creep was still further heightened for Calley's peers by the familiarity of his sliminess. It was like trying to turn Agnew into a rock star. Calley was a moral impossibility, a living satire. He made *Dr. Strangelove* look like a documentary. The authorities, in fact, seemed to have no more sense of where moral bottom was in this cesspool than those they claimed had created it.

The Nixon administration was Going Too Far.

By 1970, the extent to which military attitudes, military priorities, and military methods permeated civilian society was as much the central issue as the war. It remained unaffected by changes in the White House, for clearly the military had the same relationship with both parties and survived any form of democratic change. The militarization of society both preceded Vietnam and looked well set to survive it. The war had jogged the issue loose, but once it appeared it went beyond to the questions of why we were in Vietnam in the first place, and whether we would one day be somewhere else.

Twenty-five years of relentless insistence that the military's dualistic "Us" versus "Them" version of the world order was the only correct one, and that the nation arrange its priorities accordingly, providing a third of its best minds and a third of its annual budget for the purpose, had led only to conflict, coercion, misery, and a growing number of flag-draped boxes. The nation was no safer for all that; Vietnam demonstrated a process that recurred all over the world: that military initiatives themselves created a threat to American interests. Just as every nuclear missile added to the American arsenal actually further compromised American lives and futures, so every base and beachhead (of which Vietnam was but one) created resentment, opposition, and resistance of no value whatsoever to American political and physical security. In the neat world of military theory, the extra missile and extra base might mean national security had been increased. In the real world, where other peoples, weak or strong, friendly or not-so-friendly, had a reaction to such action, it only meant increased danger.

Unlike the young men of the fifties—men like Sahl, Bruce, and Heller, whose feelings about the military were qualified by the well-nurtured but well-founded myth of World War II camaraderie—the Boomers had only their own experience to go on. Their experience was in their own backyard, of an undemocratic force in a democratic society with a privileged call on their time, allegiance, and lives. Their faith in its ability to determine threats to the nation's welfare and respond to them was received, not experienced, passed down from the time of MacArthur, Marshall, and Eisenhower. Most retained the faith, until the military began doing the one thing no military can afford to do—lose a war. Especially this military and this war. The military's pleas that it was losing because it lacked civilian support were obviously specious. Most citizens and certainly both major parties supported the war, as the Boomers knew only too well. They could see that protesting the war year-in, year-out had no visible result, in fact Nixon had just widened it to include Cambodia, and potentially Thailand. In any case, even in the face of overwhelming opposition, this military, which had built up itself and its hardware, its reputation and invincibility, ever since they'd been born, ought to be able to make short work of a nonindustrial nation of twenty million peasants.

But they couldn't, and the faith snapped. And as happens when faith disappears, the whole canon comes into question. If Christ is not God, He is not present in the Host, the priest is a fake, and Mary is just one more teenage mother. Further, the Church's motives for building such a superstructure themselves become suspect.

What was called the peace movement sprang from this sane and proper apostasy. There was a hope, a suggestion that there might be some alternative in one's passage through life than to leave a trail of blood. Community was perhaps preferable to the solitude of victory (or defeat), stasis was preferable to conflict, living for something was better than dying for something. It was this as much as "fuck the draft" that was conveyed by the universal two-fingered "peace" gesture.

And while the hope may have been naïve, it certainly wasn't pernicious. One would never have known it from the violence of the reaction. The mere suggestion that life was not a battle was itself a challenge to battle. It made people furious. In the final analysis, all that the young demanded was the right to be left alone, to behave differently, to experiment with alternatives. They didn't seek to impose these alternatives, they weren't overrunning anyone's territory, they carried no weapons. In earlier times, far more concrete threats to American territory and culture had been treated with grumbling or amusement, ridicule or resignation, all of them arising perhaps from a still fresh sense that everyone was in the same boat. But the generation now in power wanted this incursion eliminated, eradicated, nuked. The peace movement exposed an extremism that was entirely new in American affairs. It dramatized the extent to which the military had cornered the market, not on national security so much as on national insecurity. The form it took had all the absolutism and impenetrability of military logic. This questioning of our militarism, this insistence on peace, must be dealt with militarily. "If it takes a bloodbath."

What the Boomers' attempt at disengagement taught them was an age-old lesson. Far from being the cheerful, gritty, big-hearted guys charged with doing the country's dirty work, those reluctant heroes of myth and legend, the military are, by their very nature, extremists. They are trained to see everything in terms of threat and conquest, life or death. Even Sergeant Bilko first and foremost is trained to kill. There is only one time when the military has a purpose, and that is when your country is actually physically threatened (and that means the country, not some shadowy piece of rhetoric). Then flags should snap and hearts burst with hate, and soldiers should be heroes. At all other times, they are the most dangerous men in society. For the military man there is only one fact of life, and that is death . . . as four young men and women found out to their cost one bright Ohio day in the spring of 1970.

Morning in America

Almost twenty years later, 1970 and the movement that was in full flood that year continue to haunt and frustrate those who feel they "won" the struggle. Rabid attacks on "the sixties" fill righty journals. They hammer away at the poor old period with only slightly less hysteria than they beat on the Soviet Union. The vilification takes much the same form and still demonstrates much the same logical absurdity as it did in the sixties themselves. The Boomers are still inexplicably at one and the same time "spoiled," "naïve," "Communists," and "brats"; one article depicts the clear and present danger of an entire generation deluded by radical propaganda; the next demeans a handful of snotty ignoramuses who had no effect on the moderate majority.

Just what did the sixties—that decade so much longer than ten years that stretched from Dallas to Watergate—do to deserve this opprobrium? Why is it that unlike any other decade, the sixties must be trashed, obliterated, demonized, expunged, spoken of the way one speaks of a criminal in the family, in tones of hushed and regretful horror? And why does this happen not once, but over and over again, as if like Zapata, the sixties had to be shot with a thousand rifles to make sure they're truly dead?

In less partisan times, when academia crawls out from under the rock of propaganda that has been dropped on it in recent years, someone will doubtless begin to assess this ten-year chunk of history the way any other ten-year chunk gets assessed. The Ministry of Truth being agreeable, of course.‡

The remainder of this book concerns enterprises that had their origins in this period, so a few points are worth noting before we proceed.

This is not meant as a "defense" of the "sixties"; no period of history can be defended any more than it can be attacked. On the other hand, the foam-flecked generalizations of the righties need to be met with a few of our own, if

‡ I would like to take credit for so far not having mentioned *1984* in a book about postwar satire. There is a determined effort in such periodicals as *Commentary* and certainly among the instant cultural historians of Hollywood to pretend that the sixties (1964–74) never really happened, that what appeared to be happening at the time was not really happening. By far the most enduring and brilliant aspect of Orwell's satirical masterpiece is Winston Smith's job in the Ministry of Truth, which is to rewrite history on a daily basis. His resistance to that obscene process is the ultimate sin, challenging the State's most important prerogative, that it can revise the past to fit the present. It is axiomatic in the very best circles that *1984* is about the Soviet Union. Orwell was utterly specific about the intention of his chef-d'oeuvre, that it wasn't any such thing, that it was about totalitarianism in *any* political system. Rarely in twentieth-century history has so concerted an attempt been made to historically contradict available facts and recollections as the current effort to revise this period. Norman Podhoretz may not work for the Ministry of Truth, but you can get one of its bulletins, any month, for $3.50.

only in order to understand the cultural environment of this climactic phase of Boomer humor.

Of these "sixties," it should be added, lest this is interpreted as a call for their revival, that they were unique and unprecedented (and therefore unrepeatable). Deep though their roots were in fifties dissent, the sixties were genuinely new, not a revival in turn of any other period. They were of their own making, a first time out. The sixties weren't neo-anything.

What was at stake in 1970 were the fifty-nine million minds that were somewhere between high school graduation and being firmly embedded in a career (i.e., ages eighteen to thirty-four). Certainly, not all of those minds inhaled Marcuse or Che with their morning coffee—but there were tips of other icebergs than Woodstock when it came to disaffection. (In the union movement—especially the UAW and the UMW, for example—and among young working women.) But there was one place it was glaringly evident and that was on campus, among those whom the system had already chosen to be its heirs and beneficiaries.

This disaffection wasn't confined to University of California, Northwestern, or the Ivy League schools of the East, all traditional and predictable hotspots. Kent State demonstrated the fact that campuses of all kinds and levels were seething with debate over national priorities. Instead of meekly accepting the "traditional" (which was often synonymous with "official") analyses and conclusions they were presented with in class, students were doing what came naturally—turning over the information and wondering aloud whether it really did lead to the conclusions it was supposed to. At bottom it was this lack of control that really panicked the authorities. What if the Class of 1970—and presumably every other class at least until 1974— arrived at the "wrong" conclusions? The whole massive construct that had been built, among other things on this very system of selecting its future managers, would be threatened, forced at least to confront its contradictions and inequities. It was too late to fire these future managers, for that would leave the plant either unmanned, or in charge of those already deemed incompetent. And whatever Ol' Bloodbath might say, you couldn't shoot them all.

What really got up the nose of authority about campus dissent in 1970— and continues to itch—were two things (one for each nostril). On the one side, as we have seen, was the gravity of issues that were being raised, especially where matters of authority were concerned. There was no respect shown at all, not a bit.*

But where the other nostril began to itch and burn like mad—for one nostril always works better than the other—was that these people were *kids.*

Kids, mere kids, barely out of their teens, Good Lord in Heaven! Kids

---

* In 1968, striking students occupied Columbia's administration building. Abe Rosenthal, managing editor of the New York *Times,* covered the demonstrations. He dates his disaffection with the student movement from this time, not because the students were politically or intellectually in error, but because in taking over the administration building, they made a terrible mess of the president's office.

didn't ask questions, kids learned answers. Kids were cute for a while, wore their baseball caps askew, flirted with Daddy, sulked in their rooms, then blushed, giggled, pinned each other, dented fenders, and finally either got happily married, or went happily to war, or happily to college where they drank too much. But here they were, not just the odd lefty misfit, but millions of them, refusing to do or believe anything they were told.

The long campaign waged by society's managers to stereotype and control America's young men and women ran for the first time, in the late sixties, into a brick wall. America's "kids" refused to be treated like media versions of themselves; they refused to be reassured that their misgivings were "natural for their age"; they demanded to have their questions answered, not characterized. These people insisted on being adults when their bodies said they were. These people exercised their minds at that point in their development when their brainwaves were at their most active.

The effort to create stereotypes of children, adolescents, and young adults is as old as American media and no less aggressive than the parallel attempts to stereotype the old, women, blacks, Asians, or Indians, or for that matter, bosses and workers. There were few challenges to the growing body of young adult stereotypes built up by the early movies. Vacuous "college" comedies of the mid-thirties portrayed an idealized view of harmless campus hijinx in a world where the Depression had never happened (which created at least one star in the person of Ronald Reagan); or the saccharin-cavorting of Andy Hardy.†

The origin of such stereotypes was a shared responsibility between producers and their audiences. Certainly it seemed that audiences would rather believe such fantasies, in a world where college students after 1929 were either desperately holding on to pre-Depression norms, or showing altogether too much interest in alternative forms of government; and in which adolescents tended to be hungry, homeless, and without jobs.

At a deeper level, both genres exhibited a need to regulate and normalize that wildly unpredictable period of life between puberty and the early twenties when huge personality changes can take place in a matter of months, talent and beauty appear—or disappear—overnight, when minds are at their most inquisitive and least controllable. Indeed, Ronald Reagan's second most famous role *(Knute Rockne—All American)* directly met the last problem by creating an image of college normality that sidestepped the whole issue of "fancy ideas" and the fear immigrant parents felt for this aspect of higher education. What audiences got instead was the reassuring image of gridiron warriors, for whom only team loyalty and uncritical cooperation are important.

The relationship between stereotypes of young adults and comedy is intimate. (As indeed is the relationship between all stereotypes and comedy.) By

† The popular wit and Urban Home Companion Andy Rooney derives his name from these films. It is an amalgam of Andy Hardy and Mickey Rooney.

far the greatest proportion of movies or TV series dealing with young people are comedies. The characters at their center are usually figures of fun; help-less, naïve, horny, or kooky; objects of the humor rather than in control of it. The notion that representations of youth should tend to the comedic is dan-gerously close to a law in media writing; the corollary that comedy is the exclusive property of youth is not far behind.

To a great degree Boomer humor—and the phenomenon of fifties and sixties "hip"—grew from and validated itself by resistance to such stereo-types. Both Sahl and Compass–Second City were in full flood against what college students were supposed to be like; *Mad* comics demonstrated that, far from being Seduced Innocents, the nation's kids possessed brand-new minds capable of responding to brand-new ideas. Bruce destroyed the myth of that kid-at-any-age, the stand-up comic, every time he opened his mouth, as did Gregory, Newhart, Berman, and Allen, and a few years later, Carlin and Pryor. The Smothers' rise to fame was predicated on their conforming to the stereotype of the goofy frat brothers, just as their fall was due to their emerg-ing as nonconforming politically aware adults.

The role of comic stereotypes has been rarely examined. This is alarming. Anyone with the barest knowledge of twentieth-century history should be aware of how dangerous stereotypes can be, whether friendly ("This is norm you should conform to") or unfriendly ("This is what your enemy looks like").

One of the functions of stereotypes (possibly their most important one) is as shorthand for propaganda (any selective version of reality with a moral or political purpose). By that definition, propaganda is just as much at work in the phrase "typical American teenager" and the image that comes to mind when it is uttered, as it is in the phrase "typical Russian behavior" and ditto. That is why departure from, or resistance to, such a stereotype can provoke the kind of rage it did in the sixties.

Stereotypes, in fact, say far more about those who use them than they do about the people they are supposed to represent. Polish jokes, for example, much in vogue in the sixties, were (and are) incomprehensible to Europeans. If the Poles have any national image in Europe, it is of a rather tragic and passionate people, whose nation has had a tendency to be used as a doormat by either the Russians or the Prussians. The fork in the forehead stereotype of American Polish jokes is meaningless to those with even a rudimentary expe-rience of Poland. Hence, it expresses nothing about the Poles, much less about Poland, but a great deal about fear, in an immigrant society, of newer immigrants with a predilection for hard work and ethnic cohesion. Similarly, Russian cartoon‡ versions of Americans are hilarious, but only in their out-landishness. Usually, the average American is portrayed as a stormtrooper

‡ Yes, West Virginia, there is a Russian "satire" magazine. It is called *Krokodil,* and has an official circulation of five and a half million in a population not considerably larger than our own. "I don't see you laughing, comrade, how about a subscription to *Krokodil?"*

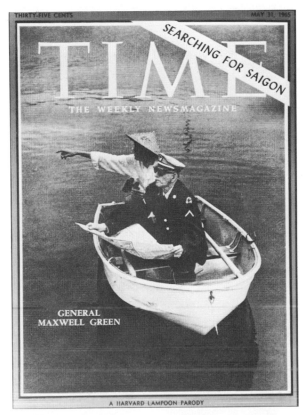

The *Harvard Lampoon* 1965 *Time* parody cover was one of the first Boomer humor reactions to the expanded war in Vietnam.

The highly successful *Harvard Lampoon* 1969 *Time* parody turned out to be a kind of final audition for *The National Lampoon*.

Ol' Bloodbath by Meyerowitz. The artist's take on Governor Reagan—the heroic battle against insignificant opponents—was unusual at the time.

Kennedy by Meyerowitz in his first re-election campaign for the Senate. Meyerowitz later drew Kennedy as the Troll of Chappaquiddick but he avoided the obvious here, concentrating more on the Kennedy team's cynical portrayal of their candidate as a tragic victim of circumstance.

EAT DEATH, BLOATED LACKEY OF THE CAPITALIST *TOY MONGERS!*

12 Free Christmas Presents Inside!
Gahan Wilson's Christmas Horrors

Gross's second cover (December 1970) was bold, bright, and innovative. It was not customary to put comic art on the cover of slick magazine.

FOTO FUNNIES

F-F-FART!

CHAUVINIST PIGS!

FART

A typical example of the sort of dumb joke "Foto Funnies" was known for. The extreme contrast between the founding editors (Kenney is on the left, Beard on the right) was never greater than in this, the first year of the magazine.

BALLS OFFICIAL PSYCHOLOGICAL TEST

IS *YOUR* DAUGHTER A HIPPIE CULT MURDERER?

50¢

A PARANOID PRESS

PUBLICATION

REAL
BALLS
ADVENTURE

SUPREME COURT
COMSYMPS LOADED MY
KIDS ON A...

BUS TO DOOM

I Survived The Attack Of The
KRAZED KENT
KAMIKAZE KIDS

Special Balls Outdoor Saga

STALKING
THE
FLEET-FOOTED
HOMO

EGGHEADS ARE
LOUSY LOVERS!

...YAWN IVY LEAGUE
CALL GIRLS

TOPLESS
NUN-SWAPPING

Latest Kick In Foreign-Run
"American" Schools

CONFESSED PINKO ODDBALL REVEALS...
THE COMMIE PLOT
TO PUT POT IN OUR
DRINKING WATER

Real Balls Adventure was the first successful appearance of a form the *Lampoon* used often—the generic magazine parody, directed less at a specific magazine than at a type of magazine, in this case the "real man" category, which ranged from *Guns and Ammo* to crime and cop titles.

An inside spread from *Real Balls Adventure*.

THE KIDDIE CAPTIVES OF PROFESSOR PERVERTO

by PERRY NOYD

NO LOITERING OR PRAYING

Folks hereabouts in Willowdale, Iowa, are a pretty trusting sort, if you know what I mean. It wasn't unusual, then, that nobody spoke up when the P.T.A. announced that kindly Prof. Perverto, here on a one-year sabbatical from Harvard, had generously offered to take over Mrs. Dunlop's fifth-grade health and hygiene class while she was in the hospital. She had been the victim of a savage rapist who left no clue to his identity except a pattern of hickeys on her body reading "Beat Yale." Well, I reckon the first inkling that something was wrong at Willowdale Elementary was when little Sally Peterson came home from school the next week with a book by Dr. Spock, the known pinko (continued on page 99)

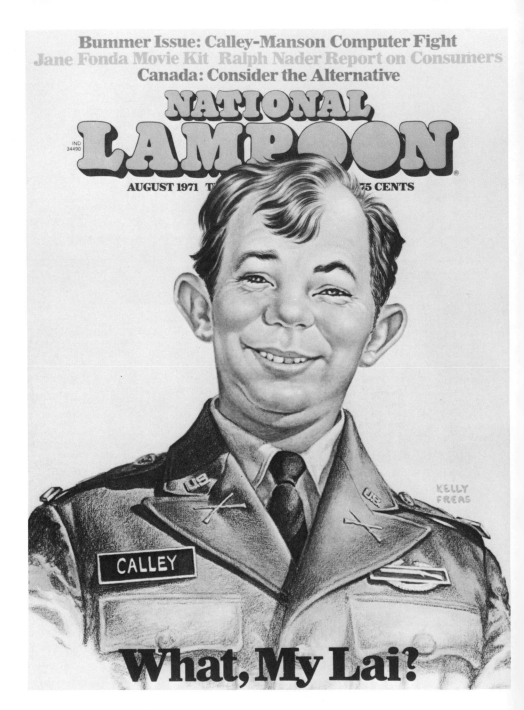

Kelly Freas's classic portrait of William Calley (August 1971), one of the best examples of the *Lampoon*'s sardonic multilevel approach to the war in Vietnam.

The last known picture of O'Donoghue and myself together—from the parody Rolling Stones album, *Rim Shot*. (O'Donoghue has the boa.)

Male Module

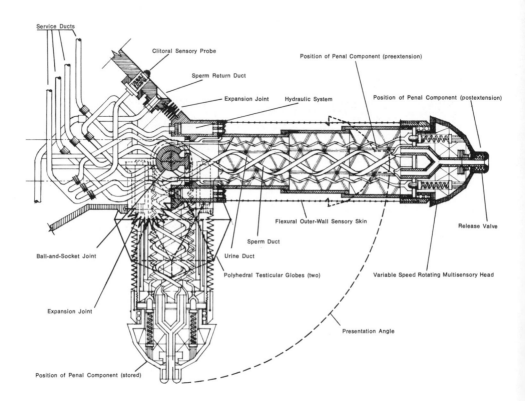

Service Ducts

Clitoral Sensory Probe

Sperm Return Duct

Position of Penal Component (preextension)

Expansion Joint   Hydraulic System

Position of Penal Component (postextension)

Flexural Outer-Wall Sensory Skin

Release Valve

Ball-and-Socket Joint

Urine Duct

Sperm Duct

Variable Speed Rotating Multisensory Head

Polyhedral Testicular Globes (two)

Expansion Joint

Presentation Angle

Position of Penal Component (stored)

Buckminster Fuller's purpose in designing human sexual equipment was, according to the accompanying copy, a profound dissatisfaction with the design concept of the human form: "The human body, in addition to its operating deficiencies, has a myriad of design flaws, among them the fact that basically the same blueprint has been in use for half a billion years, not because it represents the best possible blueprint but because in the evolutionary drawer it happened to be on top ... "

Female Module

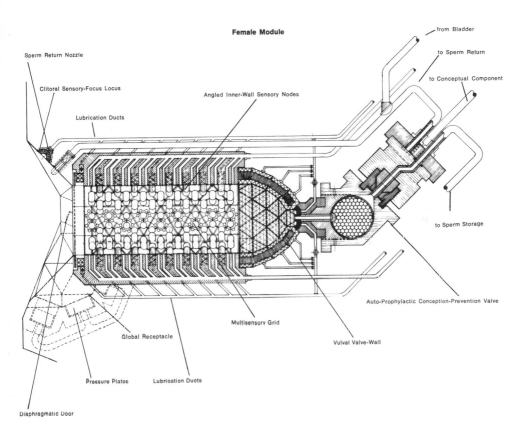

Sperm Return Nozzle

Clitoral Sensory-Focus Locus

Lubrication Ducts

Angled Inner-Wall Sensory Nodes

from Bladder

to Sperm Return

to Conceptual Component

to Sperm Storage

Auto-Prophylactic Conception-Prevention Valve

Multisensory Grid

Vulval Valve-Wall

Global Receptacle

Pressure Plates

Lubrication Ducts

Diaphragmatic Door

The RMS *Tyrranic*, which sailed Liverpool–New York–Liverpool, was, according to the *Official Ship's Guide:* "The Biggest Thing in All the World."

McCall's copy for this page ran: "Orders to Steerage: Do not make loud noises on Sundays. Remove shoes or boots before retiring. Steam smoke or heavy fumes in the steerage area should be disregarded. If sick, stay in your cot."

The Bulgemobiles (the spread included the Fireblast, Flashbolt, Blastfire, and Firewood) were, according to McCall's copy, "So All-Fired New They Make Tomorrow Seem Like Yesterday!" And "Too great not to be changed. Too changed not to be great!" Apart from "Darestreak" styling, all the Bulges boasted a "Dynajet Thunderamic 6000 Super Firebomb V-8" and "a heritage borrowed from the Grand Prix!"

DEDICATION

John F. Kennedy
1917-1963

We proudly dedicate the 1964 *Kaleidoscope* to John Fitzgerald Kennedy, whose tragic death marred the passage of this year at Kefauver High, a man whom we admired not for what he did for himself but for what he did for his country and we as citizens of it.

JFK, perhaps we learned more from you than from any other teacher in high school. You taught us the courage of action in West Berlin, the wisdom of patience in Southeast Asia, the action of wisdom in our space race, the patience of courage in desegregated schools, and the active patient wisdom of wise courageous action at the Guantánamo Naval Base. You are gone, but you have left behind a legacy of peace and prosperity at home, abroad, and in school. And, though the Presidency has passed on to other able hands, it is you who remains "President of the Class of '64" in our hearts. You who might as well have said, *"Ich bein ine Kefauver Senior."*

The Kefauver *Kaleidoscope*'s bemused tribute to their fallen President.

In Memorium

Of all the pieces that are appearing in this, the *Kaleidoscope* of this year, this is, I am sure, the saddest piece you will read and one of the hardest ones to write. As I sit here at my binder in the Yearbook Room, trying to think of what would be the right words to say, I realize that trying to say the right things about a thing like this is as hard as trying to get up in Mrs. Hampster's English class for one of her famous oral talks when she doesn't give you the topic until you're up in front of the class, and so you usually just say stupid things that you wish you weren't saying.

What I have to write about here is one of our students who is no longer with us, if you know what I mean, and it's not that he transferred or flunked out. His name was Howard Lewis Havermeyer, and most of us here on the *Kaleidoscope* staff didn't get a chance to know him too well because even when he did come to school, he coughed a lot and sometimes after coughing he made funny noises, and someone once said that Nurse Krupp told our parents that we shouldn't stand too close to him even when he wasn't coughing.

But just because we did not know him, however, does not mean that he was not a real nice guy. He used to smile at people when he wasn't coughing, and he was supposed to have been really good at baseball when he wasn't coughing. He was supposed to be good at swimming too, and he would have made the swimming team for sure if the county had given Coach Wormer permission to make the water warmer. They say he was even supposed to have been good at touch football, although he was supposed to stay away from dust, and a lot of the girls thought he looked like a Master of Ceremonies.

As I said, there isn't anything much a person can say about something like this. We all would have been a lot happier if he were still here among us, and what happened to him was certainly a bad mark on all the happy events of our young years. We had a wonderful time and wish he were here.

16

The *Kaleidoscope*'s equally baffled dedication to their fallen classmate.

Probably the best-known and most successful cover of the *Lampoon*. The shot was extremely hard to get; when the dog looked straight out at the reader he simply appeared victimized. Then someone had the notion of actually pulling the trigger. The dog reacted to the noise and this was the result.

Lampoon stalwart Meyerowitz painted the bubbling *Animal House* poster. It was credited with having greatly helped get the obscure little movie rolling at the outset. It was also widely imitated by *Animal House*'s imitators.

Above: Lieutenant Neidermeyer tries to make a man out of Flounder. *Below:* Bilevel humor: Babs and Mandy examine Mandy's relationship with Greg while Bluto examines them.

Above: Contrary to his conventional disgustoid image, Belushi was actually puckish and mischievous through much of the film—a big naughty kid. Here he is with D-day during the raid on the dean's office. *Below:* Karen Allen as Katy tells Boon he's "too well to attend" the toga party. Very faintly in the background a baby can be heard crying.

Despite the predations of Editor in Chief O'Rourke, the *Lampoon* continued to attract talented writers like John Hughes, who in turn guaranteed that the *Lampoon* would survive O'Rourke's regime. *Opposite:* The first illustration here is from Hughes's short story published in the September 1979 issue that later became the highly successful movie *Summer Vacation. Above:* The second, featuring Chase as Dad, is from the July 1983 issue after the film's release. Access to material and talent like this has helped to ensure the *Lampoon*'s continuing success and profitability as a production company.

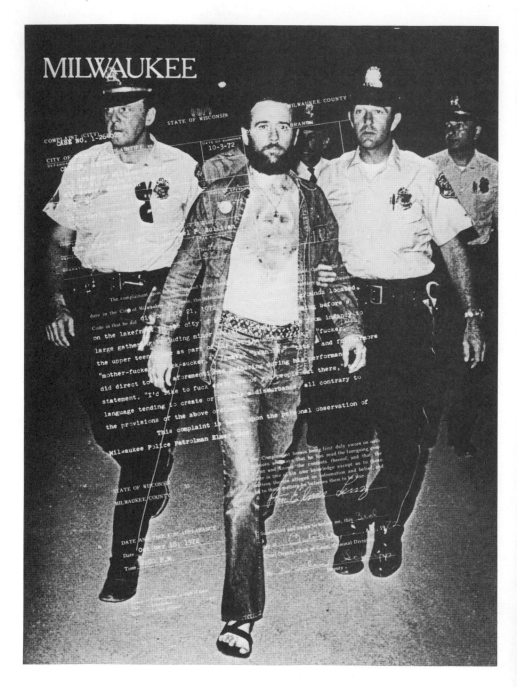

George Carlin discovers in 1972 that the "seven words you can't say on television" can't be said in Milwaukee either.

clutching a wallet bulging with dollars. (Doubtless, our own cartoon of this wildly heterogeneous people would be equally strange to them, if they ever got to see it.)

The "typical (average) American teenager" or the "typical (average) American college student" are no less demeaning and dehumanizing than the ethnic or national stereotypes. That these stereotypes are frequently presented comedically is of equal significance, because it attests to the central role "humor," or more properly ridicule, plays in public life. "The typical American teenager," whether portrayed by Mickey Rooney, Ricky Nelson, John Travolta or Lisa Bonet, however much the details may shift, always expresses the hostility and fear felt by parents for their children. Further, stereotypes of teenagers and students (or women or even bankers) express what the State wishes that citizens be in order that they can be efficiently managed. It reassures those for whom students, teenagers, women, or bankers might present a threat. Unlike the national and ethnic versions, however, these domestic stereotypes often serve as models for the very people they are aimed at. No Polish-American would ever voluntarily stick a fork in his forehead to confirm the stereotype of the Polish joke; but for a variety of reasons, chief among them to win approval, teenagers (or wives or even bankers) will try to conform to the stereotype provided for them.

And this is the point at which the insidiousness of stereotypes becomes evident. So long as they remain the stuff of entertainment, they remain relatively harmless, albeit demeaning. But when stereotype and reality start to become confused—the ultimate aim of propaganda—the damage, in human terms, begins. Since by definition a stereotype is a departure from reality, there is no way that it can become reality. There is no such thing as a typical teenager, any more than there is any such thing as a typical Pole or a typical banker. The effort to become one is bound to fail; there will always be some aspect—mental ability, motor skills, an over-large nose—that will not conform.

It is a function—perhaps *the* function—of satire to draw attention to this discrepancy. Unlike ridicule, which repeats and reconfirms stereotypes, satire seeks to destroy them. Satire's job is to remind people that stereotypes and reality just won't mix. It does this by taking on (imitating) the character, behavior, language, even the supposed "thought-process" of the stereotype and demonstrating the absurd gap between it and the real world.

Satire of course can no more prevent people's need for stereotypes than could legislation; but it is a necessary antidote. Where ridicule dehumanizes, satire rehumanizes. People need to make rules, but they also need to acknowledge exceptions. Humor in general to an extent we all recognize but have rarely considered, is the principal social glue that holds this stasis together.

Resistance to stereotype had always been a crucial element in post-war dissent, not just for the self-evident libertarian motives, but because the terrible consequences of confusing stereotype with reality lay in the dust of World War II. If what started as ridicule ended in extermination, it was time to throw away the joke book, or at least meet ridicule with ridicule. But the "friendly" stereotype—the loyal Nazi, the dehumanizing norm that ordinary Germans had tried to approximate—was just as important a component in this horror as the "unfriendly" one: their dehumanizing stereotype of the Jews. This inescapable historical fact was what fueled the passion with which fifties dissent opposed what it perceived to be efforts to regiment society, to impose conformism. It was axiomatic that when the State began to encourage stereotypes, both friendly and unfriendly, its motives were certainly suspect, and very possibly lethal. To the assertion that America was different, dissenters could point with some justice to the fact that nigger jokes and lynching went hand in hand; they could counter-assert, with less substantiation, that the organized effort to dehumanize the Russians, to create the stereotype of "Commies," was a prelude to, a prejustification of *their* elimination.

Television vastly intensified the potential for the creation of stereotypes. On the primary level, it could fit a face and behavior to them, repeat them and disseminate them; on the secondary level, it might even by its very nature depend on them. Existing media had been a crucial element in creating an image of the loyal Nazi, as well as of the evil Jew; television's ability to perform a similar function appeared to be, at least in theory, immeasurably greater.

There was no reason to suppose that it was intrinsically totalitarian, but it had all the makings of a formidable weapon for totalitarian control. Its proprietors insisted that it was art or entertainment, but it was clearly something more—a parallel reality; they insisted that when everyone had television, democracy would be enhanced, but it probably wouldn't, for viewers would still be on the receiving end, with only the narrowest of choices in those areas the medium subsumed.

All this remained conjectural, however, until the war in Vietnam. Then several things became considerably clearer. First, the war proved that once people had been dehumanized as Commies, however complex and diverse their background, history, and motives, they could be justifiably killed. Second, Boomers discovered that those stereotypes of acceptable behavior had not been escapist entertainment at all, but in earnest, and that when they departed from them, out of either moral outrage or self-interest, they were reviled. Third, when they attempted to take their case public on this "democratic medium," they were immediately stereotyped—as Commies, aliens, the enemy, indistinguishable from the Cong.

However hard the Boomers resisted stereotypes, friendly (the all-American boy) or unfriendly ("blacks are lazy"), people's need for them seemed unstoppable. Television only magnified and multiplied that need, as it multiplied and magnified so many other needs. People might even prefer its stereotypes to the evidence of their own eyes. Indeed by 1970, the Boomers had established some stereotypes of their own, both the friendly ("he/she is a real head") and unfriendly ("all cops are pigs"). The latter, in particular, had spread to include practically anyone perceived as an enemy—politicians, hard hats, civil servants, drinkers, and in one quarter, all men. Whatever satirical force the term may have had when used as a one-time metaphor (in Orwell's *Animal Farm),* its use as a stereotype was just as unfair to the diversity and humanity of cops, politicians, and so on, as any black stereotype was to blacks. (Not to mention its collossal unfairness to the diversity and porcity of pigs.)

The remaining part of the Boomer humor story turns to a considerable degree on this issue. Since there was no way to fire them all or shoot them all, the battle for Boomers' minds, their youth, and even ultimately their own recollection of it, would have to be fought. For its own survival, official America could not let this challenge to its methods happen again, or go down in the record as it actually occurred.

But for the moment the initiative was with the young, and the action was on campus. The full force of postwar dissent—artistic, scientific, and political —was cresting at just the moment that the largest college class in history was reaching awareness of itself and of the issues it would one day have to face. This generation was first and foremost, *engaged.* There may have been elements in it of violence, self-destruction, outright lunacy, but its eyes and ears were open. It dealt with matters of moment, not always sensibly, not even intelligently, but it didn't slink away into easy answers and pat conclusions, to some corner of the rug warmed by a previous occupant.

The most carefully and cogently argued of revisions cannot change the historical fact of this seriousness of purpose. Change was the aim, as it should be of any new generation; real, fundamental change, with all the good and evil that implies, change in the name of human standards, not official ones; change that would bring the machine under the control of the brain, rather than replacing it; change that would get mankind out of the rickety old junker he was driving around in, spewing parts and smoke and terror all over the planet, and get him back on his own two feet. And what was just as real was the belief that this could be done. The sense of possibility was boundless. If ever it was morning in America, it was in 1970, for morning belongs to youth, not to old men, however youthful their tans.

The year 1970 was the high noon of the sixties in all its brilliance and idiocy, glory and squalor, high ideals and cheap thrills, leaps and lurches, energy and lethargy, fierce exploration and mindless escapism, all its inimitable and unrepeatable combination of the sublime and the ridiculous. It wasn't neat and it wasn't clean, nor was it poisonous and bent on evil. Nor, above all, did it *not* happen. It happened and we're stuck with it. No amount of mature reflection, repentance, recanting, or self-imposed brain surgery will change that. We may have come a long way down the road, but the sixties remains behind us on the last crest, a wisp of smoke still curling from its communal fire. To pretend it's not there means you've been out in the sun too long.

Death, Drugs, and Daffy Doodles

The State of the Art in 1970

Death was very much in the air in 1970. But, along with the dark, there was the lighter side of death. The surprise hit of the year was an unassuming little movie called *M*A*S*H*. While it obediently followed the war movie form, it focused entirely on the grungy blood-soaked heaps of meat that were once top guns, and true grit. Although it was set in Korea, everyone knew it was about Vietnam. It was a comedy. *M*A*S*H* had two essentially straight actors, Elliott Gould and Donald Sutherland, functioning as a macabre comedy team. Humor in the shadow of death was a good bet that year, and *M*A*S*H* far outdrew the more cumbersome and cerebral *Catch-22*. (And, of course, when it hit the TV screen the next year, Compass–Second City claimed it for good in the person of Alan Alda.)

M*A*S*H was made in a hurry and on a small budget, some said to beat its elder brother *Catch-22* to market. Perhaps because of this haste, both the screenplay* and the performances had a wildness that appealed far more to 1970 audiences than the measured tread of *Catch-22*.

While *Catch-22* was packed to the rafters with the great and near-great of Boomer humor, from Bob Newhart to Buck Henry to Alan Arkin to Bonerz and Brent of the Committee, and although it was handcrafted by master film-builder Mike Nichols, it had a formal quality to it. The need to bring this classic to the screen seemed as great as the desire to depict the military stupidity that had fueled Heller's rage in the first place. Heller's book was vast, sprawling, varied in style, often internalized, its dialogue tying itself into

* The screenplay by Ring Lardner, Jr., won an Academy Award.

interminable knots of absurd logic. Bringing this to the screen was next to impossible, but what had to be translated was the bubbling seething fury which infused it all, the mad shriek of a normal man in a world of normal men gone nuts. Somehow that didn't happen. The performances—from Jon Voight to Orson Welles—were uniformly "wonderful," the movie was superbly authentic, but neither the script nor the direction connected with the lives and times of the movie's audience. It was not possible, in 1970, to do a satire on military lunacy insulated from the military lunacy people saw all around them. And yet, there just was no situation, no conflict, no relationship that seemed to ring with the necessary 1970 familiarity. It was almost as if there were a restraint at work that had decided such parallels would be unseemly.

While similarly coded in an unfamiliar war, M*A*S*H immediately rang bells. Its protagonists were powerless, separate, unable to affect the death process in any way, but expected to deal with its results. The authorities were invisible in M*A*S*H, but their will was palpable in the broken young bodies littered all over the place. No matter what you did or thought or believed in, the bodies would continue to pour in. They represented the ultimate absurdity of the generation: death and dismemberment in the supposed pursuit of life and happiness. It is from outrage that the uproarious humor of M*A*S*H springs. M*A*S*H was sick—in the classic and very best sense. But Gould's and Sutherland's antics in a sea of gore were no more sadistic than Bruce's use of the word "nigger" was racist. Nor were they fatalistic—for their sympathy for their patients remains unabated, and their repugnance at the situation manifest. No one in M*A*S*H enjoyed the gore. But its immediacy mirrored for 1970 audiences a pervasive war with immediate results, whether at My Lai, Kent State, or your local cemetery. And this was the chord that somehow Catch-22 failed to strike.

Catch-22 should have expressed the antimilitarism of the two generations it now spanned, but M*A*S*H actually did. Its success is significant. The TV series that sprang from it also says much about the mood of the country. Television's absorption of public attitudes can be deadly, but it evidences that such attitudes exist. And since M*A*S*H is one of the great success stories of postwar humor, this gives the lie to those who now maintain that such attitudes were merely the province of some discontented coterie.

The other surprise hit of 1970 was also, ultimately, about death, but about a very different kind of brutalization. It was called Joe. Joe was quasicomedic in structure, its central premise being the kind of unlikely encounter a Second City audience might suggest for an improv. It was also on occasion very funny.

The teenage daughter of a prosperous executive runs away from home to become a hippie. Her distraught father meets Joe in a bar. Joe is a hulking, simple-minded hard hat whose opinion of all hippies is that they're Commie scum, draft dodgers, and/or faggots. Despite their social and cultural divide, the basically liberal father finds his gut agreeing with Joe, and at Joe's suggestion the two set out to find the runaway in the New York underground. The resulting encounters are the bulk of the movie and Joe's menacing single-mindedness—mixed with an oddly innocent animal curiosity—drives every scene. For the most part, the underground stuff was done with restraint (there is an obligatory sex scene with Joe and a hippie seductress, which of course ends badly); eventually the two track down the daughter and her hippie lover in a commune. The movie ends as Joe and the girl's father, using Joe's hunting rifles, gun down the hippies—starting with the daughter.

Playing Joe with hypnotic intensity and a strange bilevel version of blue-collar wit was Second City and Committee veteran Peter Boyle. Boyle was actually condemned among the sillier element in radical Hollywood for creating this character, as if by merely ignoring the working class, unchic hard hats, their version of utopia could be hastened. Similarly, Joe was embraced by their opponents as signaling a "backlash" against hippies and students.

The reality was both more complex and more interesting, for Joe's character was shot through with irony. He was beguiling and terrifying. Only an actor who had played satire, who knew how to simultaneously charm and insult—a Boomer humorist, in fact—could understand that. An actor who endorsed Joe's point of view would never have been able to give him the menace that makes the movie.

But *M*A*S*H* and *Joe* were tame, compared to other forms of Boomer humor that had survived official exclusion.

The extremism at the top was trickling down very handily throughout the culture. Small wonder that the resistance took wilder and wilder forms. The most obvious example of this was a form known as "head" humor. Drug-oriented comedy ranged all over the spectrum of the drug experience, from weird personal insight to ridicule of the "straights." It was best represented by a group called the Firesign Theater who had several successful albums during this period, and by the underground comics being developed in San Francisco (which might be designated, respectively, the Southern and Northern schools of California head humor).

Rarely satirical, head humor relied largely on the curiosities of drug logic and the outlandish imagery of hallucination, along with the behavioral gap between those who were stoned and those who weren't. This appeared to be a lot like Bruce's material—remember his seminal routine about the junkie being hired by Lawrence Welk—and by 1970, Bruce had become a major figure in the pantheon of resistance saints, one of the all-time Earls of Dissent,† thanks largely to the "head" element in the movement.

It was significant that by 1970 a satirist had acquired the same standing as major musical luminaries (e.g., Dylan), but such adulation did his actual work considerable disservice. Bruce had had a highly ambivalent attitude

---

† The play *Lenny* was a hit on Broadway and books of his material, including his own autobiography, *How to Talk Dirty and Influence People*, were consistent bestsellers.

toward his own habit, and when he did talk about drugs, which was far less than people liked to think, it was the absurdities of prohibition and enforcement that concerned him, not how great and special they made the inside of your head.

Head humor, for all its surface weirdness and whimsy, its apparently delightful harmlessness, was a closed system. These artists were talking about the equipment, not making music. The wallowing in druggie states of mind seemed to have no purpose other than promotion. Head humor could be entertaining, but it was without irony. For the head humorists, far from being a means, drugs were an end.

Drugs did serve the Boomers as a legitimate experiential bond. There is plenty of moral and legal merit in the positions they could take with regard to prohibition, especially when arbitrarily applied to some substances, but not to others. And for countless numbers of people, the drug experience was a largely harmless and equally legitimate means of re-examining preconceptions and, less often, reordering their priorities. Indeed, two major Boomer humorists, Richard Pryor and George Carlin, still at the time relatively conventional comedians, both went through major transformations at this time—both the consequence of drug experiences. In the process, both converted themselves from skillful craftsmen into major artists. Carlin's account of this continues the story of his career. Once again it is typical of many people's experience of the time. Once again it is special for the insight it provides into his development as a humorist.

Carlin says: "I was aware very vividly [by 1970] that I was entertaining the fathers and the mothers of the people I sympathized with, and in some cases associated with, and whose point of view I shared. I was a traitor, in so many words. I was living a real lie for myself because I wanted to say so many different things. I'd say, 'Well that's okay, because my ends will justify the means and I'll be fine. I know who I am and my friends know. Fuck you.'

"What happened that changed everything was acid. There are three incidents that go along with the acid. Two of them happened in Las Vegas a year apart. By this time, I was an opening act in Las Vegas, and I was opening for such people as . . . try not to smile, Robert Goulet, Barbara Eden, and Al Martino. But it was horrendous! I was terribly out of place. Now I had a very harmless thing where I talked about my ass. Having no ass. This particular night, it wasn't a public show, it was some golfer assholes. The Frontier Hotel had a golf tournament. Howard Hughes owned it by this time and there was a golfer asshole convention. The eight o'clock show was delayed until about nine-fifteen because they were all drinking. As they were getting there, they were all drunk—just drunk enough to heighten their assholedom. And so I went out and did my normal show. And one of the things I'd said in the course of the show without any problem before was 'I ain't got no ass. You know, some people got an ass. I ain't got no ass. I was in the service and black guys would look at me and say, "Hey, where your ass at? Stud ain't got no ass. Where your ass at?" ' And fool around like this and boom the thing was over and I'm on to something else.

"I finish my act. I'm told in between shows that Robert Maheu [Howard Hughes keeper and right-hand man] and his wife were in the audience. Didn't like [the ass bit]. Took exception to that. And I was, at this time, suspended for the rest of the engagement, given my money, and told I could go home. I was more or less flabbergasted. That was the beginning of my Frontier experience. I had a one-year contract and I came back a year later. And I had another thing I was doing by this time. What I did was, I said, 'You know, I don't say shit. Down the strip Buddy Hackett says shit, Red Foxx says shit, I don't say shit. Smoke a little of it, but I don't say it.' This time I was not suspended. I was fired.

"Then there was the Playboy Club in Lake Geneva, where they had the whole hotel and resort. This is a great one because this was *real,*—not that I hadn't already burned my bridges, but this gave me the fuel. I needed to see that I'd done the right thing. But I remember saying at the beginning of this show for some reason, 'I'm going in a little different direction. I'm trying to go to the colleges. I'd like to work in the colleges.'

"I guess I was probably explaining myself a little too much, but I guess I felt I needed to. Now in the middle of this show, because I wasn't doing the hippie dippy weatherman, and a couple of other things that they had come to expect, I began to get catcalls and verbal things from the audience. Things like 'Where's the old George Carlin?' I remember that. These very very straight, tight asshole-looking Wisconsin people. A Milwaukee Saturday night, you know? Really rigid-looking folks, you know? At any rate, I get these things and it starts off mildly, with a little talking, you know: 'Where's our check here? Give us our check. We don't need this. We don't have to stand for this.'

"And then one guy said, 'cause I had talked about Vietnam and whatever I had said about it, he said, 'You were never in Vietnam. You were never shot at. What do you know?' I thought, 'Does he have a gun?' And it became an entire audience, maybe a hundred and fifty or two hundred people in the motions of getting up, many of walking out, fingers were being waved at me, this was something out of a movie. I finished whatever time I felt they had to pay me for and in some ridiculous act of bravado, I walked through the audience when there was clearly a wing onstage.

"About an hour later, a telegram comes to my hotel room door, which is in the Playboy Hotel, and it says, 'We cannot guarantee your safety if you remain on the premises. We are asking you to leave.' Apparently, some people had been going to the front desk and asking for my room number. So I said, 'Well, fine! I'm only ninety miles from Chicago. Hugh Hefner's mansion is there. Hef is probably home. This is a Playboy Club, freedom of speech is involved, Hef says he cares about that.' You know—pretty innocent here, pretty naïve. I said, 'Hef will back me up. And I'll get my fucking money.' So I drive down to Chicago, go to the mansion, and Hef is there with Bill Cosby.

Bill's playing pinball or some shit. And I tell Hef the whole story. And he says, 'Well, there's two Hefs, George. One of them sitting in that audience would have loved that material, loved that show. The other one' [and he was paraphrasing Lenny] 'ya gotta do business with these assholes.' And I was finally finished with that fairy tale.

"You know, there was a lot of money involved, and I was in this middle-class shit. I said, 'Fuck it.' I said, 'I just can't do it anymore. I hate these people. I don't belong with them. I'm gonna go back to the coffee houses. I know what I can do there. And if I can, I'll get on the college campus circuit. And if I can just do those two things for the rest of my life, I'll be happy.'

One of the things I did was write a form letter explaining the reasons for wanting to go to colleges and what I said was 'There are three reasons I wanted to play colleges.' I said, 'First of all because they are open to experiment and to change and willing to listen. Secondly, because they are conscious of this and that and so forth and so on, and third, there's a fortune to be made in stolen lab equipment.'

"I was rediscovering the 'Us' versus 'Them.' I was giving room to the original sense I had in that neighborhood where I grew up and attitudes that I could never penetrate. We were called, in fact, 'the street people' there, you know, when we would go crazy in Columbia and beat up a bunch of freshmen or something and steal their beanies and it would appear in the Columbia *Spectator*: 'Street Toughs Did This and That.' So my sense of 'Us' versus 'Them' was alive and well up there. And it was alive and well in the air force because I rejected everything they tried to put on me. And it began to be submerged when I got into radio and then nightclubs. The only thing that kept it alive was that I was a pot smoker all the way through and I had this playground in my head which tolerated anything that I wanted and gave me room for the rebel in me. Gave him a place to exist and look at the society and disagree with it. But that got submerged. Now I was able to exercise that part of myself again. Now, not only was it coming to life but it was gonna be rewarded. Even if that reward only came from me, feeling that sense of freedom and some of the audience liking it. A lot of people stereotyped what I was doing then or in hindsight by saying, 'Well, you just did a lot of bad drug humor.' But it wasn't all drug humor. There were things that included language, social and political ideas. Being a Catholic, I was finally purging this stuff about Confession and being a kid. There were a lot of things open to me now that had never been open before."

Carlin's voyage of self-discovery brought him to a point where he could behave, dress, speak, and think as he had always wished. Here's one of his best pieces from the period (it actually appeared on the album *Class Clown* in 1973), "The Seven Words You Can't Say on Television":

There are over four hundred thousand words in the English language, and there are seven of them you can't say on television. Three hundred and ninety-nine thousand, nine hundred and ninety-three . . . to seven.

They'd have to be outrageous, to be separated from a group that large. "All of you over here—you seven . . . BAD words!" That's what they told us they were. You know the seven don't you, that you can't say on television? *Shit, piss, fuck, cunt, cocksucker, motherfucker,* and *tits.* Those are the heavy seven. Those are the ones that'll infect your soul, curve your spine, and keep the country from winning the war. *Shit, piss, fuck, cunt, cocksucker, motherfucker,* and *tits.* Wow!

Tits doesn't even belong on the list. It's such a friendly word. Sounds like a nickname, right? "Hey, Tits, c'mon here, man!" "Hey, Tits, meet Toots"; "Toots, Tits . . ." Sounds like a snack, doesn't it? (Yes, I know it is . . .) But I don't mean your sexist snack . . . I mean new Nabisco TITS! The new *cheese* tits . . . corn tits . . . pizza tits . . . onion tits . . . tater tits . . . yeah. Bet you can't eat just one! That's true—I usually switch off . . . That word does not belong on the list. Actually none of the words *belong* on the list, but you can understand why some of them are there—I'm not completely insensitive to people's feelings . . . Like *cocksucker* and *motherfucker*—those are *heavyweight* words. There's a lot going on there, man.

Besides the literal translation and the emotional feeling . . . they're just *busy* words. There's a lot of syllables to contend with. Those *k*'s, they jump out at you. Cocksuckermotherfucker cocksuckermotherfucker. It's like an assault on you.

Now, we mentioned *shit* earlier. Two of the other four-letter Anglo-Saxon words are *piss* and *cunt,* which go together, of course . . . but forget that. (Little accidental humor I throw in.) Piss and cunt . . . The reason that *piss* and *cunt* are on the list is that a long time ago certain ladies said, "Those are the two I'm not going to say. I don't mind *fuck* and *shit,* but *p.* and *c.* are out!" Which led to such stupid sentences as "Okay, you fuckers, I'm going to tinkle now!"

Then of course the word *fuck* (Stadium cheer.) Here's some more accidental humor: I don't really want to get into that now . . . ha-ha-ha, because I think it takes too long . . . ha-ha-ha . . . But I do think *fuck* is a very important word. It's the beginning of life, but we use it to hurt one another.

People much wiser than I have said, "I'd rather have my son watch a film of two people making love than two people trying to kill one another. And that's a great sentiment—I wish I knew who said it first. But I'd like to take it a step further. Substitute that word *fuck* for the word *kill* in all those movie clichés we grew up with . . .

"Okay, sheriff, we're gonna *fuck* you now!"

"But we're gonna fuck you *slow!*"

Neither Carlin nor Pryor, for all the associations they may have with drugs, is a head humorist. Drugs allowed them to rediscover their roots. The result was some of the best humor of the seventies.

But head humor was no more interested in rediscovering its roots than it was in Scotch and soda. For all its appearance of Going Too Far, it went nowhere. In its self-absorption and exclusiveness, in fact, it reflected one of the more deadly, and ultimately fatal, aspects of the sixties manifestation of dissent—that drugs became not a banner but the battle, not a bond but the brotherhood itself. The ignorance and self-indulgence that lay behind this confusion was the most disturbing thing. For example, while heads (legitimately) complained that the prohibited substances they used were all of natural—and ancient—origin, it never seemed to occur to anyone that it does not necessarily follow that they should be a way of life. The Incas, after all, would no more have used coca to get themselves started in the morning, or maintain an erection, than Jesus would have drunk wine to get a buzz on. And further, as the grim commissars of the New Left saw much more clearly than the authorities, drugs, far from being a clear and present danger to the republic, would create a culture that left the status quo as intact as ever. Opium, too, is the opiate of the people.

In 1970, the term "head humor" was used to cover a multitude of grins. The Credibility Gap, a scintillatingly vicious group operating out of Los Angeles on radio station KRLA, were routinely referred to as "head" humorists when they were nothing of the sort. Easily the smartest outfit left in operation after the demise of the Smotherses and the decline of the Committee, the Gap were bona fide satirists, basing the bulk of their material on the day's news, creating most of it right on the air, and paying special attention to then mayor of Los Angeles, a dopey old bigot called Sam Yorty ("Just Plain Sam"), who managed to combine in one personality just about everything that was most repellent about the arsenal of democracy.‡

Although ridicule of prohibition was as much part of their repertoire as it was of any healthy Boomer, and while they undoubtedly used drugs, the Gap were the very antithesis of head humorists: well-informed, highly articulate, and tight improvisers, without question the fastest jaws in the West.

Similarly, back in New York, another very different operation was breaking some very different rules. Appearing in a dingy club on East 4th Street, in the then-genuinely bohemian East Village, a loose confederation of dunces called Channel One, held together by acid and a rotund ex-kiddie star named Ken Shapiro, was producing some very untelevisionlike television. Unlike the "oh wow!" school of alternative video (which spent its time fiddling with the color bar in order to produce visual aids to hallucination), Shapiro's crew created television you couldn't see on television. One of them, a hip preppy—a heppy perhaps—named Chevy Chase recalls what it was like:

"It was all in the Village on East 4th Street. For twenty-five dollars a week

‡ The original Gap consisted of Harry Shearer, Michael McKean, David Lander, and Richard Bebe. McKean and Lander later surfaced as Lenny and Squiggy on "Laverne and Shirley," Shearer on SNL, and McKean and Shearer as two of the stars of the film *This Is Spinal Tap*. Shearer remains one of the few genuine political satirists operating in the United States, and certainly its best political impressionist.

I stayed in the loft above the little theater, where this health guy used to do plays about health food. He died of a heart attack on a talk show—Jerome Rodale. (On "The Dick Cavett Show.") There was nothing there [except] a hundred seats and the gravel pit. No backstage, nothing. We put in a system with three monitors—Kenny had all the dough from his Milton Berle ["Texaco Star Theater"] days and I basically would run these two tape machines—Ampex 660s, two-inch tape—and also be at his house and record . . . writing was sitting around smoking pot and coming up with funny ideas and trying them out on tape, so that you could never really tell who had a big hand in it. (But it always turned out to be Ken . . .)

"We'd all live together in a one-room apartment—not Ken, he had a big, beautiful house with his wife and kids—but Lane Sarasohn, Victor Langer, and Richard Allen with our girlfriends. We'd all sleep on mattresses in one big room . . . terrible way to make a living.

"What we were doing was making fun of television. Parodying TV, doing things that you wouldn't be able to see at home on TV. That was the major point.

"There was one other group . . . with the idea to run TV in a theater. They were a bunch of psychedelic people who showed video where you'd sit on acid and watch—we were the only people doing satire.

"Shapiro was very crude; he liked to do things that were overtly sexual or scatological. One of the funny things that they did on Channel One was the Safety Sam announcement in which a penis talked to you about venereal disease, and I remember a very, very funny day or two of auditioning for the part. There were four or five of us. We each auditioned by lying upside down in an armchair with the camera focused on our genitals, and a little hat on the balls and little eyes, and to see which one looked like the most like a talking human being—or a being of some kind.

"Larry Sarasohn won, because it looked a little like a turkey, kind of benevolent-looking. You couldn't really tell what it was till you came in close.

"We wanted to shock and surprise. This was the first time [on television] anyone had done that."

The distinction Chase draws between Channel One and their psychedelic video competitors is notable. This was not humor about drugs, this was humor about television, specifically the lumbering, repressed, and repressive machine that had strangulated the Smotherses and just about anyone else who resisted its implicit politics. Crude and apolitical in content though Safety Sam may have been, the intent was therefore distinctly political. And significantly, the only place where this message could be presented and heard was the traditional locus of boomer humor—the nightclub/theater. Channel One/*The Groove Tube** was a bizarre hybrid, live from New York with the oddest vengeance.

---

* Shapiro later arranged the Channel One videotapes into a highly successful movie called *The Groove Tube* (1974).

Twenty-five years into its history, the Box had now defined itself to include certain attitudes and images and exclude others. And it had conditioned people to accept the ones it included so completely that any deviation was an almighty shock, even to supposedly unshockable youth. There was nothing new about Safety Sam—Bruce had spoken with his version of that gent fifteen years before. But to see him at home between the four walls of television in 1970 was quite extraordinary.

Many of the same ironies were at work in the weird and wonderful world of underground comics. By 1970, these had become a prosperous industry, following routes of distribution opened up by the underground press (e.g., record stores and head shops), and experiencing much the same moral indigestion. (In what sense should a free press be for free?) The appeal of underground comics was that they brought attitudes and images to a form that, since the institution of the Comics Code fifteen years before, had admitted nothing of a disturbing nature, whether sexual, criminal, or bizarre. As with Safety Sam, to see alien images within the familiar six- or eight-panel page was hypnotic, shocking, and often funny, even if the actual humor level of the concept was zero. Many underground comics were not comic, but acidic, meandering sequences of slowly unfolding images with no objective purpose, and since they were printed on newsprint in black and white, not even much use as promoters of hallucination (e.g., early Moscoso, or Rick Griffin).

If underground comics succeeded by bringing the unthinkable to a domesticated form, they also managed to bring the unreadable and the unintelligible. S. Clay Wilson's wildly energetic pseudotales of interchangeable bikers and pirates, who were always hacking up one another's salamilike penises or lapping away at various leprous sores and organs, raised a certain nervous laugh, but left you with the uncomfortable feeling that you'd just had a beer (or a jar of yak sperm) with a homicidal maniac. And if this was head humor in its purest form, at the other extreme was Gilbert Shelton's Fabulous Furry Freak Brothers. Despite the brothers' desperate yearning for dope, this was broad and traditional in its comic strip hijinx, a sitcom of the underground—Hippie Days.

Crumb in the Streets

And then, of course, there was R. (Robert) Crumb. This horny, horn-rimmed, paranerd genius personified, expressed, and commented on every paradox of his generation. He was the head humorist par excellence, creating the icons and labels of countless legions of dope suckers. But far from cauterizing his irony, drugs seemed for Crumb to heighten it. He went through drugs and out the other side. One of his most famous strips, "Stoned Agin!"—six panels of a gradually melting "head"—must have adorned tens of millions of male and female chests as a proud statement of drugginess, yet the whole strip is hilariously self-critical, not messianic.

His best-known characters, Mr. Natural, the patriarchal Zen master in army boots, and his would-be pupil Flakey Foont, are similarly observed. They exhibit that exquisite mix of the profound and the idiotic so characteristic of Boomer Bohemia. Flakey, try as he might, just doesn't get it. He cannot understand why Mr. Natural can get laid, swill beer, put his boots up on the TV, and still remain on the seventh level of understanding. (Not that Mr. Natural doesn't get his comeuppance once in a while.) Nor has Mr. N the slightest patience for Flakey. Far from floating on an unreproachful cloud of nirvana, he puts the boot in. ("Get out of here, Flakey Foont!")

Just like Bruce, Crumb's use of drugs seemed to have brought him not an obsession with the stuff, so much as a deeper understanding of the nature of obsession—of all kinds, his own and that of others. Foont is obsessed by Mr. Natural and satori; Shuman the Human is obsessed by the global horrors awaiting humanity; everyone is obsessed by big bottoms, and chowing down on each other's private parts. The perspiration of need flies off Angelfood McSpade, Eggs Ackly, Bo Bo Bolinski, Whiteman, Lenore Goldberg, Boingy Baxter, and a host of others. Crumb caught the urgency of a generation obsessed with every form of life in a society apparently obsessed with death. But there's nothing existential about it. Angst in Crumb's work could only be someone's name. His strips can barely contain their exuberance, however foul or fearsome the content of the panels. People are always striding, driving, twirling, sucking, diving, flying, screaming, "Keep on truckin'." Sometimes they simply burst into song. Quite often appliances, cars, utensils, and buildings sprout limbs and faces and join in.

His characters are always traveling vast distances—psychically or physically—moving from point A to point Z, on some trip of quest and answer. But while they pass through extraordinary adventures (Pete the Plumber passes through the waste pipes of the universe; Whiteman leaves his Winnebago to go "native" with Angelfood McSpade), they end up back where they started. And it's this—the trip, the conversion, the voyage of self-discovery—that was Crumb's central image. The trip of discovery and fulfillment, while not Crumb's only mode, was the one that stuck.†

This is crucial to an understanding not just of Crumb, but to this whole period of humor. If discovering that you were not sick and not alone had been the central individual experience of the fifties, then self-revelation, personal freedom from constraint, and private revolution were the central idea of the sixties. Whether it was achieved instantaneously or by means of a gradual journey, through the agency of drugs or a shot in the head, a Beatles song or a load of Commie nonsense, this heightened awareness of self and its possibilities crop up again and again in personal histories of the time.

And with Crumb what matters is the end result. Whatever flight of fantasy we're on, he has one foot firmly on the ground. However strange the trip may be, chances are the lady guide will have big, bouncing, grab-me buttocks.

---

† In its most extended—if not its funniest—form this appeared in the comic book *Fritz the Cat*, which later, in mysterious and possibly reprehensible circumstances, became a Hollywood movie.

There are two aspects to this, both of which tend to draw the comparison to Lenny Bruce still tighter. The first involves Crumb's style. This is inimitable, traditional, and accessible but also wildly abandoned, the familiar lines of curvature rendering everything from pants legs to car doors untidy, bulbous, and invested with personality. His line trembles with ill-concealed laughter, the excitement of getting to the good part. Whether drugs or autism gave Crumb this heightened awareness of surfaces, only God and hard work gave him the ability to render them so vividly. Thus not only do toilets talk, cars walk, and buildings boogaloo, but sometimes the simplest activity becomes an entire strip, when only energy—and the narrative preconceptions we bring to paneling—drive the action.

Crumb believed that even the most basic things were worth reconsidering. This was a real link to Bruce, who practiced spontaneity and reconsideration, let's-take-another-look. There were often darker conclusions for Bruce than Crumb, whose questioning was usually a joyous process with joyous results, but both men took the chance. And Bruce's juice, like Crumb's, was his delight in the wonderful untidiness of humanity. His command of the detail, of the tactile surface, that real touch of the real storyteller, found an echo and continuation in every line Crumb drew. Both men found people irresistible.

Not that Crumb was any Pollyanna. Sometimes the same process as "Let's Eat"—the fixation on the simplest of actions—could quickly turn the other way, as in this example from a day in the uneventful life of Potatoes Browning, maintenance man:

There no joy here; no punch line. Just ordinary life and everyday yearning. As another bent character muses, striding through battered streets and past Mr. Natural: "Is dis a system?"

It was a question worth asking. (It still is.) And the place Crumb asked it was from the street, looking up, not from the campus looking down. This is Crumb's second area of kinship with Bruce, for like him, he was a lower middle-class boy, from Delaware this time, who had avoided college, and worked at real jobs (notably at the American Greeting Card Company in the early sixties). This made him more significant and more dangerous than those who sprang from the college-educated class to which Official America insisted the revolt was confined. It meant that the skepticism spread farther and deeper than was suspected and that he had the common touch, to take it farther and deeper still.

And did he ever have the common touch. Like Bruce, he was obsessed and delighted with sub-Americana, the lumpy clothes and lumpy food, the dented cars and hubcap curbs, the gaudy cornucopia of household names, the Kresge's look. It came from him in images the way it came from Bruce in words, a whoosh from the gut, of corner bar faces, urban blight, hippie lunacy, schoolyard ridicule, Zen mastery, momma's kitchen, old radio, new theologies, the hardened arteries of Motor City, fly-blown food, transmission fluid, orange peels, grime in the streets. And with him it seemed uncontrollable, sweeping you up in its flow, so that its rules were its own, and some beery tag from a Hamtramck dive could crop up in Acidland the way cowboys suddenly turned Yiddish on Bruce. If acid did anything for Crumb, it did what the antacid boys most feared: It made him more American, not less.

By 1970, Crumb, who had by then been publishing for roughly two years, was the uncrowned king of the underground comics, which were now being drawn and published in Los Angeles, New York, and Chicago, as well as in their own capital, San Francisco. His comics, which appeared in a series known generically as *Zap Comix,* although some in the series went by other titles (e.g., *Motor City Comix, Hi-Tone Comix)* were widely sought after, and appeared as far afield as London, Paris, and Tokyo. They were also mercilessly pirated, both in themselves and as individual images, panels, or strips, appearing on unauthorized posters and T-shirts (two of the new submedia of the counterculture), often without permission. While there is no space here to explore this particular predicament of underground publishing, it was endemic to the counterculture whenever it turned creative. How was one to reach farther than one's own community and a few friendly neighborhood newsstands, but at the same time avoid cooperation with distribution or syndication companies that operated on abhorrent principles?

The rock world had already solved the problem to some extent by the industry's willingness to accept, more or less without censorship, whatever product it turned out. (Although that did not, for all its practicality, address the question of principle—exploiting rock for profit.) The underground comic press, however, was not in the same position. Because of the nature of their other business, regular distributors and syndicators would have demanded enormous and unacceptable control over the content of what the underground comics produced had they agreed to handle them. The question was academic, however, since these operators were quite ignorant of the existence, let alone the appeal of, such product as *Zap.* The underground comics had no option to "sell out." Their position was that of the sixty-five-year-old virgin. (She wouldn't let them have it, but, then, they didn't want it.)

In consequence they had to rely on their own spindly lines of distribution and endure the pirating.‡ Ironically, this unregulated capitalism probably did more to expose Crumb's work than their own efforts could ever have.

Crumb, the only comic undergrounder for whom selling out was likely to be a real moral issue, further complicated matters by being both holier than the holiest when it came to principle, and a virtual recluse. The only premenopausal virgin of the lot had a permanent period. These issues were hot ones in 1970, and once the gap was opened for humor as it had been for rock, it would become of even greater cultural significance.

The usefulness, both historically and critically, of comparing Crumb to Bruce is limited. In many ways, obvious and not-so-obvious, the two are very different. (For one thing, Crumb has not had the good sense to die. This makes him hard to deify.) One of the less obvious ways is that despite their common delight in the lumpiness of human experience and their common willingness to go as far as possible in exploring it, Crumb is too gentle and affectionate to be a genuine satirist. He doesn't—or didn't—share Bruce's rage at those humans who set out to modify, regulate, or exploit their own and others' lumpiness. Crumb is uncomfortable drawing enemies. Generally, he tends to encode them in fantasy. On the few occasions, for instance in the "Lenore Goldberg" strips, where he actually tries to depict the forces of FBI/CIA evil arrayed against the intransigent radical feminist (with the big, bouncing, grab-me buttocks), the cops are characteristically rotund and sweaty, their skin and clothing rumpled as if they had a job to do, too, and occasionally asked themselves, "Is dis a system?"

But the spirit of Bruce was alive and well in 1970, and living in Robert Crumb. Crumb was a perfect illustration of the fact that if you trod on Boomer humor it only got better. Crumb's streety roots were to his campus peers as Bruce's were to Sahl and Compass–Second City. Most ironic of all parallels between the two is that both Bruce and Crumb were, at the height of their productivity, nailed as pornographers. But where Bruce got it from a predictable quarter, Crumb got it from his own: the radical feminists of San Francisco.

As Crumb's fame grew at this time, due in large part to his typically uninhibited depictions of all kinds of sex, he became guilty of success. The public criticism of the unfortunate genius took several forms, but the one that stuck, evidently, was that his depictions of women and, in particular, his hangup with big bottoms and getting head were rabidly sexist. "Lenore Goldberg" appears to have been an attempt to placate this kind of criticism,

‡ Not surprisingly, when the San Francisco artists finally got a publishing operation together it was called Rip-Off Press.

and he appeared a couple of times in his own strips to plead his case. This, more than the criticism itself, probably did him harm, for "Lenore" is not one of his more successful strips, and no one of Crumb's talent is capable of performing ideologically. His more honest response was—probably—his most peculiar invention, the Vulture Demonesses, who both terrorized and pleasured their prey. They might have been intended as some kind of back-handed tribute to the forcefulness of the movement women. But Crumb was irrepressible. He gave them big, bouncing, grab-me buttocks all the same.

Crumb now seems as much a chronicler as a commentator. Fantasy may have loomed in his work, but he was intensely faithful to his time. He drew what he saw, and felt what was felt. For all its rep as the Mecca of substance, San Francisco was still an American city, and the gaudiest of its denizens were still Americans. Crumb delighted in the ordinariness of the places these exotics came from, but he embraced with equal gusto the sense of limitless possibility they felt at being free. They were just plain Americans, whether they toked up or sucked on foaming tankards. And whoever you were, there was always the possibility that you could be touched by the magic Meatball.

Meatball, one of Crumb's early *Zap* efforts, is an agency of enlightenment, which drops from heaven unexpectedly, bops you on the head, and immediately induces *satori*. The first two pages describe scattered instances in which Meatball struck in the early sixties; but then the pace of America's enlightenment quickens:

12

Over-the-Counter Culture:
The National Lampoon

Heresy has always been a Harvard tradition.
—JOHN REED

But for all the tumult, and the diversity of ideas and voices in 1970, there were very few overground places outside of rock music for this volcano to erupt. And certainly none with any bona fides. Television was suspect, even though television writers schooled on fifteen years of Boomer humor were finally beginning to get the clout to make themselves felt, "The Mary Tyler Moore Show" premiered in September 1970; "All in the Family" was being prepared for its premiere in January 1971. That meant one of the other traditional Boomer humor alternatives, print or the theater. The theater was actually in fair fettle comedically *(Oh, Calcutta!; Hair; Lenny),* but print was another matter. *Rolling Stone,* rolling mosslessly along by now, was of limited scope; *Ramparts,* while it employed some brilliant journalists, had an intellectual stridency that limited it as a forum.

But more important there was something missing. Something which the dissenters had always been known for. From the time of Sahl and Feiffer, one thing distinguished dissent from the jumpy hostile insecurity of the authoritarian mentality—the ability to self-criticize. With precious few exceptions* there was, in this impudent culture, very little impudence about its own leaders, its own orthodoxies, its own stereotypes.

In April of 1970 *The National Lampoon* changed all that.

The National Lampoon was not intended to be a counter-counterculture magazine; but it was not part of the underground press either. As far as the intent of its founders was concerned, it had very few of the purposes it would actually come to serve. Indeed, its basic purpose was to continue and extend

---

* "Doonesbury" appeared for the first time this year in the Yale student paper, *Bull Tales.*

the extremely pleasant collective experience producing that dean of college humor magazines, the *Harvard Lampoon.*

This august journal, which over its hundred-year history had included among its alumni such well-known humorists as William Randolph Hearst, George Santayana, and Elliot Richardson had undergone changes in the late fifties and sixties that in their own idiosyncratic way, mirrored those going on in Boomer humor at large. Though the changes started late, compared to those going on in the real world, they exhibited essentially the same dynamic, with an energetic and experimental group taking over the magazine from a moribund establishment. In the process, the group not only vastly expanded the readership but laid the foundation for later commercial success. This process really began in the same year that Second City was founded, 1959. One "reformist" who came onto the magazine in that year was Christopher Cerf, oldest son of Bennett Cerf, the founder of Random House:

"When I got to Harvard in 1959, the circulation of the *Lampoon* was, I think, 873. It had become an extremely right-wing, very preppy, upper-class, magazine. [For example] there was an issue called the 'Wonk,' issue which just made fun of everyone at Harvard who wasn't in a final club.

"They did these really nasty, vicious articles about Wonks, who were basically people with slide rules in their pockets and crew cuts, and who wore horn-rimmed glasses. I was worried that I was a Wonk—having gone to prep school, I was probably okay, and I didn't take math—it was math, science, all that stuff that was really 'bad.' There was a lot of talk that *Lampoon* was a final club, that you didn't get on to by being funny, you got on it by being well connected. People were very angry about the *Lampoon.* There was even a movement to start another humor magazine at Harvard—one that would 'respond to the needs of students' rather than just an uppercrust bunch of snotty people."

The temptations for *Lampoon* members to live a charmed life were considerable. Even within the charmed life of Harvard itself, the *Lampoon* boasted, among many traditional accoutrements, its own castle. Called, with savage wit, the Castle, this extraordinary structure is possibly one of the best jokes in American architecture. Designed by a founder, Edmund Wheelwright, in 1909, paid for by William Randolph Hearst, it is a delicious parody of the plutocratic Europhilia of early twentieth-century architectural fashion, a confusion of gables, turrets, domes, styles, and furnishings—a combination, as Cerf puts it, of a Flemish fisherman's cottage and an Elizabethan Great Hall.

The Castle is a celebration of the very opulence it parodies. It is stuffed with turn-of-the-century bric-a-brac and splendid antiques. It always has been the site of gargantuan feasts and it exudes exclusivity; the hoi polloi can have no inkling of what occurs inside its walls. This is the most elaborate treehouse ever devised, and the sign reading BOYS' CLUB—KEEP OUT is engraved on a shingle of burnished gold. The Castle symbolizes the unusual combination of wit and wealth, intelligence and opulence, that sets the *Lampoon* apart; it represents both ultra-arrogance, and ultra-tolerance, the twin peaks between which the *Lampoon* has always strung its wire.

In 1959 the wit-intelligence-tolerance side of the Castle was in bad repair. This was what Cerf and his fellows, in particular a brilliant soul named George Trow, all of them hiding in the Trojan Horse of preppiness, brought to the *Lampoon*. But what they also brought was a great desire to revivify the magazine, and in particular the regular (or fairly regular) parodies for which it had always been famed. The *Lampoon* had not done a parody since 1956 (that one was of *Newsweek*). In 1960, it was decided to parody the *Saturday Review*, a rather limited target, but since in these days the parodies were still only distributed locally, (which meant that at best they reached alumni and literati in New York, New Haven, etc.), they could afford to.

Despite the minuscule circulation, this parody was noticed by the editors of *Mademoiselle*, who decided to let the *Lampoon* editors put together their next July issue, as a parody of their own magazine—perhaps because July is a traditionally slow month in the magazine business. For this, the *Lampoon* would be paid $7,000 and allowed to insert a subscription card in the parody.

The *Mademoiselle* parody appeared in July 1961 and was an enormous success, selling over a million copies. By the standards of the time, (Kennedy's first year in office), it was fairly tame stuff ("I dreamt I was arrested for indecent exposure in my Maidenfirm bra"), hardly evincing much knowledge of the state of humor elsewhere in the land. But it had a lot going for it. For one thing, it was the first appearance of Boomer humor in the traditional magazine world. For another, it was superbly produced, all the technical and human resources of *Mademoiselle* having been placed at the disposal of the Harvard team. Lastly, it was very much in tune with the times—smart Ivy League men dealing effortlessly with Madison Avenue.

For the *Lampoon*, the immediate dividend was a tremendous surge in subscriptions. As Cerf puts it, thanks to the *Mademoiselle* parody, the *Lampoon* became what it was always supposed to be, "as much a magazine as a club." The *Mademoiselle* parody also ushered in a decade of success in the parody biz, first with a repeat in 1962 of *Mademoiselle*, then a further sequel in 1963, which was actually a parody of *Esquire* concealed between the covers of a *Mademoiselle* parody.

By the time Cerf graduated in 1963, the old regime had been solidly replaced, and the *Lampoon*'s finances were in better order. The *Lampoon* was definitely now part of the mainstream of Boomer humor—and would become more so every year. In three short years, it had undergone the kind of transformation so many others had in the previous decade, and had done it in much the same way, by rebelling against its own peculiar establishment within the Establishment.

The gutters of Mt. Arbor Street were not red with aristocratic blood; the *Lampoon* was still an exclusive club, but it was attracting wit as well as wealth. The new feel to the regular magazine, the excitement of the national parodies, and the openness to new blood of any color attracted a range of talent which would, over the next five years, enrich the *Lampoon* in every way.

In 1965 the *Lampoon* took on a perennial target, *Time,* and the result was brilliant. Its cover, coming when it did, in a desert of satiric comment about Vietnam, was a gem (see photo insert).

Despite the fact that it had only printed enough for its usual local distribution, this parody was passed along far afield, almost unintentionally becoming the first underground satire of the decade.

In 1966, the *Lampoon* went officially back to national production, this time without the help of *Mademoiselle,* and produced a parody of *Playboy.* This was a high-precision parody with an easy target (the Vargas girl, a large-bosomed pink cutie wearing nothing but green high heels, asks the immortal question, "Hi . . . How do you like my breasts?"), and a huge hit.

Newsstands couldn't keep the parody coming fast enough. It sold 550,000 copies in a week at $1.25 a piece, quite a tab on campus in 1966. Without compromising its product, censoring its humor, being "co-opted" or "selling out," the *Lampoon* managed to bring home close to a quarter of a million dollars.

The principle reason for this quantum leap in both editorial initiative and profitability was the emergence in late 1965 and 1966 of a New Wave, among whom were three young men who would become the founders of the *National Lampoon:* Henry Beard, Doug Kenney, and Rob Hoffman. The latter, who hailed from Texas, was largely responsible for putting the finances of the *Playboy* parody and therefore the whole *Lampoon* organization on a firm footing (by such rudimentary reforms as actually billing advertisers).

Another Lampooner of the time, Jim Rivaldo, recalls Hoffman: "Rob was on the business board and also started out selling ads and was conceded as the financial wiz. He was always sort of poked fun of as a Dallas tycoon. He had a very charming personality . . . (but) . . . Henry and Doug would always hold him up as the wheeler-dealer, financial wiz, and for sure he was.

But it was Beard and Kenney who were calling the editorial shots. The two could not, in many ways, have been more dissimilar.†

Rivaldo: "Henry practically lived at the *Lampoon.* He was this eternal presence around there, defiantly unstylish, wore tattered Brooks Brothers suits and big woolen sweaters that got washed every month or so. He was ruffled and professorial and wry.

"At the beginning, Doug was not around all that much. He would sort of breeze through. He was out conquering other worlds around campus. He was quite the opposite of Henry. He was always in fashion with girlfriends. He became president of the Spee Club.

"Spee was a social club. Harvard had ten clubs or so, vestiges of the social

---

† It should be noted here that Henry Beard has declined to be interviewed both here and in several other places, about the *Harvard* and *National Lampoon.*

elitism. They were not fraternities, but in reality they *were* very much fraternities. A very small number of people belonged to these clubs.

"Doug became president of the Spee Club. You know, he really climbed his way to that point through charm. He looked like a preppie, and he could pull off the act pretty well, whatever his background was. Henry just sort of cruised into it.

"I always got the impression that Doug didn't have all that much money. His father was a tennis pro or tennis instructor. [Kenney's family actually lived in a place called Chagrin Falls, Ohio.] And so he admitted that he was kind of a social climber. Henry, on the other hand, gave the impression of being an aristocrat.

"What was interesting about both of them was their military involvement. Doug was in ROTC from the beginning, and I guess he was kicked out of it and had a very bitter attitude toward military things.

"And Henry at the same time was a member of the Army Reserve, and so he always had to go out for a couple of weeks of Reserve training in the summer, along with the periodic drills once a month. Although he was never in combat, he had a real good sense of military attitudes toward things."

Beard and Kenney were not a team yet. According to Hoffman, Kenney was not around the *Lampoon* very much after his initial impact: "Doug did a very important issue in February of 1966, and it really showed his talent. He wrote, he drew, he wrote songs. Doug modeled himself after Trow, although he could draw and he was multidimensional talent. But [after that] Doug sort of went away."

This was a pattern that would recur. Kenney spent the next couple of years in pursuit of his social dreams. Beard, however, in the wake of its success, established himself as the quiet guru of the *Lampoon*. Another Lampooner who joined in 1966 was Broadway playwright John Weidman. He remembers his first impression of Beard this way: "Henry was like Bernard Baruch. Henry was the guy who sat on the park bench and told you how it was. Henry really had an aura around him. He set the tone. The resident genius. He didn't *do* anything to make himself present [but] his hero then was S. J. Perelman, and he was viewed a little bit like Perelman around the *Lampoon.*"

The following year (1966–67), the *Lampoon* devoted much of its time to spending its new wealth. One requirement was the refurbishment of the Castle, which was by then in a state of considerable disrepair; another was a certain increase in the Lampooners' standard of living.

But not all the changes were cosmetic. As Weidman points out, the *Lampoon* and Harvard itself were being transformed at the time:

"The place changed astoundingly [in 1964–68]. By 1968, a lot of the money made by the parodies had been spent on the Castle. Big Bose speakers hung from the ceiling. The *Lampoon* was, if anything, ahead of the times as far as politics, drugs, or rock and roll were concerned. Jon Cerf [Chris Cerf's younger brother] and Peter Gable had a rock group called the Central Park

Zoo, which were the hottest college rock group around Boston. They would go and play at parties for the Boston Patriots. They were really good.

"[The *Lampoon*] was certainly in step with what was happening in the larger culture. Blacks were being elected to the *Lampoon* much more quickly in those years than they were to the finals clubs around campus. It had much more to do with what was happening than . . . it did with any kind of *Brideshead Revisited* crap that may have been going on. It wasn't as though a bunch of guys in tuxedos were squinting at a joint and trying to figure out which end to put in their mouths . . . It was the best of both worlds. It was rich and it was funny . . ."

These lifestyles of the rich and funny found the traditional *Lampoon* expression in the next parody that was undertaken—Henry Luce's venerable organ, *Life*. The *Life* parody was planned for 1968. It was the first time that Beard and Kenney, who was now swinging back from his Spee persona to his *Lampoon* one, emerged solidly as the dominant voices of the group. The *Life* parody was the most ambitious, conceptually and technically, of all the *Lampoon*'s publications to date, and while a half dozen people worked on it, it was, according to Rivaldo, very much Beard's and Kenney's creation.

Rivaldo says, "Doug, the wild genius, had to be catered to. Had to be fed and clothed. Also, we all began experimenting with drugs. Doug was convinced that drugs unlocked all kinds of creativity and that much of the satire we were producing at the time was drug-induced visions. But Henry didn't. Henry never smoked dope nor took any drugs. He would just drink. I mean, I wouldn't call him an alcoholic, but, you know, at the end of the day he'd get wine and brandy. . . .

"Henry was regarded as the final arbiter of the thing . . . Doug didn't seem to care to exert any editorial executive authority."

Whatever the mix of stimuli and authority, the result was a deft and certainly unhallucinatory piece of satire.

Life was then on its last legs, a victim not just of television but of its thirty-year-old reputation as the Voice—or perhaps the Face—of America. The parody's cover story was appropriately: "The End of the World." The by now familiar satellite picture of Earth was accompanied by this caption: "Cowering timidly for satellite camera, Mother Earth whimpers her final 'Cheese' as the World hurtles toward oblivion."

There was a savage inside lead, "Organs à Go-Go," on the quest for organ donors. Despite the happy ending in which a terminally ill patient who doesn't need a heart gets one anyway, the *Life* parody reminds its readers that with all the admiration we reserve for dedicated doctors, we often tend to forget the "unsung heroes" who "donate" their innards that others might live. In this case, *Life* notes that the donor was a friendless thirty-five-year-old loner with the nickname of "Sleezy," described by the few who knew him as a "showoff" and a "lout." So not to worry.

These are not folks who like *Life* magazine very much. The parody was a far cry from the happy splashing about in the vacuities of high fashion that characterized the *Mademoiselle* series. Even the fashion spread in *Life* had obvious oral overtones. Of a model—black significantly—wearing only a bikini made of lettuce, the caption says: TOGS HE CAN SINK HIS TEETH INTO.

The *Life* parody was a new development in the *Lampoon*'s sixties parodies. True, it grew organically out of those that had preceded it, no less thorough or literate than the *Esquire* and *Playboy* parodies, but perhaps because it chose this time a magazine that functioned as an official verbal and visual version of the culture, it acquired automatically a new satiric level. In its worldliness—its careful avoidance of the usual collegiate references and academic exhibitionism—and in its equally careful attention to accuracy of graphic style, the first glimmerings of what would become *The National Lampoon* can be detected.

Another element entered the picture with the publication of the *Life* parody: a real-life Manhattan publisher named Matty Simmons. Simmons was old enough—just—to be the Harvard men's father, from the same generation as Lenny Bruce, who had hit the streets hustling after World War II. His version had taken him into publicity, specifically for various New York restaurants, and thence to a lucky encounter with the fledgling Diners Club. Helping to authenticate and expand its operations, he had become a shareholder in Diners Club, prospering with it through its phenomenal growth in the fifties and early sixties. In 1967 he sold his interest and began a magazine-publishing company, one of whose first properties was the monthly magazine put out by a new chain of reducing clubs called Weight Watchers. (The irony of moving in one's late thirties from active participation in Diners Club to active participation in *Weight Watchers Magazine,* is noteworthy.)

Simmons's other main property at the time, however, was *Cheetah Magazine.* This too had a connection, albeit more tenuous, to a chain of clubs which went by the same name. The Cheetah clubs were a bald attempt to merchandise the "psychedelic" rock and roll dance clubs that were springing up at the time, historically somewhere between the go-go joint and the disco, featuring live and recorded rock and generally repulsive light shows, intended to approximate hallucination. Since the underground was underground precisely to avoid commercialization, this was neither very smart nor very likely to succeed. For all its efforts to be hip, with it, and groovy, *Cheetah Magazine* was to the actual underground what the movie *I Love You, Alice B. Toklas* was to Haight-Ashbury.

But *Cheetah* was slickly produced, nationally distributed, and one of the very few islands of interest concerning the potential of the new generation, in an industry that seemed determined to ignore it. The *Lampoon*'s distributor, Independent News, the largest magazine distributor in the nation, was also Simmons's. They suggested a meeting between the *Lampoon* editors and Simmons, to see if the commercial potential for the expensive *Life* parody couldn't be better realized.

According to Simmons, it was too late by the time the *Lampoon* men came to him to do much for the *Life* parody, although his company sold a few ads in it. But he sensed that, with this group, there would be life after *Life*.

(For all its brilliance, the *Life* parody was a commercial flop, the first dent in an otherwise perfect batting average. The reasons for the failure were legion, but chief among them was the fact that the parody was directed at a magazine no one cared about anymore. According to Hoffman, there was also the financial aspect: "The costs were out of control. There were the same [production] costs we had in *Playboy,* although there was more editorial color. But *Playboy* sold out. *Life* cost a lot more to print: $183,000. [A staggering amount for a college parody in 1968.] The press run was 750,000, and only about half the copies sold. The project lost $75,000, and that put us in terrible shape.")

This was the summer of 1968. Beard had graduated in 1967 and gone into the Army Reserve. Kenney had graduated in 1968. It was at this time, says Hoffman, that he, Beard, Kenney, and Rivaldo decided to start *The National Lampoon.* In order to keep Beard and Kenney together, the *Lampoon* arranged to maintain them for the balance of 1968 in Cambridge while they wrote their first total collaboration, a delicious hit on the cult book of the decade, *Lord of the Rings.* It was called *Bored of the Rings* and was more properly a lampoon than a parody, taking wild and energetic swings at the original rather than guying its Druidic cuteness. The effort eventually sold 750,000 copies in paperback, and did much to earn back the *Life* debt.

Hoffman, meanwhile, disappeared to active duty in the Coast Guard in the fall of 1968, returning in March 1969 to start work on another, this time determinedly commercial parody of *Time,* Luce's other organ, and potentially a much more attractive target.

The *Time* parody would be a copublishing venture between the *Harvard Lampoon* and Simmons's company, Twenty-First Century Communications, which he owned with Len Mogel. It would also be an audition for a regular magazine, in which the New York publishers were now showing considerable interest. In early June 1969, Hoffman met with Simmons and Mogel to cut a deal for this further venture. As he puts it, the deal was a "brains and money" one, meaning Harvard brains and New York money. Twenty-First Century agreed to put up $350,000 to launch the magazine. For tax purposes, the company retained eighty percent of the stock and the Harvard men, whom Simmons then and forever after referred to as "the boys", got twenty percent. Figuring they really deserved something more like a third of the stock, Hoffman negotiated a buyout deal, to take place five years later (although within a window of a twenty-four-month discretionary period), at which time a multiple of twenty-five times their share of earnings would compensate them for the lower stock percentage. This was a Draconian—and extremely un-"boy"-like—achievement on the part of the hard-headed Hoffman, and would come to haunt Simmons later. For the moment the deal went forward (although it was not actually signed until the next spring as the first issue of *The National Lampoon* was going to press).

Meanwhile, in the summer of 1969, finishing touches were put on the *Time* parody, which in the light of these developments had assumed a lesser significance, and it was put to bed in August and September of that year. It turned out to be a tremendous success, making $250,000 profit for its publishers, digging the Castle out of its hole and certainly reassuring Simmons that he was sitting on something big. Its content was somewhat more monotonic than the *Life* parody, but vintage Beard and Kenney nonetheless. Noteworthy was its cover, which was a witty triple-decker, not only sexy in itself, but referring to a common controversy of the day (see photo insert).

A casualty of the process was Rivaldo, who, according to Hoffman, went through a considerable amount of emotional turmoil during the production of the parody. Rivaldo himself felt out of place in New York, and although he acted as art director for the parodies, was sincerely concerned that he would not be up to the task of art-directing a magazine on a regular basis. The parting of the ways between the original group was not in any way acrimonious, although the eventual founders did take the initiative in laying out their problems to Rivaldo. Rivaldo, a gentle soul, has no regrets despite what happened subsequently to the enterprise. He refers to himself ruefully as the "fifth Beatle" of *The National Lampoon*.

As soon as the *Time* parody, which was produced both in Harvard and New York, went to press, Beard and Kenney moved full-time to New York and some dingy offices on Broadway, thoughtfully provided by their new partners. Preparations for their brainchild—and Simmons's money child—began in earnest.

The chances of a new magazine succeeding are always slim. In 1970 they were positively anorexic. Television's long and pointless march had felled one after the other of the great magazines of the first half of the century, particularly those in the general interest, slice-of-culture category (e.g. *Colliers*). Unless a magazine served a particular trade or purpose, or was aimed at either homemakers or businessmen, it was probably experiencing a lot of trouble.

The problem was less one of literacy than of distribution. America had also become increasingly automotive, and that mainstay of magazine distribution —the newsstand—was one of the first things to suffer. Magazines had enormously increased their dependence for circulation on subscriptions. But the reader must be induced to buy a subscription, especially since it commits him to a set number of issues. This means bribery, which in turn means discounts. The competition for subscriptions had led to heavier and heavier discounting, so that many magazines (of which *Life* was a prime example) made no money at all on their actual subscription sales, but depended on them for their circulation figures—which in turn of course were the basis for their advertising revenue.

Television was also a formidable competitor for advertising dollars. Since television was of general interest in appeal, the hardest hit by this competition were the general interest magazines. Publishers of general interest magazines were thus faced with a nasty choice of cliff edges; in one direction, no revenue from sales; in the other, sharp drops in what they could expect from page rates.

There were a couple of somewhat rickety rope ladders leading away from this unpleasant place. First was the imminent banning of cigarette advertising on television. Magazine publishers salivated at the prospect of inhaling these carcinogenic dollars. (Cigarette advertising on TV was completely banned in 1971.) Second, supermarket and drugstore chains were increasingly beginning to install magazine racks, replacing the distribution function of the old newsstand. The day might come again when publishers could charge for their magazines what the cover said they cost.

Interestingly, two of the very few successes in postwar general interest start-ups, *Mad* magazine and *Playboy,* both had a much higher than average newsstand sale, which meant that they didn't have to entirely rely for revenue on advertisers. *(Mad,* of course, didn't carry any ads at all.) But for magazines heavily addicted to subscriptions, it was hard to be born again at the newsstand or magazine-rack—subscribers now expected to get them at cut rates in the mail.

Any way you came at it, *The National Lampoon* looked like a dog. Certainly it was aimed at a new market, but all magazines which had been aimed at this market—*Cheetah* being one of them—had crashed on takeoff. *Rolling Stone,* which was still too new to prove much, was a service magazine. For all its we-are-the-counterculture ballyhoo, it was a music magazine aimed at people who listened to music. And to be sure, the Harvard parodies had been a success and a success at their cover price on campus, one of the few places outside of cities where newsstands could still be found. But this was a magazine, not a parody, which however brilliant, always remains a parasite on the host body.

Worse still, the *Lampoon* served no purpose or trade. It was strictly for entertainment, a general interest magazine, the leper of Madison Avenue. Its chances of making any money in advertising were nil on that score and minus nil when you considered the audience it would be aimed at. There was no way of knowing if any of them had any money, and a sizable segment of them professed not to want any, ever. Furthermore, there was little hope of a prelaunch subscription campaign, for subscription acquisition means mailing lists, and mailing lists cost money, and Simmons was no Hearst. Besides, there were no mailing lists on this market, aside from the one in the Selective Service computer.

It says a great deal for Simmons that he took this chance. He had nothing to go on, other than the success of the parodies, and from a hard business point of view they meant very little. Even to survive, let alone fatten up nicely for a killing, the *Lampoon* would have to do one thing and one thing alone: be a staggering success at the newsstand. No other conventional way of making money with magazines was open to him. He would have to sell a lot of copies at full price. Their covers would have to pop. Their content would have to sizzle. To do this he relied on two recent college graduates who were neither of his generation nor his school of humor (Simmons's favorite was Alan King —a splendid humorist but hardly of the Harvard ilk). They would have to do all the things expected of comedians and all the things expected of magazines. The newsstand would be their nightclub, and they were going on without a singer.

Beard and Kenney seemed supremely unconcerned about all of this. Their principal concern was to find in the wilds of New York a group which would approximate the one up at the Castle. Nor were they very much concerned with Simmons's concerns. As Cerf recalls, "The question everyone had was who were the Weight Watchers, and why were they doing this?"

But they were doing it, and the money would be there for the printer and there would be offices to work in and coffee in the corner. The real problem was to find the right people and create the right atmosphere. Everything else would flow from that. And ultra-arrogant though this may seem, it was probably the smartest thing they did.

Beard and Kenney went into *The National Lampoon* with all the arrogance and tolerance Harvard had bred in them. They were never tempted to make the compromises which had become second nature to anyone working in the media in the sixties. They saw no need to tailor what they wrote to any particular purpose or market, or to select their writers on the same basis. As it happened, what they wrote and those they selected turned out to be just right, and the audience eventually went wild.

If they had chosen to be "professionals," worry about the market, what they wrote, subscriptions, distribution, being the lepers of Madison Avenue, and so on, *The National Lampoon* would have ended up as a Silent Scream. Instead, they did what the best of Boomer humorists had always done—and Simmons's trust in them makes him one of them: they held hands and jumped.

Throughout the fall of 1969, discussions and meetings continued. Chris Cerf figured in these, as did other *Lampoon* alumni. Cerf, in particular, was in a position to help Beard and Kenney get their bearings in literary New York; he was now at Random House editing such people as Abbie Hoffman, agitating to publish Stewart Brand and his *Whole Earth Catalog,* and serving as a link between My Father's Place and the underground.

And into his office one day came an underground writer, manic, untidy, but intensely precise, with a couple of ideas Bennett might go for. One was *The Incredible Adventures of the Rock,* in which weird epigrams accompanied a series of identical pictures of a rock, the other a children's book, written in best first-grade cyclamate, in which all the pets and little friends got gradually and horribly destroyed. Cerf loved them both, convinced Random House to publish *Rock,* and was forever under the spell of Michael O'Donoghue.

O'Donoghue was utterly one-time-only—the ultimate antistereotype. He wrote a comic strip in the *Evergreen Review* called "Phoebe Zeitgeist." It was about an excessively sexy heroine constantly embroiled in intellectual intrigue. It was deliciously drawn, and every word of every caption glittered.

He was on the cutting edge of everything below 14th Street, including his own nerves. He had staged happenings in the Electric Circus, the East Village den of Wonder Warhol. But while he was definitely acceptable to the Viva-Ultra pack, he was much too sharp to be one of them; he hung out at Max's Kansas City with Al Goldstein, whose raunchy *Screw* he perversely purported to admire. He was underground but above it, too good for it, his epigrammatic intensity cutting to the bone. He was gaunt, broke, wore a flat-peaked hat at all times, and lived along one wall of a huge loft in what was still derelict Soho. It was completely uninhabitable, lit with bare bulbs, heated by an industrial gas blower that sounded like a subway train when it was going, and full of bizarre objects, stuffed birds, legless dolls, anonymous photographs, mysterious things kept in other things, all of which became in his hands somehow hilarious. In the midst of the chaos was a filing cabinet, in which with meticulous care he kept index cards, inscribed, equally meticulously, with his "ideas"—in reality phrases which delighted him, comic *haiku* that contained within them the premise of full-blown pieces, some of exquisite horridness. All of them would somewhere, in some way get used. By inclination a poet, he was passionately concerned with the value of the words he used; each one was carefully weighed and set in place and, once in place, could not be touched by *anyone*. He felt for words the way forgers must feel for the currency they create, relishing its equal but counterfeit worth, and the trouble it will cause for those who keep the treasury.

For all his preemptive wit, he could be charming, gentle, even vulnerable. He led every group he found himself in, shimmering with manic energy, but hated leaders. He summed up the paradox of the lonely, the craving to be in, all the way inside, at the center of the innest group, jumbled with the antisocialism of "no one must touch my stuff!" Capable of monumental rage, he never laid a finger on anyone—except himself (he had a habit *in extremis* of violently punching his own thigh, as if furious at himself for letting anyone get far enough ahead of him to make him mad).

For this group, O'Donoghue was an essential ingredient, for there was nothing Ivy League about him. He came from Rochester, N.Y., and was extremely reticent about his childhood. His schooling was similarly obscure but seemed to center around art; indeed, his eye was almost as good as his ear. Questions about his background made him nervous, gave him migraines. "I'm bored now," he would say; intellectually, and probably in every other way, he didn't want to owe anyone anything. He devoured every idea that came within his ken, but better, grasped the central words at their core, which could then be made to self-destruct merely by his uttering them. Politically, his heart was in the right place, but his head was usually there first, seeking out whomever it might destroy.

He would be dubbed New Left, but it was inconceivable that he belong to any party except his own. He could only be considered left in a world where the right are those who want to define, control, and regiment and the left is those who hate their guts. For the Harvard men, O'Donoghue was something else, and something they badly needed. He was a Street Writing Man.

It seems improbable that anyone of this voltage would not eventually have come to the attention of Beard and Kenney, however the credit for the catch seems to go to Cerf and Trow. One of Cerf's mischief-making projects in the fall of 1969 was a fake baseball program to be distributed during the upcoming contest between Judge Julius Hoffman and the Chicago 7. The name of the pamphlet has not been recorded for posterity, although it was something like "The Washington Kangaroos v. The Chicago Conspirators," and it disappeared as quickly as it was put together. But O'Donoghue was invited to participate in putting it together, as was Trow, and it was here, according to Cerf, that they first met. Trow, then, brought O'Donoghue to one of the many *Lampoon* meetings that were being held all over the city.

O'Donoghue was a major addition to the group, and a welcome one, for Beard and Kenney were not having an easy time recruiting in the superheated Manhattan of the late sixties. Here their Harvardness, far from being the asset it might be on campuses across the nation, was a liability. On the one side, the liberal-left art establishment in New York, which tended to intersect with the then powerful *Village Voice* and *New York Review of Books,* did not look too kindly on anything so unproletarian as the *Harvard Lampoon.* On the other side, the New York underground press, which now boasted a comic contingent to rival San Francisco's, assumed *Lampoon*'s porcitude without hesitation. (The *East Village Other* had by now produced a number of solid comic artists, most notably Spain Rodrigues, whose postholocaust hero, Trashman, was at least a dozen years ahead of the Road Warrior; also Kim Deitch, Trina Robbins and even its own short-lived comic supplement "Gothic Blimp Works," which was inaugurated in 1969 under the editorship of Vaughan Bodé.)

Beard and Kenney may have seen the recruitment of O'Donoghue, whose East Village papers were in perfect order, as a means of infiltrating the New York underground press, but the *East Village Other*s weren't having any. Purism was rapidly developing as a terminal disease at the time: preppie Kenney and Tory Beard, along with the uptown crowd they came with—Random House, the real rip-off press, man, and Abbie Hoffman, the supposed FBI/CIA informer—didn't reassure the downtowners in the least. Beard and Kenney had greater success with the more seasoned set from the late fifties and early sixties, like Arnold Roth from Kurtzman's *Help!,* Roger Price, who had his own minihumor magazine *Grump,* and the unsinkable Jean Shepherd. And they did uncover one enormous resource in commercial artist Rick Meyerowitz, who had a hankering to do satirical material and an unsuspected talent for devastating caricature.

For the most part, though, they could not find many newcomers who fit the bill. When it came to writers, they were looking for a beast that had not yet evolved—since there had previously been no environment for it to evolve in;

such writers as there were, humorists rather than satirists, had generally found themselves a niche already and made the necessary adjustments. But there were always Cerf, the irrepressible Trow, and other *Harvard Lampoon* heavies like John Weidman. In a pinch the national version could be put out by hometeam champions.

The most significant decision they made, after the absorption of O'Donoghue, was in the art direction. Here Beard and Kenney made their first real mistake. They hired as the art directors a trio of hippie goons called Cloud Studios. Cloud Studios—aptly named since they clouded men's minds—consisted of Peter Bramley, Bill Skurski, and Michael Sullivan. They were a very genial bunch, quite funny, with modest underground credentials but not so impressive that they wouldn't work above 14th Street. Bramley was a slickish underground comic artist, and Sullivan a talented collagist. The Harvard men had their reasons for taking this tentative step into the world below the earth; they were convinced that their magazine, which was not a parody, should have an underground feel to it, to appeal to the campus audience.

While it is easy to quarterback this play from the safety of a Monday morning many years later, it was odd that they would take art direction with which their record had nothing in common. Their magazine had to have its own look, but the success of the parodies might have told them that their audience wanted graphics at least as good as those in the magazines they'd been parodying. But in 1969–70, the underground press was definitely setting the standards when it came to "artistic integrity," and it was easy to be intimidated. It was the only decision they made which was really against their better judgment, and it turned out to be disastrous.

All that the editors needed was now in place: personnel, backing, offices, art direction, distribution—and a buyout deal. Now they were on their own. Work began in November 1969, and the period between then and the appearance of the first issue was uneventful.

So was the appearance of the first issue.

Simmons must have turned white all over. The cover didn't pop; the contents didn't sizzle. And the most surprising thing about the first effort of his two whiz kids was its lack of initiative. The "theme" of the issue, or more properly its title, was "Sexy Cover Issue," essentially a quarter turn on the *Time* parody cover "Does Sex Sell Magazines?" but not half as witty. Or sexy. The unfortunate woman who graced the debut of *The National Lampoon* was clad in a skimpy leather playsuit with the top open,‡ and was being ogled by a very underground-looking animal drawn by Bramley, which was supposed to be a duck. The latter bore about as much resemblance to a duck, even a cartoon duck, as the old Fillmore posters had to legible lettering. The duck was intended to become the mascot of the magazine. In fact, it became the symbol of everything that was wrong with Cloud Studio's art direction, in

‡ There may have been some residual satirical purpose in the color chosen for the playsuit which was military olive-drab.

particular with its emphasis on the magazine looking "funny"—the print equivalent of a comedian laughing while delivering a joke.

This problem was compounded inside by simple incompetence. One of the funnier pieces of writing in the issue was by O'Donoghue and Trow, called "Mondo Perverto," a prototype for the fake magazine parody (i.e., a parody of a genre of magazine rather than a specific one) that would become a *National Lampoon* staple. "Mondo Perverto" was roughly aimed at any publication from *Confidential* to the *National Enquirer* that dealt with sensational "news." Featuring such memorable articles as "The Case for Killing Our Aged" ("You've had your fun! Now butt out!"), the piece was so full of "wacky" graphics that it was barely recognizable as a parody. The satirical point of the article—that the *Enquirer* et al. fabricate sensational features to pull in geriatric readers—was quite lost, and readers got the impression instead that the authors actually *meant* lines like "Let's give Ma Nature a hand!"

The editors went back to the Harvard well in the other main feature, a Playmate spread, supposedly from a magazine parody called *Playbore*. Like the cover it was both a good deal more tacky and a good deal less witty than its predecessor. There were some significant bright spots, however. One was a love comic called "White House Romance," starring David Eisenhower and Julie Nixon, and telling the touching story of how, although they'd been married a year, they'd not yet been to bed together. ("Don't worry, honey," says David in the final clinch. "I take those pills every day".) This too was a prototype for another *Lampoon* staple, the parody comic, which in the hands of O'Donoghue and Kenney would produce some of its best and funniest material.

In the same vein was the first episode of "Mrs. Agnew's Diary," written by Kenney, which told the story of life at the top as seen through the eyes of the Vice President's wife, Judy Agnew. Written in a gushy, breathless style of a middle-class housewife, it reduced every footfall in a corridor of power to the level of suburban gossip:

Dear Diary,
　　Today was so exciting! Pat and Dick called up this morning to invite us to lunch in the upstairs room! Spiggy [Spiro Agnew] said he thought Dick had something up his sleeve because Pat only invites us upstairs, when Dick wants to make a big deal impression. Spiggy said if he had any more of the goddamn meat loaf and cottage cheese, he'd get sick all over the rug.

This idea was taken from a similar column called "Mrs. Wilson's Diary" in the English satirical magazine *Private Eye,* describing events at Number 10 Downing Street, under Prime Minister Harold Wilson. The column was one of the few things that was immediately popular, and it eventually became the magazine's most important continuing feature.

On balance, however, the first issue was a dud. For those who had anticipated something better based on the Harvard parodies, it was a big disappointment; for those with no prior knowledge of any kind of *Lampoon,* it was not very entertaining—and even misleading, since on the evidence of the cover and a quick flick through, it looked like some oddball version of a men's magazine. At any event the issue sold in the mid-twentieth percentile.*

The picture remained very much the same for the next six months of 1970. The covers tended to be messy and unfocused, usually with far too much going on, so that there was no clear joke or image to grab the buyer. The sales remained between 22 and 28 percent, with no significant revenue from advertising. The inside was no better; it conveyed no message through its graphics and layouts other than confusion.

The editors decided on a policy of dealing with only one topic per issue. The topics (from May 1970 through October 1970) were "Greed," "Blight," "Bad Taste," "Paranoia," "Show Biz," and "Politics." It was easier to come up with material when directed toward a given subject than simply plucking a funny idea out of the ether. It also gave an intellectual cohesion to each issue and tended to intensify the satirical thrust of the magazine. By coming at one subject in a number of different ways, with a number of different styles or approaches, it was almost certain that there would be one effective piece of satire in each issue.

For all that, the first four of these subjects had a certain sameness to them —all were negative value judgments (e.g. "Blight," which was actually about the environment) and tended to be cloudy in their overall effect. In a way, the editors were making the same kind of mistake satirically that the art direction continued to make, telling the reader how to react. The last two issue subjects, however, were more neutral and more productive. "Show Biz" and "Politics" were the best issues to date. *"Show Biz"* included a brilliant photo story by O'Donoghue called "Waiting in the Left Wings" about a "radical" Hollywood film star called "Nana Bijou." It was essentially a parody of a press release and gave an account of Nana's typical day: "Afternoon finds the perky peacenik in San Diego, spitting on a Navy color guard and shouting 'No more fodder for the war machine!'—which ironically is the title of her latest Paramount movie . . ."

"Varietsky" by Beard was a supplement on show biz behind the Iron Curtain, including miniparodies of *Variety* as if it were published in Moscow ("L'grad Show Trial in 6th Boff Week"); of *After Dark* ("Your own personal guide to night life in East Berlin. Courtesy of the management of the Hotel Microphone . . .") and of a supposed *Soviet TV Guide,* including listings like "8:00 A.M. Children's Theater: Jiri Tanovic and His Puppets of the Wall Street Profiteers," and even ads: "Beloved singer Vela Vaczyscza says: "I use

---

* Magazine sales are stated as a percentage of the total press run, or number of copies printed. Distributors usually take an average of 50 percent of the cover price. No magazine usually makes any kind of profit until it breaks the fiftieth to fifty-fifth percentile, and with higher unit production costs, several points above that.

toothpaste. Why don't you?" The "Show Biz" issue ran into a major problem, however, thanks to its cover, one which both foreshadowed other similar crises and threatened to close the magazine summarily.

Simmons was desperate at this point for a cover with some oomph. He was six months into publication and still printing four magazines for every one he sold. Although the cover was usually a collective effort, this one, says Simmons, was all his—Minnie Mouse with her top off, revealing a cute little bosom and two daisy-shaped pasties. When the magazine hit the newsstands, Disney sued 21st Century Communications for $11 million.

Disney has never looked kindly on anything that infringes on the sanctity of the Godlike rodent, but the drawing of Minnie was a cartoon of a cartoon, clearly signed by the artist, and it's unlikely that an infringement of copyright suit could have stuck. Simmons, however, now bleeding in several places, was not about to take the chance. Simmons settled on a promise never again to portray a Disney character and the suit was dropped.

The affair received a certain amount of publicity, and dangerous principles had been exposed. First was the power of a much larger company—and at this point practically any company was much larger than the *Lampoon*—to control satire at its expense, whether or not they had the right to in law, merely by bringing a prohibitively large enough suit; second was the possibility that any owner of an image or even style, from "Peanuts"† to Peter Max to Andrew Wyeth, might try to prevent a parody of it. The former is a perennial problem of satire, but the latter was one peculiar to the thrust and skills of the *Lampoon*.

Another very different problem arose with the cover of the "Politics" issue. Through Cerf, the *Lampoon* had immediate access to Abbie Hoffman, and one possible idea for the cover was to use him in some way. Hoffman's reputation at this stage was ambivalent; for some time he had been regarded by the purer element in the movement as exploitative of it rather than helpful to it. (He had been unceremoniously excluded from the stage at Woodstock.) On the other hand, he had his own quite cogent ideas about the uses of the media in promoting dissent, and had certainly gained plenty of attention putting them into practice. The absurd behavior during the Conspiracy Trial of his namesake on the bench had also to a degree rehabilitated him; there was a feeling that however much the Yippies might be media hounds, it was time to stick together. (Of the loony Left notion that he was a government agent, the less said the better.)

For most people, pro or con, Hoffman was a visible, risible symbol of student radicalism. It was precisely because of this that the more conservative element in the *Lampoon* councils were very uncomfortable about any association with him, let alone an endorsement.

In the end, they decided to run Abbie, holding two hand puppets of Nixon and Agnew with the cover line "Abbie Visits 1600 Sesame Street." (This was

---

† Charles Schultz later did in fact.

something of an in-joke, for Chris Cerf had by now left Random House and was consulting for the Children's Television Workshop, the producers of the rapidly rising PBS children's program.) The puppets were made by Meyerowitz, who was becoming one of the few regular artists who delivered the goods for the struggling magazine. In the "Politics" issue he did a series of campaign posters (1970 was an off-election year), which contained caricatures of six candidates running for various offices that November: George Wallace, Ronald Reagan, Nelson Rockefeller, Edward Kennedy, Hubert Humphrey, and Arthur Goldberg. (As the intro said, "Two hawks, two doves, a parakeet, and a turkey." See photo insert.)

Beard and Kenney had, by dint of sticking to their instincts, brought the *Lampoon* a considerable distance from the "Sexy Cover" issue. The magazine had not sold out in either direction—toward safe or inconsequential areas on the one hand, nor on the other to facile identification with the movement. They weren't motivated by integrity so much as by a sense of survival. Either direction would have led to a quick and painful demise. They took their targets where they found them, and the range of their treatment was growing all the time, from the highly sophisticated and superliterate, to the broad and bawdy. The magazine was bubbling with ideas, a reflection of the welter of movements, theories, ideologies, attitudes, conflicts, and events that swirled around it, as much a forum as a nightclub, a minicampus whose entrance requirements were only that you should be overeducated and funny. It was assumed that you already had the information and were aware of the shades of attitude surrounding a given subject, whether it was the organic food movement or the Nixon administration. You didn't agree or disagree with a piece like "Waiting in the Left Wings," for the multiplicity of levels on which it worked—Hollywood's exploitation of the movement, the inanity of the movement that made it exploitable being only two of them—made that impossible. Similarly, those who thought that saying "Nixon is a pig" was funny, were themselves a subject for ridicule; indeed, it was assumed that you knew enough about Washington to realize that what John Mitchell and Henry Kissinger were up to was of considerably greater interest and significance than Agnew's manipulative mobspeak.

(Not that Agnew was off-limits: the "Politics" issue contained a long piece entitled "Eight Days That Shook Wook, Iowa," which purported to document the tragedy of Vice President Spiro T. Agnew's demise at the hands of large numbers of assassins. [More and more claimed responsibility as the eight days wore on.] This wish-fulfillment piece was also intended as a parody of the standard Kennedy assassination book, complete with a report from the whitewashing "Burger Commission" and a rebuttal from a sensationalist bestseller called *Rush to Payment.*)

To whatever extent this was "entertainment," it was not humor in the narrowly defined sense that sixties television understood it—the wacky vicissitudes of family life—nor was it *about* television. Nor was it humor in the sense that commercial print media understood it. The elephant-and-donkey school of acceptable political satire and even the more oblique stuff of "Pogo" and "Li'l Abner" were as much grist for the *Lampoon*'s mill as the two-party system itself (in fact the "Bad Taste" issue included a parody of "Li'l Abner" called "Li'l Bigmouth," in which Al Capp was revealed in actuality to be William F. Buckley, Jr.). For those in the relatively tiny world of humor writing and the even smaller one of those who wanted to write about what concerned them, the appearance of the *Lampoon* was an occasion for much excitement, an island of intelligence in a Sargasso Sea of self-censored acceptability. However hard it might be to get through visually, the range and nature of the minds that produced it was immediately apparent. And its appeal to such writers was precisely what it would one day be to its audience; that it was completely unavailable anywhere else.

13

Parodies Regained
The *Lampoon* Finds the Answer

In the first six months of its existence, for all its sorry sales percentages, desultory distribution, and compromised graphics, the *Lampoon* began to attract kindred spirits. This was just as well, for the magazine was to all intents and purposes being put out by three people—Beard, Kenney, and O'Donoghue—under their own names or pseudonyms like Fran Kafka (Kenney). This core was frequently supplemented by Cerf, Trow, and Weidman and less frequently by other Harvard alumni, but just to survive the monumental task of conceiving and writing sixty pages of editorial a month, more hands would be needed. (The masthead throughout most of this period carried only four contributing editors: Michael O'Donoghue, Christopher Cerf, Michael Frith, and "Tamara Gould," the latter a pseudonym Trow assumed lest *The New Yorker*—where he now worked—look askance at his participation.)

One of the first "outsiders" to have been attracted by plans for the magazine was Michael Choquette. Choquette was a perfect example of the odd kind of character the odd set of circumstances called the sixties created. The son of a prominent French Canadian family, he had spent much of the decade acquiring notoriety in a comedy team called the Times Square Two. This diverting duo, who dressed in Edwardian costume and performed precision-tooled versions of turn-of-the-century songs, feats of dexterity and other marvels,* were something of a cult on the folk circuit. They were also favorites of

---

* The other half of the Times Square Two was Peter Elbling. For professional purposes, they assumed the fictitious names Mycroft Partner (Elbling) and Andrew I (Choquette). This was so that they could legitimately refer to themselves as "My Partner and I." The team enjoyed modest

the Committee, perhaps because their rigidly programmed act presented a welcome vacation from improvisation.

Although he was a *Lampoon* natural—being vastly overeducated and obsessed by the need to make people laugh—Choquette never stayed in one place long enough to accomplish much. Nonetheless, his energy did serve at least one very valuable function—it forced the juice along the grapevine.

Thanks to Choquette, many people in many places were made aware of the *Lampoon* and its potential, among them three who would play a considerable role in its next few years: Sean Kelly, Anne Beatts, and me. (More of these giants in a moment.)

By far the most important addition to the team that had been made since O'Donoghue however was a young art director hired in the fall of 1970 to replace Cloud Studios. His name was Michael Gross and, like O'Donoghue, he could not have been less Ivy League. He too came from upstate New York, in this case from a small town called Newburgh, which while within striking distance of Manhattan, might, as Gross puts it, "just as well be the Midwest." Unlike O'Donoghue, Gross, at least in his own self-description was normal, conservative, an obliging go-alonger rather than original genius. While he does himself some disservice by this self-effacement (he was a talented artist in his own right), his background and previous career do provide some clues as to what he brought to the magazine and why it was of such value.

The product of a happy, if not exactly normal, childhood, Gross was deserted at birth by his natural father, whose name was Miller, and was raised in a fourteen-room boarding house in Newburgh owned by his stepfather. There were at least two consequences, both of which might have contributed somewhat to the development of a sense of humor. First, his parents neglected to tell him until he was twelve that his stepfather was not a natural parent:

"They got me into school under the name of Michael Gross, but it was not formal . . . so they were worried that I was going to have to go into the army at eighteen and they'd call up this Michael Miller and I'd say, 'Who the fuck is this?' So when I was twelve he (my stepfather) sat me down and said, 'I'm not your real father; your real name is Miller, and we gotta change your name next week.'

"I lived a very colorful childhood. [Being] raised in a rooming house is an experience. Everything conceivable that could happen to you—shootings, suicides, deaths, whores (we'd throw out the whores), people downstairs from Welfare . . .

"I grew up with the idea that when the phone rang you didn't have to answer it, because it was never for you.

"And then my father owned a bar, and he would rent rooms [to drunks]. In fact, when I was a little kid growing up, he owned a really terrible bar, so bad

---

success on the nightclub circuit, appearing on TV for a session in Greg Garrison's "The Golddiggers," a summer replacement for Dean Martin, in 1968, but then broke up.

that I used to meet other kids who'd say, 'Your father owns that bar? My mother tells me I have to cross the street when I go past that bar. Even in the middle of the day.' "

Like so many of his generation, Gross was one of the innocents seduced by *Mad* comics, and spent countless happy preteen hours rolling around on the floor at the wit and wisdom of Kurtzman, Elder, and Wood. Interestingly, he recalls that the day it turned into a magazine, he stopped liking it: "I didn't like that form, I liked it in comic form better. Jack Davis is actually the least of my favorites. I remember appreciating the subtlety of what those other guys did [Kurtzman, et al.], even at the age of ten. And I don't think my friends did, even though they laughed at the same stuff I don't think we were seeing the same thing."

This early preference for restraint and subtlety over the broad, crazy-kids-stuff approach to humor is part of what Gross means in describing himself as conservative. This quality was what would make him so essential to the *Lampoon*'s success.

Beyond this, the rest of his childhood was neither conservative nor what-ever its opposite is—he got married in high school to a girl he met there, and was admitted to the Pratt Institute of Art in Brooklyn in 1963 on the strength of an exceptional portfolio. At Pratt partly because he couldn't find a style that was his, partly because of precocious skills, he developed into what he describes as a "chameleon," capable of reproducing any style or school to which he was introduced; in what was probably a related development, he also acquired a healthy distaste for the world of "fine art."

Gross's impatience at the academic side of art was intensified by discover-ing Ayn Rand, an experience that changed the course of his life, and he dropped out in 1965, to pursue a career. Devoted to magazines, he took a number of jobs, starting in the art department at *Cosmopolitan* and ending up three years later as art director of the ill-fated *Eye* (a sort of up-market *Cheetah* that nose-dived for much the same reasons).

During this period Gross developed in a direction very different from what the late sixties designer was supposed to be: young, hip, committed, tuned-in, radical chic. Gross was less interested in the cross-currents of political or intellectual commitment than he was in precision of form, and the satisfaction of getting it right:

"Maybe because of that schizophrenia in me between liberal and conserva-tive, I wanted to be successful and commercial. I couldn't see painting in a loft because I didn't know what I wanted to say as an artist. I liked working commercially because I thought I could translate people's ideas. I wanted to do something I could go down and buy on a newsstand. And I wanted my own magazine. . . . It didn't matter to me a whole lot what I was saying or what I was doing, as long as I was translating it well."

It seems improbable that this kind of detachment from content is ever entirely possible, but there was no question that Gross's emphasis was on delivering the message as efficiently as possible rather than worrying about what was inside the envelope. Nor is there any doubt that in 1970 this emphasis on form over content made him rather unusual. The fashion of the time tended to demand that at least lip service be paid to political commitment. And he seems intuitively to have grasped that his impulse toward detachment had something in common with the position of the *Lampoon* toward the attitudes and opinions it took such pleasure in juggling:

"I went over [to *Lampoon*] for an interview. Matty Simmons interviewed me first, and basically what he was saying was 'I want it to look like a professional magazine.' Well, that was easy, that was a piece of cake. I could do that with my eyes closed.

"There was one of those *mondo bizarro* conversations with Doug Kenney. I'm not sure he knew how to ask what he was looking for. I just remember that he didn't know how to hire an art director, and didn't know exactly what I'd do, and didn't know what to ask. So he would reach into strange left field for questions that I couldn't quite answer.

"In fact I heard afterward that he went to Matty and said he didn't want me to be hired, that he didn't think I was right for it. I think he felt I was too conventional.

"It wasn't until I sat down with Henry [Beard] that I could say it in simple terms. I flipped through the magazine and there was an article about postage stamps [a Kenney piece called "America as a Second-Rate Power," a new issue of stamps commemorating modern American failures], and they were all silly underground comic drawings. I said, 'What you've done here is no different than what *Mad* magazine would do. You're doing a parody of postage stamps. They would have Jack Davis do funny drawings of postage stamps. You've got an underground cartoonist doing funny drawings of postage stamps. What you need is postage stamps that *look like* postage stamps. The level of satire you've written here isn't being graphically translated.

"Now this all seems so simple, but at the time no one understood. They thought, to be hip they just needed a hipper level of cartoon art."

In one deft example, Gross put his finger on what was wrong with the current art direction, forever cut the *Lampoon* away from the underground, and enunciated a simple principle that would give the magazine's brilliance a hard reflective surface rather than the muddy one that dragged it down into silliness. It was a principle the Lampooners knew, but didn't know they knew —it merely applied the basic rule of parody they had always followed to every graphic unit in the book. Any graphic form, and indeed any print form, had to look like the original on which it was based, whether it was a postage stamp or a Michelangelo or a menu. Only thus could the satirical intent come through with crystal clarity. Gross thus not only opened a huge graphic door to the sumptuous visuals for which the magazine became known, he also made a great deal of work for himself. From now on, the major proportion of the visuals in the magazine would have to be faithful to one or another of the innumerable personal, categorical, or historical styles, or had to reflect one or another equally innumerable print formats, through which people were accustomed to organize and receive information.

What's more, reproducing the quirks and idiocies and even prejudices built into such styles and formats could only reinforce the satire. To faithfully reproduce the visual inanity of, say, a government pamphlet, could only supplement the satire aimed at the inanity of its content, give it another level of recognition to be relished. The turn the *Lampoon* took, thanks to Gross's basic insight, helped to jack humor up to its next level, and usher in the era of modern parody—bilevel satire with an acute awareness of original form that distinguished seventies humor from its antecedents.

Beginning with the "Politics" issue, Cloud Studios was replaced, and Gross took over the art department. The importance of this move to the future success of the magazine and the subsequent course of Boomer humor is hard to overestimate. For Gross was not just a theorist; he was an experienced professional who knew how to put together a clean, easy-to-read page, and give the magazine the pace and gloss it needed to appeal to a wide audience. And by temperament—that part of himself he describes as the "chameleon" —he was open to and could reproduce a wide variety of styles. In a magazine where very different voices and approaches coexisted, that quality was of great importance. Finally, what Simmons also got for his (rather somewhat skimpy) money was a *reader*. For the first time, the team included someone who could act as an in-house test audience. Not only did Gross have no competitive need to be funny himself, but the sensibility of the boy from Newburgh and a fourteen-room flophouse was an invaluable addition to the superliterate, supereducated, superhip group.

Simmons's decision to hire Gross met with resistance from Kenney. This says a lot about how the fascinatingly paradoxical Kenney related to the underground—or to what he thought of as the underground. Gross's arrival was a double whammy in this respect, since not only had "the underground" failed to produce a cohesive magazine, but Gross, with his Madison Avenue street smarts, was in the conventional wisdom its antithesis: slick, methodical, and commercial.

For all Kenney's history of social ambition—the drive which had got him where he was, and which was entirely accepted, even loved by those into whose Castle he'd climbed—he seemed to feel a certain guilt or confusion about what he'd left below. The underground in this case didn't mean just the underground press, nor even a specific group or class of people. It meant a common sentiment rather than any identifiable individuals or theories, which encompassed sexual freedoms, drug use, political awareness, and the rejection of ambition, social or otherwise. Unlike Beard, secure in his mandarin distaste for the whole business, or O'Donoghue, equally secure in his knowledge of it and therefore able to pick and choose what was to his taste and what wasn't, Kenney bounced around in between, unsure of what he felt and just as unsure about whether it mattered. Shortly after they met, Kenney asked O'Donoghue, "Should I be for the Panthers?"

What was so captivating about Kenney was that he could both voice this guilt and know that it was absurd. Whatever Doug knew to be true, he knew that its opposite was equally and hilariously true. In fact, the remark to O'Donoghue might well have been an obscure put-on (although O'Donoghue was not someone you put on lightly, having a tendency to retaliate in a way that left you in pieces on the butcher-block), or even a complicated putdown of himself. His style reflected this; indeed his style *was* confusion, a manner of feeling a minimum of two things at all times.

Ironically, Kenney was the first beneficiary of the skills he'd resisted. The first issue Gross directed was pure Kenney: the topic chosen, given the internal politics of Gross's arrival, even had a slightly sardonic flavor. The topic didn't seem that promising at the time, but everything about the issue was new. It looked different, it felt different, it sounded different—all largely thanks to Gross. As things turned out, his debut could hardly have been more auspicious, for in the history of Boomer humor, the November 1970 issue was a major landmark. Even its juxtaposition to the previous issue, "Politics," was significant. The topic was "Nostalgia."

Nostalgia, in Kenney's ably confused hands, turned out to be nostalgia for the fifties. But not surprisingly, in Kenney's mind this was a much more ambivalent emotion than it later became. At the core of the issue were two long pieces. The first was a sparkling hodge-podge of fifties-iana called, naturally, "Those Fabulous Fifties," which opened with a wear-it-yourself Dick Clark mask, progressed through a delicious Teenage Death Song board game by Cerf (including instructions for moves like "If the Leader of the Pack's girlfriend's Dad has already said, 'Find someone new,' she picks the place where she met him to say 'We're through.' He (a) sorta smiles, (b) drives away, and (c) CRASHES FATALLY!") More goodies included a $1,200 check "for payola" made out to Alan Freed, an authentic American Communist Party card, a spread on "The Sharp Look" and the "Reet" accessories that went with it, including zip gun and comb ("a rat-tail nine-incher encased in hardened Lucky Tiger hair wax") and finally, an Iron Lung Donation Box that you could actually fold and glue to help in the fight against polio. Every artifact, mask, check, or Iron Lung fold-up was meticulously rendered, every "accessory" faithfully researched, properly lit, and shot. The mask was not a cartoon but a photograph. The check was not a funny drawing of a check, but an actual check. Because nothing "funny" stood between the reader and the author, the impact of both the images and the writing was immediate. But this was kid's stuff compared to what followed: "CatCalls, the Ezra Taft Benson High School Yearbook for 1956."

The best years of the ETBHS Bobcats' lives were immortalized in ten hilariously drab pages encased in a horrible gray-beige cover. Gross insisted on producing the back as well as the front cover of the yearbook to be faithful to the parody—in other words, he "threw away" an entire page of gray-beige leatherette (except for a sad little valedictory at the bottom: "To Mary Elizabeth: By hook or by crook I'll be last in this book, good luck in the future, Jimmy B. Arnstead").

The 1956 Bobcats start out by dedicating their yearbook to their recently deceased senior civics teacher, to whom they apologize posthumously for calling "Hacker" and "Old Croupy" and add, "We had no idea you had cancer of the trachea." They proceed to say "bye-bye" to the graduating Bobcats like Carl "Moose" Czourowski ("Spotlight on sports . . . plowed . . . fuel-injected 'vette' . . . wanna knuckle sandwich? . . . gross-out . . . future Marine . . . hates homos") and Veronica "Jugs" Weber ("Flirt . . . nice figure . . . submarine races . . . padiddle . . . built for speed . . . 'Not here!' . . . second base on first date . . . vacations in Puerto Rico . . . 'Help, Moose is after me!' "). They fondly recall the class "history":

"May found us chugging our way to Washington, D.C., where we visited the Lincoln Memorial and got photographed in front of the Capitol. Most interesting was an FBI tour that showed how the Russkies were attempting to stab this nation in the back and rob us of our priceless heritage. The real fun, needless to say, was back at the hotel, where we all got plastered. Really looped. COMPLETELY STINKO! We threw water-filled Coke bottles from the windows, Moose and Sarge beat up a few fruits, and according to rumor Jugs broke her old record . . .

"Well, Diary, I have to go now because there's so much to do, what with finals, graduation, and all. I'd like to close by reassuring our parents, who scrimped and sacrificed so we might have a decent education, that we won't let them down. Some of us have already begun shouldering our responsibilities. Moose has accepted a position as an automobile body repairman and Gus-Gus (the class clown) starts next month as credit manager trainee for a whole chain of dry-cleaning stores . . . Yours truly, The Class of 1956."

"CatCalls" ends with a class cheer dedicated to principal Ralph Krintzler, the initial letters of each line spelling out "FUCK YOU RALPH," and handwritten messages from classmates like "Dear Winki, first comes love, then comes marriage, then comes pushing a baby carriage. Veronica W. 6.23.56."

It's not easy on this side of the ocean of fifties "nostalgia" that has engulfed us in the last decade to convey quite how startling such humor was in 1970— the height of the sixties. It was new and different in two ways.

It was backward-looking and based on recognition. Familiar as this may seem now, no one in 1970, head or straight-ahead, Boomer humorist or not, based their work on that perception. "Youth" material [see Chapter 6], essentially a copy of Allen's and Cosby's work, based itself on the premise of how weird and singular one's childhood had been, not how recognizable. Even Cosby, who appeared to be doing recognition humor, was actually telling stories about his childhood, not asking the audience to identify with them. For the most part his audience was white, and his stories were about black kids; the admirable implication that childhood has a unique universality was there to be drawn, but he did not point it out. These were anecdotes, not shared memories. Cosby did not set out to say "remember what it was like then," but Kenney did.

Second, this was specifically about the fifties, and more specifically about that part of the fifties which had already been satirized by Boomer humorists of the decade itself—regimentation, indoctrination, exploitation, commercialization. There is an echo of Roger Bowen's Compass scenario "Enterprise" in the sign-off of the Bobcats as they prepare to "shoulder the burden" of auto repair and credit management—except that Kenney's humor, with the advantage of knowing how sad and drab those burdens would be, is far bleaker than Bowen's in 1955. And while Ezra Taft Benson has a certain universality—all jocks need remedial English; all teenagers are horny and have zits—this school is securely in the fifties, with its absurd civil defense drills, its hints of abortion in Puerto Rico. This is an ambivalent nostalgia. "Happy Days" it ain't.

There was nothing like this abroad in 1970. The only whiff of it was a group called Sha Na Na, who appeared at Woodstock and sang fifties-style songs, at a demented pace, clad in black-leather jackets and highly waxed DA's. But they were ersatz and deliberately so, self-proclaimed idiots, whose looks and singing style were supposed to be ridiculous, an oblique proclamation of victory by the sixties over the previous decade, which would never be again, nor be allowed to be—neither its music nor its values nor its fashions. Sha Na Na were absurd representations of the defeated Ike Age, hilarious because they were defeated, because they were so unhip. (They were also quite funny, and the closest thing Woodstock got to comedy, Wavy Gravy notwithstanding.)

True to form, Kenney expressed his confusion, thanks to Gross's attention to detail, with startling clarity. The fifties *were* fabulous as well as awful. There was love as well as disdain in those "reet accessories," in the memory of times when a zip gun was still shocking, not yet ranked by bombs in banks. There was joy as well as contempt in the sheer detail of the yearbook parody, from the authenticity of the photographs to the accuracy of the dingy mid-American proverbs scrawled in the back by the graduating Bobcats.

And that in itself in 1970 was shocking—in the age of future shock this was past shock. The sacred cow it dared to assault was the notion that the fifties were all bad and all gone.

But, in Kenney's hands, there was no obligation to choose. You didn't have to be pro-fifties or pro-sixties, a mod or a rocker, a radical or a conservative. The sixties had its drugs—and its overdoses. The fifties had its innocence—and Kennedy's assassination right under the next overpass. What became in other hands a revival—as absurd as what it was reviving—or a chic to titillate the tired, bored, befuddled masses, or worst of all a weapon of the very propaganda that had been left behind in the dust of ridicule, was in Kenney's hands a delicious dare, "remember when" as well as "thank God that's gone."

The fifties section was, also, an up-yours to both the underground and to Harvard. To the extent that there was love and knowledge in Kenney's nostalgia, it was a trip back to his Midwest roots, a return to earth from Harvard and its Castle. Beard would have been as incapable of writing the high school yearbook (he was scarcely present in the whole issue in fact), as he would have been of dropping acid. Beard could not have felt either of the conflicting emotions Kenney felt for the awful Moose—contempt for the future Marine and homo basher, sympathy for the wretched little life of grease and disappointment he was bound for. Beard simply didn't know any Mooses. At his school they were called something quite different and would one day run large corporations very badly.

And further still, said the fifties section, perhaps we don't have to grow up. Perhaps there is a way to get back homeward, *pace* the Beatles—at least it's fun to pretend. All his life Kenney had something of this—a mad bedeviled Peter Pan looking for some congenial Lost Boys (not to mention a congenial Wendy). This was something else that distinguished him from Beard, who had never been young, so it seemed, but sprang fully formed from his mother's womb, a silver pipe clenched between his teeth.

But for Kenney, behind this one amazingly simple jump in the dark, were all of these conflicting and confused motives. In many ways, at the time nostalgia seemed least likely to succeed, a personal quirk that would be funny once and pass. But Kenney's instinct here was more correct than in any other area. He wrote in many other veins of humor, but this one would produce classics every time he returned to it. It was a secret he shared with his audience, which many others would try to copy, but never with the same sense of balance, and which made him and the *Lampoon* very rich. It also opened a pinhole in a dam that would ultimately sweep away not just the dam, but the village below and all who lived there, including Kenney himself.

"Nostalgia" was, for all intents and purposes, the first real issue of *The National Lampoon*. From this point on, the magazine picked up circulation and got rolling. For roughly the next two years, the magazine went through its first great period of expansion, experimentation, sophistication, and last but not least, increasing profitability. The covers improved dramatically. December's was an O'Donoghue classic: a war-comic title panel in which a yellow-fanged Oriental Communist fighter pilot watches demonically as his latest kill, Santa Claus, falls out of the sky (see photo insert).

As if it were waking up and flexing its muscles, the magazine added names of contributing editors to its masthead for the first time since it began publication—Michael Choquette and (rather oddly, considering the number of major contributions I'd made and the fact that I lived and worked in Los Angeles) my own. John Weidman was added in January, and thereafter the list of contributing editors grew steadily.

The January issue, "Women"—actually about Women's Lib, the hot new topic on the block—saw Gross solidly in place. The cover had a gigantic 1971 Fay Wray, with tangled curls and a slit maxi, high atop the Empire State Building, carelessly holding a stuffed and shrunken King Kong.

The "Head" issue, in February, was selectively rancid about the drug aspect of the underground, and included another splendid flaunt-it piece by Gross featuring designs for legalized marijuana cigarette packs. The March issue, "Culture," kept up the pace. The cover was by Meyerowitz, a parody of Leonardo's "Mona Lisa" with a prim gorilla suppressing a mysterious smile —the "Mona Gorilla," in fact—which became one of the *Lampoon*'s most popular posters.

The magazine, in part thanks to Gross, was also becoming conscious of itself as a team. A side effect of having art direction that could render intellectual premises visually was that more group ideas were being generated— rather than written alone by individuals (and then illustrated). Also, since the "Nostalgia" issue, the magazine had seen Kenney in high gear. Sex, drugs, and (middle-class) culture were what filled his viewfinder, subjects far from Beard's expertise.

Not that Beard was idle. In December he had started a column, "News of the Month," that gave his particular talent a broad scope—discursive, intellectual, a fierce seventies Benchley. Here are two examples from early 1971:

The successful passage of the Nixon administration's sweeping District of Columbia "No Knock" Crime Bill, which makes it legal for policemen who can find "probable cause," "threat to evidence," or the telltale drip, drip, drip of stomach acid, to enter an abode (similar to a house but occupied by hippies, left-wingers, and bed wetters) without knocking, suggests some other soon-to-be-enacted anticrime provisions. In addition to knock-and-shoot (previously reported in these pages by Punji), consideration is being given to: stop-and-spit, which permits expectoration on suspicious passersby to test their potentially disruptive hostilities; kiss-and-tell, a self-explanatory provision for underground policewomen; and go fish, which gives police the power to enter a specified number of houses at random each day to see what they can find . . .

■   ■

"In the light of continued revelations of cost overruns on the C5 Galaxie, this recently discovered fragment from a Dead Sea Scroll or a Chesapeake Bay Crab, I forget which, is quite interesting:

"TO: Procurement, the Pentateuch.

"Re Your Commandment of the 14th, our Covenant 6:7:14, authorizing construction and procurement of a prototype long-range, all-weather transport, we have encountered some short-term difficulties inherent in covenants of this sort, requiring as they do a high reliance on state-of-the-art techniques. Basically, the present situation is the direct result of delivering, with inadequate lead-time and concurrent with a favorable launch-window, a hitherto untested, rain-activated, bulk carrier vessel with a random-drift capability, a forty-day/night loiter time, and an initial lift and free-float payload capacity sufficient to carry every living thing by twos. Further difficulties have been encountered in obtaining sufficient quantities of high-grade gopher wood, owing to lapses in quality control; in dealing with the Cubitic measuring system; and in fixing viable species modules avoiding lion-lamb interfaces. As a result of these difficulties, we are faced with a deferred delivery date and an escalation of prototype cost to 100,000,000 bullocks. This of course exceeds our original estimate, but it reflects . . ."

Kenney however was on a tremendous roll at the time, writing pieces that would stay around for years as "typical" *Lampoon* models, building "Mrs. Agnew's Diary" into a cult—Spiro Agnew had by now become the Ralph Kramden of the White House, loud, abusive, and crass (when flying commercial airlines, he rolled his pants legs up to his knees to try and get the Youth Fare), and the doings at the core of the Nixon administration—prophetically—got weirder all the time: "Dick came back with a Ouija Board just like the one Mel Laird [then Secretary of Defense] keeps by his globe with all the little colored flags stuck in it. Reverend [Billy] Graham showed us how it worked though he confessed he hadn't used one since he was at Ringling Brothers . . ."

Aside from this, Kenney wrote much of the "Letters" column, fast becoming another reader favorite, and the editorials.

He was becoming the dominant voice of the magazine, covering the field from the Midwest to Washington, from middle-class mores to political satire. His characteristic style—combining high Brahmin with suburban cliché or high school slang—was the one to watch, the one to learn from. He was unreliable (always late), undisciplined, a quirky editor, hard to follow, liable to praise and condemn something in the same breath, but he was unquestionably the leader.

What's more, Kenney, blondly handsome (though very unsure of the fact himself), was emerging as the magazine's star. One of his creations was yet another regular feature called "Foto Funnies," a concept using Polaroids shot in the office, and sequenced like a comic with comic balloons. The joke was always dumb, the look tacky, and that was indeed the point (see photo insert).

Gross resisted "Foto Funnies" intensely, feeling that they dragged down the design integrity. Other editors felt they were derivative, and looked like *Help!* But Kenney's instinct was unerring—readers loved them. They made the magazine less detached, more real: it was a down and dirty way for the editors to wave at the readers, and for the readers to find out what the usually faceless editors looked like.

April 1971, the *Lampoon's* first anniversary, saw the best issue to date, "Adventure." Yet again this was a Kenney choice, for "Adventure" meant pulp adventure, popular entertainment, or as the cover lines put it, "Weird Tales, Spicy Stories." The cover itself was painted by the master of comic fantasy art, Frank Frazetta, creator of the comic version of Conan, and purportedly depicting one of Rudyard Kipling's lesser-known classics, "White

Man's Wet Dream." Against the deep blue African night, a great white hunter blazed away with his revolver at naked black tribesmen, besieging an equally naked white woman, lashed to a skull-topped totem pole. Around her leg and headed for her crotch curled an intensely phallic black mamba.

Inside, O'Donoghue caught up with Kenney with a vengeance: all three of O'Donoghue's major pieces were classics in their own right (e.g., "Tarzan of the Cows," O'Donoghue's first comic, told the story of a Tarzan who grew up in southern Wisconsin farm country, speaking the language of the animals). But the centerpiece of the issue was a generic magazine parody called "Real Balls Adventure." "Real Balls" (a Paranoid Press Publication) was the *Lampoon* in full swing, an instantly accessible and hilarious vehicle for hard-edged satire (see photo insert).

Features included a story on how an undercover G-man infiltrated a hippie pad, cunningly disguised in a beatnik beret and a pair of bongos ("Beat me, daddy, eight to the bar," I whooped, slapping out a driving bongo rhythm to the lead guitar. *"Nobody here but just us wigged-out nonconformists!"*).

But the best story was "The Kiddie Captives of Professor Perverto," in which Professor Perverto—on a one-year sabbatical from (where else?) Harvard—brings sex ed and no prayer to the Willowdale, Iowa school system.

"Real Balls" was written by Kenney, O'Donoghue, Terry Catchpole (another Harvard alumnus), and a newcomer, John Boni. Boni, the next official arrival on the masthead (in July 1971) was a significant addition. A funny and prolific writer, he was the first of several who could collectively be described as of the Kenney school.

In one year, thirteen issues (or to be strictly fair to Gross, five issues), the magazine had transformed itself from the unappetizing stew of messy copy, squirly graphics, and home snapshots that made up the "Sexy Cover Issue," into a knowing, stylish, slick, and surprising package, flattering to the reader and yet packed with mind- and eye-boggling jokes.

The transformation, in the classic dynamic, had come from taking chances. Had the core team remained in the essentially detached stance of the Harvard parodies, they might have pleased readers but wouldn't have startled them; they would have confirmed what they already thought and felt about a given issue rather than changed it. Instead, they pushed readers' imaginative limits, allowed themselves to think and feel secret thoughts and feelings about the chaos around them that they had not realized up to that point they had. In many ways this was not unlike the process Shepherd and Sills and Myerson had experienced with improvisation. As a result, new areas of the common psyche were exposed, new statements were made. Openness to the welter of idea and attitude around them created a new reality. Taking leaps in the dark brought them to strange places like fifties "nostalgia" or the psychotic murk of machismo, and took them beyond the points at which their precursors had already arrived.

What's more, Beard, Kenney, and O'Donoghue were serious about their humor. They saw the world in absurd relief and relieved the resulting tension by creating words and images of what they saw. They were trying to deal with reality, not a version of it. Even the magazine parodies were increasingly less parodies than vehicles for their perceptions. It was a real war in a real place that inspired Beard; real people in a real Midwestern school that inspired Kenney. Television almost never appeared in the pages of the *Lampoon* in its first years, except in the most offhanded way, as a scene-setting detail, or in the service of some other joke (e.g. the Soviet TV listings in *"Varietsky");* television personalities appeared almost as infrequently. Beard wrote about the news, not about Cronkite; about issues, not how television presented them. The *Lampoon* was an alternative to television, another way to come at reality; and if it was a rival, why should the magazine give it the time of day?

However much Beard and Kenney had gone into this affair hoping to extend life up at the Castle, they'd ended up in the real world, grappling with real problems—intellectual, political, cultural as well as financial and personal. They were becoming aware of their audience—not only in the marketing sense, but existentially knowing that their audience was actually out there in the dark, alive and inhaling the same oxygen, listening to what they had to say, following where they led. This was no longer something they were doing to mark time until the adulthood hit, no longer a fun summer job before life began in earnest.

The *Lampoon* in 1971 was no place to become either a celebrity or rich. Rather, it was a place that urged you to take chances. The second wave of *Lampoon* editors, those who started arriving in 1971, were from other media, unlike the initial group who had always been humor writers and nothing but. All had had previous careers, many in advertising, and all found the *Lampoon* to be a breathtakingly free place to be, an outlet for ideas and frustrations long denied expression.

The next three issues—May, June, and July—began to reflect this.

June, for example, was: "Religion (for Fun and Prophet)." Kenney came through with a typically on-the-money editorial which unerringly caught the "rap" of the then-rampant Jesus freaks:

Once there was a bearded young dude with long "hippie" hair that reached to his shoulders, who hung out with streetpeople and "easy" chicks . . . the dropouts of society. Even as a kid he was "different," and in later life he was shunned by the Establishment types because of his weird clothes and working-class background. But he was popular with shy and trusting people, who followed him everywhere, even on long trips in the desert, because of his heavy raps about Love, Sharing, and other revolutionary concepts.

But not all his raps were about the ups in life. He rapped straight ahead about the bummers, too. He was hip to great hassles that were to go down in the land, and he didn't cop out when it came to putting down hypocrites. His groupies were both guys and chicks, and they grooved to his magnetic vibes and his heavy, spaced-out eyes. They really got into it.

When he split for the desert to get himself together, the straights ignored him, just another one of those "oddballs" and "kooks" common to this hot, dry climate.

But one day the Establishment got uptight. The big bust came and he was hustled in front of a judge. One of his own people had gone over to the pigs. He was accused, tried, and found guilty.

Although still in his thirties, he was sentenced to be offed, and his groupies wept for him. His gig was short, but what he was laying down will not soon be forgotten, for this dude's name was . . .

Charlie Manson.

But the "Religion" issue was more significant for the strong new voices that were beginning to be heard in the magazine's pages. Notable was that of Sean Kelly.

Kelly had been introduced to the circle by Michael Choquette and was, for *Lampoon* purposes, his writing partner. From this issue on, however, he began to appear more under his own byline. Kelly, like Choquette, was Canadian; he was also the most intellectual of all the central *Lampoon* editors, and certainly the most intellectually athletic. He had spent some time in advertising, distinguishing himself by assembling a one-minute spot for the Canadian Pacific Railroad, which consisted entirely of planes crashing. Before that he had been schooled by Jesuits at Loyola. Now, as lapsed a Catholic as only an Irish Jesuit trainee could be, he was radical, blasphemous and brilliant, and might have been expected to enliven the "Religion" issue with a little Joycean play in the fields of the Lord.

But his most significant contribution, accompanied by a finely rendered pre-Renaissance triptych of Brian Jones, Jimi Hendrix, and Janis Joplin, as John the Baptist, Saint Sebastian and a grieving Virgin, was a song called "I Dreamed I Was There in Overdose Heaven." It was blasphemous, but not about the saints of Rome. This was about the saints of rock:

> For poor Brian Jones of the rock Rolling Stones,
> Life below was a habit to feed.
> In his home in the sky, he pops stars to stay high,
> Now he knows what they mean by "God speed."
>
> I dreamed I was there in Overdose Heaven,
> Where a white boy, a black, and a girl
> Are wiped out on infinity, a new Holy Trinity,
> Brian and Jimmy and Pearl.

For the first time, a new sacred cow had been milked. In 1971, this was sacrilege of a high order. These udders were off-limits. Just as no one but Kenney could have discovered fifties nostalgia, it took a real rock-and-roller, and Kelly, aside from being a lapsed Jesuit genius, *was* a real rock-and-roller, to discover the new blasphemy. Kelly was the first Lampooner who made this particular leap in the dark, and being a fine lyricist he was able to describe very well what he found when he landed. There was, as we shall see, plenty to tell.

The "Religion" issue was actually not that religious. This might be surprising to some, for a great deal was made at the time—and in what writing has been done about the *Lampoon* subsequently—of the fact that a preponderance of its major editors were Irish or Catholic or both. (Kenney was educated at Gilmour, a Catholic prep school; Kelly we know about; O'Donoghue presumably owned somewhere in his shuttered background the odd Catholic gene; I was Catholic and an ex-monk; and several other names from the editors' line of the masthead, McConnachie, McCall and O'Rourke, although none of them evinced much feeling for the One Universal Holy and Apostolic Church, were all liable to be lumped together ethnically and theologically.)

The *Lampoon* did make several new additions to the canon of humor in the Catholic area, which had not been possible as long as Boomer humorists had been predominantly Jewish. For all the wonderful irreverence of Bruce's material (e.g., "Religions, Inc."), there is nothing blasphemous about it, whatever the Irish cops might have sworn. Only a Catholic can manage that, because only a Catholic knows that blasphemy will send him to hell. (Furthermore, only a Catholic knows that even though he doesn't believe in hell, he's still going there).

In the July issue, Kenney and the mainstream were back at their best. The title was "Pornography, Threat or Menace?" The cover was again a formal painting (as were most of the best covers of the *Lampoon*'s first period), by Dick Hess and done in a vaguely turn-of-the-century style that suggested Horatio Alger—and the accompanying morality. There were four panels, the first showing a young man in a hotel room avidly reading a large book labeled FRENCH PORNO. In the second he is hurrying out of the boarding house; in the third he is loosening his pants to a horrified young lady; and in the fourth and largest panel he is being handcuffed, looking bemused and lost, as if waking from a drug-induced dream, by two doughty detectives while the young lady is helped back to modesty by a gallant policeman. Inside, every piece looked like a winner—and indeed, it would go through the roof at the newsstand, far and away the biggest issue to date. Everyone fired on all cylinders, but Kenney came through like gang busters with: "Nancy Reagan's Guide to Dating Do's and Don't's" (reviewed by Ann Landers thusly: "Teenage questions answered with a frankness and honesty refreshing in these sniggering times").

Nancy's tips are legion: "You don't have to pet to be popular." "Playing with yourself is playing with fire!" Here are some of her more pungent musings:

Have you noticed that your body is playing little tricks on you lately? If you are a boy, you may have noticed your legs, face, arms, and chest are becoming covered with thick, black pubic hairs and your voice may be beginning to sound like a phonograph needle ruining your favorite stack of platters. If you are a girl, you may have noticed a painful swelling up here and some more funny business going on down there.

These dramatic changes can mean only one thing: cholera. If you are not among the lucky ones, then it simply means you are becoming a young man or a young woman, depending on how much fluoride they dumped in your parents' drinking water. I know that such changes can often be difficult for growing teens, but try to weather the storm and "grin and bear it." There is always impotence and menopause.

During these trying teenage years, a girl begins to "menstruate" (men-stroo-ate), and a boy begins to have "erections" (ee-wreck-shuns), normally only when called to the blackboard by his teacher. There is absolutely nothing abnormal about this, and, aside from voluntary sterilization, no known cure . . .

It is time to clear up one myth about menstruation or "the curse" as many, including myself, prefer to call it. Many girls worry because their "periods" don't come as regular as clockwork, on the first or fifteenth of the month with the rest of the bills. This is nothing more than a silly wives' tale. The "cramps" you may feel, often no more noticeable than a rhythmic sledgehammer blow to the abdomen, only mean that the two little almond-flavored organs deep in your tummy are finally getting around to preparing a little home in case a baby wants to move in. This continuing cycle varies widely in different girls and may range anywhere from fifty-three to three days, depending on whether the little almonds want their owner to bloat up like a dirigible or simply bleed to death.

This interesting process, often called "nature's egg-timer," was originally based on the lunar month of twenty-eight days. But with so many changes in our modern calendar to make way for silly things like Labor Day and Martin Luther King's birthday, the cycle is often keyed to other natural rhythms, like sunspots.

My own cycle is based on the appearance of Halley's Comet, so although I am under the weather only infrequently, I am stocking up on you-know-whats now, because when my next one comes in 1986, it's bound to be a whopper!

One more word about your period. When it finally comes, you may find it a good idea to use a "sanitary napkin" to help stanch the massive loss of precious, irreplaceable fluids from your vitals. If so, beware of fast-talking sales pitches claiming the Tampax-type tampon is preferable to the Kotex-type external napkin. The former may be somewhat more convenient, but it can lead both to unwanted feelings and risking your stock in the marriage market . . .

As for you boys, don't feel left out. If you glance down between your legs, where your vagina should be, you will see an odd-looking pink sac containing two little ugly things. Go ahead, take a look right now, but keep your hands on the book (more about that later). Quite a surprise, wasn't it? Well, the funny pink sac is called your "scrotum" (skro-tum), and the two little ugly things are called "testes" (teh-stees) and are why you can never know the ultimate, inexpressible joy of motherhood.

Believe it or not, your scrotum will respond to sudden changes in temperature, quickly raising or lowering your testes to maintain them at a constant heat level, something seen nowhere else in nature except by those few who have mastered the proper techniques of marshmallow toasting. If you don't believe me, try rubbing an ice cube against your scrotum and see what happens. Now, quickly try a lighted match. Now another ice cube. Another match. Faster. Cube. Match. Cube. Ma—aha! Didn't your mother ever tell you not to play with matches? All joking aside, this is simply another example of the wonders you can find in and around your own body, stuff that has often led to many important scientific discoveries. For example, when my husband, Ronald, was in the Boy Scouts, he used this same natural principle for a homemade thermometer and won a merit badge in meteorology . . .

Clint and Babs were returning from their church youth meeting. At her door, Babs turned and shook Clint's hand good-night. It had been a lovely date, and, thinking over the evening as he undressed back home, Clint noticed a strange feeling suddenly coming over him. In bed, Clint was still restless, puzzled by this new, overpowering sensation. Suddenly, as Clint thought of Babs's unusually warm farewell, memories of an impure picture he had once found hidden in a Gideon Bible popped up unexpectedly. As did something else. Drowsily allowing his right hand to stray under the covers, Clint sleepily took the situation in hand and, before he realized what he had done, committed an act of self-pollution. The next morning, while driving to school to be sworn in as Student Council President, Clint was struck and killed by a speeding bus.

Such stories are common in the daily papers. Every day thousands of young men and women pay tragically for a single, thoughtless surrender to temptation. But even more victims of the "solitary sin" go unrecognized, their fates mistakenly diagnosed as "poor study habits," "tennis elbow," or a "slight case of the sniffles." The list is endless. But the untold misery brought by willful masturbation cannot be reckoned by mere statistics. One has only to look at our prisons, mental hospitals, and riot-torn campuses for the real cost.

Chilling, isn't it?

There was another and soon-to-be-star—a zonked-out dropout from the advertising world, Chris Miller. His prose could take up the sexual slack of any overpolitical material, for it was so explicit it practically ran down the page. And while Miller was definitely of the "Kenney school," he was a straight-A student, a letterman, a true frat brother.

Throughout late May and early June, the July issue came together.

Lead time on an issue varied, depending on the dependability of the writers and editors, but generally it was completed roughly a month before it appeared on the newsstand. Everyone knew that "Pornography" was going to be the next notch up, a sure-fire winner, smart without pandering, right in there where the audience's attitude was, beyond the "sexual revolution," making the *Playboy* Philosophy seem as out of date as Nancy Reagan and her do's and don't's. Which was just as well because sometime in June, as the issue was being put to bed, and the final bits and pieces were being hurriedly banged out, Kenney disappeared.

14

The Years with Beard

No one knew where Doug Kenney had gone. Not Henry Beard nor Matty Simmons nor his friends—not even his wife. In 1970, Kenney had gotten married to a woman he'd known from Radcliffe, Alex Garcia-Mata. She was from the Castle end of his life rather than Chagrin Falls, smart, stylish, pretty, cosmopolitan, and well-heeled, the daughter of a prominent South American financier. They lived in the east eighties, about as far away from the East Village, Soho, and the underground as they possibly could be. (Beard lived with them for a while in a little aerie only accessible by way of a narrow circular staircase.) The situation was not a happy one, for if Kenney was married to anyone it was Beard. They were still the only two full-time editorial people at the magazine, and eighty- or ninety-hour work weeks were not uncommon. And *la duena* Alex was severe; she did not appear to find the obsessively antic Kenney very amusing. For his part Kenney was no less ambivalent about his wife than he was about anything else, although he was properly attentive to her in person.

Like any red-blooded guilt freak he did the proper thing in these circumstances—he started having an affair. The young woman in question also worked at the magazine (another clever move) and oddly enough resembled his wife somewhat. They kept the affair clandestine until sometime in the spring, when Kenney decided to take O'Donoghue into his confidence. This was Kenney's final stroke of genius, for according to John Weidman: "That was it for Doug and Michael O'Donoghue . . . apparently Michael was desperately in love with [the woman] and had no idea that Doug was having an affair with her. There were no grounds for this infatuation. On the contrary, this was all happening in Michael's head . . . [but] Doug *was* theoretically happily married."

O'Donoghue was not a good person to cross—intentionally or otherwise. As intense in his dislikes as in his likes, he had two main ways of dealing with objects of his loathing—vitriolic and highly imaginative abuse or dead silence. He chose the latter. No amount of emotional maneuvering on Kenney's part could persuade O'Donoghue to reopen lines of communication. Anything Kenney tried—cajoling, explaining, apologizing, making light of it—was met with a wall of icy, white-lipped fury. Try as he might—and try as anyone else might—to convince O'Donoghue that the primary purpose of his affair had not been to break Michael's heart, the ice would not melt. It was the first of several cataclysmic shunnings initiated by O'Donoghue, one of the bills that he routinely presented for the use of his talent. The force of his personality spread it far and wide. He was not a politicker, a whisperer behind closed doors, nor even particularly vengeful; but if he believed himself wronged, he could create a black hole of hostility that sucked everyone into it, willy-nilly.

As it became apparent that Kenney was not just taking a breather but had definitely blown the joint, it also became clear that the young woman had left with him. This didn't help matters much, if for no other reason than that her responsibilities at the magazine were not inconsiderable. (According to Simmons she returned after a while, pregnant, but whether there is a teenage Kenney somewhere in the world he does not say). But as usual with this complex man, there was a lot more to Kenney's departure than a road trip.

One was simple burnout. Kenney had been working without a break for eighteen months, every minute of it devoted to the magazine. He was not a methodical writer like Beard, who, while he worked every bit as hard, was able to lock himself away with his ancient black Remington and get on with it. Kenney had to wait until "it came," which was usually late; he was one of those writers who need to build up a head of agitated guilt before the words will start to flow. This is bad enough on a one-time basis, but when the rhythm of monthly publication makes it necessary to build up a head of guilt every thirty days, it can be a killer. Even a lapsed Catholic's resources of guilt are finite.

But guilt may have been working at another level. Kenney left when it was becoming quite clear that the *National Lampoon* would be a success.* The temper of the time militated against an uncritical view of success, especially commercial success. Even if, like Beard, you had no qualms about the worthiness of that goal, the issue was constantly in the air, and for an instinctive

---

* None of the people interviewed for this section can put an exact date on Kenney's departure. The only biographic material assembled on Kenney is an article by Robert Sam Anson in the October 1981 *Esquire*. It has Kenney leaving the magazine on July 4 weekend for Los Angeles. This may be accurate, but he had left the magazine and New York before that. I had a telephone conversation from Los Angeles with Beard in late May or early June 1971, and he was distraught over Kenney's disappearance then. Simmons cannot remember exactly when Kenney left; nor can Gross or Weidman.

doubter like Kenney, that fact alone was disturbing enough. Much of his development over the last two years had been away from the Castle's version of success and toward something with which he felt more at home, whether it was in the underground or back in Chagrin Falls. (The initial elitism of Mrs. Agnew's diary, for example—the Tupperware-is-tacky kind of humor—had given way to broad all-American farce made still funnier by the fact that the men who ran the world were engaged in it). The ambivalent sympathy of pieces like "The High School Yearbook" and "Nancy Reagan's Dating Guide" were signals that he had left the Harvard preppy far behind. Ironically, his search for a place and a voice that fit looked as if it was going to make him a very successful young man. In 1971 that was a possibly insurmountable problem. In leaving the magazine, Kenney was only doing what many of his generation were doing at the time: resisting, if not outright rejecting, the pressure to succeed; taking time off to look at the values that informed it; dropping out; splitting for the Coast. Irresponsible though it seemed—and was—it was not vacuous, or incomprehensible.

Where had he gone? According to Simmons, to Martha's Vineyard—lair of James Taylor, playground of the underground, the countercultural Cape Cod. He is supposed to have slept in a tent on the beach with his Annabelle Lee, covering himself from head to toe in the bright clay found on the island's shore.

Eventually Kenney split for the West Coast, where he spent some time with two friends—Peter Ivers, from Harvard, who was an occasional contributor to the magazine, and Ivers's friend, Lucy Fisher. Apparently, as he came through the front door of the house where they were staying, he called out: "Hi, Mom and Dad, I'm home!"†

Back at the magazine there was fear and not a little loathing. After Beard, Gross was the most immediately affected. He was the only other Lampooner who was full-time. His every move was determined by the editors, while at the other end of the process he was solely responsible for delivering the goods to the publisher, the public, and the advertisers. Simmons had a commendably hands-off attitude toward "the boys" and exhibited a tolerance about what they wrote for which he was given far too little credit. But freedom isn't free; the cost of the license Simmons gave the editors was that they delivered him a nice glossy magazine with lots of good stuff in it on time every month, and all the heat was on Gross:

"I handled [Kenney's departure] very badly. You have to remember that I was the most professional of the bunch. You have to be as art director, because you're the one who has to get the magazine *out*. You're the last guy to touch it, you gotta deliver it to the printer. So you're the one who's always saying, 'I have to have the piece by Tuesday.'

"Doug was really running the magazine, and Henry was content with that.

† This information came from the *Esquire* article also. It is hard to check as Ivers is now, alas, dead.

When Doug just up and disappeared, my feeling was that he abandoned the magazine, and he had no right to do that as a professional. And I resented it a great deal because it made life hell for me. It left us in the lurch, and I was angry. It was my magazine, too. Henry had to pick up the pieces. And no one really thought Henry *could* pick up the pieces. There was that personality of Doug's which really gave life to things, and he was a leader, a real leader; a zany one, but boom, a leader. No one thought Henry was.

"[Henry took over] beautifully. So professional. It still was never so much fun in a large sense, but his leadership qualities were entirely different."

The topic of the issue after Kenney's departure was "Bummer." (Issues in crises often had a way of sardonically reflecting the editors' collective mood.) "Bummer" didn't come anywhere near "Pornography: Threat or Menace" in pop appeal, but it would have taken Gross's lupe to spot any difference in quality. What the issue lacked in visual impact it made up for with a stunning cover, probably the best satirical cover to date: a Kelly Freas portrait of William Calley, The Mad Boomer, in full Army uniform, complete with sharpshooter medal.

What Freas had done was a superb generational joke, subtly rendering Calley as Alfred E. Neuman graced by a three-tier pun: *Mad*'s perennial "What, Me Worry?" rendered as "What, My Lai?" (see photo insert).

The centerpiece of "Bummer," appropriately enough, was a long travel-guide supplement on Canada ("The Retarded Giant on Your Doorstep"), which mined the rich vein of Canadian mediocrity, and its "Quest for an Identity":

Oh, say does that leaf-tainted banner hang pensive,
O'e the land of the discreet and the home of the inexpensive?

(Nineteenth runner-up in the federal government-sponsored National Anthem Contest, 1963.)

The piece was written by Kelly, Choquette, and the *Lampoon*'s first (and only) major female contributor, Anne Beatts.

This was by no means Beatts's first appearance in the *Lampoon*. She was another of Choquette's Canadian additions and, like Kelly, had shared a byline with him. But she too had found that actually coming to New York and being exposed to other on-the-spot contributors had been a considerable creative stimulus; she was already writing pieces with Weidman and Trow, as well as Kelly and Choquette.

An intense woman, intellectually as well as physically elegant, Beatts was typical of the first wave of new arrivals. Highly educated, but too intelligent to go where that was supposed to lead her—to academia or the media—she was a misfit who fit nowhere but the *Lampoon*. Not that she was exactly allowed to fit by her male co-misfits, something which later generated a lot of heat. Nonetheless, what she was denied in participation, she made up for in observation, and she was certainly the only woman who ever held her own in the piranha pool of day-to-day *Lampoon* repartee.‡

The *Lampoon* was becoming a group, in a time-honored tradition of Boomer humor. For the moment it was loose—and still limited by geography (the Canadians shuttled back and forth from Canada) and by economics. But the group and its collective sensibility were tangible. The *Lampoon* was becoming truly national; the trend started by O'Donoghue and Gross was now expanding to include people from all over the place. The Harvard core continued to guide it, but the Castle had been completely transformed by its new arrivals.

This emerging group helped the *Lampoon* survive Kenney's departure. For the rest of the magazine's creatively measurable life, one group or another operated it. And this was where, paradoxically, Beard's leadership was at its most functional and dramatic. For all his reserve, Beard was a group maker, a forger of collective effort. How he did this was quite mysterious. He could not have been further from either coach or symbol. This was neither Rockne nor Gandhi.

But Beard did have three things going for him: his mind, his manners, and his terrible taste in suits.

As it always had, his sheer mental ability won him respect. Living in the real world had had a considerable effect on this faculty. Through dealing with the barrage of ideas the magazine exposed him to, he had grown considerably more muscular. It wasn't just what he knew, but the way he knew it. By being forced to adapt to all kinds of ways of thinking—not the least of them those of the Nixon administration—he had become a world-class mental athlete. He made extraordinary connections, shorted-out terminals no one else would touch. His method was scientific: he mixed solutions and then displayed the crystals that were deposited.

Unlike Kenney and his ambivalence, Beard was completely secure. He was never confused about what he thought. He might not yet know at a given point what he thought, but he always seemed certain that with some vigorous research in the upper story, he could find out what it was. When the obligation arose, these habits had a surprising editorial utility. Not only was he able to adapt very quickly to widely differing ideas in widely differing areas, but could amplify them, usually at breakneck speed. (Or if he'd had a few Virgin Island rums, which was not infrequently, at incomprehensible speed).

With someone less diffident this might not have looked like good editing, so much as competing, or worse, poaching. But Beard's manners were impeccable. While it was clear that he thought about nothing but the magazine and that for the moment it fulfilled every drive in him, from sex to success, he always turned the process away from himself. You were the real author of the eighteen ideas he'd just had in as many milliseconds. (And this was reflected

‡ Someone once remarked, "if you can't stand the Beatts, stay out of the bitching." In *Lampoon* lingo, this was a compliment.

on the contents page, where he often suppressed an entirely legitimate credit).
And even if your idea stunk, and his mind could only politely look around for
something to wipe its feet on, he was gracious. He had a characteristic word
that covered all editorial situations, good or bad. "Tempting!" he would ex-
claim, pipe clenched between somewhat stained teeth.

"Tempting" meant anything from "That is the most Godawful notion that
has been proposed since postwar British socialism" to "judging by the lines of
this baby, I could be persuaded to have a prolonged intellectual orgasm."

But it was Beard's persona, his physical presence, that—oddly—exercised
the most influence. Perhaps so determinedly skeptic a group could only have
coalesced around an antileader: anyone with hard blue eyes, a firm jaw, and
an iron handshake would have been cut to ribbons in minutes. Everything
about Beard exhibited non–leadership potential. He was reserved, in a permanent state of scruffiness, bespectacled, apparently suffering from malnutrition
(although it would have been unseemly to inquire if he really was), unhealthy,
unathletic. Somehow the way he dressed expressed all of this. In a time when
even those most resistant to fashion wore myriad loose-fitting clothes and
Renaissance hair, Beard stood out like a shipment of sore thumbs. His hair
appeared to have just been chopped off by the school barber as some kind of
punishment; he dressed permanently in a charcoal gray suit (possibly always
the same one), which although it was Brooks Brothers, looked like he'd just
found it in Central Park. All this was bottomed off by a pair of loafers so
ancient they might have been used as lifeboats by small mammals leaving the
Arc.* Beard was not a power dresser.

On the very few occasions he was ragged about his dress sense, he blamed
it on his mother, and indeed his mother would show up occasionally at the
office with his clean laundry in a Bergdorf bag. From Beard's description of
this lady, one was led to expect a sort of P. G. Wodehouse aunt who'd just
come from fire-eating class; in fact she was a cheery woman who seemed
rather intrigued by the oddness of her son's surroundings and acquaintances.
From what one could piece together of his background, however, his childhood had not been a happy one. Although wealthy, his parents had had him
at an advanced age, so that his father was an old man by the time Beard
reached adolescence. Amateur psychology led to the conclusion that he might
feel emotionally deprived, and there was a verbal extremism to Beard that
seemed to spring from some profound dissatisfaction.

But words were his only weapon, and he did seem terribly vulnerable. He
looked as though he had been through a psychic hedge backward. This may
have been the key to his appeal. He elicited sympathy but so obviously had
his chops together that you had no obligation to act on it. He never asked for
help, but you wanted to help him anyway. And while you knew there was a
rod of high-grade plutonium at his core, he was utterly unthreatening.

---

* Much later, when the Greening of Beard had reached Consciousness 4 or 5, he was sometimes tempted to wear these without socks.

This at least is how he seemed to me. I had been contributing to the magazine (by long distance, because I lived in Los Angeles) since its fourth issue and had gravitated naturally to Beard. Many found him a difficult person to work with on material and preferred Kenney if they needed editorial guidance. But for an outsider like myself—especially one working from the West Coast, and often by phone—Kenney was too vague, too idiosyncratic and self-contradictory to be of much help.

Beard was formal, cut and dried, articulate. Where Kenney hinted that there might just be a certain kind of *Lampoon* material and you weren't it . . . yet . . . maybe, Beard simply seemed interested in getting it good and getting it right. His very impersonality was encouraging, where Kenney's uninterpretable looseness was not. Beard too had a predilection for political material which I shared: Kenney had that too of course, in "Mrs. Agnew's Diary," but it took a mid-American form I was uncertain of. And that part of Kenney that tended toward the underground—and he certainly looked the part of a street freak at the time—was familiar to me. Beard, though, was startling, from his rumpled suit to his spic-and-span brain, a very new voice in the mix, unashamed of its intelligence and unafraid of where it might lead. This was more than refreshing to me in 1970. It was tremendously exciting.

My career to date had been both eventful and frustrating. I was introduced to the *Lampoon* by Choquette, and in many ways our paths had been parallel. I too had been half of a comedy team (and also one which came from abroad, in this case the United Kingdom). My partner and I were called Hendra and Ullett—or, if he was giving the interview, Ullett and Hendra. We'd come to the United States in 1964, both from the Cambridge University Footlights and the class that would later form the "Cambridge Mafia" of British comedy in the sixties and seventies.†

Our joint career lasted from then until early 1969, by which time both of us had moved to Los Angeles. We'd been moderately successful, thanks in part to the Anglophilia of the times, playing most major television shows including several appearances on CBS with Mr. Edward Vincent Sullivan. Our material was, for want of a better description, bargain-basement *Beyond the Fringe*, sketches and songs with a faintly political or cultural aroma. We flew close to the flame a couple of times, once in our first weeks in New York when we opened for Lenny Bruce during his bust-ridden sojourn at the Café au Go-Go: at the "Merv Griffin Show," on which we were for a time regulars, and at the hungry i, which we played several times and thus came into extensive contact with the Committee. All these contacts however, were as much by

† The period I was at Cambridge, 1959–63, was one of Footlights' more fecund, satirically, than most. At one end were Peter Cook and Jonathan Miller of *Beyond the Fringe;* in the middle were such luminaries as David Frost, and John Cleese and Graham Chapman, later of "Monty Python." At the other end were Tim Brook Taylor, Bill Oddie, and Graeme Garden of the repellent, but immensely popular British hit *The Goodies,* which happily was unexportable; and a host of people whose subsequent influence in all media has been immense: e.g., the celebrated producer Humphrey Barclay, director Trevor Nunn, and Richard Stilgo, coauthor of *Starlight Express.*

chance as design; our chief concerns were to make a living (I had two small children) and discover what it was that made Americans laugh, which to hear TV people tell it, was not much of what we had in mind. The gap, at least for me, between the subjects that were permitted on television (or in commercial nightclubs) and what one talked about or thought about for the other twenty-three hours of the day, was by the late sixties becoming just about unbearable. It wasn't merely that "protest" wasn't allowed but that nothing from within one's generation could be mentioned, from whatever point of view. Five of your six cylinders weren't being used.

For Hendra and Ullett, there weren't even any financial rewards in the compromises. Our managers at the time (Bob Chartoff and Irwin Winkler, who later became immensely successful film producers—e.g., *Rocky)* whispered darkly to us that we'd "almost" got the slot as hosts of "Laugh-In" but were "too young." But who knew? Several other young comedy teams were probably told the same thing. There seemed no rewards for being a good little buffoon—financial or artistic.

So we broke up and for a while I tried my hand at writing television in Los Angeles—hoping, stupidly of course, that being a rung or two higher up the ladder might mean greater freedom, more access, something.

Needless to say, it didn't.

The *Lampoon* was like finding a fire hydrant after a week without water in Death Valley. Here were people who dealt first and foremost in information. They cared about it and got it right. They didn't think Agnew was Nixon's Ed McMahon—they knew he was a pretentious (and dangerous) lout who thought alliteration was talking good. They also knew what the Port Huron statement was and what it meant and where it fit, and that Tom Hayden just might be a turkey.

Most important, the whole texture of what they wrote and said, the attitudes they played with and played off, were familiar. Their referents were common ones, from Hiroshima to Chappaquiddick. And therefore their wit, their vocabulary, and the edge on it was new. Suddenly all your faculties were working, all six cylinders were being allowed to fire. The *Lampoon* was like pulling out of a muddy ditch onto the clean pavement, like walking from a dark cinema into spring sunlight.

The mysterious improvement the magazine had been undergoing since the beginning of 1971—mysterious from Los Angeles, that is—had been tantalizing me for months. The *Lampoon* seemed no longer to be just a special place a few people knew about, a little-known fat farm you could go to for a weekend and shed a few intellectual pounds—but a center of activity, a place to be.

The phone call with Beard in the wake of Kenney's departure was the excuse I needed. He didn't ask for help, but he did suggest that there was an urgent need for extra hands. Not that there was any pressing need, of course, and he knew how I was situated. There was no money . . . I had two children . . . But . . . tempting.

It was all I needed. In the last week of June 1971, I sold all my furniture, loaded my wife and kids and a few irreplaceable possessions into a VW bus, said good-bye to my Laurel Canyon neighbors, and split for the Coast.

15

O'D Heaven

I hadn't been around the *Lampoon* since the previous fall, when Beard and I had worked on the Agnew assassination piece ("Eight Days That Shook Wook, Iowa").*

What had once been a couple of guys meeting in a cheap restaurant was now a place. And the place was full of people. Chief was O'Donoghue, whom I'd never met, but whose work had me in awe, with purposes and effects I'd only come across before in novels or on film. Kelly and Beatts were there too and, frequently, Trow. Sharp-eyed people, looking for an edge, to whom the California Code of Uniform Consciousness meant nothing.

And there was Beard, courtly, delighted I could be there, promising nothing, a trifle impressed that I'd split for his coast. It was dangerous and comfortable—like coming home. And just like coming home, you were on your own.

It was O'Donoghue I hit it off with eventually. It was he that seemed to me —both as a mere reader in Los Angeles, and now as a colleague—who understood the presence of the page, the need for an artifact, words, and images working together. Beard was still a writer, whatever hoops he could make ideas jump through, as was Kenney. But O'Donoghue understood the amazing machine Gross had created, which could Xerox the most sacred images of Western civilization—practically any of them—and allow us to play with them any way we liked.

* Beard had urged me to get more and more explicit with this piece, both in its relish at Agnew's supposed demise and the sacrilegious forays into Kennedy assassination parallels. I was so scared that its appearance would mean instant deportation, I signed it with the pseudonym "Punji."

I shared O'Donoghue's fascination with the artistic end of the *Lampoon* (my father was an artist) and his intense delight in the perfectly rendered style, whether it was Norman Rockwell or an action comic. This was a new level of satire in which not just the ideas and words of your target could be made to self-destruct by imitation, but the images that were associated with them, that had burned them into people's minds.

O'Donoghue also cared about what was happening in the underground, artistically and politically. Not that he subscribed to what was happening, whether it was Warhol or the White Panthers, but he understood why it was important to others, and therefore in some circumstances why it should be attacked. O'Donoghue could spot a sacred cow on the tracks long before anyone else on the train. He was selective in this regard: just because something was sacred to someone didn't mean the magazine was obliged to attack it. But if the sins of the fathers were repeated by the sons, whatever they might be—self-promotion, exploitation, hypocrisy, gunplay—then they were fair game. If one was simply going to end up with the same combination of violence and greed, but with different faces and names, there was no point to anything. One of his favorite expressions was "rock and roll pigs," by which he meant any of our emerging "leaders" who sought to manipulate, control, divide, and diminish others, just like the last lot.

In the sanctimonious salons of San Francisco and the conspiratorial canyons of L.A., I had never heard anything quite like this. Not even the Committee had been as finely tuned about their loyalties. There had always been the possibility that someone, even if they were absurd, could be declared off-limits to satire, because they were on the "right side." But the counterculture was becoming too big, was affecting too many people's lives for that kind of hypocrisy to survive. It was necessary, perhaps even our job, to sort out the good from the bad, or the not-so-good from the not-so-bad, for *Us* to keep the new *Them* honest.

There were other bonds. Both O'Donoghue and I were provincials who'd come to the big city but had little taste for the uptown life to which Beard and Kenney, however nominally, belonged. Both of us too had had careers, albeit mini-ones, before the *Lampoon* began. Of the emerging members of the group, only Kelly so far was similar in this respect, and his academic background mitigated the similarity. Most of all, though, O'Donoghue was simply good to be around, constantly funny, with a new kind of wit, a new kind of irreverence; someone for whom nothing had to be explained, modified, censored.

I began to hang out more and more in his vast decrepit loft on Spring Street. My living arrangements at the time were difficult. My partner and I had bought a property in western New Jersey before we'd gone to Los Angeles, and my family was now living there, in a remote if beautiful old house, two hours from the city. There was no money at the *Lampoon* yet, the average price for a piece still being in the two-hundred to four-hundred-dollar range, and that only once a month (if you were lucky you might get two pieces in an issue). But the *Lampoon* was where I wanted to be—was where I knew I should be and commuting four hours each day by bus took a sizable bit out of the experience. O'Donoghue offered a ratty couch—whenever I wanted to stay in town.

Living with him was delightfully weird. He had an extremely overweight cat who got fed before he did, and an erratic sex life which occasionally meant I faced long bus rides back to Jersey late at night. The couch had a spring loose in a certain place, and the heater was ridiculously noisy (it was a cold winter). But the evenings stretching to nights were worth any discomfort, a movable feast of premise, riff, banter. Everything I cared about was suddenly realizable, expressible. The *Lampoon* was the place to do this, where everything from Lenin to Lennon could be presented and measured, but in a completely new language—satirically, the new code of the generation.

The issues that followed "Bummer" were solid and—considering Kenney's absence—remarkably successful. It was becoming clear that whatever the issue topic, perhaps even whatever the cover, people were beginning to buy the *Lampoon,* not on impulse but because it was their voice. Every step into "outrage" meant an increase in circulation. More and more, as we did what came naturally, we found that the readership agreed. We were onto something, playing the right music.

In the fall of 1971 it was decided that issues should be run by specific editors, or "guest" editors. The point was to further focus the issue topic. This was an acknowledgment that individuals with strong voices were emerging in the magazine. The first "guest editor" was O'Donoghue in November 1971. (Since the inception of the magazine, O'Donoghue had resisted coming on staff; he was still technically a free-lancer.) The topic he chose was "Horror," not a very fruitful one as it turned out, for it tended toward the campy rather than the genuinely horrific, falling from time to time into the trap of dealing with what Hollywood thought was horrible, rather than what we thought was horrible.

I did, however, get to write my first action comic for the "Horror" issue, called "Dragula, Queen of Darkness." Its premise was slight—a gay vampire terrorizes Gotham, turning all the savages gay. Having brought New York in every sense to its knees, he is finally destroyed by a large-breasted cubette reporter from that fountainhead of masculinity, *Esquire.* This was the first time I had really made use of the Gross machine: the cover was done by Frank Frazetta and the comic was illustrated by one of the foremost comic artists, Neal Adams. The thrill of seeing the panels come to life was enormous. Faces, characters, settings, movements appeared magically, not at all as I'd seen them in my mind's eye when writing, but perfect nonetheless. And the more the comic read like a real action comic, the better it got. It was like being able to direct a film.

I made use of the machine in another way that fall. There was at the time a very popular poster in circulation called "Desiderata." Purportedly this had been found in a churchyard in Pennsylvania and was set in an archaic typeface, reinforcing its immemorial weightiness. Actually, its style was suspiciously twentieth century, and its sentiments were pure *Reader's Digest.* Nonetheless it was to be found in living rooms and dorms across the nation— even more so after Les Crane, a well-known talkshow host, recorded a single of it (he spoke the words while a lugubrious group played holy-ish music behind him). This was definitely going too far. I wrote a line-by-line parody of the wretched thing and called it "Deteriorata." Gross, of course, made it look indistinguishable from the weighty original and it eventually became one of the *Lampoon*'s best-selling posters:

Go placidly amid the noise and waste and remember what comfort there may be in owning a piece thereof. Avoid quiet and passive persons unless you are in need of sleep. Rotate your tires. Speak glowingly of those greater than yourself and heed well their advice, even though they be turkeys; know what to kiss and when. Consider that two wrongs never make a right but that three do. Wherever possible, put people on hold. Be comforted that in the face of all aridity and disillusionment and despite the changing fortunes of time, there is always a big future in computer maintenance. Remember the Pueblo. Strive at all times to bend, fold, spindle, and mutilate. Know yourself; if you need help, call the FBI. Exercise caution in your daily affairs, especially with those persons closest to you—that lemon on your left, for instance. Be assured that a walk through the ocean of most souls would scarcely get your feet wet. Fall not in love therefore; it will stick to your face. Gracefully surrender the things of youth, birds, clean air, tuna, Taiwan; and let not the sands of time get in your lunch. Hire people with hooks. For a good time, call [555]-4311; ask for Ken. Take heart amid the deepening gloom that your dog is finally getting enough cheese; and reflect that whatever misfortune may be your lot, it could only be worse in Milwaukee. You are a fluke of the universe; you have no right to be here, and whether you can hear it or not, the universe is laughing behind your back. Therefore make peace with your God whatever you conceive Him to be—Hairy Thunderer or Cosmic Muffin. With all its hopes, dreams, promises, and urban renewal, the world continues to deteriorate. Give up.
—Found in an old *National Lampoon,* dated 1972

The other excitement of the fall was that in October Kenney slid back into town. He was not welcomed with open arms. Beard was clearly pleased that his friend was back, but the Harvard bonds were by now of less importance to the functioning of the magazine. A tremendous amount had changed in the few months he'd been away. The group had learned to do without him, and had transferred its allegiance solidly to Beard. Beard commanded loyalty, he had stuck it out, and he'd proven himself. In the Italianate world of *Lampoon* politics, Beard was a President everyone could agree on. Worse still, for Kenney, the magazine he had coaxed off the ground was now shooting straight up through the clouds at Mach 2. It didn't seem as though the special Kenney voice was needed in the mix—and others were exploring the territory that had been exclusively his, Miller especially. Gross says, "I was quite resentful of him. My attitude was 'fuck him.' He was gone for a long time, and the magazine was pieced together. Yes, you did miss certain kinds of Doug Kenney pieces, but it had been filled in with a lot of good material. It was a good magazine without him. And my feeling was, he doesn't have a right to do this.

"When he came back, everyone resented it. There was so much tension. Because he couldn't come back to what he was when he left. It was his magazine when he left and when he came back he was in a quiet office down the corner and one of the contributors.

"There was a great deal of embarrassment. Everybody just couldn't look him in the face. He couldn't look anyone in the face. He was embarrassed himself, so our working relationship was very nervous, and humble, and weird."

I was the next guest editor—for the January 1972 issue. To have the whole, carefully tuned, finely calibrated machinery at my disposal was excitement of a major order. I chose as my theme: "Is Nothing Sacred?" This was a rather bad choice for most contributors because it was so self-conscious. The magazine knew that nothing was sacred, and it meant very little to have said it. What I meant by it was considerably more concrete. It was time to apply the same principles to our own as we had to all others. The subtext was: Is there something or someone so sacred to us they are intrinsically off-limits?

There wasn't. Beard wrote a fine parody of Buckminster Fuller called "Repair Manual for the Entire Universe." It covered Bucky's proposals for radical redesign of fundamental objects like the northeastern shoreline, male and female sex organs (this became another famous *Lampoon* poster), and the common clam. The prose was impeccable, impenetrable Fuller. It was illustrated with exactly rendered blueprints for the various "redesigns" (see photo insert):

Kelly and Choquette introduced a new superhero called "Son O'God," a Superman-muscled Protestant whose constant enemy is Anti-Christ, a vast and delicious villain, a.k.a. the Pope of Rome. The comic was drawn by Neal Adams, and Beatts was "spiritual adviser." This was the first appearance of Son O'God (a good, if muscular dope) and the first in a long line of essentially Catholic pieces which were unique to the *Lampoon.* They got the magazine in more trouble than almost anything else it did (whatever anti-Semites may say, Jews have a minuscule influence in advertising and media compared to Catholics), and almost no other Boomer humorists ever dealt with the subject with the same intensity (except maybe for the hilarious Mr. Buckley).

O'Donoghue's hand is solidly in this issue—a topic after his own heart—but what he chose to do himself was at a slight tangent. Here was easily the best piece he ever wrote about Vietnam—possibly the best satirical piece ever written about it. It was called "The Vietnamese Baby Book," a sugary-sweet

American-style baby book, in which a Vietnamese mother has entered the life history of her child, Ngoc. Baby's first handprint has the second digit missing. The category "Feeding Baby (Breast) (Bottle)" reads: "Chose to feed bottle way because Berets of Green cut off my breasts when they interrogate me."

The categories march on: "Baby's First Word ('medic') . . ." "Baby's First Wound (Attach Sample of Dressing Here)," "Baby's First Funeral . . ." "U.S. Air Force give me condolence payment of 80 piasters, enough almost to buy another Baby Book . . ." But it was the sweetness of the format, the darling pictures of a baby doing typically babyish things like snagging his diaper on barbed wire that made the piece so riveting. In no other piece was the Gross principle so completely fulfilled as this—the cutesier and more familiar Gross made the "Baby Book," the more its horror leaped from the page.

The centerpiece of the issue was a parody of *The Whole Earth Catalog*—that Bible of the underground and counterculture. Actually it was a parody of the several supplements which had been appended to it, essentially covering aspects of the new way of living the original handbook had omitted. The most recent of these had been called *The Last Supplement to the Whole Earth Catalog.* Accordingly we called our parody "The Last Really No Shit Really the Last Supplement to the Whole Earth Catalog."

The "Supplement" was dedicated to "the Movement," represented by a grim, gun-toting radical couple (the woman with a baby on her hip)—one of the more asinine posters of the day. The "Supplement" was laid out like *The Whole Earth Catalog* itself, full of little bits and pieces of information and advice, and various musings from various gurus. Ken Kesey came in for plenty (among much else, he describes discovering the joys of Episcopalianism and bowling), as did the various branches of Buddhism. Here's Beard as Ripshit on the teachings ("Zoot Sutras") of Svi Chutni:

> Of all the "How to Do" books my favorite is *How to Know Everything, Control People, See God, Have Pleasant Reincarnations, and Make Big Karma in the Fast-Paced Mantra Field.* This stool is an old one, but the manifestation of it I use is from the commentary of Vivasectanada, and is called *The Sayings of Svi Chutni,* by Koalapanda and Goldfish, Perma Press, Hollywood.
>
> Sutra means "hair of the dog" or "any of a variety of puff-balls, especially the family Medula Oblongata," and right off the bat you get a nice feel for the role of paradox in Yoga. The sutras were composed sometime during the second administration of Grover Cleveland, around 18-something, which says a lot about the superiority of the East, considering that this obscure monk knew which end was up while our ancestors were still fooling around with gas for street-lighting. References to Yoga meditations—and the zipper, "Lincoln" logs, and the dustpan, too, by the way —can be found around A.D. 1500, and the concepts of the Godhead, the

Whitehead, and the Blackhead probably date back much earlier, but Svi Chutni restated it all for our time.

The book is in four parts: Operation of the Individual Sutra, Immediate Action for Karma Blockage, Care and Cleaning of the Chakra, and Basic Yoga Tactics. The following are an excerpt from Svi Chutni's introduction and some sutras from the first part:

My name is Svi Chutni and I am to be your principal instructor in a twenty-two-hour block of instruction on the Yoga. Yoga is your friend. You must learn to treat it right and it will treat you right. Remember, Yoga is not a "religion"; you can call it a "discipline," a "system," a "philosophy," or a "method," but never a "religion." Now for nomenclature: Yoga is an ego-feeding, brain-operated, reality-apprehending, thought-clearing, semitheocratic, living-system. Have you got that?

Response of the students: Yes, Drill Swami!

I can't hear you!

Response of the students: YES, DRILL SWAMI!

I included a message from the Weather Bureau:

The time has come for us all to face up to the facts and take the right remedy. We are all of us, black and white, brothers and sisters, pigs; and if we have any sense of cosmic rightness left in our bodies, we owe it to humanity to off ourselves.

You know this. You just don't want to face up to it. But if you need some prodding, just remember a couple of these stools from my stool-box:

• If you live *anywhere* in the North American continent, even if you poison nothing, kill nothing, contribute nothing, commune, meditate, you're living on land ripped off from the Indians. You're a pig.

• If you exhale *any* breath, it's mostly carbon dioxide, and if you don't think that's a No. 1 boss poison, try putting a plastic bag over your head sometime and see how long you last, pig.

• If you shit or piss *anywhere* on Earth you're dumping a load of ureic acid on Mother Earth, and ureic acid is one of the basic ingredients of friendly old Mr. PolyUrethane. You pig.

• If your body gives off *any* heat, it contributes to thermal pollution, which in turn is a basic energy degradation that is killing the universe. Goddamn motherfucking pig.

• You're reading this on the corpse of a tree, pig. A cow died to make your fucking belt.

Remember: if you're not part of the final solution, you're part of the problem. But don't go offing yourself half-cocked: if you take poison, it goes right into the environment; I won't even talk about guns; and there's enough gunk in the ocean without you adding to it by jumping off a bridge. I recommend hanging, with hemp, NOT NYLON, rope, over a four-foot-deep hole half-filled with active compost. If you must leave a note, write it on bark.

Of course, suicide is the ultimate ego trip. With my Sufi training I have reduced my ego to the size of the Blessed Peanut and cast it into the Lake of Denial. I am powerless to act.

What's your excuse, pig?

But probably the most interesting departure we made was a discreet ad, which of course was unthinkable in the sea-green incorruptible *Whole Earth Catalog,* called "Used Karma." "Used Karma" was the album of an in-studio concert featuring "Joan, Joni, David, Neil, James, Mimi, Kris, John, Steve, Graham, Gracie, and many good hearts." There were many great cuts on "Used Karma," including "I'm taking the Stockbridge exit off the Massachusetts Turnpike turning right onto Route 7 and going a mile down to the intersection with 102 in my mind" by James Taylor and "Coming Down from Me" by Kris "Kristofferson" Kristofferson.

But the one that went too far was a Joan Baez parody, once again not particularly fair to Baez, but taking a potshot at the well-heeled radicals of Marin and Monterey of whom she was one, and their deification of the Panthers:

Bobby Hutton was his name and his blood was like a flame
that lit the ghetto streets from dawn to dusk.
Fire with fire, eye for eye, truth for truth in the blazing sky
And he dropped the men of darkness as they came.

O pull the triggers,
Niggers,
We're with you all the way,
Just across the bay.
Whether it's in
Oakland or Marin
We're with you all the way
Across the bay.

Now Joan Baez is the name and I've a house by the sea
And though my dream is something less that don't mean I can't say
    YES
And if I can't be there it doesn't mean that I don't care
So next time, brother, off a pig for me.

O pull the triggers,
Niggers,
We're right behind you
Just across the bay.

Let us remind we're right behind you
Just across the bay.

"Used Karma" was released on Peace Now Records (A Leisure Service of Union Carbide).

Kenney contributed his first piece since his return, "Che Guevara's Bolivian Diaries," in which a dopey Che gets himself caught by the Bolivian Army, due mainly to massive incompetence and an addiction to Coca-Cola. Gross painted a faultless parody of Paul Davis's famous heroic poster of Guevara for the cover but added, splattered all over his face, a large cream pie. It too became a *Lampoon* poster.

Beatts wrote a brilliant piece about another herd of sacred cows, Native Americans, in the hushed and reverential tone peculiar to such literature, detailing the priceless legacy Indians had bequeathed to the world: the hammock, the toboggan, the decoy duck, maple syrup—and explaining that Indians never discovered the wheel because they foresaw the environmental devastation, mechanistic society, and needless suffering that would arise as an inevitable consequence.

Chris Miller did his most amazing piece of sex sci-fi to date, a highly explicit version of *Back to the Future,* fifteen years ahead of its time, called "Remembering Mama."

Gross inaugurated a section he'd been planning for some time, "The Funny Pages," six back-of-the-book pages of comic strips by a wide variety of artists, including Gahan Wilson, B. Kliban, and Jeff Jones. Gross edited this section himself, and it bore his mark, clean and spare with the emphasis on line and style rather than conventional laugh-or-else cartooning. It launched several successful careers and became probably the most popular continuing feature in the magazine.

It was a good issue, not perhaps in the continuum particularly outstanding, but certainly up to the level the magazine had established as its norm. It was intensely satisfying for me. The heft of the finished product was indescribably more pleasing than any performance I'd ever given; the originality and skill of what lay inside free to roam at will over any subject, instead of being scrunched between the terror and the greed of some faceless patsy in a boardroom.

There were some heated phone calls in the wake of the "Is Nothing Sacred?" issue's appearance, especially from the Bay Area. The prevailing tone was outrage that the *Lampoon* would play into "their" hands by hitting on the left.

That was the same kind of thinking that accused us of being Commies because we didn't like the President. We weren't Commies or playing into their hands. We simply didn't go for this "sides" business. If it walks like an asshole and talks like an asshole, it's an asshole. It was essential to make sure that our assholes got weeded out. We understood the issues involved and that qualified us to make the judgments; what exercised the outraged Left was just that—we knew and understood. We were insiders. But for us to pick and choose, to say "You fine, you asshole," didn't put us in Agnew's pocket. Agnew was nowhere in the picture—an outsider, a dog barking at a car. We were in the generation, and this generation could and would take care of itself. The complaint of the Left that the *Lampoon* was damaging its chances only revealed the poverty of their ambitions. They just wanted to get hold of the same controls: impose some other tedious morality.

The *Lampoon* shouldn't be seen as unwitting participants in the "conservative trend" that, in the face of all available historical evidence, is supposed to have started at this time. We simply knew our own, were testing them, feeling them out, just as we did one another. We didn't need Agnew to tell us who was a threat to the republic. We were quite well-informed and adult enough to know that, as he would soon find out. What we didn't need was Agnew.

Beard evidently felt that "Is Nothing Sacred?" was at least a competent issue, for after it was completed, he asked me to join the staff. I would begin in January 1972, and have the title of managing editor. Technically this made me the first full-time editor hired by the magazine's founders, although O'Donoghue had realistically been the "third" editor from the start. He'd always resisted being tied to a full-time job at the magazine, and one of my first jobs would be to convince him to take an office uptown. The group was coalescing, and this obviously had a beneficial effect on the magazine. This would never be a one-man magazine; nor would contributors, however good, be able to match our collective edge. If that was the case, it was time to start hiring, time to talk turkey.

Turkey, as it turned out, was pretty small potatoes. My starting salary would be $18,500 a year, slightly more than I'd received for my last TV writing assignment. Beard apologized for this, spread the blame equally between the magazine's constant penury and Simmons' penny-pinching, and promised that he would make sure it was made up to me "in a major way." Things were beginning to look, he said, as though they were leading to "a big payoff."

I spent a month away at Christmas banging out a screenplay for Julia Phillips, which I duly handed in and which was met with the usual resounding silence New York writers experience when they mail things to Hollywood. There seemed to be something appropriate about this—the predictably dull thud of what I'd been doing up to that point, contrasted with the high-speed, hard-edged action and reaction of the magazine.

This certainly helped inform a long piece I wrote with Kenney for the next issue up, "Escape," in March 1972. Kenney and I worked over California pretty good—Southern California mostly, since we'd given the Bay Area quite a bashing in January. The piece was in the form of a travel guide, hosted by Governor Reagan: Kenney may have found it natural to "escape" to Los Angeles the previous summer, but he'd worked up a healthy disrespect for it.

To balance things, I asked a good friend, Mike Elias, an L.A.-based TV writer-producer who'd started life in the Living Theater, to contribute some off-setting material. He wrote *"Lynch!*—a quarterly review of scholarly opinion from Whittier College," which contained studies like "Why the Soviet Union Won't Let Its Jews Leave, and If They Do Why We Shouldn't Take Them" and errata from the previous issue like: "Page 54. Harry S. Truman was the thirty-third and not the thirty-fourth traitor to occupy the White House."

Appearing for the first time in the "Escape" issue was another future staffer, Brian McConnachie, with a print piece called "Pamplemouse," based vaguely on the Dustin Hoffman film *Papillon,* about an escape from Devil's Island. McConnachie was part of the trend of that year, a completely unexpected addition to the core, a highly original and quirky talent whose indispensability could in no way have been predicted until it arrived. His route to the magazine had been via Beard, who in some ways he resembled—his dress code tended toward the rumpled Brooks Brothers, and he occasionally disappeared into the depths of the New York Athletic Club. But he was taller than Beard, gentler, and much madder.

His humor was inimitable, whimsical in a way but tougher than that, perfectly sensible and logical, provided you were prepared to accept the stupefying strangeness of his premises. One of McConnachie's best ever pieces was called "Amish in Space," a sci-fi comic in which an Amish family is in a fully equipped spaceship. But their religion forbids them to operate the spaceship, which is therefore lost and out of control. As Poppa calmly spouts biblical antimechanistic proverbs, a band of alien trolls invades the craft, strips it bare, and leaves. That's it. It was hilarious, but what it meant was anyone's guess.

McConnachie was the *Lampoon*'s Thurber. He first appeared in the magazine as a cartoonist. (In one of his cartoons a cheery nun is saying to a disappointed frog: "I'm a nun, I can't turn you into anything!") A refugee from Benton and Bowles, he had been condemned to what he called "The Floor of Lost Men"— an entire floor of people for whom the agency had no further use but were too gentlemanly to fire. His artistic abilities were nil, however, and in July we ran a collection of his cartoons called "The Worst Cartoons in the World." If McConnachie was hurt, he didn't show it—but then he never seemed to have quite the same emotions as other people. A perpetual half smile played around his lips, and his eyes twinkled wildly behind powerful glasses. Brian lived in a world of his own, but he wasn't in the least reticent about it. On the contrary he was eager to get you to join him. In *Lampoon* mythology, he eventually became the alien, trying to pass as an Earthling, who received all his orders—and pieces—from a planet called Mogdar. A delightful man, he was the one editor who survived every crisis and feud of the *Lampoon* without a blemish. He was intrigued by intrigues but never engaged in them, fascinated by malice but incapable of it.

I dived into the job of managing editor with idiot energy, rushing about "managing" everybody like a demented German shepherd and doubtless raising a few hackles. It wasn't until the issue was well along that I realized that the title really wasn't very literal, at least at this magazine. The *Lampoon* was largely unmanageable, and even more so as it came to be written more in-house; people simply established their own patterns and stuck to them, and no amount of barking would speed them up, or head them off. Gross ran every technical aspect of the book, including its scheduling. I simply got in his way. But there was one job to do immediately, and that was to get O'Donoghue signed up.

I was surprised at the degree of resistance he showed to taking a staff job. The problem was not financial—however many pieces he wrote as a free-lancer at the *Lampoon*'s paltry rates, he would be unlikely to make the same as he would on salary. If it was symbolic, the old underground-uptown conflict, then he was dead already, for he was intimately identified with the *Lampoon* and its success. Professionally, although he had written a film with Trow for James Ivory called *Savages,* neither Hollywood nor the *Playboy/Esquire* axis was exactly kicking his door in.

I had never seen O'Donoghue confused about anything. If he was ignorant of a subject, he would keep his counsel, a faintly suspicious brooding, but confusion was not his strong point. The only thing he seemed clear about was that if he took this step it would be somehow irrevocable. He could stay on Spring Street, wear his hair in stringy ringlets, be the same person in all respects, but this would be a certain door opened and another one closed. But what I think really confused him was that what he saw through the open door tempted him sorely.

It wasn't money, but it was some version of the High Life: an artistic temptation, luxuriously bohemian, part delicious decadence, part exquisitely unapproachable style. This had already started to show itself, as he got a little spending money, in a taste for expensive art deco knickknacks which were beginning to appear next to the stuffed things and headless dolls. *Savages,* in fact, was densely and, to me, quite incomprehensibly decadent, an interminable party set in an English country house, at which people you couldn't care less about descend into—you guessed it—savagery.

I was very insistent that he take the job. I thought the magazine needed his presence and his undivided energy, and that it could be taken in fascinating directions. This was partly selfish—he was exciting to be around, and if I was going to spend twelve hours a day on Madison Avenue, I wanted him to be there also. He wouldn't give me a direct answer, but did agree to talk to Beard. The next thing I knew, he was on the staff.

There were some conditions I knew about—and possibly some I didn't. One was that the magazine pursue a couple of his pet projects. The first was a notion for a film magazine to be run along the same editorial lines as the *Lampoon,* but dealing with actual releases, to be called *Rushes* (a good title, at the time). The second was that further effort be put into preparing the *Lampoon*'s first record album, something which O'Donoghue had apparently brought up several times before also, without making much headway. (The chief obstacle was that Beard was extremely reluctant for his baby to take even faltering steps into show biz.)

In the meantime, though, O'Donoghue was uptown and the "25th Anniversary Issue" was the best ever. One of the reasons was that the title was taken as an excuse for more "Nostalgia." And while the range this time was wider, the top scorers were still in the fifties, one by Kenney and one by another newcomer, Bruce McCall.

Kenney wrote "Commie Plot Comics," a brilliant evocation of fifties anti-Russian paranoia in which the Soviets succeed in taking over Pleasantville, U.S.A., through the agency of the model Jones family's malcontent brother. The Commies (who mysteriously infest Pleasantville) kidnap the brother, indoctrinate him, and before long he's infiltrating the local campus:

The local work force falls and then the school system. Model Mr. Jones smells a rat—a Commie rat—and snags his ne'er-do-well brother, but it's too late! The Red Nightmare is upon Pleasantville, and within days, the foul Russkies have crudely repainted its sign, "Stalinville." All its private enterprise is forbidden—even Junior's lemonade stand—and the Jones family is reduced to the abject misery of the workers' paradise:

Of course, it all turns out to be a bad dream on the part of Mr. Jones, but, say the publishers (The American Federation Against Communist Treachery of Dayton, Ohio), it's time for America to wake up!

"Commie Plot Comics" had as many levels as a club sandwich—every panel dripped with the drivel of America First propaganda, but rang with its authenticity. The piece was exactly like the "Yearbook"—the same kind of ambivalent "nostalgia," the unerring cliché of lunacy, the delight and relish in its never-again simplicity.

Very different in its view of the fifties, but the complement to Kenney's piece, was the debut of writer-artist Bruce McCall. His 1958 Bulgemobiles was an equally lunatic brochure on the splendiferous wagons available to the Joneses in 1958 (see photo insert). Every model included a false-perspective view of its acreage of interior space (see photo insert):

McCall was the most significant addition to the *Lampoon* since Gross. Like McConnachie, he was from the advertising world, but had stayed in it and met with modest success. (He continued to stay in it for most of his *Lampoon* career). Mild-mannered, almost compulsively self-effacing, McCall's bold, matter-of-fact humor was firmly rooted in one thing—technology. Cars were its first level, but it went beyond that to planes, ships, zeppelins, weaponry, steam engines, gadgetry, factories, inventions, and to the effect technology has on people and vice versa. He brought a clean accessible bass line to the group that was just as important as Kenney's—although it was utterly different—especially in view of the overwhelmingly male audience the magazine was attracting. McCall knew that part of the modern mind, which loves and hates its machines, is hypnotized by them and clings deliriously to the notion that whatever mess man's ingenuity has made so far, the means to clear it up is just around the corner. Once again, here was an area no one could have predicted the *Lampoon* would have tackled, but an area that was central to the concerns of the generation. McCall's special obsession and special talent, once it had arrived, was indispensable.

McCall was born in a downtrodden area of Toronto, in 1935 (making him several years older than the eldest of us—and who that is shall remain concealed forever). He wrote and drew from an early age, publishing satirical booklets for his family—a process he describes variously as "revenge" or "settling scores." Dropping out of high school, he landed a job as a commercial artist, and then as a writer, all in the world associated with cars—from Canadian auto magazines to Detroit advertising agencies (it was here that he was expected to draw the kinds of cars, and the hopes that went with them, that he later produced as the 1958 Bulgemobiles), ending up on Madison Avenue in 1964 as head writer on the Mercedes print campaigns. He kept his satirical hand in throughout the next several years, becoming class clown of the automotive magazine world, free-lancing humor articles for publications like *Car and Driver* (he created an imaginary British car called the Deadbeat, and a Deux Chevaux French economy job called the Escargot) and parodying *Road & Track* inside *Road & Track* (à la the *Mademoiselle* parody). By 1970 he had branched out into fictitious World War II airplanes, publishing an illustrated piece on this subject in *Playboy*. (It later won the moderately coveted Playboy Humor Award.)

This was enough to make him take a leave of absence in 1971 to decide what he wanted to do. He drove across the country a couple of times as everyone else seemed to be doing that year and eventually came across a copy of the January 1971 issue of the *Lampoon*.

For McCall this was Meatball: "I laughed my ass off. Suddenly in one apocalyptic moment, I said, 'There's a magazine!'

"There was a lot of political stuff I remember (which appealed to me) focusing the Nixon thing . . . using art to satirize familiar forms. It made me realize that my shy and sly, punch-pulling kind of style of dealing with the world was only the beginning of it. There was much more you could do—and get away with. (I was extremely Canadian about saying anything directly about anything . . .)"

A few months later, McCall wrote the editors, "what was probably a stiff little letter," and received an appointment.

McCall continues, "I found Henry infinitely more compatible than Doug. Henry was the science nerd, Doug was the hippie. I had nothing in common with hippies. (I was never a science nerd, but of the two extremes, Henry's side, his more bookish qualities, his seedy affability, struck me as more comfortable.) In the sense that he was revving very fast, he intimidated me, but there were very concrete elements to Henry's humor. He liked to deal with institutions, technologies, and obviously I felt more comfortable with that than the more mushy, nebulous area Doug liked.

"I discovered the satire as I worked on it ["Bulgemobiles"]. I was working from a very big quarry of images and familiarity. Any contrived bit of business that would show the desirable Middle American life. Mostly Dodge and De Soto. That 'Bulgemobiles' piece was a revenge. That's what gave it its bite; that's what gave me my energy. I just got those fuckers, got all that awful life . . . ugly American barges, huge and overdecorated . . . this was new, the first chance I'd ever had to really flex my muscles."

That Kenney seemed mysterious and incomprehensible to McCall was important to the magazine. For McCall brought none of the political, cultural, or generational preoccupations with him that most of the others took for granted.

Rock was a closed book to him, as were drugs. A Tupamaro joke left him cold. He was well informed, but his store of information was from a very different place. Part of it was Canadian, although in the *Lampoon* that was not unique; the larger part was from the common heartland culture of technology and "inventiveness," a sensibility that thinks first and foremost about how things work—and which could not have been further from what the *Lampoon*'s was supposed to be. Yet his instincts led him to the *Lampoon,* and the *Lampoon* recognized him instantly.

By the early spring of 1972 the magazine had in place the nine people who had shaped the magazine, or would continue to do so: Beard, O'Donoghue, Kenney, Kelly, Trow, Beatts, McCall, McConnachie, and myself. Another group continued to contribute heavily: Boni, Cerf, Weidman, Gahan Wilson, Meyerowitz. Chris Miller, increasingly important to the magazine, stood alone, much more than a contributor, but deliberately removing himself from the editorial process. The year also brought a host of new people, some of whom would shape the magazine in other ways, like P. J. O'Rourke and Gerald Sussman, and some of whom would blaze for a while then dim, like Ed Bluestone. But the nine were the organism Beard had created, which now had so many heads and tails that it was likely to survive the removal of any single organ, however vital it might seem.

The pace and promiscuity (figurative as far as I knew) of this group were extraordinary. Wherever two or more of these people met, the prime topic of conversation was the next issue. Ideas would flow; limits would be pushed. My impression was that all of us—with the exception of Trow, who was still at the *New Yorker,* and McCall, who was doing ad consulting—thought of little else in our waking hours. There was nowhere we would rather be than at the magazine. And the magazine didn't mean just its physical plant (thank God, since the scuzzy ill-furnished offices resembled nothing so much as a Czech unemployment office), but anywhere that two or more staff members congregated. It was said of the *New Yorker* at its height that Ross's magazine went down in the elevator every night at five P.M. That was equally true of the *Lampoon,* except that when the organism then split up and various chunks slid off into the night, the magazine continued to function and develop. It was not uncommon for people to arrive in the morning with major pieces or even entire issues which had been conceived and mapped out the evening before.

At this time—the salad days of the *Lampoon*—the number of combinations was dizzying. Almost everyone seemed able to work with everyone else. There was some shading: Trow was not altogether comfortable with McConnachie, who in turn was not quite snug with Kelly, but these problems were nugatory. The reason for this fluidity in relationships was not what might seem logical—that we were identical and interchangeable. On the contrary, the oddness and quirkiness of character and background was what fueled the urge to move around.

The language we spoke was pure Boomer. It began with a war and ended with a war. Everything in between was part of the vocabulary; we were indiscriminately educated, media-saturated, postindoctrinated. The dialects we spoke within it were legion: film cliché, literary reference, the prose doggerel of advertising, militarese, political rhetoric, jargons of all kinds from religious to scientific, every conceivable print style, apocalyptic hippie babble, mail-order catalog, rock mush, suburban gush, pop art, militant menace, street demotic—you name it. We spoke them in a practically infinite number of mixtures, in imitation, mimicry with intent to kill. This was not a parody language but a language made up of parody—dozen of parodies of all the uses to which language is put in our culture, all the tricks it is trained to perform.

In moments of lazy thinking we might even have described ourselves as cynical. But it seemed to me that far from being cynical—tired of the whole business—we were, beyond the primary objectives of entertainment and comment, actually trying to find out why we knew all this stuff. We weren't bored and listless in a place we knew too well. Far from it; we were busily and happily lost. We were playing with our knowledge, patting it, sifting it, poking it, trying to discover what it did, what its real weight and color and consistency was.

The net effect was, to some, cliquey, but we were only exhibiting the impatience anyone who speaks a certain language exhibits toward someone who doesn't. Cliques create stereotypes of themselves. But no one in this group was like anyone else; and I can't recall anyone in it ever using the term "typical *Lampoon* piece" or a "typical *Lampoon* editor." That would have been a contradiction in terms. When someone did come along speaking in a new dialect, or combination of them—Ed Subitsky, for example, who was a theoretical mathematician, or M. (Mary) K. Brown, one of the most original American comic artists since George Herriman—we stopped and listened.

There was one aspect to our language, however, which was intimidating— even to some who ended up in the cave of the Secret Nine. That was its hostility. People took this as exclusionary also—as if our fortress was bristling with verbal hardware. But that wasn't the way our hostility was directed at one another. It too was parody—a parody of hostility. Shrinks may have a field day with this, and I'm sure it sublimated real hostility, but once again it was imitation—mimicry of the hostility we felt all around us, which was the real message of the dialects we spoke, the brutalization of the society. Perhaps dimly we hoped to make the hostility self-destruct, but in any event it was fun, dangerous, playing with fire. This was called "dishing it out" (from "he can dish it out, but he can't take it"—itself an ironic use of a simplistic cliché). The aim was to be able to dish it out *and* take it—one of O'Donoghue's more sadistic assessments of a person was "He can take it, but he can't dish it out."

There was no way to keep tabs on all this activity, let alone organize it. Any attempt would have been laughed out on its ass. In any case only a fraction of it took place in the Czech labor exchange—probably the greater part went on in bars and restaurants, or wherever the magic quora assembled. But there were reasons to remember certain conversations. In my experience, a phenomenal number of ideas—often brilliant ones thrown off in the heat of some dinner, or during a visit to a neighboring office—were being wasted, simply because no one kept track of them. I started trying to keep notes of various encounters I attended (Beard had always done this at formal gatherings) and also began trying very gently to nudge people into slightly more structured gatherings.

One hangout we developed for the latter purpose was a hole in the wall called the Coral Cafe in a fleabag hotel across from the *Lampoon*. This was the kind of place where the battle between ambience and alcohol had been won hands down by Old Mr. Carbohydrate. The front contained various specimens of the melting pot in a state of premortem. The vast cavernous back, furnished in speakeasy brown, contained nothing and no one. Perfect for top-of-the-lungs political and sexual word play. The drinks cost the same as subway fare, so there was no point in going home, and the lone waitress, a dehydrated Scot who was mostly heart, poured our drinks herself. Most of them fell off the check, and they were often in multiples as big as the founders' buyout deal. (Luckily she hated the owner.) It was quite possible for eight people to drink for two hours and be presented with a check for ten dollars.

People needed little encouragement to make these activities habits. And it was easy to scoop up the reticent or the promising and let them relax a little with the people they'd been told were so scary. More good ideas came from such functions than ever came from the offices. (There was method in Simmons's drabness, though; the offices were so awful there were only two things that were fun to do there: write or leave).

Another rather more formal institution was something called the Issue Dinner. This was usually held once a month and involved the issue editor, myself, Beard, and whoever else the editor wanted to be present. The purpose here was quite specifically to brainstorm. There is an optimum number of people at such a gathering. Five is fine, six gets hard to follow, seven is too many—identical numbers, oddly enough, hold in the casting of a revue. There were sometimes two Issue Dinners a month. And when these took off, as they occasionally did, they could be tremendously exciting, since people were not randomly throwing ideas out but focusing simultaneously on a single subject. The only comparable experience I could remember was the kind of night when the Committee was really cooking, all members of the cast hitting their own styles and obsessions just right. The difference was that instead of audience suggestion governing the subject matter, there was the discipline of only one topic. Squeezing all that energy into the narrower channel made it flow even more quickly and intensely.

That's the way it was in the spring of 1972.

The first issue up after the "25th Anniversary" was Beatts's. She called it "Men!"—which in some ways meant "Women!" Beatts would have been quite capable of doing an issue about any subject, but her nature—and the times— made it inevitable that she would want to deal with the overwhelming maleness of the *Lampoon*. The issue thereby exposed some fascinating conflicts. The first was that satirical equality is not quite the same as any other kind. If men are the majority of the nitwits in power, and the magazine is doing its satirical job properly, men will be its targets more often than women. And while theoretically there was no reason why those doing the job should be of one sex rather than the other, the chances were that men would be able to get under the skin of their targets more effectively than women, simply because they knew how the nitwits worked. In this sense, every issue of the *Lampoon* was largely a "Men!" issue.

Demanding equal time on the duck shoot, however, was quite something else. Then accuracy became the issue, exposing a much nastier and certainly sexist issue—the recurrent assertion that "women aren't funny." Here Beatts was on solid ground, but it wasn't much of an issue topic. The only way she could make it work would be to find enough competent women satirists and produce a funny issue. The pressure of getting out a monthly magazine (not to mention the available staff) made this a tall order.

Then there was the further issue of how to deal comedically with women. Here too Beatts was on solid ground, for sex and sexism raised its head almost anywhere that men wrote about women. And if it came to a question of targets, the same logic that said men knew best how to satirize men should also mean that women would do the best jobs on people like Jane Fonda, Judy Agnew, or Nancy Reagan—all of them favorite Kenney targets. Men certainly had a tendency to assume that a reference to the female anatomy invalidated their opinions (or indeed demolished their credibility).

Ultimately Beatts guided her issue more in the direction of getting the men of the magazine to write about sex without being sexist, and the issue is full of short, puzzled pieces which seem to be more exercises than felt. In a couple of cases (e.g, a photo story on a transvestite called Holly Woodlawn, the result was simply kinky).

But it didn't matter. Doing the issue was fascinating, stimulating. Having to grapple with these matters was its own reward, and if we didn't make any breakthroughs here, Beatts made others, and plenty of them, later.

This magazine was a forum, not just a formula, where all the concerns that fell within its readers' ken were addressed. And beyond that, if one of the voices in the group wanted to take a solo, that was essential to the magazine's longevity. A great magazine does not live from issue to issue, cover to cover, but from the totality of what it represents. And the sequence of issues must be paced as much as any individual one.

All this functioned superbly that spring. *The National Lampoon* was knee-deep in Meatball.

So deep that even backtracking to show biz seemed like a good idea.

Man Bites Rock:
The First *Lampoon* Album,
Radio Dinner

The record album for which O'Donoghue had been pressing had become a very real possibility by the spring of 1972. There were many reasons for this. One was purely financial: comedy albums were becoming popular again, and a successful album would make the company some money, as well as opening up a new field of operation. While the magazine was doing phenomenally well at the newsstand, Simmons was still hard put to gain much advertising revenue. The project's secondary function was a promotional one. The magazine's advertising director, Gerry Taylor, felt that an album could help prove to potential advertisers the buying power of the *Lampoon*'s readership.

Taylor, an amiable but ferociously energetic salesman, had joined the magazine in mid-1971. Originally from Los Angeles, via Chicago, he had had a variegated career as an ad rep and knew the quirky campus market better than most. He had repped a couple of the Harvard parodies and published a successful giveaway magazine during the mid-sixties called *Big Ten*, one of the very few prior to *Rolling Stone* and the *Lampoon* which serviced campus readers. (It was while interviewing her for this publication that he met his then wife, Mary Travers of Peter Paul and Mary). Taylor's reaction to the panic-stricken glaze that came over advertisers' faces when *Lampoon* was mentioned, was to develop a long-range strategy aimed at reassuring them. Rather than taking a scattershot approach, begging and pleading with major advertisers (especially liquor and car manufacturers) who wouldn't come near the book on a bet, Taylor set out to build an ever expanding stable of ever more conservative advertisers. It wasn't the kind of plan to make an impulsive gambler like Simmons very happy, but as things turned out, it worked. The place Taylor started was the logical one—advertisers who were close to home and the least likely to be put off by its content: the record industry. This meant convincing them to buy space in the *Lampoon* rather than *Rolling Stone*. And that meant convincing them that *Lampoon* readers would actually buy their product; that an ad in the *Lampoon* would mean an album sale rather than simply industry promotion; that *Lampoon* readers were hipper, brighter, and more discriminating than those of *Rolling Stone*.

True or not, two things began to happen after Taylor's arrival. The first was an increasing number of record ads, the second was that the magazine began to enjoy a considerable vogue in the record industry. This was hardly surprising—among advertisers with big money, the record people were the most likely to share the *Lampoon* attitudes. If the magazine actually put out its own record, this reputation would be further enhanced. It would be something that *Rolling Stone* could only dream about.

The *Lampoon*'s first step into show business was strictly commercial. The album would probably never have been approved if it had not been useful to the advertising department. Certainly Beard, whose attitude toward show business was total Tory intolerance, would never have consented to the removal of half his staff for this purpose (O'Donoghue had suggested to Simmons that he and I do it together) had there not been a compelling argument for its profitability. I was not aware of the advertising aspect of the situation, but it would have made little difference. O'Donoghue and I weren't making money off the project, since we were both on salary, and so long as there were no constraints, we were comfortable.

O'Donoghue was uncomfortable with Taylor's involvement, however. The ad director's high-powered, well-groomed smoothness gave him counterculture goosebumps. And Taylor didn't help matters by insisting that he be the producer of the album. Doubtless he wanted to protect the project and his own reputation, and make sure the crazies didn't blow something sky high, whether it was the studio or the budget. But it was unconscionable to O'Donoghue (and to Beard) for anyone but the editors to have complete control of the album.

With the help of Jerry Weintraub, who was Mary Travers's manager at the time, Taylor set up a modest deal with RCA. The *Lampoon* would get an advance of $25,000 with the usual arrangements regarding royalties, etc. To my mind, RCA was a rather odd choice, since it was among the stodgier of labels, and we would have to use their huge antiquated Manhattan studios and be assigned union engineers (for free, however, since RCA picked up studio costs).

This didn't bode well for the elaborate aural plans O'Donoghue and I had laid, but happily Taylor came up with a further addition to the project, which considerably compensated us for this shortcoming: a brilliant young actor-singer named Christopher Guest. Guest not only had an uncanny ear for impersonation—especially of various rock stars—but was also a more than adequate musician. Although we had vaguely planned some music, this gave us a very specific and valuable capability; in turn, Guest solved a further problem by introducing us to Bob Tischler, a sound engineer at a small Manhattan recording studio which specialized in radio commercials. Now all we needed was a title, material, performers, and a great deal of luck. O'Donoghue obliged on the first score—*Radio Dinner* was to be the name of the album.

Radio Dinner was originally conceived as a "typical" issue of the magazine transferred to vinyl. But by far the most effective parts of the album however were its parodies of folk and rock. Such parodies could only be approximated on the printed page, but having a recording studio and voices at our disposal meant that we could now apply to sound, an audio equivalent of what the Gross machine brought to the printed page.

This was most important from the point of view of the *Lampoon*'s emerging reputation, for there was one area no one had yet conceived of touching, or perhaps dared to touch—rock and roll. And yet by 1972 it was well past the time to do a little constructive destruction.

The absurdities as well as the glories to which rock had soared need little detailing. Its vast range and diversity, its enormous disparities in talent and expression, its profoundly American as well as profoundly international characteristics reflected the generation spawned by World War II more completely than any cultural phenomenon.

Thus it was bound to reflect the absurdities of the generation, its pretension (political or otherwise), its self-indulgence (not to mention its occasional inordinate wealth), and its ebullient naïveté. By the beginning of the seventies, the initial impact of rock—its clear message of strength, change, and independence—had become institutional. It was assumed that dissent—good, bad, or indifferent—was transferred from mind to mind, largely by sound. Rock was the Federal Express of the counterculture and about as worthy of remark. This is not to say it had become boring, simply that its familiarity and universality were incontestable.

With this came much that was ridiculous. The idea that rock, merely by existing, could somehow "change the system"—or indeed already had—was typical. There was a distinct sense abroad that whatever system of government Nixon, Agnew, and Congress might be running, the one embodied in Mick Jagger, the Grateful Dead, John Lennon, Bob Dylan, the Doors, and the rest of the Parliament of Birds was a good deal more valid, more powerful, and more lasting. (As in the case of Nixon and Agnew, it was.) This was not entirely foolish: there was a political component, especially in the work of Dylan and Lennon, and it contributed greatly to their fame. That, though, seemed to be where their obligation ended. However much rock stars owed their success to the political content of their lyrics, their general attitude was that their fame brought with it no responsibility other than to write more songs. Exceptions were few—e.g., Baez—but for the most part, there was a double standard akin to that of "the system." They might inspire political consciousness and be the prime movers of its fervor and energy, but when asked what they intended to do with their subsequent power or what obligations it brought with it, they tended to respond that they were mere musicians. The contradiction at the core of their fame and wealth was akin to any kind of social privilege. Rock celebrities were protected in a very special way —they were sacred, oracular, unquestionable. Of all the cows in the herd, these were the most sacred of the lot.

There were five major cuts on *Radio Dinner* dealing with contemporary music—four of them actually musical. The balance of the album was a series of running jokes and character skits: a pair of inane dopers; a plangent Irish tenor singing a bastardized version of Paul McCartney's "Give Ireland Back to the Irish" and being constantly shot; O'Donoghue with some vaguely sick musings derived from his index cards; and some harmless blackouts with David Eisenhower and Julie Nixon, which explored the less Republican side of their married life. There was also an interminable and incomprehensible piece written by me about Nixon's reelection campaign—about which the less said the better.

Without question the musical numbers gave the album its notoriety. The first of these was a musical version of my "Desiderata" parody, "Deteriorata," set to music by Guest and narrated by Norman Rose, a well-known radio and TV commercial actor, who probably possesses the richest voice—in every sense—in America. He read the piece in the tone of a lugubrious deity, while behind him a sweet soaring chorus was sung by a young backup singer and friend of Guest's, Melissa Manchester. The second side began with a brilliant Guest impression of Dylan called "Remember Those Fabulous Sixties?" It was not a song but a late-night local-TV commercial that attempts to sell unwanted old records. In this case, however, Dylan was selling surplus product from all the great groups of "the fabulous decade—Purple Haze, Vanilla Fudge, Lothar and the Hand People . . . and many more." The side concluded with a hit on George Harrison, whose concert for Bangladesh was a major album at the time. In our version, a Bengali "tragedy team" performs a concert in Bangladesh for George Harrison in gratitude for his sterling efforts on behalf of their devastated country. The two tragedians, played by Guest and myself, engage in snappy back chat such as "Tell me, what do you call a Bengali woman who's been raped seven times?" "Lucky." "What do we NOT need in Bangladesh?" "After-dinner mints." And so on, all punctuated by comedy (or tragedy) stings on a sitar.

One of the best cuts was a version of the Joan Baez song, "Pull the Triggers, Niggers" from the "Is Nothing Sacred?" issue. We had planned this cut from the start, but had despaired of finding a voice to perform it. As we got more sophisticated in the business of recording parody as opposed to writing it, we became more rigorous about our requirements for absolute fidelity to the target. Approximating Baez's unique voice was next to impossible. We could not simply cheat by introducing it with "Ladies and gentlemen, Ms. Joan Baez," for that would have offended the basic purity of the attack. The voice had to be instantly recognizable as Baez for the impact of the lyrics to come through. At the last moment, Taylor found an ex–folk singer, Diane

Reed, with an obscure animus against Baez, perhaps because their voices were so similar. She sang the parody faultlessly, her voice vibrant with self-righteous restraint and concern. The difference between writing the words down on paper and hearing them sung was staggering. It seemed close to sacrilegious to hear that consecrated voice pouring forth the dread *n*-word: "Pull the triggers, niggers. We're with you all the way . . . Just across the Bay . . ."

But we had a much bigger problem; the main piece O'Donoghue had planned for the album, brilliant though it was, appeared to be unperformable. It was a parody of John Lennon called "Magical Misery Tour." Lennon was the ultimate sacred cow, a beast so holy he made Baez look like just another ordinary unconsecrated ruminant. This was for good reason. He had been the inspirer of the Beatles, the source of their wit and edge. But in the post-Beatles Yoko era, Lennon was a very different person. In 1971, deep into primal scream therapy, he had given a series of interviews to *Rolling Stone* in which he ranted on with primal "honesty" about himself, his genius, his childhood, his hatred for his co-musicians, his role in history, and much more. Nothing we could have written and put in Lennon's mouth was as outrageous as these self-revelations—not just in what he had to say about other people, but in its ominous lurch away from individuality and uniqueness and toward regimented self-obsession. Even accepting that that was his prerogative, it was a grandiose presumption on his part that the press was the proper place for so radical a therapy.

In short, he was asking for it. True to form, O'Donoghue rose to the occasion. He simply excerpted the juicier parts of the "interviews" and arranged them into rough four-line verses. There were no rhymes, no meter to speak of, and since O'Donoghue was no composer, no music. The total effect was devastating, but how to do the piece and who would do it were major problems. The original concept was simply to shout the verses out, primal-scream style, but that was too blunt, given that they were Lennon's own words; and besides there would be no parody involved, no recognizability. After all, no one had ever heard Lennon scream. Beyond that, his voice was extraordinarily distinctive—perhaps the best-known male voice in rock. But we had to do Lennon because we cared about him.

I think I felt more deeply about this than O'Donoghue, although it was his concept. His attitude was clinical; the piece was there, but if it could not be done properly, it should not be done at all. Finally, I decided I should give a try myself. In the final days of recording I made a test of a few of the lines—Tischler flattened and thinned my voice electronically, and the voice sounded at least promising. But that wasn't enough; the words had to be set to music somehow, but even the resourceful Guest had been unable to find a style that fit. It couldn't be Beatles—for what was typically "Beatles"?—and the words themselves suggested no music, quite the opposite in fact.

Enter an old hand, Chris Cerf. Cerf, who had always been intrigued by the possibilities of taking the *Lampoon* into other media, was delighted with the

Radio Dinner project and had been visiting the studio occasionally when he got off from work at "Sesame Street." He asked if he could have a crack at setting the song to music and was instantly accepted. His solution was perfect —a simple, driving "Imagine"-style piano that allowed the words to be chanted or perhaps ranted over it. He edited O'Donoghue's verses somewhat so that they roughly fit the beat, and added odd little Beatle-ish tags at the end of each. It worked perfectly.

He taught me the song, and we worked out where the beats fell in the flood of words and added some lunatic little flourishes to the tags. But my voice sounded thin and unconvincing standing next to him at the piano, and I had deep misgivings that I could pull it off.

I have never been so nervous as the night we recorded this cut. It was, to put it mildly, a high-profile assault, and I'd never had the slightest talent for impersonation. While we always had the option not to release it if it didn't work, it was a very strange sensation to be assuming one of the most familiar voices of the generation, particularly expressing such extraordinary and atrocious sentiments. I had no idea why I was doing it, only that it was right and new—another of those leaps in the dark. It was frightening even just to attempt it. Lennon might have been sacred, but I was scared.

But when I got into the booth and put on the cans (Tischler was feeding me back my own flattened and filtered voice), and when Cerf went into his piano intro, something happened. Another voice, one I barely recognized, but which sounded a lot like Lennon, a voice I didn't know was inside me, began screaming out the words in a ferocious tumble of hate and disappointment. My hatred of his words, my disappointment at his hate—all of it magically, and miserably, in his voice. My Master's Voice. I was the horn and the dog. It was an uncanny experience, like being taken over—both exhilarating and disturbing. Nor did the voice falter—it ranted on inexorably, driven by Cerf's music through the muddle of fear and loathing to a cataclysmic breakdown, one final primal grunt, and then Melissa Manchester as Yoko, whispering softly, "The dream is over."

We delivered the album to RCA in late April. With the exception of my appalling Nixon piece, it was a good album: varied, funny, well-paced, outrageous. The Lennon, Dylan, and Baez parodies alone assured that. In fact, I was secretly sure that some record people might be so outraged they would pull advertising from the magazine. (I was quite wrong, of course, for nothing outrages a record person as long as the hole's in the middle.) More importantly, first time out we had done a Gross-quality job, producing a well-performed and well-produced album, an issue of the magazine in sound. The balance of it was smart and funny, if not as pace-setting and outrageous as the parodies.

Not to us at least. At RCA, the parodies didn't even count. After a silence of some ten days, they gave us their response. Unless we excised all material relating to Nixon, David Eisenhower, and Julie, they wouldn't release the album. We refused point-blank—the agreement had stated without equivocation that there would be no censorship. That made no difference to RCA, whose parent company had just signed $180 million* worth of defense contracts with the Nixon administration.

Nixon, on the upswing of his power and arrogance as the Democrats, prepared to snatch utter humiliation from the jaws of defeat, was not to be crossed in even the most trivial of ways. The enemies' list was already operating. RCA wanted my appalling Nixon piece off the album, or no dice. On creative grounds I might have been prepared to do this, but not to save some anonymous death's-head from embarrassment. O'Donoghue was equally adamant about his David and Julie stuff, and so RCA let us go without demanding a refund of the $25,000—a minute commission for them to pay, considering the size of the defense contracts.

Taylor now went into high gear to get the album released elsewhere. He came up with an old school friend, Bob Krassnow, a man at the other end of the record spectrum from the RCA people—a super-hipster from Los Angeles who ran a small label distributed by Epic called Blue Thumb. Krassnow heard a couple of cuts and jumped in with both feet. He paid us another $25,000 in advances and set the release date for the early summer. Among other things, this meant that leaving RCA netted the company almost $40,000 as soon as Krassnow signed the check, for we had managed to spend only about $11,000 on the album. This was peanuts, but Simmons was suitably impressed at the way the cash flowed in the record biz.

Once the album had been delivered, I lost interest in it. The experience had been amusing (watching O'Donoghue relate to electronics was a treat in itself), and the exhilaration of the Lennon cut had been a revelation after years of fooling around in the claustrophobic, panicky world of television comedy. But the magazine was where I wanted to be, back in the brilliant monster that slid off into the streets of Manhattan every evening and groped its witty way back to life every noon. The album was an experience, but the magazine was a life.

New faces had appeared since we had been gone—notable among them was a zealously satirical young man called P. J. O'Rourke. O'Rourke came from the underground—sort of—a short-lived alternate newspaper called the *New York Ace,* which was attempting to upstage the *East Village Other* with two-color printing and *Lampoon*-derived cockiness. He was charming and enthusiastic in a coltish kind of way and came with the blessing of Trow, which was a heavy credential. There was something bothersome about him, though, something not quite right which put you on your guard. As managing editor I was vaguely charged with developing new talent, so O'Rourke and I hung out somewhat. Although like others I found his energy and enthusiasm captivating, I had a real sense that he was a new element. He had a way of repeating back to you your own voice, not chameleonlike as Gross did, but by mimicking your humor, parodying your parody. He was the first person who

---

* Simmons's recollection of the figure.

spoke "Lampoonese," who talked of *Lampoon* pieces as if he had carefully studied the language. He spoke it with all the ebullience of incomprehension, like a German student bellowing French at some old toper in a corner bistro. Someone—I think it was Kelly—put it another way. O'Rourke was a narc, a very good narc who hit all the right notes, but whose police-issue shoes showed beneath his bell-bottoms. This man would one day be editor of the magazine, and the only one in its history who gave himself the title editor-in-chief.

For the moment, though, such additions were just part of the daily life of the magazine. Its vitality and notoriety made it a spot that attracted all kinds of characters. A radical feminist—Shulamith Firestone—stormed into the offices one day, demanding to debate the editors on their fascistic chauvinism. Terry Southern—a minor god as far as O'Donoghue and I were concerned—appeared one day, looking frightful, and offered vague reportorial services if a mere $100 was forthcoming on a regular basis, the first payment to be made on the spot.

Perhaps the most dramatic incident occurred one sunny morning in the late spring as I was tooling around with the possibilities of my latest issue, August 1972, which was to be called "The Miracle of Democracy." O'Donoghue swung through the door and tossed a brown paper parcel from several feet away onto my desk. It was heavy and landed with a crash. "This is addressed to me," he said, "but I think it's for all of us."

I tore open the parcel to reveal nine or ten sticks of very old dynamite. O'Donoghue was fascinated, but I was not. A little experience in rural America had taught me that old dynamite is usually crystalline and liable to explode at the slightest whim. It was a miracle—of democracy perhaps—that it hadn't blown us all up when he threw it on my desk.

But O'Donoghue was intrigued by it. He picked it up and turned it over. Someone had sent him some dynamite. Not the word, not a picture. The real stuff. *His* dynamite. Great. I told him to put it very carefully back on the desk and get out of the office, just as I was about to do.

And out of the building. I didn't know what that much dynamite could do to a block of Madison Avenue, but I was taking no chances. I left the building and went around the corner for a nooner whisky and to wait for the bang. Sirens began to wail. After a decent interval I peered around the corner of 59th and Madison. The bomb squad had arrived with their great black machine (for putting bombs in), and there were cops everywhere. Two doughty Finest in heavy bomb-proof flak vests were approaching the black beast. I finagled my way through the crowd, figuring that the danger was past and went back upstairs to the *Lampoon*. There were cops and newsmen all over the place. And in the middle of the furor, crouched in his attack mode, glasses held away from his face, being restrained by everyone, was my pal O'D.: "It's my dynamite, you pigs!" he was yelling. "I want it. Give it back! It's mine!"

These were the best days of my life.

Sex Isn't Funny

And then O'Donoghue and I had a slight disagreement. Not unlike the Kenney affair, it initially involved a woman.

She and O'Donoghue had had a mad spring fling, but passion, according to him, had subsequently cooled it. They still saw one another, but (. . .) "I'm bored now."

On the night in question, several of us had dinner, including O'Donoghue and the young woman, who hung out occasionally with the movable version of the magazine and was not unadept at its games. Her code name can be "Whitefish." O'Donoghue had gone home, presumably to sleep alone. I said I might be at Spring Street later and had gone on drinking. Things narrowed down to me and Whitefish, who announced her intention of going to her apartment to smoke a joint. I could come if I liked. The night was, if not young, still under thirty, so I said okay. One thing led to another—and so to sleep. Morning. Honey in the tea. Organic muffin. Late-for-work. Push-key-under-door-when-leave.

Now in the hip happening, Going Too Far, nothing-is-sacred, dish-it-out world of the 1972 *Lampoon,* this sort of thing had happened once or twice before. Sexual traffic was increasing, as might be expected in a young, expanding, and successful group. Among other incidents was the case of another woman, who lived in Soho and whose code name shall be "Wheatjean." Wheatjean knew both Trow and O'Donoghue and still saw O'Donoghue occasionally. My marriage was not in good shape at the time, and Wheatjean and I had had a brief, happy, and not very serious affair a few months before at much the same time that O'Donoghue was spring-flinging with Whitefish. In fact, O'Donoghue had taken a more than healthy interest in this affair, in the merciless *Lampoon* manner, not the least because it was the first of my eight-year marriage. Furthermore, if Wheatjean was to be believed, it had not precluded her from seeing the sun come up with O'Donoghue once or twice. And so on. It was like that. (There was even a third woman [code-named "Rawhide"] who was known to everyone, O'Donoghue especially, and who later had a protracted relationship with, of all people, Beard.) Everybody's business and nobody's business, the line between loyalties and love were very indistinct, and claims on people made no sense.

Still, I felt stupid. Whitefish and I didn't know one another that well—we fenced more than talked, which was amusing but we had never even reached the line between loyalty and love. The whole thing had been silly and mechanical. It annoyed me that I couldn't remember how something that couldn't have been farther from my mind at midnight, had come to pass a few hours later. Smart Going-Too-Far/Nothing-Is-Sacred/Dish-It-Out-ers didn't let things happen that way. On the other hand it was not that consequential. We were supposedly "liberated"; while I wished she hadn't, and I wished I hadn't, the lady sleeps where she likes—Whitefish, Wheatjean, or Rawhide.

No, she doesn't. I had Gone Too Far. When I got to my office, there was a message for me that O'Donoghue didn't want to see me at Spring Street tonight or any other night. I called Whitefish. She claimed O'Donoghue had "forced" a confession out of her. He had lain upon his bed of pain all night, tossing and turning as the love of his life made the double-backed beast with another man. He was distraught with rage, grief, lost love, every emotion Verdi ever thought of.

He came in late in the afternoon, lips the width of piano wire, talking in some odd Englishese: "You owe me an explanation, I feel . . ." "What was the purpose of this, might I ask . . . ?" It was ridiculous. I felt like I was on the set of *Savages*. But he was obviously in the eye of some powerful emotional storm, and though it didn't look quite like hurt, I didn't want him to stay that way. If there was any wrong here, I was in it. I told him what had happened and how I thought it had happened, and said that I didn't know why it had happened, but that to whatever degree he was hurt, I was sorry and regretted it.

Nothing. My friend was looking at me as if he'd never seen me before. He was capable of staggering anger, which I had expected to have to survive, but while there was plenty of anger here, it was not the dominant emotion. Nor was rebuke. But it was intense and absolute. He sat there glaring through me, lips tight, breathing slightly too quickly through his nose. He seemed to be trying to will me to admit a wrong, a terrible wrong, an immeasurably terrible wrong, and then die.

All fault aside, as this continued it began to be a trifle absurd. Half our time was spent exploring situations this dangerous and laughing at them. And the associations of watching his face break innumerable times into a smile, or his mouth begin to curl as the right words began to form, were hard to resist. I tried to gentle him up a little. Hadn't we been talking about this just twenty-four hours before? Wasn't this part of the game? What about the ins and outs of the Wheatjean affair? What about his fancying my wife? If John Updike did it, why shouldn't we? Was this the writer of *Savages?* The rights and wrongs here were harder to find than guests for David Susskind.

Nothing. Admit it and die. All I could say was to ask that at least we talk about it again, when things had cooled some. He nodded curtly and left.

But we didn't and they didn't. I began to feel the way Kenney must have. The atmosphere in the office was as though the air had been sprayed with cyanide. The force of O'Donoghue's emotion rolled down the hallways, into other offices, other departments. People spoke in hushed tones. The copy was brought into my office as if it was a very important specimen of cancerous tissue. It felt as though someone had been assassinated. I decided to come clean with Beard. He was terrific. He didn't even appear to think I was as much in the wrong as I thought I was. He said it was not something he would have chosen to do, but . . . If he didn't use the word "injudicious," it was something to that effect and with at least as many syllables.

His main concern was with the magazine. He didn't want it torn apart.

Having been through something like this once before, he wasn't going to let it happen again. He suspected the whole thing might blow over if I kept a lowish profile. I was leaving for a short vacation in a few days, and that would help. My services on the current issue ("Boredom"—with Trow as guest editor) weren't vital, and the big piece I had planned could be finished when I returned.

My wife was very understanding; perhaps she'd expected that the heated little group was going to produce something like this, and she knew how much O'Donoghue and the magazine meant to me better than anyone.

But the days after this were awful. I was utterly miserable. O'Donoghue had one privilege to bestow on people and that was his company, and to an addict like myself withdrawal was unbearable. Things didn't cool off. O'Donoghue demanded to have his office moved away from mine (actually mine was moved away from his—one office farther away, a matter of eight feet), and walking around the *Lampoon* seemed to be a question of picking routes, checking who was in which office, timing departures so that you wouldn't give the impression of being on one "side" or the other. People scuttled out of my office lest they be seen by O'Donoghue, and be assumed to be conspiring with me. O'Donoghue would turn on his heel if he saw me in the distance.

This was now getting silly. I grabbed O'Donoghue one day and pulled him into my office. I think he thought I was going to beat him up. He had a way of taking off his glasses when attacking or being attacked—perhaps from bitter experience in the schoolyard. He took them off now and stood there looking defiant, daring me to deck him. Nothing could have been further from my mind. I begged him to cut the bullshit, and at least see if we couldn't salvage something from almost a year of friendship. And I repeated that if anyone was wrong I was, and that was our business. But now it was becoming everyone's business, and we should spare them that. As soon as I stopped standing between him and the door, he left. I never really spoke to him again.

I drank my way through the Loire Valley and a succession of M. Michelin's favorite restaurants, in an insomniac fever of worry, strategy planning, imagined dialogues, and self-recrimination. It must have been fun for my wife. I dimly hoped that when I got back, O'Donoghue would magically have calmed down, and we could grope our way back to some lesser *modus vivendi*, as he and Kenney had done.

No such luck. My office had been duly moved, people still consulted their schedules before braving the corridors, and O'Donoghue was still chain-smoking Silva Thins in his tent.

Either Simmons or Beard told me that O'Donoghue had demanded that I be fired, or he would quit. He'd been told not to be an idiot (and hadn't quit). I appreciated being told, but this remoralized me; I decided to get on with the job and stop trying to heal the wound. I completed two long pieces for Trow's issue† and stuck close to Kelly, who was doing the next issue, a sardonic "rebuttal" to fifties nostalgia called "Remember Those Fabulous Sixties."

I was damned if I was going to leave—or bust my bladder because O'Donoghue was in the men's room. As Gross had said in very different circumstances, "This was my magazine too." I would stick it out, refuse to compete or retaliate. The dinners would go on; the group would continue, the ideas begin to flow again. Anyone was welcome in my office, and if O'Donoghue wanted to bust his bladder, that was his affair. But I knew it would never be the same again.

He did speak to me once more. "Remember Those Fabulous Sixties" was a "back-to-school" issue for October. The previous year sales had been enhanced by running radio commercials for the "Back-to-School" issue, and so Kelly and I went into the studio to record one for the Sixties, a wonderful daft folksong, written by Kelly, which Guest performed in a "Sing Out"/Pete Seeger tenor. The night we were doing it, O'Donoghue was for some reason in the adjoining studio. Nobody paid much attention to this, for the tension of the situation was something everyone was becoming accustomed to, a standoff which was by now part of the *Lampoon* furniture. We took a break and came across O'Donoghue in the coffee room. In front of Kelly, Guest, Tischler, and several others, O'Donoghue snapped. He took off his glasses and went into his combative crouch. His face was distorted with indescribable rage; saliva was on his teeth even before he started in; he had no sense of his surroundings or of danger or proportion. My former friend said, "You're slime, Hendra. I hate you! You're scum, you hear? Nothing but scum, slime, ngaahh!"

That was it for Meatball.

---

† One of these was the best I was ever involved in. It was really much less mine than the artist Ron Barrett's. He had come to the magazine a few months before with some amazing photo collages of meat in various landscapes—a butterball as a mountain, meatballs as rocks, steaks as cliffs. The verisimilitude was uncanny—it really did look as though the happy tourists were Nikoning Yellowstone. We expanded the visual premise to include all kinds of other situations. The result was a stunning eight-page color piece called the "Wide World of Meat," ranging from a mouth-watering map of the Americas to a gigantified chicken leg being readied for a space shot (Pollo 1). I became quite notorious for this piece, but it was really Barrett's.

17

The Life Cycle of *Lemmings*

All summer and into the fall O'Donoghue kept it up. People were expected to choose up sides and stick to them. Some people fell for this; others had no choice. Beatts had already aligned herself with O'Donoghue, and not long afterward they began living together. Kelly, with whom I was developing a close friendship, found that the price he had to pay was arbitrary exclusion from the Presence. I learned that O'Donoghue had cut in two all the publicity photos of us from *Radio Dinner;* that he had threatened to cut down all the trees on my property. (I was an eco-nut, so this was supposed to hit me where it hurt, but it was hilarious to think of O'Donoghue—who had the muscle-tone of the average oyster—wielding a twenty-four-inch Stihl.)

What was intensely depressing was the hostility. It seemed to me that O'Donoghue and those he cowed into supporting him, had learned nothing from what he did for a living. His loathing for hatred had vanished; the mirror we held up to the hateful had shattered. Now it was just hatred, as unfunny, stupid, boring, obsessive, fearful, lazy-minded, and childish as it always is.

If we couldn't learn from our own work, what possible chance was there that our readers could? What was the point of satirizing your enemies if you behaved the same way yourself? If you possessed that knowledge but didn't act on it, felt that it and your private life were two different things? Wasn't that a form of hypocrisy as ludicrous and satirizable as our targets? If that was the case, why were we bothering? We might just as well sell out or go live in New Zealand.

For all that, what couldn't be allowed to happen was that the magazine faltered. There were dark hints from O'Donoghue's lair that he would not appear in any issues that I (or my flunkies) had any hand in, nor would I (or my flunkies) be allowed in any he edited. Beard cut this crap without ceremony. O'Donoghue appeared extensively in Kelly's "Sixties" issue* and I appeared in O'Donoghue's next one, which he chose in the best sardonic *Lampoon* tradition to call "Decadence."

Beard was undergoing a fascinating sea change at the time, which we found tempting to call the Greening of Beard. Unlike other Greenings, this hadn't meant any loss of mental acuity, but he was filling out as a person, experimenting with normality. His hair, once painfully short, now touched his shoulders; he used the occasional profanity; sex appeared to interest him, and not just as a metaphor for Republican political tactics. He was still untouchable and untouched by drugs, but he seemed to like himself better, which made you like him even more.

Delightful though this was to behold, there was one occasion on which Beard's Greening startled even me. He had developed the habit of visiting my country house fairly regularly, especially during the summer, for he seemed to have little taste for the Hamptons and other points east. My property is bounded by a large stream, which remains extremely cool all year and has many rocky pools just big enough for cooling off in the heat. A country road, infrequently used except by local traffic, runs between the stream and the house.

The *Lampoon*'s recent turmoil had not prepared me for what I saw one sweltering Saturday afternoon in the summer of 1972, as I came around the barn. Strolling down the road, hair still wet from his dip, looking cool, tan, and refreshed was our illustrious Tory leader wearing absolutely nothing but his pipe.

Beard was growing in confidence. The magazine was firmly in his hands, and nothing was going to yank it off course. He seemed to feel not just confidence in himself, but also in the extended family of the *Lampoon*, now so considerable that it could survive just about any upheaval, even an extended tantrum on the part of its star writer. Just as the magazine had survived Kenney's departure, so it would survive O'Donoghue's fury.

Kenney, as a matter of fact, had disappeared again in June, once again to go to Martha's Vineyard, and this time on a slightly more official mission—a novel he wanted to complete called "Teenage Commies from Outer Space." It was a measure of how far Beard and the magazine had come in exactly one year that his departure was scarcely noticed.

Beard held the magazine to its standards through the O'Donoghue crisis, and except for the December issue—December issues had in any case become "hodge-podge" issues, garbage pails for unused pieces and with no real theme

---

* He was even forced to *appear* with me in one piece—an album cover parody of a "long-suppressed" Stones album, *Rim Shot*. Five of us posed as the Stones in the men's room of the Plaza in full drag, O'Donoghue and I side by side, me as a French maid and he as a New York Doll in fright wig, gold lamé pasties and feather boa. Trow, who had his own theories about the bust-up, found this hysterically funny (see insert).

—maintained its continuity beyond. And if the Blob slid into the office at noon these days in two halves and stayed that way till evening, Beard was still always at the Coral Cafe, the Issue Dinners, and the ad hoc editorial meetings. Wherever he was, the magazine was, and his judiciousness carried the day. This was reassuring, for if the scintillating camaraderie of the previous twelve months was gone for good, the magazine was still intact, and that was ultimately more important than anything. Indeed, Beard's Greening might have had a benign influence in this respect. He understood my dumb behavior and O'Donoghue's dumb response better than he had the Kenney affair and was far more able to sail serenely through the squall.

Not so with Simmons, alas. The crisis down the hall seemed to bother him far more than it did Beard. He seemed to think it might be good if I took a short break from the day-to-day functioning of the magazine. This was the last thing I wanted, but there was unfortunately a fairly compelling reason for the decision. Blue Thumb—and Taylor—wanted another album, and they wanted it by the following spring. I was to put this project together. What O'Donoghue thought about this, I never found out, though I'm sure it must have galled him immensely; for my part, I didn't look forward to doing an album without him. But I'd had a lot more to do than he with the practical aspects of production on *Radio Dinner*—casting, mixing, editing, and so on—and Taylor knew this, so there wasn't much opportunity to beg off. The boss wanted an album, and the boss wrote the checks. (Minute, of course, but still checks.)

Radio Dinner had not done spectacularly well on the charts according to Simmons, though it eventually sold several hundred thousand copies and became the biggest of the *Lampoon* albums. What it had done, though, was to create quite a stir.†

More concretely, the album had worked for Taylor. What he had hoped for —solid record advertising to lead to bigger-ticket (and more conservative) advertisers—had happened. The magazine was packed with hi-fi and cigarette advertising; not only would this mean reassurance for still more conservative companies like the liquor people, it also had the effect of boosting ad revenue. From the minuscule take of 1971 ($314,000), 1972's had more than doubled (to $682,000). This was still tiny, but for a magazine as audacious as the *Lampoon,* it showed that Taylor had been succeeding when it came to reassuring advertisers. (The magazine had done nothing to accommodate them; if anything, it was becoming more audacious all the time.) Taylor said the album had been part of this process, and that another would be as effective if not more so. And so *Lemmings* was born.

Lemmings was originally conceived as a live, largely musical album. The

---

† Someone at KRLA had apparently played the Lennon cut to John and Yoko while they were promoting their latest album, and Lennon had left when it was done, without a word, several shades whiter than pale. Krassnow was the kind of person to whom this was 100 percent pure uncut joy. By late 1972 *Lampoon* was absolutely *la crème de la crème* when it came to hip, and this made Blue Thumb look terrific in just the way it wanted to be.

rock cuts on *Radio Dinner* were clearly its cutting edge—the time seemed ripe for us to take this principle further and do a whole album bringing rock down a peg or two. Beyond that, live albums were all the rage at the time, and they certainly had an excitement to them that in-studio stuff could not match. What we were doing instinctively was covering the traditional Boomer humor field. We'd conquered print, we'd done a successful comedy album; now we would tackle live performance. We would use not just one but all three of the traditional loci—and still what we did would be utterly unavailable anywhere else, especially not on television. Kelly was a natural person to work with. Not only were we becoming close personally (our common ex-Catholicism being a powerful factor), but his facility in lyric writing was staggering, and his knowledge of, and sensitivity to, rock was light-years ahead of mine. I knew what I liked and had a fairly conventional idea of what Boomers thought sacred, but Kelly's knowledge was encyclopedic from Elvis to Alice Cooper. He listened to lyrics, felt them, got their resonances. Like O'Donoghue, his first instinct was poetic, but his ear was far more complex, his word play Byzantine.

The most obvious sacred cow for us to go after was Woodstock. The rock concert was the live form of the generation, and the best means for us to throw many different performers together. Simply to parody Woodstock, though, did not seem either quite enough or very easy. There hadn't been anything very despicable about Woodstock, except perhaps the self-importance of its performers. But these performers, the words of the announcers, and all the other ancillary events had been burned into the brains of millions by a phenomenally successful album and an even more successful movie. It had taken place three long years before, and the hopes it had embodied were crumbling daily as the criminal in the White House headed toward another four years of sleaze. Why was that the case? What was going wrong? What were we doing—or not doing—that made us ultimately ineffective? What was our ge-ge-ge-generation's character flaw?

Our answer was self-destruction, Woodstock as a celebration of mass suicide. A generation hurling itself off the cliff, by every available means. The concert would be called Woodshuck—a Festival of Peace, Love, and Death. A million strong, the audience would have come for this purpose, and every performer would celebrate and encourage it. The songs would reflect the myriad ways our generation had chosen to opt out of life—to become politically ineffective, culturally impotent, personally self-obsessed, or just plain dead.

In a word: lemmings.‡

Unconsciously, though, there was a deeper warning contained in the con-

‡ In its editorial a day or so after Woodstock began, the New York *Times* referred to the audience as "lemmings marching to the sea." Just why they were lemmings was never explained; the *Times* was not talking about drugs or political responsibility. Perhaps they felt the half million young citizens could have been doing something more constructive with their time—like cleaning up the dean's office.

cept of *Lemmings,* one neither of us was aware of at the time but which is now much clearer. It was directly descended from Lenny Bruce's ferocious assault on late fifties show biz with its political orthodoxy masquerading as entertainment, its carefully packaged emotions maintained by Hollywood quality control, passing from movie to movie and mind to mind; that gradually forming crust of alternate and preferable reality—show biz reality—where everything was clearer, neater, and more familiar. For rock *was* our show biz. More even than Bruce's generation, we had put our faith in it, confused it with reality, had taken as gospel its simplistic messages of endless sex, drug utopia, and romantic revolution in which there would be no hurt or bullets, just hearts bursting with freedom and justice. In the process we had added our own vast tracts to the crust, shutting out still more light, safe in a world of electronic sound and disembodied, reassuring voices.

Such escapism was thoroughly inexcusable—knowing what we knew about how our system had been raped and twisted, and who was doing it, recognizing the corrupters for what they were, with the power and means to combat them at our fingertips, and—not the least—as privileged beneficiaries of the courageous men and women who'd taught us all this, who'd resisted the corruption from the day we were born.

The people who ran this show, although they were as deluded as we were about what they were doing, deserved no quarter—especially if our generation was going to sit glaze-eyed and slack-jawed while opportunity passed and the same bandits who'd always run the territory simply tiptoed quietly around our camp and went on their murderous way. We were not out to destroy our "leaders" in *Lemmings,* just as we'd not been out to destroy Lennon before, but to administer a large bucket of cold water where it belonged: to point out that these were entertainers, not saviors, that they wrote songs for money, that they were ordinary warty crabby men and women, that the emotions you feel during a three-minute song are not the emotions with which you confront the world, that rock reality is not reality. It was time to bring everyone, fans and idols, back down to earth.

Tall order. To accomplish it effectively we would have to assemble five or six performers into a rock group capable of playing adequately in many different styles, possessed of that extremely rare talent, impersonation—musical impersonation, at that—and just to make things a little more interesting, capable of inducing laughter.

All this had to be done in three months. What's more, since Kelly was still based in Toronto, where he was in the middle of a marital mess involving several children, I would have to do most of this alone.

Chris Guest deserves a lot of the credit for getting *Lemmings* rolling. After *Radio Dinner* he'd become one of the family and was obviously a charter member of the new cast—in fact *the* charter member. All we had to do was find five others who were as musically adept and as good at impersonation, and the Woodstock myth would be reeling.

Guest also wanted to be the musical director, as he had been on *Radio*

Dinner. This I was less sure about. To have one member of a small cast, put in charge of them was a guarantee of star wars. This touched on something else I decided on from the beginning—that whoever ended up in the cast, there would be no stars, and everyone would hit the stage equal. If the purpose of the show was to puncture celebrity, we were certainly not going to start off with celebrities.

For the time being, however, Chris was the musical director, and he set to work with Kelly working out the first songs, on the weekends when the lyric master descended from Toronto.

Among others Guest brought was Paul Jacobs. Jacobs was of a type increasingly common around New York and Boston: a precocious classical musician, whom dope, tofu, or sheer impatience had propelled into rock experimentation. He was barely out of his teens, could play a wide variety of instruments, and had an amazing facility for nonchalant and uncanny reproductions of almost anyone's style, sound, or arrangements. Chris hired his own replacement with Jacobs. Paul was faster and surer when it came to writing musical parody, and while Chris wrote some of the best songs and certainly turned in some of the best performances of the final show, the diversity of sound and the changing rhythms of its parody were mostly Jacobs's.

Another Guest contact was one of those murky people working murky comedy below 14th Street. Chris thought he'd be too broad for my sensitive tastes and too physical for the intellectual stuff of the *Lampoon.* In a small theater in the East Seventies, I watched a tall, country-club handsome young man fall all over the set of the play that was running there, belch, ogle the wings, mug, giggle at his own material, deliver a couple of excruciatingly bad news items, and then stand there looking arrogant and apologetic at the same time. I couldn't believe his name. I thought it was an attempt to be satirichip, but he insisted it was the name he'd been baptized with. He was a passable drummer and had a pleasant baritone voice, which somehow was also arrogant and apologetic. It was one of the worst comedic auditions I'd ever seen—and quite irresistible. I hired him on the spot. So now we had Chevy Chase.

Simmons pitched in with another suggestion, very good as it turned out. There was an Alka-Seltzer commercial running at the time featuring a young, very New York newlywed who'd just prepared her husband some chocolate meatballs. She was extremely funny and extremely tiny, but was possessed of a prodigious rock voice and a sizable amount of Broadway experience. She couldn't play anything, but that voice alone was a great asset; Kelly and I had an idea for a fifties death song called "Pizza Man" for which she would be perfect. In came Alice Playten.

Things were coming together. It concerned me that we were getting a strictly New York cast and satirically a rather green one. This was a very knowing group, so far, people who operated at a highly sophisticated remove from reality. Alice was Broadway, Guest had his own oddly clinical, technically irreproachable parody; even Chase's nihilistic version of the leading man—his "ingenue on acid"—was superhip, take-it-or-leave-it New York stuff. All this was fine, but we needed what Gross and Kenney brought to the magazine. Skill, experience, and something else—soul, midwestern, out of town—I wasn't sure what.

I knew that of the original Committee, Goodrow was an accomplished musician (he played saxophone) and that he was the smartest and hardest of its political satirists. He happened to be in the East and was delighted to accept. Four down.

Next I tried Ebling, Choquette's ex-My Partner, an excellent guitarist and comedian, with plenty of stage experience and an inimitable voice. He was unavailable, but he suggested that I take a look at Second City, where he'd just been taking a refresher course. There was a young kid there called Belushi, who did some musical stuff.

I didn't need to call. In my office the next day appeared a tape, mailed from Chicago, with a fulsome note from Belushi, explaining that he wanted to be considered for the *National Lampoon* revue. The tape contained a series of impressions, mostly of Brando in various roles and Truman Capote, all very tedious—and an absolutely brilliant takeoff of Joe Cocker. It was mad, out of control, impassioned, though it was recorded only with a guitar; it sounded like nothing else on the tape, and I had the distinct feeling that this voice— obviously the voice of someone who loved Joe Cocker—came from the same place my Lennon one had.

Belushi wanted this job—he called the next day. I told him I loved the Cocker and didn't like anything else. He urged me to come out to Chicago and check him out. I was reluctant to do this—for silly reasons, really. I had wanted to cast the show without returning to the motherlode of Second City. This was mainly *Lampoon* arrogance, but it came partly from a sense that Second City's comfortably established comedy would not provide the edge we needed. Time was getting short, however, and there were other people I was interested in—particularly a woman called Eugenie Ross-Leming, about whom I'd heard terrific things. And we needed another woman badly.

So I went. What I saw was outrageous. Not in any satirical sense but because Belushi inserted himself into practically every sketch in a two-hour show. Gone were any of the classic Sills precepts of improvisation. If Belushi felt like entering a scene, he did it without rhyme or reason, with irrelevant characters (on several occasions his wretched Brando), listening to no one, taking the action wherever it would leave him front and center. He fought savagely with people in scenes where there was no reason to. He broke into bravura street characters whether there was any justification or not. I pitied his fellow actors as this rolling, bearded landmine crashed through their set, threatening to destroy them if his purpose was thwarted, blow their heads off if they got in his way. Poor Eugenie was nowhere to be seen.

After a while I stopped trying to gauge his talent, which was clearly enormous, and just sat back to enjoy the audacity of what he was doing. Naked ambition, yes—but nevertheless delightful. A generation of hallowed, culturally accredited satiric theater was hanging over his head, but he didn't give a damn.

In some ways he was like Chevy, whose sheer self-confidence overrode the most minimal requirements such as excellence of material or the creation of illusion. In another he was like Kenney, simultaneously charming and infuriating. But Kenney's intention had to be filtered through the intricate grid of his education, social ambition, and self-doubt. Belushi was pure street gut. Here was the generation: raw energy and instinctive skepticism, naïve and knowing, an animal well aware that there were rules but yet to be convinced that they made any sense.

I hadn't much stomach for cramming our magazine into a theater, for parading its finely balanced multilevel savagery across the stage, but if there was any way to do it, this guy was it—the unreflecting force, the instant sense of the absurd, the intense presence and intense nihilism that reached across the footlights with those fanatic eyebrows and grabbed you by the eardrums. Belushi was the medium and message rolled into one ferocious package, rock humor, incarnate.

So in he came.

Things didn't work out with Eugenie. The cast was completed by Mary Mitchell, a distant relative in the extended *Lampoon* family who had starred in Tom Eyen's *The Dirtiest Show in Town*.

Simmons and I found a venue for this extravaganza: the Village Gate, a cavernous beat-era basement on Bleecker Street, where I had worked as comedian many times, and whose owner, the indestructible Art d'Lugoff (one of New York's True Finest), was ready with a characteristically rapacious deal (which, characteristically, he never enforced). Now all we needed was a show.

One of the consequences of deciding to put on a live show for this live record was that on top of everything else we had to mount a full-blown off-Broadway revue. People would actually pay money for tickets. We would have to assemble far more material than would normally be needed for a comedy album (usually about forty-five minutes). There would have to be a complete revue program, with a first and second act: twice as much.

One of these acts could be the Woodshuck Festival of Peace, Love, and Death. The other would have to be, so to speak, off the record. Kelly and I toyed with the idea of making the Woodstock parody the whole show, but we didn't really think the idea would sustain for ninety minutes, especially through an intermission. There was a cumulative effect to the notion of mass suicide that Coke and popcorn would somehow destroy.

Writing enough *Lampoon*-worthy material, for the first act was always the problem area of *Lemmings*—until Richard Nixon and Watergate gave us more grist than we could grind. I had had some experience of trying to adapt the magazine to performance in *Radio Dinner*. It simply didn't work, even if you went all the way back to the original comic premise. Actors just don't talk like magazines, and the stage is no place for print.

But it had to be done.

"The Ezra Taft Benson High School Yearbook" seemed like a good bet. I flew up to the Vineyard to talk to Kenney, arriving on a cold November night to find him distracted and bemused by the self-appointed task of writing the novel of his generation (*Teenage Commies from Outer Space*). It wasn't going well, he said, and he wasn't interested in the magazine, or the show. The "High School Yearbook" was just a piece he'd done long ago, and was no longer interested in; in any case it could never be converted to any other medium.

We were in rehearsal by now and it seemed logical to me, given the experience of the Committee and Second City, that the cast might generate their own material. All these people were aware of *Lampoon,* wanted to be part of it, and appeared to understand its spirit. Given their collective talent as performers, what should emerge from their "writing" together should be the stage equivalent of the magazine.

It worked but not as I'd expected. We spent a couple of weeks running improvs, hoping that the sessions would throw off some usable premises. With the exception of Goodrow, the cast were incredibly impatient with these exercises. Belushi, who'd been doing them on a regular basis only weeks before, was the most resistant to the discipline, and Chase took a devilish delight in sabotaging any illusion created in the grim rehearsal halls we worked in.

But the improv sessions paid off. Just as Compass had found that the intersection of improv and fifties dissent had generated instant comedy, just as the Committee had found that the war created satire as soon as its actors began ad-libbing, so the *Lemmings* cast discovered new territory the minute they began letting themselves go on rock. I had been wrong to expect that they would generate *Lampoon* material through improvisation for that odd combination of hypereducation and skepticism was a commodity exclusive to the magazine's editors. But rock and roll was a common language.

Playten created the ultimate megagroupie delighted that putting your ear next to a Marshall Amp could actually kill you; Chase created an Altamont Angel crazed that some fucking punk had touched his bike, leaving tell-tale fingerprints all over it. Goodrow created Max Yassir—the misanthrope farmer who's rented his land to the Lemmings. Above all, Belushi created the character of the Woodshuck emcee, a wonderfully persuasive hippie Satan, ringing every change on the announcements of Woodstock, urging the masses to self-immolate by any conceivable means, from electrocution to cannibalism.

All this flowed from them without check. There wasn't enough time or space for all the ideas and characters the cast came up with for the Woodstock parody.

Midwifed by Kelly, who had finally fled the Retarded Giant to work in New York full-time, the second act came together like a dream. The songs, almost all of them written or cowritten by him, were the most important elements. Crosby, Stills, and Nash, Dylan, John Denver, James Taylor, and Joe Cocker got theirs mercilessly, but somehow dozens of others crept in too, not in the shape of full-tilt parodies but by allusion and inclusion. One of Belushi's most inspired rants, for example, was the All-Star Dead Band. He introduced them in pitch darkness:

Lead vocals: Janis Joplin and Jim Morrison!
Rhythm guitar: Brian Jones!
Slide guitar: Duane Allman!
Lead guitar: Jimi Hendrix!!

"Okay," yelled Belushi in the black, "A one, a two, a one-two-three-four . . ."
And then the silence of the grave.
The cast of *Lemmings*—not any more than usual obsessed by music—zeroed in on rock as the metaphor and language of their comedy. It has been said that "Saturday Night Live" was as successful as it was because the generation it appealed to and who performed it were the children of television. This is the analysis of those who promote television as an alternative for reality. Left to themselves what the cast of *Lemmings*—two of whom would become by far the most significant personalities of "Saturday Night Live"—came up with was satire of their own generation that had absolutely nothing to do with television. Television was not mentioned once on the stage of this revue. And not by design, but by instinct. Television was irrelevant to our world view, a stupid drug not worthy of our consideration, neither entertainment nor culture nor information; it had nothing to do with us, was nowhere in our consciousness, not even occasionally bubbling to the surface of our collective mind. And for that reason as much as any, *Lemmings* was a hit. The poor old first act limped around, being vaguely Lampoonish, vaguely nasty, vaguely well-informed. But the minute Belushi hit the stage at the beginning of the second act, a generation began bleeding:
"All right, we all know why we came here—a million of us—we came here to off ourselves!"
The act would not stop. The self-knowledge, self-criticism, self-awareness of two decades of music flooded over the footlights. Belushi was superb. At the top of his lungs, this quintessential Boomer urged his fellows on to self-destruction, making thunder and lightning and then instructing them to climb the sound towers, directing them away from the acid and toward the belladonna, urging them to dine off one another, and above all pushing the music, those dread sounds of a generation painting itself in the corner of political and cultural impotence.

CROSBY, STILLS, AND NASH:
Between the politician's polarizing power trips,
We were just too pure and peaceful to decide.

So we got our heads together while the planet fell to bits,
Now the one side left to take is suicide.
(Chorus)
We are lemmings,
We are crazies,
We will feed our flower habit
Pushing daisies. . . .

DYLAN:
You say the world's in trouble,
You say you don't feel free,
You don't know where you're goin'—
Well, brother, don't ask me.
I don't give a darn
Out behind the barn.
(Chorus)
Oh, out behind the barn
I'm chewin' on a piece of hay,
I'm to my knees in cowshit,
I'm shovellin' my blues away. . . .

BACK TO THE LAND (John Denver):
We had time and space and freedom,
we had love and peace to spare
Though we ran out of things to smoke
and say and eat and wear.
And the morning of the avalanche,
The Yeti kidnapped Blanche
And took her to his cave up in the Rockies.
Oh, Colorado's calling me
From her glaciers and her canyons and her badlands and ravines,
And infectious hepatitis
Was all that came to stay
In January in the Colorado Rockies. . . .

TAYLOR:
Shootin' up the highway on the road map of my wrists,
Baby, I've just scratched you off my list.
I'll miss your tie-dyed bedsheets and your pretty spearmint mouth,
But my highway toes are thumbin' to the South.
(Chorus)
Farewell, New York City,
With your streets that flash like strobes,
Farewell to Carolina
Where I left my frontal lobes. . . .

COCKER:
Well, I'm standing here
Singin' my song
'Cause there's nothing to do
And all my friends are gone.
I had sunshine and a country home,
I been on the cover of *Rolling Stone.*
And it's lonely,
Oh, it's lonely.
Well, it's lonely at the bottom,
Lonely at the bottom of the barrel.
And I think of days
Of purple haze and freon
Smokin', jokin',
Doin' coke with Leon.

MEGADEATH:
Living is a bummer,
Dying is a high,
Nerves are getting number.
Die, baby, die.
Life's an antidotal gyp,
Freedom is a lie.
Dying is a total trip.
Die, baby, die.

And so on January 25, 1973, slightly shy of nine years after I'd watched Lenny Bruce be carted offstage one block away for being funny at Jackie Kennedy's expense, *Lemmings* opened. It was a hit. But in one sense it was a bomb. Everyone from the magazine—with the obvious exception—was present, and the verdict was not good. Trow tried to be nice, McConnachie was kindly but incredulous, Beard hated every second. It was depressing. I had accepted this exile and done my best to be faithful to the spirit of the magazine, knowing full well that in a funky off-Broadway theater the letter had to be different.

But they didn't get it. Or worse, didn't want to get it. However, the newspaper of record saw things differently. Said the New York *Times*: "There is a severe dichotomy in *National Lampoon*'s *Lemmings,* the musical revue that opened last night at the Village Gate. The first act, a headlong, supposedly comic assault on sex and politics, suffers from a serious case of the puerilities.

"But in the second act the show mercifully finds its wits for a wicked parody of the world of rock, spoofing the talented along with the pretenders, their absurdities, conceits and affectations."

The most immediate consequence of this was a flood of ticket sales, and a quick reappraisal by Simmons of our plans for a limited run. If it got this kind of reaction, why not run the show indefinitely? I was not happy about this. I'd hoped to get the recording done and get back to the magazine. Now it looked like my exile could become permanent. A week later the *New Yorker* review came out. It was far more explicit than the *Times*'s: "The entire second act of *Lemmings,* a new revue at the Village Gate, is devoted to something called the "Woodstunk Rock Festival (of Love, Peace, and Death)." It is, unlike the rotten first act, very, very good and very, very funny—parody so acute and audacious that it edges into satire, and so strong that one needn't know the actual rock star or group that is being mocked in order to enjoy it.

"All seven members of the company can act and sing and dance, and most of them can play musical instruments as well. The announcer for the festival, an invaluable performer named John Belushi, steps—or, rather, staggers—to a microphone with bits of information about the drugs available to the crowd: the lost insulin has been found, the strychnine hasn't been fully tested yet so can be recommended only in small quantities, and so on.

"A sodden Hell's Angel, chain in hand, reels to the mike threatening vengeance on the peace freak who touched his bike, and then bursts into tears. Funny little Alice Playten, her face a mask of feeblemindedness, comes out with her group to sing a "medley of her hits" for us, and later on does a wild impersonation of Mick Jagger.

"Christopher Guest is very funny as Bob Dylan, and funniest of all is Mr. Belushi as Joe Cocker, writhing and falling, and then back on his feet, all passion spent, in time for the closing chorus."

This review at least was a comforting endorsement. The *New Yorker* knew what the *Lampoon* was about, and that in turn meant they knew what we were up to at the Gate, profane and indecorous though we were. It was an enormous relief.

Which made me all the more furious when Walter Kerr, the *Vox Dei* of the New York *Times* theater section decided to take us to task a few days later: "One of the chief problems of the evening, for me in any case, is the company's apparent inability to distinguish parody from simple imitation. When Mary-Jenifer Mitchell, picking her way delicately through the tangle of microphone wires because she has a baby slung over her shoulder, speaks of her husband in prison as Joan Baez so often did, you do know the girl being kidded and you pick up the slant of the joke. The slant stays there, amusingly, through her chanted 'Pull the triggers, niggers, we're with you all the way' right down to her concluding lament that there are 'So many grievous wrongs/For me to right with tedious songs.' Okay parody. And good enough.

"But when the entire second half of the entertainment is given over to rock groups appearing at a Woodshock [sic] Festival, and when group after group tends to blur into the original sound with virtually no comment added or particular pretension pricked, one begins to wonder. Isn't the response coming up from the tables at the Village Gate basically nostalgic, aren't we getting simple 'recognition laughs' rather than the ribbing we've been promised? The tipoff, I'd say, comes with the absolute need to end a number of the presumed burlesques with fecal expletives, shouted over the music to get the lights down. Would we know the singers were being sassy if they didn't announce it in noisy aftermath?"

This patronizing meant that, just like the students at Columbia, we had dirty mouths and made a dreadful mess (in this case of the off-Broadway theater) and that this sort of thing just oughtn't to be allowed. That we were taking our own generation to task carried little weight with Kerr; he appeared to understand next to nothing of either the music or its targets or our methods. There was something so intransigently ignorant, and what's more, so intrinsically atheatrical, about this screed that it drove me nuts. I decided that the Cambridge Mafia would send Mr. Kerr a little something. I bought a very large bluefish, wrapped it carefully in a copy of Mr. Kerr's review, wrote "Swim with the fishes" across the review in Magic Marker and messengered it to his office.

Kerr was outraged—of course—but in that extraordinary way the *Times* has, like some great body politic that sooner or later balances everything out, a long article appeared three months later on the front page of the Sunday entertainment section entitled "Why Do Young People Love *Lemmings?*":

"National Lampoon's *Lemmings* is an enormously funny, savagely satirical revue that lays waste to, among other targets, the youth culture of the 1960s, the American Military, Bob Dylan, *Jesus Christ Superstar,* Gay Lib, Hell's Angels, a host of rock stars, and a generation of young people who adopted drugs as their salvation and headed, like lemmings, for the cliff of self-destruction.

"The second act of *Lemmings*—and the high point of the show—is the Woodshuck Festival of Love, Peace and Death, a mass suicide. It is theater turned into a rock concert (which completes the circle that began in the sixties when rock concerts became more and more theatrical).

"It takes a particular frame of reference to appreciate this sort of humor, and the people who mainly have it are between 15 and 30 years old. Of the 300 or so people who pack the Village Gate nightly to see a performance of *Lemmings,* perhaps a dozen are over 30. The other 288 are as young as 10 and seldom older than 25. Neither *Lemmings* nor the Village Gate is the kind of theater middle-aged playgoers (who are, after all, the people who keep most plays going) ever go to. Yet the show is a hit, even as it mocks and satirizes the culture and attitudes that raised its audience. Drugs and Woodstock promised a utopia of peace and love but reneged on it. Drugs turned out to be as deadly as Vietnam, even though both promised light at the end of the tunnel. The spirit of Woodstock was realized in the commercialism of the Warner Brothers film of the event, in political sloganeering ("Woodstock Nation") and in murder at Altamont.

"Everybody but the kids profited from Woodstock; the rock groups were not only paid but were also made the stars of a movie; farmer Max Yasgur made $125,000 for the use of his land (not $40,000 as his obituary in the *Times* stated), and drug dealers found their trade more respectable.

"The real message of the 60's wasn't love and peace, it was death—from needles or bullets, take your pick. Death is what *Lemmings* is about. It is also implicitly about laughter as a vital life sign."

■   ■

Okay—about the drugs. In *Wired,* Woodward has me turning Belushi on to coke during rehearsals and thus introducing him to his "drug of choice." This is like saying Kenney discovered acid in the second year of the *Lampoon*'s publication. Belushi was familiar, as was everyone else at the time, with all the staples of the pharmacopoeia, and among those staples was coke. The objective sensationalism of Belushi's "introduction" to coke might be okay in journalism, but it's not good history. Belushi knew about this drug long before he came within my purview; he might not have been able to afford it or have been very familiar with it, but the idea that I gave him his first "hit" (Woodward's term) is ridiculous.

There were drugs around *Lemmings,* and especially in the dressing rooms. The reason was simple: one of the cast members lived with a dealer. Every other dressing room off-Broadway boasted similar luxuries; the difference with *Lemmings* was that a considerable message in our show was that drugs were part of the on-going self-destruction of our generation. As the show became a bigger and bigger hit, some of the cast became more and more like what they were parodying. They really thought they were a rock group— called "Lemmings"—and were thus entitled to the same kind of self-destructive lifestyle. By the middle of the spring, when the show was at its height, packed to the doors eight days a week, beyond question the hippest show in town, each of the actors thought they had finally made their rock dream—to be in a group, with an album, and a sound, and, of course, drugs.

Belushi in particular seemed unable to put together what he did with his own life and what he satirized every night onstage. It was like O'Donoghue's inability to connect his own hatred with the hatred he was so good at mocking. I might have been expecting too much of the satire game in terms of moral self-improvement, but to satirize how drug use and rock celebrity make people absurd and then behave exactly the same way yourself was doubly absurd. Drugs as recreation was one thing; drugs as a religion was quite another. And Belushi could get himself literally legless (which I remember being from grass more often than coke and later on in the run from Quaaludes. None of us could afford much coke on the kind of salaries Simmons paid). Practically speaking, Belushi's indulgences could have appalling musical results. Belushi was the weakest of the musicians—we had tried to hide him on bass—but he was still essential to the sound, and if his timing was off, the parodies laid eggs. He insisted that he could handle it, but even when he did, it made the others, especially the fanatically precise Guest, nervous and/or furious.

There is no hiding a theatrical hit from the consequences of drugs. Especially when people like Dustin Hoffman, James Taylor, Mick Jagger, and many, many others turn up for the performance. (Taylor appeared not to get his parody at all, but Carly Simon, to whom he was married at the time, fell on the floor.) I personally didn't give a damn who was in the audience, but the value that was attached to celebrity made the cast understandably hostile and tense when anything threatened to make them look bad.

I did indulge the rock dreams on a few occasions as a reward to the cast, and later tried to contain Belushi's habits. Twice I asked for money from management to give to the cast to do with what they liked. One of these was opening night; the other, as I recall, was when the album was completed. In each case the sum was a couple of hundred dollars. I'm pretty sure management knew quite well that the money—not much among seven people—would probably be spent on illegal substances, but these were people who for the most part preferred grass to champagne and roses. They'd worked hard, they were a hit, and if that's what they wanted, they deserved it.

I also arranged advances against salaries for the various members of the cast—that was part of the producer's job. What they did with the money was no business of mine. But the clear assertion in the book that I acted as "an errand boy" for the cast is both odd and offensive. There was only one occasion when I specifically mentioned getting drugs for Belushi. He had proved himself more or less impervious to remonstrance when it came to getting high before a performance. So I decided to try and make a deal with him. If he would just stay off coke before the show, I'd get him some after it. He didn't and I didn't.

There were other temptations that spring as the show became a solid hit. The Robert Stigwood organization expressed interest in the show, as did an old acquaintance, Ron Delsener. Both wanted to tour the company—as a rock group called "Lemmings"—which would do a concert tour of the country.

Simmons resisted these offers. I'd been studying him long enough to know that the usual editorial analysis of his actions was likely to be inaccurate, but I was genuinely baffled as to why he didn't go for one of these deals. Either Stigwood or Delsener could have made the *Lampoon* a great deal richer, and could certainly have tied the brilliant cast much more irrevocably to the *Lampoon.* His stated reason was that both Stigwood and Delsener would want a fat twenty-five percent fee for organizing the tour, and that he had the know-how and contacts to do the same thing for nothing. If he did, he never used them, and the show didn't tour until much later. But his motives might have been more complex. The success of the show had been a surprise, and quite suddenly the relatively small enterprise of a second album had become a citywide sensation, turning the intention of my exile upside down. Perhaps he wanted to control the show, keep us downtown, contained, where further success wouldn't tear the magazine, the locomotive of the whole train, apart.

The magazine was doing amazingly well at the time, entering the period of its greatest circulation (1973–75) and some of its best writing. I had had little to do with it since the show had gone into rehearsal the previous winter. I kept my fingertips on the edge in the "Death" issue (January 1973),* but lost my grip more or less completely in the following months.

I made it back in briefly in June and July, but I was finding out the hard way that the magazine would do just fine without me, just as it had done without Kenney and just as it would do without O'Donoghue the next year.

O'Donoghue was not in the magazine much that year, other than with short pieces. He, Beatts, and O'Rourke spent the first half of the year putting together the *Encyclopedia of Humor.* The *Encyclopedia* was, in effect, a gigantic issue of the magazine organized around the principle of alphabetical subject order. Gross and his new assistant, David Kaestle, an old friend from Pratt, did a slap-up job of production, and the result was both a feat and a feast, containing material under its various headings ranging from one-liners to full-length parodies, the best of them (in my opinion) coming from McCall and McConnachie.

The *Encyclopedia* caused a lot of trouble for Simmons. One of the pieces was a reproduction of a then current Volkswagen ad, showing it floating in a large body of water. To this had been added the legend: "If Teddy Kennedy had been driving a VW, he'd be President today." VW got hold of this and threatened to sue the company for $30 million. But this was not the *Lampoon* of 1970, confronted with Disney. Simmons might have fought the case—it was a funny joke and the publicity for the *Lampoon* would have been formidable. Unfortunately, the basis of their suit was infringement of trademark. In their zeal, the art department had exactly reprinted the VW logo, and VW's case was iron-clad. Simmons was forced to pull the offending piece.

But the magazine's capacity to absorb this kind of problem was now considerable. Its average monthly circulation in 1973 was 724,000 (up from 1972's 445,000), and its ad revenue had doubled to $1.25 million. Much of this, Taylor claimed, came from the show biz initiatives the magazine had taken. I didn't really see how circulation could be affected by a local off-Broadway show, although he claimed that he impressed advertisers mightily by taking them to our very own hit. The albums (the *Lemmings* album was now out) had exposed the magazine where it had not been exposed before, especially by airplay. (We'd put out a single from both albums, and the second of these, Playten's "Pizza Man," actually got quite a lot of play.) Radio was certainly a natural way for us to get exposure, especially on campus, and this was an important component in the *Lampoon's*—and O'Donoghue's—next venture, "The Radio Hour."

According to Kelly, O'Donoghue was greatly incensed by the success of *Lemmings,* and as soon as the *Encyclopedia* was put to bed, he demanded his own show biz initiative. There was more to it than envy. He had, after all, been just as responsible as I for *Radio Dinner;* and he had just come off a huge print project—after working at the magazine for more than three years

---

* This was the issue which carried probably the *Lampoon*'s most famous cover (See insert).

straight. The show biz end of *Lampoon* was new and exciting, and it certainly was his turn.

In the circumstances, however, I resisted this when the project was first mooted in the early summer.

The force of my resistance came not from a desire to produce "The Radio Hour" myself, or from being a dog-in-the-manger about O'Donoghue if I couldn't. I personally didn't care if I didn't see the inside of any place of entertainment, theater, night club, or recording studio for a very long time. But it seemed to me that these projects had already made chaos of editorial cohesion that required time and patience—without making any significant profit for the company. Show biz seemed, at least in this group, to bring out the worst in people, inflating egos, mine included, creating greed for attention and credit—all of which could only exacerbate our already tense internal politics.

I'd found this out the hard way a few weeks before, after I made a dumb and extremely unprofessional mistake with regard to a piece of material in *Lemmings*.

The first act had always been a major problem in the show. We'd tried everything possible for a first-act closer but without success. Some time in March I had a very long-shot idea. Several years before, my partner and I had performed a piece (rarely, for it was extremely messy) called the "Humor Lecture." It had been adapted—with permission—from a sketch originally written by Terry Jones and Mike Palin for an Oxford University revue called *X X X X*. Originally the sketch involved a dry-as-dust lecturer and three assistants who straightfacedly demonstrated the lecturer's "history" of humor, starting from the earliest japes (getting hit in the head with planks) to the complex ones of the Industrial Revolution, (a long series of every conceivable combination of pies-in-the-face). It was very funny and very much in the current Anglophile, pseudo-intellectual style. I contacted Jones in 1965 to see if Hendra and Ullett could use it. He replied that it was fine, he and Palin had no further plans for it (although he didn't really see how two people could do it).†

He was right: two people could demonstrate the "japes," but a third was needed to lecture. Accordingly, Hendra and Ullett did it only twice—once during a tour with John Davidson and one hilarious shot on the "Merv Griffin Show," with (as I recall) Robert Goulet doing the lecturer.

I made the first half of the mistake. I rewrote this version of the sketch from memory and cast Goodrow as the lecturer, and Guest, Belushi, and Chase as the demonstrators. I must admit I had a certain proprietary sense about the piece. I thought that I at least had the right to do it, that Jones, who had by now moved on to "Monty Python," had left it long behind him,

---

† Interestingly, he said in an interview for *From Fringe to Flying Circus,* by Roger Wilmut (Methuen, 1982), "The idea for the sketch wasn't really mine, it came from Bernard Braden, I believe." Braden was a well-known Canadian-born comic who worked for many years in the U.K., chiefly during the fifties and early sixties.

and would be only too happy to get some bucks for an old sketch out of our meager script payments.

I tried out the piece to see if it was worth contacting Jones at all, and the piece was a smash, easily the funniest outside the second act, and perfect for physical performers like the *Lemmings* cast. I had meant only to try it, then take it out until I could contact Jones, but the cast, understandably, demanded that it stay in. I made the second half of the mistake. I let it go, for it certainly was nice to have a strong closing number. I made a note to contact Jones and get a check to him.

It was unprofessional certainly, a bad judgment, even a stupid gamble. What it wasn't was grand larceny, which is how the word ran around the editorial offices and the theater when it was discovered that Monty Python, just beginning their Canadian stage tour in Toronto, were closing their first act with the same custard-pie sketch.

This seemed to be something between me and Jones, and Simmons, possibly Beard, and no one else. It was my problem, and my embarrassment. All that was needed was to drop the sketch, apologize and pay the authors.‡

Instead, the word had been put out from one end of the *Lampoon* organization to the other—from stagehands to copy editors—and therefore, unpardonably, down the humor grapevine—that the piece had been directly stolen from Monty Python, that on some secret trip to Toronto or perhaps the old country I had caught the Pythons, covertly recorded their best sketch, put it in the show, paid myself for it, and taken all the credit, hoping presumably that the International Humor Branch of Scotland Yard wouldn't find out.

I was most immediately concerned with the cast and explained to them what had happened. Their reactions ranged from skepticism to lack of interest. Both Goodrow and Belushi—perhaps because they came from improv companies and were used to interchanges of material—were the most sympathetic. Their main concern was the loss of a great piece to close the first act.

In what Beard now referred to as "the snake pit" of editorial politics, however, this stuff was dynamite. The buzz was that I was finished for good, that this proved what O'Donoghue had been saying all along. I stole people's women; I stole people's material. Now there was a lovely moral basis for the whole dumb mess. I'm bound to say that I don't think O'Donoghue was behind any of this. He was not good at politics—psychowarfare perhaps but not intrigue. He talked big about "getting" his enemies, but hadn't got the busy malice needed to follow through. He just gave vent to his hostility and let the usually impressive results take their course. He got mad, but not even.

The sheer viciousness of the gossip, the concentric ripples of suspicion that spiraled from it, the way it threw everybody further apart, not only convulsed

‡ Jones and I patched this up quite amicably. He was understandably miffed that his and Palin's piece had been used without permission, but was quite content to have it dropped, be paid for its use, and that was that.

the magazine, but seemed to have no purpose other than a destructive one, to keep this deliciously negative action going. For once, it affected Beard. For the first time, Beard dipped his foot in the snake pit.

Beard accepted the gossip, At first he didn't; at first he didn't appear to want to know about the whole affair. He hated *Lemmings*. I believe he hated show business in general. It was not his affair and he kept his counsel. For a while.

He had rented a guest house on my New Jersey property for the summer of 1973. One Saturday evening there several months later, we were in the middle of a completely unconnected conversation. Beard turned to me and hissed, "How could you do it? *How could you do it?*"

And that was all. The only angry words he'd spoken since I'd known him.

I think this was the last straw for him. He'd put up with crises and intrigues for three and a half years, and whether I was guilty as charged or not, I was the proximate cause of the latest round. At least I think that's what he was saying. He certainly didn't mean the plumbing.

Beard came up with a remarkable antidote a couple of months after—a "Self-Indulgence" issue, which was to concern itself entirely with those who inhabited the masthead of the magazine. It served two functions: (1) to let all the people involved in the magazine sound off about themselves—the issue was packed with pictures of us—and (2), to clear the air by turning the malice into self-satire. What the readers thought of this is anyone's guess, but it was actually effective.

The issue was edited by McConnachie, who stood apart from all the nonsense and who had now become the Italian (or perhaps intergalactic) president everyone could agree on. No one knew who'd written what about whom. Among other appearances, I was on the cover of my own magazine, which carried several cover lines including: TONY—FAVE NASAL DECONGESTANT! TONY—LAST JOKE STOLEN! NOW ON SALE AT YOUR FAVORITE VEGETABLE STAND!

This is what we should have been doing all along. Here we were eating ourselves up, bitching and crowing over each other's madness or misfortune, calling each other lunatics, criminals, traitors when right outside our door there was—Richard Nixon.

Back at *Lemmings,* the problem of a closing number had been solved by the Chief Exec. Watergate was heating up that summer, and the cast, working with Kelly, came up with a lot of material, including the first television piece in the show, a broad lampoon of Senator Sam Ervin (Chase) and his hearings. Added to this was a piece by, of all people, Beard, called "Mission Impeachable." This was done in the black by Chase and never failed to bring the house down.

Gradually this piece evolved into an Impeachment Day Parade, which ended with an edited "speech" by Nixon himself, taken from his actual utterances on Watergate, in which he was caused to admit everything he was accused of. When the eighteen-and-a-half-minute gap was found in the Nixon tapes, this package was amplified by more Beard material (for many months Beard had been having the time of his life with Watergate in "News on the March") and was released as the third *Lampoon* album, *The Missing White House Tapes*. (Beard's material later found its way onto *The Radio Hour*.)

With Watergate providing new material daily, *Lemmings* was actually becoming interesting again, after going through the usual six-month doldrums. A juicy result was a cabaret we were asked to perform early that fall. One of the revelations of the Watergate investigations was that Nixon kept an "Enemies List," which contained several hundred names of various people who'd got up his nose, many of them prominent New York liberals and members of the radical chic. The Enemies decided to hold a party in New York and invited us to provide the entertainment. This was an odd choice, for these Enemies weren't exactly our friends, but *Lemmings* was still the hot show in town, and our Watergate material was getting talked about, especially on local media. We arrived after the show, at a large clublike place in midtown, very snooty, and filled with smartly dressed people, all of them gibbering excitedly about Watergate. The hostess—a very imperious lady who looked more like a member of Palm Beach's radical chic than New York's—treated us as the serfs we were and instructed us on length of performance and on "who-all" of great note were present.

We began to think that Nixon had a point. Just before the Impeachment Day material, Goodrow asked me if he could finish the show off by doing his impersonation of Richard Nixon. I knew what he probably had in mind, so I said yes. The set went on under extremely cramped conditions, with the audience barely inches from the performers. Nonetheless, it got plenty of har-de-hars right up to finish, whereupon Goodrow seized the mike and announced that he would now like to do his celebrated impression of Richard Nixon. This was greeted with applause. Goodrow turned around, bent over, and dropped his pants, throwing a very bony and hairless moon. A shock wave went through the dedicated Enemies, they broke up into muttering groups, and the hostess made a beeline for me. She was speechless. "Filth, disgusting . . . no idea . . . at this party of all places . . . ," she sputtered and threw us—we were of course helpless with laughter—out on the street. Nixon yes, ass no.

Lemmings had split up into two groups by the fall. One stayed at the Gate, the other went out on a short-lived and extremely ambitious tour as the road company. This was Simmons's belated answer to Stigwood and Delsener, though the moment had long passed for any such tour; also it was because Belushi was making a lot of noise about a raise and more responsibility. At one point this became loud enough for me to be told to get rid of him, which I refused to do. The eventual solution was to give him two salaries, one as a performer and one as a director, and let him put together his own company. During the summer we had been experimenting with various replacements as original cast members took breaks. These included a marvellous writer/musician from Chicago, Nate Herman; a rather dull though technically excellent musical parodist, Tony Scheuren; an intensely talented woman, Rhonda Coullet, with an Yma Sumac range who turned in, among much else, a devastating Joni Mitchell parody, written by Nate; Kay Cole, a Playten-sized singer with almost as big a voice; good old Peter Ebling, who—among much else—turned in a great parody of Donovan called "Nirvana Banana"; and Zal Yanovsky, late of the Lovin' Spoonful, who did a stomach-churning Dr. John.

Thus we had enough people to do what had a few months earlier been considered impossible: replace the irreplaceable original cast. What we didn't have was enough money (and in my case enough energy). The road company was even more expensive than the home one—because while it had to have identical sound equipment, it also had to live and travel. Belushi was soon very unhappy with the arrangement and called me constantly—he couldn't control his company; the hotels were no good, the dressing rooms were lousy; he couldn't find any drugs.

Then there was a further problem in the fall of 1973—the OPEC oil embargo. The cast traveled much of the time by bus and car, and often there was quite literally no gas available to get from one date to another.

Also, houses back in New York were getting smaller as time went on. It seemed to me I was on a very tired horse. Simmons and I started making preparations to close the show. I vowed that I would never again get involved in a *Lampoon* project involving show business in any form (a promise I kept until I left four years later). *Lemmings* had run its course, had brought into the *Lampoon* circle a dozen excellent performers, several of them potential stars, and a number of equally excellent managerial people who now had plenty of experience running, booking, and publicizing a musical show. If O'Donoghue wanted any of them for his radio show, he was welcome. I was going back to the magazine.

18

No Soap Radio:
"The National Lampoon Radio Hour"

O'Donoghue's plans for the radio show were ambitious. They faced away from the contemporary parody of *Lemmings* and *Radio Dinner,* back toward the thirties and forties, and the Golden Age of Radio. One of the first people hired to get the ball rolling was Polly Bier, a producer from "The Dick Cavett Show." She recalls O'Donoghue's description of the show when she first went to meet him in the fall of 1973: "His visions of the show sounded really very exciting. He talked about doing some very innovative stuff, about using radio in a way it hadn't been used for a long time . . . having old radio and new ideas, a place where a lot of people could try out very new stuff, as well as a nostalgia for the old days. There were a lot of pieces written that used old radio announcers, perfect recreation of the forties, perfect recreation of the fifties . . ."

O'Donoghue was not rigid about this aspect of the show—contributors remember him being anxious to get material of any kind, which was hardly surprising in light of the sixty minutes a week he had to generate. But the emphasis on the forties (strictly speaking it was more like the late thirties) gave the show a parody base from which people could write, a familiar sound and style through which up-to-date comedy could be filtered.

This was very much to O'Donoghue's taste. He had never had much interest or feeling for Kenney's Ohio reflexes, and in a way this was his answer to them. Here was his nostalgia, his Golden Age with an edge, far more stylish and knowing, more definite and fixed than ambivalent feelings about high school and the fifties.

There was something camp about this too, and it showed itself in several ways. O'Donoghue had always had a direction Gross calls "effetist." O'Donoghue would require elaborate reproductions of art deco, or forties commercial art; Gross disliked this because, as the typical reader, he didn't get what was supposed to be funny about it.

Now, however, this occasional lurch toward the effete was becoming a personal style. O'Donoghue had affected a cane and was searching about for the rest of the costume. Kelly says, "Michael always had a problem about how to dress. The problem was that he could always see through other people's style. He saw through people who wore hats; he saw through people who didn't wear hats. What could he wear that he couldn't see through? Eventually he settled on Hawaiian shirts and white suits. No one could get him for that."

O'Donoghue also required that the studio, which would be built on the ninth floor of the *Lampoon* building, be decorated in slavishly accurate forties style. It was to have a prewar, cowboy-musical cactus-and-desert theme and would eventually be called "The Radio Ranch."

O'Donoghue's approach would involve a great deal of production. Carefully crafted, stylishly dated pieces would require a certain kind of sound, appropriate music, sound effects, and above all the right kind of "radio" voices. Every piece would have to be cast, the right voice found for each period or period-derived character. This was not a situation like the Credibility Gap, where a resident group took care of all the voices, and generated material together. Scripts came from all kinds of sources, and were cast and recorded individually. There was an absolute need for a sound engineer of great range. Bob Tischler, who had engineered *Radio Dinner,* was tapped to do this, and he proved to be an invaluable resource for the show, covering the field from obscure sound effects, the right music library tape trick, or the perfect voice-over specialist with just the radio camp O'Donoghue was looking for.

Through the fall everybody in the magazine—with the exception of myself —was encouraged to produce scripts for "The Radio Hour." Many were called, many were chosen. One of the heavy hitters was McCall. The period appealed to him immensely—and more than anyone he came through on O'Donoghue's original Golden Age of Radio premise: "I was quite excited about it. I did 'Megaphone News': 'Marches across the seas, around the world, and into YOUR FACE! . . .' They did a beautiful job producing that —made my words better than they were . . .

"There were a lot of inviting things you could do in radio. I was like Marconi. I was just interested in the idea that you could throw your voice out to the public. I had 'Camera Club of the Air,' where people would try to describe their photographs to other people over the phone. It was really exciting."

"The Radio Hour" premiered in November 1973. It was distributed free to radio stations, who retained the right to sell commercial spots within the show. Thanks to an old school tie, Rob Hoffman, whose father owned the

Seven-Up bottling franchise in Texas, the UnCola became the sponsor of "The Radio Hour," and this got it off to a roaring start.

Lemmings people were not used in the first cycle of shows, except for the multivoiced Chris Guest; Bier used actors and actresses represented by commercial agencies. We had done this in *Radio Dinner* when we used Norman Rose to record "Deteriorata." He was used in many of the early "Radio Hours," as were others like Sid Davis, George Coe, and Pat Bright.

"The Radio Hour" was right up there with *Radio Dinner* and *Lemmings* when it came to innovation. Nobody had ever heard anything quite like this before. It was that special *Lampoon* mix of media skill and savage satire that topped the head-heavy whimsy of the Firesign Theater and upped the ante on anyone thinking of putting out a comedy album. Within the *Lampoon* it was the place to be in the winter of 1973, and some unlikely people were soon hanging around the ninth floor. One of them was the stately Trow, who developed a popular gossip columnist called "Mr. Chatterbox"; one of the more likely—Kenney—was always in evidence. "A lot of these people," McCall says, "were frustrated actors."

Frustrated actors themselves also hung around, according to Bier, who would often come upon Belushi and Chase loitering in the lobby when they weren't on the road, hoping to get parts. O'Donoghue began using Chase quite extensively after a while. Whatever reservations he had about using the *Lemmings*-tainted performers, he could ill afford to overlook this resource. Chase was adept at recording, not the least because of his experience with *The Groove Tube*.

But the real problem continued to be the time it took to put carefully crafted shows together. Carefully produced two- and three-minute bits were great to do, but a sixty-minute show had to be filled every week. For one person involved this seemed to be "The Radio Hour's" most difficult aspect.

Janis Hirsch had come to the *Lampoon* via *Lemmings*. She was a total devotee of the magazine while at college in Florida, regarding it as her lifeline to sanity in an otherwise dopey, preppy school—of the kind that provided its students with transportation to the beach and box lunches the day the nationwide Kent State demonstrations were called. Through her college's theater department she had gotten a job on *Lemmings* as a seller of block bookings, and then graduated to a position as super-go-fer on "The Radio Hour" together with Belushi's girlfriend and future wife Judy Jacklin. Hirsch was one of those unusual groupies who are as good, if not better, at what their idols do than they are themselves: she became one of the more delightful fixtures of the *Lampoon*.

Hirsh says, "The first year when it was Michael producing, it was so chaotic! Everybody was up all night. It was just auditioning people, and putting the show on, and booking professional voices—that was very expensive—and the show never got out on time. Duping them was a huge pain in the neck, real expensive also and time-consuming.

"But it was magic. All the pieces were real short bits. And they were hilarious. . . . The pieces were [like *Radio Dinner]* highly produced versions of *Lampoon* jokes. And it was fun for Tischler. He was doing great things, and then people would say, 'Wow—you can do *that,* Bob,' so then everybody wanted him to do everything."

But, according to Hirsch, that wasn't the only problem: "One day, we were just sitting there doing grunt work, and Michael and George began having a fight during George's recording of 'Mr. Chatterbox.'

"They were having some kind of battle, and it carried over into our office. Judy and I just dropped our pencils and watched for a while. They were fighting with words we had to look up in the dictionary. Prehistoric creatures and so on.

"And then they started throwing things. When I saw them each trying to pick up the desks, we ran into the little partition area and hid. It was really scary . . ."

O'Donoghue was exhausted by year's end and he took a break. Kelly substituted for him on the December 29, 1973 show and finally brought the *Lemmings* solidly into the "Radio Show" mainstream by broadcasting the Impeachment Day Celebrations from its first act. The show was a tour de force, hosted by Chase and Rhonda Coullet, and it celebrated not just the downfall of Nixon, but the military's ignominious failure in Vietnam. Here's Beard's "Mission Impeachable" which kicked off the festivities:

A tape recorder is turned on. An official voice is heard:

VOICE: Good morning, Mr. Hunt. Several high-ranking members of the Democratic party are attempting to seize control of the government of the United States by legitimate means. They plan to use a free press, open discussion of the issues, and the universal franchise in an all-out effort to win the presidency. Should they succeed, all our efforts to repeal the Bill of Rights, pack the Supreme Court with right-wing morons, intimidate the media, suppress dissent, halt social progress, promote big business, and crush the Congress will be destroyed. Your mission, E., should you choose to accept it, is to stop these men once and for all, by ensuring that the weakest of them, Senator George McGovern, wins the nomination—and then by sabotaging his campaign with any possible means. You will have at your disposal electronic bugging equipment, burglary tools, wigs, voice-alteration devices, a camera disguised as a tobacco pouch, forged documents, a safe house, five hundred loyal but clumsy Cubans, and two million dollars in hundred-dollar bills. As always, if any member of your CIA force is caught or killed, the President will disavow any knowledge of your activities. This Administration will self-destruct in sixteen months. Good luck, Howie.

The next day Seven-Up, calling the "Impeachment Day Parade" unpatriotic, pulled out of "The Radio Hour" for good, becoming as Kelly put it, "the
UnSponsor."

Although the show continued to prosper creatively, it was already a considerable financial drain and was taking a lot of time and energy from other
projects besides. O'Donoghue was increasingly difficult and the show became
the scene of more and more tension throughout the second series.

McCall says, "O'Donoghue was crazy. It was hard to win a fight with him,
so I didn't fight him. He was generous to me; he had that way of seeming to
be the arbiter, so if he pronounced your stuff good, you felt flattered. I needed
all the approval I could get, I guess. I found him dazzlingly funny and bright,
he seemed so sure of everything. Of course I'm the sort of guy who would
have voted for Hitler."

An unprofitable show, extreme fatigue, and egomania were a pretty explosive mix. Despite the fact that "The Radio Hour"—now half an hour long
and for a time known as the "Radio Show"—kept up its standards, things
were coming to a head. Early in the spring they did, as Simmons recalls,
"What happened is, Michael had been on the radio show for close to a year. I
thought the show was great, but it was not a money-making situation. So I
said to him, 'Michael, you've got to start working on the magazine.'

" 'Well, I don't wanna . . . I don't like this one, I don't like Tony, I don't
like Henry.' He accused everybody of stealing his girls . . . you stole this
girl, Henry stole his girl, Doug stole so and so . . . everybody was terrible.

"So one Saturday night he and I walked up and down Second Avenue for
about two hours talking. Finally he said, 'Okay, I'll start working on Monday. I'll work on the radio show too.' John [Belushi] was going to help him
take the load off his shoulders.

"That Sunday I'm home, he calls me up—and I'd just spent three tortuous
hours with the man, and he's such a difficult man. Now he's all excited.

"Anne Beatts has to have a desk in the 'Radio Show,' and she's got to have
an office. 'She must have it or else!', says Michael.

"I said, 'Michael, I'm sitting home, relaxing. I'm watching a football
game.' I felt it was something we should discuss in the office.

"So he said, 'No, we discuss it now or I quit.' I said, 'Michael, if that's how
you feel about it, you can quit.' And so he did and that was it."

This was on Easter Sunday. On Monday, as the news ran around the office,
the mood was somber. It was hard to imagine the *Lampoon* without O'Donoghue somewhere in its entrails, whether he was charming the pants off a
newcomer or punching his own thigh in homicidal rage.

A council of war had to be held to discuss what the magazine—and the
organization—would be like without him. It was a formal ritual. The meeting
was attended by all editors and by the main personnel from the publishing
and advertising sides. It was dutifully serious. We discussed who would take
over the "Radio Show" (Kelly), and what else had to be done to plug the gap.

It was a closed-door meeting—the most serious one we'd ever had, and there were the strictest instructions that we not be disturbed. Hirsch, the newest convert, thought otherwise:

"The day after Michael left the *Lampoon,* which was the Black Day when everybody was scared to go down to the editorial floor, a friend of mine had come to visit me. At that point, he was touring with Zippy the Chimp. And he brought in Zippy, who was this monkey on roller skates. So I went down to the fourth floor and Barbara (Simmons's secretary) said, 'Whatever you do, don't go in—Matty cannot be disturbed.' And I said very solemnly, 'I have to disturb him, Barbara.' She looked at me like I was committing suicide.

"So I opened the door to Matty's office, without knocking. And I have never seen so many angry male faces turn and look at me. They all said one collective 'What?' And I said, 'I've found Michael's replacement,' and they were all rising in their chairs . . . and I rolled in Zippy the Chimp!"

Kelly now took over "The Radio Show" and ran it for the next two series. Kelly refers to this period as "The Incredible Shrinking Radio Show." Sponsors would not buy time on the controversial show, and its cost was cumulatively growing. Every time Kelly went upstairs to the ninth floor, there was less furniture; another room had been rented out.

By now Belushi was a regular on the show, as was another Second City graduate, Brian Doyle-Murray. Kelly—who was running the show as well as contributing to the magazine—finally gave up after the first year of production. It was natural for Belushi to become the director of the radio program.

Belushi had been working in one *Lampoon* stable or another for close to two years. He could be trusted to put out a product worthy of the magazine, even without the guiding hand of an editor. His method, however, was quite different, and from Simmons's point of view, considerably cheaper than the sketch-by-sketch casting that "The Radio Hour" had practiced hitherto. Belushi wanted to put together a resident company which would generate and perform the show by itself.

The cast he assembled was extraordinary. Apart from himself, Guest, and Doyle-Murray there were two other old friends from Chicago's Second City, Joe Flaherty and Harold Ramis—and a wonderful loudmouth from its Toronto company, Gilda Radner. The show became the territory of this group; people from the magazine were no longer encouraged to write material for "The Radio Hour." The cast created virtually all the material themselves. Some of these shows were built around one theme and many were hilarious.

This period of "The Radio Hour" was the most complete fusion of Second City and the *Lampoon* that had occurred so far. Belushi and Doyle-Murray kept the *Lampoon* edge going, while the newcomers filled out the half hours with a group sense that the show had never really experienced before. But the show was still losing a tremendous amount of money (ultimately it would leave Simmons with a net loss of $500,000), and Simmons figured he could recoup some of this with the amazingly talented group Belushi had now assembled under the *Lampoon* aegis. He decided to start another live show, this one to be called simply *The National Lampoon Show,* which would tour campuses.

Kelly was ostensibly put in charge of this production, but it was actually run by Belushi. Kelly recalls going to see the show at a tryout in a club on Long Island called My Father's Place, and having his *Lampoon* material rejected by the cast, who'd worked out their own show and needed no help from the magazine. Kelly, exhausted from his efforts to keep "The Radio Hour" going, had no objection to a cast that "made it all up themselves" and let them go. His credit on the program read, "Entire Production Overlooked by Sean Kelly."

This cast now toured various places, most of them in the Northeast and Canada. The show was quite well received and the bookings came in. Two things happened to the show during the fall of 1974 which would have profound results for some of the cast members. First, Brian Doyle-Murray dropped out of the show. He requested that he be replaced—by his kid brother Bill, a lanky, rangy lunatic who alarmed even hardened *Lampoon* staffers by wandering around the magazine offices yelling, among other things, "I am the Honker!" Thus Bill Murray joined the cast of *The National Lampoon Show.*

Murray also joined the "Radio Show" cast when they were in town. Chris Guest and he were particularly good together. The "Radio Show" was the first appearance of several elements of Murray's repertoire—his laid-back skeptical newsman, for example, and his glutinous lounge singer. Another first appearance on the "Radio Show," according to Hirsch, was Baba Wah-Wah. Radner needed a woman reporter (there weren't too many models in 1974), and Hirsch suggested Barbara Walters, pointing out her soft "r."

Second, during a stop in Toronto, the then company manager Michael Simmons, son of Matty, was approached by another lanky, rangy person, this time as sane as he could be, who was interested in becoming in some way involved with the *Lampoon.* In Simmons's words: "This young guy walks in, and he says, 'Jesus, I've always been a *Lampoon* fan.' He was producing a show in Toronto called *The Magic Show.* He had done some triple Z movies . . . *The Beast from Under Your Armpit* and things like that. So he called me and I got friendly with him, and he came to New York. I was thinking of bringing the show into New York . . . for a limited engagement, six or eight weeks, so I said to him, 'How would you like to take the show and run it here in New York?' He said, 'Aaah—I'd do anything, I'd cut off my right arm.' I said you don't have to cut off your right arm. And that's how Ivan Reitman came to work for me."

Reitman brought *The National Lampoon Show* into New York, at a nightclub theater in the Time-Life building called the New Palladium. The show opened well to reviewers who had not seen the *Lampoon* presented onstage for almost two years, since the opening of *Lemmings.* The material was not by any means as all-encompassing conceptually as *Lemmings,* but neither was it a rerun of Second City sketches. The mix of the two schools was now generating a new kind of humor.

The cast of this show was John Belushi, Joe Flaherty, Gilda Radner, Harold Ramis, and Bill Murray. A couple of weeks into the show a young producer, Lorne Michaels, caught it. He was casting a television show called "Saturday Night."

The New Palladium was packed every night, so Reitman was happy as a clam. He'd got his in with the *Lampoon;* he was in New York instead of fooling about in Canada with his "triple Z" movies (which were actually called things like *Ilsa She-Wolf of Dachau).*

These two men were the lucky ones. Sharks had been circling the *Lampoon* for some time now, trying to work out what it was we did, what the formula was, how the ingredients could be duplicated and reassembled.

Reitman and Michaels, both of them quite unsharklike, a restless writer-producer and a mild-mannered B-movie maker, both Canadian, would become the most significant beneficiaries of everything we had been doing for the last five years.

1974—Golden Year, Golden Parachutes

The year 1974 was the second and last year of what Simmons had referred to as the *Lampoon*'s "golden age." It came in with a bang, went out with a crash, and in between had an enormous hit. As *Lemmings* wound down, and its various personnel found jobs in the organization, and as the "Radio Hour" picked up steam, the magazine emerged somehow calmer and more together, and turned out some of its best issues ever over that twelve months. Circulation figures reflected this. Average monthly circulation in 1974 was 830,000 copies, up 100,000 from the previous year. While this was not as dramatic as the 300,000 jump in 1973, it was not to be sneezed at. For a general-interest magazine, with no other purpose than to make people think and laugh, the figures were staggering. Given the pass-along rate*, which was sometimes as high as eight or ten, the number of people the magazine reached each month might be as high as eight or nine million.

Not only were Simmons's newsstand revenues very considerable, but advertising grew in 1974 to $2,153,000, up almost a million from 1973.

Two old Harvard hands returned this year, Cerf (who never really left) and Weidman, who was finishing Yale Law School and was on his way to a Broadway musical he'd written with Stephen Sondheim called *Pacific Overtures.* Beard and Cerf had become something of a team, although Beard wrote

---

* "Pass-along," a delightful creation of the print advertising community, means the number of people apart from the purchaser who read a given copy. It isn't a term usually employed until after the third martini, but in the case of the *Lampoon* it might have been more valid than usual. This was because of the high circulation on campus, where opportunities for communal use of the *Lampoon* were greater than elsewhere. Nor is this altogether hype—pass-along is actually measured and taken seriously by advertisers; total audience is usually measured as pass-along plus one, times the circulation. Hence the figures above.

a prodigious amount this year, both alone and with others. The Greening of Beard was by now practically phosphorescent. He had put on some weight, his hair was long, and he had a lover; he could be uproarious when drunk and even from time to time voiced vehement personal opinions. The days of "tempting" were gone forever. He seemed in a strange way to be getting younger as he got older. And as the boom lowered inexorably on Nixon, and the dolt who followed him walked repeatedly into it, "News on the March" got longer and funnier every month.

The January 1974 issue was "Animals," not on the face of it much of a subject, but which turned out to be one of the funniest of the lot. Beard and Weidman wrote a quite amazing long piece called "The Law of the Jungle," which dealt with the various legal institutions that had developed within the animal world, rights (particularly the right to Bare Claws), due process, and precedents ("See *Tyrannosaurus Rex vs. Canadian Ice Sheet* and other similar cases"). In a year when legal issues were in the news every morning, there was something oddly topical about it.

It was a genial issue, which largely set the tone for the entire year. The issue-editor system had long since been dropped. Issues were now loosely supervised by the editors—that is, those who graced the top line of the rigging that year: Beard, myself, McConnachie, Kelly, plus McCall, who was in effect an editor but was not on staff, occasionally Trow, and less occasionally Kenney. In very rough rotation one of us would take responsibility for a given issue, but for the first time in a while, the entire group was really "editing" in the sense of conceiving and guiding every issue.

I took responsibility for the February issue, "Strange Sex," which included a piece by Kenney called "First Lay Comics," about a nerdy pledge in a fraternity called Tappa Kegga Bru. The frat gives a pig party (for sororities like Eta Bita Pi), the nerd gets his pig drunk, a good angel and a bad angel appear on his shoulder and urge him to differing courses re involuntary sex. Later he delivers her home in a shopping cart. On the opening page, outside the frat house, a grim ROTC officer, and his Republican date snarl in disgust. This was the first known appearance of *Animal House.†*

McCall did "Travel" in April, which contained his pre–World War I advertising brochure for the Trans-Atlantic megaliner R.M.S *Tyrranic,* "The Biggest Thing in All the World" (see insert).

The magazine went on with the same basic mix as before but with a subtle shift toward restraint, toward savoring the absurdity, chewing it thoughtfully rather than ripping it to shreds or barfing it across the room.

Perhaps it was this mood that brought up "food" as an issue subject. Or perhaps it was just that we were doing a lot of eating and drinking together. In any event, this subject turned out to be a goldmine and so much material flooded out of the group and the contributors that it was impossible to do even a small portion. Yet the ideas were sensational.

† This was also the highest-selling issue to date: 860,000 copies.

It was decided that food should be the subject of two issues (the first time we'd ever taken the miniseries approach). Since the ideas fell very roughly into two categories—either about too much food or too little—the issues would be called "Food" (June) and "Famine" (July). Food contained a cornucopia of good stuff, notably a Sussman parody of that classic Time-Life high-class food-porn, "The Cooking of . . ." series. This one was called "The Cooking of Provincial New Jersey," and it showed in faultless photography the varied, mostly chemical sustenance of the Garden State. Meyerowitz did a vast parody of Leonardo's *Last Supper,* in which the table is packed with the remains of a pig-out and a horrified Jesus has just been handed the check.

Famine included a full-scale team parody of *Family Circle* called "Famine Circle," including "food" ads for things like "Mrs. Paul's Sticks" and "The Pillsbury No-Boy," and a brilliant piece about agribiz by Beard and Cerf, called "The Corporate Farmer's Almanac."

There was so much left over from these two issues that we even toyed with the idea of doing yet a third food issue called "Desserts" or "The Morning After" or some such. But that seemed like asking a bit much of the readers' digestion. Instead, McConnachie came up with the more commercial title, "Isolationism and Tooth Care," an issue dedicated to reducing America's foreign commitments in the wake of Vietnam, and at the same time avoiding cavities. This issue sold almost exactly the same number of copies as our all-time record of February (860,000), and what's more, this was in the notoriously low month of August, when we would have been thrilled with 100,000 less.

As long as we acted as a group and put out what we found funny, the readers agreed. "Food and Famine" had been very funny indeed, and the result was peak circulation in a blown-off issue. The covers in 1974 had not been classics. Yet our circulation was headed for an all-time high. This didn't mean that we could print beer stains on the covers either; it simply meant that a given issue's content could have dramatic effects, pro and con, on the issues that followed it.

On this point turned the next maelstrom the good ship *Lampoon* encountered: it was around these roiling waters that the magazine sailed forever more, and they were what eventually sank it.

Simmons saw the figures for February (the circulation high for 1974) and was anxious that we do another sex issue. If sex could do it once, sex could do it again. What's more, we were now planning our "Back-to-School" issue, by now established as the annual bestseller. What a combination—sex and back-to-school! We could break a million!

The editors resisted. First, this was not the way to pick issue topics; this was the first time Simmons had ever substantially tried to influence what topic we picked or what we put on the cover. Second, it didn't follow that sex would work twice; we were not a skin book and had never done more than one a year. We knew what our readers were interested in—sometimes sex, but plenty more besides—and had proven ourselves to be spectacularly reliable.

Third, there was an enormous amount happening in the country—a lame-duck, lame-brain President, an oil crisis, postwar economic chaos, all kinds of new cultural riptides, a tremendous anticipation for what would happen next.

The way we saw it, we were on a roll. Our "Back-to-School" issue would break a million so long as it was right. It was our time.

At least to me, there was another issue: finally, we were together again, albeit with some bruised cheeks and bandaged knuckles, nursing the magazine ever upward toward more influence and more profits. It was the worst time in the world to set a dog on us. Leave us be and there was no knowing where we would stop.

But here a personal factor entered the picture. Simmons set considerably more than a dog upon us. He set O'Rourke.

P. J. O'Rourke had been on the masthead for more than a year as executive editor. (Since the top-line staffers were simply called editors, this was something of an honorific). He had agitated periodically to be allowed to do an issue and had been turned down every time—not, as he claimed, because we were Harvard snobs (me, Kelly?) but because no one really found him very funny. He was likeable, immensely hardworking, energetic, and fast. He had done a lot of writing for the magazine, usually in collaboration (but then so did everyone) and was painstakingly loyal to a premise, turning out innumerable variations on it deep into the night. On a monthy schedule such a writer is of considerable worth. But left to himself he lurched between imitation of other styles and invective. It was like overfertilized fruit that looked right, felt right, but when you bit into it, just didn't taste of anything.

Simmons had sidestepped our refusal to give him editorial control of an issue by taking him on in 1973 as executive assistant. It was reported that the first morning he'd gone to work at Simmons's end of the office, he'd shown up in a suit and tie, and that soon afterward he'd bought a couple of hundred shares of the (now public) company.

Simmons certainly wasn't motivated by pity; O'Rourke was highly efficient and could be put on projects to keep an eye on them. It was useful to have someone reporting to him who was acceptable to the editors, especially with so many projects under way apart from the magazine. Thus after his work on the *Encyclopedia* with O'Donoghue, it was natural to put him to work on the "High School Yearbook" with Kenney. This project certainly did involve a colossal amount of organization and coordination, and by his own account O'Rourke had done the lion's share. His name even appeared before Kenney's on the credits: *"Edited* by P. J. O'Rourke and Doug Kenney."

Lower down one read "written and directed by P. J. O'Rourke and Doug Kenney."

This seemed a trifle cocky to say the least, but by the summer of 1974 the project had been put to bed—looking very good—and O'Rourke was feeling his oats. He demanded an issue; Simmons didn't see why not.

The implicit threat was that if we held out on our refusal to do another sex issue, Simmons would give the issue to O'Rourke. We did, and he did.

The issue theme ended up being "Pubescence." I refused to have anything to do with it, as did Kelly. Beard stood above it all, and although McConnachie was credited on one piece, he too had nothing to do with it.

While our refusal to participate was to some degree at fault, the issue was —in Kelly's word—"loathsome." It had practically nothing to do with pubescence other than to provide a pubescent reader with dozens of different versions of naked girls to jerk off to. In one four-page piece, in fact, three models did just that—took their clothes off in a motel room in a series of Polaroids until they were naked, explaining in speech balloons that it was all right if "you" jerked off to "us."

On every page were girls' rooms, girls' showers; vaginas were being indicated with rulers, Tampaxes were being inserted and removed, women were being mutilated and in one case flogged to death. This was not "Nancy Reagan's Guide to Dating." There was no point to it, no irony, no parody.

Worse, though, the issue was ugly. It looked ugly and its attitude was ugly. In a year which included pieces like "Law of the Jungle," "R.M.S. *Tyrranic*," "The Cooking of Provincial New Jersey," and a dozen other genial, elegant pieces, "Pubescence" was grubby and vicious. It was like watching some drunk backyard lout with a chainsaw cut up a Chippendale to settle a bet. We weren't squeamish about any of the subjects covered in this issue; we'd showed plenty and endured the criticism. What was appalling was that it made our critics right. This was simply dirty. It had no other level than that. Humor, O'Rourke's editorial appeared to imply, resided only in "your sister's cunt."

The issue sold 1,000,096 copies.

Simmons beamed; O'Rourke crowed.

The following issue was called "Civics." The cover was an official portrait in oils of President Ford; he had just planted a chocolate ice-cream cone firmly in the middle of his forehead. The issue was well up to par for the rest of the year, a little too much politics perhaps, a little too much of the kind of material that in a very short while would make Chevy Chase a star, but good nonetheless.

It sold 732,000 copies, the bottom of the pit for the year, 100,000 below the year's average.

O'Rourke crowed again. Simmons beamed somewhat less, but shook his head regretfully. It just shows. Sex sells. This political stuff . . .

The reality, of course, could not be expressed by this single-issue approach. The magazine did not sell just on its cover—though the cover could help— nor on what was inside a given issue. You couldn't flip through a *Lampoon* and appreciate the humor the way you can flip through a skin book. Humor —at least *our* humor—required more time and absorption than a vendor would allow you. The prime motive for buying a *Lampoon* was that you had liked it the last time you'd bought it. The August issue ("Isolationism and Tooth Care") with its absurdist cover and hodge-podge interior, defied both the "cover sells" and "flip-through sells" theories. It had sold as many copies as any *Lampoon* had to date. That was clearly because it had been preceded by months of consistently good issues and immediately preceded by two exceptional ones. The corollary was true. If an issue sucked, the one that followed would suffer. "Pubescence" had not only benefited by the excellent issues that had preceded it, it had disappointed a quarter of a million readers so thoroughly that they didn't come back again. "Pubescence" stripmined the readers' enthusiasm in one issue; the price had to be paid in the next. The net gain was nothing.

The argument was not one of art versus money, but of those who didn't understand the magazine's relationship to its readers, interfering with those who did. It wasn't starry-eyed editors refusing to face the harsh facts of business. This was bad business. The immediate profits were nugatory; the longer-term effects on the readers' expectations were considerable—and entirely negative. In a critical year of the magazine's development, a year of wide-ranging issues (including sex) which were driving our circulation to unprecedented heights, a year in which post-Watergate, post-Vietnam, post-Woodstock America was fascinating every mind on campus; and moreover in the most visible issue of that year—we had told upwards of nine million people that what was first and foremost on our minds was cocky-doody, peep-in-the-girls'-room, teenage smut. Our attitude faced in absolutely the opposite direction to that of O'Rourke. His thinking cut out a group of Americans called "young people," treated them like sheep who would buy what was appropriate for them or products designed for them, and who would buy it obediently, without making trouble. This was exactly the attitude toward them in fact that Kenney and supposedly he—had satirized in "The High School Yearbook."

This formula required that the *Lampoon* give young people "what they wanted": "high school" humor, boogers, cooties, lungers, sex quizzes, Indian burns, semen-soaked socks, the works. They wanted this—see, it says so here in these circulation figures. So why not give it to them everywhere, in every project we undertake, every month? They'll keep coming back for more and more—boogers, cooties, etc.—time after time because they do what they're told. That's how they've been trained. In high school.

This conflict—which can variously be stated as the editors versus the marketers, sex versus politics, stereotypes versus individuals, or even as good writing and editing versus bad—was symbolic as well as actual. Never again did *The National Lampoon* command the circulation it had built up by late 1974. And the conflict contained within it the *gestalt* of everything that would happen to Boomer humor over the next decade. The reimposition of stereotypes, where satire had smashed them; the replacement of antiauthoritarian attitudes with we-know-what-you-want formulas, patronizing and elitist; the inability to recognize differences in approach, expression, and response, and the concomitant insistence that everything be retooled to one norm. But above all, the abuse and exploitation of an audience only too willing to give its support to genuine and well-stated dissent, and the consequent shrinkage of the audience (and loss of long-term revenue) when it was disappointed. A process that might be summed up as "fooling with Mother Satire," which it's not nice to do.

Intuitively I think we foresaw that the issue was the fate of what we now did for a living. Our aim had been to create a free port outside the normal shipping lanes of public debate, where the only passports required were wit and intelligence. All this was threatened by the thinking behind the "Pubescence" issue. As it turned out, this thinking prevailed.

Later, during the period Kelly and I edited the magazine (1975–78), O'Rourke's attitudes widened beyond the merely prurient. For one thing he began presenting himself as the only member of the group who had his finger on the pulse of America. (He grew up in Ohio.) He was American Humor standing tall again; the rest of us were foreigners and Jews. In his more friendly moments, he actually tried to ingratiate himself with Kelly and me in this way, as if anti-Semitism was the only bond we Catholics of the old guard had left. More often, though, we were lumped together with the Jews we had added to the staff as whining lefties. (To his credit he was at least being original—this was in the days before people with bad eyesight, no musculature, and Gold cards began referring to their opponents as "wimps".) He also made a great deal of using racial slurs in the issues he edited. These he claimed were included to shock our liberal sensibilities, as were the various aspects of misogyny he was so expert in. What they did to those who read them didn't apparently matter.

O'Rourke seemed to believe that because the original Lampooners had been satirical at the expense of authority, they must have been liberal or lefty, and that, therefore, by being racist or sexist he would qualify as a young Turk of humor. And it was the painstaking way this appeared to have been worked out that was so laughably humorless. It was much the same with another campaign he waged—to get the editor of a righty journal called *The Alternative* somehow involved in our magazine. Even if *The Alternative* had been a hoot from beginning to end, for O'Rourke it would have been the fact that it was right-wing that qualified for inclusion in the *Lampoon,* not that it was funny. (As it was the editor in question—an odious little fruitfly named R. Emmet Tyrrell, Jr.—turned out to be a graduate of the William F. Buckley School of Humor, whose basic technique is to drape great swatches of alliterative Latinism over gutter-level bigotry. The neo-Augustan wit left us cold).

In retrospect, O'Rourke's shift might have been one of the more honest things he did at the magazine. He never did understand the ambivalence that lay at its heart; it was from this incomprehension that his conclusion, we must be lefties, came from—and, indeed, his assumption of the label "lefty" when he thought that was the thing to be. And he'd been a lefty for quite a few years now. He felt like a change. In this respect he may have been more typical of a certain element among our contemporaries than we realized at the time. He became right-wing because he was bored.

But back in the fall of 1974 we had other things on our minds. For the day of reckoning was at hand.

After October 1, 1974, Simmons and Mogel were obligated to buy out the "brains" half of the original deal: Beard, Kenney, and dark horse Hoffman. Negotiations had begun in the spring of 1974.

The curve of the magazine's success could scarcely have been less favorable to Simmons and more so to Beard, Kenney, and Hoffman. The company was earning more than it ever had. Circulation and advertising at an all-time high, anthologies and other specials had made its earnings—on which the trio's multiple would be based, higher than anyone would have considered possible five short years earlier. What the price tag came to was $7.5 million dollars.‡

This was a staggering amount for a small company to absorb; the situation was further complicated by a market that in the wake of the war and the oil embargo was all but inert. The second underwriting Simmons had depended on to finance the buyout was absolutely impossible in the then-current climate. No one was interested—and indeed it seems unlikely that even in warmer climes it would have been that attractive an offering, since the buyout could involve the loss of the magazine's two most prominent writers.

Simmons offered "the boys" everything he could think of—to spread out the expense—money down and the rest at interest in regular annual payouts, or the payout in lump sums at designated intervals, but they weren't biting.

Simmons says, "Technically, they only owned twenty percent of the magazine but the buyout was figured on them owning fifty percent . . . when we made the deal in 1970, the publishing times earnings ratio was fifteen. So in 1975, when I bought them out, fifty percent of the magazine was worth 7.5 million. [Pretax earnings in 1975 were $2 million—hence net one million, the basis for the $15 million worth]. They were very uncooperative. They demanded their money. I said, 'You can put us into bankruptcy . . . or obviously you can take over the magazine, and since we've been partners on these things, I don't think you really want to do that.'

"They said they didn't care if they did or not; they didn't care about me or who they had to hurt. The fact that I had run this magazine and made them very rich didn't matter—of course, they had a great deal to do with it—but I had a few things to do with it too. I not only put all the money up, but I ran the company. They didn't care. They demanded their money.

"I wanted to pay them out over a long period of time. I wanted them to stay. I was willing to give them a million dollars a year for seven years.

"I feel a lot of resentment. I'd always been pictured as being 'the establishment' being the tough businessman, and I don't think that I treated anybody that way.

"As a matter of fact, Doug—which I did not anticipate—was just as difficult as the others. I had been very leery of this when we first made the deal. And they had said to me, 'You're our partner. We will never hurt you.' But they did. They killed me."

‡ Advertising in 1975 ($2,258,000) and 1976 ($2,617,000) would both surpass the 1974 figure ($2,153,000), but circulation would never again reach the high of 1974.

Hoffman's account is somewhat different: "We renegotiated, renegotiated, and renegotiated. They had originally committed to put up $350,000. When push came to shove . . . they got tight on funds. They came to us in the early winter of 1970 and said, 'We don't want to have to put up the rest of the money. The magazine doesn't desperately need it, so release us from that commitment . . .' We said, 'Fine, but if you've got a certain percentage of the stock for putting up the money, and you didn't put up all the money you said, then something should have been different.'

"We got twenty percent of the stock. We felt we should get about a third of the stock. But for tax purposes they had to have eighty percent—to consolidate. So we came up with a multiple that was supposed to compensate us for the fact that we really should have owned thirty or thirty-five percent. So our multiple started out at somewhere like twenty-five or twenty-seven. Then when we renegotiated—when they didn't put in all the money—it went to like twenty-nine and thirty-one, twenty-nine in cash, thirty-one in stock.

"When it came time to sell out . . . I made so many proposals, all of which would have been better than what happened—not better for me personally, but certainly better for the magazine. One alternative was for the five of us just to buy out the shareholders and take it private. And Matty said, 'I'll never own less stock in this company than Doug.' [Laughs.] Yeah, he made a lot of nasty comments like that. Well, anyway, we had enough of those nasty comments and we said, 'Fine, okay, pay us off.'

"[The buy out] was based on a formula, but what we ultimately did was throw the formula away. 'Cause who knows what the formula was going to show? The magazine was improving. And they felt by just doing a fixed price roughly equivalent to the formula, that would protect them, in case the magazine continued to do better. We thought it would protect us in case of arguments and everything else . . . In every step of the deal it worked out better for us.

"The formula was never calculated. We [also] had some negotiations going on as to what the earnings of the company were because they took fees for this and that, and we said those fees should not be subtracted. There was some fiddling as usual with what the profits were."

According to Hoffman, the process was indeed acrimonious. He recalls a Kenney outburst but credits it with cutting through the prevarication and precipitating the deal. The deal was actually finalized by July 3, 1974, in Hoffman's recollection: "We got an installment sale. They paid down a little bit of money in 1974, a total I think of $100,000, and then they had to pay the rest of the money, I think it was on March 16, 1975."

So Simmons had until the Ides of March to come up with $7.5 million. At this point, technically, all parties obligation to one another would cease.

There was much glee in the organization that Simmons was being taken to the cleaners. Part of this was his personality, which, however far he bent over backward to give the editors freedom, retained the appearance of the guy who's only interested in a buck and where the next cigar's coming from. But for all that, though, the man, considering what he could have done, had been a remarkably easy-going steward of a very dangerous and difficult territory. Until the "Pubescence" affair, he had done no more than make loud trumpeting noises when he disapproved of, or wanted something, and had left it at that. The salaries he paid were abysmal, and he had a tendency to make definite promises of bonuses or participation that turned out to be either ephemeral or negotiable. But it was an irritation more than a felony; it was hard to get really exercised about Simmons's peccadilloes. They simply didn't hurt enough. And in his own way, he was loyal. He never fired anyone in all the editorial wars and standoffs; in his own heavy fashion he tried to solve problems rather than assign blame. And though these solutions might have made as many problems as they solved, we were not dealing here either with Machiavelli or Mussolini. Everyone still had a job.

But there was a new element at work behind the closed doors of the negotiations that winter: however much some might have relished Simmons's resultant discomfort, the editors ignored it at their peril.

The real issue was what the magazine would look like after the buyout. Kenney was on a sort of permanent in-house sabbatical, hopping from one medium to another. But what would Beard do? Characteristically, Beard kept his counsel as the time for the reckoning grew nearer. The most common prediction was that Beard would take a long, well-deserved vacation, possibly for as long as a year, and would then return to the magazine. On several occasions, he had suggested obliquely that something like this was what he had in mind, and it was hard to imagine that he could ever completely sever his ties to what was his monster.

Gross remembers him saying that he could stay with the magazine for about seven years, then hand it over to younger people, who—he hoped—would edit in a way that would be incomprehensible to him. Both Kelly and I had heard him give vent to similar opinions at one time or another. Everyone had a sense that *The National Lampoon* was set to become an institution of some sort, and that his presence somewhere in it was a foregone conclusion.

Some of this may have been wishful thinking or reading too much into inebriated assurances. But Beard was family, too. As Kelly puts it: "It was hanging out, it was getting drunk, but [it was] also Henry has no place to sleep, Henry has nowhere to go for the weekend, Henry doesn't have Thanksgiving plans, let's have Henry over for Christmas dinner . . ."

And then there were the occasional promises of financial help. These had been tastefully implied rather than promised: no one would have expected Beard to do such things any other way. Kelly and McConnachie and I had taken the promises seriously enough to begin speculating what they might entail. Since both Kelly and I had families and McConnachie was about to start one, they were a factor in the whole affair. But as the time drew nearer, the mystery only deepened. Beard's cards got closer and closer to his chest. He socialized less and turned away all questions as to his intentions. His mood seemed short and distant. McConnachie remembers criticizing one of his pieces in the November issue at a subsequent editorial meeting: "He gave me a look he'd never given me before. Like I was his faithful dog and I'd bit him."

The neat construct we'd had of the next year or so—the magazine continuing to climb in circulation, mature in content and scope, all the money tension settled and out of the way—no longer seemed so neat. The first issues of 1975 faltered badly.

Finally, the Ides of March dawned. The "boys" eventually let Simmons off the hook by deferring about $1 million of the $7.5, but got the rest immediately in cash. The split was two-two-one for Beard, Kenney, and Hoffman, respectively. We were not aware that things had been finalized until the afternoon. Kelly and I went to Beard's office. We had a vague intention of congratulating him.

Beard came into his office briskly. His eyes were uncharacteristically bright, and he had an air of tight-lipped triumph. He sat behind his desk, with us lounging about as we had countless times, morning and afternoon. We asked about the deal, although we already knew it inside and out, and Beard explained the settlement, such as it was, rather peremptorily. He then embarked on a few remarks about the rumors he'd been hearing that we were expecting a slice of the pie, which, he said, surprised him because he considered that we were more than adequately paid. There were bonuses and additional royalties from the anthologies and other projects. We really had nothing to complain about. After a few more pleasantries along these lines, the interview drew to a close. Beard leaned back, put his hands behind his head, sighed contentedly, and said something so extraordinary, so devastating—considering who he was addressing, how long we'd all known one another, what we'd accomplished, but above all in the light of what the image meant to him, its savage resonances and connotations of misery—that it took my breath away: "I haven't felt this happy," he said, "since the day I got out of the Army."

Then he left.

And—to all intents and purposes—that was the last *The National Lampoon* ever saw of Henry Beard.

20

The Gross Is Always Greener:
1964 High School Yearbook Parody,
Animal House, and "Nostalgia"

When Michael Gross went out to Hollywood in the late seventies looking for movie work, it was natural for him to look up Doug Kenney. Kenney was now cock of the Strip, one of the hottest properties in town. His first movie, *Animal House,* was the largest-grossing comedy in film history. He took the penurious Gross under his wing, settled him in, and took him around his far-flung party circuit. At one bash, he grandiloquently introduced Gross to the assembled company: "Here is the man I invented 'nostalgia' with." It was a generous gesture and a lavish claim.

It was never easy to count the layers of self-deprecation of any Kenney statement. It's likely he used the term with more than a hint of sarcasm. For "nostalgia" was by now an industry term, shorthand for a formula which movie execs could see emerging not just from *Animal House,* but from "Happy Days," *Grease,* "Laverne and Shirley," *American Graffiti,* and many lesser lights. The formula: Make it funny, make it fifties, and start baling the dough.

Kenney could certainly take the credit for discovering this gold mine—he'd been puttering about in it since the first issues of the *Lampoon* almost a decade before—a time so long ago, one could almost feel nostalgic about it. And his first two commercial forays into the past, *1964 High School Yearbook Parody* and *Animal House,* had each been enormous successes. Both had been done with substantial assistance from others: O'Rourke and art director Kaestle in the *"Yearbook"*; in *Animal House,* cowriters Harold Ramis and Chris Miller (and an ever-increasing number of others: Every time you turned around in late-seventies Hollywood, you met someone else who'd *really* been responsible for *Animal House).* But Kenney was the link, the one with the sure touch, the total and telling recall of those far-off days before the longest war in American history, before dead and deposed presidents, drugs and demonstrations, before women in the boardroom and gays in the firehouse. He was the escape artist of his generation, your trusty guide to the magic land, where all that really matters is beer, zits, and tits.

Or was he? In embracing the term "nostalgia," Kenney was doing himself a (probably deliberate) disservice. For he knew better than anyone that what he had done was not as simple as the formula. Both the million-selling book and the $100-million-grossing movie were inimitable—a unique balance of regret and ridicule. They were satirical visions of American youth as much as goofy celebrations, and wildly successful for just that reason. The formula gang had hold of only one end of the stick.

The origin of the 1964 *Kaleidoscope,* yearbook of the senior class of C. Estes Kefauver Memorial High School, Dacron Ohio (otherwise known as *1964 High School Yearbook Parody),* was the ten-page piece from Ezra Taft Benson High School in the 1970 "Nostalgia" issue of *The National Lampoon.* In several respects, the *Kaleidoscope* is an elaborate expansion of the original. There are the same quintessential high school characters, the same carefully regimented excitements, the same breathless sticky sex, the same slack-jawed bewilderment at events in the outside world. In its sheer detail—from the principal's letter to tiny items in the school newspaper—nothing is spared, and nothing is cheap. There is a line on everything, from the senior prom to the sports record (which combines appalling scores with optimistic booster-ism: "Overall it was a tough season for our board-bouncing Bucketeers, but their play was as tough as the defeats they had to face . . ." And the classic football photo caption: "Unlucky fumble gave forty-eight-point lead to Harding Hyenas"). Every sentence buzzes with instant and horrible familiarity, from the callous, offhand, tenth-rate system in which the future citizens find themselves—but which is their only standard—to the universality of the future citizens themselves. Everyone in this book is at everyone's high school, whether it's the juvenile delinquent greaser (Purdy Lee Spackle), the brain-damaged geek (Rufus "Spaz" Leaking), the class clown ("Wing-Ding" Weisenheimer), Homecoming Queen (and Future Stewardess) Amana Swansdown Peppridge (a.k.a. "Fridge"), or the Feifferesque folkie and leotard dancer, Faun Rosenberg. But perhaps the single most important achievement is the parody's style: From beginning to end it never drops that quintessential yearbook tone of parroted cheeriness, the fixed bright smile glossing over the weirdness of surroundings, taking heart in failure, hammering home the happy message that these are "the best years of our lives." Against this wall of hopeful chatter, the dreary reality of growing up Dacronian stands out like discarded streamers after a prom. But there is nothing snotty about all this; the very detail, Kenney's love of every little twist and turn of the system, the stunning familiarity of it ensures that. It's revulsion and convulsion. If we think these were the best years of our lives we're crazy, says Kenney. But they're the only best years of our lives we've got.

To make sure they were getting it right, Kenney, O'Rourke, and Kaestle—when they began working on the "Yearbook" in the fall of 1973—asked everyone in the organization to bring in their actual high school yearbooks. Some twenty-five of these were assembled, from all over the country. According to Kaestle, the startling thing about them—wherever they came from and whoever or whatever was in them—was that they were virtually interchangeable. He only had to take one at random and reproduce its layout and content to have a perfect parody.

But C. Estes Kefauver, however much it was going to look like every high school in the country, didn't exist. If its yearbook was going to look right, it would have to follow that preeminent rule of yearbooks—everyone gets their picture in—and that meant a large number of models. The other sine qua non was that every activity, organization, course, sport, and special event that occurred throughout the school year also had to get a mention, which meant creating the illusion of innumerable action shots of the school at work and play. Last, since it was a period piece, set a decade earlier in 1964, clothes and haircuts in particular had to be authentic.

In short, Kaestle, who was to photograph as well as design the book, realized that what he really had on his hands was a movie. Trouble was, hiring a cast large enough to make a convincing parody, and for that amount of time, would also cost a fortune—like a movie. What they had to do was use an actual school for the location, and an actual student body as the cast. But how could they be sure that among the latter they would find the types they were looking for, especially those obligatory ones, such as the greaser and the nerd?

Come to that, how could they be sure that high school seniors would be capable of acting out their parts?

Columbia Prep is a private school in New York City on the Upper West Side. Culturally speaking, it couldn't be farther removed from a high school in mid-Ohio. But it was a convincing vindication of the universality of the concept that when an arrangement was made between the *Lampoon* and Columbia Prep to use the school and its students, they found every stereotype they had envisaged and more. Even in weird, privileged, un-American Manhattan in a small private school, there were all-American bruisers, greasers, nerds, wonks, wimps, blimps, cockteasers, pepsters, and dogs.

Kaestle had a lot on his hands. The project needed both careful planning and on-the-spot refining; under every major heading, there were sometimes dozens of scenes and actions that had to be recreated. The students could not be expected to act or improvise the jokes required by each one. They had to be posed. Furthermore, the joke had to tread a fine line between being credible as a yearbook shot and breaking the formality enough to be funny. The zits-and-tits kind of joke wouldn't make it here, for the putative officials of Kefauver High would not have allowed such things in a yearbook. The actions had to be either minor acts of rebellion, or subterfuges shared by the seniors and the editors but not by the staff, or something disastrous that was completely at odds with the smile-button caption. All of them had to be things everyone knew from high school. Purdy Lee Spackle could make a zip gun in the Craft Club, but not a Molotov cocktail. Kenney's total recall for the details of everyday high school rebellion, failure, or frustration were thus the backbone of the book. Kaestle says: "Doug was intrinsically funny—a fast-on-his-feet creative head. Faced with a situation that was half-there but needed something, Doug could bring it the rest of the way on the spur of the moment.

"The brilliance of Doug Kenney was he never forgot anything. All those stupid things you used to yell at each other and all that stupid stuff that I somehow thought only happened in *my* high school . . . he realized that, no, it happened in *everybody's* high school. That was his genius—realizing that this went on everywhere. In that sense, the yearbook was a classic."

The photography took nine weeks, and was enormously successful. Much of this must be credited to P. J. O'Rourke. This was his finest hour at the *Lampoon.* Not only was he responsible for the organization and coordination, but in one respect the project was as perfectly suited to his talents as it was to Kenney's: for detail, consistency, the sheer wealth of information about the protagonist Larry Kroger (the book you bought was supposedly his) was an essential factor in building up both Kefauver and the Dacron in which it existed. This kind of thing had always been O'Rourke's strong suit; with Kenney's sure guidance, he could amplify and expand any premise.

One of the best examples of this team-work was a piece that appeared outside the "Yearbook" proper. (The book itself comprised not just the yearbook, but a bundle of other school-related publications—a basketball program, a literary magazine, a history book, and so on.) The piece was Larry Kroger's "Permanent Record," one of the most sinister elements in the book. The Permanent Record is officially maintained by the Dacron Public School System, and its basis is "confidential" reports by every conceivable form of official and unofficial source, including the family doctor. It comes as a completed bureaucratic form and lists absolutely everything there is to know about Larry Kroger, and his father and mother and siblings. The Dacron School System knows not just that Larry Kroger has a birthmark on his right hip, but that his family lives in a "stable" neighborhood, that his mother's "real age" is forty-one, that his father has $1,920.35 in his savings account, that he is at the "peak of earning power," and that he "failed to volunteer for combat." The source for reports on the family's "community conduct" is checked in a box marked "Neighbors." The other possible "informants" as to the Krogers' community conduct, each with a box, are: "Associates," "Employer," and something called "XEX."

Larry's childhood diseases are documented; also marked are his "Dandruff" and "Acne and Pimples" boxes. Beneath this the form asks whether the above are "Socially Debilitating." A note is made that a cousin, Sheila Kroger, gave birth in 1957 to a six-pound boy "with no arms." Larry's personal hygiene is exhaustively documented. He gets only a "Fair" in "Eyes,"

"Hands," "Eating Habits," "Desk Tops," "Gym Clothes," and "Homework." His "Locker," "Notebooks," and "Private Parts" are all "Poor."

He is lucky enough to have been inoculated against polio with the Salk vaccine. According to the other boxes, though, he could simply have been given a "Control Group Placebo."

The most telling and lasting aspect of *1964 High School Yearbook Parody,* something which distinguishes it as a work of art rather than just another "nostalgia" piece, is that it doesn't shy away from its deeper and darker implications. The year decided on for the parody—1964—provided a rich bass line to return to throughout the book. The first dead man Kefauver's seniors had to pay tribute to was John F. Kennedy (see photo insert):

> We proudly dedicate the 1964 *Kaleidoscope* to John Fitzgerald Kennedy, whose tragic death marred the passage of this year at Kefauver High, a man whom we admired not for what he did for himself but for what he did for his country and we as citizens of it.
>
> JFK, perhaps we learned more from you than from any other teacher in high school. You taught us the courage of action in West Berlin, the wisdom of patience in Southeast Asia, the action of wisdom in our space race, the patience of courage in desegregated schools, and the active patient wisdom of wise courageous action at the Guantanamo Naval Base. You are gone, but you have left behind a legacy of peace and prosperity at home, abroad, and in school. And, though the Presidency has passed on to other able hands, it is you who remain "President of the Class of '64" in our hearts. You who might as well have said, "Ich bin ein Kefauver Senior."

The very fact that Kefauver life appears to be largely unchanged by this staggering national event is the best comment of all. The theme of the senior prom is "Camelot." But the seniors haven't put two and two together yet. Camelot is a fun theme. That Camelot's hero got his brains blown out a few short months before is to them irrelevant.

Then there is, the second dedication. Nothing could be more typical of a high school yearbook than a memorial to "the dead kid." Every school had one. Here's the dedication to the dead kid, Howard Lewis Havermeyer (see photo insert):

> Of all the pieces that are appearing in this, the *Kaleidoscope* of this year, this is, I am sure, the saddest piece you will read and one of the hardest ones to write.
>
> What I have to write about here is one of our students who is no longer with us, if you know what I mean, and it's not that he transferred or flunked out. His name was Howard Lewis Havermeyer, and most of us here on the *Kaleidoscope* staff didn't get a chance to know him too

well because even when he did come to school, he coughed a lot and sometimes after coughing he made funny noises, and someone once said that Nurse Krupp told our parents that we shouldn't stand too close to him even when he wasn't coughing.

But just because we did not know him, however, does not mean that he was not a real nice guy. He used to smile at people when he wasn't coughing, and he was supposed to have been really good at baseball when he wasn't coughing.

As I said, there isn't anything much a person can say about something like this. We all would have been a lot happier if he were still here among us, and what happened to him was certainly a bad mark on all the happy events of our young years. We had a wonderful time and wish he were here.

The picture of Howie is actually Kenney photographed at his high school prom.

More insidious bits of satire run throughout the parody. Hints of regimentation, introduction, militarization are everywhere. The hall monitors wear storm trooper armbands. Carl Lepper (a.k.a. "Fungus") is one of them. He is also chairman of Locker Safety Week, gym showering monitor, and a member of the Bay of Pigs Club. His valedictory on Larry Kroger's book reads: "Don't forget ROTC in the fall. Watch yourself. Carl."

As the book proceeds, it becomes clear that the principal is a crazed coprophile who leaves turds (known to student journalists as "vandalisms") all over the school. Football coach Vernon Wormer, also scoutmaster, fondles his Scouts. All the teachers are bent some way, either sexually or alcoholically. The outlook for young women is truly exciting: they are either Future Stewardesses ("career gals on their way up in the world. They meet every Thursday evening to practice friendly grins and balance") or they can join the Future Housewives of America ("Homemaking is the oldest profession in the world . . ."). Homecoming Queen Amana Swansdown Peppridge is not only Flight Captain of the Future Stewardesses, but a third runner-up in the Miss Teenage Dacron Contest. While she is standoffish to the horny kangaroos of Kefauver—she only dates "college guys"—her life, too, is bound for oblivion. She is American suburban womanhood in all its momentary adolescent glory —the pretty vacuous face destined to either sell or buy the brand names she was christened with.

And so it goes on, this hilariously grim "nostalgia." The student council has an entry worthy of the Komsomol:

MORE STUDENT FREEDOMS MEAN GREATER STUDENT
RESPONSIBIILTY FOR DUTY TO CONSCIENTIOUS PERFORMANCE OF
SCHOOL OBLIGATIONS

One accomplishment which was very fundamental to the functioning of our democratic system upon which America was founded here at KHS was the institution of a Student Suggestion Box. Through this new institution students are now able to place "votes" (suggestions) in their own "ballot box" (the Student Suggestion Box), thereby functioning as the "legislative branch" of a democratic government. Then the Administration can either "sign the bill" (by making a suggestion into a new school rule) or "veto the bill" (by not making a suggestion into a new school rule), thereby functioning as the "administrative branch" of a democratic government.

In Robert Sam Anson's panegyric to Kenney in *Esquire* in 1981, he writes: "[Kefauver High] was a *Paradise Lost,* an untroubled heaven of top-down Chevys and bouffanted girls, a nine-to-three nirvana where quarterbacks were kings, necking was 'mellow,' and nerds never grew old. Here in the homeroom of the mind Doug Kenney was safe."

Nothing could be farther from the reality of *1964 High School Yearbook Parody.* This escapist fantasy was imposed on Kenney's first great personal triumph by many. None of them, it seems, had bothered to read what he wrote. The top-down Chevy, if you read the yearbook carefully, kills six students the night of the senior prom (where much is made of the spiked punch). There are practically no other references at all to cars, one of the mainsprings of "nostalgia." (For good measure, television, that other playground of the craze, is mentioned nowhere.) The bouffanted girls are unapproachable bitches who make poor Larry's horny little life a misery of lust and humiliation. The Kefauver quarterback's nickname is "Flinch"—and he is responsible for the fumble that gave the Hyenas a forty-eight-point lead. The nerds, far from never growing up, are the ones who will rule the world with their slide rules. The word "mellow" occurs nowhere in the *Kaleidoscope* —it would be anachronistic.

The genius of the "Yearbook" is that it accurately satirizes every aspect of a system that calls itself educational but is itself wildly out of control. One of the funniest pieces Kenney ever wrote appears in the package as part of a high school history book titled *The American Spectacle—1492 to the Present.* After tense apologies for previous editions that have infringed on copyrights all over the world, the authors—Krok and Loon—under chapter headings such as "Philadelphia, Birthplace of the Cradle of Liberty" and "Jefferson Davis and Robert E. Lee: Bitter Fruits of War," launch into a spirited minihistory of North America.

At the end there is a test. It includes questions like this:

1. What were sea dogs? Was it difficult to walk one?
2. When Patrick Henry said, "Give me liberty or give me death," was he serious?
3. If the Indians had had the atomic bomb, would they have used it? Would you?
4. Who were the Quakers? Where did they get the idea for Puffed Oats?

Was there any basic contradiction between their pacifist creed and having their Puffed Oats "shot from guns"?
5. What do you think the outcome of the Revolutionary War would have been if George Washington had been born a horse?

This was Kenney, with his pedal to the metal, putting as much distance as possible between himself and that "homeroom of the mind." Yet the myth persists that the "Yearbook" was escapist. The million or so high school graduates who bought it in the fall of 1974 weren't escaping. If the "Yearbook" had been a plangent or boisterous celebration of escapism to some pastoral age of top-down Chevys and bouffanted hairdos, it would never have sold copy one. What the high school graduates bought was the whole package, the bare-ass cheerleader on the cover, certainly, but mostly the absurd world Official America had given them to live in during their formative years.

What Kenney had in his rearview mirror was a mad system—in this case, the all-knowing, all-seeing Dacron School System, whose surrogate is indeed a madman—and what it does to people. How it turns them into stewardesses and corporate cogs, stunting them from the minute they begin to know themselves and the world; how education, Dacron-style, far from illuminating its pupils, confuses them with its mishmash of fact, prejudice, and propaganda. How the only people who learn anything at Kefauver are the technicians, the assembly line units who move smoothly from precocity to responsibility and who have no discernible childhood. The "Yearbook" satirizes savagely the insistence on a preconceived stereotype of youth; the good future citizen, the obedient clone, who looks "normal" on his or her Permanent Record, another identical product of a free society.

What makes the work so irresistibly funny is its picture of our placid acceptance of all this, our pathetic attempts to please and placate people who were once us also, and who pleased and placated their way to the grotesque shapes they have now assumed. What we're laughing at are the shapes we bent ourselves into, and the laughter is a proclamation of our freedom from them. What we're laughing at is an assault on our youth, what was done to those "best years of our lives." There is such a thing as nostalgia, and a delicious and delightful set of yearnings it can be. But this ain't it.

1964 High School Yearbook Parody has been casually lumped with other products of a very different nature, those various expressions of nostalgia for the fifties and early sixties, which have been a considerable part of our literature and entertainment for the last ten years. The very success of the "Yearbook" has been claimed through this confusion as both a part, and further validification, of the trend. But "nostalgia" has inevitably a political dimension, nonironic and revisionist. It attempts to revalidate and even reimpose the dominant values of the period it "recalls." The force of satire like Kenney's and "nostalgia," in this respect, are in head-on opposition to one another.

The values of "nostalgia" are supposed to be "traditional" or "conservative" ones, but they are not. They are the values of the Official Fifties America, which is something very different. If the "Yearbook" is arrayed against any values, it is these it finds most ludicrous and most effectively demolishes. The question then arises whether the confusion is simply an innocent mistake, the result of some sentimental sloppy thinking, or whether it is a conscious effort to defuse the force of the parody's scepticism.

With the "Yearbook," for all its success and timelessness, the question remains one of academic scope. But with its direct descendant and far more widely disseminated *Animal House,* the question becomes culturally and historically vital.

■   ■

What *1964 High School Yearbook Parody* was to the American high school, *Animal House* was to the American college. At its center is the same Larry Kroger. Larry (Delta frat name "Pinto") is the same mild, ordinary, slightly bemused character as he was in high school. In many respects, his college is a continuation of the same dull, venal system from which he has just escaped. Faber College is an anonymous, fourth-rate institute of higher learning located somewhere in the not-so-wilds of Pennsylvania, hard by a town of the same name. Both were founded sometime in the murk of the late-nineteenth century by one Emil Faber, who was a pencil magnate. On the pedestal of a campus statue dedicated to its founder, the college motto is inscribed, one that could as easily have been the motto of the Dacron School System, "Knowledge is good."

The college, like the high school, is run by a similar ogrelike authority figure, the dean, criminal rather than mad this time, who bears the same name as the fooball coach of Kefauver, Vernon Wormer. His various delegates among the student body range from nasty to nuts. The heart of the movie, the fraternity that gives it its name, is a group of highly recognizable characters, just like Kefauver's senior class. The method of the movie, the detail and recall with which it is written, echoes the "Yearbook." No stone is left unturned, and the things which live under each one are ruthlessly scrutinized.

The origins of *Animal House* within the *National Lampoon* were broader than *1964 High School Yearbook.* There were two reasons for this and their names were Harold Ramis* and Chris Miller, the other writers who collaborated with Kenney on the script.

Ramis was the first participant in the complex and lengthy process that led to the *Lampoon*'s first movie. He had come into its sphere of influence thanks to Belushi, who had called him from Second City to join the staff of the "Radio Hour" when he took over from Kelly. Ramis, like so many other figures of Boomer humor, hailed from Chicago, where he was born in 1944.

---

* Ramis, among many other credits, was the scientific genius of the *Ghostbusters* trio, Dr. Egon Spengler.

He graduated from Washington University in St. Louis in 1966, landed a brief (eighteen-month) stint as editor of *Playboy*'s notorious "party joke" page, and moved on to Second City in 1969.

A tall, bespectacled, rather diffident man, Ramis has an air of reserve that belies a formidable talent for fast, broad humor. His personality was reflected in his initial response to *The National Lampoon:* "I liked that everyone had style. And that the styles were all different. Literary values were real obvious in it—that people had read things. It was high and low at the same time. I enjoyed that. Also it didn't seem as though anyone was making concessions to the audience. The combination of freedom—or license—and the level of reference being so high, and—on the other hand—shocking crudities . . . it was really working there."

Alone in the Second City group, Ramis seemed to understand the magazine, to grasp what lay behind its appeal, and what's more to care about it, something which did not escape the attention of the editors. On the other hand, this deeper appreciation left him frustrated during *The National Lampoon Show* in 1974–75 that launched Belushi, Gilda Radner, Bill Murray, and Ivan Reitman on their various paths to glory. Ramis says: "I felt stymied during that period. I never felt we put together anything that was as coherent as *Lemmings,* nor was it as good as the very last Second City show we'd done. In keeping with what was perceived to be the *Lampoon* spirit, we'd taken a really hostile, aggressive posture in the show."

While *The National Lampoon Show* might not have been the break for Ramis it was for Radner and Belushi, his demeanor did confirm to those within the *Lampoon* organization that he shouldn't be allowed to get away. Aside from anything else, he was the only member of the Second City contingent who was a serious comedy writer. In addition, he did seem able to reflect that special *Lampoon* combination and to an editorial staff depleted by the departures of O'Donoghue and Beard, and exhausted by the various show biz ventures of the previous years, he was a valuable resource.

This was significant, for Simmons had decided that it was time for a *Lampoon* movie.

Part of Simmons's motivation for this was simply financial. The magazine by mid-1975 was in serious financial condition, thanks to the thorough cleaning administered by its founders. At the peak of its earning power, one of the more remarkable successes in modern publishing was broke, and a million dollars in debt to its own distributor (never a good group to be in hock to). The only way out for Simmons was to make some kind of big onetime killing. Since the door to television had been closed by "Saturday Night Live," the most logical road to riches was a movie.

The other factor was Reitman, who was becoming something of an éminence grise around the magazine. First and last a movie producer, it was becoming clear that this mild-mannered, self-effacing man had some extremely shrewd and well-laid long-range plans. (Reitman was known to the editors as "The Horse" because he had rather prominent teeth, which he displayed often by laughing heartily at everyone's jokes.) Reitman, it seemed, wanted out of his provincial though successful Canadian business of producing exploitation movies, and he had decided on the *Lampoon* as a vehicle for the move. In 1975 there was nothing in the current Hollywood product that suggested he might be right; and it took almost four years from the inception of his relationship with the *Lampoon* for him to prove that he was right. Along the way, he gently pushed his way into a position of major influence over a major motion picture.

But there were plenty of false starts. First, according to Ramis, Reitman asked him to try to come up with a format that could transform the material in the latest *Lampoon* show into a movie. Ramis had a better idea: "I'd always wanted to write about college. I'd had a lot of those bizarre experiences that everyone had had. And I'd been in a fraternity. So I reshaped pieces that were in the show and tried to weave them into a story about a freshman at college pledging a fraternity. And it didn't work. It didn't feel like a *Lampoon* film. It was a little too sentimental and ultimately was an antifraternity statement. I called it *Freshman Year* and sent it to the *Lampoon* to be read. It got no response whatsoever. I felt estranged from the *Lampoon*. [Ramis was working temporarily with PBS in Los Angeles.] I suggested to both Ivan and Matty that I wanted to work with an editor.

"I remembered liking Doug and suggested that maybe he'd be interested. We started talking. First, Doug and I moved briefly away from colleges. We tried a treatment on a high school movie—because of the high school yearbook. Our premise was: What was Charles Manson like in high school? *American Graffiti* had been out with a slogan: 'Where were you in '62?' Ours was: 'Where was he in '63?' Our treatment ended up being called *Laser Orgy Girls*.

"The piece ended with Manson creating a laser orgy cult in the desert. He seduces innocent girls and brings them to the desert, and they worship these flying saucers. Just as Manson is about to be caught, he's whisked away in a flying saucer, and the time control on the flying saucer is set to Dallas, November 22, 1963 . . . Doug had a Kennedy obsession.

"We told it to Ivan and he said, 'No, no, go back to college. The college idea was much better.' So Doug said all right, if we're going to do college, we've got to call Chris Miller. Doug considered Chris the resident expert on American college life."

This part of the process appears to have taken place sometime in late 1975, although as usual with anything connected with *Lampoon* outside of publication dates, everyone's recollection is hazy. Early in 1974, Miller, who had by now become the major fiction writer within the Lampoon,† began to tire of turning out individual stories and began to think about something more sus-

---

† Miller's position within the group was anomalous. His distaste for the rough and tumble of magazine politics (as he put it, "I was into being a flower child at the time"), meant that he was also left out of both publicity and whatever internal ranking went on. For readers, however, he was definitely a star attraction; when he went out on the road to do concerts in which he simply

tained. His agent urged him to write a novel and the subject they decided on was "this crazy fraternity" Miller had been in at Dartmouth. Miller wrote three chapters, submitted them to Simon & Schuster, and was met with a round "We don't think so." One story, called "Night of the 7 Fires," was more or less a documentary account of Miller's own initiation into his fraternity Alpha Delta Phi. It involved a night of prodigious drinking, in which two pledges were required to travel around the campus and its environs, from one bonfire to another, submitting to various humiliations, drinking all the time, and "booting" the results. One of the pledges is named Flounder, and finds himself unable to boot, which of course is necessary for initiation. Eventually at the last fire, a frat brother puts a raw egg in his beer. He is so nauseated that he finally regurgitates everything at once in a vast "power boot," extinguishes the entire bonfire, and thus emerges as a hero.

Another, about Miller's sexual initiation, was called "Pinto's First Lay." Miller says: "These stories were very different from the things I'd been writing up until then. They were documentary reality, rather than the wild sexual fantasies I had been writing. Doug went crazy over them. He thought they were just great. And he kept saying to me, 'You oughta do a movie on these things.' And I kept saying, 'You're right, Doug, I oughta do a movie on this . . .' but I had actually not done a damn thing about that.

"Now we are back to 1976, as Doug, Harold, Matty, and Ivan are groping around for what their movie ought to be about. Doug said something like, 'Well, I'll tell you what I think would make a great movie and that would be a fraternity house like one in Miller's stories.' I don't know exactly what went down, but one day I was up at the magazine and Doug said, 'Come in my office for a minute.' And he closes the door and he said, 'What would you say if I told you that we were planning to make the *Lampoon* movie be about a crazy fraternity house?' And I said, 'Well, I would feel real bad about that, Doug, because as you know I plan to do a movie with my stories. I don't think it would be right.'

"So Doug thought that over for a moment and he said, 'All right, how would you feel if we asked you to be the third writer?'

"And I said, 'Oooh, well! Gee! Now that sounds pretty good!'

"So basically the deal was struck and I became the third writer and *Animal House* became a movie."

The various elements of *Animal House* were now in place in spirit, and occasionally in letter. *1964 High School Yearbook;* Ramis's original college screenplay, *Freshman Year;* Miller's fraternity memories; and two comics by Kenney that had appeared earlier in the magazine—"First Lay," and "First High," both illustrated by Joe Orlando and both of which, in largely unchanged form, found their way into the final cut of the movie.

There was also a balance of skills: Ramis's experience of how to structure comedy, Kenney's common touch, and Miller's graphically authentic power of recall.‡

It was Miller's experience of all the crazy things he and his brothers had done at Alpha Delta Phi, that was the most basic "source material."

And it was in this area that such disputes and disagreements as there were during the writing of the script arose. None of these appear to have had any rancor to them, but were more a question of difference of approach on the part of Kenney, Miller, and Reitman. "Back when I was going to write my own script . . . there was going to be an upper-middle-class mean streak, because things got pretty strange in a fraternity house sometimes, and I wanted to tell that story. It was much scarier, much more *noir* . . .

"Doug had always tended toward stories which reflected a universal experience. I had always tended toward stories which were my own peculiar twist on it. *Animal House* kind of wound up going in Doug's direction . . . everybody's story."

Miller, however, fought to keep a certain authenticity to his original experience in the final version of the script. Much authenticity was lost for practical reasons, but much that remained lent a certain danger to various sequences that in turn make them the funniest. But the driving spirit of anarchy is of real origin and was the driving spirit of Alpha Delta Phi. Indeed, some of the experiences Miller actually had, far from being "everybody's story," were positively hair-raising. Miller says: "There was an upside down sense of values [at Dartmouth] . . . There was a fraternity motto, a variation of the *1984* one: 'Sickness is health, blackness is truth, drinking is strength.'

"Blackness, in this case, didn't mean being [like] black people as much as it meant black as in black humor. To behave 'black' was a compliment in my fraternity and it meant that you behaved in a perverse way. Because we were sitting there in one of the straightest colleges in the world; this is a place that turns out Republican politicians and guys who head up big companies like American Express. There was a sense that 'We got four short years here, guys, to raise bloody hell because after that every one of us is going to be working in a corporation, or sitting in a boardroom, or an officer in the Navy, and we're not going to be able to do this *ever again* . . .'

"Alpha Delta Phi had a tradition. It went back to the postwar period when the guys who had been in the service started getting out, and going to college under the G.I. Bill. So all of a sudden [from 1946 on], you got guys in fraternity houses who are not a bunch of gee-whiz kids. They were guys who had been around the world fighting and fucking . . . and they brought their behavior into the fraternity house. By the time I was in this fraternity—I joined in 1959—there was about a twelve- or thirteen-year tradition in this particular house of being the sickest, wildest, craziest house on the campus. This derived from the behavior of soldiers.

‡ The three spanned the sixties in college graduations—Miller in 1962, Ramis in 1966, Kenney in 1968.

"My fraternity had its own hierarchy of mythic figures who had moved through it in the last fifteen years. And as pledges in that house we learned about these legendary characters.

"We all listened, wide-eyed and wondering, to these tales and tried to live up to them in some way. All this is to say you kinda had to earn your wings. And I remember this one fellow . . . who had not earned his wings yet.

"We were all standing around one night in the [frat house basement] bar, and somebody turned on the campus radio station. A news bulletin said that a boy who was being held in a half-hospital, half-prison for out-of-control teenagers had escaped. He'd gotten a car and he was being pursued by the New Hampshire Highway Patrol at high speeds over winding roads. So we all drank a toast to the guy, figuring he had to be pretty cool. We could all relate to him being a crazy guy who was being persecuted. And periodically, updates would come on about this guy, and finally there was one final news item, which was that five or six miles outside of Hanover, where Dartmouth is, this boy had gone into a tree and been killed. At this point, the pledge in question said, 'Hey, I'll see you guys in a while,' filled up a beer, put a fork in his pocket, and left. We didn't think much about it. Forty-five minutes passed and he came back down with a little smile on his face.

"He said, 'You remember that guy from the crash? We all agreed that that guy sounded like a pretty sick guy, right? He'd be good in this house, right?' And we all said, 'Well, yeah . . .'

"And so he set the beer glass down on the table and it was full of brains. The brains had been scraped off the dashboard with a fork."

Miller had no illusions about writing a movie in which teenage brains were scraped off dashboards, but the hard-edged reality of what he knew (not to mention its military origins) was an essential ingredient in the final script. *Animal House* is at its best when there is danger or death involved, and in almost every case where danger or death occurs, it is the result of some authentic experience of Miller's.

The real start of work began, according to Miller, in January of 1976: "It was a joyous, happy, very excited meeting at which the three of us threw ideas around and were just thrilled—the first moment when we came to a sense of 'Oh, this is special.' We sat in a restaurant called Casey's down on Christopher Street, and had Sunday brunch and drank Bloody Marys, and ate eggs Benedict.

"And we all agreed on that day that John Belushi had to be at the center of this house. A great animal. And we came up with the name 'Bluto' then."

The three started work on the first treatment. Armed with this, Simmons flew to Los Angeles two months later. That is, he may have. From this point on, once people other than the writers begin to get involved, the story of how *Animal House* was made becomes itself a comedy, and one which would give *Rashomon* a run for its money. The differing accounts of who made the deal and how, who guided the script to its final excellence, even who hired the director and cast are unintentionally hilarious. Grosses like those of *Animal*

House are powerful magic in the movie world, and several major careers were launched, and even consolidated, by its success. Its success was unprecedented (no comedy in Hollywood history had made anything close to the $100 million plus the film ultimately took in) and was itself a major precedent, opening up a whole new branch of film comedy, including many further hits. The credit for sowing the seeds is still, even a decade later, eagerly sought.

Whoever made the first move—whether it was a low-level assistant at Universal, or Simmons dealing "exclusively with the studio heads," or any one of the several others—a minimal deal was struck with Ned Tanen, then a vice president at Universal. In the early months of 1976, Tanen called for a treatment (a prose version of a movie script anywhere from fifty to a hundred pages long) to later be expanded into a screenplay. According to Miller, the script went through many rewrites in the next year or so. Miller remembers that the source of the many changes was Reitman: "We went through a number of drafts. Each time we would complete one, we would think we had done it this time. Then a week or two would pass and we'd go up to Matty's office and sit there with Ivan and Matty. Ivan would have long lists of ideas and changes and stuff that he had in mind, and he gave the movie a lot of guidance and pushed it in certain directions, which in retrospect proved to very smart, very canny moves."

Simmons's recollection is somewhat different: "I would either talk to Ned [Tanen] or Thom [Mount, Tanen's right-hand man] or Sean [Daniel, then Mount's assistant, now the head of Universal] and basically I did what I wanted to do anyway, but I would listen to them and if their advice was good I'd do it. Reitman was involved, but not actively. The work was being done in New York and Ivan was living in Canada. There were a number of meetings with Ivan, but not on an everyday basis. On an everyday basis, I met with Doug and Chris and Harold. On one occasion a couple of the guys went to Canada to meet with Ivan. Once or twice he came to New York, but it was all almost exclusively written right in the *Lampoon* offices."

Uh-huh. Here's Thom Mount: "The script took forever to write and the guys were totally crazed and Matty was a giant pain in the ass. We all started hiding from Matty rapidly, so we could get the script written. They would come out to California and I would sneak into New York, and we'd get a bunch of deli sandwiches and we'd start working in a room where Matty could see us down the hall. And we'd talk for ten minutes about what the script ought to be, and the minute he left, we'd leave and shoot over to the hotel where we could hide and he couldn't find us."

Mount is actually one of the more intriguing figures in this mix. Starting out in 1975 as Tanen's assistant, he rose like a rocket within a couple of years to become head of production at Universal, a position he occupied until 1983, in part because of the colossal success of *Animal House.* Tall, softspoken, elegant in dress and manner, Mount could not be less the stereotype of the Hollywood mogul. He looks, talks, and thinks much more like someone you'd find at the Court of St. James than severing arteries at a major studio. The sensibility he brought to Universal in the mid-seventies, nebulous though such a quantum might be, undoubtedly helped to get *Animal House* to the screen; while he had no exclusive rights to that sensibility, only someone of Mount's particular background and awareness could have spotted the project and cared enough to see that it was made.

A native of North Carolina, Mount was founding member of an organization called the Southern Student Organizing Committee, which in the wake of Stokely Carmichael's purge of whites from SNCC in 1964, established itself as a kind of Dixie version of the SDS. Its activities throughout the balance of the sixties included civil rights campaigns, sponsorship of antiwar and poverty groups, and union organizing throughout the South. When SSOC, like SDS, began to run out of steam in the late sixties, and like SDS began to split into nonviolent and armed-militant factions, Mount left the street for the more sedentary process of learning to be an artist, first in New York and later at Cal Arts. In California, he moved on from painting to conceptual film and video, shooting a couple of guerrilla documentaries in the early seventies and working briefly for such producers as Roger Corman and David Selznick. All of which—plus a proposal for a satirical comedy by Hannah Weinstein— brought him in 1975 to Tanen's office and a job offer.

When he accepted it, Mount set himself on a track that would make him one of the most prominent members of a select Hollywood group of the seventies—ex-activists with political backgrounds who opted to redress the system from within. That, at least, was the idea—since Mount was one of the first to take this step, he was the target of considerable criticism from purer souls, like his friends Paula Weinstein (daughter of Hannah) and Mark Rosenberg (both of whom also subsequently became studio heads). Mount still justifies his subsequent activities with Fidel's old axiom "working in the belly of the beast" (though being head of production for Hollywood's largest studio was not quite what the Cuban had in mind). In a more honest moment, he says, "I've always felt it was impossible to be both politically correct and get anything done."

The skepticism inherent in that remark is Mount's saving grace. And it was this that made him able to first spot and then support *Animal House,* as no ideologue would ever have done. It's unlikely that very many people within the studio system of the mid-seventies would have been aware of the political and social edge of *Animal House.* Even if they intellectually understood it, they wouldn't have had much sympathy for it. It took someone who not only understood those attitudes, but valued them as well, to unlock the studio door and hit the lights. Mount says: *"Animal House* is a serious film, in its own odd way. It's a film *about* something. It's the story of the sixties told against the setting of a college fraternity. It's 'Us,' the smart but socially inept outsiders, versus 'Them,' the acceptable, conservative bureaucrats and their progeny. We don't get asked to the prom, so fuck 'em, we don't wanna go to the prom. We feel like outsiders in our country, so fuck 'em, we're going to redesign the country.

"Those are the underlying basic beats of this thing. It's also very soulful. You care about people when you see that movie. I think *Animal House* does a wonderful job of talking about the odd emotional dislocation of college romance and men's inability to cope with the truth of what's going on in their lives."

What on earth does he mean? *Animal House* a "serious" movie? The story of the sixties? Men's inability to cope with the truth? Redesign the country? Surely it's all toga parties, food fights, and horny adolescents peeping through sorority windows. Wasn't this the first of the youth movies? Surely the weightiest assessment you could make is that it's well done and very funny, a wacky look at those harmless, far-off, carefree days of campus hijinx.

Isn't *Animal House* just good, clean—and occasionally not so clean—fun? Isn't this the all-time escape movie, a back-to-Eden romp through golden fields of beer and Bo Diddley? Isn't Delta Tau Chi the ultimate refuge, the fantasy home away from home where no parents dare set foot, the club of every boy's dreams, the house where you can behave like animals?

It's all of those things, just as the Kefauver "Yearbook" is a loving, rollicking evocation of everybody's one-and-only high school. All these things help to give the film its wide and wild appeal. But this is not all there is to *Animal House* by a long shot. Chris Miller found that it was in this area—fraternity hijinx—that he ran into most resistance from his colleagues. Some of this was consensual, some of it came specifically from Reitman, who obviously had a clear idea both of what he wanted and why the Lampooners were the people to provide it. Miller, in fact, found that some of his cherished memories of fraternity life—and some of the points he wanted to make about it—got subordinated to the larger points of the movie.

But Miller might not have been seeing quite the whole picture himself. For while *Animal House* was about fraternity life and the ambiguities of it, exposing these ambiguities was not what the film was really concerned with. Reitman's editing and Kenney's instinct for the universal ensured that the movie would be about a lot more than fraternities.*

■   ■

The backbone of *Animal House* is its villains. It is against the dirt in high places that all of *Animal House*'s energy—sexual or alcoholic, togaed or covered with food—defines itself. This ranges from the social—the fraternity system that wants the Deltas out—to the official—the dean who is in league with the fraternity and the local Mafia scumbag who runs the town. Through

---

* Miller was further frustrated later on when one of his favorite sequences, a more or less verbatim version of his "Night of the 7 Fires" story, in which pledges engage in "power boots" after a night of chugging, was removed just prior to filming by director John Landis. It's not clear whether Landis's motives had to do with maintaining artistic balance or whether he simply had an aversion to shooting projectile vomit.

all of it runs the ROTC—the military—kicking the shit out of everyone, enforcing every detail of campus life—including its kangaroo court justice— and even willing, in the end, to gun down fellow students.

From the moment *Animal House* opens, during Rush Week at Faber, this issue is joined. From the start, its sympathies are solidly with the dorks. Larry Kroger and his large potato-shaped roommate Kent Dorfman are not the noir ambivalent rebels-without-a-course of Miller's nihilist frat, but pure Kenney everymen. Kenney had come full circle from his own social ambitions, and their fulfillment as president of the exclusive Spee Club, to solid identification with the outsiders, the kind of nonentities who would never have stood a prayer of eating Spee dinners, or for that matter, *Lampoon* ones.

Their first stop is at Faber's equivalent of the Spee Club, Omega Theta Pi. Within seconds, Larry and Kent are confronted with three quarters of "the bad guys." Omega's door is opened by a psychotic crew-cut in a madras jacket, Doug Neidermeyer, student commander of the ROTC and Omega's rush chairman. The official campus military is quickly joined by the official campus government in the shape of Greg Marmalard, Omega president, chairman of the Panhellenic Council, a smooth-as-hair-oil future business- man, and then by official campus beauty in the shape of name-tag hostess Mandy Peppridge and Babs Jansen (cheerleader captain and pep squad leader, respectively). Mandy, of couse, is Amanda Peppridge from the *"Year- book."* The two blond-bouffanted beauties snicker behind the freshmen's backs, "A wimp and a blimp!"

The Omega living room is heavily paneled, its furniture is upholstered with leather, hunting prints adorn the walls. Blacks in white jackets circulate the canapés. In the corner, a smirking Omega tickles the ivories to produce a liquid version of Pat Boone's "April Love."

The wimp and the blimp are instantly classified by Neidermeyer, and seated with the other rejects, an emaciated lad with a huge nose and a yar- mulke, an African, a guy in a turban, and a blind boy in a wheelchair. Meanwhile, the cream of the freshmen are courted by the senior Omegas, discreet, well mannered, confident, dressed like an *Esquire* back-to-college fashion spread. A prominent peak in the cream is Chip Diller, a preppy supreme with the right kind of parents from the right kind of school, confi- dent, well muscled, with a winning smile, the kind of guy who looks good in any kind of uniform. Marmalard has spotted him instantly. Definitely Omega material.

"I'm not going to say Omega is the best house, Chip, but a lot of outstand- ing guys figure they'll pledge Omega or they won't pledge anything at all."

Mandy, who also happens to be Greg's pinmate, squeezes his hand and adds: "And though Greg would never tell you this himself," she purrs, "I can tell you that there isn't a girl on campus who would pass up a date with an Omega."

Modest Greg has the clincher—straight from the "Yearbook": "We do have more than our share of campus leaders. Something that never looks bad on your Permanent Record, eh, Chip?"

Chip pledges—he is later initiated in a candlelit ceremony, in which he crouches naked but for his underpants before a black-hooded Neidermeyer, who thwacks his ass with a giant paddle. "Thank you, sir," Chip sings out gamely. "Can I have another?" He gets it.

Omega Theta Pi is the definitive picture of everything Official America deems polished and correct for its children. It could have been a caricature were it not for the details, so well observed and well balanced. There is nothing brash or broad about the way the Omegas are portrayed: Their very discreetness, their air of civilization, is their most insidious quality. Greg and Chip both have carefully styled JFK haircuts (this is 1962), but old black men hand around their appetizers. The Pat Boone tinkler is a perfect touch. These guys are "hip." They are not cartoon aristocrats, the broad-stroke "Republican" of earlier comedy—indeed, one of the exemplars pointed out to Chip is the editor of the campus newspaper. These are the future leaders and owners of seventies America and the knowledge of their methods is intimate and detailed. This is conformity masquerading as individualism. Omega is the home of "initiative and drive"—an assembly line of identical rugged individualists, identical self-starting leaders, and identical executives who think for themselves.

From the very start, therefore, Animal House is firmly in the swim of Boomer humor. It's not only conformity and authority that get cut here; the complexities of sex get it too. Sex as a threat and sex as a reward are just as carefully built into the system in the shape of the beautiful ball-breakers Mandy and Babs. There is nothing chauvinist about the treatment of Mandy and Babs; they've opted for their roles. They're willing to be victims if they can thereby victimize others, wield their own kind of power.

And if Omega is the official heights—to echo Ramis's analysis—Delta is certainly the official pits. Delta is the embryonic Woodstock Nation; rambunctious, noisy, blissfully illegal, the haven of geniuses and outsiders, wonks and weirdos, rock and rollers and rebels. At its core (actually right in its front yard, taking a leak on Larry's and Kent's feet) is the animal of the house, Bluto, Belushi playing the best version since Lemmings of what was always his finest role—himself.

Raw force, the guts of the generation, but as harmless and innocent as he seems to be dangerous, Belushi is remembered from this movie more than anything else for his disgustoid bodily emissions, but one of the most delightful things about his performance is its playfulness. Whenever Bluto moves, it is on his toes, quickly, mischievously, a fiendish, eyebrow-wagging grin on his face, as if he knew he only had a few precious seconds to break yet another rule. Whether he's dancing the slop, the bop, and the mashed potato, or darting up the steps to the dean's office, or swashbuckling his way across Main Street, Belushi is as light on his feet as Ralph Kramden, never clumsy, but always extreme. Perhaps some of his actions are gross, and why not? He's an animal. But in Belushi's naughty, big-baby hands Bluto's grossness is delicious and unthreatening. Bluto is all instinct, but his fulfillment of his urges harms no one; his satisfaction never involves someone else's loss. His energy is simply energy; neither sexual nor violent, just natural and animal, only dangerous if it is caged. Belushi is eternal youth, steamrolling convention, reinventing life, busting with sap, disrupting his surroundings by merely being alive, unsentimental, unambitious, unreflective. Bluto is the Peter Pan of *Animal House.* "Damn," he says when the Deltas are finally expelled, "seven years of college down the drain."

Inside Delta Tau Chi, beyond the bottle-chucking, rock and rolling chaos, are similar originals. "The best things in life are free" screams the jukebox, as the wimp and the blimp are sucked into a joyous madness, something the Omegas don't—and never will—understand.

There's the amazing Otter, the ultimate free spirit, smooth operator par excellence, with his bedroom eyes (and nose and tongue and lips), and his utterly amoral need to lay the entire female half of the planet. The embodiment of sexual opportunism, painfully sharp and handsome, a man who could have been an Omega, a future salesman, or even President had he not chosen to listen to his crotch. But Otter is much more than a libertine. He is the Delta's true number one, the leader of the unleadable. Not because of his sexual prowess, but because he knows all the moves, all the angles, all the clichés—and is therefore trapped by none of them. He talks *Lampoon,* the bilevel, sardonic wit that gives and takes at the same time. "We can do anything we want," he says, smiling smoothly at one point, "we're college students." "Let me handle this," he says in the Deltas' darkest hours as the Faber criminal justice system prepares to condemn them, "I'm in pre-law."

"I thought you were in pre-med," says a brother.

"What's the difference?" he replies.

Otter is that special Boomer skepticism that has been asked to believe in far more than any human ought to, and what's more, has every item down cold. When the Deltas, by now expelled, plan the final defeat of their enemies, Otter exhorts the hordes to glorious self-destruction and gets in a passing reference to Harry Truman and his defense of the bombing of Hiroshima: "We could fight them with conventional weapons," he proclaims, "but that could take years and cost millions of lives. No, in this case, we have to go all-out. This situation requires a really stupid, futile gesture."

His best friend is New Yorker Boon, the catholic hipster and drinker, lover of rock and roll, lover of the frat, lover of pleasure and good fellowship, and less certainly lover of good women. Boon is also the classic second banana who will—at least within the bounds of pleasure and good fellowship—follow anywhere Otter leads. Boon is the subtlest character in *Animal House,* for he is the truly American male, bound for nonsuccess but not failure, who drinks a bit too much, hazes the other guys, gets in late for work, prefers literal hardball to metaphoric—the seeker of everyday freedom. And who will one day be more sentimental than the rest about the good old days.

Reinforcing this is Boon's girlfriend, Katy, the prototype of the Boomer woman, already pulling away from this unreflecting male camaraderie into adulthood and independence, and as tough as the toughest of them. "I'll write you a note," she says, mock maternally, when Boon tries unsuccessfully to persuade her to go to the toga party. "I'll say you're too well to attend." But there are drawbacks to adulthood and independence too, says the movie. Think twice about throwing out those rosebuds you've gathered. The scene takes place in a Laundromat, and very, very faintly in the background, there is a baby crying. And when Katy tries to break with her Delta past and starts an affair with the only "cool" member of the faculty, English teacher Jennings, she quickly finds out that her desire for freedom is being used far more callously than anything she endured from Boon.

Jennings, although just a cameo role (played superbly by Donald Sutherland, the only star in this movie) is another razor-sharp sixties character, a jazz-loving, pot-smoking peacenik graduate student who has been to Greenwich Village and now returned to teach "while he finishes his novel." He charms his students by refusing to grade them, and disarms them with self-deprecation. "How long have you been working on it [the novel]?" asks Larry.

"Four and a half years."

"It must be very good," says Larry, much impressed.

"It's a piece of shit," says Jennings, smiling.

In a scene that is mostly Kenney's First High comic, Jennings turns Katy, Boon, and Larry on to pot for the first time ("I won't go schizo, will I?" stammers Larry), but it is not the act of selfless dope brotherhood it seems to be. For all his laid-back freedom, Jennings is a predator, feeding on the newness of his students' experience, on the youth he no longer possesses, and ultimately on Katy's beauty and naïveté.

There are others whose rightness to the time is just as perfect—Hoover, the Deltas' nominal president, completely lovable and completely ineffectual as an authority, one foot reluctantly dabbling in "the rules" and the other firmly planted in a puddle of beer. There is the marvelous D-Day, part biker, part technical genius, the Deltas' Leonardo, who knows how everything works, but will only *make* something work if it serves his purpose. D-Day looks like a Hell's Angel; he rides his bike up the Delta house stairs, but his .45 has blanks in it, and the Deathmobile he constructs for the climactic scene is not designed to kill, only to usher in glorious anarchy.

And there are still others—among them Miller, who plays a Delta called Hardbar, and Kenney as Stork, the ultimate wonk-nerd, sliderule ever at the ready, the very antithesis of his own Otterlike good looks.

All of the Deltas, but especially Otter, Boon, Katy, and the protagonist wimp and blimp (whose frat names are Pinto and Flounder) are carefully drawn originals; they could not be farther from facile, two-dimensional representations of the eternal college student. (In fact, the only eternal college student is the evil Jennings). This is no harking back to some romanticized notiop of what college ought to be, a campus *Paradise Regained,* a down-market *Brideshead Revisited.* The reason that the characters cut deep is that these people are—as Mount puts it—us. These are antistereotypes, sixties kids, a celebration of what is to come. This is not nostalgia.

Of course, there is abandon: The year, 1962, is carefully chosen, and we are supposed to revel in its preassassination, pre-Vietnam glow. (By setting their movie fifteen years before, Ramis, Kenney, and Miller neatly spanned the generation. The eldest of the Boomers had been at college in 1962 and the youngest were in college when the movie came out.) But nonetheless, the movie is about everybody's youth, not that of a given segment of the population. It is about the wild, aimless joy of the Second Age of Man and the horrible damage it does to those who think they have life down pat and their fellow citizens by the short and curlies. This is a far cry from wistful yearning for a simpler, more innocent time. Very little the Deltas do is innocent; and what's done to them is even less so. Never for all that it catches the abandon of youth does the movie make a value judgment about "then" and "now."

When it comes to the campus military, the campus government, and the campus sex system, however, the period element becomes critical. That these young people are trapped in a certain time and mentality, and are already tracked for their own individual disasters, is deftly underlined by fashion and appearance, and their obedience to the norms. *Animal House* cares most about the period it's set in when it exposes the conformity and stupidity of its villains. The Deltas couldn't care less about clothes, haircuts, and cars. They reduce poor Flounder's 1964 Lincoln to a junker in one road trip. Only the stuffy, idiotic "winners" of Omega care about madras jackets, sports cars, smoking pipes, and whether their girls are mademoiselles. When it comes to Kennedy and Kennedy-era styles, it is the Omegas who care. The Omega homecoming float has a Kennedy head with a halo labeled THE NEW FRONTIER. The Omegas are pro-Administration, whatever the Administration. Thus *Animal House* is not even nostalgic in the sense of revival, for everything that is of the period is a metaphor for what its writers (and heros) most despise. *Animal House* is far less interested in telling us what fun the early sixties were than it is in telling us where the rest of the sixties came from.

Nowhere is this clearer than in the adventures of the Deltas. For everything we like best about the movie is completely and disastrously *illegal.*

The one person who stands in the way of the Deltas' wild urges is the arch villain, Dean Wormer. Wormer is the one from whom all repression flows, who despises the Deltas on principle, and whose only goal is to see them gone and destroyed forever. To achieve this end, any means are justifiable. Wormer conforms to none of the models of the college dean that precede him; he is neither bumbling nor academic, nor even a bluenose. He has no morals, and no interest in education. Grades are simply a weapon to Wormer, part of his all-encompassing structure of enforcement which includes, naturally, the student institutions headed up by Greg and Neidermeyer. From the moment we first see him, it is clear this deliciously venal, hysterical, vicious, and manipulative slimeball is—if he is anything or anybody—Richard Nixon.

We first meet Wormer closeted in his office with Greg, the day after Rush Week. The discussion of which is the worst fraternity on campus gets Greg burbling obedient guff about "all of them being outstanding in their own ways," which Wormer abruptly ends with "Cut the horseshit, boy." The expletive is the first official one of the movie; to a mid-seventies audience, the reference to someone in high office with a dirty mouth was instantly recognizable, thanks to the scores of "expletive deleteds" from the Watergate transcripts. He does it again a few seconds later when he instructs Greg to use all means at his disposal—fair or foul—to get something on the Deltas. Greg should also involve Neidermeyer, opines the august dean, "He's a sneaky little shit, just like you." Greg, loyal flunky that he is, takes this abuse on the chin, but asks if there's any basis for the dean's extreme measures. With demonic relish, Wormer responds in the most Nixonian way possible, citing the hallowed laws of Faber College to justify his base actions: "There is a little-known codicil to the Faber College Constitution that gives the dean unlimited power to preserve order in times of campus emergency."

This has further resonance of Nixon's meretricious appeals to the Constitution to justify his illegal activities—and one which struck sixties-tuned ears with complete familiarity. The idea of a dean invoking presidential war powers to crush a dissolute fraternity is pretty funny; it works just as well if you choose to see Wormer symbolically as the man who ran the White House at both the beginning and the end of the sixties.†

The next day sees Dean Wormer in Nixonian high gear, entertaining the mayor of the town of Faber, Carmine De Pasto, re: the homecoming parade. For the use of the streets of Faber, the laconic Sicilian wishes payment. Wormer makes a jocular faux pas. "Carmine, I don't think it's fair to extort money from the college."

Replies the capo, "You use my police, my sanitation people, my Oldsmobiles [he owns the local dealership, natch], you pay. You mention extortion again, I have your legs broken."

"I'm sure I can arrange an honorarium from the student fund," purrs Wormer.

Animal House's most famous sequence, the toga party, far from being a happy wallow in the good old days—when dances were dances and girls put out on spiked punch—is a wild act of defiance, the only response the powerless Deltas have to the all-powerful dean, an out of control "up-yours" from youth to authority. Its sex is just as carefully calibrated. For far from being the orgy Katy insists to Boon it would be, the sex that actually occurs at the toga party is a further extension—in fact, a physical one—of "up-yours." There are two sex episodes at the toga party, and both are acts of revenge. Otter, who has met Marian Wormer, the dean's alcoholic wife, in a supermar-

† Wormer even has a petrified secretary who is a dead ringer for Rosemary Woods.

ket, invites her to the party and when she shows up, beds her. Pinto chats up the checkout girl in the same market and invites *her*. She shows up and although he doesn't actually get to home base, there is the appearance of his having done so when he returns the hopelessly drunk teenager to her father's home—the mansion of Mayor Carmine De Pasto.

This animal response on the part of the Deltas leads to the next escalation by Wormer of the war on puberty. The Deltas have violated both town and gown. They are to be tried by a student court, over which Greg and Neidermeyer preside. It is hopelessly rigged, of course, with Wormer calling all the shots—once again the Nixonian flavor of courtroom shenanigans where the strings are being pulled by the man at the top. Despite Otter's defense summation, the fraternity loses its charter. Their response is another of *Animal House*'s best-known sequences—a road trip.

The brothers commandeer Flounder's Lincoln and career off into the night. Their objective (or at least Otter's) is to pick up some girls at a neighboring all-girls' campus, Emily Dickinson. Emily Dickinson is the quintessential liberal arts college, and most of its students have Jewish names. One of them, Fawn Leibowitz, according to the local paper, is dead—in a "tragic kiln explosion." Otter shows up, posing as her fiancé who hasn't heard yet about the tragic kiln explosion and is treated with great sympathy by the sensitive and caring young ladies of Emily Dickinson, in particular a large-breasted young beauty called Shelly Dubinsky, Fawn's (ex-)roommate. She succors the inconsolable Otter and provides Boon, Flounder, and Pinto with further beauties from the lefty depths. They all end up in a roadhouse called the Dexter Lake Club, which is exclusively black.

There follows one of the funniest sequences of *Animal House*. Otter, who remarks upon entering the roadhouse, "We are going to die," is also keen to get under the sensitive, caring sweater of Ms. Dubinsky. He hightails it in tears to the backseat of the Lincoln and she, sensing drama, follows. She does her best to console him. Boon, who has precipitated the roadhouse crisis because the rhythm and blues group playing there is the same one he hired for the toga party, tries to establish contact with the band. "Hey, Otis, my man!" he yells at the lead singer and is met with a stone wall of black hostility.

The details of this sequence are delicious. Pinto nervously asks his nervous date what she's studying. "Primitive cultures," she snaps. Onstage, the backup group is singing a very cool chorus of "Papa-Oom-Mau-Mau." Eventually, an enormous black man appears at the liberal arts table. He asks Boon if "we" can dance with the "dates." Boon, Flounder, and Pinto don't mind at all. The liberal arts majors get to see civil rights at work in their own backyard.

Interestingly, this sequence was one of the few that involved internal disagreement at Universal. Tanen wanted it out of the final cut of the movie, claiming that it was offensive to black people and that they would "tear the seats right out of the theater" when they saw it. Mount, who had grown up, as he put it, "around many black people," insisted it stay in. It did and it has not been recorded that any black people ever tore the seats right out of any theaters.

Animal House now moves to its conclusion, thanks once more to the dean. The Deltas' grade point average is all but zero. He is beside himself with glee. Victory is within his grasp. They are all summarily expelled.

There follows a rousing speech to the inert Deltas by Bluto, which goes something like this: "What's all this lying around shit? We just gonna take this? What? Over? Nothing's over till we say it is! Was it over when the Germans bombed Pearl Harbor? Hell *no!*"

But in Bluto's rousing finale there is one phrase that stands out. It is the core of *Animal House,* the key to its attitude, the prophecy of Boomer strength, the proclamation of power: *"Nothing is over till we say it is!"*

And it isn't. From this moment out, the Delta-Boomers take over and systematically destroy town and gown. The homecoming parade is torn apart, in some cases quite literally. The Jewish fraternity, Zeta Tau Beta, for example, has a float glorifying brotherhood, a gigantic white hand, clasping a black one of equal size. D-Day's Deathmobile, a fearsome vehicle built on the remains of Flounder's Lincoln to look like something from *The Road Warrior,* rams the Jewish float, and the two hands prophetically part. The Omega float, with Kennedy's head and its halo, sports four Jackies wearing identical pink A-line suits with pillbox hats and white gloves. Two of them are Mandy and Babs. The Deathmobile rams this float too. (Babs loses her pink A-line suit entirely.) Finally, the Deathmobile rams into the reviewing stand, from which Dean Wormer—honorary grand marshal—and Carmine De Pasto, who will presumably have the dean's legs broken if anything goes wrong, watch the mayhem helplessly and sink into the splintered lumber.

Meanwhile, Stork (Kenney) has hijacked the marching band by stealing the bandleader's baton and then leading the obedient band down a blind alley and into a brick wall. The band all march, resolutely playing, into the dead end.

Back in the thick of things, as smoke bombs blind everybody and Neidermeyer's crack "Pershing Rifles" are brought low by Flounder and ten thousand marbles he has just thrown under their feet ("Get up, you faggots!" screams Neidermeyer. "Get up and fight!"), as float after float is creamed by D-Day and his Deathmobile and as scores are settled all around (Otter gets to deck Greg with a resounding left), Bluto, dressed like a Crimson pirate, cavorts on the roof of the local pharmacy, defying De Pasto's police, as Boon and Katy make up, as the movie draws to a formal big-finish ending, something very real happens.

Flounder, flushed by his sabotage, confronts Neidermeyer with a seltzer bottle. He's going to squirt his onetime nemesis in the time-honored fashion of funny fat guys. Neidermeyer, twitching with fury and frustration, reaches simultaneously into his breast pocket and produces a live round, which he slams home. Kent State lives again as he fires, point-blank, at Flounder. In his rage, he misses. The seltzer bottle shatters. But Flounder is transfixed. He is going to die. The homicidal soldier—in case you missed the Kent State reference the first time—now confirms that prophecy too by loading a second live round from his secret stash. At the split second Flounder's universe is about to go dark, the rogue black hand from the Jewish float trundles by and scoops Neidermeyer up, bearing him harmlessly away.

The rest is quite literally history. With the Omegas routed, campus military and campus government both in ruins, and town and gown in a death lock of mutual blame, the Deltas ride off into the future, triumphant. More or less. In the best comic tradition, *Animal House* doesn't end when it ends. Appended to the finale are a series of brilliant (and completely antinostalgic) subsequent histories of the major characters. Ramis, Kenney, and Miller have no illusions about who wins and loses. Nor about true love. Katy and Boon are married in 1964—and divorced in 1969.

Babs is now a guide at Universal Studios.

Otter is a gynecologist in Beverly Hills.

But the sharpest are these three:

Doug Neidermeyer, killed by his own troops in Vietnam, 1969.

Greg Marmalard, Nixon White House aide. Raped in prison, 1974.

And, just in case you had any suspicions that Ramis, Kenney, and Miller thought the system might be made to work . . .

John "Bluto" Blutarski, Washington, D.C., Senator.

Animal House premiered on July 28, 1978 in New York. Simmons held his premiere party at the Village Gate "for good luck," hoping the Gate would bring success to his movie as it had to *Lemmings.* It worked. The movie was not an overnight success, but it started well. The reviews, as is often the case with new departures in satire, were reserved, approving of its "low comedy" *(Newsweek,* Washington *Post)* and its technical prowess ("gags . . . effective in a dependable, all-purpose way"—New York *Times),* a sure sign that the reviewers had no idea what they were beholding. Charles Champlin of the Los Angeles *Times* was a little more honest about his puzzlement. He found it "paradoxically innocent and endearing" and Belushi "oddly likable," the implication being that the overall tone of the movie was sufficiently repulsive for these positive qualities to be confusing. Not a single major review even mentioned the satirical conflicts at the core of the movie; they either missed or chose to miss its political allusions, the deftness of its social observation, and its multilevel wit. To hear the press tell it, it was all about a gang of eternally childish slobs cavorting in a playpen of permissiveness. By the time Belushi had made the cover of *Newsweek* in October, *Animal House* had become "the new college humor," which amazingly was a "backlash against the seriousness of the sixties." Belushi was being pulled out of the pack as the spirit and prime mover of a film which, like other great events in Boomer humor, was quintessentially a collective achievement.

Audiences were not so dumb. They went, and they went. Young, old, collegians, and civilians. The movie was taking in $1 million a day (most films were lucky if they did this in a week). By fall, when Belushi was signed to

Universal by Mount, it had already taken in $60 million and was still climbing. It would not stop for another $40 million. Assuming that everyone went once, this means that somewhere between twenty-five to thirty million people saw the movie that year, and many, many more thereafter. It seems safe to assume to some among this group might have noticed that Dean Wormer talked remarkably like Nixon, or that Otter screwed his wife, or that Neidermeyer tried to gun down a fellow student. Sure, the toga party was great fun and, sure, toga parties were all the rage that year on college campuses (one at the University of Wisconsin according to Simmons was held for forty thousand people, an orgy worthy of Juvenal). But in screen time, these scenes were perhaps five minutes of a ninety-minute movie chock-ablock with event, conflict, surgically observed characters, and some of the best satirical writing since *Dr. Strangelove.*

You would never have guessed it, though, from the reputation makers. The secret of *Animal House*'s phenomenal success, according to them, was its grossness, its tastlessness, its willingness to go all the way, especially when it came to the Big One, sex. All the rest was edited out of the conventional wisdom. *Animal House* became a gross movie, built around the embodiment of grossness, Belushi (who was rarely gross and certainly not the center of the movie), and furthermore a youth movie, because (a) youth likes grossness, not being old enough to know any better, and (b) because since it had a lot of young people in it, it must be for young people.‡

The truth was very different. *Animal House* actually carried on and forward many of the major themes that had always preoccupied Boomer humor. Conformity, corruption at the top, the sanity of "insanity" versus psychotic "normality," sexual freedom, abiding contempt for the military and the lunacy it forces into everyday life, an intimate knowledge of the relationship between "education" and growing up American, official manipulation of friendly and unfriendly stereotypes, and finally, a clear-eyed sense of self-criticism, the redeeming ability to be hardest on your own.

True, these themes themselves had been dealt with filmically elsewhere—e.g., in *The Graduate* or *Easy Rider*—but never in their most irresistible and explosive form: satire. There had been earlier manifestations; *Dr. Strangelove* and *M*A*S*H,* for example, both maverick productions. Some cults had flourished—Putney Swope, for example; and more popularly, two of Monty Python's films, *And Now for Something Completely Different* and the superb *Monty Python and the Holy Grail,* neither of them in any way mainstream. In a different form, there was the persona of Jack Nicholson, which, from *Five*

‡ "Gross" has, since *Animal House,* largely replaced the term "sick." Both in its basic ambiguity and its use as a term of (sometimes simultaneous) approval and disapproval, it is virtually synonymous with it. There is a parallel between the urge to diminution evidenced by labeling seventies Boomer humor as "gross" and the earlier attempt to attach the term "sick" to the New Comedians of the fifties. Gross as a supposedly positive value can be found in the recent bestselling *Gross Jokes* series, essentially a regurgitation of sick jokes two decades before, and about as funny.

Easy Pieces to *One Flew Over the Cuckoo's Nest,* had a distinctive Boomer edge. Closer in were the idiosyncratic and highly personal expressions of Woody Allen's best films: *Bananas, Take the Money and Run, Sleeper,* and *Everything You Always Wanted to Know About Sex,* a brilliant string of antiauthoritarian, bohemian gems that ended abruptly with the "Me" movie of all time, *Annie Hall.*

But not until *Animal House* had a film appeared that, so thoroughly and uncompromisingly, not to mention skillfully, turned the system on its head, and wrapped up the cultural themes that had first been stated almost a quarter of a century earlier.

Certainly not until *Animal House* had such an expression been endorsed by a major studio and allowed all its resources of distribution and ancillary support.

And when this happened, when the producers let the real producers produce, stood back, and let the writers talk to the readers, the actors to the audience, the Boomers to one another, the result was more money than they had ever dreamed possible from such a venture.

But there was a price tag to this profit. The content of the movie. As Bruce had driven home twenty years before, movies are the repository of common values. The message of *Animal House* was highly disturbing. Not for nothing had the media called the *Lampoon,* in the reviews of *Lemmings,* "the heirs of Lenny Bruce." Now they were spending the patrimony—and in a manner their benefactor would have approved entirely. The *Lampoon* had brought to the movies the values—or antivalues—Bruce implied they lacked. The questions he raised in his best work, about these values and assumptions that are passed from movie to movie, were echoed by his heirs. *Animal House* turns the "moral" system upside down as surely as "Father Flotsky's Triumph" did. The delinquents carry the day, and the authorities lose. The line connecting the two—Bruce's parody and the *Lampoon*'s fulfillment of its spirit—is as clear as an interstate. Bruce would have found nothing to parody here. But more than that, Bruce would have warmed to the movie's implicit warning, the same that was at the heart of his work: Don't trust us. Do it yourself. Don't expect or allow anyone to experience life for you. And therefore, least of all, this movie. "You fucked up," says Otter gaily to his brother Flounder, "you trusted us."

But as the grosses rolled in like an oil slick off Santa Barbara, there must have been some furrowed brows in Hollywood. Here was a movie that inverted its cherished notions of morality and punishment. And no question about it, the audience loved it, soundly squelching the hoary argument for "decency" in motion pictures. Clearly, this lot couldn't care less. Or, which would be even worse, had always thought of the "good guys" as jerks, or thugs. What did that do to the next cop movie in which some guy gunned down a few dozen "bad guys"?

Conventional Hollywood insists, as does any other institution of vast cultural influence, that it simply follows where the audience leads. As Mount puts it, quoting Jack Nicholson: "We learn to surf the cultural wave." That is an oversimplification—just as it is to say that Americans like their cars and chocolate chips the cheapest ways machines will make them. Such interactions are far more complex. A dream machine the size of Universal is just as much a part of making the wave as it is at its mercy. People have to be convinced that they want their cars made of soft murderous steel, and candy in the shape of animal droppings. They probably have rather more freedom in such matters than they do in the range of ideas and emotions Hollywood feels is appropriate for them to experience.

Hollywood always tends toward what has worked in the past. "That's what they want," says the executive. "It says so here in these figures from the latest hit." "No, we don't," the audience might say—if it could. "That's what we got last time."

This process is supposed to be mitigated by the originality and audience-experience of directors and actors, and to some extent it is. What is always conveniently forgotten is that the range of choice has already been narrowed sharply by the scripts executives have bought, the "bankability" of an even narrower range of stars and directors, and by the day-to-day control most studios exercise over the course of their films through line producers and on-the-set functionaries. Claiming such a process "surfs the cultural wave" is specious. In fact, no enterprise that sets out to share its ideas and feelings with an audience is ever at its mercy. It must please them, but it cannot help leading them, even if it leads them into familiar paths. A performer is only at the mercy of his audience when he's walked off or he is doing an encore.

In the last three years of the seventies (the second half of the Carter administration), Boomer humor had overtaken rock and roll as the strongest surviving expression of the generation's ideas, attitudes, debates, and priorities. Furthermore, it was a far more comprehensive representation, since willy-nilly it dealt directly with those ideas, attitudes, debates, and priorities and with those who opposed them. In the struggle for the hearts and minds of the largest generation in history therefore, humor was a principal contender. For those with no sympathy for the positions that generation had staked out over the previous decade, it was obligatory that its humor be somehow defused, deflected, and discredited.

The history of *Animal House* and the "youth" comedies that followed in its wake is only one part of the history of the film industry in the last decade. And of course, the history of the film industry is only one part of the country's history during the same period, but it is a history in miniature of what became of a generation, and therefore of how a substantial movement of dissent in the nation that reached back to well before it was born was finally checked, dissipated, discredited, and perhaps even silenced.

The history of this period has to date been more or less exclusively written by the right wing. The basic thrust of that history is that the country was inexorably "swinging to the right" in the 1970s, and that the resulting Administration was merely reflecting its will (just as the movie industry helplessly reflects the will of the audience). The question of who did the leading and who did the following is therefore of critical historical importance. It cannot be proved that the movie industry made politically motivated efforts to undermine the ideas and attitudes, of the Boomers. But it is time we gave the issue further study than it's so far received at the hands of the power-lunch gang.

One of the more insidious axioms of what might be called "show business theory" is that, outside of those that deal directly with politicians, policy, or the major parties, its films and programs are strictly apolitical. While the election and re-election of Ronald Reagan should have demonstrated once and for all that show business and politics are intimately associated, this absurd dogma persists.

Many people interviewed for this book resolutely deny that their work has any political relevance, despite the fact that by now it is quite clear that both films and television long ago stopped being occasional entertainments for a nation whose attention was occupied elsewhere, but are instead fixed institutions in which it is engaged in ongoing and serious debates about itself. This is no less true of comedy than anything else, and especially true of movies, where character and plot and development are more concentrated and specific. The very avoidance of politics is itself of political significance—and usually impossible. Even fantasy, romance, or adventure fall within this analysis. One of the most significant hits in the seventies, *Jaws,* (written by Committee veteran Gottlieb) revolves around an official cover-up and one man's fight against it; another, *Star Wars,* bristles with politics—and religion for good measure. To call the films of Dirty Harry apolitical is laughable.

The assertion of apoliticality is itself political; it deflects both attention and responsibility from the makers and participants in the creative process. Given the analysis already offered of *Animal House,* the way in which its "imitators" dealt with its ideas, priorities, and attitudes will be seen to have a political component just as significant as its own.

Animal House (and the "Yearbook") were playing a dangerous game. Of course humor had been courting danger since Sahl first walked out onstage at the hungry i and said Joe McCarthy should zip his lip. And *Animal House*— despite the age of its characters—took some of the same chances. The leap into adulthood, where there are no friendly authorities to run to, no smiling, reassuring photos on the wall, no proud colonnades to shelter under and feel safe.

It was a dangerous game in another way also. By making *Animal House's* time and place so exact, just before the sixties proper, Kenney opened a large can of worms. And it was one that looked very appetizing to those who shared none of his ideas and attitudes.

Animal House was not the first movie that had been set so specifically— *American Graffiti* (1973) had been set in the early sixties, although it was not, strictly speaking, a comedy and certainly not a satire. It was similarly ambivalent about its time and place, and it gained much of its impact from the knowledge in its audience's mind that Vietnam and the sixties proper were just around the corner. Its television imitation, by contrast, had no such ambivalence. "Happy Days" was out in the open when it came to its opinion of the fifties. Neato! Furthermore, it tended to appeal to an audience too young to resist its simplistic Golden-Age-ism (in that respect, it wasn't nostalgic either, since its audience had no history to be nostalgic about). It was a part of an ongoing re-evaluation of the fifties that continued throughout the seventies and beyond, and which was an implicit devaluation of the cultural movements that had taken place in between.

Since, at the time, humor was acting as the most vital, continuing expression of the attitude and ideas of the sixties, whether in the wild comedy of Pryor or in the *Lampoon,* there was an effective public debate between the heirs of the sixties and the revivers of the fifties. The success of *1964 High School Yearbook* and *Animal House* seemed to ratify that "nostalgia" and Boomer humor were one and the same, when in reality they were nothing of the sort—in fact, were completely at odds with one another.

In its earliest form, the fifties revival was ironic—remember Sha Na Na at Woodstock. The revival of the fifties groups and the music that followed under the general heading "golden oldies" also exhibited a certain camp, a recognition of the music's simplicity. The same was true of using fifties elements in design or fashion, fifties clothes or hairstyles, for example, being worn with a certain irony, less a statement of style than of a sense of humor. Fifties cars were refurbished as much because of their outrageous size and shape and color as because they were antiques. And the revival of fifties films and television tended to concentrate on the truly awful—monster movies, for example—or the most banal of fifties sitcoms and adventure series. The total impression of the fifties was of a goofy Golden Age in which nothing very important happened and everyone got along with one another according to simple if wacky rules in a shiny, somewhat bulbous world.

Partly, the fifties revival expressed an aging generation's yearnings for the less complex experiences of its youth—and probably the curiosity of its kids about their parents' adolescence. Nonetheless, however much irony it contained at the outset, it was highly selective. Musically, there was no ironic revival of jazz or folk. There was no reference of any kind to the literary events of the late fifties or to the artistic upheavals. You did not hear of Beats in the fifties revivals; as Merle Haggard put it in another context: "Beads and Roman sandals won't be seen." You didn't hear of racial struggles in this rosy world, nor was there a hint of outlandish civil defense measures (except notably in *Atomic Cafe,* not one of the more widely distributed of the fifties revival movies). No hint either of its bland indoctrination, especially in its Catholic form; no pictures of Fulton Sheen adorned dormitory walls, no evocation of that most Catholic of decades, of rosary crusades and novenas unkept, made it to the screen, nor did we hear of the hysterical anticommunism of Pope Pius XII—all of it a shared and pain-filled and therefore hilarious experience of more fifties teenagers than of any other group. You could search long and hard through the various manifestations of the fifties revival without finding any reference—ironic or otherwise—to the intellectual, religious, and artistic ferment that characterized the decade.

This selective vision of America in the fifties would have been merely a charming historical footnote were it not for the fact that somewhere along the way—most probably when commercial exploitation of it began in the mid-seventies—it stopped being a joke and began to sound very much like the way things had really been. What began as an ambivalent recollection by Boomers of their origins became a simplistic celebration. It was not just "Happy Days," *Grease,* and "Laverne and Shirley," but "fifties nights," "sock hops," reissued records, "antique" car rallies, film and television festivals, even high fashion. Dion and the Belmonts were no longer the best because they were so awful; they were merely great. That top-down Chevy was no longer one of the most idiotic pieces of machinery ever to crush teenagers six at a time, but a "classic." The Bulgemobile had become a Hispano Suiza. Replacing ambivalence was a blanket revision of the fifties as terrific. What was extraordinary was that everything that was being revived was everything that had been, in the fifties, "square." Thus the idea of hip was turned—historically, at least—on its head. It was now hip to be square. Before one knew it, what had been a fond and ironic remembrance of conflicting emotions had been transformed—now it was a rerun, a revival of stereotypes.

What was being revived was not the historical fifties—certainly not those aspects of the fifties that are depicted in the first part of this book. What was being revived was a fictionalization—a version of reality that fifties humorists had already done so much to discredit. That idealized, sanitized America that had existed in 1958 in its images and sounds, in its sitcoms and beach blanket movies, in its commercials, billboards, and magazine pages, but not in its heaving social chaos and the terminal threats to its stability. An America that America might have wished existed in 1958, but which certainly didn't. A way back when that never was.

The giveaway word was "innocent." Quite respectable people began referring to the fifties as "a more innocent time." Now, one thing in the fifties that was arguably "more innocent" was television, still in what might be called its infancy, or perhaps its puberty. And it was television's "fifties" that was being revived here. Not social mores, or artistic styles, or even religious values—some of the more usual subjects of revivals, but television's intensely narrow and selective reflection of them. What people were being nostalgic about was television. Television was now not just a present substitute for reality; its history was a substitute for historical reality.

That was why in this depiction of the innocent fifties one never heard much about its innocent McCarthy hearings, or its innocent segregation, its innocent book burnings, or its innocent U-2 incident. Television hadn't known much about them in the fifties either.

Some of this has been explained by the fact that by the mid-seventies, the front end of the Baby Boomers were beginning to have their own teenage children, and these children were rebelling against the sixties look and sound of their parents. Why such children would choose to rebel by reviving the look and sounds of their own parents' youth is rather difficult to explain. It is not normal for a generation to consciously look backward for an expression of its rebellion. But to look for it in their own parents' youth makes no sense at all. The Baby Boomers did not revive the Depression "look" or sounds. They made their own. Similarly, Depression kids did not hark back to spats, burlesque, and the Volstead Act in reacting to their flapper parents. They too made their own distinctively new images and sounds.

Nor does the Baby Boomers' own participation in the fifties revival—"nostalgia"—explain why the revival has gradually been adopted by their children. Conceivably, the Baby Boomers as a generation have reconsidered their rebellion against the absurdities imposed upon them in adolescence. Conceivably, what began as a wistful remembrance of a high school prom photo has enlarged itself as a re-examination of the "values" that went with it. In that case, however, far from being rebellious, their children are the most docile in history.

What makes considerably more sense all around is that this is not just a two-generation affair. It is a three generation one. The generation against which the Boomers themselves rebelled is still very much alive, and very much a factor in the mix. The people who created the fantasy of America in the fifties, the impregnable Emerald City, bristling with weapons on the outside and well-behaved people on the inside, still retain a considerable degree of control over the nation's affairs—educationally, politically, militarily, electorally, and in the print and screen media.

The Boomers' days of raising hell lasted a mere decade. The Depression kids who fathered the Boomers and who bought and sold them the fabulous fifties were successful executives and producers and educators in the prime of life in the sixties and at the peak of their various powers in the early seventies. The truly successful and truly powerful ones are still solidly entrenched in the mid-eighties, as C.E.O.s, senators, editors-in-chief, generals, admirals, executive producers, superintendents of schools, etc., etc. It takes no conspiracy theory to explain why this generation—who had been appalled by the threat to their imminent power posed by their uncontrollable children—could hardly believe their luck when those children began sounding wistful about what they were supposed to have overthrown.

But it was more than luck. In the struggle for the future of American culture, fifties nostalgia was the point at which the Baby Boomers blinked. The minute they expressed a twinge of regret for those silly but lovable uniforms and codes of youth—wham!—they were back, and with them aggressive marketing, shameless conformism, rampant militarism. The minute they sighed over a yearbook picture, or a brown and withered corsage—wham!—yearbooks and proms were back and with them sexual repression, religious indoctrination, and grade-obsessed, get-in-line-for-a-job education. And the minute a film (albeit a low-budget, out-of-town) film appeared that seemed to celebrate those happier times of Frankie and Annette and Paul and Paula—wham!—teen movies were back and with them demeaning stereotypes, and fatuous propaganda about the family, school, the law, and filial obligation.

And it was not the Baby Boom generation this was aimed at. They had already shown themselves to be far too quirky and unreliable when it came to predictable habits. It was their children. Official America in the late seventies and early eighties was not about to let another generation pass out of its grasp. Their grandparents would show them what being young was supposed to be like, the problems they were supposed to have, the questions they were supposed to ask, the answers they were supposed to learn, the extents and the limits of their naturally high spirits. Just like it was supposed to have worked in the fifties. If, in the process, that unmentionable youth of their parents, who had dared to try to work out such things for themselves, could be expunged from history, well, son, so much the better.

With fifties nostalgia, the Boomers disobeyed that all-important dictum of Satchel Paige: "Don't look back. Something may be gaining on you." They did look back. Something was. Its name was Ronald Reagan.

The shoal of movies that followed in the wake of *Animal House* misunderstood, deliberately or not, both its structure and its humanity, what Miller calls "its redeeming sweetness." Over the next five years, such movies rang every conceivable change on words like "frat," "animal," "party," "high school," "house," "locker room," "weekend," and "beach." All the imitators exhibited a formula of a gang of horny teenagers or students, included a nerd, a blimp, and a stud, involved in getting laid, playing endless tricks with underwear and bathroom appliances, and beset by harmless authority figures. Some of them are set in the fifties—some not. Those that are are dated perfunctorily and are often full of anachronism, especially in language.

The most successful of these gang movies (actually a series of three) was the irredeemably repulsive *Porky's. Porky's* (1982) is firmly set in fifties Florida and if there is any doubt as to what the fifties revival means to its producers, it is quickly dispelled in the title sequence, during which a member of the core group wakes up and checks the length of his penis, and the following scene in which we meet three characters, one of whom is aggressively Southern and repeatedly corrects his pals when they use the term "colored man," telling them that where he comes from, the word is "nigger." He is clearly playing the word for laughs. Worse, he turns out to be the hero of the movie. Doubtless, this red-blooded and courageous expression of fifties nostalgia brought a chuckle and a lump to many a bow-tied throat.

What follows is predictable and never funny; the plot revolves around the efforts of the core group to get laid, chiefly at a neighboring whorehouse called Porky's, whose gargantuan redneck owner (Porky) is the villain of the piece. The other authority figures of the movie are the high school teachers, who are equally obsessed with sex, and the bigot kid's brother, who is the local cop and a good guy. The latter ultimately provides Porky with his comeuppance. The most celebrated scene in the movie involved peering through a peephole into the girls' showers; one of the group sticks his penis through this hole and the battleaxe girls' gym teacher grabs it and tries to pull it off. There is a minor subplot in which a Jewish athlete is subjected to anti-Semitism and is accepted, sort of, after he outboxes his tormentor. This generosity on the part of the group does not apparently stretch to "niggers" or to women. Needless to say, all the women in the movie exist to be laid; there are no friendships whatsoever between the horny teens and the objects of their nasty little wet dreams. The best the girls get to do is make catty remarks about the length of the boys' penises.

It's just about the same in the two sequels to *Porky's.* Even admitting that it was inevitable *Animal House* would be imitated, the debasement and dilution of its spirit in just three years is remarkable. At every point where its content intersects with that of *Porky's*, its values have been inverted. Blacks are not mysterious and dangerous, seductive but ultimately terrifying; they are simply "niggers," servants, and stupid ones at that. (The opening discussion of *Porky's* is about whether "colored men" know anything about cars. Later, another black man, just for laughs, of course, has to pretend to be a jealous, knife-wielding husband.) Women have no power—whether borrowed, like Babs's and Mandy's, or instinctive, like Katy's. They are pussy, which it is part of youth's right of passage to pork. The law is on your side; the villain of *Porky's* lives outside the law and the county line, where he is, alas, beyond the reach of the young bigot's heroic brother. Teachers are not sinister, merely idiots. The system that requires them, and that indeed requires young males to pork pussy, isn't mentioned. As for the student body, they are one for all and all for one, good companions or available pussy. School's fine, the law's fine, and so long as you get laid (though not by breaking the law in a whorehouse) you're fine.

The financial success of *Porky's* doesn't vindicate its content. It was aimed at male teens and was exclusively made a hit by them. The broad-spectrum appeal of *Animal House* was far different. Dollar success doesn't put every movie in the same category. No doubt many of the teenagers who paid for *Porky's* also paid for *Animal House.* They probably thought the two movies were in the same category, but the teenager could hardly be expected to catch the complex references of the latter. They might even have thought *Porky's,* which was immeasurably cruder and more graphic, a better buy. If so, the insidiousness of such a process of imitation is only underlined, for *Porky's* thus dragged *Animal House* down to its level in the eyes of its immediate audience, and in the eyes of those whom the original movie had either charmed or threatened. *Animal House's* quality could withstand the bee stings of the Frat-Weekend-Party-House kind of competition, but not the boot in the crotch of *Porky's.* If ever anyone doubted it, now they knew: *Animal House* was the gross nostalgia movie that had started it all.* Thus dissent is

* According to Simmons, a recent Harris poll actually showed *Animal House* to be still (1987) by far the most popular comedy of modern times.

contained in America by imitation, not limitation, by repetition, not repression.

Porky's also marked the end of any considerable effort to make comedies other than those directed at teens. Up to this point, there had been many other excellent broad-band Boomer comedies in the wake of *Animal House*. Monty Python's best film, *The Life of Brian*, came out in 1970, Steve Martin's *The Jerk* in the same year. *Stir Crazy*, with Gene Wilder and Richard Pryor in one of his best performances, followed in 1980, as did the lunatic and hilarious *Airplane!*, essentially the movie fulfillment of the parody line of the previous decade. Most significantly, though, the ever-shrewd Reitman side-stepped the monster he had helped create and produced two prime pieces of Boomer humor in *Meatballs* (1979) and *Stripes* (1981), both starring Bill Murray, who thus established himself not only as a major star, but as the one comic actor whose ideas and attitudes were still irrevocably those of Boomer humor. (In my opinion he remains its only standard bearer.) There were also two other excellent comedies that worked within what was rapidly becoming the dominant form of post-*Animal House* comedy: *Fast Times at Ridgemont High*, which came out the same year as *Porky's* (1982), but could not mitigate its impact, and the enchanting *Diner* (1982), set in the fifties and adolescence. *Diner* was unsentimental and adult about the fact, charged like *American Graffiti* and *Animal House* with foreboding and excitement at what is to come.

There is another line of descent from *Animal House*—the teen comedy. This variant differs from the gang comedy in the fewer number of bodies involved and the tighter focus of subject matter, usually adolescent sexuality and calf love. As with the gang comedy, however, the teen comedy exhibits the same misperceptions of the parent: first, that since *Animal House* was about young people, it must follow that it was *for* young people; second, the corollary that since young people like comedy, comedy must be their exclusive territory.

While the principle that people will only watch programs or movies about people like themselves is pervasive in modern movies and television production, it is both demeaning and absurd, and no less for young people than any others. (It would follow, for example, that *Le Misanthrope* could only be appreciated by middle-aged Frenchmen—and seventeenth-century ones at that.) The second misperception is more insidious, striking consciously or unconsciously at the heart of Boomer humor—that instinctive skepticism which marks the true adult of any age. The attitude that comedy is the way you express yourself before you know how the world works not only patronizes the young, but seeks to define all comedy, including satire, as childish. From the *Time* assessment of Bruce as a "kid" to the liberal Establishment's branding of the *Lampoon* as "sophomoric," this has been the voice of power seeking to devalue and defuse those who have its absurdities down.

King of the teen comedies is the redoubtable John Hughes *(Sixteen Candles, The Breakfast Club, Pretty in Pink,* etc.), yet another *Lampoon* graduate.

(Hughes originally came to the magazine during the period Kelly and I were coeditors, at which time he wrote prodigious amounts of material for the front-of-the-book "News" section.) While it's too soon to generalize about Hughes's work—for one thing his first hit was the highly successful *Lampoon* production *Summer Vacation,* starring Chevy Chase, a nuts-and-bolts family romp; it's for his teen films that he's best known in Hollywood.

The simplest and most important thing about Hughes's teen comedies is that they're *for* teenagers (and just for the record, white suburban teenagers). Hughes, who is a couple of decades away from his own teens, is not writing for himself here. His movies have another purpose, one all too familiar to students of Boomer humor: to create anew the stereotype of youth, to update and redesign what a thinking, feeling teen should be like. Hughes's movies are a highly sophisticated form of didacticism, a Laser Age form of patronage. They teach solutions, not questions; prime causes are rarely investigated. The misfits of *The Breakfast Club* never go beyond self-questioning to examine why society defines them as it does; this is diametrically opposite to the misfits of *Animal House,* who know beyond a shadow of a doubt where the trouble lies.

Indeed, when Hughes's comedies are compared to those of only a few years earlier, and the "values" they embody are examined, it becomes very hard not to conclude a political purpose in the narrowness of his focus. Thanks in considerable part to his influence, the assumption that comedy is for teens, and only teens will go to comedies, became by the mid-eighties almost universal in Hollywood. The teen comedy was practically the only one in which humor writers and directors could work—or, with a disrespectful glance at those who hate conspiracy theory, were allowed to work. The form became the Nativity Scene, the Annunciation of modern comedy-movie making. You could interpret it according to your lights (as Rob Reiner did, to great effect), but it had to be a Nativity scene or an Annunciation.†

The most recent deformities to claim descent from *Animal House* are the *Police Academy* movies. The first of the *Police Academy* series appeared in 1984. Incredibly, the pre-sixties extra-moral, antisocial, nonconformist frat house has now become the very bastion of authority, the college at which the upholders of law and order are trained. Every wacky guy and gal is keen to be a cop. However, these Deltas in blue only got the shot thanks to weak-kneed politicians who've lowered the entrance standards. That is the sole problem of authority—in the form of the stiff-necked but ultimately sympathetic officer in charge of their education. It leads to some real funny stuff, most of it having to do with guns. Of course, they're horny too, but not overly so, lest we lose faith in the law. And there are the usual cast of jock-wimp-stud, and so on.

---

† Mention must be made of the one *real* teen movie of the eighties, the hilarious *Repo Man.* *Repo* is brilliant satire, not because it includes the CIA in its lunatic mix, but because it gets under the Hughes stereotypes and does them and itself in, in the grand tradition. For this, its star, Emilio Estevez, is allowed to be a brat for as long as he likes.

By now, of course, the message of *Animal House* has been completely turned upside down. In effect, *Police Academy* takes the lunacy and energy of Delta Tau Phi—or at least the appearance of these things—and puts them next door at Omega. Even the Marmalards and Neidermeyers, says *Police Academy,* are Deltas at heart. Perhaps it would be best to let Mount, who conceivably, could have prevented the whole affair, to have the last word:

"It's an interesting shift in the culture—the shift from *Animal House* to *Police Academy,* the shift from a film in which an outcast fraternity, whose charter is canceled, rebels against authority that has political overtones, whether Nixonian or ROTC, to a movie in which our heroes are police trainees who want to do a good job of enforcing law and order and are prevented from doing that by an outrageous criminal element loose in the society and protected by coddling judges.

"This is a long, long decade."

■   ■

And what about Kenney? The man who—with Gross—had invented "nostalgia," the one who had taken that simple and obvious leap in the dark, back to everyone's youth? The one who knew and recalled every mad delicious detail of what it meant to grow up American in the second half of America's century?

After *Animal House,* he was lionized in the one place he saw through most clearly, hated most, and, thanks to which, his wild, supremely dumb, intensely smart vision had reached untold numbers of people. Hollywood vied for him, as it did for other principals of *Animal House,* but it was him rather than Miller, Ramis, or Belushi they most wanted. Hollywood's saving grace has always been that it knows where the true strength lies. Eventually, Kenney settled for Fox, a hot studio in the late seventies, a great deal of money, a two-year deal, and the usual accoutrements.

He then began to party. Kenney's parties tended to be either small affairs at which a few people ranted on deep into the night, or vast sprawling democratic jobs where everyone he'd met in the last twenty-four hours—from studio heads to waiters from Denny's—would boogie up, down, and sideways.

He wasn't very happy. However hot you are, a deal is a deal—and the money is for the next movie. But there was no sequel. He'd said all he had to say about growing up American. What happened to Pinto, Flounder, Boon, Otter was not sealed forever in the predictive credits at the end of the movie. Kenney's trick was recollection. And he had only one youth to recollect.

The problem was both personal and professional. Kenney had always felt a certain guilt at the success he attained by writing about what seemed to him obvious and ordinary. And from the professional point of view, there just wasn't another area of recollection that was as dynamic, comedically, as college.

He settled on a story about a country club. There was an element of recollection here, since his father had presumably worked at such places, but from the start it had none of the universality of either the *Kaleidoscope* or *Animal House*. There were only so many people who knew or cared about what happened at a country club. But it did have the potential of getting him away from recollection and into satire of suburban pretension; conceivably a country club could be a microcosm of modern American Life, the next step up for Marmalard and Neidermeyer, Babs and Mandy, once they survived Faber, and had gone on to visit their values on the big, bad world. Unfortunately, *Caddyshack*—which was actually done with Orion, not Fox—didn't turn out that way. The movie, which starred Chase and included a wonderfully lunatic performance by Bill Murray, didn't really make it. It did quite well at the box office, but was panned by the critics; more importantly, it was a creative mess that took the audience nowhere it wanted to go.

Kenney's reaction was not despair—which would fit the romantic version of his life—but rather cynicism. Weidman, who probably knew him as well as anyone, remembers two things in particular from this period. One was that Kenney had been poleaxed by a screening of the 1980 hit *Airplane!* This is understandable. It was not just that he was no longer the hot guy on the block —it was also that the movie, probably one of the best parody movies ever, owed its existence in some degree to that motherlode of parody, the *Lampoon*. The author of *Bored of the Rings, 1964 High School Yearbook,* and countless other parodies must have said to himself: "Damn. Why didn't I think of *that?*"

The other was that, before the release of *Caddyshack,* Kenney went Hollywood. Weidman recalls him calculating what grosses might be expected, and sounding a lot like any other Hollywood mogul. *Caddyshack* was by no means a financial disaster, and he had several other projects in the works.

None of which explains his death. The comforting legend is that drugs and Hollywood killed one of the better satirists of our generation. The reality is that he died as he lived and wrote, in a manner shot through with ambiguity.

In August of 1980, Kenney took a vacation in Hawaii. Part of the time his lover—actress Kathryn Walker—was with him. They spent a few idyllic days together and Walker returned to Los Angeles to organize the house they shared. Kenney was left alone.

Kenney had always done a fair amount of coke, but then so did most people in Hollywood at the time. (Something which no one now remembers, of course.) Kenney's use was heavy, but not legendary. It may or may not have had anything to do with the way he died. This explanation seems a little too pat, though—not unlike the conjecture that he had deserted the *Lampoon* back in 1971 because he'd just discovered acid. He had a career—and had survived a professional disappointment, he had a home and a beautiful lover. He had plenty of experience of what the drug did to mood.

At any event, he drove to a place called Hanapepe, about as far from the Castle or Chagrin Falls as he could be, walked down a dangerous footpath, and fell to his death. He may have jumped, he may have slipped. He may have slipped while looking for a place to jump.

His body was brought back to the mainland—not Hollywood, thankfully, but Connecticut, where his parents now lived—and an austere Catholic church. Hundreds of people showed up. Chevy Chase, who had become a good friend during the course of *Caddyshack,* gave a eulogy that was restrained and affectionate. A close friend from Harvard days, playwright Timothy Mayer, followed with another that was no less affectionate, but rather less restrained. His recollections of Kenney were often hilarious. The mourners who packed the austere Catholic church laughed, at first nervously, and then openly.

He was buried in a hillside not far away, watched by hundreds of people, most of whom in some way or another had benefited from the magazine he'd helped to found a decade earlier. One of his partners in production, Michael Shamberg, was inspired a little later to make a sometimes funny, often moving film called, quite correctly, *The Big Chill.*

21

The Morning After
the Party After Watergate:
"Saturday Night," Sunday Morning

Addiction shall be presented only as a destructive habit . . . The creation of a state of hypnosis . . . on camera, is prohibited . . .
—NBC Broadcast Standards for Television Guidelines
(General Entertainment Program Standards)

From a purist point of view, a satirical star is a contradiction in terms. Stardom is basically a technological commodity, possible only when the means exists to duplicate images indefinitely; one which is measured numerically by the number of tickets sold, sets tuned, money earned, units of entertainment completed. Stars are faces, not people—images, not presences; the very word is celestial, unreal. Stardom didn't appear as a concept until the technology to create it was invented. Personalities and entertainers up to that point might have had millions of fans (e.g., Chopin, Lillie Langtry, Oscar Wilde, Mark Twain), but the only way a fan could experience the presence of their idol was live, in a public place, in the flesh—and the opportunity to do even that came along very seldom. Such an experience was bound to be extraordinary—a once-in-a-lifetime occurrence—unpredictable both in terms of expectation and fulfillment, and human in scale.

Of none of the above is stardom made. What is awe-inspiring about stardom is that it is inhuman, mechanistic, infinitely duplicable. There is no limit to the number of times a star can be seen, or the number of people who do the seeing. While the image exists, it's not a person. None of our experiential equipment can measure it. Its ungraspable aspect is attributed to "star quality" on the part of the performer—that supposedly elusive fairy dust sprinkled on them at birth that makes them inimitable. Actually, far from being inimitable, stars are instant stereotypes, images that fall within the range of what society and its managers find acceptable and that convey attitudes that are containable.

The minute a star "emerges" from a film or a television show, or the minute a script is transformed by the presence of one, something other than art is at work. Whenever you go to see a star in a movie, you are to a certain degree, going to see something you have seen before, which mitigates the uniqueness of the experience. Whenever a star emerges unexpectedly from a movie, it is almost always—as in the case of *Animal House* and Belushi—to the detriment of the original enterprise. In either case, producers will describe the process as What the People Want, when in fact—even in the case of unexpected emergence—they have preselected all the candidates, have already measured the finalists against their standards of acceptability. That is why stars of either sex, or any supposed moral hue, are comforting rather than disturbing. Their job, even if their chosen persona is reprehensible (e.g., Peter Lorre, Joan Collins), is to be deliciously and unthreateningly familiar.

Stardom, then, with all its pomps and works, is grist for the satirist's mill. Since satire replaces the stereotype with the real, restores humanity to the unreal, stardom is, by definition, a target. To the degree that stars represent containable attitudes, and that show business is the aggregate of what is officially acceptable, satire of show business, as Bruce demonstrated, is just about obligatory.

A great deal of the resistance Boomers exhibited toward both stardom and television during the late sixties came as much from the antitechnological side of the movement as it did from any aversion to capitalism. What was disturbing about Hollywood's methods on either the large or small screen was that what it produced was not real. Not only because what it produced was intrinsically unreal—an image, not a person—but because it sought to create an alternate reality, one that did not square with experience. "Selling out," the great *crise* of the generation, was not merely about making a living, but collaborating in the creation of something at best useless, and at worst lethal. There was a certain elitist and puritanical guilt attached to making money— in some cases, any money at all, anywhere, anytime—but there was also the more positive desire to depropagandize the culture, to refuse to operate the machinery that created an unquestioned class of living myths and legends, of lies with faces. If John Wayne is America, said the Boomers, and Debbie Reynolds is the girl next door, if Jim Nabors is our Marines, and Sally Field is Catholicism, then the fault lies not in ourselves but in our stars.

Historically, the rise of Boomer humor and of television were coincident. Part of that humor's cultural role had been to offset the fantasy that television tended to create, to fragment the conformity for which it seemed to be specifically designed. Part of the reason for its peculiar intensity mirrored the intensity with which television could create fantasy and impose conformity. Television upped the ante over any previous mass medium in these areas. By the sheer number of people it could reach, the totality of its impact, verbal and visual, and its intimate, repetitive nature, television was better suited than anything that preceded it when it came to creating a single version of political events, culture, taste, morality, or any other publicly shared quantity. The element of Boomer humor that sprang from the individualist tradition, from resistance to the official and the received, was bound to be at odds with television and the uses to which television was put.

Even without the absurd and arbitrary censorship imposed by its managers, there was an intrinsic apathy between television and the humor of the first generation that grew up with it. Satire of television—meaning the satire of the conformity it promotes—has thus always been a major theme of Boomer humor.

As we have seen, one of the recurrent expressions of that spirit was for Boomer humor to find more direct, more human, less mechanistic ways to disseminate its message. Boomer humor was always at its best when it was not trivialized by inconceivably large numbers, when it was "live."* Boomer humor was not elitist about television. Often, quite the contrary. But just as often Boomer humor had no choice; it had to find a direct, live, human-sized, minimally technological forum whether it liked it or not. And as Sahl, Feiffer, Bruce, Gregory, and the improv companies discovered, impact, influence—even fame—were not necessarily coefficients of the largest possible audience. There were other roads to success and memorability than endless duplications of an image that approximated your features.

By the early seventies, Boomer humor had become so adept at finding ways not to rely on television that it was nearly independent of the Box that had once helped to parent it. Among its audience—those college-educated "future leaders" and presumably the future echelons that would support them—disaffection with television was rampant. On one side this was simply the managers' fault; they had excluded and demeaned that section of society, and they were paying the price. The fuzzy term "plastic" lumped together some very specific and well-founded misgivings about this device that had supposedly taught them what was best and most desirable about their country and its culture. On the other side, though, their victims' perception of television went beyond mere suspicion. It was television's essential nature. The fact that it was not real, except as a present object a few feet from your face. That it was not human, despite the parade of humanity across its screen. That it was incapable of spontaneity, despite its giddy changes of mood and content. That it was a machine, not a friend, a window on the world, not a means of communicating with it. Television was a technological hoax that gave you the illusion of participating in events you could never experience, but in reality

---

* Freedom of speech in the age that allows television to define the world and its standards has come to mean the freedom to speak to vast numbers of people. Far too many artists confuse success with access. As Pat Paulsen said, "Freedom of speech in no way guarantees freedom of hearing." Nor of distribution. Anyone is entitled to write or say anything they like. Getting it published or produced is quite another matter and not just for reasons of quality or merit. And the Constitution, alas, is silent on freedom of distribution.

excluded you from them, condemned you to a long-distance voyeurism, and in doing so, actually denied you the simple and mundane habit of human contact.

The people who thought this way were in the "eighteen-to-thirty-four age group." For the men who ran the networks, and the people whose inventories they were committed to reduce, the eighteen-to-thirty-fours were just about the most desirable market imaginable. Not only were they from affluence, they were likely to continue to be affluent. They needed all the things affluent Americans had always needed, plus a few new ones, like stereo systems. They were also starting out in life, which meant there was a lot to buy, both essential and nonessential. They were even tending to stay single longer, which meant every one of them needed stuff; there was less of this pairing off and sharing and making do with one car, one stereo, one apartment.

A lot of the *Lampoon*'s success in advertising—like *Rolling Stone*'s—arose from the fact that advertisers had a terrible time reaching the eighteen-to-thirty-fours on television. This wasn't because eighteen-to-thirty-fours didn't watch television. They just didn't have any respect for it, they refused to do what they were told by a box in the corner. For Boomers, TV's bona fides were "non." They might have grown up on television, but they had now also grown *out* of it. Television was for kids or cretins; at best it was a form of camp. The idea of buying what it told you and sold you was absurd.

For most of the decade that preceded the premiere of "Saturday Night Live," Boomers treated television much as they did cars or politicians. It was there, it probably had some function, but that didn't mean you had to like it. Television was fine for sports, or for major news events. (Indeed, one of the means by which television started to regain Boomer confidence was probably the Watergate hearings, and the systematic destruction of one of television's more repulsive creations.†) Beginning in the early seventies, a highly diluted form of Boomer humor began trickling down from the top, ironically most of it from CBS, nemesis of the Smotherses, whose executives had perhaps begun to realize what gold had really lain beneath those badlands. CBS was responsible for "All in the Family," "The Mary Tyler Moore Show," and "M*A*S*H" between 1970 and 1972, and much more thereafter.

But the new sitcoms weren't designed for Boomers exactly. They were more a palatable means of presenting worrisome social upheavals to television's traditional audience. As Rob Reiner points out, "All in the Family" did nothing to further any cause except Archie's. In every way, Archie, voice of the past, remained the voice of the present, reassuring in his very absurdity.

† When the Age of Television has passed, and its megasophisticated superpundits with it, one of the better books about the medium will still be Joe McGinnis's *The Selling of the President, 1968* (New York: Trident Press, 1969). The book is an account of how Nixon used television to remake himself in the 1968 campaign from a despised and ridiculed failure into presidential timber. Because it was one of the first books about this now-familiar process, it has a fresh and unapologetic incredulity about it which our latterday experts will never know. While it was intended as journalism and not satire, it is also therefore an honorary volume in the canon of Boomer humor.

Compared to the Boomers' medium of choice, recorded music, television was ridiculous. It left nothing to the imagination, as albums did or concerts. It was small and small-minded, crass and censored, incapable of conveying any message other than its own banality. And if Boomers had created a substitute star system of whose banefulness they were just beginning to be aware—a pantheon of rock images as unreal as the ones they had replaced—that didn't make television any better. No one suggested at the end of *Lemmings* that the generation's cure lay in getting back to the Box.

The National Lampoon mirrored this cultural phenomenon as it did so many others. In the five years of its peak performance, from 1970 to 1975, the *Lampoon* barely mentioned television once. There are perhaps half a dozen pieces out of as many as a thousand that deal with television in even the most oblique way. References to it, to hit shows, to characters on them, to newscasters even, are all but nonexistent. And it was not a question of snobbery. Television was not put down, looked down upon, demeaned as the opiate of people poorer or less educated, or less hip, as it was elsewhere. It just never occurred to the editors to talk about it.

In the period of the magazine's greatest influence, and highest circulation, most precipitate growth, and most numerous pass-along, when the readership could be as high as eight or nine million a month, television was to us irrelevant.

While we might be attacking the values television had taught us all, satirizing the idiotic values it helped to promote, to do this by directly satirizing, parodying, or ridiculing television was equally out of the question. The television version of reality was simply too discredited for there to be any points to be scored in making fun of it.

The significance of this is considerable. Obviously, many millions of readers agreed with us. Television as a viable part of our generation's development was dead and gone.

But this was also typical generational hubris, a naïve absolutism we showed elsewhere and in other matters. That merely by thinking something and feeling it passionately it became fact, a fatal apoliticism bred as much as anything by being raised on television, not people, from watching too many carefully refereed debates, too many ten-second news bites, too many happy endings in which truth, justice, and intelligence triumphed. We never seemed able to grasp the first law of political dynamics, that every action has an equal and opposite reaction.

Television was no more dead and gone than rock music had changed the world, any more than the military we had humiliated would now melt away, like the Wicked Witch of the West. Where money and power are involved, ideas provoke condemnation, moves mean countermoves, threats ensure entrenchment, victories ensure more battles. By doing without television, we only made television want us more. In fact, by obligingly grouping our audience in one place, we made it easier for its managers to quantify what they were missing. And it was not just a matter of the goods that could be sold. It was also a question of power; television could not afford to let us out of its grasp, could not allow so large and noisy a group to proclaim their independence, to declare publicly that they no longer needed their medium, or believed it. No, television was not dead and gone. Nor had our doing without it escaped notice.

■　　　■

The story of "Saturday Night Live" has been told, well and exhaustively, in the recent book by Doug Hill and Jeff Weingrad, *Saturday Night: A Backstage History of Saturday Night Live* (New York: Beach Tree Books, William Morrow, 1985). *Saturday Night,* the book, is comprehensive and meticulous. Every low is included and every high, all of it without bias; Hill and Weingrad's objectivity is as thorough as their research. While many people interviewed for this book were also interviewed by them, there is little that can be added here in the way of incident, and any reader wishing to know in detail the development and course of the show over the last decade is recommended to their book.

Much of what the authors deal with is, of course, available to anyone—the various casts, the material they performed, its reception and effect, subsequent careers or lack of them, and in Belushi's case, the end of it all. But their focus is so tight and their account so uncritical that the book becomes an unwitting document of decline, not just of the show, but of Boomer humor, and therefore in microcosm of the hopes and potency of the Boomers themselves.

One flaw the book shares with much writing about television is a certain sense of unreality, an attitude that nothing happens unless it happens on television. Books about what John Leonard, in his farewell to television criticism, called "the only American infinite" often exhibit this quality; one has the sensation of being harangued by intelligent but ill-informed junkies. There are vast gaps in recall, vast claims, vast achievements; vast numbers are thrown about without reserve, vast audiences, and vast reputations. None of it tends to make much more sense than the notes of an acid trip.

Thus, to hear Hill and Weingrad tell it, Boomer humor did little more than tool around on the fringes of the culture until the NBC breakthrough. No mention is made of the historical antecedents of the humor SNL purveyed. No one from the Sahl through Gregory phase is anywhere referred to; the casual reader would assume that Compass–Second City toiled in obscurity for twenty years until stars like Belushi and Radner finally bestowed on it the reputation it deserved. Even more oddly, considering the intimate relationship between the *Lampoon* and SNL, the magazine is barely mentioned either. At one point, the authors make the extraordinary statement that *The National Lampoon* was "only one of scores of humor magazines that flourished during the first half of the seventies." These magazines turn out to be the Stanford *Chaparral,* the MIT *Voodoo,* and Yale's *Bull Tales,* all of them campus humor publications with minuscule circulations.‡ Of the various *Lampoon* productions, from *Radio Dinner* through the 1974–75 *National Lampoon Show,* which provided most of SNL's original cast, there is only the merest of acknowledgments.

But if SNL's immediate antecedents are ignored, its historical ones are not. Hill and Weingrad assert:

> . . . the tenets of the show's political philosophy were that inspiration, accident, and passion were of greater value than discipline, habit, and control. "Saturday Night" was the first program of its kind to commit itself consciously to the subconscious, to emulate as much as it could the spirit of artistic abandon embodied and endorsed by the gods of twentieth-century hip. Baudelaire, William Blake, D. H. Lawrence, William Burroughs, Henry Miller, Jack Kerouac, Lenny Bruce, Ken Kesey, the Beatles, and Hunter S. Thompson were as much the fathers of "Saturday Night" as Kovacs, Carson, Benny, and Berle.

To be fair, given the authors' respect for their sources, this hilarious claim is probably not theirs but that of some member of the original group. Nonetheless, the implication that your average romantic or bohemian genius would have felt right at home with the Coneheads, or that SNL was just the first in a long line of shows inspired by *Songs of Innocence, Les Fleurs du Mal,* and *The Naked Lunch* exhibits the same crazed perception as elsewhere.

What we have here is not an incidental flaw. On the contrary, this altered state of mind is of great relevance to our story. Hill and Weingrad, like those they report on, and presumably their readers, are children of television indeed; deep enough into its alternate reality to be able to interpret all information in its terms, whatever distortions of fact or history might be involved. Within this Global Village of the Damned, values are inverted, its inhabitants unaware of the abnormality and unreality that is apparent to outsiders. How this self-delusion was accomplished and the extent to which it prevails in our society is evidenced dramatically by SNL, the book. Written from the point of view that television is morally and culturally neutral, both its method and its content demonstrate unequivocally that television is anything but; nowhere is this more apparent than in the pernicious notion that SNL, the show, was "revolutionary."

Certainly, if television is the yardstick of life and reality, SNL was innovative. But if television is viewed as just another part of life and reality (and therefore history), SNL was anything but revolutionary. It was not even subversive.

This was 1975. There was no war and no Nixon to revolt against or even subvert. In terms of courageousness, of real consequences in real life, what the Smothers Brothers had done seven years before had been far more dan-

‡ During this period, in fact most campus humor magazines were either moribund or defunct.

gerous. However paranoid Tommy might have been, the possibility of his meeting a violent end or of being a victim of violence was actual. In contrast, Hill and Weingrad quote SNL producer Lorne Michaels as saying, "The worst that can happen to us is that we never work again."

Revolution, at least of the simplistic "Us" versus "Them"—trash-the-system Jerry Rubin variety—had long been laughable. For five years, millions of *Lampoon* readers had laughed at it, and the hypocrisies of its privileged dope-sucking, two-car advocates. The networks, far from being impregnable fortresses of obscurantism, were actually moving into the *second* phase of seventies experimentation, the first of which, largely commandeered by Norman Lear and CBS, had produced a staggering run of "socially relevant" comedies. In 1975 alone, "The Jeffersons," "Barney Miller," "Welcome Back, Kotter," and "Chico and the Man," to name just the successful candidates, premiered, joining a familiar lineup of hit sitcoms that spanned all three networks, all of which had the appearance of Boomer irreverence and all of which took serious issues as the basis of their comedy. A dedicated conspiracy theorist might well conclude that NBC, having devoured every other manifestation of Boomer humor, now relished the idea of plucking the jewel from the forehead of its one remaining icon.

None of this would matter much were it not for the *claims* made, then and now, on behalf of SNL.

What is reprehensible about such claims is that they tend to muddy the historical fact: Far from being revolutionary, SNL was quite the opposite. Revolutions are beginnings. Systems change, new powers and principalities rise in the firmament, repercussions are felt long and far. SNL may have made many stars—almost every one of them for another medium—but it changed no systems and had no repercussions; it didn't even have any significant imitators. SNL began nothing. But it ended a great deal.

Examples of revolutionary activity cited by Hill and Weingrad in the early days of SNL include:
- Smoking dope in the offices of a large corporation.
- Sticking pencils in the ceiling.
- Writing on the walls.
- Stuffing the toilets up with socks and paper towels.
- Refusing to show ID to the (mostly black) security guards at Rockefeller Center, and on several occasions picking fights with them.
- Embarrassing NBC executives in the elevators.
- Routinely referring to derelicts on the street as "my agent."

"Episodes such as these," claim the faithful Boswells, "served to reinforce the belief of those on the show that they were a specially selected team of comedy commandos on a mission of truth behind enemy lines. They were united by their eagerness to bite the hand that now fed them."

Aside from the obvious observation that most of this guerrilla activity was directed at the working classes—the maintenance and security personnel at NBC—this collective attitude was prophetic. It was the appearance of abandon and anarchy that mattered, not its substance; it was the sound of dissent these people were after, not its fury. This revolution was lost the first day they showed up for work.

Appearance, not substance, was the hallmark of SNL from beginning to end; it was the means by which an unpurveyable quantity was purveyed—and squandered. Selling out is not measured by the amount of money involved, for that is always an unrealistic standard to apply to those who have to make a living. It is rather the betrayal of meaning, the abandonment of content, the trading away by the few of what belongs to the many. Ultimately, the sin of the traitor is not the money he makes, but that the enemy now possesses secrets that belonged to others—his fellows and compatriots.

To some, this was probably a welcome event; to others, it may have been an inevitable one, the evolution of dissent. But it was the first time it had happened in three decades of dissent, and it happened with the full cooperation and knowledge of the dissenters. The film industry had to find its own ways of diffusing and dispersing the impact of Boomer humor. The television industry didn't have to lift a finger.

More than anyone, the man responsible was Mr. Television the Second, Lorne Michaels. Michaels is portrayed throughout SNL, the book, as he is in the conventional legend, as El Cid of Satire, a lone crusader who invaded the Saracen fortress and, once inside, fought tooth and nail to hold the keep.

No way. Michaels was a one-man Muslim horde. In the yin and yang of television and Boomer humor, he was strictly yin. He'd gotten early training in appearance over substance as a writer for "Laugh-In"—his first American job after growing up in Canada. He had returned to the frozen North to do a two-man television show with Hart Pomerantz for the next three and a half years, and returned to the unfrozen South to write and coproduce various television comedy specials. In between, according to the authors, he ingested various substances, listened to a lot of music, and generally behaved like any other good little Boomer. If, however, he ever found any inconsistency between the latter and a career in television, there is no record of it in Hill and Weingrad. Meatball seems to have left Lorne alone.

He spent a lot of time sniffing around the various hotbeds of Boomer humor (e.g., the Committee), and complaining to everyone who would listen that television didn't speak for his generation, a common utterance of the imminent TV producer and one which could easily be answered, "So what? Turn it off."

Two things brought life to "Saturday Night" for Michaels. The first was the fact that NBC—trailing badly in the ratings—was anxious to launch a series aimed at the eighteen-to-thirty-fours. The second was that Michaels discovered New York and *The National Lampoon.* According to Hill and Weingrad, one of the first people Michaels contacted, and "ultimately one of the most important for the comedy synthesis he hoped to achieve," was O'Donoghue. They also make the revealing assertion that Michaels, "like most of those in the television business," had paid little attention to the *Lampoon* when he was in Hollywood.

Sure. Michaels called O'Donoghue (and therefore Beatts) in April of 1975, and arranged to have dinner with them at their post-everything kitsch-filled Chelsea apartment. At this time, O'Donoghue and Beatts, according to the authors, came on strong, saying they had little use for TV, and calling it "a lava lamp with sound." It was Michaels's "class" that intrigued the two Lampooners, apparently, and the fact that he took an adversary approach to the only business he'd ever worked in. When Beatts asked him why he wanted to call the show "Saturday Night Live," he answered that this was so the network could remember the night it was on.

The happy outcome of this fancy swordplay was that Michaels convinced the two supersophisticates to join his staff "and through them gained instant credibility in New York's *Lampoon*-connected underground."

Bruce McCall, however, has a rather different take on the same period. "It was the summer of 1975. Michaels had found a new interest—a new mission. We had a place out in the Hamptons, and they [O'Donoghue and Beatts] would come out and spend weekends with us. They spent all their time that summer of 1975 doing material with each other. I didn't know what the hell they were talking about. This 'new show' . . . this 'new show.' There had been no SNL—why would a show do stuff that was in the *Lampoon?*

"You couldn't do on television what you could do in the *Lampoon.* They weren't saying it in so many words, but the stuff they were doing was clearly *Lampoon* material."

The fact is that the genesis and jumping off point for SNL was *The National Lampoon.* The *Lampoon* did not want to be on television. But Michaels didn't care whether it did or not. As McCall points out, the *Lampoon* couldn't be on television. Not because of superficial matters of propriety or censorship, but because its essence was antithetical to what television demanded of humor and of humorists—repetition, familiarity, reassurance.

This is not to say that there wasn't some very good comedy on SNL. The talent it assembled included some of the best comic minds of the generation, in particular Murray and Aykroyd. What's more, some of the writing, especially the "Weekend Update" segments and various pieces by Tom Schiller, was superlative.*

But the sensibility at the top is all-important in such enterprises. Michaels, it is clear from the book, wanted more than anything to be the King of Hip, the cutting edge.

And in 1975 the cutting edge was *The National Lampoon.* What gave the initial seasons of SNL their appearance of being the cutting edge was that the series seduced—or stole—from *The National Lampoon,* not just personnel,

---

* It would be fascinating to know more of what *didn't* get on SNL than Hill and Weingrad respectfully mention. In particular, writing by the women on the staff seems to have been routinely demeaned or passed over.

but material, and not just premises, but attitudes. All of Michaels's principal stars, with the exception of Aykroyd, had been to the *Lampoon* finishing school: Chase, Belushi, Murray, and Radner. Curtin, who bloomed later anyway, had not (she came from the Proposition improv group in Boston). Newman and Morris never really bloomed. Indeed, when his stars deserted him for various other pursuits, he could not keep the show together, although he held desperately on to Radner, probably putting a permanent crimp in her career. Successful though it was in the last two years of its five-year Golden Age, SNL's material and performances deteriorated; it's interesting to note that when the sharpest tool in his case of cutting edges, O'Donoghue, left in the third season, the momentum of Boomer humor shifted away from SNL and toward *Animal House* and the movies.

This credit is reluctantly claimed. The *Lampoon,* while it had no aversion to making money, never seriously imagined that it could transfer to television and maintain any degree of comedic integrity. Not even Simmons, in the blindest of his feeding frenzies, ever thought it could be done, and as SNL proved in the worst way, both he and we were right.

But in 1975 none of this was known and one of the more revealing indications that Michaels knew exactly what he was doing is the fact that never since has he acknowledged the provenance of SNL, self-evident though it is. (This leaks into the book in the odd statement that no one in television paid much notice to the *Lampoon*—and in the authors' peculiar description of it and its offshoots as "underground.") According to Simmons, when he and Michaels appeared together once on a talk show, Michaels, in answer to a question about the debt SNL owed to the *Lampoon,* went to the absurd lengths of saying that the only magazine it owed anything to was *The New Yorker.*

But much as this adds insult to felony, the *Lampoon* in its extended family form was far from blameless. The symbiosis between key *Lampoon* performers and writers and Michaels was not unlike that between the Committee renegades and ABC five years before in "The Music Scene."

The hoary argument made by Hill and Weingrad in defense of this process is that Michaels did the Lampooners a favor by making their humor available to a far wider audience than had ever been possible before. This argument assumes that the humor remains unchanged in its widely disseminated form and that the means by which it is displayed remains neutral. And that all a middleman like Michaels has to do is bring the two together. That isn't the way it works, of course. You don't "bring" things to television, as if it were some benevolent goddess in a temple. Whatever else television is, it's a concrete technology that needs raw material like any other machine. No one who introduces this machine into a new area of the culture does anyone any favors; the best you can expect of such a person is that they're frank about their motives. And you can kiss that area of the culture good-bye as an autonomous territory. It may continue to exist, but only as a source of raw material. And, more often than not, the machine simply uses it up and moves on.

In some cases—romance, light entertainment, quotidian information, sports, even selling goods and services—the machine's end product is of little consequence, and depletes more or less inexhaustible resources. But when it mines the more serious and consequential areas of the culture, it becomes most dangerous. Because of the uniformity, utility, and inconsequential nature of what it produces, television does the culture its greatest disservice when it claims to do the most. By claiming to present vital political information when it is actually presenting a sophisticated form of sports event, by claiming to present a unique theatrical experience to "the largest audience possible" and destroying both its uniqueness and its theatricality in the process. Above all, when it begins to strip-mine intensely sensitive areas of human experience, such as religion or the learning process. The reason it becomes so dangerous is that by its very nature, it *does* strip-mine—rip off the surface of a subject, or issue, or set of beliefs, or body of achievement, and only the surface.

Boomer humor was one such sensitive area. Allowing the machine to roam freely over it was a momentous step. And much more than the *Lampoon* was involved. The whole body of Boomer humor to date was available to the new operator. There was nothing to stop any of its ideas or attitudes becoming its raw material—to disastrous ends.

Thus SNL, while it appeared to have all the qualities of Boomer humor— its willingness to Go Too Far, its antiauthoritarianism, its sexual and cultural license, its language and method, its ability to reduce the official and the stereotypical to the human—actually dealt very rarely with any of these matters. This humor had always been able to reduce propaganda and officialdom to their proper size; and the cast and staff of SNL looked and sounded just as though that's what they were doing. But they weren't.

There were many instances of this in specific material and many others in terms of policy choices. What Michaels chose to do and chose not to do are both revealing. But he never symbolically and actually summed up his entire relationship to Boomer humor, or acknowledged so clearly that he knew what he was doing as when he insisted that his show was "live." In this, Michaels implicitly acknowledged a debt that went back to the very beginnings of Boomer humor. Since it was a definitional impossibility, by insisting on it he also revealed his contempt for Boomer humor in general: The "live" of SNL was a fundamental fallacy.

Naturally, there is a difference in quality of performance when a performer is being filmed or taped in front of a live audience. It tends to be more raw, edgier, and often not as good as one designed for the camera. Direct communication with the studio audience actually tends to exclude the television viewer. Live television's advantage is all to the performer.† The urgency and danger of a truly live performance just isn't part of the viewer's experience. If this needs blunter emphasis, consider that somewhere on some channel at this very moment, you can probably turn on the TV and watch an SNL rerun from ten years ago, one of whose most brilliant performers is now dead.

Michaels was smart and hip, and a major student of Boomer humor. He knew that its origins were tiny stages in North Beach and Wells Street, that its best moments had always been those uncontrollable, unrepeatable experiences when laughter leaps from one human being to another, from living mouths to living ears, here and gone in a second, the very antithesis of technological "communication."

He was also an agent of that technology, deeply immersed in its most fundamental fallacy—that it "communicates" real experiences, at the very least approximates your being present at them, justifies its existence with the implicit assertion that a picture is almost as good as the real thing.

Boomer humor had always been uncontrollable, unrepeatable, dangerous, uncensorable, unofficial. To deliver it to television, it was essential that all these things appeared to be present. Otherwise, an extremely well-educated and skeptical audience just wouldn't buy it. What Michaels did in one stroke was to solve this impasse. He gave the audience the illusion of being present at a one-time-only performance, when in fact they were watching a carefully scripted, precensored show that rarely took any more chances than "Laugh-In" had. He gave them the appearance of danger and change, the appearance that anything could happen—when, in fact, nothing would.

Somehow it has gone down in myth and legend that SNL was constantly bucking the system, thumbing its nose, proffering its finger, farting during grace. But it's very hard to find any material in the record that lives up to these heady criteria.

Probably the most notorious episode in SNL's history was during the 1976 campaign. Chase had been developing a parody character of President Ford during the first part of the season. Ford, in Chevy's version, was an idiotic stumblebum who fell down stairs, stapled himself to things, and generally behaved in an unpresidential manner in everyday situations. Chase's technique here was characteristically and disarmingly crude. Looking nothing like Ford, and attempting nothing in the way of an impression, he simply announced himself in various ways as the President and proceeded to fall around. So total was the dislike and mistrust of Ford in the country that this met with tremendous reaction. The joke character quickly became one of Chevy's trademarks.

It also came to the attention of Ron Nessen, then Ford's press secretary. Knowing that Ford was perceived as a dolt, Nessen decided that it would be

---

† In a recent interview on CBS about his return to SNL, Michaels made an emphatic point that he has never watched his show live—he watches it on a monitor, even though he is only yards away from the live performance. The way he judges it (and to be fair, the only way he can judge it) is exactly the same way as it appears to a viewer hundreds or thousands of miles away.

neat to co-opt SNL by appearing on the show as its host. The idea was to send a message that Ford was well aware of his "image problem" and had a sense of humor about it. When Nessen actually appeared on the show, he was required to appear in a sketch with Chevy that played into Ford's stumblebum character, but little else of substance. What Michaels and his staff had decided to do instead was to "embarrass" the White House by surrounding Nessen's appearances as host with a series of sketches hinting at various forms of sexual activity.

This was the way SNL decided to take a stand against the Administration —not frontally, not fairly, and certainly not satirically. Nessen had no idea that the sketches surrounding his appearances were about douches, or curse words, or humping in bed. The media did, of course, and roundly denounced him. The show did also and claimed victory.

Whether or not Chevy damaged Ford's chances for re-election is not quite the point here. He probably didn't. It was highly unlikely that any Republican was going to be elected in 1976, in any case; a conventional militarist like Ford certainly didn't improve the party's chances. Typically, SNL had nothing to say about Ford's politics. The fact that Ford had been one of the loudest and stupidest of the prowar voices in Congress, that he was a party flunky carefully put in place by Nixon, that a deal had been struck with him to "pardon" his boss, and that, no less than Nixon, this man represented everything that the Boomers had arrayed themselves against seemed to be relatively unimportant to the staff and cast of SNL. It was far more hip to deal with the fact that Ford didn't *look* like a President. The way he moved, not the way he thought. The reason Ford should not be President, SNL seemed to say, was that he didn't make it on television.

There was an aspect to SNL's political satire of blowing away large fish in small barrels. One of the more celebrated sketches SNL's Golden Age produced was written by Franken and Davis, and centered around Woodward and Bernstein's book *The Final Days,* which recounted the last week or so of the Nixon presidency. When it came out, the book was pretty gratuitous in itself, for Nixon was long gone from the White House. But to derive a sketch from it was hardly state-of-the-art satire. The sketch was odd in that it neither parodied the book nor appeared to have much satirical thrust—it consisted mostly of a dialogue between Nixon and Kissinger, played by Aykroyd and Belushi, and its climax was a scene actually taken from the book in which Nixon gets Kissinger to kneel down with him in prayer. The assault on Nixon was so obviously out-of-date that Michaels actually prepared an intro, which read, in part: ". . . this week I had to make the toughest decision of my career: whether to ridicule Richard Nixon one more time . . ."‡

This is not to demean all the political material SNL produced; not by a long shot. But these are two of the supposed satirical high points of the show.

‡ This was dropped by the last minute and Anne Beatts substituted an intro that had Pat Nixon reading from her diary.

These may have been high-profile or high-performance pieces, but satirically they were both well out of the red zone.

On the other hand, especially in "Weekend Update," Chase, Zweibel, and later Franken and Davis often came up with savage items about the news on a routine basis. According to Hill and Weingrad, these gents were exceptions on the staff, in that they actually cared enough about politics to fight for satirical material. Herb Sargent, the Grand Old Man of American Television Satire, and *éminence grise* of this and many other shows, found the writing staff generally apolitical, in fact, noting that none of them bothered to vote when election days came around.

SNL's lack of fearlessness didn't confine itself to politics. Not only was much of the material apolitical, but it was also what might be called acontroversial. One of the more attention-getting pieces SNL presented during its first year was called the "Claudine Longet Invitational," which aired while Claudine Longet was being tried for manslaughter in the shooting of her lover, a skier named Spider Sabich. (Longet was estranged from her husband, Andy Williams.) O'Donoghue put together a videotape sequence in which skiers were shown taking dramatic falls on the slopes, each of the falls preceded by a gunshot and followed by Chase saying, "It looks as though . . . he's been accidentally shot by Claudine Longet . . ." Why this was considered controversial is hard to say. Longet was a celebrity, true, but not one particularly beloved of the American public—and no attempt had been made to cover up the sordid aspects of the affair (drugs appeared to have been involved and she'd dumped Williams for the skier). So the piece was scarcely satirical on any level. But coming from a satirist as accomplished as O'Donoghue, it was pathetic. The satirical impact of death, of which O'Donoghue was such a master, was here being squandered on nothing. Claudine was a very small fish indeed, but she was being blown away by the author of the "Vietnamese Baby Book."

Once again, it wouldn't matter, were it not for the fact that so much was made of it. Similarly, with another O'Donoghue sketch, which, according to Hill and Weingrad, "was unanimously considered . . . to be one of the best pieces ever on the show." The sketch was about the cancellation of "Star Trek" in 1969 by NBC because of poor ratings. Elliott Gould, playing an NBC programming chief, comes aboard the Starship *Enterprise* and cancels the show on the air. The sets are struck and the executive demands that various props, like phaser guns and Spock's ears, be returned to the Props Department. Kirk/Belushi and Spock/Chase remain to argue with Gould about the cancellation, and eventually only Belushi is left. He reverts to being Kirk and writes his final entry in the captain's log, which itself ends: "And except for one television network, we have found intelligent life everywhere in the galaxy . . ."

The performances were uniformly good and the Spock speeches were beautifully written, but the question remains, by what set of standards was this "one of the best ever . . ."? It wasn't about the most obviously ridiculous by-product of "Star Trek," Trekkies, because if anything it seemed to be saying that NBC's cancellation of the show was crass and simply based on greed. (An insight about as daring as saying that the Pope is really, really rich.) But the text actually tilts more toward making Shatner and Nimoy ridiculous for protesting the cancellation and trying to stay in character. And the playing with illusion seemed to have little point either. No Pirandello of video was born here.

The sketch was a skillfully disguised parody of another television show. In light of the fact that "Star Trek" hadn't been in production for seven years, it was hardly dangerous or ground-breaking satire. In fact, the book suggests that the most important concern within the show was Belushi's—that he do a "really good Kirk." This was the beginning of the end, television about television, a comic genius expending his effort on emulating a video image. In this respect, one of the "best ever" sketches on SNL got satirically whipped by its own tail, for the whole enterprise suggested that SNL and the generation it spoke to had nothing better to deify than a long-canceled science fiction series.

A mistake never made by the earlier Boomer humorists—and certainly not by its latest practitioners in the *Lampoon*—was now being made some of the *Lampoon*'s brightest lights on a routine basis. The number of sketches about television this cutting edge television show presented were legion.

Even those that appeared to be about serious matters were actually about television. Another Hill and Weingrad "high point" was Bill Murray's first appearance. He performed a sketch in which a television director is rehearsing for an execution. He was very funny, especially when trying to get the condemned man to be convincing about dying. This *appeared* to be about the horror of capital punishment, but actually had nothing to do with it. (Compare it, for example, to the Committee's long-ago sketch about a priest and warden kicking the condemned man to death because the electric chair won't work.)

It's about the heartlessness of television—something *Mad* magazine had been plugging away at for years, and a worthy target. But here a sketch about the heartlessness of television was appearing on television. What did that mean? If television was so heartless, wasn't it possible that the home audience might actually identify with the fact that the condemned man wouldn't emote properly? That, rather than hating him, the audience was cheering Murray on, were the very embodiment of the heartlessness the sketch was intended to bring home? At the very least how could anyone who'd created and performed the sketch tell?

Such material was often regarded as wildly innovative and daring, and it was—if judged by the standards of television, and especially if judged by the standards of executives delighted at watching a generation return to roost. Michaels accomplished this part of his mission, to conquer that "final frontier," to go where no television executive had gone for years, with precipitous and depressing speed.

But the corruption didn't stop there. O'Donoghue spent a lot of the second season putting himself on the air, most notably as the character Mr. Mike, who told children's stories in which various traditional characters had come to horrible ends. Once again, the satirical purpose of these tales seemed to be turned on its head from his *Lampoon* work. O'Donoghue had always had a penchant for exploring the victimization of children ("Children's Letters to the Gestapo" in the *Lampoon,* for example, a horrifying little piece in which German kids' letters revealed the degree to which they've been taught the essentials of anti-Semitism). But here the purpose had the appearance, rather, of victimizing children for their innocence, of calling them idiots for believing this drivel, or worse, wallowing in some odd form of video perversion. Mr. Mike went back over the line between satire and the old sick "Mummy, Mummy" joke.

Nor does the argument that this was supposed to offend middle-class pieties hold much water, particularly as the middle class seemed to be lapping it up. There was something rather more mundane at work than *"épater les bourgeois."* O'Donoghue, like almost everyone else on the show—with the admirable exceptions of Marilyn Miller and Aykroyd, who seemed to be trying to do what had *not* been done before—was looking to develop a repeatable character. Hill and Weingrad quote writer Rosie Shuster as saying that the cast and staff quickly cottoned on "to TV's magic formula that repetition equals success equals power."

What "worked" on SNL were the continuing characters, the safe situations, the material that reminded the audience what had "worked" last time. Emily Litella, Roseanne Roseannadanna, the Coneheads, Father Guido Sarducci, the "Samurai" series. The gradually lengthening list attested to the fact that the generation was returning home. However original the characters were in conception—Sarducci, most notably (a Catholic character was a real first)—the very fact that they became running characters diminished that originality every time they appeared. That such things are supposed to happen on TV, that the more familiar a cast of "friends" a show can develop the better, is exactly why it has never been that hospitable to Boomer humor. The only feature of the show that allowed for nonrepetitive material, "Weekend Update," was increasingly colonized by these characters as well, so that the one remaining place where some kind of savagery was possible became instead the home of the safe and predictable.

Nowhere was this more the case—and nowhere do Michaels's "Laugh-In" roots show more baldly—than in the ever-proliferating number of catch phrases. As "Never mind" and "But noooo . . ." rang around the nation, it became clear how little had changed in ten years since "Very interesting . . ." and "You bet your bippy" had been all the rage and "Sock it to me" had helped Nixon into the White House.

The answer will be heard: "So what? It all worked." The audience loved it. It was a "success" far out of proportion to its ratings—the talk of our very considerable neighborhood in the Global Village. But the audience was cheated by the appearance, not the substance, that SNL offered them. They can't be blamed for responding to the phenomenon of a cast like this "taking over" television for even ninety minutes a week; nor can they be blamed for the direction in which its leader led them. For not only did the material appear to be shocking and new—but the cast looked and sounded like them— as different as possible from previous television impersonations.

There was a further dimension to the excitement. That was that "Saturday Night" came from New York. For the print media especially—and in particular *Rolling Stone*—the fact that there was any hit TV show in New York rather than in Los Angeles was a revitalization of image for a city that had been on the verge of bankruptcy a couple of years before. SNL was a major factor in the show biz renaissance New York experienced in the second half of the seventies, one that brought executives, directors, and crews from film and TV looking for locations and talent in numbers unprecedented since the early sixties. This created a new chic, blurred the line forever between the publishing and screen worlds, gave rise along the way to the famous "bicoastal lifestyle," and did a great deal to assemble the celebrity system that dominates the eighties.

And it was celebrity as much as anything that was the downfall of this last and strongest strand of Boomer humor. But celebrity is not quite the remote and totemistic quantity the large screen bestows—it is the stardom bestowed on you by television, democratized stardom, theoretically available to everyone, whether they're an actor or a doctor, a preacher or a mass murderer. It is offered to anyone, regardless of race, creed, color, profession, talent, or beauty—to anyone capable of holding the attention of countless millions for a few minutes. It is thus far more fickle and unreliable than stardom, and even more pernicious, for it offers access to the technological hoax indiscriminately, sucks the largest possible number into the show business lie, gives everyone a chance at winning a ticket into its unreality.*

Hill and Weingrad's documentation of this process is exhaustive. It may be the first time on record that a rise and fall have been simultaneous. Chase was the first to go—he made it to the cover of *New York* magazine—thence to consideration as the next Johnny Carson. The book quotes Chase as worrying often at this time that he was becoming the very thing he'd been parodying— "a plastic celebrity." Having this self-knowledge, however, didn't stop the process; Chase was more interested in being a star than a satirist.

It didn't stop O'Donoghue either. For him, the Emmys, a limo, and some champagne—all of it in Los Angeles, one of the places O'Donoghue had once most loathed—were the point at which he "knew he'd sold out."

Not surprisingly, Michaels was the chief beneficiary of the burgeoning celebrity of his show. He had always had a taste for salons—his own and others.

* That's why, of course, film stars—real ones, as opposed to feature players who are quite commonly referred to as "stars"—now refer to themselves as "superstars."

His hot New York cult show took him to the heart of the rock and art aristocracy where he'd always most wanted to be.

Arguably, Belushi was the next to go—in 1978, the biggest celebrity yet. But by then the show was three seasons old and the cast were all celebrities anyway. One of the odder instances of what celebrity means was Belushi's celebrated impersonation of Joe Cocker while Cocker was guesting the show. Nothing brought home how far he'd come (or sunk) than the spectacle of Belushi imitating Cocker's pained contortions with the singer himself along-side, gazing in hurt puzzlement. When Belushi had done exactly the same thing in *Lemmings*, he was appearing in the context of an over-riding prem-ise, in a cocky Off-Broadway revue that attacked the very foundations of rock celebrity. Now here he was—a celebrity himself—certainly as "big" as his target. So what did this mean? How was it satirical? It certainly wasn't a compliment—it just looked absurd in itself, a sadistic video game.

The avalanche of celebrity that overtook the first cast of SNL was devastat-ing. It wasn't the drugs or the money that did them in, for drugs are never a cause, only an effect. And there's little reason to begrudge money to someone creative provided it doesn't make them uncreative. No, it was the machine that stripped their personalities from them, made them available to whoever wanted a piece, and gave them little in return except a fairly good feeling for a fairly short time.

By 1979, SNL had become a gigantic weekly party, to which anyone who was anyone from both coasts was invited or, if they weren't, wangled them-selves invitations. A year before the most dangerous President in living mem-ory was elected by the smallest turnout in living memory, the cream of the generation that knew him best thought that one of their more important priorities was to snort their brains out on the 17th floor of the New York offices of a television network. (And, for good measure, a major defense contractor.) By the dawn of the eighties, this was the cutting edge of dissent.

What was ultimately so tragic about SNL was that the cast and staff Mi-chaels assembled was so *good.* That was the real problem, the problem that both made SNL the success it was, and so reprehensible. Of no one was this more true in the cast than of Dan Aykroyd. No one performer, caricaturist, or columnist caught the gluey sanctimoniousness of Jimmy Carter as per-fectly as Aykroyd, a performance one ached to see not confined to a screen. No one could be as looney as Pa Conehead or the pitchman of the Bass-o-matic. Aykroyd was the ultimate nonstar, pure satirist, a man who became his targets so thoroughly that his own personality was irrelevant to the pro-cess. A craftsman so accurate, so reliable, you could practically see the satiri-cal tools hanging off his workbelt. And no one, therefore, who needed televi-sion less. Aykroyd was a satiric genius who would have made his name no matter where or when. The same is true—to a lesser degree—of Chase, Radner, and Belushi, and of several members of the writing staff.

The myth of inevitability now hangs around SNL like an old medal, but the truth is that it wasn't inevitable. It was only necessary to Lorne Michaels and

NBC. Two of the greatest surviving Boomer humorists, Carlin and Pryor, didn't need SNL, or to any significant degree, TV. (SNL, on the other hand, needed them—for its first and third shows—and both NBC and media revolutionary Michaels were very nervous about both of them.) Throughout the seventies, they concentrated instead on live performance and, in Pryor's case, film—too committed to their art to trust it to television.†

▪   ▪

For the successive waves of SNL cast members, the most important thing was not dissent but celebrity. While many of them were obviously very talented, the ones most worth examining are Joe Piscopo, Billy Crystal, and Eddie Murphy, for each exemplifies one stage or another of the abrupt decline of Boomer humor—in much the same manner and at much the same pace, as it occurred in movies.

Piscopo came to the show in its first reincarnation after Michaels's departure in 1980. Piscopo was first and foremost an impressionist, most notably of Sinatra, but later of many others, almost all of them television personalities like Ed McMahon, Tom Snyder, David Letterman, and so on. These were not traditional impressions in which the impressionist approximated the voice and facial expression of the target, but likenesses done with the help of costume, makeup, hair styling, and even prosthetics.

Piscopo was an imitator of celebrity, a facial and physical athlete who could reproduce, with a great deal of technical help, a famous face, a well-known image, someone who could duplicate what was already duplicated. He was the clearest example of television about television to date. Whatever this was, it wasn't satire, dissent, or even parody. Stories abounded around the staff of SNL how, once the Sinatra impression began running regularly, Piscopo would deflect suggestions for it by saying, "Frank wouldn't do that." According to some, he was so deeply into his reproduction of Sinatra that he actually thought from time to time that he *was* Sinatra. Certainly, there appeared to be a degree of wish fulfillment in Piscopo's performance of this weird clone. Piscopo didn't want to damage the image or criticize the man. He just wanted to look, sound, and be as much like him as possible.

Impressions of any kind, however uncanny, are parasitic—an acknowledgment of the superior talent or greater celebrity of their target. Unless they go further than mere impression—as Bruce's did—they become simply a debasement of the recognition factor that exists in all humor. But in the continuum of SNL, debased though it already was, the emergence of Piscopo was extraordinary. The decline was now precipitous. The most prominent member of the SNL cast was someone who intended to become a celebrity by being another celebrity.

Crystal, the most recent inheritor of this mantle, is even odder. He, also, is

---

† And it's Carlin, not Chase or any of the SNLers, who's got his pawprint in Hollywood Boulevard. True to form, George wasn't particularly grateful. He did, however, point out that when the neutron bomb dropped, this would mean his name—if not he—would live for posterity.

best known for his impressions—e.g., of Sammy Davis, Jr., and Fernando Lamas. With Crystal, a tendency has become the norm. Cutting edge satire is now the reproduction of another television personality. Crystal's impressions, equally painfully constructed and just as slavish, have no point. They are even further debased versions of Piscopo's debasement, imitations of a long-forgotten actor and a singer Lenny Bruce put on trial twenty-five years earlier.

Perhaps the public has so bought the concepts of celebrity and television that imitation of celebrity fulfills the need for attacking authority, that eternal wellspring of satire. Celebrity, as it exists in television, is authority, so by television standards this is satire. If so, the doors are now closing rapidly on the world outside—the only targets of modern humor permitted are those that television has already created or approved or, in some cases, buried.

In David Letterman's "Late Night," this construct is no problem. It's readily acknowledged by all concerned. Letterman "attacks the foibles of television" on television. In the most generous interpretation of this incestuous nonsense, Letterman is supposed to be playing a parody of himself—of talk show hosts. There the defense feels it can rest.

Letterman falls so far outside the tradition of Boomer humor that he has no measurable rating. But the Letterman audience seems to think that it is being avant-garde by watching this manipulative pap. Even when the hoax is pointed out to the average Letterman fan, he gleefully acknowledges the fact. It has become bohemian to be antibohemian. Not liking Letterman pegs you as someone for whom television is *not* the ultimate hip, for whom its triviality *isn't* the most desirable part of modern life and thought. "Lighten up," Letterman might say to Mother Teresa. "Let's throw some food around." Liking Letterman is like *Police Academy:* hip to be square, *"épater les antibourgeois."*

But the real phenomenon of the eighties is that final product of SNL, Eddie Murphy. At first glance, Murphy might seem to be in much the same bag as the Piscopo-Crystal-Letterman school of "television-is-all." Hill and Weingrad make a great deal of Murphy's impressions of Buckwheat and Gumby being possible only from a child of television. And it's true that Murphy followed Piscopo's lead in doing elaborately made-up impressions of celebrities like Stevie Wonder. But this doesn't explain the extra and vital presence Murphy brought to SNL, the Sequel. Nor does it explain his explosive rise to stardom, either on television, or subsequently in the movies.

What cut Murphy out from the pack were his welter of black street characters, like Velvet Jones, Mr. Robinson, and Raheem Abdul Mohammed. Murphy was denounced for these characters as being racist and indeed they were demeaning. And indeed Dion, his gay black hairdresser, was insulting to gays (though why it's not insulting for gays to impersonate women has never been explained). But it's also important to know that many of these criticisms were made in the name of the Golden Age of SNL. The implication was that this sort of thing would never have happened Back Then. The further implication is that Murphy speaks for the neoconservative mood in the country, for which read "neoracist." That he is, in effect, cooning it up for the Reagan era.

Neither of these criticisms is accurate. First, SNL was plenty racist. Hill and Weingrad make the substantial point that the staff were "for all their professed radicalism . . . unable to produce material that dealt with black issues in anything beyond the coarsest terms if they dealt with them at all." Garrett Morris was handled appallingly by everyone on the show. He was used, more often than not, in a dress impersonating a black singer or other stereotypical skits.

Second, although there are no doubt plenty of righty bow ties who delight in watching a black "be hardest on his own," Murphy does not speak to them. He speaks chiefly to blacks. Blacks have made Murphy's television and live careers—and, above all, his movie career.

Murphy is the last of the first wave, the Garrett Morris that never was, a wildly talented comedian who came along a couple of years too late to be exploited by Michaels but took the same route all by himself. Murphy sold out Boomer humor too—the black version—to television, and did it in acceptably racist ways so that the network could buy it. And he sold it out largely based on the work of one man, Richard Pryor. Murphy's characters are an acceptable form of Pryor's superb, gut-wrenching street characters, good enough to explode on television. Murphy delivered the undeliverable to the network as Michaels did. The street, the ghetto, Pryor, all in one neat, nondrinking, nondoping, non-gun-toting package.

■   ■

The story of SNL is the story of a generation learning to love again one of the two great technological absurdities unique to its age.

SNL made it hip once again to watch and to be on television. And while it had the illusion that it was bringing reality to television, actually it only made the illusion better. SNL helped convince us that the Box actually does reflect the real world.

We watched SNL and had the illusion that we were watching dissent, irreverence, and nonconformity finally have its way with authority's most powerful modern weapon.

Later we watched *The Day After,* and had the illusion that we really knew what it was like to live through a nuclear holocaust. (That was why it raised such Cain all over the political spectrum.)

Later still, we watched "Live Aid," and had the illusion that we really were changing the politics of famine.

Outside, though, in the real world, the fanatic brotherhood of the tribe gathered under cover of night to hatch their madness.

Outside in the real world, warheads multiplied.

Outside in the real world, little children starved to death for reasons that, had we not been so wrapped up in illusion, we might actually have been able to influence.

SNL changed nothing. It was the beginning of the end of dissent.

The odd thing was that to start thinking of the illusion as real, we had to take a step backward; to become neovideots, we had to unknow something, which from television's birth we had known. We had always been acutely aware of the illusion, even if we put it to use, amused and fascinated in the fifties, savagely skeptical in the sixties. We had always known what television did to the real world—how it took its lumpiness, asymmetry, unpredictability, and ordered it, cleaned it up, smoothed its rough edges, chopped it into chunks, shaped it into stories, gave it beginnings, middles, and ends.

We knew its need for patterns, how even random catastrophe had to become a cautionary tale; we knew how it reduced the complexities and ambiguities of democracy to black-and-white, that its version of political or social debate was fixed and that any sense that we were participating in it, or could affect its outcome, was an illusion.

The sixties had been alive with images of television as hypnosis, addiction, brainwashing, and those images had been right. We had been right, too, in thinking that television pushed us back into ourselves, off the streets, into isolation and impotence, where our political will was nil and our political clout predictable.

Above all, we knew where the illusion could lead, where its neat black-and-white morality, its totally perfect nationalism, and totally evil enemies ended up—in the hot, baffling jungles of a land for whose people they were home, not an illusion, but there to be defended to the death.

And that amazingly, those jungles had become in turn an illusion, an exciting new source of raw material for the machine, packed with photogenic gunfire, gore, and courage.

And that more than anything, the anguish and bafflement of the poor bastards who were duped or trapped into gambling their lives for this mad illusion were its victims in another, even crueler, way; for the first day they cut point, they discovered that real bullets meant real gaping wounds, real dead buddies, that little kids only asked for candy to get close enough to them to blow them to pieces, that no Bilkos were to be seen, only hard-bitten killers or shirkers and criminals, that gooks weren't actors who fell obligingly to the ground when you fired, but real men with real guns with nothing else on their minds but to kill you first.

And we knew, therefore, that we had an obligation to them, our generation, and to our brothers and sisters and children and parents to combat the illusion, wherever possible, in the streets or in print, by ridicule or song, and to try to change the system the illusion sustained, not simply exchange one illusion for another.

All this we knew. And SNL was key in convincing us that we just might be wrong.

As Saigon fell, SNL premiered.

∎   ∎

The normal field of vision for the human eye is about 180 degrees, while in a movie theater it is 45 degrees, one quarter of the norm; for television it varies according to screen size and distance of viewing, from a maximum of 14 degrees, to as little as 7, one twenty-fifth of the norm. Saccadic eye movements—the rapid exploratory back and forth motion the eye makes in a normal environment—are thus restricted when viewing television to a minute fraction of their normal range of perception, concentrated on an abnormally small area of light. This is clearly akin to standard methods of hypnosis.

But hypnosis usually stops there, at least as far as the eye is concerned. With television viewing, what happens once this state of receptivity has been induced is that cathode-ray guns powered by 25,000 volts (in the case of color TV), shoot electron streams at phosphors on the screen, which in turn project light directly into our eyes. This is not your old ambient light, however, or even deliberately directed neutral light. What is going deep into brains made passive by hypnosis is a welter of images, ideas, preconceptions, violence, sex, food, just about anything that can be seen by the naked eye and make an impression on the brain. All this is being projected directly at us, in some order of which we can never be aware and which we cannot control. And moreover, which is not real in any sense, either in that it is random and arbitrary like the real world, or a tangible entity.

This sounds a lot like hallucination, and the means by which the hallucination is induced, a lot like a mind-altering drug. It is perhaps time to look at television not as the boon to civilization that we still parrot it to be, but as a narcotic, real and hard, that is doing exactly the same damage to our minds as any other mind-changing technological discovery. That is not to say it is all bad. The human mind is no less a predictable psychological entity than any other part of our bodies. It sometimes needs a jolt to make it perceive connections it is otherwise too mundane to bother with. That is why we drink coffee in the morning and alcohol at night, and some of us, blatantly disregarding state and federal laws, use other more exotic drugs.

But the daily and incessant use of any mind-altering substance dulls, cheapens, and eventually negates any of the perceptions its initial or ritual or occasional use may induce. Furthermore, dependence on drugs leads to self-absorption, desensitization, and the inability to distinguish between inner and outer realities. And the last of these leads invariably to physical violence.

With telenarcosis, we have reached a stage of use far beyond ritual and far beyond epiphany. The beneficial perceptions that television enabled us to experience once upon a time are long gone. But we try to recapture these highs day in and day out year after year. As a result, like any addicts, we neglect human relationships, we lose touch with social norms, we forget our own history and culture, we feel we can do without love and decency. For the junkie, such vast omissions are no problem, since inside his own head, he is hallucinating all these experiences, having relationships with human beings, keeping in touch with societal norms, experiencing history and culture, feeling love, hate, fear, and other human emotions—all without the bother of getting up off the bed and going outside and dealing with the imprecision and unpredictability of the actual world.

Like junkies, we see odd connections, odd communalities. Somewhere in the ether or perhaps on the planet, all the images of telenarcosis co-exist. All the places and people that jumble for hours each day through our minds are somehow related. Those cops, newsmen, beauty queens, terrorists, wrestlers, lucky winners, killers of ten, surrogate mothers, politicians—somehow all know each other.

And as in any advanced state of narcosis, the real world becomes more and more shut out. What we loosely call television, which is indeed a communality of millions hooked by the same illusion, closes its doors on the tangible experience outside. The technodrug becomes its own world, its own justification for existence. It discusses itself, it brings us news of itself, it reminisces about its own history, revives its own past glories. The Monkees—that group despised by real-life rock and rollers—the Monkees, sighs television, were second only to the Beatles.

Sometimes it seems as though the country is in a daze. Strung out as it is, it behaves collectively like a junkie, especially in its public stance, domestic and international.

We are quick to anger, hard to please. Our attention span is short. Our behavior is unpredictable. It is difficult to convince us that being sober or straight is preferable to being stoned. We feel better this way. Being hard-core mainliners, we have constructed an elaborate system of rationales for the beneficial effects of our drug of choice, many of them extremely convincing. And sadly, probably the only way we will find out that we are not normal, not in control, strung out, is if we experience violence. Our addiction will certainly lead us in that direction. There is a stimulant effect in any narcosis—the sense of being superior, of being hip, of being capable of more than normal bozos. Junkies of any kind rarely find out the truth except the hard way. We have to wrap ourselves around a tree to find out there is no such thing as "a better driver." We have to get decked or knifed to find out just how invulnerable "the stuff" makes us.

And in political terms that means—just as it did last time—war.

Where the dissent will come from next time is hard to see. Humor is safely corralled in comedy clubs, just about live, but for the most part mere audition halls for television, their occupants as tame and distinctive as battery chickens. The obvious talent and individuality one constantly glimpses is further squeezed into the appalling stand-up-tell-a-joke form, one which was already ancient and superceded in the days of Sahl and Bruce. Not that this excuses the young men and women for practicing what Gottlieb, in a stroke of genius, called "entrepreneurial comedy." After all, the reason their assembly-line jokes stick to "Gilligan's Island" reruns and how not to make a left turn when driving down to Safeway, is because they want that Showtime special.

But they're not to be blamed for the comedy standards we bequeathed them, the systems we left behind for them to learn from. We, like the rest of our generation, turned away from sanity and human contact, away from a future in which we would not be condemned to relive history. We preferred impotence, nuclear terror, racial hatred, and our kindly old grandpa.

We turned back to television, back to celebrity, to the values that made America small.

Semi-Epitaph

The history of its humor is the history in microcosm of our generation. The wild multiplicity of character, the confusion of aims and ideals, the extreme highs, the basest lows, the willingness to take chances, the fierce integrity and utter lack of it—all these are evidenced in its humor, as they are in the generation at large.

To say that our humor is dead, is a contradiction in terms. True to form, Ol' Bloodbath never did deliver on his fighting words, and most of us are still here. (Indeed, in the case of our humorists, we can boast that the death rate is a good deal lower than that of our musicians.) But the humor celebrated throughout this book, for all that its practitioners are still alive, does seem to be half-dead or, at the very best, dormant. In the one very important respect that we don't seem to have been able to teach it to our juniors, as the fathers of Boomer humor taught it to us, it is, as John Cleese might say, deceased . . . this humor is no more . . . this is an *ex*-humor.

The reasons, we're told, that we don't hear much of this kind of humor anymore are variously: (a) there's no war, so there's no need for it; (b) people are tired of it; (c) people are more conservative now.

The first of these springs from a fundamental misreading of postwar humor. Sahl and Bruce and Feiffer needed no war to lay its foundations. What they were after were society's prevailing attitudes, among them the urge to make war. They were right. And if they couldn't either foresee the war or stop it, it was still essential that they dissent.

The second is, on the face of it, fair enough, and hard to argue with. Certainly, SNL might have depleted some of the nation's natural resources of skepticism, but in my limited experience, people's taste for humor with teeth is as keen as ever. When they can get it. And that, of course, doesn't mean that everyone likes humor with teeth. There are as many audiences for humor as there are for music. Humor has its easy listeners, and its hard rockers. But it doesn't follow that they're catered to. In fact, generalizing the audience—*all* people are tired of one kind of humor—tends to justify the production of only one kind of humor.

And it's easy listening every time.

The third of these, the mantra of the eighties, is really just another way of saying (b). It's been applied to almost everything else in public life, from dress codes to the defense budget, so there seems no reason why it shouldn't be pasted on poor old Boomer humor as well. The meaning of the phrase is mushy. (For one thing, many polls show that a considerable majority of people think of themselves as more *liberal* in general than they were ten years ago—but then what do mere people know?)

Here, however, the phrase clearly means that Boomer humor is liberal or left-wing. Since satire is neither liberal nor conservative, what this really means is that it is questioning, skeptical, disturbing. Audiences may be less open to questioning than they were, but as above it doesn't seem like it. The conclusion—those who produce and distribute humor in all media are more conservative or, to be exact, more right-wing. Here, the trend toward tightening, repression, and containment of dissent is measurable. No amount of What the People Want can obscure that. Before the public reads the book, you have to print it. And since the media are being concentrated in fewer and bigger hands (known as the Few Big Invisible Hands), with little interest in questioning and skepticism, the drive toward orthodoxy is palpable.

Boomer humor was one of its first victims, which is why after flourishing for a quarter of a century, multiplying and diversifying, gaining all the time in influence and talent abruptly, in the first year of the Reagan administration, "people got tired of it." Boomer humor was the most visible and popular expression of dissent. It was bound to be in jeopardy. Dissent means at least two ways of thinking, and any more than one is obnoxious to right-wingers in any system of government. There is one set of questions and one set of answers, one kind of behaving, one way of thinking—and one way of laughing.

And you will be laughing with me, comrade, not against me.

The smile-button Stalinism of the White House finds its echo in the *Pravda*-esque establishment of the neoconservatives, the neoliberals, and any number of other thinkers who would appropriate the ridiculous prefix. "Neo" means only—with a tip of the hat to Lampooner Santayana—that we are dealing with people who would rather relive history than learn from it. The neoestablishment condemns all of us to the neofifties, just as "nostalgia" (or, rather, "neostalgia") does, a generational snake endlessly consuming its own tail. There are no new answers, only neoanswers, pat responses to the neo-Cold War, neoracism, the same neoconformity we have all lived before. There is no escape from this closed circle. We neoparents are doomed to neoeducate our neochildren in the same neomistakes, accommodate us and them to the neo-Great Deal and the neo-Big Catch, the neo-Box and neoannihilation.

These are grim matters, we hear; not fit subjects for humor. Oh yes they are. Just as they were when they were first formed in the real fifties. And if now we have to deal not just with the idiocies of a system that has changed so little, but also with those who promote it as neo and revolutionary, fine. Satire —if its practitioners care enough—will always find a way.

The closed Soviet-Union-Threat-Or-Menace debate, which N. Podhoretz, W. Buckley, G. Will, P. Buchanan, and many others of our mirror-image *Pravda* have established as the only norm of free-society debate, is not sexy enough to appeal to an audience that has little idea who these people are. But its results in American policy, in the real eighties, are available to everyone: what we are supposed to think of the Russians, as opposed to what they're really like, now that the planet is shrinking; what our vastly corrupt defense establishment says it exists for, as opposed to what it really does, day in and day out, to our minds, our children, our future—and our standard of living; what the fundamentalist terrorists who have taken Christ hostage really have in mind for us. The list, once started, goes on and on.

What it takes, first, is to care enough. What it takes, second, is to recognize what is being done to us and our lives. What it takes, third, is not to be afraid to disagree. Dissent. Cop an attitude. And what it takes, always, is to be so good at doing them that the bastards squirm, walk out, try to get you closed down, and stop your check.

Boomer humor is not dead, any more than the generation. The great talents of the seventies, for all that may have drifted in the neofifties, are alive and well. It's hard to imagine Chase, Murray, Aykroyd, Ramis, et al., ever deciding to serve the purposes of what they instinctively distrust. Carlin lives. Pryor lives. Murphy, for all that he seems bent on achieving financial super-independence and monotonic stardom, cannot have lost his coruscating versatility, whatever ends it was put to first time out.

But of the survivors, no one more than Lily Tomlin has gone the extra step into maturity. The least compromised and most adventurous of them all, her *The Search for Signs of Intelligent Life in The Universe* best embodies the continuation of the most fundamental attitudes of the generation's humor. Its questing is instinctive, its inversion of "values" assumed, its self-awareness delicious. And it's significant that, to present her masterpiece to date, she chose the theater.

The search for signs of life in Boomer humor, as the neofifties emerge into the daylight of real time, leads to the conclusion that Tomlin might be the key to regeneration. At the outset, thirty years ago, Boomer humor defined itself in a quite unexpected way. College students and graduates invaded a turf that had been exclusively ethnic, a legitimate means for immigrant kids to achieve fame and fortune. There could have been no way of predicting this, but once it started, it seemed entirely natural. Although there is no parallel as far as conditions, the dynamic of revitalization might vest itself in women. Whoopi

Goldberg—whose one-woman show on Broadway bore many resemblances in quality, range, and edge to Tomlin's—is an obvious example; women comedians (e.g., Elaine Boozler) are almost uniformly more interesting than their male counterparts. Andrea Martin, possibly the funniest woman in America after Tomlin, has an insistent quality of hilarious skepticism. Women writers, not the least of them Tomlin's partner, Jane Wagner, seem to have an edge and commitment their male counterparts have grown bored with. And if none of this were the case, it only takes one, anyway, as Sahl demonstrated so long ago. If you want to know what works, bites, and at the same time moves an audience, look to Tomlin.

■ ■

We are the Boomers. We are a huge sprawling generation, from the days we were born held together by bonds we would be hard-put to describe, but which we know instinctively. One of the things that has held us together as much as our music has been our humor. From the minute we read our first *Mad* magazine, or saw our first improv company, heard our first Bruce or Carlin or Pryor album, saw Tommy Smothers lean into the camera for the first time, or read our first *Lampoon,* we have known that things were not the way we had been told they were. The results have been confusing and conflicting, but that is the way things in a free society are supposed to be.

Because we tried to be free, as we were taught to be, we made some bad mistakes. But it is our time now. We have another chance—in fact, we have several. Those who tried to take us back to our childhood when we did what we were told, those who tried to reimpose the control our music and our humor taught us were insane; those who are now huddled in the dandruff of a septuagenari arms salesman, watching us and wondering what we will do, have no chances left.

We are the biggest and the best and the brightest.

Remember the hallowed words of Bluto:

"Nothing's over till we say it is!"

INDEX

Index

A

B

D

E

H

I

L

M

O

P

Paar, Jack, 54–55, 158 n., 163–64, 168, 203
Packard, Vance, 154
Paige, Satchel, 418
Paley, William, 205–6, 223–24
Palin, Mike, 361, 362 n.
Palladium (London, England), 123, 165
Paris Review, 108
Parks, Rosa, 29
Parody
 Boomer humor's disdain of, 140
 Bruce's, 116
 definition of, 4 n.
 by *The National Lampoon,* 20
Pass-along rate, 374 n.
"Passionella" (Feiffer cartoon), 91–92
Pastore, John, 221, 223
Patinkin, Sheldon, 73
Paulsen, Pat, 207, 216–18, 427 n.
Peace movement, 240–41
 See also Vietnam War
"Peanuts" (cartoon), 282
Pegler, Westbrook, 163
Peppiat, Frank, 213
Perlman, S. J., 270
Peyton Place (book), 75
Phillips, Julia, 321
"Phoebe Zeitgeist" (comic strip), 276–77
Pigpen, 187
Pill, the, 147
Piscopo, Joe, 444
Pius XII (Pope), 415
"Pizza Man" (song), 349, 360
Playboy Club (Chicago), 156

Playboy Club (Lake Geneva), 252
Playboy magazine, 108, 147, 156, 163, 275, 302, 326, 394
 Lampoon parody of, 269, 273
Playten, Alice, 349, 352, 356, 360
Playwrights Theater Club, 40
Plimpton, George, 108
Podhoretz, Norman, 241 n.
"Pointy-heads," 237–38
Police Academy movies, 421–22
Polish jokes, 244, 245
Politics
 Bruce's preoccupation with, 119, 134, 137
 of the Committee, 177, 179, 182, 188–92
 Feiffer's view on, 83–84
 Gregory's involvement in, 158–60
 of "Saturday Night Live," 438–39
 show business and, 414
 Smothers Brothers and, 204, 206, 208, 212
Pomerantz, Hart, 433
Pop art, 147
Porky's (movie), 23, 418–20
Postman, Neil, 19 n.
Premise, the, 73, 150, 184
Pretty in Pink (movie), 420
Price, Roger, 278
Print media, 75–113
Prison benefit by the Committee, 182
Prison system, Bruce on, 138–40
Private Eye (magazine), 146, 280
Professionalism, rejection of, 52
Pryor, Richard, xii, 160, 172, 173, 420, 444, 446
 drug experience of, 251, 254
Psychoanalysis, 63
Pulley, B. S., 117 n.
"Pull the Triggers, Niggers" (song), 319–20, 335–36

T

U

V